Victoria Forner

PROSCRIBED HISTORY
The Role of Jewish Agents in Contemporary History

III

THE SECOND WORLD WAR AND ITS AFTERMATH

VICTORIA FORNER

PROSCRIBED HISTORY
*The Role of Jewish Agents
in Contemporary History*
III
THE SECOND WORLD WAR AND ITS AFTERMATH

Cover illustration:
"Brandenburg Gate" in Berlin.

HISTORIA PROSCRITA III
La actuación de agentes judíos en la Hª Contemporánea
La segunda guerra mundial y la posguerra
First published by Omnia Veritas in 2017

Translated from Spanish and published by
OMNIA VERITAS LTD

*O*MNIA VERITAS.
www.omnia-veritas.com

© Omnia Veritas Limited - Victoria Forner - 2025

All rights reserved. No part of this publication may be reproduced by any means without the prior permission of the publisher. The intellectual property code prohibits copies or reproductions for collective use. Any representation or reproduction in whole or in part by any means whatsoever, without the consent of the publisher, the author or their successors, is unlawful and constitutes an infringement punishable by articles of the Code of Intellectual Property.

CHAPTER X 11

ON WORLD WAR II 11

Part 1 A war imposed on Germany and the world 11
The economic miracle of National Socialism 12
Hitler's foreign policy steps: the Saarland and relations with Poland 15
Danzig 19
Czechoslovakia or the impossible state 23
The Anschluss 25
The Zionists and the Evian Conference 28
The road to Munich 31
Czechoslovakia's fiction in evidence 41
Poland's erratic policy against Germany in 1938 46
A Jewish terrorist murders Ernst von Rath: the "Kristallnacht" 50
The consequences of Kristallnacht 56
Germany seeks agreement and peace with Poland 58
Edward Frederick Lindley Wood, Earl of Halifax 61
Czechoslovakia disintegrates 64
The Tilea farce 69
Hitler's treatment of the Czechs 71
The use of Poland against Germany: the British blank cheque 73
The deterioration of German-Polish relations 78
The untenable situation of Germans in Poland 84
The situation as seen from the Soviet Union 90
General war or localised war? 97
The Ribbentrop-Molotov Pact - some reactions 103
Germany is still trying to reach an agreement with Britain 106
Halifax and Kennard farce: Poles refuse to negotiate 110
Last-ditch attempts to prevent the invasion of Poland 118
From a local war to World War II 126
Pieces and pawns of international Zionism in the British government 136

Part 2 of the early war years 140
The indiscriminate killing of the German minority in Poland 140
From war against Germany to carte blanche for the USSR 148
Red terror and Jewish terror in Estonia and Latvia 153
Beria and the Katyn massacre 159
The situation in Western Europe: Norway and the neutrals 165
The mystery of Dunkirk 170
A not very credible and unprovable thesis 174
The Armistice and the British. Jewish agents surround De Gaulle 177
The plan to exterminate the German race for good 182
Rudolf Hess' flight to Scotland 187

Part 3 Pearl Harbour: Roosevelt immolates his sailors to enter the war . 189
Roosevelt provokes Germany and puts himself at the service of the USSR 190
Japan's economic stranglehold 194
The US fleet at Pearl Harbour 196
The Purple Code 197
The hours before the attack 202

Part 4 Air terror and atomic terror 205
Germany did not prepare for this kind of war. 206

The "splendid and heroic decision"..209
The progressive destruction of Germany..212
Lindemann, Churchill's Jewish ideologue..214
Dresden, the forgotten holocaust..216
Aviation terror in Japan: atomic terrorism...225
Part 5 The Morgenthau Plan. Half of Europe for communism.................. 237
A disturbing secret document..238
The *Morgenthau Diary*. The Morgenthau Plan for Germany......................243
The Yalta Conference..255
Part 6 Immune crimes and massacres against the German people against the German people.. 268
The Nemmersdorf Prelude...268
Refugee massacres at sea: three forgotten sinkings......................................271
Königsberg..273
Two million women raped...275
German prisoners of war Eisenhower's death camps..................................277
The assassination of General Patton...285
Jewish terrorism...290

CHAPTER XI 297

THE DECISIVE POST-WAR YEARS..297
Part 1 Germany, a nation on the brink of the abyss.................................. 297
The expulsion of the Germans, an unprecedented population transfer 298
Jewish criminals in concentration camps 312
Nuremberg's disastrous set-up..318
Propaganda, denazification, punishment and looting 332
Part 2 Failure of the World Government's plan based on the monopoly of atomic violence... 337
Bernard Baruch presents plan for Global Governance.................................339
Communist Jews hand over atomic bomb secrets to USSR.........................344
Part 3 The imposition of the Zionist state in Palestine.............................. 356
Some historical events before 1936...357
The situation between 1936 and November 1947...364
From partition (29/11/1947) to the proclamation of Israel (14/5/1948) 373
Unilateral proclamation of independence and war of conquest.................381
Killings and ethnic cleansing...388
The Zionist Nuclear Golem..392
Part 4 In the United States, "witches". In China and Korea, communism 400
Harry Dexter White as head of the International Monetary Fund.............401
The cases of Harry Hopkins and Alger Hiss..406
"Such an immense conspiracy": China's surrender to communism...........412
And more of the same in Korea 431
"Witches" and "warlocks" plotting against McCarthy 434
Part 5 The Control of Communism Beria and the assassination of Stalin 454
Lavrenti Pavlovich Beria..455
The struggle for power and control of communist parties and communist countries..467
The Bulgarian crisis...477
Failed coup in Hungary..485

Stalin's "paranoid anti-Semitism"...497
The open struggle between Stalin and Beria..501
Stalin, assassinated. Beria's coup d'état..513
Germany and the end of Beria...528

OTHER BOOKS 545

CHAPTER X

ON WORLD WAR II

PART 1
A WAR IMPOSED ON GERMANY AND THE WORLD

It is not our purpose to narrate the events of the Second World War step by step, but rather to outline key facts, often distorted or falsified by official historiography, to help us understand why it happened, who forced it, and how they acted during the conflict. It has already been seen in chapter eight that James Forrestal, who suffered a campaign that ended his life on 21 May 1949, denounced the shadow powers that wanted the war. In *The Forrestal Diaries* the first US Secretary of Defence revealed that Neville Chamberlain confessed to Joe Kennedy, ambassador to London, that world Jewry and Roosevelt, its puppet, had forced Britain into war against Germany. A war that had been publicly called for by Rabbi Stephen Wise, who as early as May 1933 had said: "I am for a holy war against Hitler. I want war!" How international Zionism moved its pawns and used the suffering of its own people to achieve its aims will be seen in the pages that follow.

In 1938 preparations for war were under way and many agents were working stealthily in the various countries to bring about its outbreak. Among them, to name but a few, were Lord Halifax, Lord Vansittart, Duff Cooper, Leo Amery, Paul Reynaud, Georges Mandel, William Bullitt and others about whom there will be occasion to write later. As for the pro-war bodies and lobbies controlled by the Shadow Powers, the most prominent, of course, were Zionism, the main stakeholder; international Freemasonry, the usual instrument; and President Roosevelt's Jewish "Brain Trust". Basically, they were all the same dogs with different collars. The English Labour Party, the French Communist Party and most of the French Socialists also served hidden interests. We have seen how Negrin, Alvarez del Vayo and company, well connected with Communism and Freemasonry, based their whole strategy of resistance in Spain on the conviction that war in Europe was only a matter of time. Thus, different forces worked for war within European countries and formed a transnational warmongering party that served interests alien to those of their nations.

The economic miracle of National Socialism

Before examining the events that triggered the greatest catastrophe ever suffered by mankind, it is worth noting Germany's remarkable recovery after the Nazis came to power, as this will help to understand why German nationalism became the worst enemy of international bankers and economic liberalism. While between 1934 and 1938 the Red dictator liquidated the Jewish agents of the October Revolution and consolidated his power through purges, Hitler, the German dictator, conceived and financed to confront Stalin and to bring about an exodus of European Jews to Palestine, also consolidated his position by implementing a series of economic, social and political measures that transformed the country in four years.

In 1933 the German economy was still in a state of collapse and the population had been enduring three decades of hunger, misery and social strife, orchestrated again and again, as we have seen, by the Communist International, which saw Germany as the key to world revolution. The war reparations had ruined the population and the nation was bankrupt. Nearly seven million Germans were out of work as a result of the Great Depression. With the arrival of the Nazis everything changed as if by magic and Germany, a country that had been deprived of colonies, became the strongest economy in Europe within four years. No wonder, then, that Hitler, the man who personified this miracle, was extraordinarily admired by the Germans. How such an impressive turnaround was achieved deserves a brief summary.

First of all, the abolition of interest slavery was one of the central points of the NSDAP's programme. The party's economic ideologue, Gottfried Feder, had envisaged the nationalisation of the Reichsbank and the big banks that lent at interest. When the Nazis came to power on 30 January 1933, Feder was appointed State Secretary for Economic Affairs and set about implementing the official economic policy of National Socialism. Hjalmar Schacht, appointed president of the Reichsbank in March 1933, not only thwarted any nationalisation initiative, but also succeeded in removing Gottfried Feder from his post and became head of the Ministry of Economic Affairs, a position he held until 19 January 1939. His opposition to the granting of a series of loans requested by the state led to his dismissal. On 15 June 1939, a law was passed which made the Reichsbank "unconditionally subordinate to the sovereignty of the state". That said, let us look at some of the achievements of the so-called "economic miracle" in a nutshell.

Labour was the basis on which National Socialism built the nation. An extensive programme of public works was launched: repair of public and private buildings, construction of bridges, canals, dykes, roads, harbour facilities, etc. One of the achievements that became world famous was the famous "Autobahn", the world's first motorway system. In this way millions of unemployed people were put to work. The big question that arises is how did the Nazis pay the workers without international credit and with the country bankrupt? What they did was to replace the gold standard with the labour standard, based on the productivity of the German worker. The cost of all projects was set at one billion units of a new national currency called Treasury Labour Certificates, which were actually one billion non-inflationary bills of exchange issued by the government to pay the workers. These Treasury Certificates were used by the workers, who spent them on goods and services, thus creating jobs for more people. The certificates circulated as money and became a de facto currency. They were renewable indefinitely and were issued as bonds, for which the government paid interest to the holders.

The economist Henry C. K. Liu refers to this form of financing as "sovereign credit", no doubt alluding to the fact that it avoided borrowing money from international usurious lenders and thus avoided any kind of debt. While millions of people in the United States and Europe were still out of work and on welfare, in Germany the problem of unemployment was solved within two years thanks to this stable, non-inflationary currency. The idea of "sovereign credit" was not new: in Chapter V we have seen that when the Rothschilds and other international bankers offered loans at 24% and 36% interest, Lincoln ordered the issuance of Treasury notes, the "greenbacks", an interest-free money that had legal use in the United States. He then called for the destruction of the government that had implemented this "evil financial policy". Lincoln was assassinated by the Jewish Freemason John Wilkes Booth.

Foreign trade was also restored through the barter system. The international economic boycott decreed by Jewish organisations all over the world included the restriction of credits to Germany; but by direct exchange of goods, it was possible to avoid having to pay for financing from international banks. In October 1938, Walter Funk, Minister of Economics, travelled to the Balkans, Turkey and Bulgaria. Before a joint German-Yugoslavian committee preparing a trade agreement, Funk declared: "We can absorb in Germany everything that Yugoslavia produces. We can send to Yugoslavia everything it needs. The prices we can offer you cannot be offered by any other country. Since we are neighbours, transport costs are minimal. As we operate on a barter system, we do not need to pay for financing from foreign banks. We don't need loans. We don't need anyone. Germany offered its products to Yugoslavia, Bulgaria and Turkey, countries which thus covered two thirds of their needs. At the same time, it received the exports of these states. This created a zone stretching from the German border to the Black Sea. All this was to the detriment of the main customer and supplier of these nations, Great Britain, which could not compete, since it was subject to the credits and insurance policies of the City banks.

But barter did not only work in Europe: Brazil, Argentina and Mexico also put it into practice. On 19 January 1939, the American newspaper *Daily*

Journal World reported that Mexico had sold $17,000,000 worth of oil to Germany through the barter system. The newspaper said: "The Nazi barter system is one of the wonders of our time. Germany exchanges its products for those of other countries without any exchange of money. It is as simple as the arrangement whereby one schoolboy exchanges with another a razor with a broken blade for a live beetle in a bottle". It is clear that this kind of operation in international transactions was against the interests of the prevailing capitalist system, based on speculation and usury. The struggle between productive capital and speculative capital had already been won by the international bankers, who could by no means allow a setback that would be a serious setback for their interests.

Another important aspect of the German miracle was the protection of farmers, which became one of the government's priorities. A healthy and robust agricultural population was a prerequisite for the nation, as the Nazis attached great importance to the traditional farming family. Many farmers were among the unemployed, having been ruined in previous years by falling prices for farm produce, excessive interest rates and foreclosures by unscrupulous, often Jewish, speculators. The National Socialist government set up the National Food Agency (Reichnährstand), a public corporation comprising all those connected with food production, processing and distribution: millers, bakers, canners, middlemen, local shopkeepers.... Its role was to regulate the food market. This National Agency guaranteed farmers a market for their products at a price that was sufficient to cover production costs and prepare the new harvest, but at the same time moderate, so that buyers could enjoy reasonable prices. This created a stable market that ensured a reliable food supply for all parties. Irregular price fluctuations, often dictated by stock exchange speculators, were thus eliminated. These measures saved the German peasantry from the catastrophic fall in world prices and prevented bankruptcies of farmers: in 1932 there were more than seven thousand, but by 1933 bankruptcies had been reduced to 1,600. In 1932 Germany had imported 4.5 billion marks worth of foodstuffs, while in 1935 it imported only 0.9 billion marks. As we know, in the Soviet paradise for which workers and peasants all over the world were fighting, in 1933 millions of farmers were being starved to death in a planned manner: "Holodomor".

National Socialism's protection of workers is also noteworthy. One of the first measures of Hitler's government was to spruce up German factories, which were provided with parks or landscaped areas, swimming pools and other amenities designed to humanise the workers' environment. The programme "Kraft durch Freude", KdF, which translates as "Strength through Joy", was based on the idea that workers should not only receive wages, but that their work should be recognised by making certain enjoyments of life available to them. KdF offered workers and their families access to culture, sport and the arts. The programme had eleven sections.

One of them, "Holidays, travel and tourism", offered trips in Germany and also abroad. In three years, eleven million workers went on recreational trips by land or sea. Initially, six large ships were available in this section, which in 1935 alone made more than 100 trips across the Atlantic. In 1936 two hundred thousand workers embarked on these tourist ships. In 1935 the architect Clemens Klotz designed the Prora spa on the island of Rügen, a monumental facility for the enjoyment of German workers. The spa, overlooking the Baltic, had a vast beach of fine white sand and 350 hectares of woods and meadows. This project received the grand prize for architecture at the 1937 International Exhibition.

The issue of housing deserves praise. In order to help young married couples, neat, sturdy houses with gardens were built, which could be bought interest-free with small monthly payments. In order to encourage births, a quarter of the mortgage was paid off with each birth. Thus, with the fourth child, a couple got their home completely free of charge. This formula obviously has nothing to do with spending twenty or thirty years paying interest to a bank in order to get a decent home. As for the old flats and houses in the most run-down suburbs or neighbourhoods, the Nazis carried out renovations and modernisations in order to dignify both the slums and the houses.

National Socialism established universal and free social security. German hospitals, equipped with state-of-the-art medical equipment, provided quality care for patients, who had the right to choose their doctor and hospital. Patients could stay in hospital for up to one year and were entitled to a financial benefit. If hospitalisation continued after this period, the allowance was lost, but patients were allowed to remain in the clinic indefinitely. As for education, it was free for all eligible applicants, regardless of family origin or circumstance. These were some of the social achievements that in a few years brought an end to the nightmare of the martyred German people.

Hitler's foreign policy steps: the Saarland and relations with Poland

The Versailles "Diktat" was the cause of all evils, so the Nazis were determined to reverse its consequences for the Germans and had declared this in their programme. Territorial claims in the west were settled in 1934. Things were much more difficult in the east. Millions of Germans had been left inside the borders of the new Poland against their will. In addition, Czechoslovakia had been created, a new country in which, apart from Czechs and Slovaks, there were populations of German, Polish, Hungarian and Romanian origin who felt no connection with a state that had never existed before.

Among those affected by the Treaty of Versailles were the Saarlanders, inhabitants of the Saarland, a part of Germany handed over to the League of Nations for fifteen years. After this time, a referendum was to be held to determine whether the people wanted to become a French department or rejoin Germany. Hardly anyone in the Saar spoke French before the war, but Clemenceau had submitted a list, according to which 150,000 French people lived there. In November 1934, two months before the consultation, Germany presented a diplomatic note to Ambassador François Poncet, proposing an amicable solution. The offer consisted of an economic treaty that would allow French industry to continue to benefit from the region's resources as it had done from 1919 to 1934. The French government foolishly turned down this opportunity and sent four divisions to the border under the pretext of preventing possible mutinies, which provoked a formal protest from Hitler.

Finally, a League of Nations force secured the plebiscite, held on 13 January 1935. Despite fifteen years of French propaganda, only 0.4% of the electorate voted in favour of union with France. 90.8 per cent of the population expressed a desire to rejoin Germany. 8.8% of voters, mostly Jews or communists, called for maintaining the status quo. On 1 May 1935 the League of Nations handed over the administration of the Saar to the German authorities and Hitler declared before the Reichstag: "Germany solemnly renounces all claims to Alsace and Lorraine; after the reintegration of the Saar, the Franco-German border can be considered as definitively drawn". In other words, Germany wanted peace with France and had no further territorial aspirations: the claims in the west were over. One day after this declaration, France and the Soviet Union signed a Mutual Assistance Treaty. On 7 January 1936 Hitler let the French Government know through his ambassador that the Reich "would regard the ratification of the Franco-Soviet Pact by the French Parliament as a hostile gesture towards Germany, and incompatible with the obligations of the Locarno Pact, the text and spirit of which France would have violated". The French Parliament ratified the Pact on 27 February 1936. In response to this ratification, Hitler ordered the remilitarisation of the Rhineland on 7 March 1936.

The Saar issue was settled by a referendum, but one of Germany's disputes in the east, Danzig, was to become the "casus belli". It is therefore necessary to focus on Polish-German relations in order to get an accurate picture of what happened. An absolutely essential book is *Der erzwungene Krieg. Die Ursachen und Urheber des 2. Weltkriegs* (*The Forced War. The Causes and Perpetrators of World War II*), published in German in 1961 by the American revisionist historian David L. Hoggan. Hoggan, of which the Institute for Historical Review published an English edition in 1989. This book, whose translation into English would be of great interest, is one of our main sources. From it comes the following historical review, which is necessary for a better understanding of the facts. Dr. Hoggan's work has as its essential sources the diplomatic documents of the Western countries, which allows us to learn about texts and attitudes that shed a new light that the official historiography is blind to. We will repeatedly refer to Professor Hoggan's work throughout these pages.

With the unification of Germany in 1871, Prussia's Polish territories became part of the new German Reich. Russia and Austria-Hungary were the other two empires that held sway over Poland, although most of the territory was under Russian control, and a pro-German Polish nationalism emerged. Wladyslaw Studnicki was the main theoretician of this trend. In contrast, there was also a pro-Russian nationalism, whose most prominent ideologue was Roman Dmowski, who before the Bolshevik Revolution had attacked Germans and Jews in the Duma. While deploring the role of Jews in communist Russia, Dmowski advocated the westward expansion of Poland at Germany's expense and with Russia's cooperation. Hoggan reproduces the words of Dmowski, who in 1931 declared: "The Jewish question is the great question of civilisation throughout the world". This Polish nationalist, like Hitler, was in favour of the total expulsion of the Jews from his country, since he considered their assimilation impossible. Less important was pro-Habsburg Polish nationalism, whose representative was Michal Bobrzynski. The genuine Polish nationalist was Josef Pilsudski, who believed in Poland as a great power. Pilsudski did not share the views of the above three and rejected their approaches. However, his background was Marxist and for a time he adhered to revolutionary socialism, until he realised that its implications clashed with his nationalism.

In August 1914 Russia offered vague promises to the Poles in order to secure their support in the war. But it was Germany that proclaimed the restoration of Polish independence on 5 November 1916. General Hans von Beseler, the governor of German-occupied Poland, after announcing the agreement, ordered a German army band to play the anthem *Poland is not yet lost*, which had its origins in the Napoleonic Wars. On 6 December 1916, a Polish Council of State was established. The allied Entente countries reacted against German policy towards Poland and in the summer of 1917 dared to offer all of Poland to Austria-Hungary, to which they proposed a separate peace if it would break its alliance with Germany. Pilsudski, who was the head of the military department of the newly formed Polish Council of State, called for the immediate formation of a Polish army. The slogan of his followers was: "Never a state without an army, never an army without Pilsudski". With Germany and Austria-Hungary unable to accede to these demands, Pilsudski resigned on 2 July 1917. Arrested, he was transferred to Magdeburg, where he was comfortably installed.

With Germany's final defeat, Pilsudski became persona non grata in Versailles. The Polish National Committee was dominated by Roman Dmowski. The Jewish question was immediately put to the Polish negotiators, who had to face the demands of American Jewish groups, which infested the US delegation. They wanted the creation of an independent Jewish state within Poland. President Wilson, in the grip of the Jewish conspirators who had put him in power, expressed sympathy for these demands and argued to his English, French and Italian colleagues that "the Jews were regarded with little hospitality in Poland". In the end, the Treaty granted the Poles most of West Prussia, with a majority German population denied a referendum; and the industrially rich Upper Silesia region, although the Poles lost the plebiscite held there afterwards. A League of Nations protectorate was created for the German town of Danzig, which became a free port for Poland, thanks to the so-called Corridor. As for the borders in eastern Poland, the Allies postponed decisions, allowing Pilsudski, who favoured eastward expansion, to pursue his own plan.

In the context of the Russian civil war, the Bolsheviks, engaged in their struggle against the Whites in the Ukraine, could not prevent Pilsudski, whom Denikin unsuccessfully appealed to for help, from preparing his forces for confrontation with the Red Army in 1919, which he defeated at the Battle of Warsaw on 16 August 1920. The Lithuanians, on the other hand, saw the Poles occupy Vilna during the war, but they reacted by seizing the German city of Memel in East Prussia, which had been placed under the protection of the League of Nations. Memel eventually became part of Lithuania between 1923 and 1939. The Russo-Polish War conferred extraordinary prestige on Pilsudski, who became the undisputed leader of the army and the nation. From 1926 onwards, however, Dmowski's leadership was called into question and he became an alternative. Dmowski's programme envisaged an intensification of nationalism, improved relations with Russia, a programme for the assimilation of the various minorities that had become part of Poland, and a plan to expel the Jews. In September 1930 Pilsudski reacted by severely purging Dmowski's followers, who were interned in concentration camps. A coalition formed around him won the November 1930 elections to the Polish Parliament (Sejm). In 1935 Josef Pilsudski died at the age of 68.

Between 1919 and 1933 there was no possibility of understanding between Poland and the Weimar Republic, whose leaders always found the situation unacceptable. The Locarno Treaties (16 October 1925) guaranteed Germany's borders with France and Belgium and facilitated some improvement in relations with these countries; but the Poles did not get any guarantees regarding their borders with Germany. In 1932 Poland, in order to ensure that Stalin would not help the Weimar Republic in the event of a conflict, signed a non-aggression pact with the Soviet Union. However, shortly before Pilsudski's death and with the Nazis in power, who always regarded Pilsudski as a statesman, Berlin and Warsaw signed another ten-year non-aggression pact on 26 January 1934, which did not, however, imply any recognition by Germany of the status quo of 1919. The Polish negotiator was Józef Beck, appointed foreign minister in 1932, a post he held until 1939. He was to be one of those mainly responsible for the erratic policy that led his country to disaster. With the Soviet Union to the east and Germany to the west, the position of the new Polish state was complicated enough. The Polish historian Olgierd Gorka warned in a lecture on 18 September 1935 that an anti-German and anti-Russian policy was tantamount to suicide. With a very graphic metaphor, Gorka then equated Poland with a canary intent on devouring two cats. This was precisely the absurdity of Polish foreign policy.

In February 1936 Józef Beck began to feel out France's position in the event of war with Hitler. He was following to some extent the teachings of Pilsudski, who had on several occasions contemplated the possibility of unleashing a preventive war against Germany. Beck believed that a victory over the Nazis could confer prestige and great advantages on his country. On the evening of 7 March 1936, hours after Hitler announced the remilitarisation of the Rhineland, the Polish minister summoned the French ambassador, Léon Noël, and bluntly confessed his warmongering attitude, announcing that Poland would attack Germany from the east if France was prepared to invade from the west. David L. Hoggan writes that in response to French Foreign Minister Pierre-Étienne Flandin's refusal to trigger another war in Europe, Beck scornfully described him as a weakling and "the saddest character". Hoggan adds that the Polish foreign minister rushed to London in an attempt to influence British attitudes, but neither King Edward VIII, whom he met, nor the Conservatives took him seriously at the time. In contrast to these delusional manoeuvres by Józef Beck, Hitler sought to promote collaboration between the two countries, so in February 1937 Göring travelled to Poland and presented a plan for closer German-Polish collaboration. He met with Marshal Smigly-Rydz, from whom he asked for certain licences in exchange for concessions from the German side. He assured him, for example, that Berlin would not demand the return of the Corridor. However, the meeting did not produce immediate results.

Danzig

Danzig, founded in the 14th century west of the mouth of the Vistula, was inhabited from the beginning by German citizens. When the decision was taken to detach it from Germany, the city was the capital of West Prussia. No one thought at the time that the Poles would ask for it at the Peace Conference. President Wilson, despite knowing that the city's inhabitants were demanding that the Weimar Republic authorities reject Danzig's separation from Germany, pushed for its separation. The Treaty of Versailles gave Danzig the status of a Free City, and a League of Nations High Commissioner became the first instance of appeal in the event of conflict with Poland. Danzig's foreign relations were delegated to Poland, and the Free City was placed under the control of Polish customs. The Poles had unrestricted use of canals, ports, railways and roads for commercial purposes. Telephone, telegraph and postal communications between Poland and the port of Danzig also remained in their hands. Residents of the city initially lost their German citizenship, but it was stipulated that adults could claim it back after two years. Dual citizenship in Danzig and Germany was forbidden. The ownership of all German and Prussian administrative facilities in the territory of Danzig passed to the League of Nations. The Danzig constitution, which replaced the Weimar constitution, was promulgated on 14 June 1922. On that date, the territory of the Free City, which had become a protectorate of the League of Nations, was inhabited by 365,000 people, only 3% of whom were Polish. The League of Nations thus administered Danzig, just as it had done with Memel until Lithuania was allowed to annex it. Annexation was also the ultimate goal of the Polish authorities.

To think that a lasting settlement between Germany and Poland would be possible without resolving the Danzig question was an illusion, since the situation of the German population in the town was a source of permanent friction. Pilsudski had been in favour of the final annexation of the town, and after his death the Polish authorities followed this line of thinking. Poland also had claims to the territory of Teschen, which had become part of Czechoslovakia. Hitler contemplated German support for this claim in order to obtain some counterpart in Danzig; however, instead of taking steps to soften his attitude towards the town, the Poles became increasingly tough. In 1936, for example, they dressed their customs officials in military uniform in order to accustom the citizens to the occupation. The Danzig government protested, but, as usual, the protests were rebuffed.

On the other hand, Polish pressure groups maintained a climate of permanent agitation, supported by press campaigns. Thus a dangerous atmosphere persisted between the Free City and Poland, which did not improve despite Berlin's efforts. Jósef Beck contributed to maintaining the tension by appointing Colonel Marjan Chodaki as Polish High Commissioner in Danzig. Chodaki, a personal friend of Beck's who was a diplomatic representative in Prague, was summoned to Warsaw in December 1936 and received direct instructions from the Foreign Minister to harden the Polish position, but not to risk provoking a conflict until he had the support of France and Britain. Chodaki adopted a provocative and belligerent attitude, as will be seen below.

Another appointment, by contrast, helped to raise expectations in Danzig. The League of Nations High Commissioner, British-born Sean Lester, had on more than one occasion irritated the German citizens of the city, and they had called for his replacement. Their complaints were finally heeded and Lester was replaced by Carl Jacob Burckhardt, an eminent Swiss historian and expert on Cardinal Richelieu and the European diplomatic tradition. On 18 February 1937 Burckhardt received an appointment to the League of Nations Security Council. A second appointment for Germany was that of Neville Henderson as Ambassador Extraordinary and Plenipotentiary in Berlin. Henderson, Chamberlain's right-hand man, was a staunch supporter of appeasement with Germany. In contrast to the conspirators who followed the line set by Lord Milner, the agent of the Morgan-Rothschild-Rhodes confederacy, the 33rd degree Freemason and Grand Warden of the United Grand Lodge of England who had financed the revolution in Russia and founded the Round Table, there was a school of thought among the Conservatives that saw Nazi Germany as a buffer against Communism. At the root of appeasement was the fear of the spread of communism in Europe through a war that would only benefit the Soviet Union, a fear that was borne out by events when in 1945 half of Europe was in the grip of communist totalitarianism. On 10 May 1937, shortly before leaving for the German capital, Henderson submitted a memorandum to the Foreign Office in which he stated the following:

> "The question of Eastern Europe is neither definitely settled nor vital to British interests, of course, the Germans are more civilised than the Slavs and, ultimately, if they can be handled, they are also potentially less dangerous to British interests - one might even say that it is not even fair to try to prevent Germany from carrying out her unity or preparing for war against the Slavs, provided the British Empire is assured that such preparations are not simultaneously directed against it."

Coincidentally or not, on the same date of 10 May 1937 *The Daily Telegraph* announced that Joseph Göbbels had expressed Germany's intention to annex Danzig in the near future. Göbbels' alleged statements were false, but the news contributed to alarm and nervousness.

In September 1937 Józef Beck instructed his ambassador in Berlin, Józef Lipski, to propose to Germany a German-Polish declaration on Danzig. It was intended that the Germans would recognise in writing the status designating Danzig as a Free City. Konstantin von Neurath, Germany's foreign minister from 1932, more adamant than Hitler on Poland, ordered the German ambassador in Warsaw, Hans-Adolf von Moltke, to tell Beck again "that Germany would not recognise the peace treaties of 1919." Von Neurath rejected Beck's proposal without even consulting the Führer because he assumed there was no other possible answer.

On 18 September Carl Jacob Burdhardt, the High Commissioner, told Hitler that he expected the role of the League of Nations to be temporary and that he was confident that the final fate of Danzig would emerge from a direct agreement between Germany and Poland. Hoggan makes clear that Hitler listened to Burckhardt's point of view without offering any plan or solution and adds: "Burckhardt surmised that Hitler did not dare raise the Danzig issue because feared it might affect the Corridor, Czechoslovakia and Austrian issues." Lipski, who knew of Hitler's desire to reach an understanding, tried to soften the German foreign minister's position and on several occasions talked with him. On 18 October 1937, Neurath told him directly, "Some day an agreement will have to be reached on the Danzig question between Poland and us, otherwise it would permanently impede German-Polish relations." Von Neurath added that the restoration of Danzig's connections with the Reich could be done with Polish economic interests in mind.

Associated with Danzig was the problem of overland access to East Prussia, whose connection had been broken. In 1935, when Germany was engaged in the motorway project, Hans-Adolf von Moltke met Beck in Warsaw and informed him that Germany was interested in building a motorway through the Polish Corridor to link East Prussia with the Reich. Beck told him he would look into it, which was the excuse for a prolonged evasion. After more than two years of waiting for a response, Moltke came to the conclusion that the Polish government's attitude was negative. The plan, which envisaged the use of Polish iron for the works, would have improved the prospects of a comprehensive agreement for all mutual interests. Von Moltke, who did not want to give up on the idea, proposed to the Foreign Ministry in October 1937 that the project be launched from Pomerania and East Prussia to the borders of the Corridor without waiting for permission to proceed with the connection.

Danzig was becoming one of the centres of international attention. On 19 November 1937, Edward Frederick Lindley Wood, Lord Halifax, who was to be the prime mover in the war, visited Hitler and the Nazi leadership at Berchtesgaden on behalf of Chamberlain. According to David L. Hoggan, whose source is the minutes of the meeting, kept in the German Foreign Office archives, Lord Halifax asked Hitler if he had plans for Danzig, to which the Führer, understandably, responded evasively. However, writes Hoggan, "Halifax made no secret of the fact that he expected German action to retake Danzig." Moreover, Lord Halifax stated at Berchtesgaden that Britain recognised that there were errors in the 1919 Paris treaties that needed to be rectified.

Although Halifax's hidden agendas are not out of the question: some researchers believe that the appeasement policy was bait to deceive Hitler, the Berchtesgaden statement would imply that in 1937 Lord Halifax supported German claims and encouraged the Nazis to take the initiative in Danzig. In any case, his true intentions were later revealed. On 21 February 1938 Chamberlain appointed him Secretary of State in the Foreign Office to replace Anthony Eden, making him the right-hand man of the Prime Minister. Charles Wood, Lord Halifax's heir, had married Ruth Alice Hannah Mary Primrose, a granddaughter of Lord Rothschild, on 25 April 1936, so that Lord Halifax, thus related to the Jewish banking dynasty, became an adviser to the bank and the family's lawyer. The historian Joaquín Bochaca considers in *The Crimes of the "Good Guys"* that his alliance with the Rothschilds explains the insidious manoeuvres of this character, who, after proposing appeasement offers to Hitler, switched to the warmongering clan. His actions will be studied in detail later, and the reader will be able to judge what responsibility he bore for the outbreak of the war.

Czechoslovakia or the impossible state

Three prominent Russophile and Germanophobic Freemasons, Masaryk, Benes and Stefanik were the driving forces behind Czechoslovakia, an explosive cocktail of peoples of diverse and historically antagonistic origins who had been part of the Austro-Hungarian Empire. Another Freemason, the French Foreign Minister, Stephen Pichon, supported the claims of his brethren and alluded to "the aspirations of the Czechoslovak people for independence within its historical borders", which was colossal nonsense, since Czechoslovakia, let alone its historical borders, had never been heard of before 1919. In 1921 there were 6,727,038 Czechs, 3,122,390 Germans, 2,010,295 Slovaks, 745,935 Hungarians, 459,346 Ruthenians, 75,656 Poles, 180,332 Jews and 238,727 foreign residents living in the new state. This jigsaw puzzle of minorities scattered across a patchwork of territories claimed by neighbouring countries constituted Czechoslovakia. Considering that Germans were the second largest ethnic group in the new state, the country could have been called the Czechoslovak Republic.

After the signing of the German-Polish Pact in 1934, a press campaign began in Poland which, long before Germany did, called for the dissolution of Czechoslovakia. The leaders of both countries agreed on this. The main conflict between the Czechs and Poles was the rich industrial region of Teschen, which was in the hands of the Polish community when Austria-Hungary concluded the armistice with the Allies. With French support, Tomas Masaryk, the pro-Russian Czech president, had succeeded in bringing the territory within the borders of the new Czechoslovakia. On 26 January 1919, the Czechs made a surprise attack on the Poles living in the Teschen area in an attempt to settle the matter by force. After the military offensive ended, the Western Allies intervened on 1 February, forcing a cease-fire and referring the parties to the solution adopted at the Peace Conference. A plebiscite was proposed, but the Czechs, who supported the USSR in the war the Poles were waging against the Soviets in 1920, cancelled it thanks again to French support. Finally, on 28 July 1920, the region was assigned to Czechoslovakia at the Spa Conference. From then on, the Poles made the recovery of Teschen by hook or by crook one of their main objectives.

Alluding to the national puzzle of Czechoslovakia, Mussolini had once referred to the new state as Czech-German-Polish-Polish-Magyar-Romanian-Romanian-Slovak. When Swedish Foreign Minister Rickard Sandler asked Józef Beck in 1937 why an agreement between Warsaw and Prague could not be reached, Beck replied that for him Czechoslovakia was an artificial creation that violated the freedom of nations such as Slovakia and Hungary. Beck stressed that the Czechs were a minority in their own state and that not a single one of the other nationalities that made up Czechoslovakia wanted to be ruled by Czechs. The Swedish minister admitted to his colleague that the Czechs obviously lacked the capacity to develop good relations with their neighbours, as the country had been created out of territorial scraps from all of them.

Hitler had more reason than anyone else to maintain a very serious and pressing attitude towards the Czechs. Even before the World War, the Bohemian Germans had had to accept that the Habsburgs would grant privileges to the Bohemian Czechs in order to dampen their nationalism and keep them appeased within the monarchy. After the creation of Czechoslovakia, the Germans had had to resign themselves to being integrated into a state with which they did not identify at all. In Bohemia, Germans made up a third of the population, yet the Czechs did not see the point of granting them any autonomy - quite the contrary. In Slovakia, on the other hand, there were more Germans than Czechs. Linguistically, the Sudeten Germans were divided into four dialect groups: Bavarians, Franconians, Saxons and Silesians. This is explained by the fact that the name Sudetes comes from a mountain range stretching from the Carpathian Mountains to the banks of the Elbe.

In the 1935 elections in Czechoslovakia, the SdP (Sudeten German Party), identified with the policies of National Socialism, won the majority of the votes of the German population and became the leading party in the country. Half a million of the 800,000 unemployed in Czechoslovakia were Sudeten Germans, and they naturally expected everything from a party that claimed the policies that were ending unemployment in Germany. In the March 1938 elections, the SdP led by Konrad Heinlein became the largest parliamentary group, with 55 deputies and 37 senators. The Slovak-majority Agrarian Party, which, like the Sudeten Party, demanded internal autonomy for the various nationalities, won 43 deputies and 33 senators, making it the second-largest force in parliament. Its chairman was the Slovak Milan Hodza.

The fact that Poland and Germany had territorial claims in Czechoslovakia could be a point of convergence if an international crisis arose around Czechoslovakia, for there were many interrelationships in the complex picture that emerged in the aftermath of the calamitous Peace Conference. Irrevocably connected with the Sudeten question was the Austrian problem at the beginning of 1938. "The Czech buffer" is the metaphor used by David L. Hoggan to refer to the importance of the Austrian problem. Hoggan to refer to the importance of Austria's status for Czechoslovakia. During the winter of 1937-1938, Hoggan writes, it became clear that "the existence of 3,500,000 wretched Sudeten Germans could be ignored neither by the Czechs, nor by Hitler, nor by the world if the Germans of Austria were to unite with Germany". Aware of the situation and the hostility of all his neighbours, Czech Foreign Minister Kamil Krofta prepared a memorandum in February 1938 explaining why his country was prepared to take pre-emptive action to prevent the union of Austria and Germany.

The Anschluss

In 1938 a series of foreign policy successes enabled Hitler to liberate ten million Germans who had been denied the right of self-determination in 1919. Alan John Percival Taylor, English historian and author of *The Origins of the Second World War,* agrees with Hoggan that the policy of peaceful territorial revision adopted by Hitler in 1938 was possible and if it did not succeed it was due to the radicalism of his opponents. The first of these successes was the Anschluss (union, connection) with Austria. The detractors of this union omit that already on 4 March 1919 the Austrian Constituent Assembly had declared itself by a very large majority in favour of the Anschluss and that the third article of the Constitution recognised that "Austria was a German state".

Kurt Schuschnigg had been Austria's chancellor-dictator since 29 June 1934. His nationalist dictatorship prevented any action advocating union with Germany. Not for nothing had he declared on 29 November 1936: "The national front has three enemies: Communism, defeatism and National Socialism. Consequently, the Austrian Nazis must be regarded as the sworn enemies of the Government and the people". At the beginning of 1938 the situation was extremely tense and civil war was looming on the scene. In February 1938 Franz von Papen, the German ambassador in Vienna, arranged a meeting between Hitler and Schuschnigg in Berchtesgaden. On instructions from the Führer, Papen informed the Austrian Chancellor that German military personnel would attend the meeting, so on 12 February 1938 Schuschnigg showed up accompanied by Foreign Minister Guido Schmidt and Austrian officers.

During the interview Schuschnigg undertook to stop harassing the Austrian National Socialists and to form a pro-German government, of which the Nazi Arthur Seyss-Inquart would be its Minister of the Interior. He also agreed to allow Hitler to broadcast a radio message to the Austrians in exchange for the opportunity to address the Germans himself. As soon as he returned to Austria, Schuschnigg regretted his pact with Hitler and began to look for ways to renege on it. Finally, on 9 March he announced in Innsbruck that in four days, i.e. on 13 March, he would hold a plebiscite to find out whether the people wanted Austrian independence or the Anschluss. The irregularities of the referendum, apart from the few days between the call and the holding of the referendum, were glaring: the anonymity of the voters was not respected; the ballots in favour of union with Germany would not be provided by the government, but had to be provided by the citizens themselves and could be invalidated if they did not meet strict requirements; only members of Schuschnigg's Patriotic Front would be present at the polling stations; the counting, annulment and validation of votes offered no guarantee of impartiality; the government press, to further coerce the population, warned that a vote in favour of the Anschluss would be considered treason.

Mussolini, who had hitherto supported Schuschnigg, warned the Austrian Chancellor of the risks of the plan. Hitler turned to the League of Nations and asked it to monitor the referendum. After twenty years of intervention in the affairs of the world, the League of Nations replied that it could not interfere in Austria's internal affairs. At 10:00 a.m. on 11 March Seyss-Inquart informed Schuschnigg that he must immediately renounce the fraudulent plebiscite and call for a legal one with a secret ballot and an updated electoral roll within three to four weeks. The National Socialist leader sternly warned the Chancellor that the German army would occupy Austria if he did not accede to the request. In the absence of a reply, a new ultimatum was issued: Schuschnigg was to cede the chancellorship to Seyss-Inquart. The crisis was at its peak. The main danger for Germany was that Italy, the only major European power bordering Austria, would intervene. British diplomats in Vienna supported Schuschnigg, and Lord Halifax, who had been appointed Foreign Secretary on 21 February, did all he could to launch Italy against Germany. In London on 10 March Lord Halifax had warned Joachim von Ribbentrop, who had been the new German Foreign Minister since 4 February, of "possible consequences" if Hitler used force in Central Europe. The decisive event occurred, however, at 10:25 a.m. on 11 March: while awaiting a reply from Schuschnigg to Germany's request, Mussolini contacted Hitler and announced that he accepted the Anschluss.

Convinced that after Italian support there would be no foreign intervention, Hitler gave the order. At six o'clock on the morning of 12 March, German troops under the command of General Fedor von Bock crossed the border. The Austrian people were moved and greeted the soldiers with flowers. Those who spoke out against the union were left without arguments in the face of the enthusiasm and joy of the people,. Hitler entered his homeland to the cheers of the crowd. This triumph would never have been possible without Mussolini's renunciation of his former sphere of influence. The Führer recognised this, and on 13 March 1938 sent a telegram from Austria to the Duce with these words: "Mussolini, I will never forget this from you!" For his part Halifax, who three days earlier had tried to intimidate Ribbentrop, faced with the evidence that France remained immobile with an internal crisis and that Italy had renounced any action, opted to maintain a friendly attitude, which was greeted with jubilation by the Nazi leaders, who again and again declared their desire for understanding with Britain. Halifax's double-dealing was already beginning to show, but the Nazi leaders preferred not to see it. Ribbentrop then remarked to Göring,

"Chamberlain seriously contemplates an understanding." The latter replied, "I am convinced that Halifax is also a reasonable man."

Through a simultaneous referendum on 10 April 1938, Austrians and Germans were consulted by Hitler on whether or not they wanted the Anschluss. Germany informed the League of Nations, France, Britain and Italy of the plebiscites and invited observers to monitor the democratic legitimacy of the process; but the offer was not accepted. However, the most important international agencies sent their correspondents to report on the events. The final result in Austria was 4,443,208 votes in favour of union with Germany and 11,807 against. In other words, 99.73% of the population voted in favour of linking the two nations. The turnout was 99.71%. In Germany the results were very similar: 99.55% of the citizens went to the polls and 99.02% of them were in favour of the union of their country with Austria. In terms of turnout and political consensus, these figures show that the Anschluss of Germany and Austria is an event without equal in history.

The consequences of the Anschluss on European politics were predictable and were not long in coming. Curiously, on 10 April 1938 Edouard Daladier became Prime Minister of France. The fall of Léon Blum and the Popular Front came despite the efforts of Winston Churchill and Henry Morgenthau, who opposed Chamberlain's policy of appeasement. Both wanted to rely on France to bring about a change in London's policy, but with Daladier this would be more difficult, as the new prime minister favoured appeasement with Germany. The new foreign minister, Georges Bonnet, had served until 1937 as ambassador to the United States and was one of the leading advocates of the moderate tendency, and was therefore in favour of seeking peace through a permanent policy of appeasement with Hitler. Bonnet, who had the support of many of the Cabinet ministers and was encouraged by important French economic groups, had great influence over Daladier.

Bonnet left France towards the end of the war and settled in Geneva. The fact that many prominent politicians were arrested and imprisoned in his homeland for no apparent reason advised Bonnet not to return to France, where the communists proceeded with a severe purge that liquidated 100,000 French citizens. A Parliamentary Committee was set up in France in 1946 to investigate the causes and events of World War II. Bonnet did not return until he received assurances that he would not be arrested. The former foreign minister testified in 1951 before the Committee and had to defend himself against accusations that he was a fanatical supporter of the Germans. Before testifying before the Parliamentary Committee, Bonnet wrote a memoir in which he made many interesting points. Among other things, he expressed his conviction that a lasting Anglo-German settlement was possible if the British had been sincere and genuinely wanted it. A view shared by Hugh Wilson, the US Ambassador in Berlin, who in February 1938 sent Washington a report by an Embassy expert, which concluded: "An Anglo-

German understanding is the first objective of Hitler's diplomacy in 1938, as it was in 1934, or in 1924, when he wrote *Mein Kampf*".

After the Anschluss, of course, turmoil and jubilation broke out in the Sudetenland, which came to the forefront of the political scene. The Czechs sent Jan Masaryk to London, who returned to Prague on 16 March 1938. David L. Hoggan writes that in his report Masaryk claimed "that the British tended to regard an Anglo-German war as inevitable, but that it was evident that they did not contemplate such a conflict in 1938." On 31 March the German legation in Prague informed Berlin that Konrad Heinlein, the leader of the Sudeten German Party (SdP), pleaded that propaganda to encourage the Sudeten people be curtailed because they were already sufficiently aroused. In collaboration with Ribbentrop and Ernst Eisenlohr, the German Minister for Czechoslovakia, Heinlein helped draft the famous Karlsbad Decree, which set out the demands for Sudeten autonomy.

In a speech by Heinlein on 24 April, the demands of the document were made public. The Czech Foreign Minister, Kamille Krofta, again sent Jan Masaryk to London with the task of asking for military aid to confront the Germans. On 3 May 1938, Masaryk again reported in writing that Lord Halifax had not guaranteed British intervention. However, on 21 May the Foreign Secretary sent instructions to Sir Neville Henderson, the British Ambassador in Berlin, to hint to the Germans that the British "might" fight if the Germans entered Czechoslovakia. Henderson was instructed to add that there was the possibility of French intervention and that "Her Majesty's Government could not guarantee that they would not be forced by circumstances to become involved as well." Henderson reported days later that the British military had inspected the German-Czech border and had detected no German troop concentrations.

The Zionists and the Evian Conference

In the midst of the turmoil in Europe over the union of Austria and Germany and following the electoral success of the Sudetenland Party (SdP) in Czechoslovakia, the Evian Conference (France) was held from 6 to 15 July 1938. Its initiator was President Roosevelt, who was concerned that Jews emigrating from their homeland should be able to transfer their belongings to the host countries. The idea was that the Haavara Agreement, signed on 6 August 1933 between the Nazis and the Zionists, could be extended to other countries. Delegates from 31 countries attended the conference. Germany sent an observer who confirmed that Germany wanted to encourage the emigration of German Jews and was willing to transfer their globally assessed assets. Germany offered 3 billion marks, which could be given to the Red Cross or the League of Nations, which would divide the sum among the countries interested in receiving them.

It has been seen above that while Talmudist Jews all over the world had declared war on Germany in 1933, the Zionists collaborated closely with the Nazis. It is understandable, then, that the World Zionist Organisation refused to participate in the Conference, since it was not at all concerned about the possible suffering of European Jews, but quite the opposite: for its purposes the danger was that they would be comfortably resettled in Europe or the United States and not emigrate to Palestine. Douglas Reed quotes in *The Controversy of Zion* a few sentences by Stephen Wise, which show that the rabbi was swimming between two waters. In 1949 Wise acknowledged that before the war they feared "that their Jewish brethren in Germany might be inclined to accept a peace settlement which would mitigate or ameliorate their ills..., that the Nazis might decide to avoid some of the evil consequences of their regime by palliative measures which might disarm the world-wide outcry." In other words, instead of welcoming policies that would spare their co-religionists afflictions, the Talmudist and Zionist leaders wanted the persecution to continue. In 1934, in the context of the World Jewish Conference, Rabbi Wise was quoted as saying: 'To die at the hands of the Nazis is cruel; to survive by their grace would be ten times worse. We will survive Nazism unless we commit the inexplicable sin of making pacts with it in order to save a few Jewish victims". In 1936 Wise insisted on the same ideas: "Without a second thought, we rejected with contempt any proposal that would guarantee the safety of a few Jews in exchange for the shame of all Jews."

In reality, what Wise, Baruch, Brandeis, Untermayer and company really rejected was the opposite, i.e. the security of the majority of Jews in exchange for giving up the interests of the few. In *The Hidden History of Zionism*, the Jewish anti-Zionist author Ralph Schönman denounces Rabbi Wise, who, as leader of the American Jewish Congress, wrote a letter in 1938 opposing any change in US immigration laws that might facilitate a haven for Jews: "It may interest you to know," the text quoted by Schönman said, "that a few weeks ago representatives of the leading Jewish organisations met at a conference.... It was decided that no Jewish organisation would, at this time, sponsor a law that would modify the immigration laws in any way.

At the beginning of 1938, in defiance of all the campaigns describing Germany as a hell for Jews as a result of the Nuremberg Laws, doctors and dentists of Jewish origin were participating in a compulsory health insurance programme (Ortskranken-kassen), which guaranteed them a good number of patients. Hugh Wilson, the American ambassador to Berlin, informed Secretary of State Cordell Hull that in 1938, ten percent of the lawyers in Germany were Jewish, even though only one percent of the population was Jewish. Roosevelt, in his zeal to defend Jewish interests, opposed a German law of 30 March 1938 that deprived the Jewish church of the right to collect taxes paid by citizens, a prerogative it had hitherto shared with the Protestant and Catholic churches. In practice, the situation created by the new German law was similar to that in Great Britain, where taxes went to the Anglican Church and Jewish synagogues received nothing. On 10 May 1938, Ambassador Wilson warned that the State Department's continued protests and accusations against Germany were not doing any good.

Objectively speaking, it is incomprehensible that the president of a Christian country would object to a sovereign nation depriving Judaism of taxation. Roosevelt, so demanding of respect for Jewish rights in Germany, had had no problem in 1933 with recognising the USSR, a country where atheistic communists had savaged Russian Christians and dynamited churches and cathedrals. At a time when Roosevelt was worrying about German synagogue revenues, religious persecution in Spain had been going on for years: nearly 8,000 Catholic priests had been murdered and thousands of church buildings had been burned or destroyed without Roosevelt expressing the slightest condemnation.

While a barrage of public accusations continued to fall on Germany, not a word was heard about Poland's hostility towards its Jews, a country which in December 1937 had asked Yvon Delbos, the French Foreign Minister, "whether he would agree that all Polish Jews should emigrate to Madagascar". On 14 March 1938 Summer Welles, the American Under-Secretary of State, privately complained to the Polish ambassador to the United States, Jerzy Potocki, about the treatment of Jews in Poland. Potocki knew that anti-Jewish policies in his country were harsher than those in Germany, yet he responded without shrinking from the fact that "the Jewish question in Poland was a real problem". In April 1938, Colonel Beck, the foreign minister, decided to withdraw Polish citizenship and not to renew the passports of all Polish Jews living abroad. Many of them were in Germany, and the German authorities were quick to announce that they would not tolerate Jews without valid passports staying in Germany. The fact was that as long as their Polish papers had not expired, these Jews were protected from Hitler's racial laws, so they could legally leave Germany and go to a country other than Poland. Following Colonel Beck's decision, a flood of Polish Jews entered France from Germany before their passports expired.

The Evian Conference was indeed a shattering spectacle, for not only did it show once again that the Zionists' only concern was to achieve their state in Palestine, but it also demonstrated the hypocrisy of countries such as Britain, which sought to charge £1,000 cash for every Jew expelled from Germany. The 3 billion marks offered by Germany to take the Jews was equivalent to about a thousand dollars a head at the time, which was a considerable sum. Had Germany accepted the amount demanded by the British, the total amount would have been 17 billion marks. In the absence of the World Zionist Organisation, the Zionists were represented at the Conference by the Revisionist Zionist Organisation, which demanded as the only possible solution the admission of 200,000 Jews into Palestine, which was unacceptable to Chamberlain's Conservative government, which since the Great Arab Revolt of 1936 had been under continuous pressure from the Palestinians in protest at illegal Jewish immigration. After nine days of fruitless discussions it emerged that, with the exception of the Dominican Republic, no country was willing to extend its immigration quotas for Jewish refugees, which, apart from pleasing the Zionists, allowed Chaim Weizmann, Israel's future first president, to make a pained statement in which he once again portrayed the Jews as poor victims and eternal victims: 'The world seems to be divided into two parts,' he told the *Guardian* journalist. One where Jews cannot live and the other where they cannot enter".

Before the end of the year, on 7 December 1938, David Ben Gurion, prime minister of the Zionist state in 1948, spoke much more clearly and with less hypocrisy to the Zionist leaders of the Mapai (Labour Party). All the fanaticism of the Zionist movement is reflected in this sentence: "If I knew that it was possible to save all the children in Germany by bringing them to England and only half of them by transporting them to Israel, I would choose the second solution". These words leave no room for doubt: a year before the outbreak of war, Zionism was prepared to sacrifice part of its own people to achieve the goal of a racist Jewish state in Palestine.

As will be seen throughout these pages, the promoter of the Evian Conference, Franklin D. Roosevelt, Honorary Grand Master of the International Order of Molay, was the catalyst for the war desired by Zionism. He and Lord Halifax, who was also a Freemason, were the two essential engines used by the Occult Power to set the disaster in motion. On 3 January 1936 Roosevelt had already accused Japan, Germany and Italy of militarism in an address to Congress. On 25 November of the same year Japan responded by signing the Anti-Komintern Pact with Germany. On 5 October 1937, the US President delivered the famous "Quarantine Speech", in which he threatened the three nations with economic reprisals. The aim was to quarantine the three countries and "preserve the human community from contagion". According to Roosevelt, Germany, Japan and Italy were "destroying the whole international order and all fairness to the 88% of the world's citizens who love peace, security and freedom. Italy, which for no apparent reason was included among the "stinking states", acceded on 6 November 1937 to the Anti-Komintern Pact, which gave birth to the "Axis" Berlin, Rome, Tokyo. Thus, in the guise of this moral superiority, Roosevelt called together in Evian the countries supposedly in favour of justice and peace in the world.

The road to Munich

As soon as the Evian Conference was over, at which, as we have seen, the Zionists fought at all costs to ensure that the right of asylum could be offered to the Jews, the Sudetenland of Czechoslovakia again came to the forefront of international attention. On 20 July 1938 Lord Halifax informed the French government that a mission headed by Lord Runciman would travel to Czechoslovakia. The announcement was made official on 26 July. After the Sudeten electoral victory in the March elections, Edvard Benes had shown complete intransigence to Konrad Heinlein's demands for internal autonomy, and the situation had rapidly deteriorated. In the face of Benes' threats to arrest the Sudeten leader,, the continuing unrest turned into a full-blown riot. It was in this context that the British government imposed, "nolens volens", the dispatch of a fact-finding and, eventually, arbitration mission, which was not at all to Benes' liking.

On 3 August Walter Runciman arrived in Prague, but the ill will of the President of the Republic forced him to interrupt his work and leave the country on 10 September. By then, the Sudeten Germans had already moved from demanding autonomy to demanding incorporation into the Reich. On 21 September, Lord Runciman delivered his mission report to Downing Street. In *Les causes cachées de la 2éme Guerre Mondial*, a special issue of *Lectures Françaises* edited by Henry Coston, Jacques Bordiot reproduces in an extensive article some passages of the report, in which Runciman considered the Sudeten complaints justified and denounced the absurd attitude of the Czech government for not taking any action:

> "It has become absolutely clear to me that these border districts between Czechoslovakia and Germany, where the Sudeten population is in a large majority, must immediately obtain the right of autonomy. If a concession is unavoidable, and I believe that this one is, it had better happen quickly and without delay. There is a real danger, and even a danger of civil war, in the continuation of a state of uncertainty. Consequently, there are very powerful reasons for a policy of immediate and forceful action. Any plebiscite or referendum would, I believe, be a mere formality as far as these German-dominated areas are concerned. A large majority of their inhabitants wish to merge with Germany. The inevitable delays which a plebiscite would entail would only excite popular feelings, with very dangerous consequences.
> I therefore consider that these border districts should be transferred immediately from Czechoslovakia to Germany, and, furthermore, that measures for a peaceful transfer, including regulations for the protection of the population during the period of transfer, should be taken at once by agreement between the two governments...".

By the time Lord Runciman submitted this report, the crisis was already at its height. On 12 September Hitler, in response to a defiant speech by Benes two days earlier, denounced in Nuremberg the policies of the Czech Government and promised the Sudeten people that he was ready to take up arms to help them. As for France, which because of its commitment to Czechoslovakia might be tempted to intervene, Hitler recalled that for the sake of Franco-German friendship he had given up Alsace and Lorraine, including the former German city of Strasbourg, so that there was no dispute between the two countries. A few hours after the Führer's speech, all the Sudeten territories were in revolt against the Prague government. On the 13th it was reported that violent clashes between Czechs and Germans had taken place during the night, resulting in 25 dead and about 100 wounded. On 14 September the British premier requested an interview with Hitler, who received him in Berchtesgaden the next day. Chamberlain then offered to hold a plebiscite. This position was supported by Mussolini on the 17th in a speech in which he said: "In consideration of the problem which is agitating Europe at this moment, the solution consists of a single word: a plebiscite for all the nationalities which ask for it, for the nationalities which were coerced into what was intended to be Greater Czechoslovakia".

Neither Hungary nor Poland could miss the opportunity to make their territorial claims in Czechoslovakia known. As soon as they heard of the meeting between Chamberlain and Hitler in Berchtesgaden, they sensed possible British complicity in a future partition of the country, and both approached the British on 16 September to ask for British support for their aspirations. The British ambassador in Warsaw, Sir Howard Kennard, informed London that the Polish government was preparing a note calling for self-determination for the Polish Teschen minority in Czechoslovakia. Clearly, acceptance of a plebiscite in the Sudeten region would lead to the acceptance of others: Benes feared above all that Slovaks and Ruthenians would take advantage of this to secede, which would mean the ultimate breakdown of the artificial state.

The World Jewish Congress, as soon as it learned of the meeting between Hitler and Chamberlain in Berchtesgaden on the 15th, hastened to send to the British Prime Minister a resolution voted on the 18th, which was published on 19 September 1938 in the London *Jewish Chronicle*. Its text was as follows:

> "It is our duty to share with you the growing anxiety experienced by millions of Jews in the face of Germany's attempts to acquire new territories inhabited by Jews. The Jews of the whole world have not forgotten the inhuman treatment inflicted on the Jews of the Saar and of Austria. The Executive Council of the World Jewish Congress therefore begs you not to accept any agreement which does not fully safeguard the rights of the Jews."

On the same day, 18 September, the head of the French government, Édouard Daladier, and Georges Bonnet, his foreign minister, travelled together to London and reached the following agreement with the British:

> "All districts in the Sudetenland with a German majority of more than 50% of the population will be returned to the Reich without popular

consultation. An international commission in which there will be a representative of the Czechoslovak state will verify all borders and will be responsible for the evacuation and transfer of the populations. The British government would agree, like France, to give its guarantee for the new Czechoslovak borders."

Also on 18 September Julius Lukasiewicz, the Polish ambassador in Paris, had presented a note to Bonnet "categorically demanding that if a plebiscite were to be organised for the German minority in Czechoslovakia, a plebiscite for the Polish minority should be agreed at the same time". Once the Franco-British agreement was known, the Polish ambassador directly demanded the return of the Teschen district to Poland on the 20th. On the same day, Hungary informed France that it supported Poland's actions and made the same demands for Ruthenia. In these circumstances, on 21 September Prague gave its assent to the Franco-British agreement; but at 10.30 p.m. on the 23rd, on the advice of Georges Mandel[1], the French Minister of Colonies, whose real name was Jeroboam Rothschild and who was the natural son of a Rothschild, Benes decreed a general mobilisation in Czechoslovakia.

On Thursday 22 Chamberlain travelled to Godesberg to present the Franco-British plan to the Germans. The idea of an international commission as it had been put forward in London by the French and British did not please Hitler, for he believed that it would support the Czechs in fixing the new borders. Hitler proposed the immediate occupation of the Sudeten territory and only accepted a plebiscite in districts where there was doubt about the sentiment of the population. In his article "De l'Affaire des Sudetes aux Accords de Munich", published in the special issue of *Lectures Françaises* mentioned above, Jacques Bordiot writes that Chamberlain protested strongly and retired to his hotel, where he spent the whole of the 23rd and refused to meet Hitler again. On the 24th, after a passionate discussion, Hitler presented the British Premier with a Memorandum accompanied by a letter specifying the regions to be abandoned by the Czechs within forty-eight hours and those to be submitted to a plebiscite.

While they were meeting, a telegram reached Godesberg announcing that the Czech Government had decreed general mobilisation. Although they

---

[1] Georges Mandel's real name was supposedly Jeroboam Rothschild, although some sources give the name Louis George Rothschild. Mandel was to be appointed Minister of the Interior by Paul Reynaud, who replaced Daladier as Prime Minister on 21 March 1940. Both worked feverishly to bring about the outbreak of war. When Winston Churchill, representing the warmongering clan in London, learned of the Franco-British plan, he rushed to Paris to meet with Mandel and Reynaud to draw up an alternative plan. Although not officially considered to be related to the bankers, Georges Mandel, nicknamed "the ruthless Jew" by his detractors, worked for them and was in their orbit, living in luxury and undisguised ostentation.

both feigned astonishment, the news came as no surprise, since Chamberlain knew of it and had given his approval the day before, while Hitler was also aware of it through his espionage services, and also knew that the French Council of Ministers had decided to call up a million reservists. In *Les responsables de la Seconde Guerre Mondiale*, Paul Rassinier transcribes the Führer's words to Chamberlain: "Despite this unheard-of provocation, I stand by my proposal not to take any action against Czechoslovakia during the negotiations, or at least, Mr Chamberlain, for as long as you are on German territory". Chamberlain undertook to deliver the Memorandum to Benes, and Hitler extended the deadline for evacuation to 1 October.

Meanwhile, Lord Halifax's disloyalty to his prime minister began to show. Andrew Roberts, author of *The Holy Fox. A Life of Lord Halifax*, a biography that resembles a panegyric, for in it vileness becomes virtue and duplicity becomes shrewdness, writes that while Chamberlain sought agreement, Halifax, who had remained in London, received an avalanche of "letters, calls and visits from old friends whose opinions he respected, such as George Lloyd, Leo Amery, Oliver Stanley". The names are significant enough: Lloyd George had already been used by Zionism during the First World War; Leo Amery was the secret Zionist Jew who had drafted the Balfour Declaration; Oliver Stanley was to be appointed Secretary of War in January 1940. All called on him to make no further concessions to Germany. In other words, Halifax had become the politician on whom the warmongers pinned their hopes.

After receiving Hitler's Memorandum, Prime Minister Chamberlain returned to London on 24 September. At the Cabinet meeting on the 25th, Chamberlain saw for himself that his Foreign Secretary not only did not support him, but was openly in favour of war as a means of overthrowing Hitler. Overnight Halifax had changed his mind. Chamberlain sent him a pencilled note that amounted almost to a threat of resignation. It is reproduced below from Roberts' work:

> "Your complete change of viewpoint since I saw you last night is a terrible shock to me, but of course you must form your own opinion.
> It remains to be seen what the French say.
> If they say 'they will go in', I don't think I could accept responsibility for the decision.
> But I don't want to anticipate what has not yet emerged. N. C. (Neville Chamberlain)

Halifax responded to these words with another note of reply in which he wrote the following: "I feel like a brute - but I was up all night, tormenting myself, and I was unable to come to any other conclusion at this time on the matter of coercing Czechoslovakia. E. (Edward). Chamberlain replied on another underwhelming note, not without some bitterness: "Conclusions at night are seldom reached with the proper perspective. N. C."

The allusion to France's position in Chamberlain's note was relevant because during the Government's deliberations Halifax had said that if France decided to support the Bene" government, Britain should support it. Halifax maintained this position despite the fact that only a day or two earlier he had received a telegram from his ambassador in Paris, Eric Phipps, in which Phipps urged the Foreign Office minister not to support the "small but noisy and corrupt war party" in France. In the same telegram, also quoted by Andrew Roberts, the ambassador said: "The best of France is against the war at almost any price".

On 26 September Chamberlain informed Hitler in a personal letter hand-delivered in Berlin by Sir Horace Wilson that the Czech Government rejected the Memorandum. Chamberlain invited him to agree to continue negotiations without recourse to force and stated: "In the event of France being drawn into hostilities with Germany in execution of the obligations arising from the decrees, the United Kingdom would feel obliged to come to her assistance.

Simultaneously, the Poles were playing the cards of their own game. On 21 September Poland announced that it would take measures to ensure the welfare of the Poles in Czechoslovakia. Bonnet, the French foreign minister, then suspected that Beck had made a deal with Hitler and wanted to clarify this. On 24 September the French ambassador to Poland, Léon Noël, was received in Warsaw by Marshal Edward Smigly-Rydz, who, on Beck's instructions, assured him that Poland had no agreement with Germany on Czechoslovakia, confirmed that its aspirations were limited to the Teschen area, and announced that his troops would enter Teschen if the Czechs did not accept Polish claims. Bonnet was quick to press President Benes to make concessions to the Poles.

David L. Hoggan reports a letter from Benes to Beck, delivered in Warsaw on 26 September 1938, in which he "agreed in principle" to cede Teschen to Poland if the Poles supported Czechoslovakia in a war against Germany. According to Hoggan, the Polish Foreign Minister declared indignantly that Benes' "agreement in principle" was not worth the paper it was written on; however, since Poland was acting in contact with the French, he decided to make an effort to reach agreement with the Czechs along the lines proposed by Bonnet. Beck informed Benes that if they returned Teschen to Poland without delay, they could count on Polish assistance against Germany, provided that France maintained its obligations to the Czechs. President Benes, who was insincere in his offer to Poland, made the flimsy excuse that the railway network in Teschen territory was central to his operational plans against Germany, and insisted that Teschen could not be handed over until Germany had been defeated in the war. Beck immediately broke off the negotiations.

Chapter Eight has already introduced William C. Bullit, the American Ambassador to Paris, whose maternal grandfather was the Jew Jonathan

Horowitz. It will be seen below that Bullit, a close friend of Roosevelt's, with whom he conversed daily, was an instrument of those behind the scenes who were pushing for war. It is interesting now to note an interview he had on 25 September 1938 with the Polish ambassador in Paris. Lukasiewicz told him that the Polish government had changed its mind about the crisis and that the war would take place. The Polish ambassador revealed to Bullit that if Germany moved against the Czechs, Poland, in addition to Teschen, would invade Slovakia. The conversation with Bullit shows how wrong the Polish leadership was in its analysis and forecast of events. Lukasiewicz posed the conflict as a religious war between fascism and Bolshevism and pointed to Benes as an agent of Moscow. He noted that the first objective would be to establish a common front with friendly Hungary. Hoggan writes: "The Polish diplomat believed that a Russian attack on Poland would follow this move, but assured that Poland was not afraid. He predicted that within three months Russia would be defeated by Germany and Poland and insisted that the Soviet Union was a hell of warring factions. Bullit accused Poland of betraying France, but Lukasiewicz denied it. He said that Poland would not make war on France, but that if France, Britain, and the United States supported the Czechs, the Western powers would be the tools of Bolshevism." It must be considered that both the leaders of Poland and Germany hated the communist system and what it meant. If Britain had not torpedoed German attempts to establish with the Poles a common front against the Bolsheviks, a solution involving peace between the two nations and a common opposition to the Soviet Union would have been reached, as Lukasiewicz envisaged.

Bonnet's efforts to reach an agreement between the Czechs and Poles failed. Benes, who on 21 September had shown himself resigned to ceding territory to Germany, was unwilling to hand over Teschen to the Poles. On 28 September, the most pessimistic forecasts were about to come true. At 11.30 a.m. Chamberlain contacted Mussolini and asked him to try to do something. While François-Poncet, the French ambassador in Berlin, made a new attempt and held an interview with Hitler, the German Chancellor interrupted the conversation with the French diplomat to receive an urgent communication from the Italian ambassador, Attolico, who asked him on behalf of the Duce to postpone the general mobilisation for 24 hours. At 3.15 p.m. Neville Henderson, the British Ambassador, telephoned London to announce that Hitler wished to invite Chamberlain, Daladier and Mussolini to Munich the following day to discuss a peaceful solution to the Czech problem. The British Prime Minister received the news in the House of Commons, where he had made a highly charged speech on the imminent danger of war. In announcing Hitler's invitation and his decision to accept it, he received one of the loudest ovations in the history of the British Parliament. The whole world received the news with a sense of relief and hope. No one, except the usual regulars, wanted war. The citizens of Munich, enthused by the desire for peace, greeted the European leaders with euphoria when they arrived to negotiate on 29 September.

The four protagonists of the Munich meeting sought to avoid war and achieved a temporary peace. The conference began at 1 p.m. and ended at 1.30 a.m. The Czech representatives in Munich were informed of the proceedings but were not allowed to take part in the deliberations. The Czech representatives in Munich were informed of the progress of the talks, but were not allowed to take part in the deliberations. Neither Poles nor Hungarians were present in Bavaria. Mussolini's moderating role was crucial, and an agreement was eventually reached on the basis of a draft submitted by the Italian delegates. On some points the conditions demanded by Hitler at Godesberg were improved. The date set for the occupation of the Sudeten German territories was 10 October. In some districts (where the Germans were to gain a majority) a plebiscite was to be held. The new border was to be determined by an international commission that included a Czech and a German representative. France and Great Britain offered to guarantee the new borders against any unprovoked aggression. The same powers guaranteed Czechoslovakia a settlement of the problem of the Polish and Hungarian minorities. The agreement stipulated that if a solution had not been found for these regions within three months, a new meeting of heads of government would be held.

As early as the following day, 30 September, a number of political consequences followed. Chamberlain proposed a private meeting with Hitler. It took place in the Chancellor's flat in Prinzregentenstrasse. Only Paul Schmidt, Hitler's interpreter, was with the two leaders, who discussed the general situation in Europe. In his book *Temoin sur la scène diplomatique* (*Witness on the Diplomatic Stage*) Schmidt records excerpts from this interview, some of which are commented on by David L. Hoggan. Chamberlain said he hoped there would be no air strikes on women and children if the Czechs resisted. Hoggan, cannot help but comment on Chamberlain's concern: "This was ironic when one considers that Chamberlain knew that the British Air Force, in contrast to the German strategy of tactical air support to ground forces, was basing its strategy in a future war on concentrated air attacks on civilian centres." Hitler assured that he was completely opposed to such attacks and that Germany would never employ them except in case of retaliation. As the conversation ended, Chamberlain asked Hitler if he would sign a declaration of Anglo-German friendship, which was presented to him in English. This is the text of the agreement:

> "We, the German Führer and Chancellor and the British Prime Minister, have held an additional meeting today and have agreed to recognise that the question of Anglo-German relations is of the greatest importance for both countries and for Europe.

We look upon the agreement signed last night and the Anglo-German naval agreement as a symbol of the desire of our two peoples never again to go to war against each other.
We are determined that the method of consultation shall be the method adopted in dealing with matters which may concern our two peoples, and we are determined to continue our efforts to settle possible causes of differences and thus to contribute to securing peace in Europe".

This important agreement, which was accepted by Hitler without reservation, should have become the pillar for the preservation of peace in Europe and for the defence of the Continent against communism.

Another consequence of the Munich Pact, also on the 30th, was Poland's ultimatum to Czechoslovakia. In the evening, Józef Beck summoned the German ambassador in Warsaw, Hans-Adolf von Moltke, to tell him that he had just sent an ultimatum to the Czechs. He wanted to know whether Germany would maintain a benevolent attitude in the event of a Czech-Polish war. He added that he wanted German support in case the Soviet Union attacked Poland. Beck demanded that Prague surrender the town of Teschen and its district by noon on Sunday, 2 October. He also demanded the surrender of the rest of the territory claimed by Poland within ten days. Beck warned that if the Czech note of agreement was not received by noon on 1 October, "Poland would not be responsible for the consequences". The Czechs, whose President Bene" was to resign on 5 October to go into exile in London, were quick to capitulate before the deadline. The new president of the Republic, Emil Hácha, simply stated that the Munich signatory powers would not intervene despite the brutality of the approach and that the Poles would not seek his cover. Only France sent a demarche to Warsaw protesting the Polish ultimatum. Germany, for its part, offered Poland the protection it wanted in the event of a Soviet attack. Czechoslovakia's unviability was becoming increasingly evident, and it was clear to all that it would only survive as long as the Slovaks did not decide to secede from the Czechs.

On 30 September Daladier and Bonnet landed at Le Bourget airport, where they were greeted by an enthusiastic crowd. The crowd, spontaneously decked out and in tune with the majority of European peoples who rejected another war, took to the streets along the route to Paris and demonstrated their joy and gratitude to the politicians who had preserved peace for France. In his *Memoirs* Winston Churchill describes those who applauded Chamberlain and Daladier as "vociferous mobs". Perhaps he would have preferred a reaction like that in the USSR, where Chamberlain was burned in effigy in Red Square, a ritual in the official presence of the Foreign Commissar, the Jew Maksim Litvinov (Meyer Hennokh Moisevitch Wallack), despite which there was no note of protest. It is not difficult to imagine the international uproar that would have ensued if Ribbentrop had publicly supported the burning in effigy of President Roosevelt in Germany.

A few days later, on 5 October, the French Chamber of Deputies ratified the Munich Agreement by 535 votes to 75 (73 Communists). The Mandel-Reynaud tandem and their team as well as Léon Blum and his supporters, though disgruntled, considered it politically inopportune to confront public opinion. Among those who played along with the Communists and rejected the Munich agreements were two famous painters, the Jew Marc Chagall and Pablo Picasso. The latter, who declared himself a pacifist and communist, had already been in the hands of Jewish dealers such as Daniel-Henry Kahnweiler and the Rosenberg brothers[2] for thirty years. Both artists returned their decorations to the French state in protest. It is not without regrettable sarcasm that Picasso, whose Guernika passes for a plea against war, protested against peace in Europe because of its political servitude.

The House of Commons was also in session on 5 October 1938. Paul Rassinier writes in *Les responsables de la Seconde Guerre Mondiale* that during the debate Chamberlain "committed a blunder that was to have repercussions on Hitler's subsequent behaviour". Whether it was a blunder or a forced concession to cajole opponents of his policy, the fact remains that the prime minister linked the Munich agreements to a massive armaments programme for all three armies. He emphasised the investment for the Air Force, which was to build 3,000 aircraft by the end of the year and another 8,000 during 1939. The programme was unanimously accepted; but as Chamberlain prepared to explain his position in Munich, Churchill took the floor to denigrate his policy and the agreements, which he called "a disaster of the first magnitude". Churchill openly pointed to the aspirations of the international powers that wanted war, and spoke of the need to end Nazi power through an alliance comprising France, Britain, the Soviet Union and the United States. The fact that to liquidate Germany Churchill and Roosevelt wanted to ally themselves with a ferocious communist dictatorship that had starved to death (Holodomor) seven million Ukrainians and since 1917 had caused the deaths of twenty million people can only be

---

[2] Picasso was discovered in 1905 by the Steins, a wealthy Jewish family. Leo and Gertrude Stein were in charge of finding works of art and Michael Stein was the financier. In 1907 Daniel-Henry Kahnweiler, who was a member of a family of Jewish financiers, became acquainted with the Cubists and the "Fauves" group. In 1909 Picasso became engaged to Kahnweiler, to whom he sold his entire output. A second, more formal contract was signed for three years on 18 December 1912. Two other Jewish brothers, Léonce Rosenberg and Paul Rosenberg, appeared during the war and took Kahnweiler's place. Léonce Rosenberg set out in 1916 for Picasso's international launch. "Together we will be invincible," he told him. You will be the creator and I will be the action. Paul Rosenberg took over from his brother in 1919. Through the Rosenbergs, Picasso entered the closed circle of the great art dealers, usually members of powerful Jewish families connected with banking, and his works passed into American museums and collections. In the 1920s the agreement with the Rosenbergs was only verbal and Picasso also worked with other Jewish representatives such as Wildenstein, Loeb and again Kahnweiler.

explained by the reasons we have been setting out throughout this book. Churchill's speech was applauded by all 137 Labour MPs and by leading supporters of the war, including Sir Vansittart, Hore Belisha, Anthony Eden and others. The Munich Agreement was passed in the vote by 369 votes to 150, one of whom was the First Lord of the Admiralty, Alfred Duff Cooper, a member of the government who resigned. In resigning, he uttered the following choice: "War with honour or peace with dishonour". Again, the opposite was true, especially considering that sixty million human beings were to be the victims of such an honourable war.

What had happened in the House of Commons had put Hitler on his guard. After the declaration of friendship signed a few days earlier, more restraint on the part of the British leaders, at least, was to be expected. On 9 October he made a speech in Saarbrücken in which he said: "The heads of government opposite us claim that they want peace, and we must believe them. But they govern countries whose structure makes it possible at any time to replace those who want it with those who do not. It would be enough for a Duff Cooper, an Eden or a Churchill to take Chamberlain's place to bring about a second world war at once, for that is their intention. They do not hide it: they proclaim it openly." The German press denounced with indignation that it was inexcusable for members of the Chamberlain Government to propagandise in favour of rearmament on the grounds of German danger.

Czechoslovakia's fiction in evidence

After the Munich Agreement, the last Polish ultimatum, the occupation of Teschen and the resignation of Benes as president of the Republic, political chaos was generated day by day in Czechoslovakia. The anti-German propaganda has been blaming everything on Hitler, generally presented as an insatiable expansionist. The facts, however, show that Poland's proposals and demands were less moderate and more aggressive, yet the German chancellor tried until the last moment to agree with the Poles on a policy of cooperation in all the disputes that arose. Poland's aspirations for Czechoslovakia were not limited to Teschen, but had other goals, one of which was a break between the Czechs and Slovaks. Although the Slovak nationalist movement had been ruthlessly suppressed by President Thomas Masaryk from the very birth of Czechoslovakia, the Poles made no secret of their commitment to an independent Slovak state.

In 1938 Monsignor Józef Tiso, a Catholic priest who became the first president of the Slovak state in 1939, and Karol Sidor, also a Catholic politician and supporter of the Poles, were the two main leaders of Slovak nationalism. Most Slovaks opposed Czech rule and were in favour of ending it; however, they were politically divided into several conflicting groups. The most influential group wanted Slovakia to return to Hungary, but Budapest was unwilling to compromise and offered no effective support. Another group was the Sidor group, which favoured a partnership with Poland and even envisaged a Polish protectorate for Slovakia. It should be noted that customs, temperament and cultural relations were links that naturally brought Poles and Slovaks closer together. Monsignor Tiso was the prominent leader of the third grouping, which called for full independence for the Slovaks, even if initially they had to rely on one of their powerful neighbours to achieve it. Finally, there was a pro-Czech movement. With these ingredients, most international observers predicted that a Slovak crisis was imminent. If Hungary did not dare to support his supporters, Jozef Beck, the Polish foreign minister, was prepared to promote Slovak independence. Monsignor Tiso advocated strong protection for Slovakia, and Germany was the only alternative if Hungary and Poland refused responsibility.

Poland had two other targets in Czechoslovakia: one was Zips-Orawy, a region in the Carpathian Mountains bordering Slovakia that Poland and Hungary had disputed since the Middle Ages. Beck was tempted to take advantage of Czech weakness to seize this disputed territory. Another was the elimination of Czech control in Ruthenia, a region in the southern Carpathian Mountains inhabited by a million people that had been awarded to Czechoslovakia in 1919. If there was a split between the Czechs and Slovaks, it was unthinkable that the former could continue to hold this territory. The thesis of the Polish leaders was that Ruthenia had belonged to Hungary for hundreds of years and should be returned to Hungary, a country mutilated at the Paris Conference, which had lost two thirds of its population and three quarters of its territory. One of the Poles' fears was that a hypothetical independent Ruthenia might fall into the hands of the communists.

The Czechs were quick to accuse the Poles of seeking chaos in Czechoslovakia. On 3 October, Czech Foreign Minister Kamille Krofta informed the British that the Czechs were withdrawing smoothly from Sudeten territory, but complained strongly about the Poles, whom he accused of plotting and organising propaganda in Slovakia. Krofta expressed to the British his fear that Czech weakness could be exploited "to spread suggestions that Slovakia would be better off if it were associated with Poland." In David L. Hoggan, Krofta harboured such fears because he was aware of "how deep was the hatred of the Czechs in Slovakia, so deep that the Slovaks preferred almost any association to that of the Czechs." Krofta added that he "wished above all" for French and British help against the Poles, but that he also hoped that "Hitler could perhaps help to resist Polish ambitions."

In Munich, it had been stipulated that some areas would be handed over to Germany within ten days and that others would be occupied by an international police force, pending a plebiscite. The British ambassador to Germany, Neville Henderson, a convinced supporter of the appeasement policy, worked closely with the French minister, Bonnet, to facilitate the implementation of the agreements and avoid disputes. Henderson, according to Hoggan, "was considered the most promising of young British diplomats when he was sent to Berlin in 1937; but because of his dedication to these principles, unconvincingly maintained by his bosses in London, he was soon isolated and in an unenviable position in the British diplomatic service". Henderson found that the Czechs were seeking needlessly to obstruct the implementation of what had been agreed at Munich, where it had been agreed that areas where there was more than 50% German population would be handed over to Germany without plebiscite. The Czechs wanted to raise the percentage to 75%. Halifax supported the modification of the agreement in favour of the Czechs until the last minute, but had to give in to the French and Italians, who opposed it and insisted on the need to "respect the spirit of the protocol". Halifax thought that the Czechs could be helped in areas where a plebiscite was to be held, but President Beneš, convinced that there was no longer any way to oppose Germany, resigned in indignation on 5 October.

The Czech Communist Party had forced the resignation of Milan Hodza's government on 22 September, and a provisional government headed by General Jan Syrovy succeeded him. After Benes' resignation, Syrovy served as interim prime minister and president of the Republic until Emil Hácha was appointed to the second post. Foreign Minister Krofta was replaced by Franti"ek Chvalkovsky. The enthusiasm of the Western powers for the new government was not excessive and the idea of sending troops to supervise the plebiscite began to be questioned. Roger Makins, a Foreign Office expert working on the International Commission to delimit the Czech border, announced on 6 October that he shared his Italian colleagues' view that the Czechs would gain nothing from a referendum. The Czechs themselves realised that a vote would do nothing to further their cause and could, on the contrary, demonstrate their alarming weakness, so the Czech delegate to the Commission informed the Germans on 7 October that his government would prefer to forget the plebiscite. Germany, which had the right to demand the plebiscite in accordance with the Munich agreement, postponed its decision for a few days.

On 11 October, Neville Henderson confided to Halifax that there was a large pro-German groundswell in Bohemia-Moravia and that the Czechs could lose Brno (Bruen), the capital of Moravia, if the referendum were held. This was an alarming prospect for the Czechs, as they would be virtually cut off from Slovakia. For his part, the British ambassador in Warsaw, Howard Kennard, explained to Halifax that the Poles were in favour of the expulsion of the Czechs from Slovakia. Finally, on 13 October, Hitler agreed to annul the plebiscite and to keep his troops in the occupied zone. Hoggan writes: "The discussion of the plebiscite began with Halifax's idea that it could be used as an instrument against the Germans. It ended with a sign of relief in London when the Germans dropped the idea."

Simultaneously, Hungarians and Czechs began negotiating an agreement on the ethnic claims of Hungarians in Slovakia. Polish Foreign Minister Józef Beck feared that the Hungarians were not exerting enough pressure and asked to discuss the matter. On 7 October Budapest sent Foreign Minister Count Istvan Csaky to Warsaw. The Polish press had launched a strong campaign for the annexation of Ruthenia to Hungary, and Beck proposed to the minister that he claim the entire province; but there were 14,000 Romanians in Ruthenia, and Csaky expressed his fear of an attack from Romania if he did so. The German ambassador to Poland, Moltke, informed Ribbentrop on the 8th that Hungarian fears about Romania worried Beck. To further muddle the territorial gibberish, the Italians did not look favourably on Poland's intended patronage role. Italy understood that the Poles intended to create a bloc of independent countries between the Axis and the Soviet Union and therefore supported Slovakia's independence. Negotiations between Hungary and Czechoslovakia broke down without agreement on 13 October.

Meanwhile, the situation in Slovakia was becoming increasingly confused: the pro-Czechs had virtually disappeared from the scene and the other groups were at least demanding autonomy. On 8 October a Slovak local government had been formed and on 22 October a constitutional amendment allowed the Slovak Autonomy Act to be passed. Autonomy was to be short-lived, for from this moment on public opinion began to move unequivocally towards independence, which was welcomed by the Poles, who were still determined that Hungary should annex Ruthenia. On 11 November 1938, all parties managed to unite in the Slovak National Unity Party.

Subcarpathian or Transcarpathian Ruthenia, although administered by Hungary for centuries, was an ethnically diverse region inhabited by Ukrainians, Hungarians, Romanians, Bulgarians, Russians and other minorities. In 1945 it became part of the Ukrainian Soviet Republic. Beck was particularly fearful of the policy Germany might adopt on the Ruthenian question, so he warned them through the Polish ambassador in Berlin, Józef Lipski, not to encourage the nationalist ambitions of the Ukrainians. It should be borne in mind that millions of Ukrainians in eastern Poland had come under Polish control. On 18 October Lipski expressed to German State Secretary Ernst von Weizsäcker the desire for a policy of friendly cooperation in the Hungarian-Slovak affair. Weizsäcker informed Ribbentrop that a policy of concessions in this matter could be useful for a policy of understanding with Poland. On 19 October Ambassador Moltke informed Berlin that the Poles feared that Ruthenia might endanger their control over the Ukrainians living in their territory, who, encouraged by the self-determination processes in Czechoslovakia, had provoked riots in Lwow.

After a trip to Bucharest to try to influence the Romanians on the Ruthenian question, on 22 October Józef Beck ordered Ambassador Lipski to inform the Germans that Poland wanted their support in bringing the entire province of Ruthenia under Hungarian control. Lipski requested that the Polish government be kept informed of Germany's plans regarding the Hungarian border question. Hitler then felt that the time might be right to raise German claims regarding Danzig, and instructed his Foreign Minister to let the Poles know that German support would depend on the degree of cooperation between the two countries on the proposed questions of the connection with East Prussia through Danzig.

On 24 October Ambassador Lipski had lunch with Ribbentrop in Berchtesgaden. This date marked the beginning of German attempts to reach an agreement on Danzig through bilateral negotiations. Lipski admitted that Beck's efforts in Romania had failed. Ribbentrop pointed out to him that Poland's plans for Ruthenia entailed some difficulties, since the Ruthenians were unlikely to vote in favour of union with Hungary in a plebiscite. There was also the attitude of Romania, with which Germany wanted to improve trade relations through the barter system. Ribbentrop, at in any case, assured that this was not a refusal and offered some ideas. Over lunch Ribbentrop asked Lipski to pass on an invitation to Minister Beck to visit Germany in November 1938. Hitler's plan for Danzig immediately came up in conversation. Germany was going to ask Poland to allow the annexation of the town and planned to ask permission for the construction of a motorway and a railway line to connect with East Prussia through the town. Obviously, there would have to be a "quid pro quo" and Germany was prepared to make many concessions: Poland would be guaranteed a permanent free port in Danzig and the right to build its own motorway and railway connection to the port, the area of which would be a permanent free market for Polish goods. Germany also offered recognition of existing borders, including the 1922 boundaries in Upper Silesia. Ribbentrop claimed that Germany had more ideas and more proposals and suggested a new treaty between the two countries that would contain a general agreement and a non-aggression pact for no less than 25 years.

Leaks about this conversation spread rapidly through Europe. As early as the next day, Ambassador Kennard, who claimed to have obtained the information from various sources, told Halifax that Germany and Poland were negotiating a general agreement in return for the common Hungarian-Polish border. Beck understood, however, that he would not receive German support for his plans for Ruthenia unless he adopted a positive attitude to German proposals for collaboration. He knew that Britain wanted to support Poland against Germany, but at the same time he realised that the British were playing for time. His conviction that Britain would oppose Germany," Hoggan writes in *Der Erzwungene Krieg*, "prevented him from seriously considering the German offer. His realisation that the British needed time to prepare for their war induced him to adopt a delaying tactic in his negotiations with Germany." Beck had already decided that he preferred to risk Poland's future to the outcome of a pre-emptive war by Britain against Germany, rather than seek an agreement with Hitler, so he gave up seeking their co-operation in Ruthenia. The lure of an Anglo-Polish alliance prevented Polish leaders from seeing the practical advantages of an understanding with the Germans. Hoggan puts it this way: "An alliance with Britain would make hostility from both the Soviet Union and Germany inevitable, without giving Poland the slightest military advantage. An alliance with Britain would be tantamount to a death sentence for the new Polish state..... Poland had no chance of establishing cordial relations with the Soviet Union. Her only hope of achieving national security lay in a pact with Germany, and Poland was lost unless she understood the necessity of such a compromise."

Poland's erratic policy against Germany in 1938

Convinced that Germany's defeat in a new war served Poland's interests, Polish leaders rejected the peace that was repeatedly at their fingertips. In March 1938 the Polish Foreign Ministry saw the terror unleashed in the USSR by Stalin's purges as a sign of internal weakness and decline. The facts soon showed that the stupidity of their approach meant that their country was the pawn used by the pawns of the Hidden Power that was driving the war. In his *Memoirs*, Winston Churchill himself declared with his usual cynicism: "There never was a war easier to avoid than the one which has just devastated what was left of the world after the preceding conflict. Since stubbornness on the Danzig issue was the trigger for the conflict, a brief review of German-Polish frictions during 1938 is in order before we go on to narrate the events chronologically.

Among the most outrageous and intolerable policies for Germany was the persecution of the German minority in Poland. Although the German authorities tried to coordinate with each other to solve minority problems, the Poles considered cooperation unnecessary. *Gazeta Polska* argued in a June editorial that minority issues were an internal matter for each government. The fact that the Polish minority in Germany was insignificant compared to the German minority in Poland led Polish leaders to disregard Poles living in the Reich. On 8 July Germany drafted a memorandum containing the main complaints about the mistreatment of Germans in Poland. A land reform law for 1938 severely damaged German interests: more than two-thirds of the land to be confiscated in Posen and West Prussia was to be handed over by German farmers who owned property in these provinces. The memorandum accused the Polish authorities of tolerating and encouraging a boycott of industrial enterprises employing Germans. Eighty percent of German workers in eastern Upper Silesia were unemployed, and young Germans were being denied apprenticeships that could enable them to find employment. The Poles had intensified their programme of closing down Elamannian schools. The memorandum, which summarised the overall situation, concluded with the suggestion that future concessions to Poles in Germany would depend on improved conditions in Poland.

In a report dated 2 September 1938, Ambassador Moltke explained the increasingly unfavourable situation of the German minority. Moltke pointed to the OZON group (National Unity Group), founded by Colonel Adam Koc. This was an officially funded group designed to foster the rise of anti-German sentiment and to secure a broad base of popular support for government policies.. Following German successes in Austria and Czechoslovakia, the Poles adopted a policy of intimidation. Moltke reported that an increasing number of Germans were being sentenced to prison terms by Polish courts for making comments such as: "The Führer will have to put things in order here" or "Soon it will be Poland's turn". Ambassador Moltke was concerned about the indifference with which the Polish government viewed the growing number of anti-German and anti-German demonstrations. Without police intervention, German consulates were harassed by groups of Poles, who sang an anti-German folk song saying that God would reward Poles who hanged Germans.

As soon as Teschen was occupied by Polish troops in October 1938, German persecution was a constant. Although Hitler had given full support to Poland in its claim to this territory from the Czechs, the Poles proceeded to treat the Germans and pro-Germans as enemies. The measures began already with the military occupation of the area. All German schools were immediately closed. The next step was directed at the parents of the children, who were threatened with unemployment if they did not send their children to Polish schools. German teachers were dismissed and it was announced that Polish was the only official language. Lawyers and doctors were told they could not practise if they did not learn Polish within three months. Bank deposits were frozen for a long time and Germans' pensions and payrolls were reduced. During the first month, 20% of the district's German population fled and accommodation had to be provided for 5,000 refugees in camps in western Upper Silesia. Notes of protest from the German authorities were to no avail. At the end of the year Moltke met with Beck in Warsaw and complained bitterly about the situation in Teschen. The ambassador expressed to the minister the despair of the Germans in the territory, who had come to regard the twenty years under Czech rule as a paradise compared to Polish oppression. In his reply Beck insisted that this was a local phenomenon.

In West Prussia, new censorship measures were also adopted in schools, where the list of banned books was expanded: the heroic poem *Nibelungenlied*, books of poems by Goethe, Defoe's *Robinson Crusoe* and others were censored. The main charitable organisation in the town of Graudenz was closed and its property confiscated. In the small town of Neustadt, even its regular Christmas play was banned. The Young Poles'

Association launched a boycott campaign against German companies in Polish West Pusia, and in January 1939 they began picketing without any intervention by the Polish authorities. Nevertheless, Polish sources refused to acknowledge the facts and insisted that the persecution of Germans was entirely "imaginary".

We have already noted in the section on the Evian Conference that the Polish foreign minister decided in April 1938 to withdraw the citizenship of Polish Jews living abroad. This provoked a crisis with Germany, which we will now explain in more detail. Germany was supposedly the malevolent country that did not want Jews on its territory, so Jewish organisations all over the world had organised an international boycott against it and openly called for war against Hitler. However, and official historians say nothing about this, many more Jews had emigrated from Poland than from Germany between 1933 and 1938. A report by the Institute for Contemporary History in Munich cited by Hoggan shows that during these years an average of 100,000 Jews emigrated annually from Poland, while only 25,000 to 28,000 emigrated from Germany. Moreover, as we know, most of these German Jews voluntarily left for Palestine with their assets thanks to the Haavara Agreement reached with the Zionists. By 9 November 1938, 170,000 German Jews had left the country; but in the same period of time 575,000 Polish Jews had emigrated from Poland. In addition, thousands of Jews who had left Germany in 1933 had returned in 1934, while hardly any Jews had returned to Poland. Jerzy Potocki, the Polish ambassador to the United States, in March 1938 made it clear to Summer Welles, the American Under-Secretary of State, that Poland wanted to increase the emigration of Polish Jews, and Welles offered to help settle them in Venezuela and other Latin American countries. A special Polish mission headed by Michal Lepecki had been sent in 1937 to Madagascar to study the possibilities of shipping Polish Jews to this rich and sparsely populated French island in the Indian Ocean.

On 28 March 1938 the American ambassador in Warsaw, Angier Biddle, reported that many Polish Jews would welcome a new war in Europe. According to Biddle, the destruction of the new Polish state could improve the condition of the Jews, and many of them believed that the Soviet Union was a real paradise compared to Poland. The ambassador added that the situation of Jews in Poland was increasingly unfavourable, which increased Jewish disloyalty towards Poland. On 29 March Biddle announced that the Polish Parliament (Sejm) was passing a large number of new anti-Jewish laws. A law passed in the Sejm in March 1938 outlawed 'kosher' (Jewish-friendly) food, even though two million Polish Jews ate only kosher meat. Another law also passed in March allowed the Polish authorities to withdraw citizenship from Jews who had been out of the country for five years by not renewing their passports. Many of these Jews were in Germany: approximately 70,000 Polish Jews had been living in the Reich since the end of the World War. On 15 October 1938 a new decree implemented the law, so conflict with the German authorities was inevitable.

The German Foreign Ministry tried in vain to persuade the Warsaw authorities of the need to cancel the decree, which was intended to get rid of all Polish Jews not living in Poland. Ambassador Moltke made a last attempt on 26 October, three days before the rule invalidating Jewish passports was to come into force automatically. Finally, in the face of futility, Moltke warned Jan Szembek of the Polish Foreign Ministry that Germany would expel all Polish Jews who sought to endorse them unless they received a satisfactory response. At the announcement of this measure, Szembek expressed his astonishment, and Moltke explained that the matter could easily be settled if the Polish government agreed that the decree would not apply to the territory of the Reich. Moltke offered a second solution: that Polish citizens in Germany should be allowed to return without the special stamp validating passports. Józef Beck personally made it unequivocally clear that there was nothing to negotiate on the matter.

After this refusal, the Germans set to work. On 28 October, two days before the deadline, between 15,000 and 17,000 Polish Jews, mostly men, were transported to the border. Years later, the American journalist William Shirer wrote a fictional story, according to which the transport took place in cattle cars and under inhumane conditions. In reality, the German authorities took great care to ensure the good treatment of the travellers, who were provided with ample space, good food and medical care, as Red Cross personnel travelled on the trains. The first convoys passed the border without the Poles knowing about it and being able to stop them. When they realised what was happening, the police tried to prevent entry, even though the decree could not be enforced until 30 October. Soon thousands of Polish Jews were being held in small towns near the Upper Silesian border, and trouble began. The German police then decided to smuggle as many Jews as possible through the forests and along unguarded trails. The Poles counterattacked and expelled to Germany a few Jews from the west of the country who had retained German citizenship since the end of World War I. The Poles were forced to leave the country. On the same day, 30 October, the authorities of both countries suddenly agreed to halt the deportations. It should be noted that the German authorities made it clear to the expellees that there would be no objection to their return as soon as they had obtained new, valid passports. Interestingly, after the Anschluss between Germany and Austria, more Jews had entered Germany than had left it in five years: in Berlin alone, according to a report by Ambassador Hugh Wilson, 3,000 Jews had entered in May 1938.

A Jewish terrorist murders Ernst von Rath: the "Kristallnacht"

It was in this context that on 7 November 1938 a seventeen-year-old Jew, Herschel Grynszpan, murdered the third secretary of the German embassy in Paris, Ernst von Rath. Once again, as usual, a Jewish terrorist committed a crime with wide historical repercussions. Some have sought to see in this attack the same significance as the Sarajevo assassination by the Jewish Freemason Gavrilo Princip. Joaquín Bochaca recalls in *Los crímenes de los buenos* that von Rath was one more of the Nazi officials murdered by Jewish terrorists. We will mention only the case of Wilhelm Gustloff, founder of the NSDAP in Switzerland and distributor of the book *The Protocols of the Elders of Zion*, who on 4 February 1936 was assassinated at his home in Davos by the Jew David Frankfurter, who shot him at point-blank range. In the book *Les vengeurs*, by Michel Bar-Zohar, the terrorist recounts in the first person how he murdered Gustloff: "I shot... once, twice, three times, four times.... All the bullets hit, in the head, in the neck, in the chest.... He collapsed. In the 1960s, Bar-Zohar interviewed Frankfurter in Israel, portraying him as a vigilante avenger. There he worked as an employee of the Ministry of Defence. Sentenced on 12 December 1936 to eighteen years in prison, this criminal was released in 1945.

Grynszpan's family was one of those who had been deported, so his criminal attack has been explained as an act of angry revenge. One of the most widespread versions is that Grynszpan's intention was to assassinate Ambassador Welczeck, but because he could not identify him, he shot von Rath. It has also been written that the young man wanted to kill himself in front of a portrait of Hitler in order to become a symbol of the Jewish people. Ingrid Weckert published the book *Feuerzeichen* in Germany in 1981, the English version of which appeared in the United States in 1991 as *Flashpoint: Kristallnacht 1938: Instigators, Victims and Beneficiaries*. This book provides a detailed investigation of Kristallnacht (the Night of Broken Glass). Herschel Grynszpan, who had left his family in Hannover at the age of 14, provides some very interesting facts about his father, a Polish Jew. His father was a Polish Jew who had moved to Germany after the World War. The young Herschel, who did not like to work, lived with his aunt and uncle in Brussels and Paris, where the French authorities refused to renew his residence permit because his passport had expired. His Parisian uncle asked him to leave because he did not want legal problems. Although he had no job and no money, Herschel moved into a hotel. The information provided by Ingrid Weckert from this point onwards is very significant. The hotel where Grynszpan settled was located next to the headquarters of an influential French Jewish organisation, the International League Against Anti-Semitism (LICA). Weckert asks: "Who maintained him from February 1938 and who paid for the hotel accommodation?". Another question is why did the hotel allow him to stay for so long if his papers were not in order? Although he had no money and lived with an expired passport, Grynszpan was able to buy a pistol costing 250 francs on the morning of 7 November 1938, with which he killed von Rath an hour later.

Arrested at the scene of the crime, the murderer was taken to a police station. Although the thesis has prevailed that Grynszpan was an obscure Polish Jew acting alone and on his own initiative, a few hours after his arrest, one of France's most famous criminalists, Vincent de Moro-Giafferi, appeared at the police station and told the police that he was his lawyer. Weckert asks again: "Why was he so interested in defending a young foreigner? Who was going to pay his fees?" Moro-Giafferi looked after Grynszpan for the next few years. Before he could be tried, war broke out. The French authorities handed the criminal over to the Germans, who took him to Germany and interrogated him, but never tried him, as Moro-Giafferi remained his lawyer from Switzerland, where he lived during the German occupation of France.

Years after the war, the case file became available, and among hundreds of pages there was a note explaining that the trial would not be held for "unofficial reasons". In other words, the regime that was supposed to have committed the greatest crimes against the Jews was unable to bring von Rath's murderer to justice. After the war, Grynszpan returned to Paris, where he received identity papers granting him a new name. The Grynspan family also survived the war. After being deported to Poland, they managed to emigrate to Palestine, where the father testified in Jerusalem at the trial of Adolf Eichmann. Weckert believes that the answer to the Grynszpan mystery is Moro-Giafferi, who was legal advisor to LICA, founded with Rothschild funding in 1933 by the Jew and Freemason Bernard Lecache, a warmonger who in 1938 proclaimed the need for a merciless war against Germany.

It so happens that Moro-Giafferi had also appeared in February 1936 in Davos (Switzerland) to defend David Frankfurter, the Jewish criminal who, as mentioned above, murdered Wilhelm Gustloff. During the trial, which began on 8 December, it was proven that Frankfurter had been hired by an influential organisation to carry out the attack. All clues pointed to LICA; but Moro-Giafferi did not allow the name of the International League Against Anti-Semitism to be uttered by his defendant. The pattern or model of the answers of Frankfurter, who testified in court that he had acted on his own initiative, was exactly the same as that used by Grynszpan.

Ernst von Rath did not die on the spot, but on 9 November, the day that ended with the "Night of Broken Glass", images of which have been shown regularly for eighty years to remind the world of the hell in which Jews lived in Germany. On the night of 9-10 November, a series of violent riots against Jews took place in large German cities and in some smaller ones: the windows of their shops were smashed, many of their homes were broken into or destroyed, and some synagogues were demolished and flooded. Many

Jews were assaulted and several murders took place. Of the 1,400 synagogues in Germany, 180 were razed or damaged. It is not true, therefore, that "all synagogues" were attacked, as has been claimed. Nor is it true that all shops were attacked: 7,500 of the 100,000 Jewish-owned shops had their shop windows smashed. Hermann Graml of the Institute for Contemporary History in Munich is an example of how Kristallnacht has been used in propaganda. This prominent historian wrote: "Every Jew was beaten, persecuted, robbed, insulted and humiliated. The SA tore Jews from their beds, beat them mercilessly in their homes, and then chased them almost to death.... Blood flowed everywhere.

On the same day, after von Rath's death, Goebbels made an anti-Jewish speech in Munich, which has been considered the trigger for Kristallnacht. However, it is fully established that none of the NSDAP leaders ordered violence against Jews. In fact, the widespread riots surprised them all when they gathered in Munich to commemorate the 1923 putsch. There Goebbels was informed by telephone of the serious anti-Jewish demonstrations taking place in the major German cities. After dinner, Hitler left the premises at about 8 p.m. and retired to his flat. Shortly afterwards, at about nine o'clock, Göbbels rose to address the gathering. Among other things, he declared that the days when Jews could kill Germans with impunity were over, and that legal measures would henceforth be available. He pointed out, however, that von Rath's death should not be used as an excuse for private action against Jews. Ingrid Weckert considers it impossible that Goebbels' allegedly inflammatory words could have been what incited the pogrom, since action against the Jews had already begun and Göbbels therefore spoke them after the event.

The fact that the riots took place simultaneously in all places obviously indicates that it was not a spontaneous reaction, but a well-prepared one. The secret societies had already demonstrated in the French Revolution, which broke out in numerous cities at the same time, their mastery in the execution of this type of action. Let us recall that agents of illuminated Freemasonry spread the "Great Fear" throughout France after the storming of the Bastille. Ingrid Weckert argues that something similar happened on Kristallnacht. In order to establish responsibility for what happened, the NSDAP commissioned an investigation by the Supreme Party Court. In February 1939 the chief judge of this internal court, Walter Buch, sent the results of his investigations to Hermann Göring. On the basis of Judge Buch's report, the examination of documents from a number of post-war trials of alleged Nazi criminals, and the testimony of thousands of defendants and witnesses, Weckert developed his thesis of what had happened.

According to these sources, on 8 November, the day before the pogrom, strangers who had not been seen before suddenly appeared in several Hessian towns near the French border. They addressed the mayors, district party leaders (Kreisleiters) and other prominent people in these towns. They asked what actions were being prepared against the Jews. Surprised by these questions, the officials replied that they knew nothing of such plans. The strangers feigned astonishment when they heard the answers and shouted for some reaction against the Jews. This same stratagem was used in 1789 in France: then supposed emissaries of the monarch toured towns and cities with a false edict calling for the destruction of castles that did not belong to the king. Some people approached by these individuals reported the facts to the police or discussed them with friends. They were generally thought to be disturbed anti-Semites. In one case, two men dressed in SS uniforms presented themselves to an SA colonel and ordered him to destroy a nearby synagogue. Weckert considers this absurd and unthinkable event to be proof that the strange characters were foreigners who did not know how these German entities functioned, since the SA and the SS were completely separate organisations, and a real SS would never have tried to give orders to an SA unit. Therefore, the Colonel (Standartenführer) refused the order and reported the incident to his superiors.

Since provocations with local officials did not yield the expected results, the tactic of emboldening the people directly on the streets was used. Two men appeared in a marketplace and began speeches intended to incite the people against the Jews. When some hotheads finally attacked the synagogue, the provocateurs disappeared. Similar incidents occurred in several cities: unknown persons suddenly appeared, made speeches, started throwing stones at shop windows, started attacks on Jewish buildings: schools, hospitals or synagogues, and disappeared. These events took place on 8 November, before von Rath's death was announced, and were only the beginning. Well-organised incidents and widespread began in the evening of 9 November. The anti-Jewish demonstrations were particularly significant in Hesse and the Magdeburg area, although they also occurred in large and small towns throughout Germany. Groups of five or six young men armed with sticks and truncheons, without showing the slightest emotion or anger at the murder of the German diplomat, went through the streets of the cities, methodically smashing shop windows. However, since violence begets violence, a certain number of individuals, angered by the destruction, joined in the riots: in this way, large groups of people took part in the riots.

During the trials before the Supreme Party Court, it was found that telephone calls woke up local or regional NSDAP leaders in the middle of the night. Someone pretending to be speaking from headquarters or regional party offices would ask what was going on in the city. If the officer replied that all was calm, then he was told in slang language that they had been ordered to give the Jews their comeuppance that night. Some thought it was a joke and went back to bed; others, half asleep, did not even understand what was going on; some sought confirmation of the order and contacted the office from which the voice had said it was calling. The presiding judge concluded that there had been confusion in the chain of command.

The German authorities realised that what was happening could only be detrimental to Germany, so they immediately tried to restore order. As soon as Goebbels had finished his "inflammatory speech" in Munich, the district chiefs (Gauleiters) and the head of the SA telephoned their subordinates and ordered measures to be taken to stop the violence and restore peace. Particular emphasis was placed on the fact that under no circumstances were demonstrations to be tolerated. These telephone instructions were written down by those on duty at party headquarters and sent by telex to the various district offices, so that they were archived and can be examined. The SA chief, Viktor Lutze, ordered his subordinates (Gruppenführers) in Munich to contact the barracks and to warn that under no circumstances were members of the SA to take part in anti-Jewish demonstrations, but that, on the contrary, they were to intervene to stop the disturbances which were in progress. The police and the SS also received orders to the same effect. The telex sent by Himmler to Heydrich ordering him to protect the Jews and prevent the destruction of their property is still in the archives of the International Military Tribunal in Nuremberg.

Hitler learned at about 1 a.m. that violent anti-Jewish acts, including the burning of a synagogue, had taken place in Munich. He immediately made an angry call to the chief of the Munich police. He ordered him to put out the fire immediately and to ensure that there were no more disturbances in the city. He then contacted police chiefs and party officials throughout Germany to ascertain the exact extent of the disturbances. Finally, the following message was drafted for all Gauleiters: "By express order of the highest authority, fires against shops or other Jewish property must not take place in any case and under any circumstances".

Ingrid Weckert wonders: "Despite these categorical orders, how is it possible that so much damage and destruction could have been done with the participation of SA members? According to written records, at least three SA groups did not obey Lutze's orders and sent their men to destroy synagogues and other buildings. At the trials between 1946 and 1952, the report of Karl Lucke, head of the 50th Brigade, was read out at 8:00 a.m. on 10 November. Lucke stated that at 3:00 a.m. he received the order to burn all the synagogues in his district. In his extensive account, submitted by the prosecution in Nuremberg, he included the list of synagogues destroyed by members of his brigade. The alleged order to burn down the synagogues must have emanated from Herbert Fust, the head of the Mannheim SA group, who was in Munich with the other SA leaders and, like the others, correctly passed on the orders of his chief, Viktor Lutze. The telephone operator on duty at the Mannheim barracks confirmed that he had understood the message and hung up; however, instead of relaying the order to the group leader, who was in the nearby town of Darmstadt, he called Oberführer Fritsch and showed him a piece of paper with notes that all the synagogues in the Mannheim district were to be destroyed. At 3 o'clock, when the work was already being completed, the man on the telephone called Karl Lucke and passed on the false order. At the same time he informed him that the action had been under way for several hours. Lucke then ordered the colonel of his brigade to proceed with the destruction in the Darmstadt district. No judge was interested in the identity of the telephone operator on duty, who, in Weckert's opinion, was an agent of those behind the whole Kristallnacht plot.

Early in the morning of 10 November, Propaganda Minister Joseph Göbbels announced over the radio that actions against Jews were strictly forbidden and warned that those who did not obey this order would be severely punished. He also explained that the Jewish question would be solved only through legal measures. Nevertheless, Hermann Graml, the historian quoted above, accuses Dr. Goebbels of having directed the agents provocateurs without presenting any evidence. Indeed, when Göbbels was asked to explain himself, he argued that the German people had been so angry about the murder of Ernst von Rath that they wanted to punish the Jews. Ingrid Weckert considers that he did not believe what he said, and adds that Göbbels expressed to several people his suspicion that a secret organisation must have been behind it all, since it could not be that something so well organised could have been a spontaneous popular outburst.

The NSDAP leaders were initially at a loss to explain what had happened. The first thing they did was to look for those responsible within their own organisation, and they began to point the finger at possible culprits. Hitler himself came to believe that Göbbels had been the instigator. The SA members who took part in the pogrom were denounced in the courts of justice by various Jewish and German witnesses. Some of them were charged with murder, others with looting, assault and other criminal acts. Hitler, however, wanted the Party to conduct its own investigation and postponed the trials until the accused had appeared before the Supreme Party Court. A good number of them were expelled, so that when they were tried by the ordinary courts of justice they were no longer members of the NSDAP. In *Les responsables de la Seconde Guerre Mondiale* Paul Rassinier quantifies the number of people who were tried and convicted for their participation in the events as 174.

On the 12th Göring, on Hitler's orders, summoned the chief ministers concerned to discuss what had happened. Gentlemen," the Führer told them, "enough of demonstrations which do no harm to the Jews, but to me, the highest authority for the economy of Germany. If today a Jewish shop is destroyed, if its goods are thrown into the street, the insurance company will pay the damage to the Jew, so that he will suffer no harm..." Since the destroyed goods were heavily insured, in order to compensate for the amounts that the German insurers would have to pay, it was decided to impose a very heavy fine on Jews who had assets of more than 5,000 marks.

This measure has been unanimously criticised; but the Nazis argued, among other things, that because of the boycott and the declaration of war by the Jews, the Reich was short of foreign currency, so that now the Jews who had instigated the boycott could help their co-religionists to pay. The companies were ordered to pay the amounts demanded for damages without delay, and then some of this money was allowed to be used for payment of the fine, which was to be paid in four instalments: 15 December 1938, 15 February, 15 May, and 15 August 1939.

However, there was a second part to this affair. Nahum Goldmann, president of the World Jewish Congress, appealing to what he called the "historical truth" about Kristallnacht, demanded in 1952 that Chancellor Konrad Adenauer pay 500 million dollars in reparations for the damage caused that night. Adenauer demanded a justification for such a large sum. Goldman himself writes in *The Jewish Paradox* that his reply was: "Look for the justification yourself. What I want is not the justification, but the money." Naturally, Goldmann received the money he demanded.

The consequences of Kristallnacht

It is reasonable to assume that the LICA and those who prepared in the shadows the assassination of Ernst von Rath had much to do with Kristallnacht. Even before the Bolshevik Revolution, pogroms had been organised in Russia by Jewish groups seeking to profit from them. One fact to note is that in 1938 the number of Jews entering Palestine had fallen to the lowest level since the migration of Zionists from all over the world to the Holy Land began at the turn of the century. A revival was imperative, and Kristallnacht was it. It has already been noted that, despite the Nuremberg Laws, European Jews who had to leave Poland or other countries preferred Germany as a place to live and work. What happened on the night of 9 November was something exceptional and had nothing to do with everyday behaviour. The anti-Jewish pogrom was rejected by German public opinion, which was largely horrified by events that went against its sense of decency and order.

Inevitably, an international press campaign took it upon itself to portray the situation of Jews in Germany as a daily hell. In the United States, it was used as an opportunity to proclaim to the four winds that nowhere in Europe were conditions for Jews worse than in Germany. On 14 November Cordell Hull ordered Ambassador Wilson to leave the country and forbade him to leave on a German ship. On 15 November it was the German ambassador in Washington, Dieckhoff, who wrote to the German secretary of state to let him know the extent to which hostility towards Germany had flared up in American public opinion. Even more worrying was the animosity of President Roosevelt himself, who called on his countrymen to boycott all German products. Roosevelt announced that he was going to study the immediate implementation of a project for the construction of 10,000 aircraft and, in addition, pressured Britain to renounce its policy of conciliation with Germany. Paul Rassinier quotes a text from the Polish ambassador in Washington, sent to Beck on 12 January 1939, in which Potocki explains the extent to which Kristallnacht served as a pretext in the United States for attacking Germany:

> "The anti-Semitic excesses which have recently taken place in Germany have unleashed an anti-German campaign of rare violence here. Various Jewish intellectuals and financiers, Bernard Baruch, Supreme Court Justice Frankfurter, Secretary of State for the Treasury Morgenthau, and others who enjoy Roosevelt's personal friendship have taken part in it. This group of persons occupying the highest positions in the American Government is indissolubly connected with the Jewish International."

Although neither the German government nor the NSDAP instigated the riots, things were not going to be the same in Germany either. The idea of removing Jews from the country was greatly accentuated as a result of what had happened. Hitler ordered the creation of a central agency to organise the emigration of Jews from Germany as quickly as possible. Göring then created the Reich Central Office for Jewish Emigration (Reichszentrale für die Jüdische Auswanderung), whose director was Reinhard Heydrich. Although the conditions of the Haavara Agreement were very favourable, fewer Jews emigrated to Palestine than the Nazis and Zionists desired. In the summer of 1938, an Intergovernmental Committee for Refugees, headed by the American lawyer George Rublee, had been founded. This Committee and the German government signed an agreement in January 1939 whereby all German Jews could emigrate to the country of their choice. Thanks to this 'sensational agreement', as Rublee himself described it, different governments set up reception camps to provide job training for Jewish emigrants in order to facilitate work in their new countries. German Jews over the age of 45 could thus either emigrate or remain in Germany. Those who chose to remain in the Reich could live wherever they wished with guaranteed social security, like any other citizens. The clauses or provisions of the Rublee plan served as the basis for the Reich Central Office. In addition, a parallel Jewish organisation, the Reich Union of Jews in Germany (Reichsvereinigung der Juden in Deutschland), was set up to advise Jews. Both agencies worked together to facilitate emigration. On the other hand, the SS and other National Socialist organisations collaborated with Zionist groups to encourage as many Jews as possible to leave Germany. With the help of the Rublee Plan and the Haavara Agreement, hundreds of thousands of Jews emigrated from Europe to Palestine. In September 1940 "Palcor", the Jewish news agency in Palestine, reported that half a million Jewish emigrants had arrived from the German Reich and occupied Poland.

Germany seeks agreement and peace with Poland

Poland's inability to adopt a positive attitude towards Germany led to increased friction in late 1938. The planned seventy-five kilometre motorway from Buetow (Pomerania) to Elbing (East Prussia) via Danzig was only to run through forty kilometres of Polish territory. Germany, which had offered Poland compensations and territorial concessions of great interest to Poland in exchange for the return of Danzig, had been waiting for a reply since 24 October, the date of the meeting between Lipski and Ribbentrop. The Germans remained hopeful that an agreement was possible. However, the lack of a reply from Beck was a bad sign, so Ribbentrop decided to summon the ambassador on 19 November 1938 for the sole purpose of asking him whether he had received instructions from Beck about the German offer. Lipski replied in the affirmative and gave a half-hearted assurance that an agreement for a motorway and railway line through the Corridor was possible. However, he recalled that the maintenance of the Free City was vital to Poland's interests and announced that Beck had instructed him to make a counter-offer, the main point of which was a treaty recognising the permanent independence of Danzig. Ribbentrop made no secret of his disappointment, although he assured that he would consult with Hitler. Three days later, on 22 November, Ambassador Lipski returned to Warsaw to discuss the Danzig issue. It then became clear that the hint of a possible agreement on the motorway and railway line had merely been a ploy to appease the Germans. The Polish leaders agreed that they would make no concessions on either Danzig or the transit lines in the Corridor.

An explanation for this intransigent position is once again offered by David L. Hoggan, who reports on a very eloquent report telegraphed the previous day, 21 November, by Count Jerzy Potocki, the Polish ambassador to the United States. Given the interest of this revealing document, we reproduce the text:

> "The Polish Ambassador was informed by William C. Bullitt, the American Ambassador to France who was visiting the United States, that President Roosevelt was determined to involve America in the coming European war. Bullitt explained to Potocki that he enjoyed the special confidence of President Roosevelt. Bullitt predicted that a long war would soon break out in Europe. Of Germany and its Chancellor, Adolf Hitler, he spoke with extreme vehemence and resentful hatred. He suggested that the war might last six years, and advocated that it should be fought to such an extent that Germany could never recover."

Potocki, Hoggan continues, did not share Bullitt and Roosevelt's enthusiasm for war and destruction:

"He asked how this war could come about, since it seemed extremely unlikely that Germany would attack Britain or France. Bullitt suggested that a war would break out between Germany and some other power, and that the Western powers would intervene. Bullitt considered a war between the Soviet Union and Germany inevitable and predicted that Germany, after an enervating war in Russia, would capitulate to the Western powers. He assured Potocki that the United States would participate in this war if Britain and France made the first move. Bullitt inquired about Polish policy, and Potocki replied that Poland would fight rather than allow Germany to alter the western frontier. Bullitt, who was a strong supporter of Poland, was convinced that Poland could be trusted to stand firm against Germany".

It is astonishing to note that Bullitt, the roving ambassador of the war party and agent of the international conspiracy, knew perfectly well how events were going to unfold, for things happened as he had announced them to the Polish ambassador.

The American revisionist historian's source is *Polish Documents on the Causes of War*. In a lengthy note, Hoggan explains that both Bullitt and the US State Department initially denied the legitimacy of these documents. However, their authenticity was confirmed by diplomat and professor Waclaw Jedrzejewicz of the Józef Pilsudski Institute in New York, author of *Poland in the British Parliament, 1939-1945*. The controversy over the authenticity of the so-called "Polish Secret Papers" deserves further clarification, which we offer below from Mark Weber of the Institute for Historical Review.

These documents were captured by the Germans when they took Warsaw in September 1939. An SS brigade commanded by Baron von Künsberg attacked the Foreign Ministry by surprise as they were about to incinerate the incriminating documents. On Friday, 29 March 1940, sixteen documents were published by the Nazis under the title *Polnische Dokumente zur Vorgeschichte des Krieges (Polish Documents on the Background of the War)*. In Berlin, journalists from all over the world, after having access to the originals, which they were allowed to examine, received facsimile copies of the documents as well as German translations. The Foreign Office edition was entitled *German White Book No. 3*. The book appeared in several languages in Berlin and other capitals. An edition was published in New York by Howell, Soskin and Company under the title *The German White Paper*. Naturally, the ambassadors involved, notably Bullitt and Potocki, denied the authenticity of the documents. However, Edward Raczynski, the Polish ambassador to London, confirmed in 1963 in his diary, which appeared under the title *In Allied London*, that the documents were genuine. In his entry of 20 June 1940 he wrote: "the Germans published in April a White Paper containing documents from the archives of our Foreign Ministry, which contained reports by Potocki in Washington, by

Lukasiewicz in Paris and by me. I do not know where they were obtained, since we were told that the archives had been destroyed. The documents are certainly authentic, and the facsimiles prove that the Germans had the originals and not mere copies."

Ambassador Jerzy Potocki was convinced that Roosevelt's belligerent attitude was a consequence of the Jewish environment around him. Potocki repeatedly informed his government that American public opinion was simply the product of Jewish machinations. In Potocki's view, Jewish influence on American culture and public opinion was absolutely preponderant. On 9 February 1938 Potocki reported to the Polish Foreign Ministry that Jewish pressure on President Roosevelt was growing: 'The Jews are now the leaders in creating a war psychosis which would plunge the whole world into war and bring about a general catastrophe. This feeling is becoming more and more evident.

Of all the *Polish Documents on the background of the war*, one of the most revealing is Potocki's secret report dated 12 January 1939, which describes the situation in the United States and the campaign against Germany. Propaganda," wrote Potocki, "is for the most part in the hands of the Jews, who control one hundred per cent of the radio, the cinema, and the daily and periodical press". Also very revealing is a passage on the treatment of the USSR: "It is interesting to note that in this extremely well-planned campaign directed above all against National Socialism the Soviet Union is completely excluded. If it is mentioned at all, it is always in a friendly way, and things are presented as if Soviet Russia were working in the bloc of democratic countries. All this confirms for the umpteenth time that Franklin Delano Roosevelt's governments were controlled by Jewish agents. Roosevelt himself, as we know, was Jewish, since his mother Sara Delano came from a seventh generation Sephardic family. Moreover, F.D.R. was married to his cousin Eleanor, another Jew seriously committed to Zionism.

The other figure who, like Bullitt, was also determined to prevent any agreement between Germany and Poland was the ineffable Lord Halifax, the Foreign Office Secretary, whose ambassador in Warsaw, Kennard, met in November 1938 with Jacob Burckhardt, the Swiss diplomat who was acting as the League of Nations High Commissioner in Danzig. The High Commissioner expressed his conviction that the Poles would be willing to cede Danzig to Germany. When discussing the situation with Burckhardt, Kennard made no secret of his hatred of Germany. The ambassador's haughty attitude displeased the High Commissioner, who saw fit to inform the Germans of the British diplomat's ill-disposition. From this moment Hitler and Ribbentrop knew that the man who enjoyed Halifax's confidence in Warsaw was an enemy of the policy of appeasement. Learning of the contents of the conversation between Kennard and Burckhardt, Lord Halifax feared that the Polish might be concealing their true intentions and contemplated the possibility that the High Commissioner might identify with

Germany's position. Halifax warned Kennard that Burckhardt possessed "exceptional diplomatic and political skills" and could not be taken lightly.

Fearful that Poles and Germans might go behind his back, Halifax met the Polish ambassador, Edward Raczynski, in London on 4 December to clarify Poland's real intentions. The Foreign Secretary asked him bluntly whether Hitler had recently raised the issue of German claims to Danzig. The ambassador answered evasively, stating that Poland's biggest problem at the moment was to get international help to get rid of the Jewish population. Raczynski assured Halifax that the Jews were "a huge problem" in Poland. Halifax, annoyed, understood that Beck had not authorised the ambassador to provide further information about the German-Polish negotiations, and ordered Kennard to use every means to find out Beck's real intentions.

Edward Frederick Lindley Wood, Earl of Halifax

At this point, before moving on, a few lines should be devoted to the Earl of Halifax, Lord Halifax, a Rothschild man whose brazen actions led to the outbreak of war. Edward Frederick Lindley Wood was born without a left hand and with an atrophied left arm on 16 April 1881 and died on 23 December 1959. He entered the House of Commons as a Conservative MP in 1910. In his inaugural speech he emphatically denied that all men are created equal and called on the English people to remain true to their vocation as a "master race" within the British Empire. Viceroy and Governor-General of India between 1926 and 1931 and Secretary of State for War for five months in 1935, the 1st Earl of Halifax was Secretary of State at the Foreign Office between 21 February 1938 and 22 December 1940. When he left office, it was to go as ambassador to the United States, where he remained until 1946.

As head of British diplomacy he played a double game that invites one to consider him a dishonest and hypocritical man. As soon as he was appointed Foreign Secretary, Chamberlain's figure began to be dwarfed by the personality of his minister, whom Hoggan describes as a "self-seeking, ruthless, clever, self-righteous, self-righteous, sanctimonious, sanctimonious diplomat". His political perfidy earned him the nickname "The Holy Fox", an appellation bestowed on him by Winston Churchill. His biographer Andrew Roberts chose this epithet as the title of his book, *The Holy Fox. A Life of Lord Halifax* (1991). It is, as we have already hinted above, an uncritical biography in which Hitler is presented as the usual bad guy who wants to expand the Reich and dominate the world, while the figure of Halifax is haloed with a nimbus of moral and intellectual superiority, supposedly putting Britain's "honour" before any other consideration.

A politician of little weight within the Conservative Party, Halifax was commissioned by Chamberlain to visit the Führer. He made his first appearance before the German leaders on 19 November 1937, when he visited Hitler in Berchtesgaden before being appointed a minister. At that time his son Charles had already married Lord Rothschild's granddaughter. As a calling card, Halifax brashly told the Nazi leaders that he "expected German action to recapture Danzig". Three months later, Lord Halifax, Edward Wood, replaced Anthony Eden as Foreign Secretary, and within a few months his views on the Danzig question had taken a 180-degree turn.

On 21 May 1938, however, Burckhardt, the High Commissioner for Danzig, still informed the Germans of the Foreign Office Secretary's readiness, which had been expressed in an interview a few days earlier. Lord Halifax," Burckhardt was quoted as saying, "has described Danzig and the Corridor as an absurdity. During the conversation the head of British diplomacy acknowledged to the High Commissioner that this was probably the greatest stupidity of the Versailles agreements and expressed the hope that a change in the "status quo" could be achieved through bilateral negotiations between Poland and Germany. To top it all off, Lord Halifax suggested to the Swiss diplomat that Britain would be willing to mediate between Germany and Poland if there was an "impasse" in the bilateral negotiations. Naturally, this news was greeted with the greatest interest in Germany.

And even in July 1938 Halifax was still apparently in favour of the policy of appeasement. At ten o'clock on the morning of the 18th he received Fritz Wiedemann, Hitler's personal envoy to London, at his residence in Eaton Square. Alexander Cadogan was present at the interview and acted as translator. Wiedemann, author of a work on Hitler, *Der Mann der Feldherr werden wollte* (1964), received the following message from the Secretary of the Foreign Office: "Tell your Führer that I hope to see, before my death, the realisation of the goal of all my efforts: to see Hitler received by the King of England and acclaimed by the London crowd on the balcony of Buckingham Palace". It is understandable that, in the light of these words, some authors consider that Halifax was simply trying to trick Hitler into taking the bait of appeasement.

After the Munich Conference, everyone understood that Anglo-German relations were the basis on which peace and security in Europe could be built. The declaration of Anglo-German friendship signed on 30 September 1938 in Hitler's Munich flat was a document of hope. However, as we have seen, on 5 October Churchill and Duff Cooper immediately lowered expectations in the House of Commons. Nevertheless, a few days later, on 12 October, Lord Halifax took tea with Kennedy, the US ambassador, and presented him with a satisfactory picture of European policy. According to *US Foreign Relations*, 1938 documents cited by Hoggan, the Foreign Office secretary admitted to the ambassador that anyone with any influence knew that Hitler did not want war with Britain, and added that just because Britain was increasing its air power did not necessarily mean that it planned to interfere on the Continent. Halifax told

Kennedy that he expected Hitler would make a proposal for the annexation of Danzig and Memel and suggested that Britain would not intervene.

When Kennedy and Halifax met again two weeks later, on 28 October, something had already changed. Lord Halifax told the ambassador that, as he had predicted, Hitler had asked to obtain Danzig. In this second conversation, Halifax gave a grim account of the German Chancellor's attitude to Britain and also offered Kennedy a great deal of unreliable information about Hitler's supposed attitudes to current affairs on the Continent. A few weeks later he assured Kennedy that Hitler was consumed by a seething hatred of Britain and was planning to tear the Soviet Union to pieces in the spring of 1939. According to Hoggan, the motive for these fallacious tactics was to prepare for a possible British attack. It can be said that from this point onwards the reins of British policy passed progressively into the hands of Lord Halifax, and Prime Minister Chamberlain was to become a puppet under his Foreign Secretary.

One issue of concern to Halifax in the aftermath of the Munich Conference was the improvement of relations between Germany and France. With the prospect that France might be able to shake off its ties with Britain and come to an independent understanding with the Germans, Halifax gave specific instructions for action to his ambassador in Paris, Sir Eric Phipps. On 1 November 1938 he warned him that "the French Government might be tempted to disavow Her Majesty's Government because of German intrigue". On 7 November, informed of ongoing negotiations for a Franco-German friendship pact, similar to the one signed by Hitler and Chamberlain at Munich, Halifax gave further instructions to Phipps. The Foreign Office feared that this rapprochement could destroy the British system of "divide et impera" on which its theory of the balance of power was based. British leaders," Hoggan opined, "thought that their position in the world depended on the endurance of rivalries and divisions on the Continent".

On 21 November, two days before the Franco-German agreement was approved, Ambassador Robert Coulondre replaced François-Poncet, who had been held in high esteem by Hitler, in Berlin. The final text of the declaration was ratified by the French Council of Ministers on 23 November, the day Chamberlain and Halifax went to Paris for talks with the idea of receiving assurances that would reduce the importance of the treaty. An anti-British demonstration greeted the British politicians with jeers. Finally, on 6 December, a large German delegation led by Ribbentrop went to the French capital to sign the Franco-German Friendship Pact, which contained a declaration of non-aggression and recognised the borders set by the Treaty of Versailles as final. Lord Halifax received assurances from his colleague Bonnet that there were no secret agreements in the treaty, which was rejected by both Roosevelt and Stalin.

Czechoslovakia disintegrates

One after another, the German, Polish and Hungarian minorities freed themselves from Czech control. On 9 October 1938, the Kingdom of Hungary initiated talks with the Czecho-Slovak state over the Hungarian-inhabited regions in southern Slovakia, which led to armed clashes between Hungarian paramilitaries and Czechoslovak troops. Eventually the two countries asked Italy and Germany to arbitrate, with the tacit approval of France and Britain. Lord Halifax confidentially informed Budapest that arbitration could easily be proposed without Britain and France, who thus disengaged themselves from the territorial dispute.

Taking advantage of the Czech-Magyar discord and the weakness of Prague, the Polish government presented new territorial claims. The Poles demanded six districts in the Carpathian Mountains bordering Slovakia. On 31 October, they sent a new ultimatum threatening the Czechs with attack if they did not receive an affirmative reply the same day. After realising that the British would do nothing against Poland, they capitulated at 5 p.m. on behalf of Slovakia, despite the monumental anger of Monsignor Tiso, the leader of the Slovak nationalist coalition, who for the first time asked for German protection because he believed that Polish claims were not ethnically based. The whole episode served to reaffirm Tiso's thesis that Slovakia needed the protection of a powerful neighbour in order to gain independence from Prague. The events also contributed to the undermining of Poland's esteem among Slovaks.

On 2 November 1938, the first Vienna arbitration transferred to Hungary a 10,000 sq km territory of southern Slovakia, whose population of one million people was almost exclusively Magyar. This left three major ethnic groups within the Czechoslovak state: the Czechs, who numbered some six and a half million; the Slovaks, some two million; and the Ruthenians, who numbered close to half a million. Polish claims that Ruthenia should also pass into Hungary were welcomed by Halifax, who felt that a common border between Hungary and Poland would increase both countries' opposition to Germany. Although Britain had pledged at Munich to be a guarantor of the agreements, Foreign Office policy increasingly disregarded the interests of the Czechs, and Halifax was therefore disinterested in arbitration, although he was later surprised by the success of Italy and Germany.

Józef Beck, for his part, was disappointed that the Ruthenian question had not been resolved in the Vienna arbitration between Ribbentrop and Ciano. On 22 November 1938 Moltke, the German ambassador in Warsaw, was instructed by Ribbentrop to let Beck know that Germany would not support a revision of the Ruthenian agreement unless a German-Polish pact was reached. Moltke let Beck know that Ribbentrop had asked the Hungarians not to object for the time being to what had been conceded in

Vienna. Moltke, on the other hand, let slip that Ribbentrop had told him that Germany did not envisage that the Ukrainian question could cloud German-Polish relations and that there was no intention of stirring up Ukrainian nationalism. It seems clear that this was an insinuation that Beck no doubt understood.

In addition to Britain, the Soviet Union had also lost interest in Czechoslovakia, as it saw no possibility that it could act as a barrier against Germany. Sir Basil Newton, the British ambassador in Prague who was very critical of Poland's policy towards Czechoslovakia, expressed his opinion to Halifax that the Czechoslovak state would not last long. Newton felt that, with Karol Sidor as a supporter of association with Poland, Beck had wasted the chance to play an influential role in Slovakia. Moreover, Newton condemned the Poles for "the utterly ruthless policy towards the Czech population" in the regions they had gained. The ambassador denounced that "the Czechs were not the only victims, as the Germans were also often mistreated". The Poles, on the other hand, had in Ambassador Kennard their staunchest advocate and, of course, more in tune with the Foreign Office Secretary.

Seeing that the disintegration of the state was becoming more and more likely, on 11 December 1938 the Czechs showed Ambassador Newton their irritation and bewilderment at the impasse over the Munich guarantee issue. Foreign Minister Chvalkovsky admitted to the British Ambassador that the internal situation was very delicate and that they would welcome any kind of guarantee. Chvalkovsky realised that Britain and France were reluctant to take the initiative. Hoggan reveals why France did not intervene to prevent the collapse of Czechoslovakia either. According to this historian, when Chamberlain and Halifax travelled to Paris on 24 November before the signing of the Franco-German Friendship Pact, they discussed with French leaders the guarantee given at Munich regarding the new borders and ethnic minorities. Daladier and Bonnet saw no reason not to launch the guarantee process if Germany and Italy did not object. The French were astonished to find that the British did not share their view. Halifax proposed that the guarantee should not be operative in the event of a German violation, unless Mussolini was prepared to support France and Britain against Germany. Bonnet thought this was a joke, so the French objected that such a guarantee would be sterile and futile, for it was unreasonable to think that Mussolini would oppose Hitler on behalf of the Czechs. If the four powers did not accept this formula, Halifax replied undaunted, there would be no guarantee. The French leaders never knew why Halifax would not commit himself, so they concluded that the British wished to avoid any guarantees to the Czechs. Newton enquired about the matter from Prague, and Halifax replied that the French had rejected the British proposal.

On 22 December 1938 Henderson and Coulondre, the British and French ambassadors in Berlin, announced that London and Paris would approve a separate German guarantee to the Czechs. Logically, the Germans did not see why they should take the initiative in guaranteeing a state that had repeatedly acted against them if France, the Czechs' ally, was unwilling to do so. Initially, they surmised that the British and French would take up the initiative and propose some solution along the lines of the Munich agreement, but they did not. On 21 January 1939 Chvalkovsky travelled to Berlin for talks with Ribbentrop, who raised his objection to the Czech-Soviet alliance and the excessive size of the Czech army. Chvalkovsky demanded that Germany take the initiative for a territorial guarantee of Czech territory before seeking to reduce its army. While these talks were taking place, on 24 January 1939 Lord Halifax sent a message to President Roosevelt denouncing Hitler's disturbing intentions. Halifax said that Hitler had guessed that "Britain was now the main obstacle to the execution of his new ambitions". Finally, the German-Czech communiqué issued on 28 January 1939 made it clear that the Berlin negotiations had not borne fruit. Germany did not accept that unilateral action on the guarantee issue should be demanded of it.

While Franco-British disagreement on the guarantee issue persisted, on 8 February 1939 Ambassador Coulondre let the Germans know that France was ready to listen to any German suggestion. Ribbentrop discussed the matter with the Western ambassadors and asked for time to study the issue before making a proposal. Both he and Hitler concluded that France and Britain were disengaging because they were not really interested in the problem. In February, reports grew that Slovakia wanted to end its subjugation to the Czechs, and Ribbentrop received confirmation that the Slovaks wanted independence.

On 12 February, a meeting took place between Hitler and Adalbert Tuka, a veteran leader of the independence movement, who told the Führer that the union of Czechs and Slovaks was already impossible for economic and moral reasons. Tuka confirmed to Hitler that the rest of the country's leaders were determined to achieve independence. The situation of the Czechs could not have been more insecure, since they received no support from anyone and were unable on their own to control the internal situation. Hitler's response was logical: he decided that he was not prepared to support the Czecho-Slovak state and would help the Slovaks. On 22 February the Czechs presented the four powers at Munich with an "aide-memoire", a sort of memorandum, but a shorter one, containing a demand for territorial guarantees. The Czechs would renounce their alliances and declare themselves neutral in exchange for these guarantees. On the 26th, British diplomats reported from Bratislava to their government that Slovak dissatisfaction with the Czechs was at an all-time high and that German influence in Slovakia was increasing. The next day, 27 February, Halifax was quick to inform the British Ambassador in Washington, Sir Ronald Lindsay, that he had received information "pointing to the possibility of a military occupation of Czechoslovakia". On 28 February Germany sent notes to the British and French governments announcing its position against the guarantee.

This was the state of affairs when, on 1 March 1939, Hitler received the diplomatic corps accredited in Berlin on the occasion of the annual luncheon. The German Chancellor met Henderson, the British Ambassador, in the presence of other diplomats. He publicly expressed to him that he "admired the British Empire" and made a point of stressing that there were no major points of conflict in relations between the two countries. Henderson had no instructions to raise the Czech question and the matter was not discussed, indicating that Halifax was continuing his tactic of showing disinterest. It was not lost on anyone, however, that the situation on the ground was very tense. During the first week of March, the Czechs and Slovaks were engaged in important negotiations on the economic issue and reached an impasse. On 6 March, the Czech authorities reinforced their military presence in Ruthenia and dissolved the self-government. Newton immediately informed Halifax and assured him that the crisis was over. Another British ambassador, Kennard, reported from Warsaw on the 7th that a Slovak delegation was expected to arrive imminently to ascertain what the Polish position would be in the event of a declaration of independence. Kennard expressed the view that Poland's favourable position on Slovak independence was due to its interest in settling the Ruthenian question.

On 9 March, the event that finally triggered the crisis between the Czechs and Slovaks occurred. The Prague government dismissed the four senior ministers of the local government in Bratislava. The editor of *The Times* of London, Geoffery Dawson, who had been Lord Milner's man in South Africa and was in tune with Lord Halifax, despite noting in his private diary on the 12th that Czechs and Slovaks were fighting in the streets of Bratislava, followed a reporting line that presented a calm situation in Europe. Ambassador Henderson, on the other hand, reported from Berlin on 11 March that the Czech-Slovak dispute was being covered by the press. German newspapers reported that Bishop Tiso had asked the German government for help. Poland, which was concentrating all its attention on Ruthenia with the aim of its annexation by Hungary, learned on 13 March that Hitler would not oppose the invasion of Ruthenia by Hungarian troops. Miklós Horthy, the Hungarian regent, sent a message of thanks to the German Chancellor on the same day. Also on the 13th, Monsignor Tiso arrived in Berlin and obtained a German commitment to support Slovak independence. Events moved quickly and on 14 March the Slovak Diet approved secession and proclaimed independence, which was protected by the Reich. On the same day, Hungary presented a 12-hour ultimatum to the Czechs, who submitted. The Hungarian army began the occupation of Ruthenia on the same day.

Without instructions from the Foreign Office, on their own initiative, the British ambassadors in Berlin and Prague undertook important demarches on the same day. Neville Henderson contacted the Czechs and suggested that Foreign Minister Chvalkovsky travel to Germany to discuss the situation with Hitler. The Czechs responded favourably to Henderson's suggestion. Newton, working closely with his colleague, reported from Prague shortly afterwards that President Hacha and Chvalkovsky were expected in Berlin. The Czech leaders left by train at 4 p.m. on 14 March 1939. Welcomed on arrival with military honours, as this was a visit by a head of state, Hitler offered Hacha's daughter, who was travelling on the train, flowers and chocolates. The meeting began at 1:15 a.m. on 15 March and ended an hour later. Hitler was accompanied by Ribbentrop, Göring, and General Keitel. President Hacha called for the continuation of an independent Czech state and offered to reduce the army; but Hitler refused the request and announced that German troops would enter Bohemia-Moravia the same day and were prepared to crush any resistance. Hacha, who had heart problems, had a mild heart attack during the session, from which he quickly recovered after being treated by German doctors. Everyone breathed a sigh of relief, as they thought with dread what the international press would have said if Hacha had died in Berlin. The Czechs agreed to telephone Prague to order that any resistance be prevented.

Germans and Czechs living in the industrial centre of Morava-Ostrava had feared since October 1938 that the Poles might occupy this vital Moravian enclave. To prevent this eventuality, Hitler had ordered German units to enter the area in the evening of the 14th. The Czech population understood the move and there was no violence. This was an exceptional measure, since the German advance did not take place until the negotiation of the details of the agreement, which lasted until the 16th, had been concluded. Instead of assuming its commitments, British policy on the Czech question had been so murky and equivocal since Munich that complaints or grievances could hardly be made to Germany about Hitler's solution of the Czech problem. Halifax had shirked his responsibilities in both the Czecho-Slovak crisis and the Czech-Magyar question. In fact, by disinterested in the fate of Czechoslovakia and inhibiting himself during the frantic final weeks, Halifax had encouraged Germany to seek a unilateral solution. Ambassador Henderson, who knew of German intentions, had informed London before the arrival of the Czech politicians in Berlin. Halifax ambiguously implied that Britain had no intention of interfering in matters in which other countries were more directly concerned. Henderson therefore thought that his government's reaction would be mild, but it was not: Hitler's entry into Prague was to be the signal for the British to definitively abandon the policy of appeasement, as the warmongers had been demanding.

Another episode in March 1939 was to make it abundantly clear that Halifax's conduct was intended to unleash a public campaign aimed at the destruction of Germany. Despite the fact that there was no challenge to British interests and that Hitler was absolutely pro-British, the British took a series of steps aimed at making war inevitable. Halifax and his colleagues, moreover, had planned a conspiracy to shift all the blame onto Germany.

The Tilea farce

On 15 March Halifax told the House of Lords that he had made unsuccessful efforts to the Munich powers to support the British in securing the Czech state. He admitted that the events in Prague had met with the approval of the Czech government, but regretted that the spirit of Munich had been violated. Between 15 and 20 March 1939 the British took three unscrupulous steps which transformed the policy of appeasement into a policy of war: they asked the USSR to sign an alliance against Germany, an ominous and dangerous step which could mean Bolshevism's hegemony in Europe; they offered Poland military protection if it rejected the agreement with Germany; and they perpetrated a blatant lie about Germany's intentions to occupy Romania. All this was accompanied by a disinformation campaign to convince the British public that Hitler was a fanatic intent on world domination. Alan Campbell Johnson, a staunch admirer of Lord Halifax, refers to these steps as the "Halifax diplomatic revolution".

On 17 March 1939 Chamberlain, despite his mistrust of Stalin's play in Europe, made a historic speech in Birmingham, prepared by his Foreign Secretary. The Prime Minister presented himself as a naive and innocent person who had been a victim of German duplicity. He declared that he would never again believe in Hitler. He admitted that Britain should have assumed its obligation with regard to the guarantees given to Czechoslovakia, but that this had been impossible because of the collapse of the state. He then warned that Germany was trying to conquer the world and expressed faith in Britain's military power and in the ability of its leaders to manoeuvre in the diplomatic arena. Chamberlain announced that they would not wait for Hitler's next move, but that his government would immediately implement a series of measures against him.

Among those who celebrated the change in British policy as a victory were Sir Robert Vansittart, Permanent Under-Secretary in the Foreign Office, and Sir Alexander Cadogan, who succeeded him in 1938. Both hated Germany. The Zionist Leopold Amery, who drafted the Balfour Declaration, was also still at the Ministry. Another figure who welcomed Halifax's March U-turn with enthusiasm was William C. Bullitt, Roosevelt's ambassador-at-large. On 17 March Bullitt sent a report to the American President announcing that there was no longer any possibility of a diplomatic settlement in Europe. Halifax asked President Roosevelt to join Britain in demonstrating "the extent to which the present German rulers offended the moral sense of civilisation". Halifax was promised that the Secretary of State for the Treasury, the Zionist Jew Henry Morgenthau, would deepen his economic policy of discrimination against Germany.

With all this support, Halifax set his war policy in motion with one of the most brazen intrigues in modern diplomacy: the Tilea farce. The Germans were negotiating a trade treaty with Romania that threatened the City's interests in Romanian oil and other industries when Halifax accused them of trying to take control of the entire Romanian economy. Despite the fact that Germany has no common border with Romania, the Foreign Office invented a non-existent military threat from Germany to Romania. The tool was Romania's London-based plenipotentiary envoy, Viorel Tilea. Robert Vansittart was the one to brief him. Before Hitler marched on Prague, he was led to believe that Britain would oppose Germany. In November 1938 King Carol of Romania had travelled to London to negotiate a loan to buy arms, but had failed. Halifax, in return for cooperation in his anti-German plan, offered Tilea the loan and the elevation of the Romanian Legation in London to the rank of Embassy. On 17 March 1939, Tilea made public a conveniently prepared report that Germany had presented Romania with an ultimatum. Vansittart rushed this "big news" to *The Times* and *The Daily Telegraph* before Chamberlain made his speech at Bimingham. Millions of readers were shocked to see that Hitler's rapacity knew no bounds, and hostility towards Germany soared.

So brazen was Lord Halifax that he dismissed the repercussions the affair might have in Bucharest. On 18 March Reginald Hoare, Envoy Extraordinary and Minister Plenipotentiary to Romania, pleaded with Halifax to stop broadcasting Tilea's irresponsible statements and to stop alluding to them in official communications. This urgent request had no effect in London, so Hoare, fearing that the whole affair could seriously damage British prestige, proceeded to contact the Romanian Foreign Minister, Grigore Gafencu, so that he could explain in detail to the Foreign Office the absurdity of Tilea's claims. Gafencu let him know that questions were pouring in from all sides about the German ultimatum, reported in *The Times* and *The Daily Telegraph*, and expressed his bewilderment that the negotiations with Germany were being conducted "within the parameters of absolute normality between equals".

David L. Hoogan puts it this way: "Hoare assumed that his report would induce Halifax to repudiate Tilea's deception. Nothing of the sort happened. Hoare, who had been surprised when Halifax accepted Tilea's story without consulting the British Delegation in Bucharest, was astonished when Halifax continued to express his faith in the authenticity of the story after its falsity had been demonstrated." For his part, the French Foreign Minister, Georges Bonnet, summoned the Romanian ambassador in Paris, M. Tataresco, to ask for clarification. In his book *La Défense de la Paix*, Bonnet reproduces what Tataresco told him: "The German-Romanian talks have resulted in a trade agreement whose signature is imminent". Tataresco assured Bonnet that the alleged ultimatum had never existed.

Naturally, the Germans were also perplexed by the conspiracy hatched in London, so they wanted to make sure for themselves that the Romanian authorities disapproved of Tilea's slander. Gafencu assured them that their official's accusations regarding German claims on Romania were completely unfounded and were disapproved by the government. The foreign minister also had to explain himself to the American diplomats in Romania, whom he assured that negotiations with Germany were proceeding normally. Gafencu complained that Tilea's false report "had been exploited by the Jewish-controlled Western media". Despite being outraged at Tilea, the foreign minister did not dare to withdraw it from London for fear of offending Halifax.

The British Foreign Office Minister had not forgotten either the Poles, who were part of all the assumptions he was making for precipitating war in Europe, or the Soviets. Halifax contacted Ambassador Kennard in Warsaw on 17 March. He wanted to know as soon as possible Beck's position on his plan to transform the anti-Soviet Romanian-Polish alliance into an anti-German alliance. He asked him to tell Beck that he was discussing this possibility with Tilea. Józef Beck met with Kennard on the 18th and by then had his own reports, received from London and Bucharest. King Carol himself had assured the Polish diplomats that there was no threat from Germany. Although the story had been floated by the Foreign Office, Beck could scarcely believe that Tilea had made the statements attributed to him. He told Kennard that he rejected the idea that there was any threat from Germany to Romania and showed no interest in the Halifax plan.

Although Romania had never asked for it, Lord Halifax, without the slightest consultation with the Romanians, informed the Soviet Union that the Germans were seeking control of Romania and asked them to defend it in the event of German aggression. Halifax cared little for Moscow's scepticism, since ultimately he could always claim that he had been misinformed by the Romanian plenipotentiary in London. In the end, his request to the USSR for protection for Romania was a secondary issue, since what he was after was an Anglo-Soviet alliance. Tilea's fraudulent history served as a pretext for him to approach the Soviet Union.

Hitler's treatment of the Czechs

Hacha, the Czech president, and Chvalkovsky, his foreign minister, signed a document on 15 March in which they placed "in the hands of the German Führer the fate of the Czech nation and people". Hitler pledged to "take the Czech people under the protection of the Reich and to guarantee an autonomous development inherent in their national peculiarities." On 16 March 1939, the Protectorate of Bohemia-Moravia was proclaimed. Baron

Konstantin von Neurath, former German Foreign Minister, was appointed "Reichsprotektor". The obvious danger of war between the Czechs and Slovaks and the ensuing bloodshed had been averted by this solution. In Winston Churchill's *The Gathering Storm* (1948), the former British premier confesses that on 15 March Halifax met Herbert von Dirksen, the German ambassador in London. Drawing on this source, Hoggan writes that Halifax told Dirksen "that he could understand Hitler's taste for victories without bloodshed, but he promised the German diplomat that Hitler would be forced to shed blood next time".

On 15 March Ribbentrop addressed a letter to French Foreign Minister Bonnet, justifying the German policy in Prague as a necessary step to preserve order and avoid bloodshed. On the 16th Bonnet tried to take the initiative by proposing a soft Anglo-French protest to avoid a violent British reaction. Finally, on the 18th, the French and British ambassadors in Berlin handed their formal protest to Secretary of State Ernst von Weizsäcker, who avoided any sign of disturbance at Lord Halifax's words to Ambassador Dirksen and confined himself to defending Germany's policy on the Czechoslovak state crisis with composure and conviction. In Berlin it became known that Halifax intended to recall the ambassador for an indefinite period. On the 17th Weizsäcker had met with Henderson, and the Briton had asked the German Secretary of State to provide him with all possible arguments and information for use in London against the enemies of the policy of appeasement. Weizsäcker knew that in private Henderson had agreed with the analysis of the situation. The German Secretary of State informed Henderson and Coulondre that he refused to accept their notes of protest because the German Government considered that the Munich agreement had been overtaken by events. On 19 March both ambassadors were recalled for consultations and left Berlin.

Nevertheless, Germany was prepared to deal with the new situation by adopting a series of measures to make things easier. A few days later, on 24 March, Bohemia-Moravia was established as an area with its own customs. On 27 March it was announced that Czech would remain the official language in Bohemia-Moravia. On 16 April, after a month of German rule, it was decided to lower the German flag flying over Hradschin Castle in Prague. General Walther von Brauchitsch ordered the German garrisons to concentrate on areas populated by the German minority in order to avoid friction between the soldiers and Czech civilians. President Hacha formed a new Czech government on 27 April 1939. The new Czech administration retained the Departments of Transport, Justice, Interior, Education, Agriculture, National Economy, Public Works and Social Service. The Ministries of Foreign Affairs and Defence were dissolved. As early as April Hitler was keen to let the British know that the articles that had established the Protectorate did not necessarily apply and that Germany was prepared to negotiate the Czech question and the future of the Czechs through the channels of conventional diplomacy.

On 1 June 1939 the Reichsprotektor von Neurath drew up a report on favourable conditions in Bohemia-Moravia, and on 7 June Hitler granted an amnesty for all Czechs imprisoned for political reasons, both in the Sudetenland and in the Protectorate. During the same month, the Czech government in Prague negotiated a series of trade agreements with delegations from foreign countries. On 23 June, a Czech-Norwegian trade agreement was signed, and the following day another agreement was reached with the Netherlands. The cooperative attitude of the Czech leaders and population predisposed Hitler to make further concessions, and in July he allowed the Czech government a military force of 7,000 soldiers and some 300 officers from the former Czech army. It was agreed that only Czech nationals could serve in this force.

The use of Poland against Germany: the British blank cheque

The Polish ambassador in Paris, Julius Lukasiewicz, was the subject of special attention from William C. Bullitt. Documents from Ambassador Lukasiewicz cited by Hoggan reveal that on 19 March 1939 these two diplomats assured the Polish Foreign Minister, Józef Beck, that President Roosevelt was prepared to do everything possible to promote a war between Germany and the Anglo-French front. Bullitt admitted that he remained suspicious of Chamberlain's policy and still feared that the British government might try to settle its differences with Hitler. Bullitt promised Lukasiewicz that Roosevelt would vigorously resist any British moves in this direction.

Since Chamberlain had caved in to Lord Halifax, there was little or nothing to fear about Britain's political intentions. Halifax informed Paris, Moscow and Warsaw on 20 March that he wanted an armoured pact of Britain, France, Russia and Poland against Germany. This offer of alliance was the culmination of five days of frenetic activity that transformed the policy of appeasement into a policy of war. From this moment on, the Poles decided to defy Germany, whose foreign policy continued to bear fruit without bloodshed: in that dizzying March 1939, Lithuania agreed to the return of the German territory of Memel, which became part of East Prussia without Polish opposition.

Poland was ready to take on Germany, but wanted nothing to do with alliances with the Soviets. On 21 March Kennard, the British Ambassador, was informed that Warsaw refused to enter into any alliance that included the USSR, much to the displeasure of the Foreign Secretary. Lord Halifax discussed his proposed alliance with Ambassador Kennedy on 22 March and complained bitterly about the Poles' attitude to his planned alliance. In any case, he let Kennedy know that he was determined to continue his anti-

German policy and that hostilities in Europe could soon break out. Halifax asked him to advise Roosevelt to concentrate the US fleet at Pearl Harbour as a measure to protect Australia and Singapore from a possible Japanese attack.

However, the Polish ambassador in Berlin, Józef Lipski, understood that a policy of cooperation with Germany was in his country's best interests. In fact, Ribbentrop was able to win him over with his proposals. On 21 March the two diplomats met in Berlin. The German minister was aware of the offer Halifax had made to Poland the day before, and warned the Polish ambassador of the dangers of such an alliance. Lipski showed Ribbentrop his country's interest in Slovakia and confessed that they hoped that agreements with the Slovaks would not lead to a military occupation of the country. The German foreign minister pointed out to the Polish ambassador that the Slovaks had asked for the protection of both countries and that the German-Slovak negotiations were not directed against Poland. Ribbentrop assured Lipski that Germany was prepared to discuss how Poland could have the same influence in Slovakia as Germany, which required a climate of trust and cooperation between the two countries. Once again Joachim von Ribbentrop stressed the need for an agreement between Germany and Poland and deplored the treatment of the German minorities. The German Foreign Minister again presented a carefully prepared plan with convincing arguments, including the renunciation of German possessions in the Corridor. Ribbentrop reminded Lipski of the terms of the agreement presented on 24 October 1938, in which they sought only the union of the National Socialists in Danzig with those in Germany and the connection with East Prussia. Ribbentrop had the feeling that he had convinced Lipski of the advantages of collaboration and agreement. For his part, the ambassador promised to travel to Warsaw to try to convince his minister.

On 22 March the Polish ambassador was already in Warsaw and took part in meetings at the Foreign Ministry to reconsider the Polish position. Lipski presented a personal report on the German offer, which was met with hostility from Beck. Germany was accused of enveloping Poland, and Lipski accepted that Ribbentrop's proposal could be understood as an ultimatum. It was decided to retain the ambassador to Poland until a detailed reply to the Germans had been prepared. Because of his position in favour of a pact with Hitler, Lipski's reliability as a negotiator with the Germans was questioned. Jean Szembek, Polish State Secretary for Foreign Affairs, writes in his *Journal, 1933-1939* that Beck decided not to allow Lipski to meet with Ribbentrop again to discuss a settlement. Count Michal Lubienski went so far as to accuse Ribbentrop of having succeeded in demoralising Lipski. The Polish ambassador learned that his appeal for an agreement had been rejected and that he no longer enjoyed Beck's confidence, so he expressed his wish to resign from his post.

In deliberations at the Foreign Ministry, the Halifax proposal for a pact with the USSR was rejected outright, but Beck was confident that he could opt for an Anglo-Polish alliance. So convinced were the Polish leaders that Germany's proposal was an ultimatum that on 23 March, in agreement with the military leaders, Poland decided on a partial mobilisation. The strength of the Polish army was doubled with the call-up of 334,000 reservists. Along with this measure, the plan for waging war against Germany was distributed to the main commanders. After learning of the surprising partial mobilisation of the Poles, Hitler consulted the Commander-in-Chief of the Army, General Walther von Brauchitsch, to whom he explained that important negotiations with Poland were in progress, and that he did not wish to see Germany involved in a conflict.

Much more alarmed was the German ambassador in Warsaw. Increasingly sceptical of Polish intentions, Moltke attached particular importance to the arrest of Stanislav Mackiewicz, a prominent Polish journalist and editor of *Slowo* (*The Word*), who had long been in favour of a German-Polish agreement. Finally, Moltke reported that Lipski would return to Berlin on 26 March, so both Hitler and Ribbentrop were hopeful that there was still a chance. Before Lipski closed the door on the German-Polish agreement in Berlin, Lukasiewicz informed Bullitt on the 24th that his country would formally reject an alliance integrating the Soviet Union that same day. The Polish ambassador told his colleague that Poland preferred a unilateral alliance with Britain. The American ambassador was convinced that the British would accept the proposal.

When the Polish ambassador in London, Edward Raczynski, went to Halifax to reject the quadruple alliance, he told him that the Polish government believed that a pact with the USSR could "provoke a catastrophe". Raczynski developed Beck's thesis that an alliance with the Soviet Union would unduly threaten peace. The ambassador added that he was authorised to propose an Anglo-Polish alliance. Halifax immediately admitted his interest in the proposal. "With unbounded hypocrisy," writes Professor Hoggan, "he declared that he would not object if Poland and Germany could negotiate satisfactorily on the Danzig question." According to Hoggan, "the fact that Halifax felt it necessary to make this point demonstrates his tactical skill as a diplomat. He did not wish to give the Poles the impression that he was pushing them into war." The next day, 25 March, Bullitt informed Lukasiewicz that he had asked Ambassador Kennedy to let Chamberlain know that the United States looked favourably on Poland's position in relation to the alliance. On the 26th Bullitt contacted Kennedy again: he wanted him to tell Chamberlain that the United States expected Britain to go to war with Germany if the Danzig question led to an explosion between Poles and Germans. Bullitt met again with the Polish ambassador and expressed his conviction that the British response to the Polish proposal would be in the affirmative. For his part, Lukasiewicz confided that Lipski would reject the German proposal the same day.

When the Polish ambassador announced his country's categorical rejection of the negotiating proposals, the Germans were shocked. The Polish counter-proposals ignored the German demand for the return of Danzig and the connection to East Prussia. Germany's offer to secure the borders was also ignored. Ambassador Lipski submitted a written memorandum to Ribbentrop, which the German minister read with astonishment. He made no attempt to conceal his surprise and regretted that Poland's refusal to allow the annexation of Danzig would ruin any chance of a German-Polish agreement. Lipski replied that "it was for him a painful obligation to draw attention to the fact that any attempt by Germany to implement these plans, especially as far as the return of Danzig to the Reich was concerned, meant war with Poland." Ribbentrop, unable to maintain his usual composure on this historic occasion, could not contain a feeling of despair. He tried futilely to nullify the consequences of the Polish communiqué and told Lipski that Germany was in no hurry to settle the Danzig problem and that perhaps Poland could reconsider the whole matter when the general situation was calmer. The Polish Ambassador referred to his government's written note and asked whether Germany could not, after all, give up its Danzig aspirations. Lipski assured Ribbentrop that Beck would visit Berlin again gladly in response to this German concession. The German Foreign Minister would have abandoned efforts with the Poles had it not been for Hitler, who was stubbornly convinced that a German-Polish agreement was worth every effort.

Lord Halifax met with his diplomats on 27 March and informed them of his decision to prioritise the alliance with Poland. On the same day he sent a telegram to Kennard, announcing the decision and expressing his confidence that a new alliance proposal could be presented to the Soviet Union later in the day. On 30 March he informed Kennard that the guarantee given by His Majesty's Government to Poland would be laid before Parliament the following day. Halifax wryly informed the British Ambassador in Warsaw that the American Embassy had bombarded him with assertions that Ribbentrop was pressuring Hitler to invade Poland before the British would make any commitment. Halifax let Kennard know that he had decided that engagement would not be restricted to cases of unprovoked aggression. Hoogan, who has a wealth of diplomatic documents on the matter, writes: "He told Kennard that he had decided to ignore the question of the aggressor. He did not want to remain neutral in case the Poles forced Germany into war." The British telephoned the Polish president, Ignacy Moscicki, and Marshal Smigly-Rydz to announce their decision, to which they agreed.

Conservatives, Liberals and Labour readily accepted the unilateral guarantee to Poland when it was presented to Parliament on 31 March. In his speech in the House of Commons, Chamberlain explained the commitment in these words: "...in the circumstance of any action which clearly threatened Polish independence, and which, in consequence, the Polish Government considered it vital to resist with its own national forces, His Majesty's Government would consider itself bound at once to give the Polish Government the fullest possible assistance. An assurance to this effect has been given to the Polish Government." Chamberlain's speech was broadcast by radio to the Continent at four o'clock in the afternoon of 31 March. When Viscount Jacques Davignon, the Belgian ambassador in Berlin, learned of the text, he exclaimed in alarm that the British commitment was tantamount to a "blank cheque". He is therefore the author of the metaphor.

On 2 April 1939 Józef Beck left Warsaw by train for London. He was accompanied by Józef Lipski and Colonel Szymánski, a military attaché in Berlin whose wife, Halina Szymánska, was a Polish spy who during the war acted as a contact for Wilhelm Canaris and was one of the most efficient agents of British MI6. A German Foreign Office protocol chief welcomed her at the Berlin station on the morning of the 3rd. Despite the events of the past few days, Beck had been expecting Ribbentrop; but the German Foreign Minister did not show up, which was clear evidence that Germany's attitude towards Poland had changed.

The Polish delegation arrived in London late at night, so formal talks were held on the morning of the 4th. Beck promised Halifax that in the event of direct conflict between Britain and Germany, Poland would fight the Germans. This amounted to an offer of a reciprocal guarantee. Halifax accepted the offer, but added that it was insufficient for his needs, as he wished to obtain further commitments from Poland. Beck was surprised and asked the Foreign Office Secretary what he had in mind. Halifax calmly said that he wanted Poland to agree to go to war if Germany attacked Holland, Belgium, Switzerland or Denmark. Surprised by the far-reaching nature of the request, Beck replied that he would need some time to think it over. The second major issue of the meeting was the Polish refusal to join the quadruple alliance. Lord Halifax asked for an explanation of the reasons for the refusal. Once again, the Polish foreign minister argued that such an alliance could be dangerous and even fatal for Poland. Beck's reasons did not satisfy Halifax, who made it clear that he was extremely disappointed by the Polish position on his alliance plan. The future of Poland," writes Hoggan, "was indifferent to him. The new Polish state was merely a pawn in his game." Yet, to the astonishment of British and European public opinion, by handing over the "blank cheque" to Poland, Britain, for the first time in its history, was leaving it to another power to decide whether or not to go and fight outside its own country.

Roosevelt's ambassador-at-large, William C. Bullitt, hurried to meet Beck, with whom he was on friendly terms. He was expecting him in Lille. The Polish foreign minister confirmed that he was satisfied with the atmosphere in London and confided to Bullitt that Halifax had sought to oblige Poland in case Germany attacked other neighbouring countries. Beck's main interest, however, was in Germany's reaction, so he speculated with the American ambassador about Hitler's possible reactions in response to his trip to London and the assurance obtained from the British. Beck thought that Germany might break off diplomatic relations with Poland.

At eleven o'clock on the morning of 7 April, as soon as he had taken leave of Beck, Bullit sent a message to President Roosevelt, confirming that Beck had returned very pleased with the understanding and degree of compromise reached in England. The report included allusions by the Polish minister to Hitler and Ribbentrop, whom Beck described as a 'dangerous imbecile'. As Beck and Bullitt surmised, the German leaders' disappointment at the impossibility of reaching an agreement with the Poles was all too evident. The confirmation that Britain had offered unlimited military support to Poland was greeted in Germany with great concern and provoked Hitler's reaction, who proceeded to order the drawing up of plans for an eventual conflict with Poland. The "Fall Weiss" (Operation White), the military code name for preparations for a possible German-Polish war, began to take shape.

The deterioration of German-Polish relations

Despite the fact that a German-Polish non-aggression pact had been in place since 26 January 1934, Józef Beck, who knew full well that Halifax's plans included the destruction of Germany, agreed to place his country at the centre of British and American warmongering policy, which was tantamount to breaking the pact. As much as Halifax said he would not oppose an agreement on Danzig, Beck knew it would have been the Foreign Office Secretary of State's greatest disappointment. Now, the British needed France and counted on it in their war plans against Hitler. The Poles also knew how important it was to have the French on their side, so on his return from London Beck tried to improve relations with Paris. Poland expected France to support the blank cheque unconditionally, but Bonnet, who was also interested in the four-way alliance proposed by Halifax, initially delayed a direct interview with his Polish colleague. Meanwhile, Bullitt continued his pro-war work in Paris: the tenacious American ambassador remained in constant contact with Poland's Lukasiewicz, and on 9 April 1939 he told him that he expected France to attack Germany from Belgium in the event of a conflict.

On 7 April 1939 the Italians occupied Albania, and European diplomacy temporarily focused on the situation in the Balkans. President Roosevelt took advantage of the circumstances to send letters to Hitler and Mussolini, which were released to the American public on 14 April and received by their addressees on 15 April. Roosevelt, in the service of the

Jewish lobby which had elevated him to the Presidency, was one of those who worked hardest for war; yet he appeared to international public opinion as a generous and disinterested peacemaker who worked with all his energy for peace. In these messages he held Italy and Germany exclusively responsible for all threats to peace in Europe. He asked Hitler and Mussolini to declare that they would abstain from war under all circumstances for twenty-five years. "Are you willing," Roosevelt asked, "to guarantee that your armed forces will not attack or invade the territory or positions of the following independent countries?" He went on to list twenty-nine countries, including Russia. Interestingly, it demanded that Italy and Germany sign non-aggression pacts with Syria and Palestine, which were not independent and were under French and British mandate. The references to Palestine must have been a demand of the Zionists who made up the Brain Trust.

In these circumstances, Romanian Foreign Minister Gafencu arrived in Berlin on 18 April after stopping his train at the Polish border to meet Beck. On 19 April he met Hitler and began the conversation with a lengthy recapitulation of his recent meeting with the Polish Foreign Minister. The German Chancellor criticised Beck for accepting the British guarantee and complained that he could never understand the change in Poland's attitude. He confided to Gafencu that he had planned to denounce Polish policy towards Britain as an intolerable violation of the 1934 Pact, which he considered broken. Hitler lamented to Gafencu that the Polish leaders did not appreciate his intentions to respect Pilsudski's Poland, with its borders and the absurd Versailles Accords. "I have restrained the press," Hitler was quoted as telling him, "from speaking out against the scandalous treatment of the German minority." He contrasted this attitude with the constant attacks on Germany in the Polish press. On the possibility of war with the United Kingdom, Hitler predicted: "In the end we would all end up, victors and vanquished, under the same ruins; and the only one to profit would be Moscow." The Führer admitted to Minister Gafencu that he was accused in Germany of being an unrepentant admirer of the British Empire, and confessed to him that this was true. He assured him that only an inhuman fate would compel him to conceive of a conflict with the British and added that "he had been a great Anglophile from his earliest youth."

A few days later the Romanian diplomat, who had travelled around Europe throughout April trying to seek conciliation and avoid war, arrived in London. He had been informed in advance that the Tilea issue would not be accepted as a subject for discussion. The first meeting with British diplomats took place on 24 April. The Foreign Office Secretary was surprised to find that Gafencu avoided discussing the USSR issue and instead took the initiative with a plan of his own for resolving European differences. Convinced that the main obstacles to solving the problems lay in Britain and Poland, Gafencu had received German support for his peace plan and was determined to present it to Halifax with the utmost vigour. The Romanian diplomat explained his conversation with Hitler, whom he described as "a force of nature". Gafencu told the British that the German Chancellor had evidently spoken to him with the fact that he was travelling to London in mind. After admitting that, following his interviews with Beck and Hitler, he was convinced that the German-Polish situation was hopeless, the Romanian foreign minister enthusiastically announced that he had a plan that the German leaders fully accepted.

This plan envisaged a new agreement for Bohemia-Moravia, which could be devised in such a way as to reduce tension on the other issues and bring about a general agreement. Naturally, the British, who had made the events in Prague the main pretext for action against Germany, did not like the plan at all. Halifax immediately asked whether the Germans would restore the Czech state, and Gafencu replied that they would, since Germany approved of the plan. Sir Alexander Cadogan then replied that "the restoration of Prague would hardly be a compensation for Poland." Gafencu conceded this, but flatly denied that Hitler wanted war and added that the world was waiting for an alternative, which could be generated if Germany was offered some proposition on to negotiate. At the end of the talks, the Romanian minister had the impression that he had failed to convince his hosts.

While Gafencu was in London trying to find a way to peace, it had already been decided four months in advance that war would take place. In an extensive article entitled "President Roosevelt's Campaign to Incite War in Europe: The Secret Polish Papers", Mark Weber, director of the Institute for Historical Review, explains that on 25 April 1939, Ambassador Bullitt called journalist Karl von Wiegand, chief European correspondent of the International News Service, who presented himself at the embassy. The words he spoke to him were reprinted in the *Chicago Herald American* on 8 October 1944 in an article entitled "Von Wiegand says". They are: "The decision on the war in Europe has been made. Poland is guaranteed the backing of Britain and France and will not yield to any of Germany's demands. America will be in the war soon after Britain and France enter it". One can only ask: Who had made the decision?

Sir Neville Henderson, after being held in London for forty days, was allowed to return to Berlin. On 20 April Halifax announced to the House of Lords that the ambassador would shortly return to Germany, which he did on 26 April. On 27 April Henderson visited the Foreign Office and met the Secretary of State, Ernst von Weizsäcker, to whom he admitted that he had suffered a great loss of face in the Foreign Office. Henderson, who knew that Hitler's willingness to negotiate on Prague's status had been rebuffed, was informed that the Führer was preparing to make a speech to the Reichstag in response to Roosevelt's accusations. On the same day, the Foreign Ministry issued two notes announcing the abrogation of the 1934 non-aggression pact with Poland and the 1935 Anglo-German naval pact. The atmosphere in

Berlin was heating up, and meetings and talks between diplomats followed one after the other. Coulondre discussed the situation with Poland's Lipski. The French ambassador regretted that the European scene was so confused, and admitted that it was largely due to the fact that British diplomacy moved abruptly from one extreme to the other. Lipski explained in detail the content of the German offer that had been rejected by his country. Both ambassadors agreed that the proposal was remarkably generous.

The German Reichstag met on the morning of 28 April to hear the Führer, who carefully sought to leave open the door to negotiations with Poland and Great Britain. In his speech he reviewed German policy from his accession to power in 1933 until the occupation of Prague in March 1939. He recalled that the Czechs and Hungarians had turned only to Germany and Italy to mediate in the dispute, although it had been decided in Munich that mediation was the obligation of all four powers. It was at in the second part of the speech that he referred to President Roosevelt's policy. He ridiculed Roosevelt's call for non-aggression pacts with countries on other continents and with countries that did not even enjoy independence. He referred to Roosevelt's constant efforts to provoke him. Referring to his allegations of alleged German interventions abroad, he concluded that "from a military point of view they could only be generated in the imagination of a madman"[3]. In his speech, the German Chancellor paid, as usual, a tribute of admiration to the British Empire and insisted on his desire for a permanent Anglo-German friendship. On Poland, he said he respected its maritime interests, praised Marshal Pilsudski for his desire to improve German-Polish relations, and described in detail the points of the offer he had made to Poland. He deplored the acceptance of the British guarantee and announced that Germany was no longer prepared to maintain the proposal made in October 1938 as a basis for an agreement with Poland, which was a clear step backwards. Raising his tone, he explained that he had abrogated the 1934 pact with Warsaw, which he had earlier offered to extend to twenty-five years, because the Poles had violated it by seeking the British guarantee, which, he said, did not mean that Germany was unwilling to assume new contractual obligations towards Poland.

The German Chancellor's speech was followed with expectation throughout Europe. In Poland, of course, there was a hostile reaction in the government and in the press. Göbbels felt compelled to respond in the German press, asking in an article in *Der Angriff* (*The Offensive*): "Do they know what they are doing? In France, however, the moderate tone of the speech reassured French leaders, and in London, too, the conciliatory tone

---

[3] Hitler was somewhat accustomed to provocations and insults of the most serious kind coming from the United States. Fiorello La Guardia, a Zionist Jew who was mayor of New York from 1934 to 1945, used to insult the German Führer: "savage murderer", "depraved", "drunkard", "sodomite", "madman", "driver of a herd of sheep" were some of the adjectives chosen by La Guardia in his public speech at a rally in 1937.

of Hitler's words was appreciated. In Hungary, too, the peaceful intentions expressed in the Führer's speech were welcomed. On the other hand, the Italian ambassador in Berlin, Bernardo Attolico, informed German diplomats the next day that his country was prepared to exert pressure on Poland to accept a reasonable settlement of the differences between the two countries. Weizsäcker welcomed the offer with gratitude, but expressed fears that any demarche would be futile. The reaction in the United States was another matter, where President Roosevelt was furious after reading the English translation of the speech, in which Hitler ridiculed his policies. From this moment on, Roosevelt personally hated Hitler: "This personal factor," writes Hoggan, "was added to the other motives which gave Roosevelt the desire to destroy Germany".

In Poland, Lipski formally resigned on 1 May 1939. The Polish ambassador informed Beck that it was impossible for him to remain in Berlin under the present circumstances. Nevertheless, the foreign minister did not accept his resignation and ordered him to return to Germany. Moltke, the German ambassador, also returned to Warsaw on 4 May after spending a few days in Berlin. In the shuttling back and forth of diplomats, there was a significant change at the head of the USSR Foreign Commissariat: on 3 May 1939 Maksim Litvinov was dismissed as Commissar. The fact that this Polish Jew was replaced by Vyacheslav Molotov did not displease the Polish Foreign Ministry. It was known in Warsaw that Molotov was very close to Stalin and that both were married to Jewish women.

In response to Hitler's speech, Józef Beck appeared before the Sejm on 5 May 1939. Prior to his speech, the embassies had been instructed to criticise Hitler's address. Beck's aim was to convince public opinion that he was able and willing to challenge Hitler. Beck prepared his speech in the knowledge that London would be unreservedly supportive of his words, which allowed him to go as far as he wished. After beginning by acknowledging that this was a decisive moment, he analysed his foreign policy steps. Mentioning the agreement with Britain, he confirmed that Britain had agreed to fight for Poland and that, in return, Poland had pledged to support the British in any conflict. Despite knowing that he was acting as an accomplice of Britain, which was seeking a pretext for war, Beck claimed that Anglo-Polish interests were based on a complete lack of aggressive intentions and accused Hitler of having unjustifiably exploited the British guarantee to Poland to scrap the 1934 pact. Surprisingly, although Sir Alexander Cadogan had confessed to Joseph Kennedy that the guarantee to Poland was unprecedented in the history of British foreign policy, Beck declared that there was nothing extraordinary about the British guarantee, which he described as a normal step in the pursuit of friendly relations with a neighbouring country. Disdaining any historical rigour, since West Prussia had been colonised by Germans and before the war almost 70 per cent of the inhabitants were German, he called the word "Corridor" "an artificial invention, since it was a former Polish land with a negligible number of German settlers". These words amounted, once again, to a disparagement of Hitler's generosity, who was prepared to accept permanent Polish rule over this former German territory. Although Lipski had acknowledged that only Hitler could have made such a generous offer, Beck claimed that Germany had offered no concessions and was only making demands. The Polish minister's speech, which branded Hitler a liar, was peppered with impudent lies from beginning to end. He went so far as to admit that the German Chancellor had offered to recognise the present frontier with Poland; but, and here we quote Professor Hoggan, "he took a position unprecedented in the annals of European diplomacy on the grounds that such a promise was utterly worthless." Shamefully, Beck insisted that Hitler had assaulted Poland's honour with his overtures and rejected those who preferred peace to national honour. At this climax of the speech, an angry voice shouted: "We do not need peace. On leaving the rostrum, Beck received a thunderous ovation.

The Polish foreign minister's parliamentary intervention dealt a severe blow to hopes for peace in Europe and was widely recognised as such. Naturally, Beck's intransigent words were backed by Halifax, and King Carol of Romania concluded that Beck's speech made war inevitable. Weizsäcker, State Secretary at the Foreign Ministry, tried to avoid an alarmist attitude by a circular letter to the German embassies, in which he dismissed Beck's speech as "a petty dictum of a weak government". In France, however, Foreign Minister Georges Bonnet did not welcome Beck's speech with the enthusiasm desired by the warmongers, who were jubilant. Bullitt and the Polish ambassadors to France and Britain, Lukasiewicz and Raczynski, agreed that Bonnet was the leader of the struggle for peace in France. Bullitt promised to do everything in his power to discredit him to Daladier.

On 6 May the American ambassador in Paris was pleased to inform his friend Roosevelt that Prime Minister Daladier had less and less confidence in Bonnet. Bullitt was betting on Champetier de Ribes, who advocated war, as Bonnet's replacement. William C. Bullitt's mother was the daughter of Jonathan Horowitz, a German Jew who had emigrated to the United States. The American ambassador belonged to a family of prominent Philadelphia bankers. Bullitt, who had assisted President Wilson at the Versailles Peace Conference and had urged recognition of the communist regime in Russia from the outset, was President Roosevelt's voice in Europe, hence he travelled to the United States several times a year to participate in White House Councils.

The untenable situation of Germans in Poland

Following Lord Halifax's instructions, Ambassador Henderson delivered an embarrassing threat to Germany in Berlin on 15 May 1939. The Foreign Office, following Beck's speech, officially warned that the British Empire would fight with the aim of destroying the Third Reich should Hitler try to recapture Danzig. Meanwhile, the situation for Germans living in Poland continued to worsen. From the end of March, they not only received threats, but also became victims of persecution and terror unleashed by alleged Polish patriots. The Polish authorities themselves acted against the German minority, many of whose members were arrested for no apparent reason. Complaints by German leaders about their treatment were to no avail.

Even before the blank cheque was issued, violence against the German minority had broken out in various regions without the Polish authorities heeding the consuls' protests. Incidents on 30 March in Bromberg in the Pomeranian region prompted Ambassador Moltke himself to protest to Polish Deputy Minister Szembeck. On the same day, a German citizen who owned a restaurant in Jablonowo was beaten up and his business destroyed. The police had been alerted but did not show up. In Posen (Poznan) German establishments were regularly stoned and insurance companies refused to pay compensation, so Consul Walther sent a diplomatic note to Ribbentrop denouncing assaults on German citizens in a dozen towns and villages. On 4 April Moltke sent a communiqué to Ribbentrop denouncing that ten paramilitary associations had issued a public appeal calling for a boycott of German trade and handicrafts. It also called for a ban on German-language films and for restrictions on the number of schools and on the publication of newspapers and books. On 18 April the German Chargé d'Affaires in Warsaw, Krümmer, officially complained that Germans had been deprived of their right of citizenship during the municipal elections, prevented from standing as candidates and denied the right to vote. Throughout April, aggression and excesses of all kinds continued without any intervention by the Polish police. In May, while the stonings of shops and private homes continued, the Polish authorities began to take action against German schools and to seize newspapers and publications.

A wave of rioting began on 13 May in the Lodz region. Tomaszow Mazowiecki, a town of 40,000 inhabitants of which some 3,000 were German, was the epicentre of the vandalism. Many Germans were injured and one woman died. During the two-day riot, most German property in the area was damaged or destroyed. Polish factory owners were forced to dismiss their German employees. Other violent incidents took place in the province of Poznan and in Eastern Upper Silesia. On 15 May the German Foreign Ministry discussed the possibility of reprisals against the Polish minority in Germany; but it was decided to reject this idea as harmful, useless and senseless. The Polish authorities banned the German-language press from reporting on the incidents against the German minority, and when German newspapers began to denounce what was happening, German journalists were restricted from entering Poland. The German authorities concluded that the best source of information about anti-German incidents was their consular representations, so in the months that followed many consuls began to be arrested. In Berlin, Weizsäcker appealed in vain to Henderson and Coulondre for their governments to exert pressure on the Polish government to prevent a repetition of these outrages.

On 21 May, a serious incident occurred in Kalthof, in the territory of the Free City of Danzig, near the East Prussian border. On 20 May, local German inhabitants demonstrated to show their indignation at the arrogant stance of Polish customs inspectors in Kalthof. Polish High Commissioner Chodacki was in Gdynia when the customs authorities called him to say that they feared an assault on Polish facilities. Councillor Perkovski was in charge of the High Commissioner's Office in Chodacki's absence, so he ordered the Danzig police to intervene. Hours later, Perkovski, an assistant and his driver, a former soldier named Zygmunt Morawski, approached Kalthof and found that it was quiet and that the customs officers had gone home. Perkovski ordered Morawski to stay in the car, parked about a hundred metres from the customs building. It was 12:50 in the morning, yet Morawski left the high beams on. Soon a car approached from the opposite direction, returning to Danzig from East Prussia. Its driver, Grübnau, stopped to ask the Polish driver to turn off his lights. Morawski's response was a pistol shot that ended Grübnau's life. After committing the murder, Morawski abandoned the vehicle and, in order to leave the territory of the Free City, sped on foot towards the Polish border.

The High Commissioner was returning to Danzig when Perkovski told him by telephone what had happened. As soon as he arrived, Chodacki ordered all Poles to go to Dirschau (Tscew) in Polish territory. Perkovski, who was the president of the Polish railway company in Danzig, went with his assistant to the station, which was near the customs house, and returned by train to Poland. On the same day, the 21st, Chodacki presented a note to the president of the Danzig Senate, Greiser, in which he protested against the demonstration in Kalthof and referred to the murder of Grübnau without apology. Greiser reminded Chodacki that the sovereign power in Danzig was the League of Nations, not Poland, and demanded that Perkovski, his assistant and the Polish chauffeur be returned to Danzig for trial. Chodacki arrogantly rejected the demand and, in a demonstration that the Poles in Danzig considered themselves above the law and despised the jurisdiction of the Free City authorities, Józef Beck himself defended Chodaki's high-handed attitude.

The fact that an innocent German citizen was murdered on the territory of Danzig without any apology from the Polish authorities infuriated Hitler, who sent a personal funeral wreath to Grübnau's funeral. Göring warned Ambassador Henderson that Germany would intervene in Danzig despite Polish and British opposition. Henderson replied grimly that the Poles would regard any intervention in Danzig as a threat to their sovereignty and that Britain would immediately come to Poland's aid with the full strength of its armed forces. Burckhardt, the League of Nations High Commissioner, informed the Germans that on the same day, 21 May, Halifax had said in Geneva that the British would fight for Poland against Germany without considering the origins of the conflict. On 24 May the British Parliament discussed the Kalthof incident, but Chamberlain confined himself to commenting that a Danzig citizen had been killed and that an investigation was under way.

Tension in Danzig was mounting after the Kalthof incident, aggravated by the contemptuous and inadmissible response of the Polish authorities. The chairman of the Free City Senate, Arthur Greiser, submitted two protest notes on 3 June: the first was a refusal to allow Grübnau's murderer to stand trial, the second was a protest against the steady increase of Polish customs inspectors on Danzig territory. The Polish High Commissioner, Colonel Marjan Chodacki, ignored both protests. On 6 June Burckhardt, the League of Nations High Commissioner, met with Greiser and reported on a recent interview with Ribbentrop, who had told him that Germany was still committed to a settlement with Poland, but would accept the risk of war to liberate Danzig if the Poles refused. Burckhardt confessed to Greiser his conviction that the Soviets were delighted at the prospect of a suicidal internal conflict in Western Europe. On 11 June the Polish authorities, again in uncompromising tones, announced that they would accept no more complaints about their customs inspectors and warned that they planned to increase the number of officials.

In Berlin, Weizsäcker met with the British Ambassador on 13 June to discuss the crisis in Danzig. Henderson confirmed that Halifax's official line, which advocated the need to encircle Germany, remained unchanged. Neville Henderson confidentially expressed his personal disagreement with Halifax's policy. He considered the blank cheque to Poland to be highly damaging and also expressed his opposition to a military alliance between Britain and the USSR. "Henderson knew," writes Hoggan, "that he was overstepping his authority in making these remarks to the German Secretary of State, but he could not tolerate that the Germans might think that he agreed with Halifax's war policy. It was clear that he was not the right man to represent Halifax in Berlin." As if the situation was not tense enough, on 17 June Joseph Göbbels turned up at Danzig on the pretext of attending the Danzig Cultural Exhibition, which commemorated the historical role of the Baltic port. In a theatre in the city he delivered a provocative speech in which he announced that Danzig would return to the Reich. Days later, on 20 June, the *Poiska* gazette defiantly retorted that Poland would never bow to German pressure.

The person primarily responsible for the security of the German minority was the head of the Department of the Interior, Waclav Zyborski, who on 23 June 1939 agreed to discuss the situation with Walter Kohnert, one of the leaders of the German minority in Bromberg. Zyborski admitted that the Germans in Poland were in an unenviable situation, but recommended that they complain to Hitler about their predicament. He claimed that the Germans were disloyal and added that Poles in Germany were also being mistreated. Zyborski accused Kohnert and his friends of being under the influence of National Socialism and warned that the time had come for the fight that had long been in preparation. He ended by telling his interlocutor frankly that his policy called for harsh treatment of the German minority and made it clear to him that there was no possibility that the Germans in Poland could alleviate their harsh fate. In fact, the authorities were closing down German companies and businesses and confiscating buildings belonging to the German community.

On 6 July Rudolf Wiesner, leader of one of the German parties in Danzig, appealed to Polish Prime Minister Slawoj-Skladkowski, citing violent attacks against Germans in various cities. He referred in particular to the wave of attacks between 13 and 15 May in Tomaszow near Lodz, to another anti-German pogrom carried out on 21 and 22 May by uncontrolled mobs in the Lodz region, namely in Konstantynow, and to a third wave of violence in Pabianice between 22 and 23 June, where the Institute, a trade union of German Christians, bookshops and other buildings had been attacked. The consuls reported that some Germans, frightened by death threats, poisoning of dogs, felling of fruit trees, theft of timber, arson and other intimidating acts, left their homes and tried to cross the German border. Many of them were arrested and imprisoned on charges of illegal migration for attempting to cross into Germany without permission. Wiesner's protest did not produce any results, so the leaders of the German groups had to recognise that they had no chance of influencing the Polish authorities to provide protection.

Coincidentally, on the same day, 6 July, Józef Beck had a meeting at the Foreign Ministry with Jerzy Potocki, the Polish ambassador to the United States, who was in Warsaw. The two discussed the critical situation and Potocki told him that he had returned to Poland to propose a change in Polish policy. He denounced to his superior that both the United States and Britain had a war psychosis. He insisted on denouncing the role played by Jewish bankers and capitalists and warned that the Western armaments factories were united in a solid front for war. The ambassador tried to make Beck see that they were delighted to have found their pretext in the Danzig issue and in Poland's defiant attitude. Potocki bluntly charged that to Western usurers and speculators the Poles were merely black slaves who were required to work for nothing. He also warned Beck that it was an illusion to expect the Americans to intervene in Europe to defend Poland.

These arguments, whose relevance was obvious, had no effect. However, Potocki was not the only diplomat who disapproved of Józef Beck's line: the Polish ambassador to Ankara, Sokolnicki, a close friend of Jan Szembek, the state secretary for foreign affairs, supported Potocki's efforts. Both were certain that Szembek would have accepted his position had he been in charge of the Ministry. On 14 July Sokolnicki met Franz von Papen, the German ambassador to Turkey, in Ankara. As Hoggan writes, again citing diplomatic archives, "Sokolnicki confessed to him that he would like a negotiated settlement between Germany and Poland before the Jews and the Freemasons had convinced the world that a catastrophic conflict was inevitable". Potocki returned to the United States after his failed demarche to Beck. *The New York Times* reported the diplomat's comment on 8 August: "Poland prefers Danzig to peace".

Among these Masons was Bullitt, who kept warning his brother Mason in the White House that the French foreign minister was working for peace. Bullitt could not get Bonnet to give Poland a blank cheque as well. This lack of conviction on the part of the French foreign minister to support the war was a setback. In July, in the midst of escalating tension between Poland and Germany, Bonnet received Neville Henderson, the British ambassador to Germany, in Paris. Both agreed in condemning Halifax's war policy. Bonnet thought that an Anglo-French war against Germany was absolutely unnecessary and told Daladier that he would rather resign than have any responsibility for such a disastrous conflict. Daladier expressed his understanding for Bonnet's attitude and begged him to remain in his post and continue to fight for peace.

A new incident in Danzig almost brought the outbreak of war forward. On 25 July a Polish soldier, Budziewicz, was killed in strange circumstances in the territory of Danzig. The murderer, a customs officer named Stein, swore that he had acted in self-defence, which did not prevent his arrest and the charge of reckless homicide. The Danzig authorities apologised to Chodacki and promised to pay compensation. The contrast between this attitude and that of Poles in the Grübnau murder case is obvious, but the Polish press concealed these facts from the public and propagandised that Polish personnel in Danzig were being indiscriminately attacked and that Budziewicz had been killed unprovoked on Polish territory.

Four days later, on 29 July, the Free City Government submitted two protest notes regarding illegal activities and hostile economic measures by Polish customs inspectors and border officials. The protest threatened retaliatory measures. The Polish government turned a deaf ear and on 1 August abolished the export to Poland of herring and margarine, two duty-free products that constituted 10% of Danzig's trade. The newspaper *Danziger Vorposten* (*The Danzig Sentinel*) reported that in ten years the number of Polish inspectors had been increased by 400%, despite the fact that the level of trade in Danzig in 1939 had even decreased compared to

1929. The cost of this increase in personnel was borne by the impoverished Danzig community, so the newspaper proposed in its editorial article reprisals against the Polish customs inspectors. This suggestion was used by Chodacki to humiliate the Free City: with Beck's permission he presented on 4 August an outrageous ultimatum to Greiser, the president of the Senate, who received an official notice that in the early hours of 5 August the Danzig borders would be closed for the import of all foreign goods unless the Free City government promised by 6 p.m. never again to interfere with the activities of the Polish customs inspectors. This was a definite threat, since Danzig was barely producing food and its livelihood would have been strangled. The League of Nations High Commissioner, Jacob Burckhardt, was not even consulted, and only on the 6th did he receive official notification from the Polish authorities, which was a slight on his authority.

On 7 August a shocking report appeared in Krakov's *Illustrowany Kurjer*. Polish censors allowed the publication of an extraordinarily imprudent article, which admitted that Polish units were constantly crossing the German border to destroy German military installations and confiscate German military equipment. The Polish government was unable to prevent Poland's most widely circulated newspaper from announcing to the world that Germany was suffering violations of its border with Poland. Polish leaders were marching blindly into a forced and totally unnecessary conflict that would mean their ruin and were unable to understand that they were being used by Halifax and those working to unleash a war against Germany.

In Berlin Hitler and Ribbentrop concluded that Poland was trying to precipitate the conflict, so they advised Greiser to accept the terms of the ultimatum at once: on the morning of 5 August Greiser called Chodacki to announce that they were capitulating to his demands. On 9 August Weizsäcker read a note verbale to the Polish chargé d'affaires, Prince Lubomirski, which contained the warning that Germany rejected any responsibility for the consequences of further action against the Danzig inhabitants. Lubomirski asked for a written copy of the note. Weizsäcker explained that he was not authorised to submit a written note, although he gave him permission to make his own copy of the original text. Jozef Beck, who had informed Ambassador Kennard on the 4th that the Polish government was prepared to take military action against Danzig if the terms of the ultimatum were not accepted, considered the note verbale an insult to Poland, so he responded on the 10th with another note verbale warning that the Polish government refused to accept any responsibility for the consequences if Germany persisted in protecting Danzig. It added that any intervention against Polish interests in the Free City would be considered an act of aggression.

Germany's preparations for a possible war with Poland, begun after learning of Britain's blank cheque, were virtually complete. The overriding concern in Berlin was to prevent the intervention of the Western powers through diplomacy. Economically and militarily, Poland was a poor and weak country that could not sustain the arrogant and overbearing policies adopted by its rulers. Forty percent of its population were not Polish. The large Jewish minority was treated worse than in Germany; but international Jewry was willing to ignore this and "defend" the country that most rejected them. On the other hand, in addition to the German minority, there were the Ukrainians, whose readiness to rise up against the Poles in the event of war was highly regarded by Hitler. The country chosen as a "casus belli" was in fact hated by almost everyone, and most especially by its eastern neighbour, the Soviet Union, whose alliance was sought by Britain and France.

The situation as seen from the Soviet Union

As has been seen in the study of the Stalinist purges, between 1934 and 1938 Stalin was convinced that Trotsky's powerful friends and certain Western powers were trying to use Germany to unleash a war against the USSR, which was to be used to replace national communism with the internationalist communism advocated by the Trotskyists. In fact, Hitler had been financed for this purpose by the Wall Street bankers. If the aim was to wipe out both communism and fascism, a war between the two would have made some sense. However, the aim was not communism, but Stalin. Nevertheless, the facts were to show that given the choice between Stalin and Hitler, the conspirators behind the war preferred Stalin. It was not for nothing that communism had been established and sustained with the support of international Jewish capital. The Hidden Power was confident that after the war Stalin could be replaced by one of its agents, the Georgian Jew Lavrenti Beria, one of history's great criminals, a cover-up who had remained in the shadows until he replaced Yezhov as head of the People's Commissariat for Internal Affairs (NKVD) on 25 November 1938.

Throughout this work, sufficient evidence has been provided to understand that communism was a tool designed to quickly grab the resources of Russia and other countries that fell under its rule. Without the massive help of the Jewish capitalist bankers who implanted it in Russia it could never have survived. The fact that, freed from the gold standard and through the implementation of the "barter", the eastward orientation of German policy, "Drang nach Osten" (eastward thrust), was becoming a reality was a cause for alarm. Countries such as Hungary, Yugoslavia, Bulgaria, Romania and Turkey could form a political and economic axis which, as well as being a barrier to the USSR, challenged the interests of the City, whose interests Britain defended. If Poland had been able to properly understand the advantages of joining this group of nations, the pressure on the Soviet Union would have been complete. For all these reasons, France, the United States and Britain, whose traditional policy was based on the balance of power on the Continent, were to be used as instruments of opposition to a Germany that challenged the economic order of the international bankers imposed through liberalism.

The Soviet leaders were delighted with Halifax's determination to foment a war against Germany with or without the participation of the USSR, since it was the greatest conceivable contribution to their possible future westward expansion. In April 1939 the Soviet Union was under no obligation to participate in an Anglo-French conflict against Germany for the benefit of Poland, a fact known to Bonnet, France's chief diplomat. The Soviet Union had an agreement with France that obliged it to assist France in the event of German aggression, but could stand aside in the event that France attacked Germany in a conflict between Germany and any other country. This situation led to a sharp confrontation between Bonnet and Halifax. The French disapproved of the prospect of a Stalin looking at war in Europe with his arms folded and did not share the Briton's idea of going to war in these circumstances. The Soviets knew that Britain had weakened its military and political position by offering the guarantee to Poland.

Another fact that demonstrates the double standards with which the so-called democracies acted in Europe is the indifference with which they regarded the expansionist pretensions of the USSR, which aspired to annex important European territories, with which they viewed. While any German claim was considered unacceptable, however justified it might be, British diplomacy was eagerly seeking alliance with the Soviets, even though countries such as Romania, Finland, the Baltic states and Poland itself feared that an alliance of the Soviet Union with the Western countries against Germany would allow the Red Army to penetrate into the heart of Europe, as it eventually did during the World War. As early as April 1938, Soviet diplomats had begun to discuss with the Finns their territorial aspirations in the Land of a Thousand Lakes. Finland refused the military cooperation demanded by the USSR, which sparked a campaign against it in the Soviet press. On 5 March 1939, the Finns again refused a request from Litvinov, the Jewish Foreign Commissar, to install Soviet bases in Finland. The Finnish leaders were well aware that the Soviet Union was determined to re-establish Russian domination over their country; but no one was offering them protection, let alone blank cheques.

On 10 March 1939 the 18th Congress of the Communist Party opened in Moscow. In his opening speech Stalin predicted the outbreak of a new imperialist war between fascism and an Anglo-French-American alliance. True to the approach used at the Moscow trials, Stalin claimed that France and Britain were seeking to pit the Soviet Union and Germany against each other in a war and accused the Western press of trying to poison German-Soviet relations since the Munich conference. Stalin was quoted as saying: "We will not allow our country to be dragged into conflicts by warmongers who are accustomed to using others to pull their chestnuts out of the fire." Joseph E. Davies, a Zionist friend of Roosevelt who had replaced Bullitt as ambassador to Moscow, a post he held until June 1938, wrote in his diary on 11 March 1939: "Knowing Russia as I do, I feel that this is discouraging and really ominous for the negotiations taking place between the British Foreign Office and the Soviet Union in connection with the guarantees to Poland." Friedrich Werner Count von der Schulenburg, who had represented Germany in Moscow since 1934, also understood like his American colleague that Stalin's speech marked a new direction in Soviet foreign policy, and so reported to Berlin on 13 March. The German ambassador announced that Stalin's animosity was now directed against Britain and emphasised that for the first time he had ridiculed the allegation that the German Reich had aspirations in the Soviet Ukraine. The implications of Stalin's speech did not go unnoticed by Ribbentrop either.

Once the negotiations with France and Great Britain had begun, Litvinov was replaced as Foreign Commissar. Maksim Litvinov (Meyer Hennokh Moisevitch Wallach-Finkelstein) had been the Bolsheviks' unofficial ambassador to London in 1917 and, it will be recalled, was arrested and exchanged for Alfred Milner's man Bruce Lockhart after the attempted assassination of Lenin. The Jew Litvinov had endeavoured to encircle Germany by means of a crushing coalition. Stalin must have felt that he shared too many affinities with the British, and on 3 May he was replaced by Vyacheslav Molotov, whom Stalin ordered to purge Jews from the Foreign Commissariat, where they were in the majority in leadership positions as well as among ambassadors. The dismissal of Litvinov, who between 1941-43 held the all-important post of ambassador to the United States, caused a great sensation among the Diplomatic Corps, as no one thought that he would be dismissed in the midst of the talks. It was interpreted that Stalin had definitely decided to improve relations with Germany. In *Mission to Moscow* Davies summarises various opinions of two unnamed diplomatic experts on Russia. According to these interpretations, Stalin did not trust either France or Britain and suspected that they wanted to involve him in a European war in order to leave him in the lurch. This interpretation would confirm once again that Stalin still had in mind the plan to get him out of the way through a war with Germany, as laid out in the Moscow trials.

On 16 May Moltke reported to Berlin from Warsaw that Beck was firmly opposed to an agreement with the Soviet Union, which meant that an Anglo-French agreement with the USSR on Poland was highly unlikely; however, it was feared that an Anglo-Soviet agreement might be forged. Ribbentrop instructed Ambassador von Schulenburg to discuss the situation with Molotov in Moscow, but all his attempts at rapprochement were unsuccessful, which was interpreted in Berlin as a lack of confidence by Soviet diplomats in the German aristocrat. The man chosen by Molotov to convey the USSR's attitude was the Bulgarian representative in Berlin, Parvan Draganov, who on 15 June informed Ribbentrop that the Russians were undecided, but added that they preferred peaceful relations with Germany to an alliance with Britain. Draganov implied that the Soviet Union required certain guarantees in order to clarify its position. The German leaders thus understood that it would be necessary to reach a specific agreement with Stalin to secure the neutrality of the Soviet Union in the event of war with Poland.

Hitler brooded over the matter for several weeks before instructing Joachim von Ribbentrop to take the necessary steps to reach an understanding. Naturally, he knew that a pact with Stalin would allow the expansion of the USSR, which the Führer was repulsed by; but in July 1939 he concluded that such an agreement would be decisive in preventing the outbreak of a full-scale European war. The German government had no doubt that the Soviet Union would settle accounts with Poland in the event of a German-Polish war. Unlike Hitler, who had offered to respect Poland's borders, Stalin had never shown any inclination to accept the existing borders between Russia and Poland. Nor were the Germans unaware that Moscow had other territorial ambitions, one of which was Finland. Finnish diplomats found to their horror that both were seeking agreement with the Soviets at the expense of neighbouring countries.

At the same time, while Draganov was confirming to the German Foreign Ministry the USSR's interest in an agreement with Germany, Lord Halifax decided to pursue the pact with Stalin with determination, and sent William Strang, head of the Central Division of the Foreign Office, to Moscow, who arrived in the Soviet capital on 14 June. Strang discovered that the French ambassador, Paul-Emile Naggiar, was likewise actively seeking an agreement in principle with the Communists. Both diplomats concluded that acceptance of the terms presented by the Soviets committed them to support Soviet intervention in Romania, in the Baltic states or in the very Poland they sought to protect.

David L. Hoggan explains in *Der Erzwungene Krieg* (*The Forced War*) how Molotov conducted the negotiations with the British and French representatives: "He was seated at a desk placed on a dais; the Western negotiators were placed in a semicircle without tables on a lower level. The new Russian attitude of contemptuous arrogance was the inevitable consequence of the British guarantee to Poland. Molotov knew that the Soviet Union now had a much stronger negotiating position than the British Government". Although Halifax instructed Strang to move closer to the Soviet positions on the decisive issues, the USSR's position remained unchanged for the next few weeks. On 20 July 1939 Strang complained to Halifax about the "humiliating negotiations". Finally, the parties accepted Molotov's suggestion and decided on 23 July that, although there was a virtual political agreement, it was necessary to await the outcome of the military talks before proceeding to signature.

President Roosevelt intervened in the negotiations between the Soviet Union and the Western powers through the new ambassador to Moscow, Lawrence Steinhardt, a Zionist Jew to the core who was the nephew of billionaire Samuel Untermayer, the advocate of Germany's destruction who in 1933 had called on Jews everywhere to declare holy war on the Germans. Steinhardt, who had replaced Davies, received on 15 August a confidential letter to Molotov dated 4 August 1939. The letter had been sent through Bullitt and was therefore eleven days late arriving in Moscow. It recalled that the interests of the United States and the Soviet Union were identical in promoting the defeat of Germany and Italy in a European war. Roosevelt, anxious to unleash war, urged the USSR to enter into an alliance with Britain and France and implied that the United States would eventually join this coalition. Steinhardt presented Roosevelt's letter to Molotov on 16 August, when the military delegations of the three countries were meeting.

Almost two weeks earlier, when tension between Berlin and Warsaw was reaching a peak because of the treatment of the German minority and the factional attitude of the Poles in Danzig, the Germans took the decision to tolerate Soviet aspirations in the Baltic area in exchange for neutrality in a possible war with Poland. On 3 August 1939 Ribbentrop informed Schulenburg that he had informed the Russian representative in Berlin, Astakhov, that Germany wished to reach an agreement with Russia on all matters of interest, and asked him to reiterate the offer to Molotov personally. Thus, when the British and French military missions arrived in Moscow on 10 August to study the military aspects of the agreement with the USSR, they were received with little enthusiasm, which did not prevent the Germans from demanding clarification of the meaning of these delegations. They were assured that contacts with Germany had changed the Russian attitude towards Britain and France, but that it had been decided to continue the negotiations because they could not be broken off without reasonable explanations.

The Soviet military delegation led by Marshal Voroshilov held its first meeting with the French and British military teams on 12 August. The Soviets were outraged that the British intended Russia and France to bear the brunt of the war that Halifax sought to provoke against Germany. Voroshilov insisted on specific promises of back-up in the event of possible Soviet operations in Estonia, Latvia and Lithuania. On 14 August the Communists introduced the fundamental question of military operations in Poland and Romania. Voroshilov argued that both countries would be defeated by Germany in a short time if they did not accept Soviet military collaboration. As far as Romania was concerned, this assertion was absurd, since there was not the slightest possibility of conflict between Germany and Romania. As for Poland, Britain and France were prepared to accept its occupation by Russian troops; but the problem was to obtain Polish consent. Voroshilov argued that in the event of Germany attacking France, the USSR could not counter-attack unless the Soviet offensive through Polish and Romanian territory had been agreed.

Sir William Seeds, the British ambassador to Moscow, warned Halifax on 15 August that the talks would fail unless Britain and France secured Polish consent. Seeds was confident that Beck and the Polish military could be persuaded to agree to a secret pact and went so far as to present his thesis to the French military delegation. Daladier and Bonnet were informed of the impasse that had been reached. Voroshilov demanded a definitive answer to this fundamental question as soon as possible. Bonnet decided to contact Lukasiewicz, who turned up at the Quai d'Orsay on the evening of the 15th. He bluntly put to him the two alternatives: if the Russians did not receive permission to operate on the territory of their neighbours through the military pact with Britain and France, they would sign an agreement with Germany. The Polish ambassador replied that Beck would never allow Russian forces to enter Polish territory. Bonnet dared to remind him that Hitler had announced that he would defeat Poland in three weeks and went so far as to add that he shared this view. Lukasiewicz was indignant and angrily declared: "On the contrary, it is the Polish army that will invade Germany from the first day". The French minister realised that the fatuity of the Poles was contumacious and gave up trying to amend the ambassador's delusions with arguments of a military nature.

France was obviously more at risk than Britain in the event of a war with Germany without the support of the USSR. On 16 August the French Foreign Minister informed his British colleague about the meeting with the Polish Ambassador and asked for his cooperation in making the Poles understand that the right of intervention in Poland and Romania was the "sine qua non" condition for Russia's participation in any war that might break out after the outbreak of a German-Polish conflict. On the same day, on the 16th, Molotov received Roosevelt's letter from Ambassador Steinhardt, and the two men proceeded to study its contents. The American diplomat had to hear from the Soviet Foreign Commissar that the British and French military missions had come to Russia to discuss military collaboration in terms that Molotov described as "vague generalities". He went on to regret that these delegations were unable to respond to the specific points Russia had raised.

On 17 August Halifax instructed Kennard to reprimand the Poles for their refusal to cooperate with the Soviet Union and to explain to them that military considerations made the use of Polish territory by Soviet forces inevitable. Halifax refused to accept that the USSR was a greater threat to Poland than to Germany. In Hoggan's view, British leaders were incapable of understanding that their policy "was promoting the spread of communism rather than British imperialism". Although perhaps they did understand and did not care, since they were blatantly acting as agents of the covert forces that had implanted communism in Russia and desired a second war in Europe to complete their design for global domination.

It is recorded in US Foreign Relations documents in 1939 that Prime Minister Daladier met with Bullitt on 18 August and repeated three times, outraged by Warsaw's stance, that he would not send a single French peasant to give his life for Poland if the Poles refused Soviet aid. Bullitt was greatly alarmed by this violent reaction, which he considered anti-Polish, as it indicated that France would not support a war against Germany if the Moscow negotiations failed [4]. Roosevelt was informed of Daladier's attitude and feared that Halifax was prepared to abandon his plan for war against Germany if he did not get the support of the Soviet Union or France. The Foreign Office, however, had a certain advantage, for it knew in advance that the German-Soviet pact was going to be signed thanks to two traitors, the brothers Theo and Eric Kordt. Theo was Chargé d'Affaires at the German Embassy in London; Eric was Weizsäcker's right-hand man at the Foreign Ministry in Berlin. At the end of June Eric Kordt had warned Robert Vansittart about the contacts between Germany and the USSR. Halifax foresaw from these spies that the Anglo-French negotiations with Molotov would ultimately fail because the Russians preferred an agreement with Hitler. This allowed him to prepare his strategy for dragging France into the war. Professor Friedrich Lenz, in his article "Worm in the Apple", quotes Vansittart's words to Theo Kordt on 31 August, the day before the invasion of Poland: "England will fight this war to the end, and like Samson in the Bible will pull down the pillars of the temple and bury everything under the rubble.

The last meeting between the military delegations in Moscow took place on the evening of 21 August. Voroshilov announced that he was responsible for the Red Army's autumn military manoeuvres,. He was therefore going to request a suspension of the meetings in order to devote his time to this task. Once again, the Soviet Marshal expressed his astonishment to the Western delegations that they were seeking to negotiate an agreement without a clear commitment on the important question of the right to

---

[4] The head of French military intelligence, Colonel Maurice Gauché, had repeatedly expressed his irritation at the Polish position to Daladier and Bonnet. He considered the Poles to be extremely boastful about their army's capabilities and told the prime minister that if negotiations in Moscow failed, France should let Hitler settle accounts with Poland. Gauché felt that they should not feel obliged to Warsaw, since the Poles had signed the pact with Germany in 1934 without consulting France. He also felt that the Polish ultimatum to Czechoslovakia in October 1938 had ignored French interests. He also denounced the fact that in March 1939 the Poles had recognised the German protectorate over Bohemia-Moravia without consulting the French government. Colonel Gauché was also highly critical of Halifax's policy. He warned his superiors that, although he did not want war, Hitler was not bluffing and would risk war before capitulating to the extravagances of the Poles. It seemed obvious to the head of French counter-espionage that his country should abandon war plans in the event that the Russians refused to join the Anglo-French front. These views were shared by Bonnet, who proposed to act accordingly.

manoeuvre on Polish and Romanian territory. No sooner had the session ended than the British and French military learned from the press that a non-aggression pact was planned to be signed between the USSR and Germany. The fact that the public knew the news before the Franco-British delegations had been informed was a deliberate affront which did not go unnoticed in diplomatic circles. Ambassador Henderson expressed his outrage in a cable sent to Halifax on 22 August: "The treacherous cynicism of Stalin and company towards our military missions negotiating in Moscow is incredible". Henderson, who had always opposed an alliance with the Soviet Union, quickly realised that Stalin had played on circumstances to inflict maximum damage to British prestige.

However, Henderson imagined how far the British and French were willing to go in their negotiations, and how little they really cared about Poland. Early on the morning of the 22nd, General Doumenc informed Marshal Voroshilov that he had received authorisation to support Soviet military operations in Poland. Doumenc assured him that he had full powers from Daladier to sign without reservation a pact that included other Russian interests and wishes. That is, the British and French were willing to promote the communists' westward expansion as long as they signed up for the war against Germany. Voroshilov replied that Poland was a sovereign country and that plans for Soviet military operations on its territory could not be decided without its consent. As late as the afternoon of the same day, the British ambassador in Moscow, William Seeds, accused Molotov of "bad faith" during the negotiations. The Soviet commissar coolly told him that the "insincerity" of the British leaders deprived them of any valid basis for such an accusation. On the 23rd Seeds cabled Halifax to maintain the mission in Moscow in case the negotiations with Ribbentrop failed. Even after the pact was signed, Halifax gave intsructions to Seeds to assure the Soviets that he fully shared that their military operations in Poland were indispensable and that he was prepared to support them fully, which amounted to pledging British support for the Communist invasion of Poland while insisting on declaring war on Germany over Danzig, which did not even belong to Poland.

General war or localised war?

Hitler contemplated the possibility that the setback in Russia might change Anglo-French warmongering policy, and he sought to contribute to this through diplomatic measures and new proposals. Despite his Anglophilia, he understood that it was the French who showed a more reasonable attitude, in contrast to Britain's exaggerated desire for war. If one considers that the French leadership could not conceive of confronting its German neighbour without an Eastern front opening up, it must be admitted that the USSR's signing of a neutrality pact with Germany made conflict in

Europe more unlikely than if the Soviets had contracted an alliance with the Western powers. Indeed, if was to spare Europe from catastrophe, it was enough to pressure the Polish leaders to negotiate, rather than to support them in not doing so.

On 11 August Hitler met with Jacob Burckhardt, to whom he confessed that it was impossible for him to be more patient with the Poles, so he asked the High Commissioner to explain the situation to the French and British and to remind them that Germany did not want a conflict with the Western powers under any circumstances. Burckhardt promised to comply. Beck told Szembek that he was indignant with Burckhardt for agreeing to meet Hitler under the present circumstances. This fateful politician for his country and for Europe feared that the Swiss diplomat might make a desperate effort to reach an agreement. In Basel, the High Commissioner informed representatives of France and England of the humiliations and abuses suffered by the German minority and asked them to work for a negotiated settlement; but Halifax merely instructed Kennard to tell the Poles that they must improve their tactics if they were to avoid the impression that they were guilty of provoking the war. Halifax also advised the Poles to cease their provocations at Danzig and to restrain the press.

Those who also wanted peace in Europe were the Italians. Their Foreign Minister, Count Galeazzo Ciano, arrived in Salzburg on 11 August to meet Hitler and Ribbentrop at the Führer's residence in the Bavarian Alps the next day. On the morning of the 12th Ciano held preliminary talks with Ribbentrop, who, in an extremely serious mood, filled him in on the recent atrocities against the German minority and intimated that war between Poland and Germany was inevitable, although he expressed his conviction that it was possible to restrain the conflict through diplomatic action. Ciano was surprised to discover that Ribbentrop was confident of Russian neutrality in the event of a German-Polish conflict. The German foreign minister told his Italian colleague that he hoped Russian neutrality would be decisive in deterring Britain and France. Mussolini had instructed Ciano to try to convince the Germans that a general war in Europe must be avoided, as it would be catastrophic for Italy and Germany. The Italian Foreign Minister disagreed with Ribbentrop's analysis, stating that he and the Duce were convinced that the British and French would use any pretext to launch military operations against Germany, which was why conflict with Poland must be avoided at all costs. Ciano told Ribbentrop that if Germany was attacked by France and Britain, Italy would not enter the war.

In the afternoon Hitler arrived and they met with him for an intense conference that lasted more than three hours. Ciano repeated to the Führer that war with Poland had to be avoided, and suggested that the Axis countries should call for an international conference. The German Chancellor carefully considered the Italian diplomat's arguments and views, but did not agree with them. It was therefore agreed to hold a further meeting the following day. On the 13th Ciano expressed his fear that Britain and France would attack Germany even if a Russo-German agreement were reached, and noted that both countries were well advanced in their military preparations, so that a war in the present circumstances would be to their advantage. He predicted that a war in 1939 would shatter German and Italian relations with the United States and allow Roosevelt to win a third term as President. Ciano insisted that Italy was not prepared for war. Despite his initial position, however, Ciano realised that Hitler's approach made a great deal of sense, and when he returned to Italy he explained it to Mussolini, thinking that the Duce might, perhaps, share it.

In short, what the German Chancellor had told him was as follows: 1. The Russians seemed willing to cooperate with Germany because they were confident that a German-Polish war would enable them to obtain eastern Poland. 2. Stalin would not support Germany in the international conference on Danzig proposed by Italy, since it would only serve Germany, did not suit its expansionist intentions, and could only lead to a lasting Anglo-German agreement, which was anathema to the Soviets. 3. Germany and Italy could try to persuade France and Britain to admit Spain to the discussions in order to gain more support, but they would still be in a minority against an Anglo-French-Russian-Polish majority. 4. Nothing would be achieved at such a conference precisely because of Soviet influence. 5. The Führer asked the Duce to reconsider his position of not supporting Germany, since Italy's defection greatly increased the danger of war. 6. Hitler was convinced that a strong German-Italian front, coupled with a Russo-German pact, would break the unity of thought in France and Britain.

It seems that Ciano came away quite convinced of the logic of the Führer's arguments and even went so far as to pledge his word on the maintenance of Italian-German solidarity. In the book *Profesora Mercedes Vilanona: a contracorriente*, a work by several authors published by the University of Barcelona, it is stressed that, although Ambassador Attolico and Ciano himself had asked Hitler not to publish anything until the Duce had been informed, the Germans wanted to take advantage of the opportunity to strengthen their position, and so on the 13th itself, two hours after the Italian diplomat left Salzburg, La D.N.B. (Deutsches Nachrichtenbüro) announced: "The Italian-German talks have covered all the current problems, in particular the Danzig question. The result has been a complete identity of views between German and Italian foreign policy. Not a single problem has been left in abeyance". This communiqué did not please Attolico, who asked permission to travel to Rome, where he arrived on 15 August. He expressed to Mussolini his opinion that Italy should not support Germany in the event of war breaking out in Europe. Although the chargé d'affaires at the embassy in Berlin, Count Massimo Magistrate, contacted Rome on the 15th to report that the Germans had told him that confirmation of a pact with the USSR was very near, Attolico convinced both Ciano and Mussolini that it was inadvisable to support Germany in the event of a general war. Weizsäcker learned that Attolico had gone to Rome for the express purpose of convincing the Duce of the necessity of not committing himself to Germany, and the German leaders were extremely concerned.

Ciano spoke twice on the 18th with the British Ambassador to Italy, Sir Percy Loraine, with whom he agreed to discuss the meeting with the Nazi leaders. The first time, Ciano told Loraine that he had verified information about the reckless Polish violations of the German border, which naturally caused great indignation in Berlin. The ambassador concluded that Italy would stand by Germany. At the second meeting, however, the Italian Foreign Minister confessed to the British Ambassador that Italy had not agreed to support Germany in the event of war, and added that it had no intention of doing so. Ciano's indiscretion had a very damaging effect on Germany, weakening the impact that Hitler wanted to make by announcing the pact with Russia. Hoggan writes: "French military leaders later claimed that they would never have risked a Franco-German war had it not been for Italy's promise of neutrality". This confession by the Gallic military supports the relevance of Hitler's presentation to Ciano on 13 August: a firm Italian stand with Germany would have done more for peace in Europe and for Italy's interests than the indecision and weakness shown by Ciano to Percy Loraine.

On the same day, 18 August, Attolico met Ribbentrop in Salzburg on Mussolini's behalf, and made it clear that Italy knew that war with Poland would not be localised because France and Britain would intervene. The ambassador insisted that his country could not accept a war before the end of 1940. In view of the news from Rome, Halifax was quick to take advantage of the situation to intimidate the Italians: on 20 August he sent a message to Ambassador Loraine to be delivered to Ciano. It warned Italy that Britain would attack it immediately if it joined Germany as an ally in a future war. This threat had a huge impact on the Duce, who reaffirmed his plans for an international conference. The Germans were not informed of the British ultimatum.

The decision to seek the pact with the USSR was taken during the days when terror against the German minority had gone rampant and Beck had presented an outrageous ultimatum to the Free City of Danzig. Instead of decreasing, the anti-German measures increased day by day. On 14 August, the East Upper Silesian authorities launched a campaign of mass arrests against Germans, which was accompanied by the confiscation or closure of social facilities and businesses that remained open. During the first phase of the arrests, a young German shot and wounded a police officer, Viktor Szwagiel, which only served to further enrage the Poles. Arrested Germans were not interned in the area, but were forced to march into Poland in prisoner columns. Thousands of Germans tried to avoid arrest by crossing the border into Germany. Human traffickers took advantage of the situation and, in exchange for money, helped the fugitives escape through passes far from police control. The agitation and fear of the Germans in those days led them to believe that in the event of war the Poles would murder them en masse. On 16 August, Senator Rudolf Wiesner, one of the most prominent German minority politicians and leader of the "Jungdeutsche Partei" (Young Germans' Party), was also arrested. On the same day, Chodacki had met with Senate President Greiser and announced that the boycott of German goods would continue until Danzig recognised the unrestricted right of Polish inspectors to carry out their duties on Free City territory. Shortly afterwards Chodacki flew back to Warsaw to discuss the situation with Beck and receive instructions.

The situation of the German minority in Poland continued to deteriorate. On 17 August the German consuls in Teschen and Kattowice (Upper Silesia) informed the Foreign Ministry that hundreds of German citizens were being arrested. The consul in Teschen claimed that the wave of arrests was aimed at taking hostages. On 18 August, it was the German chargé d'affaires in Warsaw, Wühlisch, himself, who warned the Foreign Ministry that the Poles had launched a massive campaign of arrests against the German minority in the areas of Posen, West Prussia, Central Poland and Eastern Upper Silesia. The Political Department of the German Foreign Office published on 20 August a list of 38 Germans who had been wounded, mistreated or killed. The list included some women who had been raped.

On 21 August, an astonishing event took place: Rudolf Wiesner, who had been arrested five days earlier, showed up in Danzig after having managed to escape from Poland. On the 22nd he met in Danzig with representatives of the Reich and gave them an account of the events. Wiesner claimed that it was impossible to establish loyal relations with the Poles because they were incompatible with the fact that they were ethnically conscious. Wiesner claimed that since the spring of 1939 the German minority had been experiencing a disaster of "inconceivable magnitude". He denounced that Germans had been dismissed from their jobs without justification and had been deprived of unemployment assistance, and were suffering from hunger and deprivation of all kinds. Welfare institutions, cooperatives and trade associations had been destroyed. In recent weeks, mass arrests, deportations, mutilations, beatings and other violence had reached unprecedented levels. Nevertheless, Wiesner insisted that the leaders of the German minority continued to hope for a peaceful solution between Poland and Germany that would restore peace, remove the spectre of war and preserve the right to live and work in peace. German diplomats and the Danzig authorities discussed the advisability of publishing Wiesner's exhibition, but Albert Foster, the local leader of the National Socialist Party, convinced them that it would serve no purpose and advocated a policy of firmness with the Polish inspectors and customs officials, whose actions should be confined to the areas stipulated in the treaties. This was the state of affairs in Poland and Danzig when it became known that the signing of a Russo-German pact was imminent.

It was at a secret Politburo meeting on 19 August 1939 that Stalin announced that the Soviet Union would definitely sign a non-aggression pact with Germany. On the same day, 19 August 19, the Germans and Soviets had signed a trade agreement they had been negotiating since 1938. The next day, a report in *Pravda* warned of major differences in the negotiations with the Western military missions. Naturally, Stalin did not envisage the possibility that the agreement with Germany could be used by Hitler to achieve a negotiated, peaceful settlement with the Poles: without a German invasion, Stalin would not have been able to enter Poland in turn. One of the advantages of the pact was that it would greatly facilitate Soviet expansion with Berlin's consent, whereas the pact with the Western powers would have involved a desperate struggle with Germany. Unlike the Nazis, the Communists also did not expect the pact with Hitler and the rejection of the alliance with Britain and France to involve a localised war. Stalin expected that Halifax and company would not shrink from Germany, since in order to expand at the expense of its six Western neighbours, general war would have to break out.

On 20 August Schulenburg received a telegram from Hitler to Stalin, which he presented to Molotov on the 21st. In it, the Führer informed the Soviet leader that Germany accepted the Russian outline for a non-aggression pact and explained: "The tension between Germany and Poland has become intolerable. Polish behaviour towards a great power is such that a crisis could occur at any moment. In the face of this audacity, Germany is determined from now on to look after the interests of the Reich with all the means at its disposal ". The German Chancellor proposed that Ribbentrop should fly to Moscow on the 22nd, although he added that the 23rd would also be an acceptable date, and informed Stalin that the tense situation would prevent Ribbentrop from remaining in Russia for more than a day or two. The text concluded with these words: "I would be glad to receive your prompt reply.

On the 21st Stalin responded cordially and proposed that Ribbentrop travel to Moscow on the 23rd, while requesting that a special communiqué announcing the pact be issued on the 22nd. The die was cast: Germany was no longer a buffer for the states bordering the USSR, which were thus at the mercy of Soviet expansionism. It was obvious that France and Britain would do nothing to protect Eastern Europe against communism, and the facts proved it. Poland itself had its best shield against the Bolsheviks in Germany, but Beck's blindness went so far that on the 22nd he told Ambassador Kennard that the pact made no difference to Poland because, unlike Britain and France, he had never counted on Soviet help. He added that the understandable disappointment in Paris and London was the price they had to pay for having had false hopes in the USSR. It seems clear that the Polish foreign minister was a gloomy incompetent lacking in the least bit of sanity.

Kennedy, on the other hand, quickly realised the delicate situation in which Poland was placed and discussed the matter with Chamberlain, who was fatalistic and unable to ask Halifax for restraint. The British Prime Minister admitted to the American ambassador that they would not encourage the Poles to make concessions to Germany. Kennedy personally believed that, under the new scenario, Poland would eventually agree to resume negotiations with the Germans and was disappointed to discover that neither Chamberlain nor Halifax was prepared to urge Poland to change course. Here is his suggestion to the State Department, contained in the 1939 U.S. Foreign Relations papers handled by Hoggan: "If President Roosevelt contemplates any action for peace, it seems to me that the place to work is over Beck in Poland, and to be effective it must take place quickly. I see no other possibility."

The Ribbentrop-Molotov Pact - some reactions

Joachim von Ribbentropp flew to Moscow on the 23rd in a Condor transport plane accompanied by thirty-two experts. The reception was extremely hospitable. Talks began the same day in the afternoon. The Soviets immediately asked the Germans to tolerate their plans to establish military bases in Estonia and Latvia. As for Finland, they insisted that they wanted a free hand. They also asked for Germany's neutrality in the conflict they planned to initiate with Romania in order to regain Bessarabia for the USSR. Although the Führer had given him full powers, at 20:05 Ribbentrop telephoned Berlin to make sure that Hitler accepted Stalin's aggressive plans for these countries, which were to be the unfortunate victims of the disastrous warmongering policy orchestrated by Halifax with Roosevelt's backing. At 23:00 the German Chancellor gave an affirmative answer. The Reich would not oppose the westward advance of communism. Hoggan writes: "To be precise, Germany was not handing over nations to Russia, since she was under no contractual obligation to these countries, except the promise that she herself would not attack them.... The Russo-German agreement of 23/24 August 1939 concerned the delimitation of interests rather than active collaboration between the two countries. These facts were ignored by irresponsible Western propagandists, who without the slightest basis insisted that an alliance had been concluded between Germany and the Soviet Union."

The pact contained a secret protocol recognising a Soviet sphere of interest in Eastern Europe; but this recognition was conditional on the outbreak of war between Poland and Germany. Ribbentrop informed the Soviets on the 23rd that the decision to respond to Polish provocations with a military campaign was not irrevocable. Hitler and Ribbentrop made it clear that Germany would not be forced to recognise these aspirations if a settlement of the German-Polish dispute could be reached. For their part, the Soviets announced their intention to intervene in Poland in the event of war. The line formed by the Vistula River and its tributaries Narew and San was drawn, which was to delimit the zones of military occupation on both sides.

This unnatural pact stunned millions of people on both sides around the world. Hitler, financed by Wall Street to take on Stalin in order to put Trotsky back in charge of the USSR, had just destroyed his entire course of action by a desperate pact which he himself would later call "a heinous crime". The Führer, the champion of anti-communism, was thus dynamiting the Anti-Kommintern Pact of 1936 at a time when Japan had its army in Manchuria. It was a high-risk gamble that could have served to avert war in Europe. If Italy had played its cards as Hitler had hoped, it is very likely that France would have backed down rather than play along with Britain. Stalin, too, had calculated his expectations. By overestimating France's military potential, he thought that the situation of the First World War could be repeated. His idea was to intervene militarily against Germany when all combatants were exhausted, which would allow him to complete his westward expansion.

During the crucial stage of negotiations between the USSR and Germany, the British Ambassador in Berlin, increasingly alarmed by the foreseeable catastrophe looming over Europe, was working hard for peace. Fully aware of the role of the press, he denounced it as a tool in the hands of the forces demanding war and assured Lord Halifax that Hitler sincerely desired an Anglo-German agreement. Neville Henderson deplored the attitude of Kennard, the ambassador in Warsaw, who deliberately refused to acknowledge the desperate plight of the German minority in Poland. Henderson went so far as to ask Halifax to reconsider the plan that Gafencu, the Romanian foreign minister, had presented in London. Since his demands to Lord Halifax to seek reconciliation with Hitler before it was too late were to no avail, Henderson made representations on his own initiative to the Polish and Italian ambassadors, Lipski and Attolico. Henderson hoped that the Italians would come forward with proposals to seek a diplomatic settlement.

Another diplomat aware of the change in the European situation after the Ribbentrop-Mólotov pact was Bonnet. The French foreign minister did not see why France could not reach a separate agreement with Germany if the USSR, its main ally in the East, had done so. From the very 23rd Bonnet began to look for ways of freeing French foreign policy from British tutelage. But if Henderson denounced the use of the press by the warmongers, Bonnet could have done the same for the French media, where a shameful campaign in favour of the war was orchestrated. In the third volume of *The Hidden Face of Modern History,* Jean Lombard provides precise data on the ownership and financing of the main agencies and publications in France, most of which were controlled by Jewish agents. In the *Protocols of the Elders of Zion*, the importance of controlling the press and literature had been analysed in detail. Protocol XII reads:

> "Our press will represent aristocratic, republican, revolutionary, conservative and even anarchist tendencies. Like the Hindu god Vishnu, we too will have a hundred hands, each of which will take the changing pulse of public opinion in the direction that suits us, because an excited person easily loses his judgment and becomes subject to all sorts of influences. These fools, who think they hold the opinion of their paper, will in reality only hold our opinion or one that is convenient to us. They will think they are following their partisan publication, and in reality they will only follow the flag we will fly before them. To lead our army of journalists in this direction, we shall have to organise with very special care. Under the name of the Central Press Association we shall bring together the writers' associations, in which our representatives will inadvertently issue the slogan and the battle cry."

In France, the spectrum ranged from the Communist newspaper *L'Humanité*, which was full of Jewish editors, was loyal to the Communist Party and defended the German-Russian pact (which is why it was banned by Daladier), to the news agencies. In January 1939, to cite just one example, the Jewish journalist Emmanuel Berl accused Robert Bollack, also Jewish, director of the Fournier Agency, of corrupting French journalists to incite them to go to war against Germany. In April 1939 Charles Maurras confirmed that American Jews had sent three million dollars to Bollack to finance the warmongering campaign.

With or without the support of the press, Bonnet was convinced that France and Europe had to be spared war, so he asked Daladier to convene an emergency meeting of the Defence Council, composed of the military chiefs and the most senior ministers in the government. His plan was to get the military to corroborate that French hopes for a war against the Germans were doubtful without the support of the Soviet Union. The head of French diplomacy knew that the British would not maintain their opposition to Hitler without French support. The meeting began at 18:00 in Daladier's office and the attendees sat in a semicircle around the prime minister's desk. It soon became clear that Count Ciano's indiscretion about Italian neutrality played a part in the conference. Both General Gamelin, Commander-in-Chief of the Army, and Admiral Darlan, who assured that the Navy was ready, stressed that Italy would almost certainly be neutral in the event of general war in Europe. Gamelin explained that Italian neutrality would relieve the army's work in the Alps. Guy La Chambre declared that aviation was in full swing. Bonnet was annoyed by the excessive importance these military leaders attached to Italy's attitude. Impatient, he asked General Gamelin how long he estimated the Poles would hold out against the Germans. Solemnly,

Gamelin assured that the Germans would be unable to defeat the Poles before the arrival of the rainy season and predicted that by the spring of 1940 the fighting in Poland would be in full swing. On the basis of these calculations, the Army Chief declared that it would be time for the French army, reinforced by British troops and possibly some thirty Belgian and Dutch divisions, to break through the Siegfried Line. Interestingly, a year earlier Gamelin had claimed that this defensive line would withstand the French assault for two years. Bonnet was stunned when he heard that French preparations for a war against Germany were already adequate. Bonnet's main argument for suggesting a change in policy towards Poland, France's dangerous military situation, was thus undermined by the French military.

For their part, the Poles reacted to the announcement of the Russo-German Pact by intensifying their propaganda campaign against Germany and encouraging abuse and mistreatment of the German minority under the false pretext that hundreds of acts against the Polish minority were occurring daily in the Reich. The *Gazeta Polska*, an official newspaper, claimed on 24 August that the pact was a failed bluff because it had not produced any effect on the nerves of Poles, French or English. For the conservative *Czas*, it was a hoax perpetrated by "the new Berlin comedy". *Kurier Warszawski* triumphantly announced that the new pact was proof of the weakness of both partners. A Polish journalist told *The New York Times* that the pact had no military value for Germany. To top it all off, in a clear desire to provoke war, Polish batteries opened fire on German airliners flying over the Baltic on 24 August, an aggression that was formally protested by Germany on the 25th. The Poles only admitted to firing on one German plane that had been sighted over Polish territory. Meanwhile, some 80,000 German refugees had managed to cross the border.

Germany is still trying to reach an agreement with Britain

After Halifax's failure to build the Grand Alliance against Germany and the signing of the German-Soviet Pact, Hitler tried to regain the diplomatic initiative from a more advantageous position. The German Chancellor was still confident that London and Paris would withdraw their support for Poland. The opportunity to seek agreement with the British arose as early as 23 August, when Henderson travelled to Hitler's Berghof on the Obersazlberg to hand him a letter written by Prime Minister Chamberlain, warning that the UK would intervene in the event of war despite the pact with the USSR. The Führer did not miss the opportunity and wrote a letter in reply on the 23rd, in which he placed special emphasis on the suffering of the German population. He recalled that prominent British personalities had recognised the Danzig problem in recent years and that the Poles had closed the door to negotiation because of the British blank cheque. The day ended with an evening conference at the Berghof with the top Nazi leaders.

Although on the 18th Herbert von Dirksen, the ambassador to London, had flown to Berlin to warn that the British would support the Poles even if they initiated hostilities without provocation from Germany, Hitler expressed at the conference his confidence in a rational policy on the part of Britain, which "had no need to declare war and consequently would not declare war".

Göring, however, did not share Hitler's point of view, so, with the Führer's permission, he had turned to engineer Birger Dahlerus, an important Swedish businessman with good contacts in England and Germany, who had already been acting as an unofficial negotiator since July. On 23 August Dahlerus was in Paris and in the evening received a call from Göring, who asked him to return to Berlin immediately. On the morning of the 24th the Swede arrived in the German capital, where he assured Göring that he was prepared to devote himself with full dedication to the task of achieving an Anglo-German agreement that would preserve peace. Dahlerus was instructed to travel to London as soon as possible in order to convey to the British leadership an important personal promise from Hitler. From the British Embassy in Berlin, contact was made with the Foreign Office, and Dahlerus obtained permission to report to London, where he arrived on the morning of the 25th. There he began negotiations that were to continue for a week, until his services were abruptly rejected by the British. During those seven days there were comings and goings, twists and turns from London to Berlin and from Berlin to London. Halifax admitted to the Nuremberg tribunal that sentenced Göring to death that the Swedish negotiator had done all he could to keep the peace during the final crisis that preceded the outbreak of World War II.

On 24 August, there were many different reactions on the various stages. In France, for example, leading personalities urged Daladier's government to put pressure on the Poles in the interests of peace. Bonnet, who was keen to seize the first opportunity to release France from its military obligations to Poland, reported that Beck had agreed to have his ambassador in Berlin make representations to the German leadership. Göring pleaded with Lipski to ask his superior to try to defuse the tension. However, on the same day and at the same time, tension in Danzig continued to rise. Chodacki threatened the Danzig authorities with immediate reprisals if Albert Forster, the National Socialist leader, was appointed head of the Free City State, a decision taken unanimously by the Senate which Greiser had communicated to Burckhardt. The Swiss diplomat, increasingly concerned, warned that the appointment could only inflame tempers. Forster favoured a hard line with the Poles after the breakdown of negotiations with the customs inspectors. His intention was to confiscate the Poles' weapons in Danzig and arrest them, measures which Hitler rejected on the grounds that they could be an excuse for precipitating the conflict.

At 15:00 on the 24th Chamberlain addressed a special sitting of the House of Commons. Noting that the situation was getting progressively worse, he warned MPs that there was a danger of imminent war with Germany. Chamberlain admitted that he was not in a position to judge properly the allegations of aggression against the Germans in Poland. "In Berlin," he said, "the announcement of the pact was hailed with extraordinary cynicism as a great diplomatic victory which removes any danger of war, since we and France will probably no longer be able to fulfil our obligations to Poland. We feel that our first duty is to reject this dangerous illusion." He then added brazenly : "Nothing we have done or proposed to do threatens the legitimate interests of Germany. It is not an act of menace to prepare to help friends to defend themselves against force." Of course, Chamberlain knew that only a day earlier his Government had offered the Soviet Union entry into Poland without the consent of the Polish Government and that it was not at all prepared to defend its "friends" against Communist invasion. Naturally, Chamberlain could never admit that Danzig and Poland were merely a pretext for destroying Germany. To cap all this idle talk, the Prime Minister declared that the main objective of British foreign policy was to avoid needless bloodshed in foreign countries.

On the same day, Ribbentrop, having just arrived from Moscow, was instructed by Hitler to try to strengthen Germany's position by obtaining a declaration of support from Italy. To this end, the German Foreign Minister telephoned Ciano in the evening and asked him for a decisive and conclusive statement on the Italian position. Count Ciano did not want to say that the Italian reply would be negative, and promised that Germany would receive a reply the following day. However, Percy Loraine, the British ambassador in Rome, learned that after the session in Parliament Halifax was under pressure to modify the position he had committed himself to at Danzig. There is documentary evidence that the Foreign Office Secretary confided to Loraine that the cession of Danzig to Germany might ultimately have to be considered as part of an international agreement. The ambassador, who had received a further call from the Duce that same day for a diplomatic arrangement, was puzzled by this information and wondered whether Halifax was trying to encourage Mussolini to take the initiative for an international conference to enable Britain to resolve its difficulties. Henderson also decided to contact Halifax on the 24th, to whom he frankly warned that German complaints about abuses against the minority in Poland were fully confirmed. On the same day Halifax relayed the complaint to Kennard and asked him to urge caution on the Poles, but the British ambassador, who fully supported Polish intransigence, dismissed Henderson's allegations.

Finally on the 25th Hitler summoned Henderson in order to offer an alliance to Britain. The German Chancellor told the British Ambassador that the Danzig question would be settled and that his pact with the USSR ruled out the danger of a German-Soviet war. In Ribbentrop's presence, he reminded Henderson that Germany had no aspirations in Western Europe and that he wanted the British Empire to remain prosperous and strong. As for the problem of the colonies lost twenty years earlier, he proposed relegating it to the distant future and argued that it was foolish to discuss such matters before Britain and Germany had reached agreement on arms reduction. The Führer immediately informed the British diplomat that he was going to make him a formal offer of an Anglo-German agreement. Germany wished to supplement its pact with the Soviet Union by signing a friendship treaty with Britain. Hitler assured Henderson that he was prepared to take the necessary steps to avoid the catastrophe of war. The desire for peace with Britain led Hitler to make an unprecedented commitment, never before offered by a political leader: Germany, at the demand of the British Government, was prepared to place the entire power of the Reich at the service of the defence of the British Empire anywhere and at any time. Germany, as it had already offered, guaranteed Poland's new borders in the west. All this in exchange only for London's convincing Warsaw to return the Free City to the Reich after a plebiscite, and for the construction of a motorway and a railway line through the Corridor. Of course, respect for the German minorities in Poland had to be guaranteed. The meeting with Hitler and Ribbentrop moved Neville Henderson, who deeply desired the Anglo-German agreement. The British Ambassador prepared to travel to England the next day to convey the offer to his superiors.

The plan to invade Poland was ready for 26 August, and everything depended on the outcome of these last diplomatic efforts. Shortly before 15:00, Polish telephone communications through Germany were interrupted by order of the military authorities. This alarmed Foreign Minister Beck, who, instead of thinking of an attack, concluded that it was part of a war of nerves. In mid-afternoon, the British radio announced the signing of a formal Anglo-Polish alliance. The alliance treaty contained a secret protocol stipulating that it would apply exclusively against Germany, i.e. the British were disengaging from the defence of Poland against the USSR.

This fact first came to light almost two months later, on 19 October, when Rab Butler MP made it public in the House of Commons. The British had undertaken only to consult with the Poles in the event of Soviet aggression in Poland. It had been stipulated in the treaty that Britain would not recognise the annexation of Polish territory by a third power without obtaining the consent of the Polish leadership. This clause led during World War II to tremendous pressure from Britain on Polish leaders to accept the annexation of eastern Poland by the Soviet Union. Shortly after this news, Mussolini's response to Ribentropp, promised the day before, arrived: Italy was not ready for war and would only be ready for war in 1943. Italy would remain neutral, as it lacked arms and raw materials. In a letter, Hitler asked the Italians for a list of the most urgent needs.

Before the treaty with Poland was signed, Halifax received two urgent calls from Henderson. In his first contact, the ambassador was absolutely in favour of accepting Hitler's offer of a settlement and urged the Foreign

Office Secretary to give it serious consideration. The second contact was to report further atrocities perpetrated against Germans in Poland. Henderson, claiming that his source was absolutely reliable, reported that in Bielitz, in Eastern Upper Silesia, Poles were deporting Germans from the area and forcing them to march into the interior of the country. Eight Germans had been killed and many others wounded during these actions on 25 August 1939. Henderson, who deplored the passivity of his government, feared that Bielitz would be the last straw and that Hitler would order the invasion. He would have been more worried if he had known that the Poles had committed another massacre in Lodz, where 24 Germans had been shot that very day. Nevertheless, at 18:30 the Führer ordered General Keitel to suspend preparations against Poland, pending a response to Ambassador Henderson's offer.

Halifax and Kennard farce: Poles refuse to negotiate

On 25 August 1939, President Roosevelt received a communiqué from the President of Poland, Ignacy Moscicki, which he forwarded to Hitler. Roosevelt assured the German Chancellor that Moscicki had promised to enter into direct negotiations with Germany. With hypocritically charged theatrical dramatics, Roosevelt added: "Everyone is praying that Germany will accept it too." The Nazi leaders, accustomed to Roosevelt's gestures to the gallery, knew that this was mere propaganda to accuse Germany of rejecting peace in order to discredit it, so they continued to pin their hopes on the British response. Evidence of the American president's dishonesty is offered by Eric Phipps, the British ambassador in Paris, who reported to London that Bullitt had been instructed by Roosevelt to seek greater coordination against Germany. He proposed to intensify propaganda against the National Socialist regime in order to portray Hitler as solely responsible for the war. Before midnight on that Friday, 25 August, Colonel Beck assured the American ambassador in Warsaw, Biddle, that war was inevitable and that his country had a legal basis for declaring war on Germany if Germany did not take the initiative against Poland within the next few days. Incredible as it may seem, Beck was anxious for the war to begin. Reports from Noël, the French ambassador in Warsaw, confirm that Beck was very ill in those days because of fatigue from tuberculosis and his addiction to stimulants. Noël, who detested Beck, did not refrain from expressing his opinion that Beck was morally and physically decadent. In 1944 Beck died of tuberculosis in Romania after the British authorities refused him permission to enter Britain.

At 19.40 on the 25th Hitler, deeply disappointed by Italy's position, telephoned personally to Hans Georg von Mackensen, the German Ambassador in Rome, and asked him to inform him what the specific requirements were regarding armaments and other materials. Four hours later, at 11.30 p.m., Mackensen reported that the next day Mussolini would send the Führer a precise list, which was indeed received in Berlin at 12.10 p.m. on the 26th. Among the Italian requests were: six million tons of coal, two million tons of iron, seven million tons of oil, one million tons of wood, and many tons of copper, sodium nitrate, potassium salts, rubber, turpentine, lead, nickel, tungsten, zirconium and titanium. The Italians also asked for 150 anti-aircraft batteries and ammunition. Hitler replied a few hours later that Germany could supply Italy with coal and iron, but could not supply it with oil, copper and other materials in which it too was deficient. Nor could it deliver immediately all the anti-aircraft batteries requested. At 18:42 Mussolini insisted to Hitler that a peaceful solution was essential for the people of Italy and Germany.

Before flying to England, Henderson wrote a personal letter to Ribbentrop at 7.30 a.m. on Saturday 26 August. He told him that he was about to leave for London to explain the "great proposal" for an Anglo-German agreement which Hitler had made to him the day before. He expressed once again his conviction that the agreement was necessary for a peaceful settlement of the Polish question. He emphasised to Ribbentrop that "for four months Herr Hitler had shown great fortitude in his patience" and hoped that he would be able to maintain it because of the enormous risk involved. He also asked him to inform Hitler that it would be an indignity on the Ambassador's part if he did not return to Berlin the same day or the next, and begged him to trust in his good faith. The letter concluded with the assertion that a new Anglo-German war would be the greatest catastrophe that could befall the world. Halifax did not authorise the ambassador's return until the afternoon of the 28th.

While Henderson travelled home in renewed spirits, Halifax contacted the ambassador in Warsaw, Kennard, in the morning, who rejected the possibility of reopening negotiations between the Germans and Poles. The Foreign Office Secretary suggested that Polish leaders should be wise to ask the German government to approve the expulsion of the entire German minority from Poland. Halifax thought that this would deprive Hitler of constant complaints about the Poles' mistreatment of the Germans. One might wonder whether Halifax was also proposing to expel the population of Danzig, which did not belong to Poland and was inhabited almost entirely by German citizens. However, the Poles were not prepared in principle to consider this solution, as they feared that the German government might take a similar measure against the Polish minority.. *The Times* of London reported in its 26th edition on Henderson's peace efforts, and reported on the ambassador's conversation with Hitler the previous day. In the face of the interest aroused, Kennard and the Poles looked on with alarm at the contacts between London and Berlin.

The British Ambassador arrived at Croydon aerodrome and left immediately for London. The text of the peace offer in his briefcase had been telegraphed the night before, so that the Cabinet had had time to examine it. Chamberlain and Halifax were waiting for him at 10 Downing Street. Henderson tried for three hours to convince them of the significance of the moment for Britain and for Europe. When the ambassador left the meeting for Buckingham Palace, Chamberlain and Halifax stayed together for another hour. King George VI talked with his ambassador for a long time, and when the interview was over, a Council of Government was convened, in which Henderson participated. The British Cabinet remained in session until after midnight, when the meeting was adjourned after ministers decided to reconvene the following day. In the German Chancellery, the anticipation of news from Henderson was at its height. At last came the news that the Chamberlain government had suspended its deliberations until the following day. More patience was called for, even though there had been another serious provocation during the day: a Polish warship had fired on a German civilian transport plane carrying Wilhelm Stuckart, State Secretary of the Reich Ministry of the Interior, who had come to the Free City to discuss the legal problems involved in Danzig's proposed return to the Reich, from Danzig to Berlin.

At the same time, Birger Dahlerus was still working to get the British to be reasonable and force the Poles to negotiate. After Henderson's arrival in London, the Swedish engineer had been received by Halifax at 11:00 on the morning of the 26th. The Foreign Office secretary handed him a personal letter for Marshal Göring, recommending direct negotiations between Poland and Germany. Dahlerus decided to fly immediately to Berlin, where he arrived at 5:30 p.m. in order to deliver the letter. During the night of the 26th, the Swedish businessman had his first meeting with the Führer before having a long conversation with Göring. On the 27th Dahlerus returned to London, where British leaders assured him that a reply to Hitler's proposal submitted by Ambassador Henderson would be forthcoming during the day; but this did not happen, and a formal reply was delayed until the afternoon of 28 August. However, through discussions with Chamberlain and senior Foreign Office officials, the Swedish negotiator came to the conclusion that Britain would favour any further attempt by Germany to settle differences with Poland through negotiations. Once this obstacle had been overcome, the way would be clear for the Anglo-German agreement. With this information, Dahlerus decided to return to Germany.

Hitler was pleased to hear the message, but the crucial question immediately arose: the British had to persuade the Poles to negotiate, for without negotiation nothing could be achieved, war would be inevitable, and a golden opportunity for understanding between Britain and Germany would be lost. Dahlerus contacted British diplomats at the embassy in Berlin, whose chief representative in the absence of the ambassador was the chargé d'affaires, Sir George Ogilvie-Forbes, and informed him that Hitler was prepared to refuse aid against Britain to any power, including Italy, Japan and Russia. The German Chancellor believed he was entitled to make this offer because his only ally, Italy, had refused to support Germany against Britain and France. However, despite the disappointment that his position had aroused in Hitler, on the 27th Count Ciano personally called Halifax to try to influence his decision. The Italian Foreign Minister, on the basis of the friendly relations between the United Kingdom and Italy, pleaded that the British Government give the highest consideration to Hitler's offer of an Anglo-German agreement. Ciano asked Halifax to encourage the Poles to negotiate with Germany.

After so much effort, everything still depended on Poland agreeing to a reasonable negotiating process, which in turn still depended on the UK seriously demanding it. But while Ambassador Henderson did not share Halifax's warmongering line and sought a peaceful solution, his colleague in Warsaw, Kennard, was working for war in perfect harmony with the Foreign Office Secretary. The British ambassador in Warsaw had detailed reports on the unbearable plight of the Germans in Poland and knew they were mistreated, but preferred to ignore it and lie cynically: "As far as I can judge, the German allegations of massive mistreatment of the German minority are gross exaggerations, if not complete fabrications".

Finally, before the Henderson returned to Berlin with his Government's official reply to Hitler's offer, the Foreign Office Secretary, urged by Dahlerus, who had returned to London, and by Henderson himself, contacted Kennard by cable at 14:00 on 28 August. Halifax alluded to the recent communiqué to Roosevelt from Polish President Moscicki indicating that the Poles were prepared to negotiate directly with Germany. Halifax told Kennard that Britain naturally expected the Poles to act accordingly. The British ambassador, who was opposed to further talks, decided not to put pressure on Poland, and the same evening responded with indifference and nonchalance that Beck was prepared to enter into direct negotiations with the Germans at once. The absence of details or any specific proposals clearly indicated to Halifax that no serious British demarche had been made in Warsaw. Halifax did not make the slightest effort to demand that his ambassador undertake a genuine démarche (direct démarche) in favour of negotiations. However, the Foreign Office Secretary informed the British embassies of his dialogue with Kennard and a state of confusion was created, as the hoax spread that London was exerting pressure on the Poles. Significant of the lack of rigour and seriousness in the actions of Halifax and Kennard is that the Foreign Office did not even instruct Sir Eric Phipps to brief Bonnet on the British "demarche" in Warsaw. Had he done so, the French foreign minister would no doubt have seized the opportunity to demand that Halifax put pressure on the Poles.

In contrast, the Swedish negotiator Dahlerus, as proof of how seriously the Germans were taking the possibility of finally negotiating an agreement with the Poles, informed the British on the evening of the 28th about the basic outline of the offer they were going to make to Poland (it would go down in history as the "Marienwerder" proposals). Göring thought that the fact that the British knew that Germany maintained a moderate position would help the negotiations. Göring had even scouted out the venue for the negotiations. He had asked Dahlerus to tell the British that, in order to prevent the Poles from having any objections to going to Germany, he had planned to hold this important conference in the Baltic Sea, some distance from the Polish coast, on the luxury yacht of the Swedish industrialist Wenner-Gren, chairman of the Electrolux corporation, who had offered it for the occasion. Göring was confident that this information about a neutral venue for talks would be passed on to the Poles; but Halifax did not consider it of interest, and all he passed on to Kennard was that the SIS (Intelligence Service) had reported on the German Army's military preparations. Of Halifax's attitude, Hoggan writes: "Halifax knew that the emphasis on military preparations, not to mention Germany's desire to negotiate with Poland, would be the greatest possible stimulus to further drastic measures to increase the danger of war and reduce the chances of a negotiated settlement".

At 17:00 on the 28th Henderson finally flew to Berlin with the official British reply to Hitler's offer. Before leaving, he sent a cable requesting an interview with the German Chancellor as soon as possible. Anticipating that Hitler would summon him without delay, he warned that he would need time to translate the text into German at the British Embassy. The official note said that the British Government noted that Hitler's offer was conditional on a settlement of the German-Polish dispute. The British insisted that any settlement would have to be subject to the international guarantee of a number of powers, including Germany and Poland. Halifax told Hitler that the Polish government had declared its readiness to negotiate directly with the German government. The document reminded Hitler that an Anglo-German conflict as a result of failure to reach an agreement "could plunge the whole world into war. Such an outcome would be a calamity unparalleled in history". In other words, the British were admitting that they would seek to involve the rest of the world in the conflict, despite recognising that it would be the greatest disaster in history. It is absolutely baffling to see that Halifax could avert the apocalypse he announced by putting effective pressure on the Polish government.

At 22:30 Henderson called Hitler to announce that he had the translated text. The meeting took place during the night of 28/29 August and the atmosphere between the two was very friendly. The German Chancellor, hoping that the British would not wish the tragedy they themselves foresaw, outlined to the Ambassador the new proposals he would present to the Poles, about which the British leaders had been fully briefed by Dahlerus. Hitler announced that the negotiating document would be drawn up on the 29th and that he would reply to the official British note on the same day. Henderson, fearing that he had given the impression that he expected his reply without delay, told the Chancellor that there was no need to hurry: "We are taking two days," he said, "to draft the note. I am in no hurry." Then Hitler replied with extreme seriousness, "But I am." After the receipt of the British note and the conversation with Henderson there followed an interlude of optimism and hope, which seemed fully justified by the fact that the British announced that they had induced the Poles to agree to new direct negotiations, which, as has been seen, was not true. It may be argued," writes Hoggan, to whom we turn once again, "that Hitler and his entourage were extremely naive in believing promises coming from London. This was undoubtedly true, but Hitler simply did not see clearly that the British had anything to gain by giving a false picture of the Polish position. Hitler, in his enthusiasm for the British Empire, was inclined to give the British leaders more credit for intelligence and integrity than they actually deserved."

In fact, the day of 29 August 1939 allowed an interval of optimism in all countries. Ribbentrop contacted Attolico and told him that after Hitler and Henderson's meeting they believed that an agreement was possible. Foreign Minister Bonnet, too, although France, like Poland, had practically completed its mobilisation, was encouraged by the news from Berlin, which raised hopes for the preservation of peace. After a telephone conversation between Ciano and Halifax, hope also reached Rome. Mussolini sent a message to Hitler at 4.40 p.m. in which he considered the British note of the previous day as a suitable basis for a satisfactory agreement. Henderson was also optimistic when he transmitted shortly after noon additional information to Halifax about the new proposals to the Poles and announced that the official German reply would be forthcoming that same day. Henderson added that Göring was anxiously awaiting some indication of Poland's attitude to the new negotiations and warned London that Göring was wary of Warsaw's stubbornness.

As the day wore on, optimism began to wane, as the news everyone had been waiting for was not forthcoming. The first to suspect that something was amiss was Henderson himself, who had hoped during the day for some indication from his government that the Poles had been pressed to negotiate. The British Ambassador knew that if Halifax had not taken action in Warsaw the disappointment would be great. As late as the afternoon of the 29th he decided to contact London to plead with the Poles to insist that they should negotiate with Germany. He again stressed to the Foreign Office Secretary of State that Hitler preferred a negotiated settlement to any war, including a local war. Henderson made a second call minutes later to emphasise that the French should be asked to join Britain in applying strong pressure on Poland. Henderson rightly suspected that Halifax had not made the slightest effort to obtain French support, which he would have been quick to offer.

Shortly after Henderson's second call, whose requests were obviously ignored by Halifax, a telegram arrived in London from Kennard. The ambassador wished to inform Halifax that the Polish Government had decided on a general mobilisation, which, according to military plans, was only to be ordered in the event of war. Evidently, the architect of this Polish decision which practically made war inevitable was Halifax, who, instead of communicating Hitler's wishes for negotiation and peace, had informed the Poles that German forces would be in position for operations against Poland on the night of 30/31 August. Halifax, rather than pressuring Warsaw to accept negotiation, had hinted that it should prepare for invasion. Kennard also made a second call to London, which somewhat eclipsed the prospect of mobilisation: rumours that Poland would be asked to negotiate with Germany had reached Beck, who had decided to announce in advance that they were refusing to do so. Beck stated flatly to Kennard that he was not prepared to make any concessions and saw no reason to negotiate. He explained to Kennard that he would not accept any of the proposals he had already rejected in March 1939. Halifax received this communiqué with satisfaction and, instead of playing the role expected of him, renounced any further dealings with Warsaw for a prolonged period. The Foreign Secretary knew that Kennard would resolutely support Beck's intransigence. These facts were ignored in European capitals, where cautious optimism remained. Halifax, despite knowing that the Poles were doomed in advance in case of war, ignored a third attempt by Henderson in the form of a telegram, in which he insisted that it was vital that Poland accept Germany's invitation to negotiate without delay.

For his part, Hitler had already put the finishing touches to the text of his reply to Britain. Late on Tuesday evening, 29 August, Henderson was received by Hitler, who at 7.15 p.m. presented him with the official note. In it Germany accepted that the dispute with Poland had become crucial to Anglo-German relations, and confirmed its desire for a peaceful settlement and its readiness to negotiate. Hitler asked the British Government to advise Poland to send an emissary the following day, Wednesday, 30 August. The urgency was emphasised because of the pressure of events, and it was reported that Germany expected the Polish representative to arrive no later than midnight on 30 August.

A few minutes after the note was delivered to Henderson, Dahlerus telephoned the Foreign Office from Berlin to reiterate that Hitler and Göring were positive about the British attitude towards Germany that had emerged from the note of 28 August. Shortly after this contact, Kennard sent London a further communiqué: although Bonnet had instructed his Ambassador Noël to protest strongly against the general mobilisation, the Poles intended to announce it publicly the next day, as these events could not be kept secret. Kennard bluntly told Halifax that he could hardly ask the Poles for restraint now when he himself had prompted the decision to mobilise by providing information about Germany's plans. Beck, now in his role of fighting cock, informed Halifax through Kennard that only an explicit statement from

Hitler announcing that Germany was abandoning Danzig once and for all and would never again insist on improving its communications with East Prussia through the Corridor could prevent the general mobilisation, scheduled for 8:00 the next day. Still, Beck was prepared to receive and study the full text of Hitler's reply to Britain, despite his announcement that he would not negotiate with Germany.

After his interview with Hitler, which was stormy as the Chancellor was outraged at the news of the latest mass atrocities against the German minority, Henderson immediately contacted London and again asked Halifax to spare no effort to convince the Poles to accept negotiation on the terms presented by Germany. At 21:15 on 29 August, the Foreign Office received Hitler's reply text. There was therefore time for the British Government to contact Warsaw and for the Poles to send a plenipotentiary to Berlin. Henderson did not attempt to deny that the German note smacked of an ultimatum, but reported that Hitler had expressed his willingness to consult with Stalin about the possibility of an international guarantee for Poland.. As evidence of these intentions, Ribbentrop contacted Soviet Chargé d'Affaires Ivanov before midnight on the 29th, informing him that Germany would favour USSR participation in an international settlement over Poland.

Henderson set about taking every step in his power to prevent the terrible outcome he so feared. He first hastened to contact his French colleague in Berlin, Coulondre, whom he quickly convinced that Hitler's plan was worth supporting. Coulondre contacted his superiors in Paris and urged that maximum pressure be put on Poland to send an emissary to Berlin in time. After midnight on 29 August, again on his own, without waiting for instructions from London, the British ambassador met with his Polish colleague in Berlin, Lipski, to whom he expressed his conviction that Poland could and should dispatch a plenipotentiary to Germany. The Polish ambassador was quick to inform Beck of Henderson's demarche, and the Polish foreign minister in turn immediately called Kennard. Also, shortly after midnight on the 29th Halifax forwarded to his ambassador in Warsaw the full text of Hitler's reply and merely commented that it "did not seem to close all the doors", so Kennard told Beck that he had received no further instructions from London and proposed to let the night pass in anticipation of further contact from Halifax the following day.

In the early hours of 30 August, Neville Henderson passed on valuable information to Lord Halifax, which was expected to be used to convince the Poles of the need to negotiate. The ambassador insisted that Birger Dahlerus was ready to fly to London at any time. The Swedish mediator was instructed to tell the British that midnight on 30 August was not a deadline for the arrival of the Polish plenipotentiary and that Berlin was not necessarily the place for the meeting. Henderson reminded Halifax that the possibility of holding the conference on the Swedish industrialist's yacht off the Polish coast remained open. In the early hours of the 30th, therefore, peace was still possible, since the Germans assumed that Britain was putting pressure on Poland. However, the Nazi leaders were unaware that Halifax had at no time seriously asked the Poles to negotiate, so the Poles remained steadfast in their refusal to accept it. They were also unaware that the Foreign Secretary had supported the general mobilisation in Poland and that the British Ambassador in Warsaw had advised the Poles not to negotiate with Germany. For several days the British Government had fostered the false impression that it favoured direct negotiations between Poland and Germany when in fact it was applying the favourite stratagem of its diplomatic tradition: blatant duplicity.

Last-ditch attempts to prevent the invasion of Poland

For Ambassador Henderson the fateful 30th had begun at four o'clock in the morning, when he received a telegram from Halifax sent at 10.25 p.m. the previous day. It told him that the German note was under consideration, but that the British Government could not be expected to be able to get a Polish plenipotentiary to Berlin within twenty-four hours. He was asked to warn the Reich authorities. An hour later, at 5 a.m., Dahlerus left Tempelhof airport for London, where he arrived at 8.30 a.m., shortly after Halifax had received confirmation that the Poles were proceeding with the general mobilisation. The Swedish envoy meticulously explained to Chamberlain and Halifax Hitler's proposals, which, unlike those made on 24 October 1938, no longer simply ceded the Corridor to Poland, but provided for a plebiscite. At 12.30 p.m. Dahlerus telephoned Göring to tell him that the British felt that Hitler was putting too much pressure on the Poles with his plan. Dahlerus asked Göring whether it might not be possible for Lipski to receive the proposal and take it to Warsaw. Göring did not dare to support this idea without the Führer's permission, so he asked for some time to discuss it with the German Chancellor. At 13:15 Marshal Göring contacted Dahlerus again and informed him that Hitler rejected the plan to hand over the proposals to Lipski for him to present them in Warsaw, as this was not an indication that Poland accepted the negotiation. It was not a matter of demanding unconditional acceptance of the proposals, but of using them as a basis for negotiation. Hitler was prepared to accept that a special envoy should go to seek the proposals, provided that this implied acceptance of the proposals as a starting point for negotiation. At 15:00 Dahlerus telephoned again to say that the British did not like Hitler's new plan and insisted that the Polish Ambassador be allowed to travel to Warsaw with the proposals. The key idea that the Poles should show at least some willingness to negotiate was thus ignored. Göring, enraged, refused to repeat the consultation with Hitler and insisted on the proposal made by the Führer.

Already in the afternoon Halifax told Kennard vaguely that the Poles should be encouraged to enter into negotiations, but explicitly informed him that Britain would never require Beck to submit formal proposals for a settlement with Germany. Hoggan notes the following fact: "Ten days earlier the British had pressed Poland to accept the penetration of Soviet troops into its territory; but they refused to put pressure on the Poles to resume direct negotiations with Germany. This seems especially grotesque if one remembers that the Poles regarded the Soviet Union as their main enemy and that Halifax had assured Germany that Poland was prepared to resume negotiations." Halifax's overriding concern was to blame Germany for the eventual conflict with Poland, so he asked Kennard to tell Beck that he should in principle accept direct negotiations with the Germans because "they should be given no opportunity to lay the blame for the conflict on Poland." These instructions make it clear that Halifax never seriously contemplated a peaceful settlement of the crisis.

At 5.30 p.m. on 30 August Henderson informed Ribbentrop that he had received a message from Chamberlain to Hitler. The British Prime Minister wished to let the German Chancellor know that the official reply to the German note of the 29th would reach Berlin before midnight. Ambassador Kennedy in a report to Roosevelt issued on the same day, 30 August, wrote that Chamberlain stubbornly refused to admit that Britain might advise the Poles to make some concessions to Germany. Chamberlain admitted to Kennedy that it was the Poles and not the Germans who were unreasonable. Kennedy's exact words were: "Chamberlain is frankly more concerned about getting the Poles to be reasonable than he is about getting the Germans to be reasonable". Hoggan finds Chamberlain's demonstration of impotence pathetic.

On the other hand, the position of the USSR in these hours of maximum tension was one of uncertainty, for the Communists feared that Germany's diplomatic efforts would succeed, which would prevent a German-Polish war and make their plans for westward expansion impossible. The Tass news agency, the Soviet press and radio stations announced on the evening of 30 August that the Soviet Union was massing its armed forces along the Polish border. This announcement, made before the general mobilisation in Poland became known in Moscow, was apparently intended to encourage the Germans to take a harder line with the Poles.

The fact that the UK Prime Minister privately admitted that it was the Poles who were intransigent justified Henderson, the ambassador appointed by Chamberlain to underpin the policy of appeasement, in continuing his efforts for peace. Henderson learned from Halifax that Dahlerus would be flying from London to Berlin on the evening of the 30th. The ambassador took the opportunity to denounce once again to his superior that atrocities against Germans in Poland were increasing in number, and that this was an enormous risk factor in the precarious situation. Henderson hinted that Pius XII would be prepared to employ special nuncios in an effort to intercede on behalf of the German minority; but Halifax dismissed this suggestion by the ambassador, who deeply deplored Britain's attitude to the barbarities of the Poles against the Germans. At 6.50 p.m. on the same day, 30 August, Halifax sent dire instructions to Henderson. In them was the reply to the German note of the previous day: the British leaders flatly rejected Hitler's proposal that they advise the Poles to send a plenipotentiary to Berlin for direct negotiations. Halifax called the German proposal "totally unacceptable". Ambassador Henderson was therefore to tell the German authorities that Britain would not advise the Polish Government to go along with Hitler's plan.

Shortly before midnight on 30 August Ribbentrop received Henderson, who handed him the British reply, which began with these words: "His Majesty's Government repeats that the wishes of the German Government for an improvement in relations are reciprocal, but it must be recognised that they cannot sacrifice the interests of other friends in order to achieve this improvement. The note showed no interest in persuading the Poles to negotiate. After reading the text carefully, the German foreign minister informed Henderson in dismay that they had prepared proposals for a diplomatic agreement which they intended to present to the awaiting Polish plenipotentiary. Increasingly tense, Ribbentrop proceeded to read slowly through the sixteen points of the Marienwerder proposals and to explain each of them in detail. It called for the return of Danzig to the Reich on the basis of self-determination and envisaged, after a temporary period of twelve months from the agreement, the holding of a plebiscite in the northern region of the Corridor, from west of Marienwerder in East Prussia to Schönlanke in Pomerania. Ribbentrop, who spoke English, read in German, as Henderson had asked the minister to use his own language in his discussions.

Interpreter Paul Schmidt, who was present in order to clear up any possible misunderstandings, was surprised when Henderson asked for a copy of the proposals and Ribbentrop replied with a faint smile: "No, I cannot give you these proposals. Hitler had instructed the minister to give the proposals to the ambassador only if the British offered any indication that the Poles would negotiate. Henderson, stunned, thought he had misunderstood and repeated the request: "In any case," Ribbentrop replied angrily, "this is all behind us, since it is now past midnight and no Polish negotiator has come forward." Indignant, Henderson noted, "This is therefore an ultimatum." Thus the conversation ended, and the British ambassador withdrew in silence, convinced that the last chance for peace had vanished.

Göring learned of the abrupt end of the Ribbentrop-Henderson meeting in the company of Dahlerus, who had just returned from London. Alarmed, he immediately went to Hitler and asked him to hand over the text of the proposals to Henderson. The Führer agreed. At 1 a.m. on the morning of the 31st Dahlerus phoned the British Embassy and read the proposals to Ogilvie-Forbes over the telephone, but when the business manager sought out the Ambassador to hand him the text, he found that Henderson had gone out without saying anything. Ogilvie-Forbes could only leave the note on the table in his office. Ambassador Henderson, despite the stormy meeting with the German Foreign Minister, had gone to the Polish Ambassador's house and asked him to propose to his government a meeting between Göring and Ridz-Smigly, the Marshal who was acting as head of the government. Having experienced Ribbentrop's mood, Henderson allowed himself to add that any negotiations under the aegis of the German Foreign Minister had little chance of success. Henderson asked Lipski to claim the proposals from the German Government and hand them over to Warsaw; but the ambassador let him know that his demarche was not in Warsaw's favour and that he could not take the step without instructions from Beck.

At 9:15 on the morning of 31 August, Henderson cabled Halifax that if nothing happened in the next few hours, Germany would declare war on Poland. Following this desperate warning, a telegram was received at the Foreign Office from Kennard, who expressed his satisfaction that Britain had refused to press Poland to negotiate with Germany. Beck had let the British Ambassador know that he was holding a consultation meeting with the Polish Government and that some kind of statement would be sent to London by noon. Kennard assured the Foreign Secretary that Beck would do nothing to reach an agreement with the Germans.

Dahlerus, Henderson and Ogilvie-Forbes reported at 10:00 at the Polish Embassy in Berlin. The Swedish emissary, whom Henderson had called after finding the note in his office, had a copy of the proposals with him and read them to Lipski in German. Dahlerus had the impression that the Polish ambassador did not realise their importance. Meanwhile, Henderson telephoned the German Foreign Ministry and let Weizsäcker know that he was advising Ambassador Lipski to negotiate with Germany. Ambassador Henderson tried once again to make his colleague understand that the proposals offered a good basis for beginning a negotiation that would allow a settlement between Poland and Germany. Henderson told him that it might still be possible to get things back on track if he agreed to receive them. Lipski was not hopeful, since he had lost his influence in Warsaw since March 1939, when Ribbentrop had convinced him of the need to negotiate on the basis of the October 1938 proposals. Finally, Lipski, thoroughly agitated, told the British Ambassador that he had no reason to negotiate with the German Government, for if war broke out, he knew that a revolution would break out in Germany and that they would march on Berlin. Henderson, saddened, then realised that there was no point in discussing the matter further with the Polish ambassador.

The Italians, too, who were not informed of the events described above, again tried to make representations to the British Government. Attolico called Weizsäcker at 11:30 on the 31st to inform the German leaders that Mussolini had advised London to put pressure on Poland to accept

Dänzig's return to Germany. After contact with London, the Duce had been under the impression that the Poles had agreed to negotiations. He soon learned from the German ambassador, Mackensen, that the situation was not as he had thought it would be. After learning of the Marienwerder proposals, which had been sent to the German Embassy in Rome, Mussolini instructed Attolico, who visited Ribbentrop in the afternoon, to advise the German leadership to receive Lipski as a last means of achieving contact.

As for the French, a key player for Halifax, Bonnet was still trying to prevent France from being dragged into an imposed war that he saw as absolutely unnecessary. The French foreign minister found Poland's delaying tactics unjustifiable and inexplicable. Bonnet pressed Halifax for France and Britain to make the Poles understand that they must do something to avoid a European war. The Foreign Secretary had little interest in preserving peace in Europe; but he could not turn a deaf ear to the French minister's plea. Consequently, he decided to make a face-saving gesture. Informed in advance by Kennard that Beck had formally expressed his gratitude for the British decision not to respond in any way to Germany's proposals, Halifax decided to instruct the British Ambassador, accompanied by his French colleague, Ambassador Noël, to ask Beck to notify the Germans of his readiness to accept direct negotiations. On the afternoon of the 31st, both ambassadors called the Polish Foreign Minister and asked him to authorise Lipski to receive the German proposals and bring them to Warsaw.

Beck had previously sent precise instructions to Ambassador Lipski not to accept proposals and not to enter into negotiations with the German government. The telegram was intercepted and decoded by the Reich's telegram decryption and communications surveillance services. The text, quoted by Dahlerus in his statement to the Nuremberg tribunal, is as follows: "Do not, under any circumstances, allow yourself to be drawn into technical discussions. If the Reich Government makes oral or written proposals to you, you will state that you have absolutely no full powers to receive or discuss these proposals, that you are only empowered to pass them on to your Government and to ask for further instructions". Before the Nuremberg tribunal Dahlerus related that, after receiving the text of the telegram, Göring realised that there was no longer any hope unless a change of attitude could be brought about on the part of the Polish. Dahlerus stated that, overlooking the fact that Germany knew Poland's diplomatic code, Marshal Göring showed him the telegram and even considered showing it to the British.

The Anglo-French demarche did not upset Beck, who knew that the British had agreed to take the step with France as a mere formality. More difficult for him was the approach of the papal nuncio, Filippo Cortesi, who on behalf of Pius XII urged Beck to accept negotiations with Germany on the basis of the Marienwerder proposals, which were already known in the Vatican. Beck himself later admitted that no event in the final phase of the crisis irritated him as much as the Pope's insistence in his attempts to persuade him to negotiate. The scene between Cortesi and Beck is recorded as reaching extremely tense levels. The Polish foreign minister went so far as to accuse the nuncio of working for the Germans and warned him that Pius XII wanted him to surrender to Germany. Cortesi did what Britain supposedly should have done if it really intended to put pressure on the Polish government to avoid war; however, the fact that Poland was staunchly Catholic, which gave the country special consideration from the Vatican, did not help Cortesi's mission to succeed.

Pius XII's goal was to save Poland from the disaster to which it was heading because of the erratic decisions of its leaders. Giovani Pacelli had been elected Pope by the College of Cardinals in March 1939. His great diplomatic experience had been decisive in his election. As will be recalled, Pacelli was in Munich in 1919, where he was led at gunpoint to the Jewish Max Levien, who ruled the city. There he experienced Communist dictatorship in the Soviet Republic of Bavaria, imposed by Jewish revolutionaries close to Trotsky and Lenin. Pius XII had begun his peace efforts in May 1939, when he realised that the British intended to sacrifice Poland as a pawn in the war against Germany. Even then, the Pope proposed an international conference, which Beck rejected. On 24 August Pius XII had appealed to the world not to start a war over Danzig. On 31 August, in desperation, he summoned the representatives of Great Britain, France, Italy, Poland and Germany to an audience. Dr. Kazimierz Papee, the Polish diplomat at the Vatican, was unable to assure the Pope that Poland would negotiate with Germany. In the well-founded fear that Beck was refusing to negotiate, Pius XII decided to commission Nuncio Cortesi to go to the Polish foreign minister.

Among the last efforts to keep the peace was also the mediation of Italy, seconded by Bonnet. At 11:00 on the morning of the 31st, Count Ciano, alarmed by the gravity of the situation, telephoned Halifax to ask him to persuade the Poles of the need to negotiate and promised that Mussolini would use his influence with Hitler to keep him patient. François-Poncet, the French ambassador to Italy, contacted Minister Bonnet at noon to inform him that Mussolini believed that if the Poles agreed to return Danzig to Germany, all other issues could be settled without pressure afterwards. The French foreign minister was encouraged by the words of his ambassador in Rome and decided to play his last card for peace by supporting the Italian efforts, which called for a diplomatic conference.

Italy's ambassador in Paris, Raffaele Guariglia, who was on very good terms with Bonnet, informed Ciano that France gave full support to Italy's mediation. Guariglia, a prestigious career diplomat whose appointment as ambassador in November 1938 had been warmly welcomed in Paris, was an astute observer who deplored the warmongering activities of the American ambassador, Bullitt. The Italian diplomat was convinced that Roosevelt and

Bullitt's campaign to unleash a war in Europe was in the interests of the Soviet Union. The ambassador believed that Halifax was blind and, in his intention to destroy Germany, disregarded Britain's real interests. Guariglia knew that the British could not offer immediate help to Poland and deplored the fact that delusions about their future greatness prevented the Poles from understanding the gravity of the Ribbentrop-Molotov Pact of 23 August 1939. Ambassador Guariglia understood that France was having difficulty escaping the British encirclement and hoped that Ciano could convince French leaders of the need to adopt a foreign policy independent of Britain.

Ultimately, then, Italy, France, the Vatican and Germany were trying to make the Poles understand once and for all that Danzig, a German-inhabited town that did not even belong to Poland, did not deserve a European war. Unfortunately, the Foreign Office ignored all calls for Britain to join the cry for peace. By contrast, Halifax and the British pawns working in the interests of the Hidden Power driving the war were increasingly outraged by the tenacity with which European politicians fought to avoid conflict. Such was Halifax's desire to avoid negotiation that he went so far as to severely reprimand Ambassador Henderson for giving Dahlerus the Embassy telephone in Berlin to lobby London, and disavowed his initiative to Ambassador Lipski. Halifax made it clear to Henderson that he rejected the German proposals as a basis for negotiation and warned him that he and Dahlerus maintained "an obstructionist attitude towards the Polish Government."

In his anxiety to hasten the invasion of Poland, Halifax even regretted ordering Kennard to join Noël in asking Beck to authorise Lipski to receive the proposals, which was a minor gesture that did not involve negotiation. According to David L. Hoggan, Kennard went so far as to assure the Polish foreign minister privately that Britain did not want Lipski to receive the German proposals and that the Anglo-French demarche had been prompted by the need to offer a gesture of appeasement to France. In reality, Kennard, whose greatest concern was that a last-minute demarche might ruin all the war effort, was not informed that Beck had received the Marienweder proposals hours earlier.

Hitler, who for days had been enduring in anger the continuing provocations of the Germans in Poland, had already ordered the attack for 1 September at 12.40 p.m.; but there was still a possibility of cancelling the operation provided the order was given before 9.30 p.m. on the 31st, since the invasion was scheduled to take place at dawn. The text of the order was headed by these words: "Now that all possibilities have been exhausted of bringing a peaceful end to the situation on the eastern frontier, which is intolerable to Germany, I have decided in favour of a solution of force". Despite the obvious danger that Britain and France would declare war on Germany after months of aggression and savage persecution of the Germans, Hitler, who had been telling his generals for days that he would continue to wait for a favourable gesture from the Polish authorities, decided to intervene in Poland.

On the evening of 31 August, the German Foreign Ministry received from Göring a copy of Beck's instructions to his ambassador in Berlin not to negotiate anything. Despite this, Ribbentrop received Lipski at 18:30 on the evening of 31 August. Fifteen minutes earlier, at 18:15, Kennard had informed Halifax that Lipski would meet Ribbentrop, although the ambassador had been forbidden to engage in talks and, above all, to receive any proposals. Lipski read to the German minister the contents of a note from Beck, in which he reported that Poland had just learned of recent talks between Britain and Germany, which had begun on 23 August. The note stated that the Polish Government's disposition regarding possible negotiations between Poland and Germany had not yet been decided, although it was favourable in principle. Finally, the German Government was informed that the Polish Government would soon inform the British Government of its position on such negotiations. Beck was not in a position to say whether Poland was in fact ready to resume talks with Germany. Ribbentrop was saddened by the double-speak and calculated ambiguity of the Polish note. Ribbentrop then told Lipski that he had hoped until the last moment that he would come with full powers to negotiate. The ambassador replied that he had only been instructed to contact the Foreign Ministry and present the note. He was not authorised to give any guarantees or make any statements. In these circumstances, the interview ended immediately. Still, as he dismissed Lipski, Ribbentrop asked him if he personally believed that his government might reconsider the decision and allow him to negotiate. The Polish diplomat evaded the question and repeated that he had not received full powers.

At 21:00 on the 31st, German radio broadcast the news that Poland had refused to consider the Marienwerder proposals. Between 21:00 and 22:00, Weizsäcker summoned the diplomatic representatives of France, Great Britain, Japan, the United States and the USSR to give them the terms of the proposals, which were accompanied by a diplomatic note explaining the latest German policy and emphasising the fact that Hitler had waited in vain for two days for some indication that Poland would negotiate with Germany. Two hours later Polish radio gave a distorted version of the German offer, concluding: "Words can no longer conceal the aggressive plans of the new Huns. Germany is seeking to dominate Europe and is annulling the rights of nations with unprecedented cynicism. This insolent proposal clearly shows how necessary the military orders issued by the Polish Government were." The epithet "Huns" (Asian people of uncertain ethnic origin) for the Nazis was coined by the Jew Léon Blum, who had alluded to Hitler as a "mechanised Attila". Later, in a radio message broadcast on 7 June 1940, after Hitler had incomprehensibly allowed the evacuation of the British expeditionary force at Dunkirk, Churchill used the same epithet and referred to the need to "destroy the mechanised Attila".

From a local war to World War II

Operation White was launched: German troops began the invasion shortly before five o'clock on Friday, 1 September. Fifty-three divisions out of Hitler's 120 attacked with unstoppable thrust, and three hours later the Polish front was collapsing everywhere. The air force began to pound ammunition depots, airfields, stations, railway and communications junctions, and other targets of military interest, including the Polish air force, which was to be almost completely destroyed in the first thirty-six hours. At 8 a.m., amidst indescribable enthusiasm in the city, the Danzig Senate proclaimed Danzig's reincorporation into the Reich. At 10.10 a.m. Hitler made a speech before the Reichstag, in which he reminded the deputies that Danzig "was and is German". He said the same thing about the Corridor, which, for the sake of peace and cooperation, he had been prepared to give up in favour of Poland, just as he had given up Alsace-Lorraine and South Tyrol.

But it is the political and diplomatic activity that interests us, for it shows that, with the exception of Britain, the European countries did not want war. The Foreign Office Secretary, Lord Halifax, once again had in his hands the possibility of stopping almost immediately what was in principle a localised war; but, predictably, all his activity was aimed at provoking the escalation that was to trigger World War II. When Neville Henderson heard on German radio that the Marienwerder proposals had been rejected, he contacted Halifax to express his conviction that Beck had made a blunder, since they were a good basis for negotiations. Halifax himself had admitted to Kennard his concern about Poland's refusal to receive the proposals, although the reason for his dismay was quite different: he feared it might be "misinterpreted by world opinion". Henderson sarcastically observed that for Warsaw the proposals were virtually identical to those of October 1938, since the Poles had asserted quite firmly that "90% of the Corridor was Polish from the beginning of the world", so they were assured of victory in the plebiscite.

On 1 September Henderson rejected the propagandists who, on the grounds of the immorality of the National Socialist regime, justified British intervention in the war: he considered an ideological crusade against Germany in a world threatened by communism to be ridiculous. As is evident from his writings in numerous dispatches, Henderson also contested the balance of power argument in Europe as an alibi for a war he considered "completely unjustifiable". Obviously, Henderson could not be unaware that in March 1933 Judea had openly declared "holy war" on Germany. Recall that the Jewish newspaper *Natscha Retsch*, quoted in chapter eight, had in

1933 announced the aims of international Judaism in these words: "... the war against Germany will ideologically promote and enliven our interests, which require that Germany be completely destroyed".

Nor could the French Foreign Minister accept the instructions Beck had given Lipski before being received by Ribbentrop. Bonnet asked Ambassador Lukasiewicz to inform Beck that France insisted on the need for direct negotiations. Bonnet, given the ambiguity of Britain's approach, felt, however, that a general conference, as proposed by Italy, might be more fruitful. The French ambassador in London, Charles Corbin, warned him a few hours before the outbreak of the German-Polish war that the British were prepared to spoil any attempt at a conference by demanding German demobilisation beforehand. Despite this information, Bonnet recommended to Daladier that France should support a conference in which, without excluding direct negotiations between Poland and Germany, all European problems could be dealt with. Daladier argued that the conference could always be called off if Hitler demanded too much. The French government was therefore ready to support the conference, so Bonnet telephoned London to instruct Corbin to inform the Foreign Office of France's latest decision.

As soon as it became known in London that Germany had attacked Poland, the British demanded an Anglo-French ultimatum; but Bonnet, convinced that France should not go along with Halifax's warmongering policy, replied that he could not take such action without consulting Parliament. Nevertheless, Daladier convened the Council of Ministers, which met at 10:30 on 1 September and ordered a general mobilisation. At 11:50 Bonnet informed François-Poncet that the government had authorised him to support the Italian initiative to convene an international conference, and he instructed the ambassador to inform Mussolini of France's position. Halifax immediately realised that, following Bonnet's refusal to support the ultimatum, he had to focus his efforts on disrupting the Italian mediation effort, which with French support constituted the greatest threat to his war plans. The Foreign Secretary instructed Sir Percy Loraine, after thanking Mussolini's mediation efforts on behalf of Britain, to insist with the utmost vigour that the outbreak of war in Poland made Britain's military intervention against Germany inevitable.

At 14:00 Kennard cabled Halifax that Beck was expecting British air protection that afternoon. At 17:00 on 1 September, while the British Parliament was in session, Halifax telephoned Bonnet to advise him that the ambassadors of their respective countries should immediately demand the surrender of the passports. Halifax said it would be more effective for Britain and France to declare war on Germany that very day. The French foreign minister flatly refused to go to war with Germany in such haste, but Halifax reiterated his demand for an urgent response. After an arduous discussion, Bonnet, demonstrating his diplomatic agility, imposed on his counterpart a solution that resembled an ultimatum, but was not, since there was no limit.

Halifax had no choice but to accept that a joint Anglo-French "ultimatum" be presented in Berlin, with no expiry date. It was always better than nothing. At 17:45 he hastened to instruct Henderson to present the Anglo-French "démarche": both ambassadors were to advise Germany that commitments to Poland would be implemented unless they received satisfactory assurances about the suspension of "all aggressive action against Poland." Bonnet had carefully worded it in these words in order to omit the requirement that the Germans must withdraw from Poland. The absence of a deadline allowed France time for negotiation.

Italy's mediation efforts were thus to be decisive. In the skill of the Italian Foreign Minister, Galeazzo Ciano, lay the last chance of avoiding a general war in Europe. At 13:00 on 1 September, the ambassador in Paris, Guariglia, informed Ciano that Paris wished to endorse a diplomatic solution. Two hours later, the Italian ambassador sent Mussolini a request from Daladier for Italy to organise a conference. Both Paul Rassinier and David L. Hoggan consider the sincerity of the French leaders' efforts to avoid war to be obvious. Both consider it obvious that French and British attitudes to the crisis were different. Hoggan believes that Ciano failed in his efforts because he was unable to take proper advantage of these differences to put pressure on the British and force them to accept a compromise.

On the morning of Saturday, 2 September, the situation of the Poles was desperate and the pressure on France was mounting. At 8 a.m., the Havas agency published the following communiqué: "The French government, like several other governments, was informed yesterday of an Italian proposal aimed at settling the European difficulties. After having discussed it, it has given a positive response". At the Quai d'Orsay the Foreign Minister was thus awaiting further indications from Ciano on the organisation of the conference. Ciano and Mussolini had decided that, before approaching the British and French again, it was essential to make sure that Germany was prepared to support the conference. At 8.30, Count Ciano telephoned his ambassador in Paris to find out whether the note presented the night before to Ribbentrop had the character of an ultimatum or not. At 9:00 Ambassador Lukasiewicz called Bonnet and asked him directly that France enter the war in favour of Poland. The French minister, who later complained that the Polish ambassador had been excessively "impatient" during the conversation, managed to avoid any kind of commitment.

Through Ambassador Attolico, at 10:00 a.m. Ciano sent a message to Hitler informing him that the French leaders had requested Italian mediation in favour of a diplomatic conference. In *Les responsables de la Seconde Guerre Mondiale* Paul Rassinier reproduces the text, taken from Documents on German Foreign Policy:

> "By way of information and leaving the decision to the Führer. Italy makes it known that it would still have the possibility of getting France,

England and Poland to agree to a conference on the basis of the following propositions:
1. An armistice that would leave the armies in the positions they currently occupy.
2. The convening of a conference to be held within two or three days.
3. A solution to the German-Polish conflict that would necessarily be favourable to Germany, given the present situation.
France has been particularly favourable to the Duce's idea.
Danzig has now returned to Germany, and the Reich now has sufficient guarantees to ensure the realisation of most of its demands. Moreover, it has already obtained moral satisfaction. If the Führer were to accept the draft conference, he would achieve all his objectives and avoid a long and widespread war.
Without wishing to exert the slightest pressure, the Duce considers it of the utmost importance that the present communiqué be submitted immediately to Herr von Ribbentrop and to the Führer."

Immediately informed, Hitler welcomed the initiative with enthusiasm and ordered the Foreign Office to sound out the British ambassador. Henderson reluctantly admitted that the British leaders would probably not accept the solution without the prior withdrawal of German troops to the border, which discouraged the Nazi leaders. Attolico appeared at 12:30 in Wilhelmstrasse, where Ribbentrop explained to the Italian ambassador that he was preparing to reply with a negative to the French and British ambassadors' notes received the previous day. Ribbentrop admitted to Attolico that he wanted to postpone the reply, but that in order to do so he had to make sure that they were not "ultimata". Attolico informed Ciano at 15:15 that Hitler had decided that it was impossible to proceed with plans for a conference until the French and British clarified the ambiguity of their notes.

Bonnet, still waiting for news, was delighted when he received a phone call from Ciano, who announced that the mediation effort had begun. The Italian foreign minister told Bonnet that the Germans needed to be assured that the previous day's notes were not "ultimata". Bonnet, the author of the two texts, gave Ciano absolute assurances that they were not. Knowing that the British would be obliged to accept his opinion, the French minister added that he would take the precaution of consulting Daladier and Halifax. For his part, Ambassador Loraine admitted to Ciano in Rome that the British Government had not yet presented Germany with an ultimatum. This important issue clarified, Hitler welcomed Italy's mediation plan and agreed to suspend military operations in Poland. At 16:00 on 2 September Attolico sent a cable to Ciano informing him that Germany was in favour of the Italian proposal. Ribbentropp asked Ambassador Attolico to announce to Italian leaders that Germany was ready to announce the plan to end the war in Poland by noon on Sunday, 3 September.

With Germany's acceptance of the Italian plan, everything depended on whether Minister Ciano could handle the disagreements between France and Britain properly. Shortly after 16:00 Bonnet and Halifax had a conversation that made it clear that the Foreign Office Secretary was prepared to kill the conference plan before it was presented to the Poles. Halifax insisted that the Germans must complete their full withdrawal from Poland and Danzig before Britain and France would agree to consider the Italian conference proposal. Bonnet knew that no power could accept such a deal and replied to Halifax that his proposal was unacceptable and unrealistic. The French minister considered the German concession to halt their advance on the spot to be adequate; but Halifax rejected this view. Despite the obstructionist attitude of the British minister, Bonnet decided to continue his efforts for peace. An hour later, at 17:00, British pressure continued with a call from Sir Alexander Cadogan, Permanent Under-Secretary at the Foreign Office, who with astonishing cheek acknowledged that the British demand for troop withdrawals limited the chances of a diplomatic conference and insisted that the time had come to go to war. Cadogan announced that Halifax was asking for a joint Anglo-French ultimatum to expire at midnight on 2 September. Bonnet insisted that complete German withdrawal from Poland could not be a sine qua non for a conference, and replied that he intended to wait until Italy specified its plan for an international conference.

Shortly after this conversation between Cadogan and Bonnet, Ciano telephoned Halifax. The Italian Foreign Minister listened in astonishment to the intransigent words of the Foreign Secretary, who repeated what he had told his French colleague: the British Government would not consider the Italian plan for a conference until Germany had completely evacuated Polish territory. Ciano was astonished to find that Halifax was unaware of Hitler's willingness to suspend hostilities. The Italian minister pointed out that Germany was prepared to stop the war on the 3rd and come to the conference the next day. As Bonnet had done, Count Ciano insisted that demanding the complete withdrawal of German troops was totally unacceptable and would destroy all chances of a peaceful settlement. Percy Loraine also reported from Rome to Halifax that Hitler had agreed to an armistice and an international conference. The German Chancellor had declared that he would be able to stop operations in all sectors by noon on Sunday, 3 September. Loraine confirmed to Halifax that, according to Ciano, France was pleased to see the possibility of stopping the war in less than twenty-four hours.

Meanwhile, the French foreign minister unilaterally tried to persuade the Poles to agree to a conference and sent instructions to his ambassador in Warsaw. Kennard indignantly informed Halifax that Noël had been ordered not to reveal the contents of Bonnet's latest directives. The British Ambassador decided to obtain the information from Beck himself, who confirmed that France had asked him to agree to a five-power conference, which would include Britain, Germany, France, Italy and Poland. Hitler was not afraid of being left in the minority with Mussolini's support alone, as he relied on French backing for an agreement. Kennard advised the Polish Foreign Minister to reject the French proposal; however, he admitted to Halifax that Beck had refused to reveal his attitude to the conference plan, but Kennard was confident that the Polish response would be negative. The Polish Sejm convened a special session on 2 September, and the Ukrainian representatives declared themselves terrified at the prospect of a Soviet invasion from the east as a result of the Ribbentrop-Molotov pact.

The French Chamber of Deputies and Senate also met from 3 p.m. on 2 September. The government intended to give the chambers carte blanche to make the decision that could lead to war or peace. However, both Prime Minister Daladier in Parliament and Vice-President Chautemps in the Senate made moderate speeches in favour of a peaceful solution to the crisis. Pierre Laval spoke in the Senate and warned that it would be unconstitutional to enter the conflict without requesting a declaration of war from Parliament. Laval shared Bonnet's view that Poland had breached its obligations to France and persisted in warning Daladier that an unjustified declaration of war against Germany would be suicidal for France.

Every hour of the afternoon of 2 September could be decisive for the future of Europe, and the Foreign Secretary was well aware of this, increasingly alarmed by the French government's position, which was giving rise to serious doubts in London. Halifax cabled Phipps, the British ambassador in Paris, to make an extra effort: "We will be grateful to you," he said, "for all you can do to give Mr Bonnet courage and determination. Ambassador Phipps informed the Foreign Office that the French were prepared to consider a joint note if Italy's mediation efforts were unsuccessful, in which case they favoured offering forty-eight hours before the expiry of the possible ultimatum. From Warsaw Kennard repeatedly demanded that Britain and France attack Germany immediately. Absurdly, the British ambassador went so far as to sound out Soviet diplomats to find out whether the USSR would be prepared to offer military supplies to the Poles.

Late in the afternoon of 2 September the French government, under increasing pressure from the British, was holding a decisive meeting. Ambassador Phipps, in constant contact with the Foreign Office, confirmed to Halifax that the prevailing sentiment was to seek agreement to avoid war and that it was hoped that between 20:00 and 21:00 the Council of Ministers could have reached a decision. The Foreign Office Secretary, who feared that Foreign Secretary Bonnet would be able to impose his views, decided to telephone Ciano in order to undermine his mediating role. The call came at exactly 18:38, the time when the French government was deliberating. Halifax, according to Hoggan, misled Ciano by not only telling him that there could be no conference without the withdrawal of German troops from

Poland, but by adding that France and Britain had reached full agreement on this important issue. This led Ciano to believe that Bonnet had accepted the British imposition, even though the Council of Ministers was still meeting in Paris.

At 19:30 Chamberlain presented to Parliament a distorted version of the peace efforts underway. The British Prime Minister, following the line of lies devised by the Foreign Secretary, declared that Britain could not accept negotiation at a conference while Polish towns were being bombed and the countryside overrun. Chamberlain, who knew full well that Hitler had agreed to suspend hostilities on the spot in order to hold the conference, followed the instructions of Halifax, whose primary objective was to end the last chance of averting the war that was to devastate Europe. For his part, Halifax addressed the House of Lords, where he repeated that "cities were being bombed".

Unfortunately, Halifax's strategy vis-à-vis Ciano paid off and Mussolini concluded that the cause of peace was lost. Hoggan believes that the Italians made an unforgivable mistake, since Britain would never have gone to war alone against Germany. Here are his words:

> "There was no justification, despite his confused approach to the subject, for believing any of Halifax's statements without first checking their accuracy with other sources. Both Ciano and Mussolini knew that the history of British diplomacy was peppered with deception and lies. The Italian leaders naively believed that no European leader, including Halifax, could be so ruthless as to provoke a world war after the recent bitter horrors of WWI. Their judgement was also clouded by vanity. Halifax had for several years cleverly combined flattery and threats in his dealings with Italian leaders. It was especially tragic that Mussolini, who was a shrewd and competent leader, was not then more critical in his assessment of Ciano. He realised later that Ciano was not sufficiently qualified for such an important post, but then it was too late."

At 20:00 Kennard communicated for the umpteenth time that Beck was asking Britain to send air support immediately. The Polish leaders had not yet understood that London would not help them. Kennard, who could have interpreted it, nevertheless sent these words to Halifax: "I trust that we shall receive confirmation of our declaration of war as soon as possible and that our air force will make every effort to show activity on the western front in order to relieve the pressure there". Kennard seemed to be unaware that his country was in no position to do anything to help the Poles in the West.

Ciano's catastrophic instructions to Attolico reached Berlin at 20:20 on 2 September. He announced to his ambassador that Mussolini had withdrawn his offer of mediation. Ciano added that it was futile to pursue peace efforts when both Britain and France insisted on the withdrawal of German troops as a necessary condition for acceptance of the conference.

Hitler was advised to abandon his plan for an armistice, as the plan for a conference had been dropped. However, by 8.20 p.m. the French Government had momentarily adjourned its meeting without having reached a decision on the conditions for acceptance of the conference. Bonnet, still hoping to convince his colleagues, was stunned to learn that the Italians had abandoned their efforts. At 8.30 p.m. he telephoned Ciano and made it clear that France had not yet accepted the impossible condition demanded by the British. The Italian minister listened dumbfounded to the words of the head of French diplomacy and confessed that he did not see how Italy could correct the mistake it had made. Anatole de Monzie, Minister of Public Works, a pacifist convinced of the need for an alliance between France and Italy to avoid war, implored Bonnet as soon as he heard what had happened to resume efforts for the conference on condition that Germany stopped the advance, but the foreign minister told him that he no longer saw this as feasible.

Finally at 9.30 p.m. the British Ambassador in Rome contacted the Foreign Office by cablegram, the text of which read: "the Italians do not consider it possible to press the German Government to continue to accept the recommendations of Signor Mussolini". Halifax was delighted to hear this news and was determined to launch his offensive against the French Government. At 9.50 p.m. Chamberlain telephoned Daladier and, again misrepresenting the facts, complained that he had suffered a "vexatious scene" in Parliament when he announced that he was still consulting with France on the presentation of an ultimatum. In reality there had been no more vexatious scene than the Zionist Jew Leopold Amery, the draftsman of the Balfour Declaration, who had complained that Chamberlain had not been sufficiently belligerent in his speech. In *The Holy Fox. A Life of Lord Halifax* Andrew Roberts reproduces this moment from the Commons session: ".... When the leader of the Labour Party, Arthur Greenwood, rose to speak, Leo Amery shouted: 'Speak for England!' Greenwood told the House: 'Every minute's delay now means... endangering our national honour.'"

Chamberlain told Daladier that he wished to inform the British public before midnight that at 8:00 a.m. on 3 September France and Britain would present an ultimatum to Germany, the deadline for which would expire at noon. In other words, Chamberlain, with absolute impudence, gave Daladier two hours to comply with his demands. The head of the French government, astonished at the British premier's hysteria but convinced that London had won the game, refused the request on the grounds that Ciano could resume mediation. Daladier advised against any diplomatic action before noon the following day. In London, Daladier's response to Chamberlain did not please Chamberlain, so Halifax, aware that without Italian mediation France was already very weakened, decided to telephone Bonnet at 22:30 in order to make a very risky gamble.

The Foreign Office Secretary announced to the French Foreign Minister that, regardless of France's attitude, the UK would present its ultimatum at 8 a.m. the following day. Halifax took the lead during the telephone conversation and eventually imposed his demands on Bonnet. He subsequently drafted a memorandum on the dialogue with his French colleague, in which he wrote that Bonnet, after some hesitation, "finally agreed". At 23:50 Halifax, although he knew he would not present the ultimatum until the following day, instructed Henderson to warn Ribbentrop that he could ask to see him at any time, which amounted to blatant disregard. Shortly afterwards, around midnight, Bonnet had a long conversation with the Italian Ambassador Guariglia, in which he admitted his capitulation. Both agreed that Britain's lack of cooperation had made the conference impossible.

Andrew Roberts writes in *The Holy Fox* that once the government had taken the decision to reject the conference and sent an ultimatum the next day that was to expire in just two hours, Halifax returned to the Foreign Office after midnight in the company of Sir Ivone Kirkpatrick, who had been First Secretary at the British Embassy in Berlin until 1938. Kirkpatrick, whose words are reproduced by Roberts, recalls that, once all the telegrams had been sent, Halifax "seemed relieved that we had made our decision.... He ordered beer to be brought to him, which was served by a sleepy resident clerk in his pyjamas. We laughed and joked, and when I told Halifax that news had arrived that Göbbels had forbidden listening to the radio broadcasts, he replied: 'He should pay me to listen to this. The scene could not be more reassuring: while Minister Bonnet and Ambassadors Henderson and Guariglia have been striving to avoid war, aware of the hecatomb it would be for tens of millions of people, Lord Halifax, relieved to have achieved his goal, is drinking beer and having fun with a colleague like a vulgar braggart. In the biography we have been consulting, Halifax's petulance is variously displayed. Roberts, quoting Polish Ambassador Raczyinski as a source, relates, for example, that when Hitler offered Germany's readiness to guarantee the British Empire, the news was regarded as an insult by Halifax, "on whose face he sneered".

Henderson delivered the ill-fated ultimatum to Dr Paul Schmidt, the German interpreter, at 9:00 on 3 September. Ribbentrop, probably annoyed by Halifax's discourtesy the previous evening, had avoided the British Ambassador on the grounds that he was in no mood to receive "ultimata" that day. Schmidt presented the document to the Führer's office in the Chancellery. When the interpreter entered, silence reigned in the room. Hitler was seated at his desk and Ribbentrop was standing at a window. After calmly reading the note, there was a moment's pause, and then the German Chancellor thoughtfully asked himself, "What now?" There was another pause, and Ribbentrop said quietly, "I suppose France will deliver a similar ultimatum in the next few hours." Schmidt came out of the Führer's office and remarked to a group composed of important leaders: "Within two hours Germany and Great Britain will be at war." In his eagerness to make war inevitable, Halifax, who days earlier had deemed twenty-four hours insufficient for Warsaw to send a plenipotentiary to Berlin, gave Germany only a two-hour deadline to capitulate. Göring solemnly told those present: "Heaven have mercy on us if we lose this war."

At 11:20 on 3 September, shortly after the ultimatum had expired, Ribbentrop received Ambassador Henderson and handed him the reply to Chamberlain and Halifax, which began: "The German Government and the German people refuse to receive, accept, much less comply with, the demands in the form of an ultimatum made by the British Government". The note alluded to the unacceptable conditions suffered by the German minority and ended with these words: "The German people and their Government do not, like Great Britain, claim to rule the world, but they are determined to defend their own freedom, their own independence, and above all their lives." Before withdrawing, Henderson merely said that history would judge on which side the real responsibilities lay, to which Ribbentrop replied that history judged already that no one had worked harder than Hitler for the establishment of good relations between Germany and Britain.

In London, at the same time, by 11:12 a.m. it became clear that there was no official reply from Berlin, so Chamberlain and Halifax drafted the communication they were to present to Parliament at noon. Halifax personally announced the declaration of war in the House of Lords. In the Commons, Winston Churchill referred to the impending war with a phrase supposedly for history: "Our hands may be busy, but our consciences are at peace". It is difficult to understand how it is possible to keep one's conscience at peace when an indecent decision has been taken that will unleash the greatest carnage in human history. Andrew Roberts comments on Churchill's quote : "Britain's clear conscience was a fundamental value for the war, obtained through the unstinting efforts of her Foreign Secretary to secure peace, even after his own personal hopes had been reduced to nothing". These words constitute a culminating example of the falsification of reality and put the author to shame.

The French ambassador went to Wilhelmstrasse at 12:30, where he was met by Weizsäcker. Coulondre's ultimatum expired at 17:00 on the same day. Ribbentrop, who was receiving the new USSR ambassador, had asked Weizsäcker not to let Coulondre go, as he intended to talk to him. The German Foreign Minister arrived promptly and had a brief and serious discussion with the Ambassador, whom he reminded that on 6 December 1938 France had signed a declaration of friendship with Germany. Coulondre simply stated that he had always feared that his diplomatic mission in Berlin would end in this way.

The fate of the European peoples, condemned to the worst tragedy in their entire history, was sealed. Absurdly, despite the efforts of many peace-seeking leaders, the Halifax war policy, supported by President Roosevelt, ultimately triumphed. Whichever way you look at it, there was no justification for British and French declarations of war when Hitler had accepted the armistice just after the invasion had begun. As Paul Rassinier points out, "there is no example in the history of warfare of the power being asked for an armistice having withdrawn its troops to its frontiers before negotiations had begun. The cessation of hostilities is done with the troops immobilised on the spot and only withdrawn once the armistice has been signed, according to plan".

The blank cheque given to Poland by Halifax, who shamelessly advised Polish leaders to refuse negotiations, was the determining cause of Polish defiance of Germany and constituted a decisive impulse towards war. As for the blindness and incompetence of the Warsaw leaders, suffice it to say that they did not even understand what the British refusal to guarantee Poland's security in the event of USSR aggression meant. There is not the slightest doubt that the Poles were unceremoniously used as an instrument of Britain's warmongering policy, which was fervently supported by the United States. Both countries were the indispensable tools of Zionism and international Jewish banking since 1917, when they had served to guarantee the creation of the state of Israel.

Pieces and pawns of international Zionism in the British government

Apart from Lord Halifax, who, as noted above, was related to the Rothschilds through the marriage of his son to a granddaughter of Lord Rothschild, other agents of Zionism held important positions of power in the British government that declared war on Germany. Of particular note is Winston Churchill, who was appointed First Lord of the Admiralty on 1 September 1939 and was to become Prime Minister on 10 May 1940. Martin Gilbert, Churchill's official biographer, published in 2007 the book *Churchill and the Jews. A lifelong friendship*, in which he exposes with the utmost naturalness that the British premier was a Zionist.

We already know that Churchill's paternal ancestor, John Churchill, 1st Duke of Marlborough, when he was head of the army in 1688, was bribed £350,000 by Medina and Machado, two Sephardic Jewish bankers from Amsterdam. The Duke of Marlborough betrayed his sovereign James II and joined the forces of William of Orange. In gratitude for services rendered, Solomon Medina rewarded him with an annual allowance of £6,000. It has also been noted that, as first Lord of the Admiralty in 1915, Winston Churchill, in cahoots with Colonel Mandell House, sought to precipitate America's entry into World War I by facilitating the sinking *of the Lusitania*. We will now add some information from the above-mentioned work to show the extent to which Churchill was committed to international Zionism.

"For more than half a century," Gilbert writes, "Churchill's life was intertwined with Jewish affairs." The relationship began in his teens, for even then his father, Lord Randolph Churchill, brought him into contact with the Rothschilds. When in 1937 the Peel Commission proposed the partition of Palestine into two states, Churchill, with categorical disregard for the rights of the Palestinian people, declared that he was not in favour of partition and that the Zionist state should get all of Palestine. 1938 was a bloody year in the "promised land", where nearly fifteen hundred Arabs were killed. On 19 May 1939 the Chamberlain government, unaware that one of the fundamental aims of the war was to provoke a mass exodus of Jews to Palestine, published the so-called MacDonald White Paper, which the Zionists called the Black Paper. This document called for a Palestine governed jointly by Arabs and Jews and limited immigration to a maximum of 75,000 Jews over the next five years, thus ensuring an Arab majority in the future state. Before the debate took place in the House of Commons, Churchill invited Chaim Weizmann and other Zionist leaders to lunch and read them the speech he was about to make. Such was their servility that Weizmann himself acknowledges in his memoirs that Churchill offered to change it as he saw fit. On 23 May 1939, during the debate, Churchill accused the government of betraying the *Balfour Declaration*: "Now there is a break," he said, "a breach of promise, there is an abandonment of the Balfour Declaration, there is an end of the vision, of the hope, of the dream". Martin Gilbert's work, in short, demonstrates with crystal clarity that Britain's premier during World War II was a key player in international Zionism.

The great debate ended in victory for Chamberlain and his White Paper by a majority of 268 to 179; but there were 110 abstentions. Among other things, the debate showed that the Labour opposition supported the Zionists and was the first warning to the prime minister that his own party could replace him. From this moment on, the figure of Winston Churchill, a politician whose decline had been steady for ten years and who, according to his biographers, suffered from depressions because he believed he was politically 'finished', emerged as if by magic thanks to the support of international Zionism, whose leader Chaim Weizmann appeared in the office of the newly appointed First Lord of the Admiralty as soon as the war broke out.[5]

---

[5] There has been controversy over the origin of Churchill's mother, Jenny Jerome, whose real name would be Jenny Jacobson/Jerome, since Moshe Kohn noted in an article published in *The Jerusalem Post* on 18 January 1993 that she was a New York Jew. If so, Winston Churchill himself would be Jewish. Historian David Irving also alluded in *Churchill's War* to Churchill's Jewish ancestry, although it seems that his source was the aforementioned Moshe Kohn. Other authors, however, deny that Jenny Jerome was Jewish. In any case, what is relevant is not whether Churchill was Jewish or not, but

Another example is Isaac Leslie Hore-Belisha, son of Jacob Isaac Belisha, a Jew who was not born in England. A member of the Liberals, Hore Belisha succeeded in getting Chamberlain to appoint him Secretary of State for War between 1937 and 1940. Conservative MPs reproached their leader for entrusting such an important post to a warmonger, whom they nicknamed Horeb-Elisha, a pun alluding to his Jewish origin (Mount Sinai is Hebrew for Mount Horeb). Many Conservatives accused him of being more concerned about the Jews than the British and of wanting to precipitate war against Germany. In order to control the armed forces, the new minister proceeded to dismiss three prominent members of the General Staff. One of them, Field Marshal John Vereker Gort, Lord Gort, could not bear to be in a room with Hore Belisha. Hore Belisha soon brought many Jewish co-religionists into the Ministry, for example three names: Sir Isidore Salmon, whom he made a deputy adviser; Humbert Wolfe, an intellectual who drew up for the Minister a list of writers who could serve as propagandists; Lord Stanhope, First Lord of the Admiralty. Soon the feeling of outrage descended into the lower ranks of the army and into public opinion. British soldiers sang in the early months of the war a 19th century song entitled *Onward, Christian Soldiers*, which translates:

> "Forward forced army,/ You have nothing to fear,/ Isaac Hore-Belisha/ will lead you from the rear,/ Dressed by Monty Burton (Montague Maurice Burton, actually Moshe Osinsky, a Lithuanian Jew who owned the largest chain of clothing shops),/ Fed by Lyons cakes (a Jewish-owned restaurant chain);/ Fight for Yiddish conquests,/ While the British die./ Forward forced army,/ marching to war./ Fight and die for Jewry,/ as we did before (allusion to the Balfour Declaration)."

The Chancellor of the Exchequer, the man who negotiated the multi-million dollar war loans with the bankers, was Sir John Simon, friend and protégé of Sir Philip Sassoon, a Jewish financier and Zionist leader related to the Rothschilds who died prematurely on 3 June 1939. The Sassoons, Jews of Iraqi origin enriched by the production and export of opium, are predominant in banking in China and India. It was Philip Sassoon's father, Sir Edward Albert Sassoon, who married a Rothschild. On 15 February 1939, the Chancellor of the Exchequer, Sir John Simon, declared in the House of Commons that the Treasury intended to double public borrowing to buy armaments from £400 million to £800 million. Simon was for a time considered a Jew in Germany; but it seems that the Nazi authorities themselves later disavowed this.

Numerous secretariats, under-secretaries, councillorships and even a few other ministries in the Cabinet that declared war on Germany were in

---

whether he was a Zionist who served the cause. There is no doubt about that, as has been explained.

the hands of Jews, Freemasons and Gentiles married to Jewish women. The marriage of Jewish women to wealthy or influential Gentiles became common practice from the 19th century onwards. "Do not marry them. Your daughter do not give to their son, and their daughter do not take for your son." This prohibition, which comes from *Deuteronomy*, is not often applied for reasons of interest. Since it is the mother who determines Jewishness (one is Jewish by right when born to a Jewish mother), many women began to marry aristocrats, scientists, intellectuals, wealthy men or influential politicians. Lenin, Stalin and Molotov, as we know, married Jewish women.

Part 2
Relegated events of the early war years

We will devote this second section on World War II to the little-reported events of the Second World War. Some are ignored or concealed, while others that are known do not receive the attention they deserve and are deliberately forgotten. The first of these, which will be discussed below, is the massacre of German minority civilians in Poland, the best-known episode of which is the so-called "Bloody Sunday" of Bromberg. As early as 19 September 1939, Hitler denounced some of the events in a speech in Danzig. The German Chancellor, after expressing his appreciation of the Polish soldiers who had fought bravely on the battlefield and criticising the Polish army commanders for their incompetence, reported that 300,000 Poles had been taken prisoner, 2,000 of whom were officers. He then went on to denounce that thousands of people, many of them women, young girls, children and old people had been brutally murdered in a savage manner. He described the events as the foulest seen in centuries and claimed that, as a soldier on the western front during the First World War, he had never seen anything like it. After denouncing the silence of the so-called democratic countries, so often deplored earlier by Ambassador Henderson, he claimed that he had nevertheless ordered the Luftwaffe to act only against military units. Hitler referred to the criminals as "sadistic beasts who had let themselves go and allowed their perverted instincts to run riot while the sanctimonious democratic world looked on without a hair's breadth".

The indiscriminate killing of the German minority in Poland

In 1940 the text *Dokumente Polnischer Grausamkeit* was published in Berlin, which can be read in English on the Internet Archive under the title *The polish atrocities against the german minority in Poland*. It is a book compiled from the criminal records of the special courts of justice that were set up in Bromberg and Posen, the reports of the police commissions of enquiry, the testimonies of medical experts from the Health Inspection Department of the Military High Command, and the original documents of the Military Commission under the High Command, which was set up to investigate violations of international law. These courts of justice established in Bromberg and Posen were ordinary courts, which administered justice on the basis of the Criminal Code of Germany and the jurisprudence of the Reich Supreme Court. The report, edited and published by order of the German Foreign Office, thus contains a wealth of documentary evidence compiled by various agencies. A second work on the gigantic pogrom against the Germans in Poland was also published in 1940 by Edwin Erich Dwinger under the title *Der Tod in Polen. Die Volksdeutsche Passion* (*Death in Poland. The Passion of the German Minority*).

By 1 February 1940, 12,857 bodies had been identified by the authorities, but no trace had been found of the 45,000 members of the German minority who were still missing and presumed dead, so they were added to the total number of victims, which thus stood at around 58,000. It has already been seen in the preceding pages that the expulsions, mass deportations and murders of the ethnic German minority had begun in Poland long before the invasion took place. Despite this, and despite repeated allegations that in the event of war with Germany all Germans were to be killed and the farms burned down, most of them, rooted in their homes and property, which in many cases had been acquired by their ancestors hundreds of years before and inherited from generation to generation, decided to remain in their homes, since they could not believe that the threats of murder would be carried out.

As soon as the war began, on 1 September, a password was officially given over the radio, which was the order for a criminal campaign against German civilians, planned in advance by the authorities, to begin. This radio broadcast is clear evidence that this was an organised genocide. According to the testimonies of Mrs. Weise, wife of a prestigious doctor who worked at the Protestant Hospital in Posen, and of Dr. Reimann, the message began with these words. "Hello! Hello! Germans, Czechs and Bohemians! Carry out order number... at once." Neither of these two witnesses was sure of the exact number given; but another witness, Konrad Kopiera, director of the Schicht Centre in Warsaw, recalled that the number of the order was 59. Another neighbour from Posen (Poznan), Mrs. Klusseck, reported a second order which she heard over the radio on the evening of 1 September. Like the previous one, it was to be executed immediately and was addressed to all courts, prosecutors and other authorities. It ended with a code containing more than seven numerical digits, some letters and other signs, which could not be deciphered by the German authorities, who were still investigating it when the book was published.

The period from 31 August to 6 September was the height of the violence against German civilians, which reached its climax on 3 September in Bromberg, a town on the Brahe River that was renamed Bydgoszez after the war. There, as the photographs attached to the *Dokumente Polnischer Graumsamkeit* show, men, women and children were massacred with horrifying cruelty and sadism. The victims included Protestant priests, teenage girls, often raped, young children, the elderly and even pregnant women. An example of such pregnant women is Helene Sonnenberg, who was murdered in Rudak along with Martha Bunkowski and others. Helene was the wife of the Protestant sacristan of the Rudak parish, Albert Sonnenberg. On 1 September, the pastor was taken from his home at bayonet point. Helene, who was away with her three-year-old son Heinrich, decided not to return. No one wanted to protect them, and they spent six days hiding in barns and brickworks. On 6 September she met Martha Bunkowski, a single woman who, like her, was hiding from the mobs. On the 7th Martha went to fetch clothes for little Heinrich. When she returned, she was accompanied by soldiers. On 8 September, both women were found dead in the pigsty of the sexton's house. Dr. Panning's medico-legal report stated the following: "The fact that the remains of the foetus were found not in the mother's body but between the thighs is due to a known process called 'bier delivery'. That is, the expulsion of the child's body from the mother's womb in such cases occurs as a result of putrefaction...".

Polish witnesses Maria Szczepaniak and Luzia Spirka, both neighbours of Bromberg who had hidden in a cellar, testified that German citizens were killed indiscriminately, regardless of age, religious creed or sex. No social class or rank, these witnesses confirmed, was spared the slaughter: peasants, farmers, teachers, priests, doctors, merchants, workers or businessmen were murdered, tortured to death, beaten and stabbed for no reason. Paul Zembol, a witness from Pless (Pszczyna), a town in southern Poland close to the Czech and Slovak borders, said: "Never before had I seen faces so distorted by fury or bestial expressions. They had certainly ceased to be human beings".

Bodies shot or beaten to death were found unburied scattered everywhere: on doorsteps, in yards and gardens, along roadsides, sometimes covered with leaves and branches, in field ditches, on the banks of rivers and lakes, in the vicinity of forests. In almost all cases they had suffered gruesome mutilations: eyes gouged out of their sockets, teeth smashed out, brains oozing from skulls, tongues cut out, abdomens slit open, intestines out, legs and arms broken, fingers and toes amputated, castrations, women with breasts severed.... Sometimes the bodies lay on the ground tied in twos, threes or in rows with their hands tied behind their backs.

The "Bloody Sunday" in Bromberg took place before the German troops could report to the town, which they entered on Tuesday, 5 September. The perpetrators of the killings were policemen, retreating Polish soldiers en masse, and the brutalised populace. In order to illustrate the dynamics of the crimes, we will recount the case of the Schmiede family, for which we have two sources: the testimony of Mrs. Irma Ristau, a 25-year-old Protestant woman who lived at 10 Kartuzka Street in Bromberg, who gave a sworn statement before a military judge, and the version of events in the second chapter of Edwin Erich Dwinger's aforementioned work. Merging the two texts will enable us to obtain a more complete picture of the facts.

In court, Mrs. Ristau, whose maiden name was Bloch, stated that her husband worked in Bromberg for a master gardener, Mr. Schmiede, and that on Saturday, 2 September, her husband called the Schmiede's to confirm whether he should come to work as usual. Mrs. Ristau accompanied her husband because the day before she had been threatened and beaten with an iron bar at her workplace and was afraid to be left alone. In addition, a neighbour named Pinczewski who lived at 8 Kartuzka Street had accused them the day before of being "two Hitlerites" and threatened to cut them up as soon as the war started. The Schmiede family had six small children, and Irma Ristau had been helping out in the family's kindergarten for some time. The Ristau couple spent the night at the Schmiede teacher's house, whose gardens were on the outskirts of the city.

At lunch the next day, says E. E. Dwinger, an apprentice entered the room where the couple and their six children were eating. The master gardener asked him what the news was: "Just the same call," he replied. It's been going on for an hour! I don't understand what you mean." With a glance Mr. Schmiede imposed silence; but Mrs. Schmiede noticed this and asked, "Are you sure they are not scheming some mischief?" Mr. Schmiede tried to reassure her. "What could they do to us? We are civilians! We have always fulfilled our obligations and paid our taxes faster than the Poles themselves, we have served as soldiers in their army.... Perhaps they will drive us out of the city if Bromberg has to be surrendered to the Germans, that is to be expected, of course." Increasingly frightened Mrs. Schmiede suggested whether it might not be better to flee. At this point Irma Ristau, who was present, recounted the threats she had received from her neighbour Pinczewski. "Calm down," Master Schmiede cut them off, "Besides, it's already too late, the troops are retreating, and standing in the way now is more dangerous than staying in the house."

Shortly afterwards, thousands of retreating Poles flooded the streets of the city and advanced towards the centre. Like a fiery stream of molten lava," Dwinger writes, "they filled roads and alleys, and rushed feverishly into every house inhabited by Germans. The core of these masses were soldiers, accompanied by rabble and students who showed them the way to their targets. A group of soldiers entered the Schmiede's house with bayonets drawn. The frightened master gardener could not express himself in Polish. You don't know Polish, you son of a bitch," a soldier shouted, "but you've got a gun. The invitation to search the house was of no avail, the soldier ordered him to take three steps back and shot him. Mrs. Schmiede fell to the ground next to her mortally wounded husband. Miraculously, none of the three shots fired at her hit the target (the criminals were probably drunk). She jumped to her feet and, screaming madly, managed to get out with the children before the soldiers had time to fire again. Outside, they ran to a cellar that served as an air raid shelter, where Mrs. Schmiede locked herself in with her children and other employees, including Irma Ristau and her husband.

The Poles then surrounded the house and set it on fire. Panic ensued in the cellar and, fearing that they would burn or suffocate to death, some tried to get out, but the entrance was on fire, so the only way out was through a window. The first to try was an apprentice, but he was shot in the head as soon as he set foot outside. The next to risk it a little later were the Ristau family. Irma Ristau testified as follows:

> "My husband and I climbed up and managed to get to the street. We raised our hands in the air and told the Poles that we were surrendering and not to shoot, but the civilians shouted: 'You must kill them, they are Hitlerites and spies'. Then a Polish soldier fired and my husband collapsed with a bullet in his head. I fell to the ground amidst the noise and lost consciousness in terror. When I came to my senses there was a soldier with a bayonet next to me, who took my husband's wedding ring, his watch and 45 zlotys. My husband's shoes, which he had only worn at our wedding and for a few days, he handed over to the civilians. He grabbed me by the hair and lifted me up, but I fell back to the ground next to my husband. When I asked the soldier to at least leave me the ring as a souvenir, he hit me with the butt of his rifle on my neck and back with such violence that even today I can hardly move."

Irma Ristau, in pain and impregnated with her husband's blood, ended up in a barracks, where she begged to be killed, as she no longer wished to live. "It's a pity to waste a bullet on you," said one of the soldiers, "go to hell." Thus Mrs. Ristau returned to where her husband's body had been left, where she saw how soldiers and civilians were dismembering him. We will only add how E. E. Dwinger concludes the account of Mrs. Schmiede, of whom Imma Ristau gives no further information in her statement. According to this author, she saved her children's lives by placing towels soaked in vinegar in their mouths and protecting them with her own body from the gunfire that entered the cellar through the window. In the evening, the inceded house collapsed and the mob dispersed. The next day they dared to come out of the cellar and, although they were arrested, fortunately saved their lives.

Practically every house in Bromberg where Germans lived was attacked, and entire families were killed. None of the city's neighbourhoods was spared the pogrom. We could present hundreds of cases listed in the *Dokumente*, for it is an exhaustive report of more than 400 pages, but that would only add to what has already been said. However, it may be of interest to reproduce at least one complete statement verbatim. We have chosen Paul Sikorski's for two reasons: it is brief and allows us to appreciate the extreme cruelty of the criminals. We deduce that Sikorski, a man of thirty-five years of age, was taken for a Pole because he spoke Polish perfectly; however, he declared under oath that he was a Catholic and that he belonged to the German minority:

> "On Sunday, 3 September 1939, at about six o'clock in the morning, I went to the mill to turn off the light and the turbine. On the way, I

suddenly heard loud shouting coming from the station. About ninety metres away I saw near the platforms a group of railwaymen, civilians and military, beating seven people between twenty and sixty years of age with rifle butts, bayonets and sticks. They had surrounded the victims. I approached and heard them shouting in Polish: 'let's kill the Germans'. Even from a distance, I saw the blood spurting out. I turned around when I realised that the horde wanted to come towards me. I returned at nine o'clock and examined the bodies. Two of them had had their eyes gouged out with bayonets. The eye sockets were empty and there was only a bloody mass. Three other bodies had their skulls split open and the brains were a metre away. The other bodies were blown apart. One of them was completely open. I knew two of the victims, they were Leichnitz, a butcher from Jagershof, and Mr. Schlicht.

In the afternoon, between three and four o'clock, a group of soldiers and railwaymen came to my mill and brought eighteen Germans with them, tied in pairs. I saw them perfectly from my garden. The eighteen were shot two by two and when they were lying on the ground they were beaten. Among the dead were a fourteen-year-old boy and a woman. Everything had to be done quickly on this occasion, for they left immediately. I then inspected the bodies; they were there for three days.

On Monday morning, when the Polish soldiers were said to have evacuated the town, two soldiers brought in an elderly couple. In front of me they placed them next to a wall in the mill. I rushed over to the soldiers, knelt before them and begged them in Polish to release the old men, who were about sixty-five years old. However, I was pushed away with the butt of my rifle by one of the soldiers, who said, 'Let these damned Germans die.' Before I could get up, they were both shot down and their bodies fell into a ditch...".

Before the invasion, columns of German minority arrestees were increasingly frequent into Poland. Numerous people testified in court about their experience of these marches, which became widespread as soon as the war began. A detailed account before a military tribunal was given on 15 September by Gotthold Starke, editor-in-chief of the *Deutsche Rundschau* in Bromberg. He recounted his experience from 1 September, when he was arrested at his home and placed in an orphanage together with other people of German minority and German nationality, such as Consul Wenger, his secretary, and other officials of the Consulate General in Thorn. According to this witness, lists of persons to be arrested had already been drawn up at the end of April and the beginning of May. There were three types of detainees, who were classified into three groups by means of coloured tickets: red, pink and yellow.

A brief summary of the account will give an appreciation of the hardships of these marches. Starke reports that on 2 September more prisoners arrived at the orphanage. At five o'clock in the afternoon they were assembled in the courtyard and separated into two tiers. Then began the march through the streets of Bromberg amidst insults and spitting from the Polish population. The detainees, including children, women and old people, were to be taken to Thorn, thirty-six miles away. On 4 September they were marched from Thorn to Ciechocinek, where they were accommodated in camps for young people and separated by gender. Those who had not provided themselves with something to eat, who were the majority, had already gone for days without food. On 5 September, they left Ciechocinek for Wloclawek and at noon, under a scorching sun, camped at a rubbish dump in Nieszawa. There they were joined by a large group of prisoners from Pomerelia, including old men and women in terrible conditions. They were all locked up in a gymnasium upon arrival in Wloclavek, where they were not even given water. The next day, 6 September, they set out for Chodsen, where they were joined by new columns of prisoners from Pomerelia. According to Starke, the prisoners now numbered about 4,000, of whom between 600 and 800 came from Bromberg. Among them were about a thousand Poles: social democrats, convicts and other shady-looking individuals. In short, the march continued on successive days until on 9 September they reached Lowitsch under German artillery fire, whereupon the Polish guards abandoned them. Of the 4,000 detainees, only 2,000 remained. The 1,000 Poles were gone. The prisoners began to disband, many of whom reached the German positions. Since leaving Bromberg they had travelled on foot some one hundred and fifty miles.

 Let us now take a closer look at one of these marches through the account of Herbert Mathes, owner of a furniture factory in Brombreg, who, under oath, told the court what happened to 150 Germans who marched to Piecki near Brzoza. His son Heinz Mathes confirmed the statement. Herbert Mathes and his two sons, aged thirteen and fifteen, were arrested in Bromberg on 3 September by four men armed with axes, who handed them over to the soldiers. With their hands tied, they were bundled into a group of a hundred well-known citizens of the town and taken to the station barracks. On the way, they were beaten, spat on and threatened with knives and axes. More detainees, including other parents with their children, gathered at the station. In total there were about four hundred people, of whom the luckiest were taken aside to load ammunition and saved their lives. The rest marched towards Brzoza. "The old men who could not go on," Mathes declared, "were wounded with bayonets and some died. Shortly afterwards beyond the town the word 'halt' was given and we were fired upon from the front and the rear. Many were killed in this bestial manner." A convoy of about one hundred and fifty people was then organised. "I protected my children," continues the witness, "and was wounded with a bayonet in the thigh." During the march, those who could not continue and sat down "were shot with a rifle butt because after about two hours the lieutenant forbade firing." At five o'clock in the morning only forty-four people were still alive when they were allowed to rest in a stable. Heinz Mathes, who understood Polish, informed his father that they had gone to look for petrol to burn them there, although the children were to be allowed to return home. Finding no petrol, at half past seven in the morning the soldiers ordered the prisoners to line up in threes. The first three were shot, and the story goes like this:

> "This was repeated up to six times. Heinz bravely pleaded that neither he nor his brother Horst should be killed; he received a bayonet wound in his right shoulder. 'Another three'. Heinz then told me that the corporal had said it was a waste of good cartridges and that the remainder should be knifed. 'Oh my God!' He could just hear himself. Those who were not silent received the deadly muffled blows of the butts. We three were next, there were five others behind. We went out hand in hand, but were pushed aside to the left. Two soldiers, corporals, grabbed us and pushed us a few steps forward. They were the robbers whom Heinz had shrewdly told during the day that we possessed valuables and money. We then gave them everything we had and they began to fight over the distribution. At which point we took the opportunity to run away.... We wandered around all night; it was Monday night. Heinz was bandaged with a piece of my shirt. We were in our shirts, our shoes had been taken off in Bromberg. On Wednesday night our situation was disastrous, we saw a lot of soldiers in the vicinity and we had to avoid the danger. Isn't it better to die?' Horst asked. Our tongues were swollen and quite white, our lips thick and crusted. Rescue came: a heavy dew settled on the leaves of the trees, we licked it greedily and ate a frog 'more delicious than wine', said Heinz. Horst, who had said goodbye, came back to life...".

On Thursday, 7 September, Herbert, Heinz and Horst Mathes met German soldiers. Once back in Bromberg, they were able to embrace Mrs. Mathes, mother and wife, who could not believe that such a miracle had taken place.

Many of the mass murders were confirmed by the discovery of the numerous mass graves where the bodies of the victims were buried: in the suburb of Jagershof, near Bromberg, sixty-three people were shot. In Slonsk, in the south-east of Thorn, a town inhabited for centuries by Germans, a grave was found with 58 bodies of members of the German minority. The largest mass grave was located on 14 October 1939 near Tarnowa, north of Turek, where the bodies of one hundred and four ethnic Germans were found, many of whom had been cruelly mutilated. In December 1939 mass graves were found in Klodawa and Krosniewice.

There are two statements about the 63 corpses found in the mass grave at Jagershof: one tells how eighteen people were shot; the second testifies to the murder of another twenty victims who ended up in the same grave. We will end this section on the massacres of the German minority in Poland with a brief account of the first of these two statements. Among the eighteen people shot was the Protestant pastor Kutzer, the father of four children between the ages of three and fourteen. In his house, this sexton was sheltering other German refugees from other parishes. At 3 p.m. on 3 September, the pastor and his seventy-three-year-old father Otto Kutzer, two young men, Herbet Schollenberg, aged fourteen, and Hans Nilbitz, aged seventeen, and three other refugees were arrested. They were all taken to an embankment near the parish, where they joined twelve other detainees, including a woman, Mrs. Kobke. Placed in a line, twelve soldiers shot them one by one from a distance of seven metres. After witnessing the first execution, Mrs. Kobke fainted. When the executions were over, they untied the woman's hands and, after making her look at the corpses lying on the ground one by one, they let her go. The "spectacle" was witnessed by about two hundred people.

From war against Germany to carte blanche for the USSR

The Poles were unable to establish a front in any of the areas through which German troops entered Poland, so by 6 September it was clear that they had lost the war. In *Hitler's War* David Irwing confirms the following: "Hitler's territorial plans for Poland were still undetermined. He had hoped that he would be forced to accept Italian mediation and an eventual armistice, and to improve his position at the negotiating table he had captured as much territory as possible in the first few days". After Ciano's failure, Hitler hoped that the invasion of the Soviet Union would force Britain to declare war on Moscow as well. However, as we know, a secret clause in the treaty signed in August by Beck and Halifax stipulated that London was only committed to defend Poland from a single "European power", which was unknown to the Nazi leaders.

Stalin, who had not yet moved his army and was still waiting in the wings, informed Berlin on 9 September of his intention to occupy that part of Poland which was to be returned to the USSR in accordance with the terms of the pact signed on 23 August. Under the pretext of "coming to the aid of its Ukrainian and Byelorussian blood brothers", whom it considered threatened by the "disintegration of the Polish state", the Red Army entered Poland on 17 September 1939. By this time Beck had resigned and Sikorski, the head of the Polish government, in a pathetic gesture asked the British and French to declare war on the USSR. Naturally, the Poles finally understood that they had been sold out, since no one had lifted a finger to help them. Marshal Rydz-Smigly, Chief of Staff, ordered his units not to fight the Soviets, who, except for occasional resistance from a few enraged Poles, encountered almost no opposition. Roosevelt had the gall to justify the Soviet invasion of Poland as "an action to prevent the whole country from being occupied by the Germans". After the communist invasion, 230,000 soldiers, of whom 15,000 were officers, fell prisoner to the Soviets. The debacle had been consummated. Before long, Poland was no longer on the map of Europe.

On 28 September Ribbentrop travelled to Moscow and reached an agreement with Stalin and Molotov to push the initially planned German border over the Vistula to Bug. In return, Germany allowed Lithuania to fall into the Soviet sphere of interest. The Soviet Union annexed 180,000 square kilometres populated by twelve million Ukrainians, Belarusians and Poles, territories that were integrated into the Soviet republics of Ukraine and Belarus. Of course, no one in Europe objected in the slightest. That is, Britain and France, despite knowing that the German minority was being subjected to all sorts of injustices and atrocities in Poland, declared war on Germany because they did not consent to Danzig, a German-populated town, being reintegrated into the Reich; yet they readily accepted Stalin's coming "to the aid of his Ukrainian and Byelorussian blood brothers" and annexing half the country.

Official historians are unwilling or unable to explain adequately why the famed democracies gave the USSR carte blanche to act as it pleased. Only the line of interpretation of the historical facts that we have been maintaining throughout this work can adequately clarify what happened and what was to happen. In the desire to completely destroy Germany, Britain and the United States, the supposedly subservient democracies, subject to the shadow powers that imposed the war, were, as is well known, going to allow communism to occupy half of Europe and reach as far as Berlin. It is worth remembering once again that the Soviet Union was a ruthless communist dictatorship that denied traditional Western values. Since 1917, millions of opponents had been murdered and the Judeo-Bolsheviks had carried out the greatest plunder in history for their masters. Communism, as we have seen, had been consolidated with the approval of the United States and Great Britain through bloodthirsty terror. Its crimes, committed over a period of 22 years, had broken all records in 1939.

After "coming to the aid of his blood brothers" and setting in motion plans to annex Polish territory, Stalin turned his gaze to the Baltic republics, whose foreign ministers were summoned in turn. One after another they came to Moscow and within two weeks, from 26 September to 10 October, were forced to grant military bases to the Soviet Union through the imposition of mutual assistance treaties. In October 1939, 25,000 Soviet troops were stationed in Estonia, 30,000 in Latvia and 20,000 in Lithuania. These troops outnumbered the armies of each country, so the military deployment effectively ended the independence of these countries. On 11 October, Beria, the new strongman of the NKVD after the fall of Yezhov, ordered the "extirpation of all anti-Soviet and anti-social elements" in these republics: officers, officials, adverse intellectuals and other hostile elements were arrested.

The next step was to be Finland. On 5 October 1939, Molotov asked the Finnish ambassador in Moscow to send a plenipotentiary to Helsinki to discuss "concrete political questions". The Finns, who were already aware of the demands made of the Baltic republics, viewed the summons with suspicion. In order not to be taken by surprise, the government took the precaution of calling up reservists for extraordinary manoeuvres and to increase defensive preparedness. Thus began the path that was to lead to the outrageous aggression of the Soviet Union, which intended to annex Finland. Since the Finnish case is very significant and exposed the double standards and hypocrisy of the Western democracies, let us dwell on it for a moment and give it a little more attention.

It all began in April 1938, when the Finnish foreign minister, Rudolf Holsti, received an unusual visit from Boris Yartsev, a Jew of Ukrainian origin whose real name was Boruch Aronovich Rivkin. This character, who had worked since 1922 in the secret police (OGPU) and in 1945 was an agent at the Yalta Conference, was a personal envoy of Stalin's placed in the Helsinki embassy as second secretary. Yartsev wanted Finland to agree to a military pact, since, he said, Germany intended to attack the USSR using Finland as a springboard. Holsti assured him that they had no intention of dissociating themselves from Nordic neutrality, let alone ceding their territory for aggression against Moscow. Despite the insistence of Stalin's envoy, who met twice during the summer with Prime Minister Aimo Cajander, the Finnish government remained firm. At the end of August 1938, Yartsev was told that his claims were an attack on Finnish sovereignty and went against the Nordic line of neutrality. The new foreign minister, Eljas Erkko, did not change the Finnish government's position one iota when a second emissary of Jewish origin, Boris Yefimovich Shtein, tried to persuade him to persuade Finland to lease the islands east of the Gulf of Finland to the USSR.

When Molotov's request was received on 5 October 1939, the Finns decided not to send the foreign minister to Moscow, but to appoint Paasikivi, an excellent Russia specialist, to the mission. Juho Kusti Paasikivi took a few days to prepare for his mission, and on 9 October the Finnish delegation, greeted at the station with demonstrations of patriotic ardor, left by train for Moscow. In the Kremlin, Stalin and Molotov proposed to the Finns a mutual assistance treaty similar to those they had just imposed on Estonia, Latvia and Lithuania, but Paasikivi refused to play along. Then, citing the security of Leningrad, the Soviets proposed a long-term lease of the Hanko peninsula, the gateway to the Gulf of Finland, in order to establish a naval base in the port of Lappohja. They also asked for the concession of part of the Karelian isthmus and some islands. The Finnish delegation stood firm, arguing that their government had forbidden them to make territorial concessions.

As the crisis deepened, the Nordic heads of state and foreign ministers met in Stockholm on 18-19 October. King Gustav V of Sweden informed

Finnish President Kyösti Kallio that Sweden would not provide military assistance to Finland in the event of a conflict. Thus, when Paasikivi returned to Moscow on 23 October to resume negotiations, he knew that his country was on its own and could not count on Nordic assistance. Although the Finnish negotiators made some concessions, a new round of talks between 2 and 4 November 1939 showed that the renunciations announced by the Finns did not meet the USSR's demands. With the negotiations stalled, the Paasikivi delegation returned to Helsinki on 13 November without a new date being set for the resumption of negotiations.

During the autumn the Soviet Union had been massing troops along the border. Suddenly, on 26 November, Molotov accused the Finnish army of artillery fire on the town of Mainila, where the shells were said to have caused casualties among the soldiers stationed there. To avoid incidents, Finland was required to withdraw its troops 30 kilometres from the border line. The accusation was false, but the Finnish government was willing to look into the incident and discuss a reciprocal withdrawal of troops in the border area. Moscow then publicly accused Helsinki of threatening the security of Leningrad and denounced the non-aggression pact that had been in force until 1945. Diplomatic relations were broken off, and on 30 November about half a million Red Army troops began an invasion of Finnish territory from various points along a 1,000-kilometre front. At the same time the air force bombed the main urban centres, especially Helsinki. The declared aim was to conquer the country quickly, in two weeks if possible, and to put an end to its independence.

Stalin and Molotov camouflaged their aggression with a crude excuse: after setting up a puppet government in Terijoki (Karelian Isthmus) led by the communist Otto Kuusinen and composed of Finnish communists exiled in the USSR, they claimed that the troops had entered Finland in response to a call from this government, which they recognised as legitimate. On 2 December the Soviets concluded an assistance treaty with the "Terijoki People's Government". Communist propaganda announced that the Finnish capital would soon be taken, that the Finnish people would be liberated from White terror and that a people's republic would be created in Finland. This was intended to explain to the foreign powers that the Red Army was not attacking the Finnish people, but was liberating them at the request of the People's Government. The fact is that the Finnish people had overcome the civil war of 1918 and were perfectly united. L. A. Puntila in *Histoire politique de la Finlande de 1809 à 1955* writes: "the great internal reforms accelerated by economic development since 1935 had improved the condition of workers and peasants, education had been intensified and the work of the cultural societies had borne fruit. National sentiment had been consolidated and people had learned to appreciate independence".

The Finnish armed forces, which had been on manoeuvres since early October, were not surprised by the attack. A feeling of deep emotion overwhelmed the whole country, and in the first hours of the war Marshal Mannerheim was appointed commander-in-chief of the armies. The Soviets put 1,000 aircraft into combat, but Finland was only able to counter them with 150 aircraft. Compared to the 2,000 tanks deployed by the communists, the Finns had only 50 tanks at their disposal. The country's hopes rested on 330,000 relatively well-trained men with a patriotic sentiment more decisive than any armament, the famous Winter War spirit, which underlined the Finns' unshakeable will to defend their country against the invader. In the poem *The Weary Soldiers*, Yrjö Yylha describes in a moving way the almost religious spirit that animated the Finnish fighters. In a few lines of the poem, at the end of their strength, the soldiers ask to be promoted to the heavenly legions. God answers them: "My army is on earth, / Whoever lays down his arms I do not know".

The Russians concentrated their offensive on the Karelian isthmus and during December 1939 launched offensive after offensive to break through the Finnish lines. The first massive attack was carried out at the beginning of the month and the second in mid-December, both of which collided with the defenders. The attackers then tried to open a gap north of Lake Ladoga, but the Finns won several battles in Tolvajärvi that boosted the morale of the population and impressed abroad. At Christmas the Reds tried again to break through the Karelian isthmus front, but the result was another defensive victory. Further north, the Ilomantsi, Lieksa and Kuhmo positions also resisted the onslaught of Soviet troops. The attempt to split the country in two around Oulu also failed and the communists suffered a humiliating defeat at Suomussalmi, where the Finns resorted to encirclement tactics and won a significant spoil of war.

After a month of hostilities, all Red Army attacks had been repulsed. Naturally, Finland's human resources were limited and the situation of the Finnish army was delicate, but not hopeless. The Soviet Union, while sending hundreds of thousands of new fighters to the battlefield, finally decided in January to open negotiations with the legitimate Finnish government, which meant the end of the Terijoki government. Moscow's demands were unacceptable to Helsinki, so in February 1940 the Red Army launched a new offensive on the Karelian Isthmus, where on 11 February it finally succeeded in breaking through Summa. At the end of February the Finnish troops were forced to retreat to the second defensive line west of the isthmus. Fighting again raged at Viipuri. Forced by circumstances, Prime Minister Risto Ryti travelled to Moscow on 7 March at the head of a delegation to seek as painless a peace as possible, which, despite the harsh conditions, was signed on 12 March 1940. After 125 days, the Winter War was over.

The terms of the Moscow Peace entailed significant territorial cessions, including the Petsamo Corridor, which gave Finland an outlet to the Arctic. Public opinion was shocked and Finnish flags flew at half-mast throughout the country. Most of Finnish Karelia was handed over to the USSR and more than 400,000 people fled or were expelled. This was one of the least known population transfers of World War II. The Karelians left their homes in 1940, returned to them in 1941 when Finland joined Germany in the invasion of Russia, and left them for good in 1945. At the end of the war there was the incredible transfer of sixteen million Germans, who were also expelled from their homes, but this is a matter for another chapter.

In short, the Finns were left to their own devices. Only eleven thousand foreign volunteers came to fight alongside them against the communists. Seven thousand of them were Swedes who stood in solidarity with their neighbours despite their government's official position. The remaining 4,000 volunteers were Danish, Norwegian, Hungarian and American. Although Finland enjoyed the sympathy of international public opinion, the Soviet Union acted with impunity, as its expulsion from the dying League of Nations was no more than a joke. The whole world was unmoved, ready to accept that Finland, a country of enormous strategic importance, would move into the communist orbit of influence. A few months earlier, however, Danzig, a city inhabited by about half a million Germans who wanted to return to the Reich, had been a casus belli.

Red terror and Jewish terror in Estonia and Latvia

Stalin's criminal actions did not end in Finland. Before the occupation of Estonia, Latvia and Lithuania, between 15 April and 10 June 1940, Stalin began to concentrate millions of soldiers along the Romanian border. On 26 June, shortly after the surrender of France (22 June), Molotov presented an ultimatum to the Romanian ambassador in Moscow, Davidescu, demanding the immediate "return" to the USSR of Bessarabia, a region in eastern Romania that had belonged to the Tsarist Empire. In addition, he also demanded the handover of Northern Bukovina. On 28 June, on the advice of Germany and Italy, the Romanian government capitulated and evacuated the army and administration from these two regions. The Soviets also occupied the Hertza region without explanation. Bukovina and part of Bessarabia were incorporated into Ukraine, and the rest of Bessarabia became the Republic of Moldova, from which more than 30,000 anti-Soviet elements were deported, plus another 12,000 from Bessarabia incorporated into Ukraine. In this way, while Germany was at war with Britain and France, the USSR continued to expand without any problem.

The strategy for the final incorporation of the Baltic states into the USSR was launched in June 1940. Under the pretext of "provocative acts against Soviet garrisons", hundreds of thousands of soldiers occupied Estonia, Latvia and Lithuania in application of the Treaty of Assistance. The institutions of the three Baltic countries were dissolved and their representatives arrested. In *The Black Book of Communism*, Nicolas Werth claims that between 15,000 and 20,000 people were arrested and gives the figure of 1,500 opponents executed in Latvia alone. On 14 and 15 July 1940, elections were called in the Baltic republics, in which only candidates from the communist parties contested. A period of arrests, deportations and executions followed in all three countries: some 60,000 Estonians were deported or executed; in Latvia, some 35,000; in Lithuania, more than 30,000. Estonian author Jüri Lina provides a detailed account of what happened in his native country. In *Under the Sign of the Scorpion*, Lina devotes some twenty pages to denouncing the criminal role played by Marxist Jews in Estonia during the communist takeover. We therefore draw mainly from this source.

The occupation of Estonia began on 17 June 1940. The President of the Republic, the Freemason Konstantin Päts, and the Commander-in-Chief of the Army, Johan Laidoner, who was also a Freemason, decided not to resist. Two Jewish, supposedly cultural organisations played a key role in the imposition of communism in Estonia. One of them, "Licht" (light), founded in 1926, was based in Tallinn and collaborated with the International Red Aid and the Estonian Communist Party. The second, "Schalom Aleichem" (peace be upon you), operated in Tartu and was also instrumental in introducing Bolshevik communism to Estonia. Most of the members of Licht, whose chairman was Moses Sachs, were Zionists or communists. Three Jewish communists connected to Licht, Leo Aisenstadt, a bank manager, Ksenia Aisenstadt and Sosia Schmotkin, printed the *Kommunist* newspaper in the former's house. Another member of the Aisenstadt family, Hirsh, was an official of the Jewish Agency in Estonia and under the name of Grigori Aisenstadt was an NKVD agent in charge of one of the so-called "extermination battalions". A large number of Licht's members took part in what was officially called the "socialist revolution of 1940". Two of them, Viktor Feigin and Herman Gutkin, son of the wealthy Jewish merchant Heinrich Gutkin, lowered the Estonian flag and raised the red flag on the Tall Hermann tower on 17 June. Another Estonian author quoted by Jüri Lina, Olaf Kuuli, notes in *The Revolution in Estonia 1940* that Viktor Feigin was appointed warden of Tallinn's main prison and led a terrible organisation, the RO (Rahva Omakaitse), which translates as People's Guard, at the head of which he spread terror in Tallinn. Arnold Brenner, another Licht member who was a former NKVD commander, and Viktor Feigin were, according to Kuuli, involved in the Spanish Civil War.

Jüri Lina quotes a report published on 24 June 1940 in the *Chicago Tribune*, whose correspondent Donald Day reported the events. The journalist reported that Jewish extremists led by Herman Gutkin had marched through Tallinn to the Soviet embassy, where the Jews tore up the Estonian flag. In his memoirs, Donald Day notes that the newspaper's editor deleted the words "the Jews", which did not appear in the printed text. As for the seizure of Tartu, Estonia's second city, it was organised by Schalom

Aleichem in coordination with the Communist Party. A Schalom Aleichem militant, Selda Pats (Zelda Paatz), and her brother Jaakov Pesah coordinated the activities. On 22 June Selda herself founded the Revolutionary Youth Committee with Moisei Sverdlov.

The terror against "class enemies" was orchestrated by Estonian and Russian Jews working in coordination with the Soviet occupiers. Lina singles out Hans Grabbe (Hasa Hoff), a leading member of the cultural organisation Licht, as the greatest criminal in modern Estonian history. Grabbe became one of the heads of the NKVD and was one of the main persons responsible for the deportations and atrocities of the communists. According to Lina, Grabbe ordered "the mass execution of Estonian officers." A Swedish Secret Service report cited by the Estonian author states that almost all Jews were in one way or another in the service of the NKVD. The same document states that during the Soviet occupation the judicial system was reorganised and many Jews and other individuals with murky pasts were appointed as judges.

The Finno-Ugric languages, to which Estonian belongs, are not part of the Indo-European languages. They are agglutinative languages that hardly anyone is interested in because, apart from the fact that they are spoken by few people, they are very difficult to learn. The fact that Jüri Lina has access to written sources in the Estonian language is very interesting, as few scholars have access to them. He refers to his research at the National Archives in Tallinn in 1993, where he had in his hands documents proving that many Licht members were part of the Soviet militia. Foreign diplomats and military observers noted in their reports that Estonian Jews had suddenly become political commissars and executioners for the NKVD. Among the most important Jewish criminals who betrayed their country and cruelly tortured Estonians, Lina cites Dr. A. Tuch and Dr. B. Glückmann, both related to the NKVD. Glückmann, both related to Licht; the dentist Budas, who in the town of Kuresaare on the island of Saarema used to scald the feet and hands of his victims in boiling water; the prosecutor Stella Schliefstein, a hunchback known as "the spider" who was an expert at breaking the muscles of legs and hands into a thousand pieces. Other Jews denounced by the Estonian author are Manne Epstein, Hirsch Kitt, Gershom Zimbalov. A Jewish source, Professor Dov Levin, confirms that Leo Aisenstadt and Sosia Schmotkin became important Soviet officials. According to this source, Leo Aisenstadt and another Jew, Dr. Gens, became part of the puppet government in Moscow.

Before the Soviet occupation, during the period of Estonian independence, Estonian Jews had enjoyed unlimited freedom: almost half of the shops in Tallinn were run by Jews, they had their own organisations, their own schools where the *Talmud* was taught, their own newspapers, and even a chair of Jewish studies at the University of Tartu. According to the extensive essay *Eesti Juudi Kogukond* (*The Estonian Jewish Community*), written by Eugenia Gurin-Loov and Gennadi Gramberg and published in Tallinn in 2001, in addition to various cultural associations, there were Zionist political organisations in Estonia, political Zionist organisations existed in Estonia, such as the WIZO (Women's International Zionist Organisation), "Beitar", a Zionist youth movement founded by Vladimir Jabotinsky, and "Hashomer Hazair" (The Youth Guard), another Zionist youth movement with a socialist tendency. In 1924 Päts, the Masonic president, presided over the opening ceremony of a Jewish secondary school in Tallinn. On 12 February 1925, the Cultural Autonomy Act of the Estonian Republic was passed, and in June 1926, Jewish cultural autonomy was enacted, with the Jewish community electing its Council of Cultural Autonomy. According to the authors of the article, "the cultural government itself was of great importance for the Estonian Jews and constituted a unique phenomenon in the history of European Jewry". Moreover, so strong was the Zionist movement in this Baltic Republic that David Ben Gurion visited Tallinn in the 1930s.

Between July and August 1940, Licht was responsible for compiling lists of Jews unwilling to collaborate with the communists and the new Soviet authorities. On 7 September 1940, this organisation began publishing for Estonian Jews the weekly *Na Leben* (*The New Life*), whose editor-in-chief was Simon Perlman. Licht, under the leadership of Moisei Scheer and Leo Epstein, chose to close down all Jewish organisations that were adverse to them and seized their funds and resources. Soon after, Licht's Marxist revolutionaries abolished their own organisation, and the Soviet authorities ended the cultural autonomy that Estonia had granted to the Jews. Subsequently, despite the above, propagandists such as the writer Max Isaac Dimont, a Finnish-born Jew and author of the book *Jews, God and History*, spread the falsehood that there was no democracy in independent Estonia between the wars and that anti-Semitism prevailed in the country. According to Dimont, Jews were persecuted in Estonia and anti-Semitic legislation was on the rise. They were thus grateful for the very special treatment accorded to them by the Estonian people.

After the beginning of the German attack on the USSR on 22 June 1941, following a Beria decree issued on 24 June, General Konstatin Rakutin, who commanded the NKVD border troops in the Baltic, ordered on 26 June the formation of special extermination battalions, each of which consisted of three hundred and twenty members. According to Jüri Lina, the Lithuanian Jew Michael Pasternak, who had a street named after him in Tallinn, exercised supreme command over these battalions. Josef Goldman, a member of Licht, commanded one of the most brutal extermination battalions in July 1941.

In 1993 Mart Laar, while Prime Minister of Estonia, published the book *Metsavennad* (*The Brotherhood of the Forest*), a title that alludes to a partisan movement of opposition to the Soviet invasion and occupation that arose in the three republics. In this work, Mart Laar reveals that one of the extermination battalions was composed exclusively of Jews. Jüri Lina, for his part, has established that many members of Licht were members of these battalions, which are an infamous memory for so many Estonians. Lina cites the following list of the most active criminals: Zemach Delski, Jakob Vigderhaus, the brothers Moisei and Gerschom Zimbalov, Refoel Goldmann, Isaak Halupovitsch, Schimon (Semjon) Hoff, Simon Strassman, Abram Vseviov, Isaak Bulkin, Meier and Issak Minsker, Moisei Schimschelevitsch, Leo Epstein and Boruch Schor. Some members of Schalom Aleichem in Tartu voluntarily joined the extermination battalions, among them Josef Mjasnikov, founder of the Estonian Zionist movement "Netzach", and the aforementioned Selda Pats and Jaakov Pesah.

According to a report in the *Eesti Ekspress* newspaper of 7 June 1991, there were at least five hundred and forty Jews in these ruthless units. The extermination battalions," writes the Estonian author, "were known for their indescribable brutality and cruelty, especially towards women and children. The victims were thrown alive into the fire, parts of their bodies were amputated, they were nailed to the walls...". Thousands of opponents were imprisoned or eliminated during the two months of the Red terror, which only ended on 28 August 1941 with the Germans' entry into Tallinn. Jüri Lina locates the criminals in the areas they terrorised. Thus, he places Boris Friedam in the town of Voru; Jakob Jolanski in Pärnu; Shustov in Kuresaare. The actions of the murderers are well documented. There is, for example, the case of twenty Estonians arrested at the railway station, who, after interrogation in Tallinn, were executed in the Liiva forest on the orders of L. Rubinov, the Jewish battalion commander. Here is a brief account of another case as written by Lina:

> "Josef Goldman, who commanded one of the extermination battalions, ordered that all women and girls found on the roads, on the farms or in the fields should first be raped, then their breasts were to be cut off and finally they were to be burned alive. Men were also treated in a similar way: first they lost their genitals, then their eyes, after which their stomachs were cut open and they died as slowly as possible".

Lina cites in her work the names and surnames of some of the victims and the way they were tortured and killed, for example Anna Kivimäe and her daughters. The mother's head was smashed in and the daughters were raped and then had their eyes gouged out. Gardener Albert Palu was burned alive in Helme on 5 July 1941. The same thing happened to Albert Simm and his wife in Pühajoe. On the same day a fourteen-year-old teenager, Tiit Kartes, was arrested in Aseri: after torturing him and cutting off his genitals, he was murdered and his corpse was left in a forest. Sometimes the exterminators skinned their victims alive. Mart Laar, the aforementioned prime minister of Estonia, described some of the crimes of the extermination battalions in an article entitled "The Time of Horrors". Laar recounts the dehumanising destruction of three Estonian villages and all their inhabitants: children were nailed to trees and pregnant women were beaten to death. In the village of Ehavere, babies were smothered against their mothers' breasts with bayonets; women's tongues and breasts were amputated. Jüri Lina adds that he was personally able to find information showing that pigs were sometimes fed with the bodies of Estonian Brotherhood of the Forest guerrillas and attributes the ultimate responsibility for these crimes to the Jews Hans Grabe (Hasa Hoff) and Michael Pasternak.

The Estonian researcher constantly relies on Jewish sources to support his assertions. Thus, for example, Irina Stelmach admitted in the 17 December 1993 edition of the newspaper *Hommikuleht* that there were many of her fellow Jews in the extermination battalions. Augustina Gerber, editor of the Jewish newspaper *Hasahar* claimed that Soviet Estonia had become the "promised land of the Jews". Jüri Lina confirms that this was so, since "Jews became high-ranking heads within the Soviet apparatus in occupied Estonia." The Latvian Jew Idel Jakobson was the number two in the NKVD Research Department. In April 1942, Jakobson signed an execution order for six hundred and twenty-one Estonians held in the Vostok-Uralsky camp in the Siberian town of Sosva, which did not prevent Jakobson from dying in Tallinn at the age of 93 without ever having been tried for his crimes, reports Lina.

In Jewish hands was the control of the media, the recording industry, scientific development and everything to do with propaganda. The main radio commentators were the Jews Herbert Vainu, Gabriel Hazak and Simon Joffe. Lina also mentions the name of the Jewish Marxist in charge of falsifying history, Herber-Armin Lebbin, who continuously spread lies about Estonia's willingness to join the Soviet Union. As usual, many Jews held important positions in the political police. Among them, the Estonian author mentions the businessmen Epstein, Mirvitz, Bakszt, Kofkin, Himmelhoch; the lawyers Markovitch and Kroppman; the photographer Schuras. At the head of the Prison Department, he cites the Jew Feodotov; the Russian Jew Lobonovich was vice-chairman of the Commissariat of Internal Affairs.

In Latvia, where the occupation was celebrated by many Jewish communists who took part in the riots when Soviet tanks rolled into Riga, Jewish activists also played a leading role in the terror against the 'enemies of the people'. Prominent among the Jewish heads of the NKVD in Latvia were Simon (Semion) Shustin, Alfons Noviks and Moses Citron, a troika joined by Isaac Bucinskis, head of the Latvian militia. The first two organised the deportation of Latvians on 13 and 14 June 1941. At the stations, men were grouped together on one side and women and children on the other. On these two days alone, about 16,000 people were deported, many of whom died before reaching the camps, and others during the first winter.

Simon Shustin came to Latvia from Moscow, where by Lavrenti Beria's decree he had been appointed Commissar of Internal Affairs in Latvia. Many of his henchmen in the NKVD were local Jews. After the Soviet withdrawal, documents were found showing that the execution of Latvian patriots began as soon as the occupation began. Before fleeing to Moscow, Shustin signed Order No. 412 on 26 June 1941, ordering the execution of seventy-eight people, six of them women. In red ink he wrote: "Considering that they constitute a public danger, they must all be shot". According to Jüri Lina, Shustin, who was known as the "executioner of Latvia", eventually emigrated to Israel in the 1970s; but this fact could not be verified. According to other sources, on 8 February 1996, the Latvian Prosecutor's Office brought charges against Shustin for crimes against humanity and it was learned that he had lived in Kolpino (St. Petersburg district) between 1960 and 1972. During the investigation, the Latvian Prosecutor General found a letter addressed to Alfons Noviks dated 12 July 1968. The investigation finally discovered that he had died on 3 August 1978, and the case was closed on 30 June 1997.

Alfons Noviks, head of the NKVD in Daugavpils, Latvia's second city, was arrested and brought to trial, where he and his colleague Moses Citron wreaked terror. His criminal career in Latvia had two stages: with the arrival of the German troops he fled to Moscow in July 1941; but he returned in 1945 and was appointed Commissar of Internal Affairs and head of State Security. As established in the judgment of the Riga court which sentenced him on 13 December 1995 to life imprisonment for genocide and crimes against humanity, between 1940 and 1953 he participated in the deportation to Siberia of about 100,000 Latvians. The Riga court also found him guilty of the torture and execution of numerous political prisoners (according to several witnesses who testified against him, Noviks tortured and beat with extreme cruelty during his interrogations). In 1949 alone, he personally ordered the deportation of 41,544 people, for which he was awarded the Red Flag medal. The court found that some 150,000 Latvians and Lithuanians had to go into exile because of his policies. Alfons Noviks was living quietly in Riga when he was arrested in March 1994. He was imprisoned for only a short time, as he died on 12 March 1996.

Beria and the Katyn massacre

The Red Army's entry into Poland was followed by NKVD units charged with eliminating the Polish leadership and deporting hundreds of thousands of civilians living in the newly occupied territories to labour camps. The Soviet occupation prompted elements of ethnic minorities who hated Poles to settle scores with them. Labour Guards Units were formed in the cities and Peasant Guards Units in the countryside, mostly composed of enthusiastic Jewish collaborators who provided the NKVD with information about the Polish resistance and denounced members of the army, police and other "enemies" in hiding. They were instrumental in drawing up lists of people to be arrested. NKVD General Ivan Serov appointed the Jewish Colonel Semion Moiseyevich Krivoshaynin to carry out the task of liquidating those who opposed Soviet authority. Krivoshéin has already appeared in this work: he was the chief of the tankmen who loaded the Banco de España's gold reserves onto the ships that transported them from Cartagena to Odessa. In the Battle of Madrid Semion Krivoshéin commanded the tanks of the Republican Army and was known to the Spaniards as "Melé".

No reliable data are available on the arrests and deportations of civilians carried out by the Soviets in Poland between September 1939 and January 1940, but figures are available on four subsequent major deportations: the first three were carried out in the first half of 1940 and the fourth in the summer of 1941. Polish historians put the total number of deportees at over a million, but other sources put the figure at half a million. In any case, prisoners of war must be counted separately, who, as mentioned above, numbered 230,000, of whom only 82,000 survived in the summer of 1941. Among these prisoners were 25,700 Polish officers and civilians whom Beria proposed to shoot, as recorded in a letter to Stalin on 5 March 1940. Once the crime, which has gone down in history as the Katyn Forest Massacre, was committed, the Soviets blamed it on the Germans with the complicity of the British, who, despite knowing the truth, concealed it and helped to spread the false claim of responsibility for the massacre.

On 11 October 1951, a US Congressional Committee held the first public hearing on the Katyn war crime in Washington. The investigation continued in 1952 with further hearings in Washington (4, 5, 6, and 7 February), in Chicago (13 and 14 March), in London (16, 17, 18, and 19 April), in Frankfurt (21, 22, 23, 24, 25, and 26 April), and later. At these hearings, some 100 witnesses testified before the Committee. It was unanimously considered proven that the massacre of the Polish army officers was the responsibility of the NKVD, i.e. the People's Commissariat of Internal Affairs, whose commissar was the Jew Lavrenti Beria. The Committee concluded that already in the autumn of 1939, shortly after the invasion, the Soviets planned the extermination of the Polish leadership. According to the findings of the Investigative Committee, there can be no doubt that the massacre was a planned plot to eliminate all national leaders who would later have opposed Soviet plans to establish communism in Poland. Exactly the same thing had been done in Russia, as the reader will recall, where the Judeo-Bolsheviks eliminated the country's "intelligentsia" with the same intention.

From September 1939 to March 1940 the NKVD executed a perfectly organised plan to separate Polish officers and intellectual leaders from the rest of the prisoners. Those selected: army chiefs and officers, lawyers, doctors, priests, technicians, civil servants and intellectuals were interned in Kozelsk, Starobelsk and Ostashkof, three camps on the territory of the Soviet Union. According to the Committee of Inquiry hearings, 5,000 prisoners were interned in Kozelsk near Smolensk; 4,000 Polish officers were interned in Starobelsk near Kharkov; 6,000 prisoners were interned in Ostashkov near Kalinin. *The Venona Secrets*, to which we will return in the next chapter, reports that on 31 October 1939 Vassiliy Zarubin arrived at the Kozelsk camp. Zarubin, a secret agent who in the United States later used the name Vassiliy Zubilin, behaved as if he were the camp commandant. It was he who selected the prisoners to be sent to the Lubyanka in Moscow for thorough interrogation. Zarubin determined which Polish officers were to be severely punished for their past anti-Soviet activities and which could be recruited to become Soviet agents.

Through the testimony of 26 people who had been in these three camps, it became known that the Soviets divided the Poles into groups: senior military personnel were interned in Kozelsk together with doctors who were army reservists; non-commissioned officers, political leaders and teachers were grouped in Starobelsk; finally, border guards, policemen and other officials were interned in Ostashkov. Religious leaders were divided between the three camps. The total number of detainees in the three facilities was fifteen thousand four hundred, and their custody was entrusted to selected NKVD personnel. During their internment, each was observed and interrogated to see if there was any possibility of converting them to communism: only six agreed to join the Soviet forces. In March 1940 the interrogations were terminated and it was announced that the camps would be closed. A rumour began to spread among the prisoners, encouraged by the camp authorities, that they would be sent home. During the evacuation, which lasted until mid-May 1940, groups of two or three hundred people left every day or every other day to be killed. Only four hundred prisoners survived. These were taken to Pavlishev-Bor, another camp where the NKVD continued to interrogate them in order to try to convert them to communism. The Poles massacred in the Katyn Forest came from the Kozelsk camp.

The "very secret" text of the letter sent by Beria to Comrade Stalin on 5 March 1940 appears in full in *The Black Book of Communism*. Beria reported that in the POW camps there were 14,736 officers, officials, landlords, policemen, gendarmes, prison officials, settlers in the border regions and intelligence agents. The final part of the letter follows:

"... Included are:
- Generals, colonels and lieutenant colonels: 295.
- Commanders and captains: 2,080.
- Lieutenants, second lieutenants and trainees: 6.049.
- Police, customs and gendarmerie officers and non-commissioned officers: 1 030.

- Police officers, gendarmes, prison officers and intelligence officers: 5,138.
- Officials, property owners, priests and settlers: 144.

In addition, 18,632 men are detained in prisons in the western regions of Ukraine and Belarus (of whom 10,685 are Poles).

Included are:
- Former officers: 1,027.
- Former intelligence, police and gendarmerie officers: 5,141.
- Spies and saboteurs: 347.
- Former real estate owners, factory owners and civil servants: 465.
- Members of counter-revolutionary resistance organisations and other elements: 5,345.
- Deserters: 6.

Since all these individuals are bitter and irreducible enemies of Soviet power, the NKVD of the USSR considers it necessary:

1. Order the NKVD of the USSR to try before special tribunals:

(a) 14,700 former officials, civil servants, property owners, police officers, intelligence agents, gendarmes, settlers in the border regions and prison officials detained in POW camps.

b) As well as 11,000 members of the counter-revolutionary organisations of spies and saboteurs, former real estate owners, factory owners, former Polish army officers, civil servants and deserters arrested and confined in prisons in the western regions of Ukraine and Belarus to be given the ultimate penalty - the death penalty by firing squad.

2. The examination of individual files shall be conducted without the appearance of the detainees and without an indictment. The findings of the indictment and the final judgment shall be presented as follows:

(a) In the form of certificates issued to individuals detained in POW camps by the USSR NKVD administration for POW affairs.

(b) In the form of certificates issued to the other persons detained by the NKVD of the Ukrainian SSR and the NKVD of the Byelorussian SSR.

3. The files will be examined and the sentences passed by a tribunal composed of three persons, Comrades Merkulov, Kobulov and Bashtakov.

People's Commissar for Internal Affairs of the USSR L. Beria".

The executions began on 5 April 1940. From this day until 14 May, 6,311 prisoners of war and policemen were systematically shot in the back of the head in the cellars of the NKVD prison in Kalinin. The massacre was personally directed by three NKVD chiefs, Vasily Blokhin, Mikhail Kriwienko and Nikolai Siniegubow. The former has gone down in history as one of the most prolific executioners in history, credited with personally executing tens of thousands of people in the course of his bloodthirsty career. In relation to Polish prisoners, he is said to have killed 300 in a single night, one every three minutes. The bodies were then loaded onto trucks and dumped in mass graves about thirty kilometres from the town of Mednoye. At another NKVD centre in Kharkov another 3,820 prisoners of war were executed and trucked to nearby forests to be dumped in pits.

Also used for the mass murder of prisoners was a method that has already been discussed twice in this work: the sinking of barges full of prisoners. As will be recalled, the first to use this method during the French Revolution was a criminal called Carrier, who sank large rafts loaded with people in the Loire. This method was taken up again in 1919 in Astrakhan by the Bolshevik Chekists. Thousands of detainees were then thrown into the Volga from the boats with a stone around their necks. On what happened in April/May 1940, Adam Moszynski, a prisoner in Starobelsk and author of the most complete list of the names of the prisoners interned in the three camps, stated the following before the Committee of Inquiry: "As far as I know, based on substantial research on the matter, the prisoners in Oshtakov were placed on two large, very old barges and, after being towed to the open sea, were destroyed by artillery fire". Allegedly, these prisoners were taken to work in coal mines on one of the Arctic islands.

The Katyn Forest Massacre was the only known massacre during the war. There, 4,421 Polish prisoners of war, who had been unsuccessfully sought by the Polish authorities since the summer of 1941, were buried in mass graves. A chronology of events will help to understand the dynamics of the events. Following Germany's attack on the USSR on 22 June 1941, Poland and the Soviet Union signed an agreement on 30 July 1941 that allowed them to resume diplomatic relations. As a result of this agreement, all Poles still held in camps were released by the Soviets. On 14 August 1941, the Poles and Soviets signed a military pact, and on 16 August General Wladyslaw Anders began the futile search for his murdered comrades.

On 13 April 1943 the Germans announced the discovery of the Katyn graves near Smolensk, where Polish army chiefs and officers, members of the intelligentsia, government officials and priests were buried. On 15 April 1943 the Polish government in London asked the International Red Cross to send a delegation to the site to investigate the truth about what had happened. On 26 April the USSR again broke off diplomatic relations with Poland over the fact that it had requested a neutral investigation by the Red Cross. On 30 April 1943 a medical examination commission headed by Dr. François Naville, Professor of Forensic Medicine at the University of Geneva, and composed of leading jurists, doctors and criminologists from twelve European universities and neutral countries produced a unanimously approved report stating that the Poles buried in the graves had been massacred in the spring of 1940. On 24 January 1944 a Soviet Special Commission issued its own report on what happened in Katyn, according to which the Germans had committed the atrocity in August 1941. It was not until 1992 that the USSR acknowledged its responsibility for the elimination of the Polish elite in 1940.

On the body of Major Adam Solski, one of the victims buried in the Katyn graves, a diary was found, the entries of which enabled the Congressional Commission of Inquiry to learn the dates on which the massacres took place. The last words were written on 8 and 9 April 1940. On the 8th he wrote: "Since twelve o'clock noon we have been standing at a dead end in Smolensk". On the 9th he wrote twice. In the first entry he said: "A few minutes before five o'clock in the morning reveille on the wagons and preparations for departure." The diary ended with the second entry on the 9th. Here is what was written: "Already at dawn, the day started strangely. We left in vans with small prisoner cells (terrible). We were taken somewhere into the woods, some summer camp. Here, a thorough search. They took the watch, which read 6:30 in the morning, asked for my wedding ring, which they kept, rubles, my belt and a pocket knife." This diary was brought by General Bor-Komorowski to the sessions of the Committee of Inquiry held in London in April 1952.

Before the Germans discovered the graves in April 1943, General Anders had personally met with Stalin. In December 1941 Anders, accompanied by General Sikorski, head of the Polish Government in exile, enquired with Stalin about the whereabouts of the missing officers. The reply was that they were not and had not been detained. General Anders testified before the Committee in London and reproduced the dialogue with the Soviet leader: "We asked: 'Well, where could they have gone?' To which Stalin replied: 'They escaped. We tried to find out: 'Where could they have escaped?' Stalin replied: 'To Manchuria'. I said this was impossible. On 18 March 1942 Anders had a second meeting with Stalin in the Kremlin and presented him with a list of the names of the missing officers. He insisted that none of them had yet established contact with the Polish army. Stalin said, "Well, what use would they be to us? Why would we want to keep them?" During this second interview Stalin let it slip that they may have fled separately when the Germans invaded Russia.

On 13 April 1943 there was a radio broadcast in Berlin which, in addition to shaking international opinion, served to stop the Poles from searching for their missing servicemen:

> "From Smolensk comes news that the native population has revealed to the German authorities. Mass executions were carried out there. The Bolsheviks murdered ten thousand Polish officers. The German authorities made a horrible discovery. They found a pit twenty-eight metres long, sixteen metres wide and twelve metres deep, in which lay the bodies of three thousand Polish officers. Uniformed, sometimes in chains, they all had gunshot wounds to the back of their necks. The search for and discovery of other graves continues."

The announcement was followed by an intense propaganda campaign to try to exploit the discovery politically. The Nazis made desperate efforts to have the International Committee of the Red Cross conduct an impartial investigation. Hitler personally instructed the German Foreign Ministry to make every effort to obtain such an investigation. The Polish Red Cross was informed by the International Committee that an investigation could only take place if all three nations involved participated. When the Poles requested the investigation, the Soviets reportedly accused the Poles of "collaborating with the Nazis" and abruptly broke off diplomatic relations.

In London, Sikorski met with Churchill on 15 April 1943 and told him that the evidence he had found indicated irrefutably that the Soviet Allies were to blame for the mass murders. As Lord Cadogan wrote in his Diary, Churchill told Sikorski: "The revelations of the Germans are probably true. The Bolsheviks can be very cruel." Despite this admission, he ended up advising him that the matter was best forgotten, since nothing would bring the murdered officers back to life. Anthony Eden, the Secretary of State in the Foreign Office who had replaced Lord Halifax, appeared before the House of Commons on 4 May 1943 and reported that the British Government would lay the blame for what had happened on the common enemy. Eden added "that he deplored the cynicism with which the German Government was accusing the Soviet Union, with the veiled purpose of breaking unity among the Allies". Of course, F. D. Roosevelt, too, knew the truth of what had happened and concealed it from the public. Recently declassified documents from the US National Archives reveal that Roosevelt knew in 1943 that the Soviet secret police had shot 22,000 Poles, the country's military and intellectual elite, in the back of the head. Winston Churchill himself had sent him a detailed report written by Owen O'Malley, the British ambassador to the Polish government-in-exile in London.

The situation in Western Europe: Norway and the neutrals

With the Sudetenland issue settled, Hitler had declared actively and passively that he had no further territorial claims in Western Europe and that France could rest easy about Alsace-Lorraine. However, after Britain and France declared war on Germany, few countries could avoid becoming embroiled in the conflict, which eventually spread inexorably across the Continent. The Allies' propaganda, disseminated through the world press, imposed an idea that has prevailed: Germany attacked neutral countries because it wanted to dominate the world, and they, on the other hand, acted as disinterested saviours of the peoples under attack. The reality, as we have seen, was quite different, for neither the United Kingdom, France nor the United States lifted a finger to defend the Eastern European countries attacked for no reason by the USSR, whose westward expansion did not seem to be of the slightest concern.

The King of Belgium and the Queen of Holland offered their good offices in November to restore peace. They asked President Roosevelt to assume the leadership of a League of Neutrals and proposed that he support a protest against the violations committed by the USSR in invading Poland, subjugating the Baltic countries and attacking Finland. Naturally, Roosevelt, despite his hypocritical speeches in favour of peace, refused to associate himself with the efforts of the two monarchs. Lord Halifax, for his part, in a public speech that Ribbentrop described as "brazen", took it upon himself to rule out any possibility of negotiations. David Irving makes it clear in *Hitler's War* that the rejection of peace was because "London was subject to a lunatic Jewish-controlled minority against which Chamberlain was a spineless and impotent man". Holland and, above all, Belgium were in an impossible position if war broke out between France and Germany. However, when on 19 October 1939 Hitler gave the first directive to prepare the massive attack on France, "Operation Case Yellow" (Fall Gelb), he believed that it would be possible to avoid hostilities with the Netherlands, provided the British respected their neutrality and did not land in the country. The German generals presented the Führer with their scruples about violating Belgian territory, and this led to repeated delays in the execution of "Fall Gelb", which was due to begin in November.

The fact that, except for the Flemish minority, the sympathies of the Dutch population were with the Allies meant that the armed forces of both countries were concentrated almost entirely on the German border. The Nazi leadership especially feared that the British and French might overnight join the Belgians in attacking Germany's "Achilles heel", i.e. the Ruhr industrial area, which would have been a severe blow. On the other hand, the British were constantly violating the neutrality of the Netherlands by overflying RAF aircraft, so it was clear by November that when the operation, which had been postponed to 3 December, began, the Netherlands would have to be invaded.

In December 1939 Admiral Erich Räder alerted Hitler to the dire strategic position Germany would be in if the British occupied Norway. Evidence that Räder's fears were justified came through Rosenberg's contact in Norway, Major Vidkun Quisling, who had been Minister of Defence until 1933. Quisling, a convinced anti-Communist who had founded the "Nasjonal Samling" (National Unity), an anti-Jewish party akin to National Socialism, had conclusive evidence that London was planning to control the country with the support of Carl Hambro, the Jewish Speaker of the Norwegian Parliament, who, according to Quisling, had allowed the British Secret Service to infiltrate the Norwegian Intelligence Service from cover to cover. The press was also in the hands of friends of Hambro, a hugely influential figure, the scion of a powerful Jewish banking family.

Hitler wanted to form a personal impression of Quisling, who on 14 December presented himself to the German Chancellor in the company of Viljam Hagelin, a businessman. During the conversation, the Führer stressed emphatically that his political preference was for Norway and the whole of

Scandinavia to remain neutral, and that he had no intention of expanding the theatre of war by involving more countries in the conflict unless he was forced to do so. Quisling, however, informed Hitler that he had two hundred thousand followers, some of them very well placed, ready to seize power when the Hambro Government, which had prolonged his term of office, was illegally kept in power from 10 January. Quisling suggested overthrowing him and then asking Germany to send troops to Oslo.

In January 1940 the German Intelligence Service confirmed that Belgium, despite increasing concentrations of Anglo-French troops on its border with France, was only fortifying its border with Germany. Moreover, the authorities were encouraging the fraternisation of Belgians with the French and British. Moreover, the Belgian Gendarmerie had received orders to facilitate the invasion of France, and signposts to that effect had even been erected in the west. The evidence that the Allies were preparing their offensive through Belgium was clear. With the exception of one division, all mechanised infantry, armoured and cavalry forces were deployed on the German border.

On 17 February 1940, the *Altmark*, a 15,000-tonne supply ship, sailed unarmed through Norwegian waters under the flag of the German merchant navy. On board were some 300 British sailors, who had been rescued from the sea by the cruiser *Graf Spee* after the British ships they belonged to had sunk. The *Altmark* supplied the famous cruiser in South Atlantic waters and had received these prisoners before the *Graf Spee*'s captain, Langsdorff, ordered them sunk in the estuary of the Río de la Plata to avoid capture. Two Norwegian reconnaissance torpedo boats interrogated the captain of the *Altmark*, who did not reveal that he had any prisoners on board, although if he had, his legal position would have been no different, and proceeded to escort him. The British cruiser *Cossack* and six destroyers were in the vicinity and were ordered to seize the German ship, even if this meant violating Norwegian territorial waters. On sighting the British ships, the captain of the *Altmark* sought refuge in the Jössing Fjord. The Norwegian torpedo boats authorised this and kept the British at bay until nightfall. Finally, the British ships forced their way into the fjord and boarded the German ship. The *Altmark*'s report described how the boarding party seized the wheelhouse "and began firing like blind fanatics at the German crew, who, of course, had not a gun." Six men were killed, many more were wounded. Some crew members tried to flee over the ice surrounding the ship and others threw themselves into the sea. The Norwegians later testified that the British had also shot the defenceless men in the water. The prisoners were released and the ship and crew were looted. The Germans did not fire a single shot.

Naturally, the Norwegian reaction was one of outrage. The act of war inside the fjord was a flagrant violation of Norway's neutrality that could not be tolerated, and the government in Oslo lodged a strong diplomatic protest.

For his part, Hitler learned from communication signals decoded in Berlin that the captain of the *Cossak* had even been ordered to open fire on the Norwegian torpedo boats if they resisted action against the *Altmark*. In Germany, the media reported the incident and there was a public outcry. From this point on, although neither in his directives to the Wehrmacht nor in his speeches to his generals had Hitler predicted the occupation of Scandinavia, the occupation of Norway began to be considered. It was on 1 March that the German Chancellor signed the first instruction for the planned occupation of Norway and Denmark. By this date, RAF aircraft had already violated the airspace of Denmark and Norway, as well as Belgium and the Netherlands, on countless occasions in order to evade German anti-aircraft defences.

Since Winston Churchill published *The Gathering Storm* in 1948, *it has* been known that the British naval authorities' plans to attack Norway had begun to be outlined in September 1939. On 16 December 1939, when he was not yet prime minister, Churchill had already submitted a memorandum to the government pointing to the need for action in Norway. Small nations must not tie our hands," he said. On 6 February 1940 the British War Council approved the plan, which involved the seizure of Narvick and the occupation by force of northern Norway and Sweden. In the latter country the seizure of the Baltic Sea port of Lulea was contemplated. The secret name of these plans was "Operation Stradford". Thus, in March 1940, both the United Kingdom and Germany were preparing to land in Norway, but the British plans were much further advanced.

At the beginning of March, the diplomat Walter Hewel sent numerous telegrams to the Führer from Helsinki, Trondheim and Oslo, denouncing that the British intended to intervene in Scandinavia under the pretext of helping Finland. Ribbentrop also received information from Quisling showing that the British and French invasion plans were already well advanced. When it became known on 12 March that Moscow and Helsinki were negotiating an armistice, the Allies realised that they had to intervene immediately if they were to use the alibi of the Russo-Finnish war to legitimise their landing. London," writes David Irving, "made desperate efforts to prolong the war for a few more days. Winston Churchill had evidently flown to Paris on 11 March to inform the French government that on 15 March his expeditionary force would sail for Narvik". This British revisionist historian notes that the "Forschungsamt", the German intelligence service specialising in decoding communications, had on 12 March decoded an urgent telephone call from the Finnish ambassador in Paris to his foreign minister, announcing that Churchill and Daladier had promised help if Finland asked for it without delay. In other words, after more than three months of a war of aggression against Finland, they were suddenly in a hurry.

Operation "Case Yellow", meanwhile, had continued to be postponed. The strategic importance of Norway and Denmark in safeguarding

Germany's back was obvious, so securing these countries was becoming a priority. The fact that the ports were frozen in March made it advisable to wait until April. On 28 March 1940, the Allied Supreme War Council decided to launch a two-stage operation in early April. The plan was to first mine neutral waters to provoke Germany into a rush to occupy southern Norway, which would justify a large-scale landing at Narvik in the north to seize control of the railway lines carrying iron ore from Swedish mines, vital to Germany, to this port. The imminence of the British operation was again confirmed by Quisling, who warned of the arrival of British and French agents who, disguised as consular officials, were setting up in key locations in Norway. Admiral Räder pleaded with Hitler to launch the invasion as soon as possible and proposed the date of 7 April.

The British plan was put into action on 5 April. The Germans detected that some major manoeuvre had begun thanks to the "Forschungsamt", which decoded a communication ordering some 20 U-boats to begin operations. The possibility was then considered that the British had detected the German invasion plan and were deploying to abort it; but German naval experts correctly deduced that the enemy intended to lay a barrage of mines in preparation for an intervention in Norway. On 8 April it was confirmed that British warships were laying a mine curtain in Norwegian waters, which was an unquestionable violation of the Scandinavian country's neutrality. During the night of 6-7 April, the German fleet had begun the operation that had been planned since early March. Battleships, cruisers and destroyers sailed for the Norwegian ports of Narvik, Trondheim, Bergen and Oslo. Hitler could present his seizure of Norway as a response to the Allied action. On 9 April, 24 hours after the British had mined the territorial waters, German forces landed in Norway and occupied Denmark, whose government had surrendered without resistance.

It is no longer necessary to describe the operations in Norway. We will only say that the German navy suffered significant losses: many ships were sunk and human losses were considerable. The Norwegian shore batteries and the action of British submarines and other ships operating in the area inflicted very significant damage on the landing forces. The British made landings at Namsos, south of Narvik, and at Aandalsnes, south of Trondheim. Some 12,000 British, French and Poles also landed at Narvik, trying to recapture this port where Swedish iron was being shipped to Germany. Two thousand German and Austrian soldiers had settled in Narvik unopposed, thanks to the cooperation of a commander close to Quisling. This strategic enclave became the main theatre of a struggle that lasted several weeks. By early May 1940, the British had evacuated their forces from Namsos and Aandalsnes, and only the troops fighting to recapture Narvik were still fighting.

Important British military records were seized in Norway. An infantry brigade fighting south of Aandalsnes was forced to flee before the advancing

Germans, who captured significant documents, the importance of which was soon realised. The brigade commander had received instructions aimed at the occupation of Stavanger. The orders were dated 2, 6 and 7 April, i.e. days before the German invasion. Other documents showed that landing operations were planned for Bergen, Trondheim and Narvik. In addition to these documents, files were found at the French and British consulates in Oslo that proved beyond doubt that the Allied plan to invade Norway had been scheduled in January and that certain Norwegian leaders were cooperating and working to ensure that there was no resistance. At noon on 27 April Ribbentrop distributed these incriminating documents to the foreign diplomats who had been summoned to the Foreign Ministry. In the afternoon, a radio broadcast that could be heard all over the world denounced Britain's bluffs and blathering about the small neutral countries. Ribbentrop published a White Paper on the Norwegian documents that shocked international public opinion. In conclusion, Admiral Räder was sentenced to life imprisonment in Nuremberg for planning and directing a war of aggression against Norway.

The mystery of Dunkirk

On 10 May 1940 came the long-delayed "Operation Yellow", i.e. the Wehrmacht's general attack along the French front and the invasion of Holland, Belgium and Luxembourg. The French defensive lines were unable to stop the breakneck offensive and within ten days it was clear that Germany had defeated France. On 20 May, German generals found that at least twenty enemy divisions were trapped north of the Somme. In the evening, General Brauchitsch telephoned Hitler to tell him that his tanks had reached Abbeville, a town ten kilometres from the mouth of the Somme at the English Channel. The Germans could begin the second phase of the Campaign, codenamed "Red", which consisted of a sweep south towards the Swiss border. Before this, however, it was necessary to capture the 340,000 or so British and French troops who had been bagged up north of the Somme. This did not happen because of "Halt Befehl", Hitler's halt order that halted the advance towards Dunkirk, a momentous decision that allowed Britain to recover and led to Germany's subsequent defeat.

One of the military geniuses behind this spectacular victory was General Heinz Guderian, who in 1937 had published *Achtung Panzer!*, a work that laid the foundations for the "Blitzkrieg" or lightning war, first applied on 1 September 1939 in Poland. Guderian's theory of a military tactic of such a rapid and devastating advance that a country could be conquered in a few weeks was confirmed. Those who attributed the success of the blitzkrieg to the Polish army's lack of substance found on 10 May 1940 that the Allied high command, anchored in the theories of the war of attrition they had experienced in the First World War, had no answer to a war of sweeping movements, based on large, self-sufficient tank units concentrated at the "Schwerpunkt", the essential point of the battle. With the defences razed to the ground, the enemy's logistical and command centres were left to the mercy of the armoured units, which moved freely in the rear awaiting the arrival of the infantry to finish off the victory. To understand the consequences of the "Halt Befehl" (halt order), it is necessary to consider that mobility was one of the keys to the Blitzkrieg conceived by Guderian. The assault was directed towards the enemy front lines and was not to stop until, due to the disorder generated, operational response capabilities were nullified. Air support was then provided to protect the Panzers and prevent any possibility of reorganisation.

So clear was victory, that on 21 May Admiral Räder, faced with the evidence that the bulk of the British army was trapped, privately revealed to the Führer that he had been studying the problems of a sea invasion of the British Isles from November onwards. Hitler refused at first to consider the plan without explanation, and days later rejected the idea again when Jodl insisted on the advisability of preparing the invasion. On 22 May, after two days of deliberation, Churchill, who had been appointed Prime Minister of the United Kingdom on 10 May, decided to withdraw the British Expeditionary Force (BEF) from France. For this reason, on 22 May, Lord Gort, head of the BEF, ordered the withdrawal from Arras to the coast without informing the French command, to which he was subordinate.

Seeing an unusual number of troop transports heading out to sea, the Germans interpreted this as the British intending to evacuate their Expeditionary Force. Generals Brauchitsch and Halder, without informing the Führer, ordered General Fedor von Bock to advance from the south to complete the encirclement. On 23 May, the three divisions of Guderian's Panzerkorps took Boulogne and Calais, two of the three ports for a possible British evacuation, and were preparing to march on Dunkirk, the last point through which the Allied forces, which were fighting against General von Bock's group of armies and retreating, could flee. At this point Guderian was closer to Dunkirk than the entire British army and nothing stood in the way of his advance. Had Guderian reached Dunkirk, the Anglo-French armies would have been completely surrounded and would have had only two options: surrender or annihilation.

In the early hours of 24 May Hitler, accompanied by Generals Jodl and Schmundt, reported to headquarters in Charleville, where, supported by Field Marshal Gerd von Rundstedt, the most conservative general in the Wehrmacht, he cancelled the order Bock had received. Hitler apparently relied on Rundstedt to enforce his decision to halt the advance towards Dunkirk. Displaying an unwarranted state of nerves, which may well have been theatrical, he demanded that Rundstedt assess the threat posed by the French army from the southern flank. Rundstedt, understanding that the Führer was suggesting prudence, proposed to halt operations and allow the

Panzers to enjoy a few days' rest. Hitler agreed wholeheartedly. The possibility that the British might escape to England was not even discussed. On the evening of the 24th Guderian received a telegram from Rundstedt HQ which read: "Armoured divisions are to remain within medium artillery range of Dunkirk. Permission is granted only for reconnaissance and protective movements." Guderian, who knew that in the Blitzkrieg it was essential not to lose "momentum", was stunned by this order. Since he could not understand it and was given no arguments to justify it, he chose to ignore it and continued his march to Dunkirk, which was only eighteen kilometres away. Then came a second order, backed by the Führer's authority, repeating that the advance must not continue and that he must withdraw to the previous lines.

In *The Other Side of the Hill*, Captain B. H. Liddell Hart, a renowned military critic, studies the German invasion of France and analyses the events at Dunkirk in a chapter entitled "How Hitler Defeated France and Saved Britain". The British historian reproduces the words of Gunter Blumentritt, one of Rundstedt's staff generals who met with Hitler on 24 May:

> "He then left us in awe as he spoke with admiration of the British Empire, of the necessity of its existence, and of the civilisation that Britain had brought to the world. He compared the British Empire to the Catholic Church, saying that both were essential elements for stability in the world. He said that all he wanted from Britain was for it to recognise Germany's position on the Continent. The return of lost German colonies would be desirable, but not essential. He said he would even offer to support British troops should they get into difficulties somewhere. She ended by saying that her aim was to make peace with Britain on grounds which she considered compatible with her honour."

Some historians try to justify the "Halt Befehl" from the point of view of military logic. They argue that it was necessary to preserve the tanks for the offensive to the south, that the mud of the Flanders marshes was a danger to the armoured vehicles, that Rundstedt's decision was the most prudent one.... All these reasons are extremely weak. Other historians point out that the BEF was able to escape because of the inability of Göring and the Luftwaffe. Hitler allegedly supported Göring's claim, who boasted that the air force was sufficient to prevent the evacuation. If so, this was an incredible misjudgement, since most German aircraft were based at airfields in Germany, while the RAF operated from across the Channel. Guderian himself wrote in his memoirs that Hitler's and Rundstedt's fears that the Panzers would get stuck in the mud were unfounded. Bevin Alexander, author of more than a dozen books on military history, a specialist in military strategy who is considered one of the most prestigious military historians, writes in *How Hitler Could Have Won World War II* that a great opportunity to defeat Britain was lost at Dunkirk.

British propaganda, instead of admitting Hitler's quixotic gesture, created the myth of the "Miracle of Dunkirk" or the "Spirit of Dunkirk". In reality the only prodigious thing had been an incomprehensible decision that undoubtedly had miraculous effects for the British troops trapped at Dunkirk. Contrary to the opinion of most of his generals, who were almost unanimously in favour of closing the pincer, Hitler prevented the tanks from completing the encirclement and surrounding the BEF and the best units of the French army. On 26 May General Halder noted with disappointment in his diary that the tanks remained "rooted to the spot". The Luftwaffe could see from the air that the beaches were becoming increasingly crowded with soldiers. David Irving refers to the human tide flowing into the harbour and notes that "the roads were jammed with columns of lorries fifteen miles long".

It was not until the evening of the 26th that Rundstedt authorised the advance to continue; but the momentum had already been lost. On 27 May the Germans realised that in the almost three days they had been at a standstill the British had had time to organise a strong defensive cordon that served to stop the penetration and allow "Operation Dynamo", the code name for the evacuation, which began on 27 May and was suspended at 0230 on the morning of 4 June 1940, the day Guderian's Panzers arrived in the harbour. In these eight days some 226,000 British and 112,500 French troops were able to leave France. Another 40,000 remained on the ground and surrendered. Seven hundred tanks, 2,400 guns and 50,000 vehicles were abandoned.

The facts being stated, it is inevitably clear that Hitler's unhealthy Anglophilia was the cause of serious damage to Germany. It is not understandable, in our opinion, that Hitler continued to pursue towards Great Britain a strategy which the facts had repeatedly disavowed. It is not understandable why, having the bulk of the enemy army in his hands, he refused to consider the suggestions of Räder and Jodl for the final defeat of Great Britain. If the British Expeditionary Force had been destroyed in France, Italy and Germany would have been able to take Gibraltar and control North Africa and Mare Nostrum. The threat of invasion would have prevented the British from holding on to the Mediterranean. Nor can it be understood that Hitler acted as if he did not know that the Rothschilds and other Jewish bankers controlled England and the United States, whose governments were in the hands of their agents. The Dunkirk mystery is, however, just one more of those surrounding the enigmatic figure of Hitler.

Chapter 8 has already dealt with the numerous contradictions and inconsistencies that punctuate Adolf Hitler's life and political activities. The enigma begins with his paternal grandmother, Maria Anna Schicklgruber, whose son Alois (Hitler's father) was a bastard, supposedly conceived as a result of illegitimate relations with the wealthy Jewish Frankenberger. Fritz Thyssen, one of Hitler's financiers, reveals in *I Paid Hitler* that grandmother

Schicklgruber became pregnant while serving as a maid in Salomon Rothschild's house in Vienna, which is why some authors see Frankenberger as a front man for the banker. 2. In 1909 Hitler befriended the founder of the magazine *Ostara* and the ONT (Order of the New Templars), a Gnostic Kabbalist named Adolf Josef Lanz, who concealed his Jewish origin and was in reality a Zionist claiming Palestine for the Jews. While preaching racial purity, Lanz married the Jewess Liebenfels, and thus became known as Georg Lanz von Liebenfels. 3. In 1920 two Jewish friends of Hitler, the British double agent Moses Pinkeles, alias Trebisch-Lincoln, and Ernst Hanfstängl, "Putzi", who became Roosevelt's wartime adviser, provided most of the money that enabled the NSDAP to buy the *Völkischer Beobachter* newspaper. 4. Between 1929 and 1933 Hitler met three times with James Paul Warburg, son of Paul Warburg and representative of the same Jewish bankers who had created the Federal Reserve cartel and financed the Bolshevik Revolution. As a result of these meetings, the Nazis received funding from Wall Street. Hitler evidently knew that he was receiving money from the most powerful international Jewish bankers and allowed himself to be used. 5. Let us also remember that Hitler's collaboration with the Zionists was instrumental in laying the foundations of the future Jewish state. While Judea declared war on Germany, a proclamation that appeared in a seven-column headline on the front page of the *Daily Express* on 24 March 1933, the Nazis and the Zionists signed the Haavara Agreement, which allowed some sixty thousand German Jews to emigrate to Palestine with more than $100 million, then a fortune. Zionist writer Edwin Black admits that this agreement was "indispensable" to the creation of Israel. 6. We will end this recapitulation by recalling that the very powerful B'nai B'rith lodge was able to carry out its conspiratorial work in Germany until 1939.

A not very credible and unprovable thesis

In 2005 Greg Hallett published the book *Hitler Was a British Agent*, a work that insists that Hitler was a puppet in the hands of the conspirators who provoked World War II, who used him as a scapegoat. Without providing any definitive proof, Hallett claims that Hitler was a British agent, as was Wilhelm Canaris, the head of the military secret service (Abwehr). Of Canaris, Bernard Fay, who worked on Petain's orders between 1940 and 1944 with Masonic documents in France, says in *La guerre des trois fous* (*The War of the Three Fools*) that "he fought Nazism like a crusader intent on destroying an infectious monster", and adds that "a few days before the offensive of May 1940 he had warned the British General Staff." Greg Hallett, who warns that we cannot normally accept the truth because it does not pass the filters placed on it through education, relies on testimonies of retired intelligence agents; but also on texts and statements that can be verified. According to Hallett, historians and even Hitler's biographer John Toland have ignored Hitler's stay in England.

Hitler's sister-in-law, Bridget Hitler, née Bridget Dowling, published *The Memoirs of Bridget Hitler* in 1979. The book is of no interest, but in it Bridget certifies that her brother-in-law Adolf Hitler lived in her house in Liverpool. We have a copy of the book and can see how this woman, who was seduced by Alois Hitler, a half-brother of Hitler's whom she met in Dublin in 1909, recounts her personal experiences with the future Führer. To begin with, it should be noted that Hitler concealed his stay in England in *Mein Kampf*. In his autobiographical account he says that he left Vienna in May 1912 for Munich, but Bridget Hitler's work shows that this is not true: it was not until May 1913, a year later, that he arrived in Munich from England, not Vienna.

Here is a brief account of Hitler's stay in England, where he arrived at the age of twenty-three. In November 1912 Alois and Bridget went to Liverpool's Lime Street station to meet Angela Hitler and her husband Leo Raubal, a customs official in Vienna. Both had been invited to spend a few days with them. Instead of Leo and Angela Raubal," Bridget writes, "a poor-looking young man approached and shook hands with Alois. It was my husband's younger brother, Adolf, who had come in his place." Alois's indignant reaction startled his wife: "He was furious, disregarding the place, spoke so harshly and loudly that all the people looked at us in astonishment." At first, the newcomer endured the rebuke without complaint, but soon began to retort even more vehemently. At the height of the argument, Bridget continues, "Adolf moved closer and grabbed Alois' coat by the lapels. For a moment the tension was so high that I thought about leaving; they had forgotten I was there. I left them. This is how Bridget recounts in her book the first meeting with the future chancellor of Germany.

Both brothers did not turn up until the evening at 102 Upper Stanhope Street, Princes Road, a three-bedroom flat, where the guest was accommodated in the room prepared for the Raubals. The anger between the two was gone and their mood was friendly. "Adolf, however, was completely exhausted. His pallor and lassitude were so marked," writes the narrator, "that I feared he was ill. Immediately after dinner he retired." Bridget explains that she then took the opportunity to reproach her husband for the scene at the station and explains that when Alois replied he did so sarcastically by saying, "You don't understand. If you knew everything you would feel as I do.... I had invited Angela and her husband. I had not invited that useless Adolf. He is a disgrace to all of us. I don't want to have anything to do with him". Let us now look at an excerpt selected by Greg Hallet:

> "My brother-in-law stayed with us from November 1912 to April 1913, and I cannot imagine a less interesting and unpleasant guest. At first he stayed in his room, sleeping or lying on the sofa which he used as a bed

most of the time. I had the impression that he was sick, so bad was his colour and so strange was his look. I felt sorry for him despite what Alois had told me. When I washed his shirt - he hadn't brought any luggage - the collar was so threadbare that it wasn't even worth turning it inside out. I persuaded Alois to give him some things and he didn't mind doing so. In fact I think he would have been more willing to help Adolf if Adolf hadn't been so ungrateful and complicated. Adolf underestimated everything we did."

Hallett attributes the bad colour and peculiar look in his eyes to the brainwashing he was subjected to by MI6 during the months he was indoctrinated, but this is obviously only a personal interpretation.

Bridget tells how Adolf would go to the kitchen, accompany her while she prepared the food and play with her little boy, William Patrick. There he expressed to her the great disappointment he felt at not being able to enter the Academy of Art in Vienna. Alois took him to London several times; "but he soon began to move about on his own and did not return," Bridget notes, "until late at night. Although it has been said that Hitler learned English during his time in England, his sister-in-law denies this. According to her, he knew only a few words. Another interesting piece of information in Bridget Hitler's memoirs concerns astrology. She claims that it was in Liverpool that Adolf's interest was awakened. An astrologer, Mrs Prentice, "did his horoscope over and over again."

Tired of his brother's presence, Alois proposed that he go to America and even offered to pay for the trip. At first," says Bridget, "Adolf was enthusiastic, but within a few weeks his interest waned. He argued that he should first learn English." As the stay in the Liverpool house dragged on, the brothers' relationship became strained and the hosts began to think about how to get rid of the embarrassing guest who was disrupting family life with his presence. When it was hinted to him that he should leave, his words were: "You cannot expect me to go until I can stand on my own feet. Surely this is not asking too much of a brother." At last Alois, after angry discussions, finally convinced his brother that he should travel to Munich and bore the expenses of the journey. "When I think of his departure," Bridget writes, "I see again the pale, thin face and haggard eyes of my brother-in-law as he hurriedly kissed me and Alois before boarding the train. Leaning out of the window as the train was leaving the station he shouted something that ended 'Zukunft wirst du erstatten von mir erhallten'." The translation would be: "In the future I will repay you for what I have received". Words that were unwelcome to Alois, for, he told his wife, they had a double meaning. When Adolf Hitler arrived in Munich in May 1913, he had just turned twenty-four.

Another surprising statement in Hallet's work concerns the death of Adolf Hitler, who, according to the author, did not commit suicide in the Berlin bunker. Once again, there are very interesting testimonies that make it possible, at the very least, to consider this contingency. One of the texts that cast doubt on the official version was written by US Secretary of State James Francis Byrnes, considered one of the all-powerful Bernard Baruch's men in Washington, who, in his book *Speaking Frankly*, published in 1947, recounts a conversation he had with Stalin on 17 July 1945 in Potsdam. Here is an excerpt:

> "... The President (Truman) quite informally asked Stalin, Molotov and Pavlov, the qualified Soviet interpreter, to stay and have lunch with him. They agreed. The conversation was of a general nature and very cordial. The President was favourably impressed by Stalin, as I had been at Yalta. Speaking of our visit to Berlin, I asked the Generalissimo (Stalin) his opinion of how Hitler had died. To my surprise he said that he believed Hitler was alive and that it was possible that he was in Spain or Argentina. About ten days later I asked him if he had changed his mind and he said he had not."

That is, the person who was supposed to confirm that Hitler was dead, since it was Red Army soldiers who arrived at the bunker where he supposedly committed suicide, instead of giving news of the discovery of the body, twice told Secretary of State James F. Byrnes that he believed Hitler was alive. To refute Soviet insinuations that Hitler was not dead and had been protected by the Allies, Hugh Trevor-Roper, who worked for British Military Intelligence during the war, was commissioned by the government to investigate the death of Adolf Hitler. In 1947 he published the book *Hitler's Last Days*. Trevor-Roper was a friend and colleague of the famous Soviet spy Kim Philby, whom he accused after the war of preventing Admiral Wilhelm Canaris from overthrowing Hitler's regime in order to negotiate with the British government.

We cannot, of course, accept without significant hesitation the theories of Greg Hallett, who believes that British agents got Hitler out of Berlin at the last moment; nevertheless, since the "Halt Befehl" was an order bordering on treason, we wanted to provide them so that the reader can judge for himself whether or not they deserve any credibility.

The Armistice and the British. Jewish agents surround De Gaulle

After Dunkirk, Ribbentrop asked the Führer if he should draft a plan for peace with Britain. David Irving quotes Hitler's reply: "No, I will do that myself. It will be only a few points. The first is that nothing must be done which might in any way hurt Britain's prestige; secondly, Britain must return to us one or two of our former colonies; and thirdly, we must reach a stable modus vivendi with Britain." A few days later, on 10 June 1940, Italy officially declared war on France and Britain. A day earlier, the front had completely broken down and the Germans had launched themselves in pursuit of the French troops, who were fleeing in disarray amidst a tide of millions of refugees.

On 11 June Churchill landed in France aboard his Flamingo aircraft, which was escorted by eleven Hurricane fighter planes. With him were Anthony Eden, appointed Secretary of State for War, and Generals Dill, Ismay and Spears. The latter, described by the French diplomat Paul Cambon as "an intriguing Jew who was getting in everywhere", was the son of Isaac Spiers and Hannah Moses and had changed his surname in 1918 to hide his Jewish origin. This delegation held a decisive meeting with members of Paul Reynaud's government, including Marshal Petain, who on 17 May had left the embassy in Madrid to take over the defence portfolio; Jeroboam Rothschild, alias Georges Mandel; Brigadier Charles De Gaulle; and Maxime Weygand, a general of Belgian origin who on 17 May had replaced Gamelin. General Weygand was considered the natural son of King Leopold II of Belgium and had been raised by a wealthy Sephardic Jew with far-reaching business and international connections, David de Leon Cohen, an adviser to the monarch. The meeting took place at Muguet Castle, Weygand's headquarters. In the course of the talks Churchill tried his best to keep France fighting and proposed an all-out resistance, but offered no effective help.

On 12 June, the French Council of Ministers met in the afternoon at the Château de Cangé, the residence of Albert Lebrun, President of the Republic. Petain insisted on the need to ask for an armistice, so the Council decided to summon the British for the following day, 13 June. Churchill was accompanied by Lord Halifax, Lord Beaverbrook, a Jewish newspaper magnate whom Churchill had just appointed Minister for Aircraft Production, Alexander Cadogan, and Generals Ismay and Spears. President Lebrun received them, accompanied by the new Foreign Minister, Paul Baudoin, and asked the British to allow France to disengage from its commitments. Churchill pointed out that President Roosevelt had to be informed first and awaited his reply; but he eventually said that he understood the French position and resignedly left the chateau with his delegation. Weygand and Petain, who refused to leave France to go to Africa, as the Prime Minister proposed, asked Reynaud to request an armistice, which he did on 15 June, with the French capital already occupied by German troops.

The Council of Ministers, meeting on the afternoon of 15 June 1940 at Petain's request, took the decision not to move to Africa unless the armistice conditions were truly unacceptable. Admiral Darlan raised the question of the navy, whose possible surrender to the Germans so worried the British that at 1330 hours on the 16th they demanded that the fleet sail for British ports before negotiations with Germany could begin. Reynaud himself considered London's request reasonable, since, he pointed out, the fleet was essentially protecting the Mediterranean. At 15:45, the British made a new demand: that the air force should take off for England or North Africa. Faced with these demands, Marshal Petain threatened to resign.

Jean Lombard Coeurderoy explains in *The Hidden Face of Modern History* that London then decided to offer an astonishing solution: nothing less than the union of the two Empires with a common Parliament. The text of the proposal, approved by the British government, was drafted by three personalities who were to hold important posts in the post-war period: the financier Emmanuel Monick, René Plevén and Jean Monnet, the last two of whom were trusted by the Lazards, Jewish bankers based in Paris, London and New York who were part of the founding cartel of the Federal Reserve in 1913. At the outbreak of World War II, Monnet had been appointed head of the Franco-British Economic Coordination Committee. The vice-president of the French government, Camille Chautemps, flatly refused to accept that his country should become a British "Dominion". When the proposal was put to a vote, the French Council of Ministers backed the Vice-President and rejected the British proposal by 14 votes to 10. At 19:30 on the same day, 16 June, President Reynaud resigned.

On 17 June, Marshal Petain formed an eleven-member government and, with the mediation of the Spanish ambassador in Paris, José Félix de Lequerica, and the Vatican nuncio, asked Germany for an end to hostilities and the terms of the armistice. On the same day, General Spears left France, taking with him in his plane Brigadier Charles De Gaulle, who the night before had surreptitiously asked him for a seat in his plane. De Gaulle, in addition to voluminous documents, took 100,000 francs of secret funds with him to London. On the 18th and 19th he gave vibrant radio addresses over the BBC microphones, addressing the French people with these words: "I, General de Gaulle, am conscious of speaking on behalf of France".

The Germans had seized a document dated 9 November 1939 which discussed the reparations France would impose on Germany after Hitler's defeat. Despite the harsh terms of the armistice contained in this document, the conditions offered by Hitler were extremely flexible. On 20 June, Admiral Räder asked Hitler if Germany would demand the surrender of the French fleet, which was the third largest in the world. The Führer replied that the German Navy had no right to demand the French ships since they had not been beaten. Moreover, the fleet was beyond their reach and the French should retain it to preserve their colonial interests. On the 21st the German Chancellor went to the forest of Compiègne to sign the armistice in the same wooden dining car that had been used by the French in 1918. General Keitel read a preamble that had been drafted by Hitler himself, from which the following extract is taken: "After heroic resistance, France has been defeated. Therefore Germany has no intention of conferring on the terms of the armistice or the negotiations an abusive character on so gallant an enemy. The sole aim of the German demands is to prevent any resumption of war, to provide Germany with the necessary safeguard for her continuation of the struggle against Great Britain, and to make possible the dawn of a new peace, the main element of which will be the rectification of the brutal injustices imposed on the German Reich ".

On the evening of 22 June 1940, the armistice was signed, which provided that the Germans would occupy the northern part of France, including Paris, as well as the entire Atlantic coast up to the Spanish border. The French government would cooperate with the German forces and have administrative responsibility for the whole country. The French Government would have to pay for the support of the occupying troops. All French troops would have to be demobilised, but the French Empire would remain intact. Germany did not even reclaim Cameroon and Togo, colonies that France had taken from it at Versailles. Henry Coston, author of the five-volume *Dictionaire de la politique française,* quotes Marshal Petain's words to General Alphonse Joseph Georges on the generous terms of the armistice: "In granting us this armistice the Germans have made a great mistake. We had nothing to defend ourselves and if they had demanded the fleet we would have had to give it to them." Four years later, in 1944, Churchill confessed in Marrakesh to this same general that "Hitler had made a mistake in granting the armistice to France." As Churchill told General Georges, "he should have marched into North Africa, seized it and gone on to Egypt."

After Reynaud's resignation, the President of the Republic considered Marshal Philippe Petain the most suitable person to head the government and he was voted in by the National Assembly. The Vichy government, with the exception of Great Britain, was thus recognised by all the countries of the world, including the United States and the USSR. The armistice did not require France to break off relations with London, so it must be made clear that it was the British who did not recognise their former ally. On 27 June Churchill ordered "Operation Catapult". On 2 July 1940, ten days after the armistice was signed, a Royal Navy fleet left Gibraltar for the Algerian port of Mers-el-Kebir in the Gulf of Oran, where part of the French fleet was stationed, including four battleships, four cruisers, a super destroyer division and a flotilla of destroyers. British Admiral Sommerville demanded that Admiral Gensoul hand over all the ships, i.e. the surrender of the fleet. When he refused, at 16:53 on 3 July, the British opened fire on the French ships, most of which had their guns pointed towards land and their engines switched off, so that only a few of them managed to get out to sea. To prevent them from leaving the bay, British aircraft lit the harbour with magnetic mines. 1,300 French sailors were killed and several hundred wounded. The British lost only four aircraft and two torpedo boats. Necessarily, France broke off diplomatic relations with the UK. It can be said that Mers-el-Kebir was the French Pearl Harbour.

French public opinion thus saw that its former ally, contrary to what Germany had done, was demanding the surrender of the fleet. The fact that the attack had been carried out treacherously and without any justification provoked a growing sense of Anglophobia among the population. In the face of French bewilderment, on 8 July de Gaulle justified the action and declared that the French government had consented to hand over the ships to the enemy, who would have used them against England or the French Empire. De Gaulle stated bluntly: "Well, I will say it bluntly, it is better that they were destroyed". It must be said that on 23 June 1940, as punishment for his speeches from London, the President of the Republic had signed Charles de Gaulle's dismissal from the Army, and the following day, 24 June, Foreign Minister Baudoin sent the following message to the Foreign Office: "The French Government considers it an act of enmity to allow a French general to launch on British radio a call for revolt against its decisions."

The French National Committee was born in London, which initially served to proclaim that the Vichy government did not represent France and to justify actions such as that of Mers-el Quebir. It later became the French National Liberation Committee. As early as 1944, this body became the provisional government. De Gaulle was soon surrounded by a host of politicians and agents of Jewish origin. From the outset, two heavyweights stood alongside him: Maurice Schumann and René Samuel Casin. The former became the head of Propaganda from July 1940 and spoke on more than a thousand occasions on Radio London. Schumann, indispensable to de Gaulle, took advantage of his conversion to Catholicism to serve as a link between the French Zionists and the Vatican. The latter was a Zionist member of the Universal Israelite Alliance who achieved international fame as a jurist. Casin went into exile in London with de Gaulle in 1940 and was one of his spokesmen. There he laid the foundations of the Constitution of the Fourth Republic. In 1943 he represented the Liberation Committee on the War Crimes Commission set up by the Allies, and in 1944 he worked at the Ministry of Justice to enable the French military justice system to try the Nazis.

Among the most prominent Jews placed in General de Gaulle's entourage were the following: Hervé Alphand, a commercial expert who was in charge of economic and financial matters. René Mayer, son of the Grand Rabbi of Paris Michel Mayer and agent of the Rothschild banking interests, was in charge of Communications and was a member of the Liberation Committee until de Gaulle appointed him Minister of Transport and Public Works in 1944. He was later Vice-President of the Universal Israelite Alliance. Daniel Mayer, who founded the Socialist Action Committee in January 1941 and received orders from the General to unite the groups operating in France into a single organisation: the CNR (Conseil National de la Résistance). Marie-Pierre Koenig, a general who was at De Gaulle's side from the beginning and later became Minister of Defence. Admiral Louis-Lazare Kahn, who on behalf of General de Gaulle's government participated with the Allies in the anti-submarine struggle in the Atlantic. Georges Boris, a British liaison officer evacuated from Dunkirk, was appointed by de Gaulle to be in charge of Free French contacts with the BBC. Some saw him as the Bernard Baruch of France, having been an adviser to several French prime ministers. Pierre Mendès France, a Sephardite of Portuguese origin, arrived in London in 1941 and in 1943 de Gaulle appointed him Finance Commissioner of the French Committee of National Liberation. In 1944 he signed the Bretton Woods agreements, which were to shape post-war world economic policy, and in 1953 he became prime minister. André Diethelm, who became Vice-President of the National Assembly in the post-war period, held a number of commissionerships until 1944, when he was appointed Commissioner for Production of the Liberation Committee and in the same year became Minister of War. Jean Pierre-Bloch, a Freemason of the "Liberté" lodge and president of B'nai B'rith France after the liberation, arrived in London in 1942 and became head of counter-espionage. Marc Bloch, chairman of the Liberation Committee whose nom de guerre was "Narbonne", was in charge of preparing the Allied landing in France. He was eventually discovered by the Gestapo and shot. Carole Fink, author of *Marc Bloch. A Life for History*, reveals the names of a string of Jews who led the Resistance. Among them are Raymond Aubrac, Maurice Krigel-Varlimont, Max Heilbronn, Jean Pierre Lévy, Georges Altman, André Kaan, Georgette Lévy, Léo Hammon, Jean Maurice Hermann, André Weil-Curiel, Jacques Brunschwig-Bordier, Robert Hirsh, who in 1951 was appointed Director General of National Security by De Gaulle.

The plan to exterminate the German race for good

Instead of disseminating them properly, official historians have preferred to bury texts such as Theodore N. Kaufman's *Germany must perish*, Henry Morgenthau Jr.'s *Morgenthau Diary*, or Michel Bar Zohar's *Les Vengeurs* in oblivion. We will be presenting them in due course in this book. It is now time to turn our attention to Kaufman's book, since chronologically it is the first to appear. Before commenting on it, it is useful to situate it in the time when it was written and published, by outlining in a few paragraphs the war situation and Hitler's illusory plans.

After the quixotic gesture at Dunkirk and the signing of the surprising armistice with France, Hitler set out to return to Berlin in order to make a public peace offer to Britain in the Reichstag. Admiral Räder insisted on the need to attack the main naval bases at once and prepare for the invasion; but the Führer did not want to unleash the Luftwaffe and had even forbidden any attack with threats of court martial, which he felt might provoke irreparable hatred. Incoherently, he still believed that after the defeat of France the British would listen to reason. In his peace plans, Hitler had thought of a solution to the Jewish problem. His plan was to ask France for the island of Madagascar to accommodate the European Jews. During the summer of

1940, Foreign Office experts worked intensively on the deportation. Reichsführer SS Heinrich Himmler issued corresponding instructions to the police generals in Eastern Europe, and Hans Frank, the Governor General, was relieved to receive the order to stop the transfer of Jews to the General Government of Poland. All Jews, including those already on Polish territory, were to be deported to Madagascar.

It must be stressed again that these plans were made on the assumption that London would eventually accept them. What is surprising is how unrealistic were the premises on which this hope was based. Documents captured in France by the German occupiers demonstrated unequivocally the kind of war the British were preparing. A secret document from 1939 clearly stated that Germany was to be defeated and dismembered. David Irving reports that among the written records of the Supreme War Council he found one dated November 1939, which stated that Chamberlain had unveiled the plan for the destruction of the Ruhr by long-range bombers. Aerial photographs had been taken and models of the entire industrial region had been built. The British Prime Minister himself had admitted the havoc the bombing would wreak on the civilian population. In fact, the order to implement this plan was given on 11 May 1940, two weeks before Dunkirk. The first secretary of the British Air Ministry, J. M. Spaight, called the order a "splendid decision", as reported by Frederick John Partington Veale, author of *Advance to barbarism*, a remarkable work on air terror and other crimes of the victors, to which we shall return when we study the Dresden Holocaust.

Hitler returned to Berlin on 6 July. On 14 July he made a statement to the United Press declaring his readiness to accept any mediation that would lead to a settlement with the United Kingdom. On the 16th he half-heartedly accepted an outline from General Jodl ordering the Wehrmacht to prepare for the invasion of Britain "should it become necessary". On 19 July 1940 the long-awaited speech before the Reichstag finally took place, in which the German Chancellor, despite the fact that since May the British had begun a night-time air offensive which had caused great unrest in German cities, appealed to "Britain's common sense" and offered peace and a return to the 1939 borders in the West and an agreement with Poland. While in Europe Germany was still looking for ways to prevent the extension of the war, in the United States Roosevelt had begun to prepare his future intervention. On 16 May 1940, in a message to Congress, he set a target of 50,000 aircraft per year. On 31 May the Supreme Council of the Scottish Rite, meeting in Washington, pledged to promote intervention.

On 3 August 1940 Churchill rejected the good offices of the King of Sweden, which were the last attempt at mediation before the Battle of Britain began. From 8 August until 5 September, the Luftwaffe attacked ports, airfields, aircraft factories and other military targets. On 27 August, however, RAF planes bombed Berlin, and during the following nights the attacks became increasingly virulent. German cities in the Ruhr had been under bombardment for three and a half months. With the bombs falling on the Reich's capital, Hitler finally opened his eyes and ordered night air raids on London. If they proclaim that they will launch full-scale attacks on our cities," he said angrily, "we will wipe out their cities. Nevertheless, he did not allow saturation bombing raids on the residential areas of the English capital, as Jeschonnek, Göring's chief of staff, had requested. The main targets were to be railway stations, industry, gas and water reservoirs, "not the population for the time being". From 7 September to 2 November 1940, London was bombed nightly, the most deadly of which was the industrial centre of Coventry.

On 28 October 1940 Italy attacked Greece from Albania, a declaration of war. This action was to provoke the extension of the European conflict to the Balkans in the early months of 1941. It was against this background of war that *Germany must perish*, the work by Theodore N. Kaufmann, which we now turn to, was published. Kaufman, a Manhattan-born Jew who was president of the American Federation for Peace, proposed in his work the systematic sterilisation of the entire population of Germany in order to exterminate it forever. The text was printed in late 1940 or early 1941. A second edition was published in March 1941 by Argyle Press of Newark, New Jersey. It was not until July 1941, however, that the Nazis discovered the book and, in addition to being shocked, decided to use the pamphlet for propaganda. On 23 July, an article appeared on the front page of the newspaper *Der Angriff* with the headline "Diabolical Plan for the Extermination of the German People", calling the work an example of "Old Testament hatred". On 24 July, the *Völkischer Beobachter, an* NSDAP newspaper, also published on its front page an article entitled "The product of Jewish criminal sadism". The newspaper claimed that Kaufman was an associate of Samuel Irving Rosenman, the conspicuous ideologue of the Brain Trust and advisor to Roosevelt in the White House. Excerpts from the book appeared on 3 August in the weekly *Das Reich*, which was published nationwide. Joseph Göbbels ordered the book to be translated and printed about a million copies with Roosevelt's picture on the cover. This translation was distributed to German soldiers in order to make them aware of the terrible fate the Jews had foreseen for them if they lost the war.

Although it has been said that the book had much impact in Germany and very little in the United States, major Jewish-owned newspapers such as *The New York Times* and the *Washington Post* devoted to it commentaries that are not to be sniffed at. The former called it "a blueprint for permanent peace among civilised nations". The latter referred to Kaufman's proposal as "a provocative theory presented in an interesting way". According to the *Times Magazine*, the project was "a sensational idea!" The *Philadelphia Record*, that city's leading newspaper, felt that the work of Kaufman, who was a member of the American Jewish Congress, "presented with complete sincerity the dreadful undercurrent of the Nazi soul." It should be noted that *Germany must perish* appeared almost a year before the United States entered the war and that the Auschwitz prison camp was not even open.

The sterilisation plan was presented in the book as the most practical way to exterminate the German race, since a massacre "was impracticable when it had to be carried out on a population of seventy million people". Kaufman regarded his proposal as a "modern method" that science called "eugenic sterilisation", the best way to "rid mankind of its misfits: degenerates, insane and hereditary criminals." He warned that sterilisation should not be confused with castration, as it was a much simpler and quicker operation lasting no more than ten minutes, although he acknowledged that in the case of women it was somewhat more complicated. The sterilisation of the German people, according to Kaufman, was a health measure that should be "promoted by mankind in order to immunise itself against the virus of Germanism". To implement his plan he proposed the following methodology:

> "The population of Germany, excluding annexed and conquered territories, is about 70 million, almost equally divided between males and females. To achieve the purpose of the extinction of the Germans it would be necessary to sterilise only 48 million - a figure which excludes, because of their limited power to procreate, males over sixty and females over forty-five. With regard to the males subject to sterilisation, the army corps, as organised units, would be the easiest and quickest way to operate. Taking 20,000 surgeons as an arbitrary figure, and assuming that each of them performed a minimum of twenty-five operations a day, it would take no more than a month at the most to complete sterilisation. Naturally, the more doctors available, and there could be many more than 20,000 available considering all the nations that could be called upon, the less time would be required..... If it is considered that the sterilisation of females needs a little more time, it must be calculated that the females of Germany could be sterilised in a period of three years or less.... Of course, after complete sterilisation, there would no longer be a birth rate in Germany. With a death rate of 2 per cent a year, life in Germany would decrease by one and a half million people a year....".

Again and again Jewish authors such as the aforementioned Kaufman, Morgenthau, Bar Zohar emphasised unequivocally that the war was not against the Nazis, but against the German people. Before the Nuremberg laws and almost two years before the war, the Zionist leader Vladimir Jabotinsky had clearly announced this in January 1934 in an article published in *Mascha Rjetsch*:

> "The struggle against Germany has been unleashed for months now in every Jewish community, at every conference, in every trade union of

workers and by every Jew throughout the world. There is every reason to accept that our participation in this struggle is of general importance. We will start a spiritual and material war of the whole world against Germany. Germany is striving to become a great nation again, and to regain its lost territories as well as its colonies. But our Jewish interests demand the complete destruction of Germany."

Theodore N. Kaufman repeatedly insists on this idea in the book we have just reviewed: "This war is fought against the Germans. It is they who are responsible. It is they who must pay for the war. Otherwise there will always be a German war against the world. And with this sword hanging permanently over the civilised nations, however great their hopes and however arduous their efforts, they will never achieve permanent peace." Despite the fact that it was the international Jewish organisations that in 1933 declared war on Germany, Kaufman places all the blame for bringing the world to war on the Germans. In fact, this has always been taught in high schools and universities around the world, especially in Germany, thanks to the role played by official historiography. Kaufman was particularly furious with the German soul, which he compared to that of wild beasts, which can only live in the jungle:

> "I feel no more personal hatred for these people than I could feel for a herd or for wild animals or for a group of poisonous reptiles. One does not hate those whose souls cannot exude any spiritual warmth; one only feels pity. If the German people want to live by themselves, in darkness, it is strictly their own affair. But if they make constant attempts to wrap the souls of other peoples in the fetid wrappings that cover their own, the time comes when they must be expelled from the realm of civilised humanity, among which they can have no place or right to exist."

At the end of September 1941 Wolfgang Diewerge wrote a booklet of some thirty pages entitled *Das Kriegsziel der Weltplutocratie* (*The War Aim of the World Plutocracy*), published in Berlin by the NSDAP publishing house. It insisted that Theodore N. Kaufman was not a Talmudic fanatic acting alone, but moved in the circles of Jewish advisors to President Roosevelt, hence he presented himself as a pacifist patriot, philosopher and anthropologist seeking the good of mankind. In 1944, in order to stimulate resistance in the face of the inevitable defeat, the Nazis published a four-page pamphlet entitled *Never!* recalling Kaufman's genocidal plan and other dire threats made by the Allies against Germany.

Rudolf Hess' flight to Scotland

Almost coincidentally with the appearance in the United States of the plan for the extermination by sterilisation of the Germans, Rudolf Hess made his famous flight to Scotland. Plans for the invasion of Russia had been under consideration since the early months of 1941, and Hitler still longed for peace with Britain so that he could concentrate the full power of the Wehrmacht on attacking the Soviet Union. It was in this context that the last attempt to stop the war with the British took place. At 17:40 on 10 May 1941 Rudolf Hess flew from Ausburg to Scotland to offer Churchill's government a peace plan supposedly drawn up in October 1940.

In *Hitler's War* David Irving seems to give credence to the idea that Hess travelled at his own risk to Glasgow to meet the Duke of Hamilton, a true friend of Germany whom he had met in 1936. Irving recounts the scene of Hitler's astonishment before General Karl Bodenschatz, Göring's representative, when an aide to Hess burst into the great hall of the Berghof and handed the Führer a thin envelope. The General opened it and handed the two pages it contained to Hitler, who put on his spectacles and began to read listlessly. Suddenly he stood up and exclaimed in a voice so loud that it could be heard throughout the house: "Oh my God, my God, he has flown to Britain!" Numerous onlookers flocked into the room and Hitler angrily asked Hess's adjutant why he had not reported it earlier. His reply was that he had not done so out of loyalty to his boss. The Führer then addressed the Bodenschaft: "Why, General, did the Luftwaffe allow Hess to fly even though I had forbidden it? Let Göring come forward!" It seems clear to us that Hitler was overreacting to hide from his sceptical generals that for the umpteenth time he was seeking a pact with Britain. We do not find it credible that Rudolf Hess would have taken such a momentous decision without the Führer's permission. Logically, the German Chancellor knew that to announce that Rudolf Hess had travelled officially with a separate peace plan between Germany and the United Kingdom was tantamount to breaking the Axis and leaving his allies in the lurch.

Whatever the case, the BBC finally announced on the 12th that Rudolf Hess had parachuted into Scotland and little else. It is to Hess's credit and courage that, after avoiding anti-aircraft fire and Spitfire pursuit, he parachuted, although he had never parachuted before, resulting in a sprained ankle. Naturally, his mission was unsuccessful. Through the mediation of the Duke of Hamilton, Hess planned to meet King George VI and Churchill to convince them that the Führer did not want to continue the "senseless war" and that "the real enemy was Russia". As is well known, Rudolf Hess did not talk to the king or to Churchill, who, unaware that Hess had come to propose peace, did not allow him to return to Germany and had him imprisoned. Churchill later wrote that he had not been "directly responsible for the manner in which Hess was treated". The notorious Spandau prisoner would die in prison in 1987 at the age of 93, a victim of the victors' "justice". The British government seized the documents Hess was carrying with him and decided that they would not be made public until 2017, which suggests that their contents may reveal some interesting information.

Part 3
Pearl Harbour: Roosevelt Immolates His Sailors to Enter the War

Although polls revealed that Americans were stubbornly hostile to their country's entry into the war, Roosevelt's anti-German manoeuvres increased as the conflagration progressed. In June 1940 only 14% of the population supported intervention. A year later the percentage had risen to 21%, and by September 1941, despite an intense press campaign, those in favour of abandoning neutrality stood at only 26%. In September 1940 Henry Ford, Charles Lindbergh, General Robert Wood and Douglas Stuart Jr. had founded the anti-war America First Committee, which was supported by the *Chicago Daily Tribune.* Nearly a million people were active in this Committee, which was openly opposed to the "Fight for Freedom" Committee. The latter had been launched on 19 April 1941 by the interventionist lobbies and was formed on the basis of the "Century Group", a creation of the "Council on Foreign Relations", which, as is well known, is a very powerful power structure of the "Round Table" which shapes US foreign policy. The warmongering Committee included such figures as Paul Warburg, the alma mater of the Federal Reserve; Lewis Douglas, another Wall Street luminary linked to the Round Table; Dean Acheson, a member of the CFR; and publicists such as Joseph Alsop, editorial writer for the *Herald Tribune*; Henry Luce, a think tank magnate who was a member of the secret society Skull & Bones and publisher of several publications; Henry Luce, a member of the secret society Skull & Bones and publisher of several publications; and the American media. Bones secret society and publisher of several publications; Elmer Davis, who five times a week indoctrinated Americans in favour of the war on CBS and was appointed by Roosevelt as director of the United States Office of War Information; and other pawns at the helm of major media outlets.

As early as September 1940, the US president violated the Neutrality Act, which prohibited the export of war materials to countries at war, and persuaded Congress to allow him to transfer fifty destroyers to the UK in exchange for the use of eight bases in the Western Hemisphere. This enabled the British fleet to make up for the losses it had suffered in its clashes with the German navy. Having won a third re-election in November 1940 on promises to keep the United States out of the war, Roosevelt asked for full powers, which alarmed much of the country. Clyton Morrison, editor of *The Christian Century,* sensed the intentions of the president's request and wrote: "It will not be a war of the nation, but a war of the president. History will one day judge severely Roosevelt's attitude at this critical time of the world." On 10 January 1941 Roosevelt replaced the "Cash and Carry" formula, which authorised the sale to belligerents of goods without military interest, provided they were paid for in cash and transported on ships of the purchasing countries, with the Lend Lease Act, which allowed sales on credit to Britain. Furthermore, in flagrant violation of neutrality, the goods were transported on American ships under the British flag.

On 29 March 1941, Franklin D. Roosevelt ordered the seizure of German and Italian ships in American ports, a measure that was seconded by Mexico and Cuba. This action, a true act of piracy unbecoming of a neutral country, showed definitively that the United States was preparing to intervene in the war in favour of Britain. A few days later, on 9 April, the Danish ambassador in Washington, Henrik Kaufmann, nicknamed the "King of Greenland", signed an agreement with the United States allowing the occupation of Greenland without Copenhagen's authorisation. The Danish government overruled Kauffmann, dismissed him and prosecuted him for treason, but Roosevelt ignored Danish protests and occupied Greenland, from whose shores he could control naval traffic in the Atlantic.

Roosevelt provokes Germany and puts himself at the service of the USSR

Roosevelt's provocations to the German navy in the Atlantic, seeking a reaction that would justify US entry into the war, intensified as soon as "Operation Barbarossa" began. On 22 June 1941, with the invasion of the United Kingdom definitively ruled out, Hitler ordered the action that all but Stalin had been waiting for: the invasion of the Soviet Union. It was what the Jewish bankers who had brought the Nazis to power had originally intended. Studying the Moscow trials, it has been seen that a German attack on Stalin was supposed to trigger a war that would allow Trotsky to be reinstated in power. By 1941 Trotsky had already been assassinated, so the Jewish Communists proliferating in Roosevelt's "Brain Trust" were confident that after the war Stalin could be replaced by more trusted agents who would enable them to regain absolute control of the vast resources of Asia and of Communism, whose tentacles, as Trotsky had intended in 1918, were to reach all the way to Berlin. The second major objective of Hitler's financing was to unleash the persecution of the Jews, which was to enable Zionism once and for all to create the state of Israel after the war.

Embroiled in a war that encompassed almost all of Europe and had already spread to North Africa and the Middle East, Hitler began on 22 June a headlong flight forward that would have catastrophic consequences for the German people. A week into the invasion of the USSR, Roosevelt sought to hasten the immediate entry of the United States into the war and ordered the deployment of naval patrols in the North Atlantic, which were to detect German submarines and ships. At the end of July 1941, patrols were intensified and orders were given to protect ships sailing in the area, regardless of their flag. In other words, the squadron of a neutral country was to watch, inform on and even attack German warships that might intercept convoys carrying arms and supplies to the Soviet Union and the United Kingdom.

After the attack on Russia began, Roosevelt had sent Harry Hopkins, his right-hand man, to London and Moscow. Paradoxically, he was a Soviet agent, specifically agent "19", as demonstrated in 1995 by the "Venona" documents, about which more will be said later. In mid-July Hopkins met with Churchill in London, where there were numerous American Lend-Lease Act missions arranging the delivery of all sorts of materials, such as the B-17 flying fortresses, which were to kill hundreds of thousands of German civilians in the aerial terror that was to be practised on a massive scale in the years that followed. Hopkins and Churchill signed a joint action agreement that provided for multiple assistance and support in the war against Germany and, although the United States was not yet at war, made a commitment not to negotiate any separate armistice or peace treaty. Robert E. Sherwood recounts in *Roosevelt and Hopkins. An Intimate History* that Hopkins showed Churchill a map on which Roosevelt himself had marked in pencil a line in the Atlantic Ocean, west of which the US navy and aviation would patrol, "thus leaving British escort ships free for service elsewhere, particularly the Murmansk route".

From Scotland Hopkins flew to Archangel and from there to Moscow, where he spent three days. On 30 July he had his first meeting with Stalin, to whom he passed on a message cabled to him by Acting Secretary of State Benjamin Sumner Welles, a Zionist committed to the creation of the State of Israel whose family was related to the Roosevelts. The text, reproduced in Sherwood's work, demonstrates the extent to which the American president, five months before bringing his country into the war, was prepared to defend communist totalitarianism in Russia:

> "The President wishes you, when you first see Stalin, to convey to him the following message on behalf of the President himself:
> Mr. Hopkins is in Moscow at my request to discuss with you personally, and with such other officials as you may designate, the vitally important question of how we can effectively and expeditiously deliver the aid which the United States will render to your country in its magnificent resistance to the treacherous aggression of Hitlerite Germany. I have already informed Mr. Umansky, your ambassador, that the United States Government will give all possible assistance as regards the shipment of ammunition, armaments and other supplies necessary to meet your most urgent requirements and which may come into use in your country during the next two months. We will discuss the details of these matters with the mission which, headed by General Golikov, is now in Washington. I understand that Mr. Hopkins' visit to Moscow will be invaluable, since it will indicate to the United States what your most pressing needs are, so

that we can arrive at the most practical decisions on simplifying and speeding up the delivery of what is requested.

By next winter we will be able to complete whatever material, however much, your government wishes to obtain from this country. Therefore, I believe that the main interest of both governments should concentrate on the material that can arrive in Russia within the next three months.

I ask you to treat Mr. Hopkins with the same confidence that you would feel if you were talking to me directly. He will communicate to me, also directly, the views you put to him and tell me what are the most urgent problems in which we can be of service to you.

Let me express, in conclusion, the great admiration we all feel in the United States for the bravery displayed by the Russian people in defence of their freedom, and in the struggle for Russian independence. The success of the Russian people and of the other peoples in opposing Hitler's aggression and his plans for the conquest of the world has greatly encouraged the American people."

We note the fact that the ambassador to the United States, Konstantin Umansky, was once again a Jew, as was his successor, the ubiquitous and indefatigable Maksim Litvinov, who, after handing over the Commissariat for Foreign Affairs to Molotov in 1939, was sent to Washington in November 1941 to replace Umansky. We already know that the Soviet ambassador to London during the war, Ivan Maisky, was also a Jew and a Zionist. Maisky, as mentioned above, became a close friend of Negrin's and was the man Beria had in mind for the post of Foreign Commissar after Stalin's assassination in 1953. Also the US ambassador in Moscow, Laurence A. Steinhardt, was a Jew. Steinhardt, was also a Zionist Jew. It has already been stated in chapter eight that Steinhardt was the nephew of Samuel Untermayer and was active in the Federation of American Zionists.

Steinhardt was with Hopkins at the Kremlin meeting with Molotov and summarised the interview for the State Department. From his words it is known that Hopkins assured Molotov that Washington would not tolerate any Japanese venture into Siberia. Hopkins' own report confirmed Steinhardt's testimony, for in it he confirms that Molotov told him that if the President (Roosevelt) could find "adequate means of directing a warning to Japan" he would be prevented from attempting any aggressive move. Hopkins writes: "Although Mr. Mólotov did not express himself in the following terms, the implicit meaning of his words was that the warning should include a warning that the United States would come to the aid of the Soviet Union if it were attacked by Japan.

If in 1938 and 1939 Stalin had been suspicious of the intentions of Britain and France, when the invasion began on 22 June 1941, he may have thought that the plot he had fought against in the Moscow trials was returning. He probably feared that this was the first step in a plan with the West to get rid of him, which is why he left his post in fear and left the country and the army without his supreme leadership. This is the only way to understand his attitude and the fear that gripped him. It was Beria who reacted and went looking for him. Khrushchev recounts that when Beria asked him to resume command, Stalin replied, "All is lost. I surrender." Hopkins' visit confirmed to him beyond doubt that things were quite different: he could rely on the United States, since their unconditional help was coming when his country was being invaded. Two months later, on 28 September, William Averell Harriman, a partner in Kuhn, Loeb & Co, a member of the CFR and "Skulls & Bones", arrived in Moscow to set up a new supply programme.

Roosevelt was anxious to start the war against Germany as soon as possible, so incitements soon followed in the Atlantic: US naval patrols were provoking German U-boats by dropping depth charges, but the U-boats were reluctant to respond to the attacks. Hitler had told Admiral Räder that under no circumstances did he want to "provoke an incident that would result in a declaration of war by the United States". A mishap occurred on 4 September that Roosevelt tried to exploit. British aircraft pinpointed to the US destroyer *Greer* the position of the German submarine U-652, which was operating in the sea blockade zone. The *Greer* attacked with depth charges and the U-boat responded by firing two torpedoes that missed the ship. As soon as news of the confrontation reached the United States, Germany was accused of piracy and of attempting to sink a destroyer on its "harmless patrols". Admiral Harold Stark, Chief of Naval Operations, issued a detailed report stating that both the British aircraft and the *Greer* had harassed the submarine for hours, and that both had attacked it with depth charges. On 11 September, President Roosevelt gave the order to "fire on sight". Hitler declared, and I quote: "President Roosevelt has ordered his Navy to fire on sight as soon as they discover our ships. I forbid my commanders to do the same, but I order them to defend themselves if they are attacked. Any officer who violates this order will face court martial."

The paradox of 16 September was that British-flagged convoys were sailing under the protection of warships from a neutral country. Senator Wheeler therefore recognised that Germany had every reason to attack his country. Hopkins put it another way: "If Hitler were inclined to declare war on us, he already has every conceivable excuse." Finally, on 17 October 1941, what Roosevelt had been wishing for happened: the destroyer *Kearny*, escorting a convoy, attacked the German submarine U-568, which in turn had attacked British merchant ships. The U-boat responded with a torpedo that hit the American ship, killing eleven crew members and injuring twenty-two others. Although there were casualties on this occasion, Roosevelt again failed to get the House of Representatives to authorise a declaration of war. As for public opinion, Hopkins lamented that the incident was "taken as a matter of course by the people of the United States". No doubt this was so because Americans knew that it was their president who was exposing

American ships and the lives of seamen. The *Washington Times-Herald* went so far as to report that the families of the victims were receiving painful messages that tortured them: "Your dear son," one said, "was sent to his death by the criminal imbecile at the head of our Government".

A few days after the attack on the *Kearny*, General Robert E. Wood, a member of the America First Committee, publicly requested that the President appear before Congress and ask for a definitive vote on whether or not the United States should enter the war. Robert E. Sherwood writes the following about it in *Roosevelt and Hopkins. An Intimate History*:

> "This was precisely the same demand for swift and bold action which had been advised to Roosevelt by many people, such as Stimson and others, both inside and outside the Government, during the last six months. But the very fact that such a proposal should now come from such a staunch isolationist champion, sufficiently confirmed Roosevelt in his conviction that, if he did as he was told, he would meet with disastrous and certain defeat."

Robert Sherwood and Samuel Rosenman, a Jewish Supreme Court Justice close to arch-missionary Louis D. Brandeis and adviser to Roosevelt, wrote the President's speeches. The words quoted, therefore, come from a very authoritative source. Despite the relentless press campaign in favour of intervention, Roosevelt knew with certainty that public opinion was against the war. Hence, it took an event like the Japanese attack on Pearl Harbour to change the American people's sentiments. Rosenman and Sherwood were the authors of the famous speech of 28 October 1940, in which Roosevelt said the following during the campaign for his third re-election: "I have said this before, but I will say it again, and again, and again, and again: your boys will not be sent to any foreign war.

A few days after the *Kearny* incident, on 31 October, the destroyer *Reuben James* was sunk when another German submarine, U-552, repelled the attack. A torpedo hit her bow and the shell magazine exploded. The ship sank and one hundred and fifteen crew members perished, including all the officers. This time too, Roosevelt did not get permission for a declaration of war. Contrary to expectations, public reaction was increasingly adverse. Sherwood wrote at the time: "There was a sort of tacit understanding among the Americans that none of them should be indignant even if the Germans sank our ships with their submersibles, for such indignation might lead us back to war.

Japan's economic stranglehold

As it became clear that it was impossible to lead the country into war because of the incidents with the Germans in the Atlantic, Roosevelt stepped up measures to economically strangle Japan, which had been engaged in a costly war in China since 1937. In this context, the United States had already decided in 1940 to cut off oil supplies to Tokyo, which had to find other suppliers if it wanted to continue the fight against the Chinese. Initially, the Japanese were able to buy crude oil from Mexico and Venezuela. They also had the alternative of sourcing supplies from the Anglo-Dutch colonies of Burma and Insulindia, which usually supplied the Japanese with oil, rubber and other raw materials without any problems. Roosevelt and his clan of Jewish advisors then decided to pressure Britain and Holland to go along with his oil embargo on Japan. For its part, Standard Oil, of the Rockefeller and Jacob Schiff trust [6], which owned Venezuela's oil, announced that it was suspending shipments. Mexico, under pressure, did the same.

At the time of the German attack on Russia, Japan contemplated taking advantage of the opportunity presented by the invasion of the West to attack the USSR and land troops in Siberia in order to seize the oil fields, which would have been catastrophic for Stalin and helpful to Hitler. Ribbentrop was pushing in this direction; but the Soviets knew this and maintained substantial garrisons of troops there. When Roosevelt received reports warning of Japanese intentions in Siberia, he was quick to issue a warning message and sought assurances from Tokyo that the attack would not take place. Shortly afterwards, as seen above, came the arrival of Harry Hopkins in Moscow, where Molotov expressly requested that the United States let Japan know that it would come to the aid of the Soviet Union if it was attacked. As if that were not enough, on 26 July 1941 Roosevelt ordered a freeze on Japanese funds in the United States, which paralysed Japan's import and export financial operations, most of which worked with American financial institutions. The British and Dutch governments, the latter in exile in London, followed in Roosevelt's footsteps. Thus, with its assets frozen, the Japanese economy was strangled.

Crisis was inevitable. Consequently, the Japanese offered to withdraw from their bases in Indochina in return for the lifting of the embargo and the return of their seized assets, but Roosevelt and Churchill rejected Tokyo's proposal. Nor did they accept Japan's offer to withdraw its troops from China, which, deprived of crude oil, iron and rubber, could not really continue the war. By November 1941, Japan had endured Roosevelt's

---

[6] Standard Oil had been one of the great beneficiaries of the revolution of the Jewish-Bolsheviks, who, despite having nationalised oil, sold it a chain of wells in the Caucasus. Standard Oil built a refinery in Russia and sold Russian oil to European countries. In 1927 the banking firm Kuhn Loeb & Co, owned by Jacob Schiff, the Jewish banker who had financed the revolution, granted the Bolsheviks a new loan of $65 million. In 1928 Rockefeller's Chase National Bank was selling communist state bonds in the US. Between 1917 and 1930 the Rockefeller trust built nineteen large refineries in the USSR, whose industrial equipment and machinery came from the United States. In return the communists granted American companies gold mining rights in Russia.

blockade for four months, and was therefore forced to go to war in order to survive. The British ambassador in Tokyo considered the most likely target for a future Japanese attack to be the Dutch East Indies, where the oil fields could be seized. A secret US Navy report suggested that Japan could attack Russia or the Anglo-Dutch colonies. Attacking Pearl Harbour was an option that did not seem to be contemplated. Even the British Prime Minister, who between 9 and 12 August had held the Atlantic Conference in Newfoundland with the American President and received assurances that the United States would enter the war, was not informed that the attack would take place there.

The US fleet at Pearl Harbour

Under the pseudonym Mauricio Karl, Mauricio Carlavilla published in Madrid in 1954 *Pearl Harbour, Roosevelt's betrayal,* a book containing extremely revealing information about the Japanese attack on Pearl Harbour on Sunday 7 December 1941. There are numerous books and articles written by revisionist authors on Roosevelt's attitude. The first to spark controversy was John T. Flynn, who as early as 1944 published *The Truth about Pearl Harbour,* in which he charged that Roosevelt and his cronies provoked the attack. Today there is no longer any doubt that there was no surprise at Pearl Harbour, but a criminal act, an act of infamy by Roosevelt, who had no qualms about sacrificing some 2,500 Americans in order to involve his country in the Second World War. The merit of Carlavilla's book lies in the fact that he was one of the first writers, perhaps the first in Spanish, to denounce what happened. His work will therefore be used in the following pages, as well as several articles published in *The Journal of Historical Review.*

The squadron's presence at Pearl Harbour was questioned as early as April 1940 by Admiral James O. Richardson. Richardson, who by 1958 had completed his Memoirs. The book, which appeared under the title *On the Treadmill to Pearl Harbour: The Memoirs of Admiral James O. Richardson (USN Retierd),* was published by the United States Navy. *Richardson (USN Retired), As Told to Vice Admiral George C. Dyer (USN Retired),* had to wait until 1973 to see the light of day. This was apparently due to criticism of Admiral Harold Stark, the Chief of Naval Operations, who did not die until 1972. During these fifteen years official historians had more than enough time to distort and obscure the truth about what happened at Pearl Harbour.

At Admiral Richardson's suggestion, the Pearl Harbour fleet was to return to the west coast of the United States in May 1940; but plans changed and Richardson was ordered to remain in the waters off Hawaii. In his Memoirs, he writes: ".... The decision to keep the fleet at Pearl Harbour in May 1940 was made, in my opinion, on a completely false premise. The premise that the fleet positioned there would exert a coercive influence on Japan's actions.... In 1940 the foreign policy makers of the Government - the

President and the Secretary of State - thought that by positioning the fleet in Hawaii they would coerce the Japanese. They did not ask their military advisers whether it would actually accomplish this objective. They imposed their decision on them.

Admiral Richardson jeopardised his career by twice travelling to Washington to personally oppose the president's decision to keep the fleet at Pearl Harbour. On his second visit, he told Roosevelt verbatim: "Mr. President, I feel I must tell you that we in the Navy senior command do not have the confidence in the civilian leadership of this country which is essential to the success of a war in the Pacific." Among other things, Richardson insisted that the ships were not well equipped to go to war and that the fleet was too exposed on those islands, as the defensive elements there were insufficient to protect it from potential attack. The admiral asked the president whether the United States would declare war on Japan if it invaded the Anglo-Dutch colonies. Roosevelt responded evasively, noting that he was not sure the Americans would be willing to fight for such a reason. The position at CINCUS (Commmander-in-Chief, U.S. Fleet) was normally held by its incumbents for a period of between eighteen and twenty-four months; but Richardson was removed on 31 January 1941, barely twelve months after taking up the post. His replacement was Admiral Husband E. Kimmel.

Instead of heeding Richardson's complaints about the defencelessness of the fleet at Pearl Harbour, in March 1941 the order was given to withdraw one aircraft carrier, three battleships, four light cruisers and eighteen destroyers from the base, leaving it in a severe disadvantage vis-à-vis the Japanese fleet. This imbalance prevented Admiral Kimmel from making pre-emptive scouting moves away from the base. The units evacuated from Pearl Harbour were sent to the Atlantic, where the British squadron was already enjoying an increasingly clear superiority.

The Purple Code

In the aforementioned work, Mauricio Carlavilla (Mauricio Karl) devotes a chapter to explaining that American espionage had managed to decipher a highly secure Japanese code known as the "Purple Code", which was encrypted by a very sophisticated machine that allowed an enormous number of variations in the dispatches. The Americans "succeeded in deciphering the Japanese Purple Code," writes Carlavilla, "and even managed to build a model of a machine that deciphered the dispatches as easily as the apparatus installed in the Japanese Embassy in Washington. The Purple machine established the key to each cipher by means of its own mechanism. Without possessing a twin machine, it would have been impossible to decipher any Japanese message....". The Americans gave the name "Magic" to their system. Five such machines were built, none of which, significantly, were installed at Pearl Harbour. Thus the base could only know what Roosevelt and his minions wanted to communicate to it. After the attack, a Commission of Inquiry was set up to investigate what happened. Government representatives testified before the Commission that the naval base was deprived of "Magic" to prevent it from being identified by the Japanese.

Even if this were true, there was nothing to prevent the Pearl Harbour commanders from being informed of all the information being gathered in Washington, or at least of the relevant data affecting the safety of the fleet based there. In fact, Admiral Kimmel had asked twice, on 18 February and 26 May 1941, to be kept informed. His request was as follows: "May I suggest that it should be an essential principle that the Chief of the Pacific Fleet should be informed with the utmost urgency of all important developments as they occur and by the most rapid means available". In June Kimmel met personally with Admiral Stark, who assured him that he would be provided with the information he required.

For two or three months the promise was kept; but suddenly, during the three months before the attack on Pearl Harbour, Kimmel stopped receiving reports of interest that would have enabled him to deduce what was in the works. Among those who regularly received Magic's decrypted messages were President Roosevelt; Chief of Staff George Marshall; Secretary of the Navy Frank Knox; Admiral Harold Stark, nicknamed "Betty"; Secretary of State Cordell Hull, who like his counterpart Molotov was married to a Jewish woman, Rosalie Frances Witz, daughter of banker Isaac Witz.

The US Ambassador to Tokyo, Joseph Grew, sent a telegram to the State Department on 3 November 1941, warning that "Japan would risk a national harakiri rather than yield to foreign pressure." Grew, an honest diplomat, was no doubt unaware of Roosevelt's wishes, for he ended his telegram with these words: "My purpose is only to insure against my country's entry into war with Japan because of a misconception of Japan's ability to plunge headlong into a suicidal conflict with the United States." Although the ambassador did not suspect it, those were exactly the words the American president wanted to hear, i.e., confirmation that Japan would attack.

Since April 1941 Japan had been desperately trying to reach an agreement with the United States that would salvage relations between the two countries. On 5 November a message from Tokyo to the Japanese Embassy in Washington was decoded, urging the ambassador to make "maximum efforts" and to act with "maximum determination" to reach an agreement. On 12 November the State Department decoded a message received by the Embassy the previous day stating that the date was "absolutely immovable". Faced with the stalemate in the negotiations, the Japanese government dispatched a special envoy, Saburo Kurusu, to

Washington, who arrived in the US capital on 15 November. On 17 November Magic transcribed the first message received by Kurusu, in response to a message previously dispatched from Washington by the special envoy. The text ended as follows: "See that time is short. For this reason do not allow the United States to go out of its way to delay the negotiations any further. Apprehend them for a solution on the basis of our proposals and do all you can to arrive at it". Let us now look at a longer text, transcribed by Mauricio Carlavilla, which was sent from Tokyo to the Embassy on 22 November and deciphered on the same day:

> "It is terribly difficult for us to vary the date I set in my 736, you know this. I know you are working hard. Stick to the policy we have set and do everything you can. Spare no effort and try to reach the solution we want. Your expertise allows you to surmise why we need to re-establish American-Japanese relations before the 25th; but if within the next three or four days you can finish your talks with the Americans; if the signature can be achieved by the 29th, which I reiterate to you - twenty-ninth; if the relevant notes can be exchanged; if we can achieve intelligence with Britain and the Netherlands; and, in short, if all things can be completed, we have decided to wait until this date, and we say that this time the dead line cannot be changed. After it things will happen automatically. Please give this your careful attention and work even harder than you have worked so far. For the time being this is only for the information of you, the two ambassadors."

Four days later, on 26 November, a new message was transmitted from the Washington Embassy to Tokyo, which was deciphered two days later. It spoke of "complete failure and humiliation". Ambassador Nomura and Kurusu had met with Secretary of State Cordell Hull, who had rejected the latest overtures made by the ambassadors on 20 November and presented them with an absolutely outrageous and unacceptable nine-point proposal. The reply from Tokyo was sent on 28 November and decoded the same day at the State Department:

> "Well, you two ambassadors have made superhuman efforts, but in spite of this the United States has gone ahead and put forward its humiliating proposal, completely unexpected and extremely regrettable. The Imperial Government can on no account take it as a basis for negotiations. For this reason, and with a report of the Imperial Government's views, which I shall send to you, the negotiations will be broken off de facto; this is inevitable. However, I do not want you to give the impression that the negotiations are broken off. Tell them only that you are awaiting instructions, and that, although the views of your Government are not clear to you, to your way of thinking, the Imperial Government has

always made just claims and has made great sacrifices for the cause of peace in the Pacific....."

With the obvious aim of catching the Americans completely off guard, the ambassadors were not expected to break off negotiations and to delay the talks as much as possible. Finally, we will refer to two other messages sent on 30 November that were decoded by Magic on 1 December. The first was sent from Tokyo to the Japanese Embassy in Berlin. It was instructions to the ambassador to "very secretly" inform Hitler that talks with Washington were broken off and that war between the Anglo-Saxon nations and Japan could break out "suddenly by a coup de force which could come more quickly than anyone could imagine". The second was to the Washington Embassy. It noted that, well past the deadline, the situation was becoming increasingly critical, and so, in order to prevent the Americans from becoming suspicious, the press and other sources had been told that, despite major differences, negotiations were continuing.

Messages encrypted with the Purple Code in relation to the Pearl Harbour base, more and more numerous as the date of the attack approached, were intercepted and decrypted by Magic. The contents of these initially concerned the division of the waters between the islands into zones and subzones, the number of ships, their location: whether they were anchored or moored, the movements of units, and so on. All these preliminary enquiries clearly indicated that the attack being prepared was aimed at the US naval base in Hawaii. The orders to destroy the codes, an obvious symptom of the imminence of the war, were issued in late November and early December.

On 25 November 1941 Roosevelt met with Secretary of State Cordell Hull, Secretary of the Navy Frank Knox, Admiral Stark and Secretary of War Henry Lewis Stimson, a member of the secret society "Skulls & Bones", the Brotherhood of Death at Yale University founded by William H. Russell and incorporated into the Russell Trust Association as an appendage of the Illuminati. Stimson would years later be an outspoken advocate of dropping atomic bombs. The President informed them that the Japanese could attack within a week. On 27 November the Navy Department sent a dispatch to Admiral Kimmel, which was "to be regarded as a war warning". It informed him that negotiations had ended, and that a Japanese attack was expected, which could well be against the Philippines, Thailand or Borneo. Kimmel was ordered to make a defensive deployment, even though the potential targets were thousands of miles away.

In December 1941, shortly after the attack on Pearl Harbour, the Roberts Commission, appointed by President Roosevelt, was formed. Admiral Kimmel testified before this Commission that during July 1941 he received seven Japanese dispatches intercepted and coded by Washington, but that during August he no longer received any information on the tension between the United States and Japan following the economic blockade decreed by Roosevelt on 26 July. Regarding the dispatch of 27 November, he told the Commission as follows:

> "The report addressed to me by the Navy Department, telling me that negotiations had ceased on 27 November was a pale reflection of the real situation and as biased as if it had been written to mislead. Diplomats had not only stopped talking, they were with their swords pointed at their chests. As for Japan, the talks that followed after 26 November - as it transpired - were pure comedy. They were a ploy to conceal the coup Japan was preparing. Such a ploy did not fool the Navy Department. The Navy was well aware of the plan. The squadron was exposed in the face of the Japanese manoeuvre because the Navy Department did not communicate to me the reports in its possession about what the Japanese were up to."

The Roberts Commission, as reported by Admiral Richardson in his Memoirs, was created at the suggestion of Felix Frankfurter, a conspicuous Zionist placed by Roosevelt on the Supreme Court, who had introduced into the Administration and the Judiciary a legion of Jewish judges and lawyers who acted under his orders. Richardson explains that the Roberts Commission was shaped by carefully designed principles: it was a joint commission composed of members of the armed forces and a council of civilians, headed by a member of the Supreme Court. It was not governed by the rules of evidence that prevail in civilian or military courts of enquiry. In Richardson's view, the Roberts Commission report "was the most biased, unfair and dishonest document ever printed". Richardson found that military members of the Commission "were later rewarded for their services with advantageous postings and promotions." The fact that the Roosevelt Administration, having betrayed Admiral Husband E. Kimmel and Lieutenant General Walter C. Short, the base commanders, sought to scapegoat them and blame them for the Pearl Harbour debacle outraged Admiral Richardson, who wrote in his Memoirs that the country had never been treated to a more ignominious spectacle than that represented by government officials who refused to accept responsibility for Pearl Harbour.

In 1995, Captain Edward L. Beach, a seafarer of distinction, published *Scapegoats: A Defense of Kimmel and Short at Pearl Harbour,* a defence of Kimmel and *Short,* who were dismissed and retired early with loss of rank. Until his death in 1968, Kimmel worked tirelessly to clear his name from history. Shortly before his death Kimmel stated the following in an interview: "They made me a scapegoat. They wanted to get America into the war.... Franklin D. Roosevelt was the architect of the whole plan. He gave orders - although I can't prove it categorically - that only Marshall could send reports to Pearl Harbour on the movements of the Japanese fleet, and then he told Marshall not to send anything." Kimmel thus directly accused President Roosevelt, George C. Marshall and "others in the High Command" of having brought about what Roosevelt himself called "a date that will remain in infamy." Captain Beach presents sufficient evidence in his book to show that Kimmel and Short were wrongly accused of the felonies of Roosevelt and company.

The hours before the attack

In the early hours of Saturday 6 December, the so-called Japanese "pilot message", sent to the Washington Embassy, was captured. By 6 p.m. it had been deciphered, and shortly afterwards copies were distributed to Magic's usual recipients. It was a long communiqué in fourteen parts, to be delivered the next day to Secretary of State Cordell Hull. It provided a historical justification for the attack that the war would bring. The second part accused the United States and Britain of having "resorted to every possible measure to prevent the establishment of a general peace between Japan and China". The ninth part alluded to Roosevelt's desire to attack Germany: "The American Government, obsessed with its own views and opinions, may be said to be planning the extension of the war. While on the one hand it seeks to secure its rear by stabilising the Pacific area, on the other it is busy helping Great Britain and is preparing in the name of self-defence to attack Germany and Italy, two countries which are struggling to stabilise a new order in Europe...". The last part of the message stated that it was "clear the intention of the American Government to conspire with England and other countries in order to obstruct Japan's efforts for the consolidation of peace." The text concluded with these words, "The Japanese Government regrets to have to inform the American Government that, in view of its attitude, we can only consider that it is impossible to reach an agreement by further negotiations." This message was not to be delivered until a new dispatch ordering it was received, a clear allusion to waiting until the aggression at Pearl Harbour had begun. This order, which was also deciphered by Magic, arrived on the same day, 7 December, and the time coincided with the time of the attack.

General George Marshall, who should have immediately called General Short, was the subject of a legendary disappearance that has gone down in the history of his country. As he testified under oath before the Roberts Commission on 10 December, he could not remember where he had spent the afternoon/evening of 6 December, just four days earlier. His wife Katharine Tupper Marshall helped him to refresh his memory and stated that he had been with her. In fact, no evidence was produced to show where General Marshall had been between 6pm on the evening of 6 December and 9 or 10am on the morning of 7 December. Among the many explanations, the most striking is the one that was spread orally in retired military intelligence circles, according to which Marshall was a secret dipsomaniac and on the night of 6 December 1941 was being treated at Walter Reed

Hospital, having given a false name at the reception desk. Mrs. Marshall wrote in her book *Together* that on Sunday 7 December he had breakfast in bed with her. Another version explains that General Marshall had breakfast only an hour later than usual. Both accounts agree that after breakfast, while everyone was trying to reach him, the General went for his usual Sunday horseback ride in Rock Creek Park. At 11:20 a.m. Marshall finally showed up at his office.

As for Admiral Stark, it is known that he arrived home from the Navy Department at about seven o'clock on the evening of the 6th and went quietly to the theatre with his wife and some friends. When he returned, a servant informed him that he had been summoned from the White House, so he went up to his office and spoke to the President that evening. Since both he and Roosevelt had received the latest report decrypted by Magic, Stark could have warned Admiral Kimmel of the impending attack at that very moment; but, probably on President Roosevelt's instructions, he did not do so. At 9:25 a.m. on the morning of the 7th Stark arrived at his office. It was then five o'clock in the morning in Hawaii. It was still more than two hours before dawn broke over Pearl Harbour. Stark had on his desk all the information he needed to know with almost absolute certainty that the attack would take place as soon as the sun rose. A phone call could have saved many of his subordinates' lives; but instead of keeping the loyalty he owed them, he chose to become an accomplice in one of the worst crimes in American history.

Captain Wilkinson suggested to Admiral Stark that a warning dispatch be sent to the Pearl Harbour squadron; but it was not until twelve noon that the message drafted by General Marshall was ready for the figure. In Hawaii it was 7:30 and the first waves of Japanese aircraft were already approaching the base. Marshall arranged for the cipher to be sent by ordinary means, so it was transmitted from Washington to San Francisco on the Western Union line and from there to Honolulu, where General Short was based, who received it six hours after the attack, while Admiral Kimmel received it eight hours after the military disaster. General Marshall had the transpacific telephone. Had he used it, Short and Kimmel would have had at least half an hour or three-quarters of an hour to take defensive measures. There is no historical precedent for a state with so much information about an enemy attack to stand idly by and let itself be surprised.

Nearly 2,500 dead and 1,200 wounded was the price Roosevelt paid for his "day of infamy" to end American resistance to involvement in the global conflict. In the years that followed, humanity was subjected to increasingly brutal warfare, which crescendoed into unparalleled extremes of barbarism. The localised war that could have been stopped in two days if Lord Halifax had accepted the armistice proposed by Italy and accepted by Germany and France became definitively global. The whole of the Far East and the Pacific became the scene of an apocalyptic planetary war that ended with a death toll of 60 million after the genocidal bombs were dropped on Hiroshima and Nagasaki in August 1945. The entry of the United States into the war allowed Stalin to withdraw permanently from Siberia the troops that were indispensable on the Western Front, where the Germans had reached the outskirts of Moscow.

In connection with this withdrawal of Soviet troops from Siberia and their dispatch to the Western Front, Roosevelt's priority objective, it should be added that one of the most famous Soviet spies, Richard Sorge, who worked at the German Embassy in Tokyo and whose code name was "Ramsey", had sent Moscow on 15 October 1941 a message of extraordinary importance: "Kouantoung's army will not attack Siberia. Japan has decided to attack only the United States and England. I repeat: Japan's neutrality assured. Will not attack Russia. Five months earlier, on 20 May 1941, Sorge and his operator Max-Gottfried Klausen had sent the following message: "Hitler is concentrating one hundred and seventy to one hundred and ninety divisions. The attack will be on 20 June and his immediate objective will be Moscow." On that occasion Stalin dismissed the information and two days after the announced date the invasion took place. The mistake made then was not to be repeated, for a month after Sorge's message, Marshal Eremenko's army, deployed in the Far East, was sent to reinforce Moscow and thus prevented the fall of the Russian capital. Three days after transmitting the information to the USSR, Richard Sorge's espionage network was discovered.[7]

---

[7] Richard Sorge has been considered one of the greatest spies in history. Incomprehensibly, the Communists rewarded his services by allowing the execution of the man who had warned them of the German attack and that Japan would not attack the USSR. Arrested in 1941, Sorge was executed on 7 November 1944. On as many as three occasions the Japanese proposed to the Soviet Embassy in Tokyo that they exchange him for a Japanese prisoner. All three times the reply was the same: "We know of no man named Richard Sorge". Born in Baku to a German father, a mining engineer, and a Russian mother, Richard Sorge was the grandson of Adolphus Sorge, who had been secretary to Karl Marx. He had an extraordinary capacity for languages: in addition to German, English, French, Japanese and Chinese, he spoke Russian, but few of the Germans and Japanese who came into contact with him ever knew it. In January 1929 Sorge met Agnes Smedley, the famous American journalist who was also a Soviet agent, in China. With her he built up a spy ring in Shanghai that spread throughout the Far East and ended up concentrated in Japan, for in 1932 Sorge received instructions from Moscow to establish himself in the Japanese capital. In May 1933 he travelled to Berlin to build up his cover. There he managed to join the Nazi party and was given a job as a correspondent for *the Frankfurter Zeitung*, which had Agnes Smedley as its China correspondent. Sorge travelled to Japan via Canada and the United States, where he made contact with other Soviet agents. He landed in Yokohama on 6 September 1933. At the German embassy he met Colonel Ott, a military attaché who was soon promoted to general and later became ambassador. Ott, who knew nothing about the Far East on his

Part 4
Air Terror and Atomic Terror

Among the least reported and publicised crimes of World War II was the aerial terror over Germany, a terror that was also put into practice in Japan, where it reached its final apotheosis with the dropping of the atomic bombs on Hiroshima and Nagasaki. Not even this unspeakable crime perpetrated on the orders of Harry Solomon Truman, the Jewish, Zionist, 33rd degree Freemason president who ordered this holocaust when Japan was totally defeated, has been considered sufficient to place this political leader among the worst criminals of all time. On the contrary, it has been claimed that Truman went down in history as a democratic president who made the decision to save an invasion that would have cost the lives of a million Americans. There will be time later to tell the story of nuclear terror, for now it is time to denounce two other Zionist Freemasons, Roosevelt and Churchill, who were ultimately responsible for the aerial terror over Germany, culminating in the Dresden holocaust.

The general public has been inculcated with the idea that it was the Germans who mercilessly bombed the United Kingdom. The famous Battle of Britain has gone down in the annals of history as the ultimate example of the suffering of the English people. However, the reality is quite different and the figures prove it. In two months, between 7 September and 2 November 1940, German bombing raids on London resulted in some 14,000 dead and 20,000 wounded. Total casualties from German bombing raids on UK cities reached 41,650 dead and 48,073 wounded in May 1941, when the Luftwaffe attacks ended. These figures, painful enough, were multiplied by a factor of three or four in a single night in Dresden, where, according to the most conservative estimates, 135,000 people died between 13 and 14 February 1945. Twenty-five German cities with more than half a million inhabitants were razed to the ground by the RAF. In Hamburg, to cite now another example, more than 700 British bombers carried out over several nights "Operation Gomorrah", named after one of the cities inhabited by sinners and criminals that Jehovah, the God of the Jews, exterminated with a rain of fire and brimstone. In Hamburg, during three or four nights in late July and early August 1943, bombing raids caused a firestorm that killed some fifty thousand people and wounded more than one hundred and twenty thousand. Nearly one million Germans living in the city were displaced to other parts of the country and even to Poland.

This way of waging war against civilian targets did not come about overnight, but was conceived beforehand. Before soldiers start firing the first

---

arrival, found in Sorge an assistant who gradually became an indispensable adviser. This gave the Soviet spy access to official sources of information.

shot, wars have been launched in offices long beforehand. As early as 1933, international Jewish organisations had already called for a "holy war" against Germany. F. J. P. Veale states in *Advance to Barbarism* that in 1936, in the course of a meeting at the Air Ministry, the British decided that in the event of a future war, non-military targets should be bombed. Britain was thus sticking to its tactic of provoking civilian casualties, for it should not be forgotten that during World War I the main cause of death among the German population was the British blockade, which continued for almost a year after the armistice was signed and resulted in the starvation of nearly a million non-combatant civilians.

Germany did not prepare for this kind of war

Winston Churchill and other warmongers spread a lot of nonsense about Germany's armaments programme that was seized upon by British leaders to justify their own armaments programme. Churchill's perverse intentions were exposed in several works by Francis Neilson, a multifaceted character and author who in 1915 resigned his seat in the British Parliament. In 1950 Neilson published *The Makers of War,* a book denouncing Churchill's lies and presenting various studies and reports on the arms expenditure of belligerent countries. It is generally accepted that since coming to power the Nazis concentrated their efforts on improving the internal situation. The social and economic achievements of the first four years of National Socialism in Germany have already been noted. However, in contrast to these policies of economic growth, neighbouring countries such as France and Czechoslovakia were taking steps that could only provoke suspicion and mistrust in Germany. A brief outline of events related to armaments and defence policy is given below.

On 2 May 1935 France and the USSR signed a Treaty of Mutual Political and Military Assistance. On 15 June of the same year the Soviet Union and Czechoslovakia concluded a similar agreement. In February 1936 the French Parliament ratified the Pact with the USSR and Germany denounced it as a hostile gesture incompatible with the Locarno Treaty. Before ratification, Hitler believed that hesitant French parliamentarians could prevent it, so he tried to dissuade France by directly addressing French public opinion through an arranged interview with Bertrand de Jouvenel of *Paris-Midi.* Here is Hitler's reply to a question from Bertrand de Jouvenel: "You want Franco-German rapprochement. Won't the Franco-Soviet pact compromise it?"

> "My personal efforts towards such a rapprochement will always remain. However, in practice, such a pact would naturally create a new situation. Don't you realise what you are doing? You are allowing yourselves to be drawn into the diplomatic game of a power which wants nothing more

than to put the great European nations in a mess from which it will benefit. We must not lose sight of the fact that Soviet Russia is a political element which has at its disposal an explosive revolutionary idea and gigantic arguments. As a German, it is my duty to consider such a situation. Bolshevism has no chance of success among us, but there are other great nations less cautious than we are against the virus of Bolshevism. You would do well to give serious thought to my offers of agreement. Never has a German leader so repeatedly made such proposals to you. And from whom do these proposals emanate? From a pacifist charlatan who has made up his mind about international relations? No, but from the greatest nationalist Germany has ever had at the helm? Let us be friends!"

It seems that due to government pressure, reported by some authors, this interview did not appear in *Paris Midi* until the day after the vote in the French Parliament, which took place on 27 February 1936. The Treaty of Mutual Assistance between France and the Soviet Union was adopted by 353 votes to 164. In response, Germany remilitarised the left bank of the Rhine on 7 March, restoring German sovereignty over the entire territory of the Reich, but in violation of the Treaties of Versailles and Locarno, which had previously been violated by France.

Moreover, a few months earlier, on 18 June 1935, Germany had signed the Anglo-German Naval Agreement with Britain, which regulated the size of the Kriegsmarine (Navy) in relation to the Royal Navy. Germany pledged that the size of its war fleet would permanently be 35% of the tonnage of the British fleet. This was an agreement without a quid pro quo, as Britain was not committing itself to anything. On 28 April 1939, following the granting of the blank cheque to Poland, Germany denounced this agreement.

On 19 March 1936 Ribbentrop, invited to appear before the League of Nations, recalled from the rostrum all the proposals for peace made by the German Chancellor which had been rejected. Among them he mentioned: general disarmament; parity armament based on armies of 200,000 or 300,000 soldiers; an air pact; a proposal to adopt a set of measures to ensure peace in Europe, an offer made in May 1935. In this speech Ribbentrop denied that Germany had unilaterally violated the Locarno Treaty. Months later, on 31 March 1936, Germany submitted a memorandum suggesting the creation of an arbitration tribunal to resolve possible conflicts between nations. It insisted on proposals for a non-aggression pact. Among the proposals directly related to air terror and warfare in general were the following: prohibition of dropping poison gas bombs and incendiary bombs; prohibition of bombing open cities or villages beyond the medium range of heavy artillery or battle fronts; prohibition of bombing with long-range guns of cities more than twenty kilometres from the battlefield; abolition and prohibition of the construction of tanks of the heaviest type; abolition and prohibition of artillery of the heaviest calibre. Germany declared itself ready to implement this regulation if it had international backing. The Netherlands welcomed the proposals and asked France to put pressure on Britain to accept the memorandum at least in part. Some time later, on 14 February 1938, Chamberlain declared in Parliament that "His Majesty's Government was not prepared to restrict the activity of its air forces.

David L. Hoggan corroborates that British leaders were not simply interested in an air force capable of defending against a possible German air offensive. According to Hoggan, British strategy from 1936 onwards was based on the doctrine of massive attacks on targets far from the front line. Their strategy," Hoggan writes, "contrasts with that of the Germans, who expected that aerial bombardment would in the event of war be restricted to actions on the military front. The difference in strategy was reflected in the types of aircraft produced by the two countries. Germany built many light and medium bombers for tactical operations in support of troops on the ground; but the British emphasised the production of heavy bombers to attack civilian targets far from the front. The British Defence Requirements Committee decided as early as February 1934 that the greatest potential enemy in the event of war would be Germany". In the spring of 1938, the British had planned to produce 8,000 warplanes a year from April 1939, a target that was even exceeded. In addition, during the war, through the Lend-Lease Act, Roosevelt supplied Churchill with long-range heavy bombers, the B-17 flying fortresses. [8]

During the first thirty-six hours of military operations in Poland, the Germans destroyed almost the entire Polish air force. President Roosevelt, a paragon of hypocrisy, on 1 September 1939 appealed to Germany and Poland against the bombing of civilians. Lord Lothian, British Ambassador in Washington, explained that Roosevelt was making the appeal on behalf of the Poles and that the President had declared that the bombing of civilians in recent wars "had sickened the hearts of all civilised men and women." On the same day 1 Hitler replied to Roosevelt that his message coincided with his views and therefore proposed a public declaration by belligerent governments in any war condemning air raids on civilians. The German Armed Forces High Command also issued a communiqué on the matter in the afternoon/evening of 1 September. The authorities indignantly denied reports in the servile Western press that Germany was bombing open cities. The German military insisted that the air raids had been exclusively against military targets; but this statement received little attention in the newspapers, which instead published pictures of murdered members of the German minority, presented as innocent Polish victims of the air war.

---

[8] This powerfully armed bomber was a four-engine, high-altitude, long-range bomber that could stay aloft for six to ten hours with a heavy bomb load. Its price was exorbitant, costing some $240,000 at the time. Despite this, more than 13,000 were produced during the war.

Swedish negotiator Birger Dahlerus, although he was about to retire from the diplomatic scene, made a last call to the Foreign Office on the afternoon of 1 September to offer Lord Halifax his willingness to continue the mediation. Dahlerus used this last contact to convey Göring's promise that Germany would never bomb open cities if the British agreed to refrain from this practice. Halifax must have listened dismissively to the proposal, for he knew that the bombing of open cities would be a basic formula for victory in the war they intended to declare against Germany.

The "splendid and heroic decision"

In April 1944, when the Luftwaffe was virtually paralysed for lack of fuel and the outcome of the war was already clear, *Bombing Vindicated*, a work by James Molony Spaight, who until 1937 had been the principal undersecretary of the Air Ministry, was authorised for publication in Britain. Spaight explains in the book that on 11 May 1940, the day after the start of the German offensive in France, the Air Ministry took the "splendid and heroic decision" to launch the strategic bombing offensive on civilian populations in Germany, which destroyed or seriously damaged seven million homes and killed, at the lowest estimate, six hundred thousand people, although some authors, including F. J. P. Veale, put the figure at two million, a figure that is supported by many researchers. The English historian David Irving puts it at two and a half million. To these should be added millions injured, maimed and chronically ill as a result of carbon oxide poisoning, most of whom were elderly, women and children.

The first chapter of *Bombing Vindicated*, "The bomber saves civilisation", seeks to justify the slaughter of hundreds of thousands of innocent civilians on the pretext that "civilisation would have been destroyed had there been no bombing in the war. It was the bomber," Spaight pathetically writes, "which, more than any other instrument of war, prevented the forces of evil from prevailing". J. M. Spaight, with bleeding gall, besides admitting that the responsibility for bombing civilian populations lies with Churchill's Government, insists that all the credit for having conceived and carried out this practice must go to Britain. Spaight vehemently confirms that the "splendid decision" was not taken thoughtlessly or spontaneously, but can be traced back to a "brilliant idea" that British experts had in 1936 when the Bomber Command was organised. Spaight asserts that "the whole raison d'être of Bomber Command was to bomb Germany if it became our enemy". He goes on to say that it was obvious that Hitler realised what the intention of the British was in the event of war and was consequently anxious to reach an agreement with Britain "which would limit aircraft action to the battle zones."

In *Advance to Barbarism*, a seminal work of historical revisionism published in England as early as 1948 under the pseudonym of "a jurist", the

English historian F. J. P. Veale extensively paraphrases *Bombing Vindicated*. Veale comments in his magnificent work on an article that Air Marshal Arthur Harris, Commander-in-Chief of Bomber Command, known in the press as "Bomber" Harris and in the RAF as "Butcher" Harris, published in *The Star* on 12 December 1946. Harris agrees with Spaight in disparaging the short-sightedness of professional soldiers around the world and particularly in Germany for failing to realise in 1939 that heavy bombers would be a far more effective weapon against civilians than against fighting forces. Let us read the words of F. J. P. Veale:

> "He (Harris) states that Germany lost the war because, when, in September 1940, it was forced to conduct blitzkrieg, it discovered that the generals who controlled the Luftwaffe and contemplated the bomber simply as a long-range artillery for use in battle had neglected to equip the Luftwaffe with heavily armed heavy bombers designed for blitzkrieg. The Germans, writes Air Marshal Harris, had allowed their soldiers to prescribe the entire Luftwaffe policy, which was expressly designed to support the army in quick offensives.... Too late in the day they saw the advantage of a strategic bomber force.... The result was that the German Army had been deprived of air cover and air support on all fronts to provide any kind of defence for Germany against independent strategic action in the air."

In other words, Harris, who also published the book *Bomber Offensive*, criticises the Germans for lacking heavily armed heavy bombers that would allow them to attack the enemy's civilian population and protect themselves from attack from the air. Had the Germans been able to persist in their attacks," Harris writes, "London would have suffered irrevocably the terrible fate that Hamburg faced two years later. But in September 1940, the Germans found themselves with almost unarmed bombers.... Thus in the Battle of Britain the destruction of the bomber squadrons was something akin to shooting cows in a field."

Captain Liddell Hart in *The Revolution in Warfare* (1946) soberly singles out Winston Churchill as the man primarily responsible for the bombing of civilians. When Mr. Churchill came to power," writes Liddell Hart, "one of the first decisions of his Government was to extend the bombing to non-combat areas". In an address on 21 September 1943 to a complacent House of Commons Churchill was quoted as saying, "In extirpating Nazi tyranny there are no limits of violence to which we will not go." On 6 July 1944 Churchill addressed a secret four-page memorandum to his Chief of Staff, General Hastings Ismay, which in 1985 was reproduced by *American Heritage* magazine and also by Mark Weber in the *Journal of Historical Review*. The world's great icon of democracy proposed the following project:

"I want you to reflect very seriously on the question of asphyxiating gases. It is absurd to take morality into consideration in this matter when the whole world put them into practice during the last war without any protest from moralists or the Church. On the other hand, at that time the bombing of open cities was forbidden, and today everyone practises it as a matter of course. It is simply a fashion, comparable to the evolution of the length of women's skirts. I want a cold look at how much it would cost to use asphyxiating gases. We must not let our hands be tied on silly principles. We could flood the cities of the Ruhr and other cities in Germany in such a way that most of their populations would be in need of constant medical care. It will be necessary to wait perhaps a few weeks or even a few months before Germany can be flooded with asphyxiating gas. I wish that this question would be examined coolly by sensible people and not by a team of uniformed psalm-singers, spoilsports whom one comes across everywhere."

Perhaps Churchill had read *Last and First Men*, a novel published in 1930 in which Olaf Stapledon predicts the advent of genetic engineering and describes a devastating war in which squadrons of bombers drop huge shipments of poison gas on the cities of Europe. Also H.G. Wells, a member of the Fabian Society who has already been introduced in previous chapters, wrote a screenplay for the film *Things to come* (1936), based on one of his novels, which anticipates what was to come. The action is set exactly in 1940. The war surprises ordinary people who live carefree lives. Aeroplanes destroy cities and murder civilians with poisonous gases.

Apart from the science fiction novels that predicted what was to come, Edwin Baldwin, three times Prime Minister of the United Kingdom between the wars, made a speech to the British Parliament in 1932 entitled "A Fear for the Future", in which he starkly expressed his view of what was to come. On 18 February 1932, a year before Hitler came to power, Germany had submitted to the Conference on Disarmament in Geneva a proposal calling for the elimination of combat aviation. The British delegate to the Conference gave assurances that it would be considered. On 9 November 1932, Baldwin acknowledged in Parliament that large armaments inevitably led to war and said the following:

"... I think it is also good for the man in the street to realise that there is no power on earth that can protect him from being bombed. Despite what people may tell him, the bomber will always get through. The only defence is in the offensive, which means killing more women and children than the enemy, and more quickly if we want to save ourselves.... If the conscience of the young people should come to feel, in connection with this instrument (bombing) that it is evil and should be abandoned, it will be done; but if they do not think in this way..... well, as I say, the future is in their hands. But when the next war comes, and European civilisation is annihilated, as it will be, and by no other force than that force, then do not let them blame their elders. Remind them that they, chiefly, or they alone, are responsible for the terrors that have fallen upon the earth."

Clearly, it is unacceptable and outrageous that Baldwin should seek to shift the responsibility for the possible use of the terror of aerial bombardment onto the younger generation for not having opposed it. Germany's proposal had been made and it was up to the political leaders who in 1932 had the power to accept it.

The progressive destruction of Germany

The "splendid decision" to bomb German cities was taken on 11 May 1940. On the same day, the RAF dropped its first bombs on Freiburg, a city far from the front. With no war-related industries and no targets of military interest, Freiburg was the first city to be attacked from bombers flying at high altitude. According to a Red Cross report published in *The New York Times* on 13 May, fifty-three people, twenty-five of whom were children playing in a public park, were killed. One hundred and fifty-one other civilians were wounded[9]. The Luftwaffe could have responded with a similar attack, but was not instructed to do so. It was almost four months, during which attacks on German cities continued, before Hitler ordered retaliatory bombing raids on England. Thus began the destruction of Germany from the air: some sixty cities with more than 100,000 inhabitants were priority targets for attack. Some of these major urban centres, such as Cologne, were repeatedly attacked from 1940 to 1945.

The case of Cologne illustrates the systematic strategy of death and destruction implemented by Churchill and his advisers, to which we will devote the attention they deserve below. First bombed in May and June 1940, Cologne, as a communications centre on the Rhine, was easily identified by the pilots, who dropped bombs on it free of charge on their return journeys to their bases, so that until April 1942 it was not bombed en masse on numerous occasions. As a result, its 800,000 or so inhabitants were not often alarmed. That all changed on the night of 30-31 May 1942, when, under the code name "Millennium", more than 1,000 bombers of all types dropped 1,500 tons of bombs on the city, two-thirds of them incendiary. A year later, between 16 June and 9 July 1943, Cologne suffered four massive bombing raids. One of these alone, carried out on the night of 28 June by some 600

---

[9] On the Freiburg bombings, David Irving supports the theory that it was the Germans themselves who bombed the city by mistake. According to him, Heinkel 111s that had taken off from Lecheld, near Munich, to attack a French air base in Dijon got confused and dropped the bombs on Freiburg.

four-engine bombers, killed nearly 4,500 people and left 230,000 homeless. In 1944 Cologne was bombed twenty-eight times during the month of October. From 28 October to 1 November, nine thousand tons of bombs fell on the Rhine district. On 2 March 1945 the city was bombed for the last time by some 900 Lancaster and Halifax bombers. The dead were left unburied in the streets because the population had already left the city. By the time the Americans entered Cologne on 6 March, the old town had been almost completely destroyed, but ten thousand people remained.

The first of the large-scale bombing raids was carried out on Essen and began on 8 March 1942. Between March and April the city was attacked six times by more than 1,500 bombers. In the same month of March, on Sunday the 29th, Lübeck, one of the Hanseatic Baltic cities of no military or industrial interest, was bombed, although its port was a gateway for supplies from Norway. More than 3,000 buildings were severely damaged or completely destroyed. The entire historic centre of the city, known as the "Queen of the Hansa", was practically reduced to rubble. From 1942 onwards, this so-called "strategic" bombing, a euphemism for "strategic" bombing, gradually increased in number and intensity. The dreadful destruction of Hamburg is a special mention.

As the campaign progressed, the bombing became more and more deadly, as experience and improved techniques increased their destructive power. Hans Erich Nossack, author of *The Sinking. Hamburg, 1943*, bears witness to the largest urban bombing ever carried out, an unprecedented and devastating air raid. Nossack watched the destruction of Hamburg as a spectator from a cottage fifteen kilometres southeast of the city. "Everything seemed bathed in the opalescent light of hell," he writes. The terror began on 24 July, when the UK and US air forces launched "Operation Gomorrah", involving Lancaster, Halifax, Stirling and Wellington bombers, some 800 in all. As they approached the coast, they unloaded tons of small aluminium strips that jammed German radar. That night 2,300 tons of incendiary bombs fell on the city. On the 25th another 2,400 tons of bombs were dropped on Hamburg. On the third day, although Hamburg continued to burn, American planes carried out another bombing raid, raising the temperature to over 1,000 degrees Celsius. The flares reached hundreds of metres in the air. Explosive bombs had previously destroyed roofs, doors and windows, and the super-heated air sent streams of fire at 240 kilometres per hour into tornadoes that penetrated everywhere.

The firestorm ("Feuersturm") is produced by a convection effect that causes hot air to suck in air from the sides and rise creating currents that reach thousands of degrees Celsius at speeds of hundreds of kilometres per hour. The area is desiccated, oxygen is sucked out and this further accelerates the hot air storm that sweeps everything away. On the 27th another seven hundred RAF heavy bombers dropped more incendiary bombs: the oil set the canals on fire, the asphalt melted and the defenceless inhabitants could not breathe for lack of air and could not even throw themselves into the canals to escape the blast furnace their city had become. Reconnaissance planes flew reconnaissance missions on the 29th and checked on Hamburg. It must not have seemed enough, for in the evening another 800 heavy planes were ordered to take off and drop their bombs on the burnt-out city. The terror did not cease until 2 August, when 740 bombers attacked for the last night. In all, 8,621 tons of incendiary and explosive bombs fell on Hamburg. With the nightmare over, Nossack, in a refugee truck, describes his entry into the city as an apocalyptic pilgrimage.

Figures for the dead, wounded and displaced in Hamburg have already been given above. There is, however, one interesting account of the state of the city in March 1949, almost six years later. In *Memoirs of a Diplomat* George F. Kennan writes:

> "I was taken by car on a tour of Hamburg, visiting especially the areas devastated by the bombs. It was not a pleasant sight to see or to think about. Everything was razed to the ground, mile after mile. It had all happened in three days and three nights in 1943. Seventy thousand human beings had perished in the bombing. It was estimated that there were still more than three thousand corpses in the rubble. I had personally experienced the first sixty British air raids on Berlin and had seen - since the end of the war - many ruins, but these made a special impression on me".

There is no shortage of historians who insist on justifying aerial terror as a response to the bombing of London and even as a retaliation for the bombing of Warsaw or Rotterdam. J. M. Spaight, author of *Bombing Vindicated,* personally rejects such comparisons. When Warsaw and Rotterdam were bombed," Spaight writes, "the German armies were at their gates. The aerial bombardment was part of an offensive tactical operation". Liddell Hart also shares this view, noting, "The bombing did not take place until the German troops were fighting their way into the cities, so they conformed to the old rules." As for Hamburg, however, Spaight insists that "the loss of valuable lives must be contemplated as the price to be paid to gain a military advantage." It can hardly be admitted that any military advantage was gained by continuing to massacre the inhabitants of Hamburg when there was nothing left to destroy.

Lindemann, Churchill's Jewish ideologue

Winston Churchill himself acknowledges in his Memoirs that the instigator of the air terror over Germany was Lord Cherwell, Frederick Alexander Lindemann, his Jewish adviser, close friend and right-hand man, a Baden-Baden-born physicist who proposed the areas of Germany to be destroyed. Although the Wikipedia article tries to conceal his Jewish origin: "it has sometimes been thought that he was Jewish", the prestigious encyclopaedia reports, "but he was not", the truth is that the "Oxford Chabad Society", whose aim is for Jewish students at Oxford University to deepen their Jewish identity, proudly claims him as one of the Jewish professors at Oxford, where he was professor of experimental philosophy and director of the Clarendon Laboratory, where Jewish physicists from the University of Göttingen, whom he helped to enter England, came together. Lindemann is described in Wikipedia as an insensitive elitist who despised the working classes, blacks and homosexuals. A proponent of eugenics, he supported the sterilisation of the mentally incompetent. The authors of *The Semblance of Peace*, J. W. Wheller-Bennet and A. Nicholls, reveal that "Lindemann's hatred of Germany was pathological and an almost medieval desire for revenge was part of his character". Perhaps that is why, after planning the airborne terror that cost the lives of two million people, Lindemann supported the plan for Germany of his Jewish colleague Morgenthau, about whom we will write a few pages later.

F. A. Lindemann, whose private secretary was David Bensussan-Butt, also of Jewish origin, was the chief scientific adviser to Churchill's government and attended meetings of the War Cabinet. In November 1940 an aerial reconnaissance unit was set up to study the true extent of the bombing raids on Germany. Photographs taken during the summer of 1941 were carefully studied by Bensussan-Butt in order to improve effectiveness. At the end of 1941 Lindemann presented Churchill with an initial plan to destroy 43 German cities with a population of 15 million people. The plan stipulated that it would require four thousand bombers, a number that was not yet available to the RAF.

On 12 February 1942 Lord Cherwell presented Churchill with a more elaborate plan for massive saturation bombing raids on German cities in order to "break the spirit of the people". His proposal stated: "The bombing must be directed on the houses of the working classes. The houses of the middle classes have too much space around them and bombs can be wasted." On 30 March 1942, he submitted a memorandum to the Prime Minister in which he raised the possibility of using up to ten thousand bombers, whose bombs could fall on the densely populated neighbourhoods of the German working classes. Research seems to show," he said in the memo, "that having one's own house destroyed is most damaging to morale. People seem to care more than having their friends or even their relatives killed." Churchill considered Baron de Cherwell one of his oldest and best friends. According to General Hastings Ismay, Lord Cherwell had access to the most sensitive intelligence information, dined with Churchill regularly and accompanied him to his meetings with Roosevelt and Stalin.

Another Jewish professor, Solomon Zuckerman, also worked with Lindemann in preparing the studies and reports that were then submitted to

Churchill. Zuckerman and Bensussan-Butt, Lindemann's Sephardic secretary, studied scientifically how to kill and destroy with maximum effectiveness. In his studies, Solomon 'Solly' Zuckerman concluded that one tonne of bombs killed four people and left 140 homeless. However, it seems that Zuckerman did not entirely share the strategy of saturation bombing of large urban centres of Professor Lindemann, the great scientific guru who eventually imposed his criminal doctrine. Zuckerman considered saturation bombing too expensive and wasteful. In 1943 Solly Zuckerman drew up the bombing plan prior to the Allied landing in France, which was presented to Dwight D. Eisenhower. The Americans discussed it for a year, preferring to bomb the fuel factories rather than attack the transport networks, as proposed in Solly's draft.

President Roosevelt supported the strategy of bombing German cities with his statements and through prestigious propagandists. The White House Press Secretary, Stephen T. Early, personally defended the necessity of the bombing. Two other journalists of Jewish origin, William L. Shirer and Walter Lippmann, argued in their articles that there was no alternative. Walter Lippmann was America's most influential journalist. Born in New York, he was the son of Jacob Lippmann and Daisy Baum, both German Jews. Dr. Caroll Quigley singles him out in *Tragedy in Hope* as one of the organisers of the Round Table in America. "Lippmann," writes Quigley, "has been from 1914 until now the authentic mouthpiece of American journalism in international affairs, in the service of the 'Establishment' on both sides of the Atlantic." A theorist in public opinion, Lippmann wrote twice a week articles that appeared in hundreds of American newspapers, copyrighted by *the Herald Tribune* in New York. In an article in the *Sunday Times* on 2 January 1944, Lippmann, who was part of Roosevelt's Brain Trust, wrote: "We should be ashamed of ourselves and our cause if we could not in good conscience accept our moral responsibility for the destruction of German cities". Yet, while civilian populations were being bombed with absolute moral responsibility, German industry managed to reach its highest production levels in mid-1944.

Dresden, the forgotten holocaust

On the night of 13-14 February 1945, the largest indiscriminate massacre in history took place in Dresden: the murder in a single day of at least 135,000 people, most of them, as usual, women, children and the elderly. Nothing can explain or justify the brutal extermination perpetrated in fourteen hours in the capital of Saxony, one of the most beautiful cities in Europe, for which it was once known as the Florence of the North. Germany had already lost the war and hundreds of thousands of people from the eastern provinces were fleeing in terror from the Red Army. The roads around the city and the streets through it were filled with crowds moving westwards. In Dresden, some one hundred and twenty kilometres from the front, more than half a million refugees, helpless civilians unable to fight, had gathered. This crowd had overwhelmed all possibilities of reception and was in addition to the more than six hundred thousand inhabitants of the city. All the public buildings were crowded with these unfortunate fugitives who had lost everything. Dresden had no barracks, no weapons factories, no military targets. On the contrary, there were numerous hospitals with huge red crosses painted on their rooftops. Despite all this, the British and Americans incomprehensibly decided to launch a massive air raid or saturation raid on the Saxon city.

Even "Bomber" Harris did not seem to understand the reason for the attack. In his book *Bomber Offensive* there is some hesitation or hesitation about the bombing of Dresden on the night of 13 February. Marshal Arthur Harris leaves us with these revealing words: "I will only say that the attack on Dresden was then considered a military necessity by people far more important than myself." In *Advance to Barbarism* F. J. P. Veale does not fail to appreciate that behind this confession lies a desire to disassociate himself and writes: "It may be noted that the Air Marshal explicitly refrains from endorsing the opinion of these important people." In any case, Harris refrains from revealing the identity of the people who ordered him to destroy Dresden, and he keeps the loyalty he supposedly owed them.

As David Irving's *The Destruction of Dresden* provides a detailed account of this incredible episode of World War II, readers are encouraged to refer to it as a good source of information. According to Irving, on 7 October 1944, some 30 American bombers had attacked the Ruhland refinery near the city and took advantage of the situation to bomb the industrial area. More than 400 people were killed, mostly factory workers. It was the first time Dresden had been attacked, and the inhabitants of the city, where French, Belgian, British and American POWs worked, thought it was an isolated event that would not be repeated. The good relations between these POWs and the population are the subject of the British historian, who reproduces the words of a British prisoner written on 24 December 1944: 'The Germans who live here are the best I have ever seen in my life. The commandant is a gentleman and we have extraordinary freedom in the town. The sergeant has taken me to visit the centre of Dresden. Dresden is undoubtedly magnificent and I would like to see much more of it. The fact that the city had been so long away from the theatre of war perhaps contributed to these friendly relations and explains why in February 1945 there were not even any anti-aircraft defences, which could not have been ignored by the Allied leaders. There had been, but when it was realised that they were of no use there, the regional command felt that they would be more useful in the Ruhr or other areas. Thus a widespread legend was born among the citizens that Dresden would never be attacked. Perhaps some of the outlying industrial districts would, but not the centre.

The first refugees had arrived in Dresden in October 1944, when the Soviet offensive threatened the heart of East Prussia. In *Memoirs of a Diplomat* George F. Kennan refers to what happened there in these terms: "The disaster that befell this area with the entry of the Soviet forces was unparalleled in the history of modern Europe. In large sections of it, judging by the evidence, hardly a man, woman or child of the indigenous population was left alive after the Soviets' initial passage; and it is hard to believe that they all managed to flee to the west". The columns of East Prussian refugees who fled south before the arrival of the Red Army consisted mostly of women, children and invalids from the rural regions, who had been evacuated en masse (some six hundred thousand people) to the Saxon cities and also to Thuringia and Pomerania. It should be noted that among the mass evacuees were also Russian and Western prisoners of war. More than four and a half million Germans lived in Silesia, the province to the east of Saxony. When news began to spread in the first weeks of 1945 that the Soviets were preparing a new offensive against the German lines on the Vistula, the need for a new evacuation became urgent. Some of the people who fled went southwest to the mountainous area between Bohemia and Moravia, but others emigrated to Saxony, so that Dresden had to receive a new wave of refugees. News of the treatment of the Germans who had not left East Prussia had spread throughout Germany, so that the people of Silesia often did not wait for the order to evacuate. As is well known, in the areas of Silesia through which the Soviet hordes passed, there was a frenzied orgy of murder, rape and arson.

On 16 January 1945, Dresden was unexpectedly bombed again: some 400 US Air Force "Liberators" attacked Dresden's refineries and junction stations unopposed. The attack resulted in some 350 casualties, including the first British prisoner, who was working in an "Arbeitkommando" (work group) and died while being transported to hospital. Irving again emphasises the exquisite treatment of the British POWs and relates that while the German dead were buried in a mass grave in a city cemetery after a mass funeral, 'the Dresden Captaincy, with surprising respect for the Geneva Convention, ordered a parade to take place with representation of the various forces of the city, and the unfortunate British soldier was buried with full military honours, a British and a German picket giving him guard of honour in the military cemetery of Dresden-Albertstadt'. This information came from the head of the prison camp, who gave notice of this to the victim's parents. Shortly after the destruction of Dresden, the British Government published a dossier on the officially known prison camps, nineteen of which were in transit at the time of the attack. A Red Cross report put the number of Allied prisoners concentrated in Dresden at over 26,000, of whom 2200 were Americans.

The first officially organised evacuee trains began arriving in Dresden on 26 January. Waiting for them at the central station were over a thousand girls from the Girls' Youth of the Reich Labour Service. Their job was to help the elderly and invalids down, carry their luggage, find them shelter and provide them with food. Once they had been evicted, the trains returned to the east in search of new batches of refugees, who arrived in the city for weeks on end. The work of the girls of the Labour Service was such that they had to be reinforced by the Hitler Youth, the German Girls' Youth Union and other women's associations ("Frauenschaften"). Primary and secondary schools were converted into military hospitals, so the pupils also helped to receive the thousands of evacuees entering the Saxon capital every day. Along the railways and roads leading to Dresden, the party's social organisations managed to set up relief and supply stations at regular intervals in order to alleviate as far as possible the ravages of hunger and the bitter cold of winter.

In Wroclaw, the capital of Lower Silesia, Wehrmacht troops were surrounded and put up heroic resistance from 13 February to 6 May 1945, when the city surrendered only after Berlin had done so. As the thunder of artillery sounded closer, fear gripped the city's population, and on 21 January the evacuation of women, children, old people and invalids remaining in Breslau was ordered. Since the rail services could not cope, more than 100,000 people fled on foot, as wagons had been used to evacuate the rural population. It took weeks for the fugitives to reach Saxony. By the time the siege of Breslau began, there were barely 200,000 inhabitants left in the capital. In their flight into the Reich, many exhausted people chose to stay in Dresden, which had become the main hub for refugee traffic.

Fugitives from Silesia accounted for three-quarters of those taken in at Dresden, with the remainder coming from East Prussia and Pomerania. David Irving estimates the total population before the bombing at between 1,200,000 and 1,400,000. On the evening of 12 February, with the arrival of the last convoys of refugees, Dresden reached its highest density of inhabitants per square kilometre. The stations were overcrowded with people staying with their belongings. In the next few days, trains were scheduled to leave for the west in order to relieve as much of the city's congestion as possible. Right up to the last moment, floods of people continued to pour into the streets on foot or in crowded carts. Since the public buildings were already full of cots and beds, tents had been set up for tens of thousands of people in the city's largest park, the "Grosser Garten", where thousands of them died in the bombardment. Mixed in among the civilians were also wandering soldiers whose units had been scattered along the front. The field gendarmerie directed them to areas on the outskirts, as the local roads were blocked by the caravan traffic of wagons and horses.

Irving confirms that the appearance of Dresden's name as a specific target came as a surprise to the Bomber Command, as it had never appeared on the weekly target lists. Several objections were raised against the inclusion of the Saxon capital on the list, including, for example, that there was nothing to suggest that it was a city of great industrial importance, or that there were large numbers of prisoners in the region whose camps were not well located. Arthur Harris ordered Air Marshal Robert Saundby, who reported to him, to ask the Air Ministry to reconsider the matter. The decision having been referred to "higher authorities", Sir Robert Saundby was informed days later by private telephone that the attack was part of a programme in which the Prime Minister was personally interested. The response had been delayed, he was told, because of the absence of Churchill, who was in Yalta at the time. Sir Charles Portal, a crypto-Jew of Huguenot descent who had been appointed Chief of the Air Staff on 25 October 1940, was also in Yalta accompanying the Prime Minister. Charles Portal, temporarily appointed Air Marshal in October 1940 and confirmed in the rank permanently in April 1942, was one of the leading advocates of Lindemann's doctrines of mass bombing strategy.

The Yalta Conference, held between 4 and 11 February 1945, ended without the destruction of Dresden, which had been ordered days earlier. The reason for the delay was the foggy weather that had settled over central Europe. Finally, on 12 February, the weather forecast showed good weather conditions. On the morning of 13 February 1945, fast reconnaissance planes appeared over the city, which lies on a meander of the Elbe. Rather than fear, they aroused curiosity among the inhabitants, who remained convinced that Dresden would not be attacked. The pilots were able to observe as much as they wished in absolute safety, so that they must necessarily have seen the tide of fugitives flooding the roads, which could in no way be mistaken for columns of retreating soldiers.

It was several hours after nightfall when the people of Dresden began to hear the sound of "Mosquito" locators, flying six hundred metres above the rooftops of the city. Their mission was to fire red illuminating rockets that signalled targets to bombers approaching at high altitude. At 22:07 the pilots of these planes received the last words from control: "Finish spotting soon and get out of there". Informed of the threat hanging over their heads, the population rushed to the shelters. At 22:13 on the night of 13 February, the first explosive bombs began to fall, gigantic bombs weighing two and four thousand kilos, bursting everything and tearing off the medieval roofs of the old city of Dresden. The Lancaster squadrons passed one after the other, and soon the lightning flashes of the big bombs were spreading throughout the city. Thus began the most bestial bombardment in history, which was to continue for fourteen hours and fifteen minutes.

Since Dresden was a target far away from the bases, the bombers had to return to England as soon as they had emptied their bellies of the deadly cargo they were carrying. After the first squadrons had withdrawn, rescuers, even from neighbouring villages and towns, dared to come to the aid of the casualties; but at 1.30 a new wave of over five hundred Lancasters arrived, preceded by fighter squadrons equipped for night fighting and strafing

German airfields. These bombers were loaded with explosive bombs that spread the fires and prevented any action by German firefighters and soldiers. This second "raid" was followed by a new group of bombers in two formations: in the first, the planes carried a two-thousand-kilogram explosive bomb and five incendiary bombs weighing three hundred and seventy-five kilos; in the second formation, the explosive bombs weighed two hundred and fifty kilos and the rest of the load was incendiary bombs with no ballistic qualities, which meant that they were dropped without any precision. Since the aim was to set fires of enormous proportions, these incendiary bombs scattered over the city served their purpose perfectly. In total, the Lancastrians dropped 650,000 incendiary bombs (1,182 tonnes) and 1,478 tonnes of explosive bombs on Dresden.

German night fighters were hardly able to take any defensive action and the ground defences remained completely mute. David Irving, who interviewed numerous pilots involved in the destruction of Dresden, writes that "many Lancaster crews were almost ashamed of their lack of opposition and many of them deliberately circled the burning city several times without being disturbed by any kind of defence". So much so that for ten minutes a Lancaster equipped with cameras flew over the dreadful scene filming for the RAF Film Department. This 250-metre film," writes Irving, "now in the archives of the Imperial War Museum, is one of the most sinister and magnificent testimonies of the Second World War. But it provides irrefutable proof that Dresden was not defended, for not a searchlight, not a single anti-aircraft battery appears in the entire length of the film." Irving offers the following testimony from a Lancaster pilot who had been left behind:

> "A sea of fire of, in my opinion, about sixty-five square kilometres covered everything. From our plane, the heat of the brazier was perfectly perceptible. The sky had stunning scarlet and white hues, and the light inside the plane was reminiscent of a strange autumn sunset. We were so stunned by the spectacle of the terrifying bonfire that, despite being alone over the city, we flew over it for several minutes before making our way back, subdued by the terror we imagined below us. We could still see the glow of the holocaust thirty minutes after leaving the place.

Another returning pilot, impressed by the reddish glow, checked the aircraft's position with his navigator and found that it was more than 150 miles from Dresden. The Air Ministry itself, noting the magnitude of the blaze over Dresden, announced in a communiqué that the flames were visible "almost three hundred kilometres from the target." The British also reported that 1,400 aircraft had taken part in the operation and that they had lost only six Lancasters, as ten others that did not return to their bases had managed to land on the Continent when they had run out of fuel.

As far as British terror was concerned, it was planned that the Americans would also do their bit. It was up to them to continue the slaughter. Ten days earlier they had shown their competence in Berlin, where on 3 February they had launched a devastating attack on "railway and administrative areas" that had killed 25,000 Berliners in a single afternoon. The crews of 1,350 flying fortresses and Liberators were briefed at 4:40 a.m. on 14 February. It fell to the 1st Airborne Division to continue the massacre. At 8:00 a.m. 450 B-17 heavy bombers, those capable of carrying the heaviest bombs of 4,000 and 2,000 kilograms, took off for the Elbe city. Another 300 flying fortresses of the 3rd Airborne Division were to attack Chemnitz. The targets for the lighter aircraft were Magdeburg and Wesel. Dresden was still burning and hundreds of thousands of wounded were still untreated in the rubble when the third massive attack in less than fourteen hours began. At 12:12 another deluge of bombs finished off the incomprehensible crime that the British had begun the night before. In all, the Americans dropped 475 tons of high-powered bombs and 297 tons of incendiary bombs in packets and bunches. The medieval and baroque areas of the city were prime targets for bombing.

With the bombers' work done, the thirty-seven P-51 fighters, whose mission had been to protect the flying fortresses, and three other groups of fighter planes taking part in the operation, realising that they were unopposed, turned to strafing the columns of people who had survived and were trying to escape the inferno. Ambulances, fire engines, cars and any vehicle moving on the roads were targeted by the American pilots, who flew almost at ground level. However, the Dresden-Klotzsche airfield, full of fighters, was not attacked. The units' flight crews had been evacuated, as they were night fighter squadrons and the airmen could not participate in daylight operations. These German pilots, not understanding why the fighters and transport planes stationed at the airfield were left untouched, watched helplessly as strafed civilians from fields to the west of the city.

As for the attack on Chemnitz, a city thirty-five miles from Dresden and one hundred and eighty kilometres from the Soviet lines, the three hundred B-17 flying fortresses that bombed it on the morning of 14 February did only the first part of the job. Sir Arthur Harris had planned for the British to finish the job in the evening. So, at 3pm on the afternoon of the 14th, the Lancastrian crews who had ravaged Dresden, after just six hours' rest, were called in for a briefing for another long raid. At Chemnitz, explains David Irving, there was a tank factory, large textile and uniform factories, locomotive repair shops and other clear targets. However, intelligence officers at different airfields repeated the same instructions, which had nothing to do with the destruction of these targets. The crews of Group 1 were told: "Tonight your objective will be Chemnitz... you are to attack the concentrations of refugees who have gathered there after the last raid on Dresden. Irving transcribes the following extract from the briefing given to Group 3, at another airfield: "Chemnitz is a town about thirty miles east of Dresden and therefore a much smaller target. The reason for going there tonight is to wipe out all the refugees who have managed to escape from Dresden. They will carry the same load of bombs, and if tonight's attack goes as well as last night's, they will not visit the Russian front again." At these words, adjectives and comments are superfluous. Fortunately, the predicted weather conditions did not come true, the clouds completely obscured the city, and the attack could not be as deadly as desired.

A British prisoner in Dresden wrote that the city burned for seven days and nights. The authorities estimated that eighteen square kilometres were devoured by flames. The same phenomena described in the account of the Hamburg bombings were repeated in Dresden, and even more frightening. The tornadoes caused by the firestorms engulfed people, throwing them into the air along with objects of all kinds lifted up by the whirlwind of fire. People who fled along the railway embankments," Irving explains, "the only path not blocked by debris, reported that cars in the most exposed areas were lifted up by the hurricane like a sheet of paper. Even open spaces, such as large squares and extensive parks, offered no protection against the tornado. We will spare the reader the recounting of more Dantesque scenes, for they are easily imaginable.

The claim to "break the spirit of the people", formulated by F. A. Lindemann, Lord Cherwell, was fully achieved with the destruction of Dresden. Reports of the death toll circulated in Berlin, and there was talk at that two or three hundred thousand people had been annihilated in a single night. Public opinion, aware of Theodore N. Kaufman's plan to exterminate the German people, began to think seriously that the Allies had decided to extinguish the German people. The Morgenthau plan, which was already known to the government and to the NSDAP, confirmed the worst omens. Some German leaders recognised that air terror and indiscriminate killing had disintegrated German morale.

The total number of dead in Dresden will always remain a matter of speculation. Circumstances prevented the authorities from continuing the work of identifying the victims and carrying out a reliable count. The fact that temperatures of over 1,000 degrees Celsius were reached in the Dresden blast furnace meant that tens of thousands of bodies were completely charred, making it impossible to identify them. Nevertheless, on 6 May 1945, it was officially announced that 39,773 of the dead had been identified. At the end of February, the "Abteilung Tote" (Section for the Dead) considered that the identification work was delaying the burial of the corpses and risked epidemics. Decomposing, broken, headless, charred or burnt to ashes bodies had to be buried as a matter of urgency, hence the proliferation of mass graves. For days the survivors tried to locate their missing relatives in order to avoid burial in a mass grave. While they searched for a wheelbarrow, rescue teams frequently arrived and took the corpse of their relatives piled on carts to the eucalyptus and pine forests on the outskirts of the city. SS and police units trucked piles of corpses to Berlin's cemeteries.

Two weeks after the disaster, the authorities considered the endless caravans of corpses to the forests north of the city to be a danger of typhus and other epidemics, and decided that the thousands of bodies still lying in the rubble, cellars and streets of the city centre would no longer be moved to the mass graves in the forests. Access to the city centre and the Old Market was then closed to the population. From then on, lorries full of corpses were handed over at the edge of the forbidden zone to Wehrmacht officers, who drove the vehicles to the centre of the Old Market Square and dumped their contents on the ground. Large iron beams placed on stone blocks formed large grills about eight metres long, on which bodies were piled five hundred at a time, with piles of straw between each layer. Wood and straw were placed under the grills and a fire was lit. This rudimentary method was used to incinerate the corpses, a task that took all the hours of a day. Once the bodies had been cremated, the soldiers placed the ashes in trailer trucks and transported them to the cemetery at Heide, where they were buried in a grave eight metres wide and sixteen metres long. Nine thousand corpses were cremated in a single day.

It is understandable, therefore, that under these conditions it was impossible to accurately count the number of dead. In Berlin, official sources estimated the number of casualties after the bombing at between 180,000 and 220,000. The International Committee of the Red Cross, on the basis of reports provided by the authorities, gave the figure of 275,000 dead in the entire Dresden area in 1948. In 1951, Axel Rodenberger published *Der Tod von Dresden*, a hard-hitting book that sold more than a quarter of a million copies and remained a landmark in the Federal Republic until the mid-1960s. According to the author, the death toll was between 350,000 and 400,000. These figures tend to be considered excessive because, instead of relying on documents, the author relies on his own experience, eyewitness accounts and information from the Propaganda Ministry. In *Advance to Barbarism*, the work by Frederick John Partington Veale cited above, the death toll is estimated at well over 300,000. To justify such a high death toll, he recalls that every house in Dresden was packed and that public buildings were overcrowded with the unfortunate refugees, many of whom had even camped out in the streets. In Irving's work, which we have used as our primary source, the original English edition of which was published in 1963, the death toll is estimated at between 135,000 and 150,000. However, ten years later, in 1973, the German historian Hans Dollinger insisted that 250,000 people lost their lives in Dresden. In 1974, Rolf Hochhuth, the German writer and playwright famous for his play *The Vicar* (1963), a drama in which he denounced the attitude of Pius XII towards Nazism, based his source on the research of David Irving, gave the figure of 202,000 dead. Of the wounded and mutilated, of whom little is said, it is estimated that there were 300,000.

What is most shocking about this whole affair is that instead of seeking ways for Germany to publicly acknowledge and honour the Dresden dead, Chancellor Angela Merkel, the daughter of a Polish Jew named Herlind Jentzsch and remarried to Jewish professor Joachim Sauer, has sought to minimise what happened. A commission of "historians" commissioned by the city of Dresden itself established in 2009 that between 18,000 and 25,000 people died in the bombing. In other words, they do not even want to acknowledge the almost 40,000 dead who could be identified. The relatives of the dead and other German citizens who try to demonstrate annually on 13 February to honour the memory of the victims of the Dresden Holocaust have in recent years been insulted by socialist and communist counter-demonstrators and must therefore be protected by extensive police deployments. While the genocidal perpetrators of the criminal bombing of Germany and Japan have passed unblemished into history, non-Genocidaires who had the misfortune to be guards at Auschwitz in 1944, such as Oskar Gröning, who at the age of 93 was arrested in March 2014 and was to be tried for war crimes in 2015, are being prosecuted in Germany. More on this in a later chapter.

Aviation terror in Japan: atomic terrorism

Air terror reached its most nauseating expression with atomic terrorism, which was preceded in Japan, as in Germany, by the destruction of almost every major Japanese city. The ultimate expression of non-nuclear air terror was reached in Tokyo, which suffered devastating attacks from March to July 1945. Both the bombing of the Japanese capital and the dropping of the atomic bombs on Hiroshima and Nagasaki were gratuitous and could have been avoided, since Japan had long since lost the war and had already spent half a year in the search for peace. Since it has already been explained how aerial terror was practised in Germany, we will devote most of this section to commenting on little-known, because hidden, aspects of the decision to use nuclear terrorism. First, however, we must write a few lines about the Tokyo bombings.

The conquest of the Mariana Islands in the summer of 1944 allowed B-29 flying fortresses to take off from bases closer to Japan. By the end of the year, the first attacks on Tokyo were carried out. By March 1945 more than 300 heavy bombers were operating from the Marianas and massive bombing raids began. In March alone, more than 100,000 tons of bombs were dropped on 66 Japanese cities. Particularly deadly were the attacks on the capital, which on 9 March 1945 was subjected to a massive carpet bombing, which, as in Germany, combined explosive and incendiary bombs in order to cause as much destruction as possible. Of the 2,000 tonnes of bombs dropped on Tokyo, half a million were incendiary napalm and magnesium. It should be noted that typical Japanese houses have wooden roofs and walls, and inside there are plenty of tatami mats and rice-fibre or rice-paper-lined panels. The bombing was carried out by some 350 B-29s and began well into the night. To the misfortune of the unfortunate inhabitants of the city, shortly before the attack, a strong gale arose, which further accentuated the effects of the firestorms. So brutal were the effects of these storms that a waterspout of air reached a height of ten kilometres and the bombers themselves were thrown hundreds of metres upwards by the hot air currents. It took the Japanese authorities almost a month to remove all the charred bodies from the rubble. The bombing killed more than 100,000 people and nearly 400,000 were badly injured, most of them badly burned and maimed. Some 280,000 houses were destroyed and at least one million Tokyoites were left homeless.

Two days later, on 11 March, General Curtis LeMay ordered the attack on the urban area of Nagoya, which was bombed at low altitude by nearly 300 aircraft. Two nights later it was the turn of Osaka, Japan's second largest city in terms of population and industrial production. Thirteen hundred more B-29s dropped 1,700 tons of bombs on Osaka, which again generated air currents so intense that, as in Tokyo, they rose up to the planes. On 16 March 1945 Kobe was LeMay's fourth target: three hundred and seven B-29s dropped two thousand three hundred tons on the city, which was razed to the ground. 250,000 people, a third of the population, lost their homes and tens of thousands were killed and wounded. We could go on listing the exploits of the Americans through aerial terror, but we think it is no longer necessary. In Washington,, General Norstad told a conference about the damage done to the Japanese during the bombing raids of March 1945. In his own words, it was "the greatest damage that has ever been inflicted on any people in the history of the world in such a short period of time".

Atomic terror will occupy the rest of the space of this fourth part of the chapter on the Second World War. The atomic bomb was a Jewish bomb from beginning to end: it was intended or desired by Jews; Jews were the ones who proposed its manufacture to Roosevelt; Jews were Roosevelt and Baruch, who ordered its production; Jews were the ones who manufactured it at Los Alamos; Jewish Wall Street banks financed the "Manhattan Project"; and Jews were Truman, who authorised the dropping of the bombs on Hiroshima and Nagasaki. The connotations and implications behind the decision to premeditate this unspeakable mass murder are far-reaching. That is why we will return to the subject later, in a second section on the monopoly of nuclear violence, which will form one of the parts of the next chapter, the eleventh of this work of ours, which is getting longer and longer for the writer and for the readers, should we ever have them.

The first thing to note about the development of the atomic bomb is that research into the development of nuclear fission was well advanced in Germany and Japan, and scientists needed only financial and political support to develop the atomic weapon. However, neither the Emperor of Japan nor the Chancellor of Germany, where the universities of Göttingen,

Berlin and Munich had been the world's leading centres of modern physics between 1920 and 1930, were prepared to take the plunge, as both had ethical objections. Hirohito made it known to the Japanese wise men that he would not approve of such a weapon. Hitler, for his part, considered such bombs inhumane. National Socialism claimed an "Aryan science" as opposed to "Jewish science", which was characterised by a materialism that had to be dispensed with because it threatened to corrupt everything. The two most prominent advocates of Aryan science were Philip Lenard and Johannes Stark (Nobel laureates in physics in 1905 and 1919). These two scientists believed that a symbiosis had to be created between spirit and matter. According to them, nature is essentially mysterious. Man had to recognise the limits of his knowledge and was not allowed to delve into certain mysteries, but to respect them.

It seems that the philosophical basis for the prudent and humble attitude of these German scientists could be the Greek "hybris". A pre-Socratic concept that alludes to the punishment imposed by the gods on those who acted without moderation, with arrogance and immoderation. The transgression of the limits imposed on men, a frequent theme in Greek mythology and tragedy, led to hybris. Those protagonists who were unaware of their place in the universe and defied the gods by their actions were inexorably punished. In a September 1945 article in *Politics magazine,* Dwight Macdonald, editor of this pacifist publication, quoted Albert Einstein's words shortly after the dropping of the atomic bombs: "No one in the world should have any fear or misgivings about atomic energy because it is a supernatural product. In developing atomic energy, science simply imitates the reaction of the sun's rays. Atomic power is as natural as when I sail my boat on Saranac Lake". However, when asked about the unknown radioactive poisons that were beginning to alarm even editorialists, he replied emphatically, "I will not talk about this." Albert Einstein would no doubt have angered the Greek and Roman gods of antiquity, who would have punished him for his impertinent arrogance.

In January 1939, the scientific community learned that German physicists had discovered nuclear fission, which meant they could theoretically split the atom. Niels Bohr, a Danish physicist of Jewish origin, whose mother Ellen Adler belonged to a very important Jewish family in Danish banking, thought he understood from a conversation he had in Copenhagen with Carl F. von Weizsäcker, son of the State Secretary for Foreign Affairs and a pioneer of nuclear research in Germany, that German physicists were working on the atomic bomb for Hitler. In reality this was not true, as the goal of building a nuclear weapon was never a priority for the Nazis and always remained on the back burner. Bohr contacted Edward Teller, another Jewish physicist of Hungarian origin who had emigrated to America, where he was in turn in contact with Leó Szilárd and Eugene Wigner, also Jewish physicists who came from Hungary and lived in the

United States. These three scientists persuaded Albert Einstein to warn President Roosevelt about the information Bohr had passed on to them.[10]

On 2 August 1939, on the outline of a text drafted by Szilárd, Einstein signed a letter that he delivered to Alexander Sachs, a Russian-born Jewish economist who acted as an unofficial advisor to Roosevelt and who had worked with Justice Brandeis for the Zionist Organisation of America. In the extensive 1998 article *The Secret History of the Atomic Bomb* (accessible online in PDF), Eustace Mullins writes the following about this character: "Sachs was actually a Rothschild courier who regularly delivered large amounts of cash to the White House. Sachs was an adviser to Eugene Meyer, to Lazard Frères International Banking and also to Lehman Brothers". Einstein could have presented the letter to Roosevelt himself, for when he arrived in the United States in 1933 he was invited to the White House and immediately became involved in Eleanor Roosevelt's campaigns. Alexander Sachs was chosen, however, and on 11 October 1939 he personally delivered Einstein's letter to Roosevelt. The letter asked the president to promote the nuclear fission programme in the United States in order to prevent "the enemies of mankind" from doing so first. Mullins believes that the fact that Sachs was chosen to present the letter was a clear indication to President

---

[10] Einstein arrived in the USA with a halo of prestige. Supposedly, he was committed to peace and disarmament projects, which did not prevent him from calling for the manufacture of the atomic bomb. The facts show that in reality, Einstein was a convinced Zionist and a racist. Chistopher Jon Bjerknes, a Jewish dissident who on his website *Jewish Racism* unequivocally denounces Zionism and the conspiracy surrounding it, is the author of *Albert Einstein the Incorrigible Plagiarist* (2002) and *The Manufacture and Sale of St. Einstein* (2006). In these works, which are excerpted on his website, he exposes the set-up behind Einstein's fame, accusing him of being an unscrupulous, compulsive plagiarist who always took advantage of the work and efforts of others without citing them. Among the scientists plagiarised by Einstein are Robert Brown, a researcher who worked on particle motion in fluids; Jules Henri Poincaré, the first to demonstrate that time and space can only be relative; Hendrik Lorentz, whose theories on the conversion of matter into energy and vice versa were only reinterpreted by Einstein, a fact that Max Planck and Walter Kaufmann felt obliged to denounce; Philipp von Lenard, who discovered the photoelectric effect in cathode rays; and Friedrich Hasenöhrl, the Austrian physicist who was the creator in 1904 of the basic equation $E=mc^2$ and who died a year before Einstein appropriated the formula.
Philipp Lennard claimed that the famous equation should be attributed to Hasenöhrl, as he had written it a year before Einstein. Before he died in the war in 1915, Hasenöhrl left his work at the Patent Office in Bern, where the ineffable plagiarist worked. Einstein read the theory there and, after Hasenöhrl's death, published it in the same year 1915 without having the honesty to cite the author. At a lecture on 24 August 1920 in Berlin, the physicist Ernst Gehrke accused Einstein of plagiarising Lorentz's mathematical formalisms for the theory of relativity and Melchior Palagyi's concepts of time and space. In front of all present, he personally addressed Einstein, who was unable to reply. Stephen Hawking in *A Brief History of Time* confirms that Einstein has been given credit for a theory already anticipated by Poincaré, Lorentz, Hasenöhrl and others. In short, the whole scientific community knows the truth and only the general public is being misled.

Roosevelt that the Rothschilds approved of the project and wanted it carried out quickly. The nuclear programme could not have happened without the backing and sponsorship of Wall Street: the Federal Reserve banking cartel contributed more than $2 billion to the Manhattan Project.

Eustace Mullins, disciple and friend of Ezra Pound and author of *The Secrets of the Federal Reserve*, became in his long and prolific writing career one of the most lucid authors in exposing the conspiracy of the illuminati bankers. In *The Secret History of the Atomic Bomb* Mullins out Bernard Baruch, whom Henry Ford considered the Consul of Judah in America, as America's grey eminence for the atomic bomb programme. Baruch, for decades the undisputed factotum of US policy, was the great New York agent of the Rothschilds, for whom he had been scheming since the early 20th century. Among other services to this Talmudist banking dynasty, Mullins credits Baruch with setting up the tobacco and copper trusts. It was Baruch himself who chose the Jewish physicist Julius Robert Oppenheimer as scientific director of the Manhattan Project at the Los Alamos laboratory in New Mexico. In the Nagasaki Atomic Bomb Museum, inaugurated on the occasion of the 50th anniversary of the dropping of the bomb, the portraits of Einstein and Oppenheimer, the so-called "father of the atomic bomb", are prominently displayed, thus singled out among those responsible for the nuclear genocide.

Jack Rummel reveals in his biography *Robert Oppenheimer Dark Prince* that in 1926 Oppenheimer began seeing a psychiatrist because of his emotional problems. A few months earlier, at Christmas 1925, he had unprovokedly tried to strangle his friend Francis Ferguson in Paris. The psychiatrist diagnosed him with dementia praecox, the term then used for schizophrenia. Oppenheimer's diagnosis, according to the psychiatrist, was not favourable. At that time, dementia praecox was considered an incurable disease that would eventually require permanent hospitalisation. Three years later, at Berkeley, Oppenheimer showed signs of his imbalances in public by behaving in a haughty and extremely disrespectful manner towards a former Jewish professor from Göttingen, James Franck, who had won the Nobel Prize for Physics in 1925. "Tragically," writes Rummel, "Oppenheimer recognised his self-destructive character, which he called 'bestiality', but often could not help falling into it." In 1936 he began to become involved in communist organisations and to work for left-wing groups. "Oppenheimer," Rummel notes, "read avidly about politics. One book that particularly impressed him was a work by Sidney and Beatrice Webb entitled *Soviet Communism. A New Civilization*, which praised the achievements of the Soviet Union." The FBI kept him under surveillance for a long time, as they had discovered that his former girlfriend (Jean Tatlock), his wife Kitty, his brother Frank and his sister-in-law were or had been members of the Communist Party. In November 1940, before being appointed scientific director of the Manhattan Project, Oppenheimer had married Kitty Puening, a woman who had had three husbands, the second of whom, Joe Dallet, a member of the American Communist Party and a fighter in the Spanish Civil War in the ranks of the Lincoln Battalion, had died in 1937 at Fuentes de Ebro.

The main scientists Oppenheimer requested for the Manhattan Project were almost all Jewish or married to Jewish women. The aforementioned Edward Teller, who would later be considered the father of the H-bomb (hydrogen bomb), collaborated from the beginning, although in 1954 he would end up testifying against Oppenheimer when he was accused of spying for the Soviets, a circumstance we will discuss in the next chapter. The first group to work on the design of the bomb included Hans Bethe, a Jewish physicist of German origin who later became the head of the Theoretical Division at the laboratory. Alongside him were John von Newman and Richard Freyman. The former, a Budapest-born mathematician, was the son of a Jewish banker named Max Newman and Margaret Kann, who was also from a wealthy Jewish family in Pest; the latter was born in Manhattan to Jewish parents. Another physicist recruited by Oppennheimer to work on the bomb design was Robert Serber, whose wife Charlotte, Jewish like him, became head of the lab's technical library. Both were controlled by the FBI, which suspected them of being communists. Oppenheimer himself, as we have noted, was spied on because of his relationship with the Communist Party: his telephone was tapped, his correspondence opened, and intelligence agents disguised as bodyguards watched him. Although Intelligence Colonel Boris Pash requested that he be "completely removed from the project and dismissed from the job by the US Government", he managed to keep his job, not least because Bernard Baruch was his mentor.

Felix Bloch, a Zurich-born Jew who won the Nobel Prize for Physics in 1952, was also part of the group when the Los Alamos National Laboratory was opened in March 1943, officially inaugurated on 15 April. In addition to the above, other Jewish scientists recruited by Oppenheimer joined the Manhattan Project at Los Alamos. Among the most important were Victor "Viki" Weisskopf, George Kistiakowsky, Stanislaw Ulam, Emilio Segré, Otto Frisch. The most important and prestigious of the non-Jewish physicists who collaborated with Oppenheimer on the bomb was Enrico Fermi, who had been married to a Jewish woman, Laura Capon, since 1928. Winner of the 1938 Nobel Prize in Physics, Fermi had built the first nuclear cell at the University of Chicago before arriving at Los Alamos. In December 1942, Fermi achieved the first controlled nuclear fission chain reaction. Niels Bohr and his son also joined the laboratory in late 1943 or early 1944 to work on the construction of the bomb.

After the terrible bombings in March, Japan called for an end to the war. By May the situation was untenable: more than half a million people had been burned to death by bombing and firestorms and nearly 20 million

Japanese had lost their homes. General MacArthur acknowledged that in the spring of 1945 Emperor Hirohito himself was leading a coalition seeking a negotiated peace that would end the nation's agony. Only four Japanese cities had not been destroyed in the bombings: Hiroshima, Kokura, Niigata and Nagasaki. Little did their inhabitants suspect that the reason for the immunity was that these four cities had been chosen as targets for atomic bomb testing. In *Hiroshima's Shadow* (1998), Dr Shuntaro Hida, who treated some victims of the atomic holocaust, confirms that they found it strange that B-29s passed over the city every day without ever attacking it. Only after the war," he says, "did I learn that Hiroshima, according to American records, had been left intact in order to preserve it as a target for the use of nuclear weapons.

On 25 April 1945, a preparatory conference for the founding of the UN was convened in San Francisco, attended by delegations from fifty countries. The Americans included seventy-four members of the Council on Foreign Relations (CFR), a key body of the Round Table, the secret society founded by Rhodes and Milner in collaboration with Rothschild, Morgan, Rockefeller and others. The head of the American delegation was Secretary of State Edward Stettinius, son of an associate of J.P. Morgan who had been one of the great arms dealers in World War I. Stettinius convened early in the Cold War and was the first American to meet with the US delegation. Stettinius summoned a select group of four members of his delegation to the Garden Court of the Palace Hotel in early May to discuss the situation caused by insistent Japanese demands for an end to the war, which posed a problem: the bomb would not be ready for months and could not be tested on the previously chosen cities, which had been deliberately kept intact.

Mullins reproduces the following dialogue between the meeting: "We have already lost Germany," said Stettinius. If Japan surrenders, we won't have a population on which to test the bomb". Alger Hiss, who had attended the Yalta Conference as an adviser to Roosevelt while at the same time being an agent of the Soviet KGB, replied, "But Mr. Secretary, no one can ignore the terrible power of such a weapon." Stettinius insisted: "Even so, our post-war programme depends entirely on the ability to terrorise the world with the atomic bomb." John Foster Dulles, a future Secretary of State and CFR member who in 1933 had travelled to Cologne with his brother Allen to secure funding for Hitler, coolly added: "To achieve this goal you will need a very high count. I would say a million." Stettinius confirmed: "Yes, we reckon about a million, but if they surrender we will have nothing." "Then," said Foster Dulles, "you must keep them in the war until the bomb is ready. It won't be a problem. Unconditional surrender. Let us prolong the war three months longer and we can use the bomb on their cities; we will end this war with the brutal fear of all the peoples of the world, who will then submit to our will." It is clear, then, that the United States intended to maintain an exclusive monopoly on atomic terror in the post-war period. The fourth person attending the meeting was Averell Harriman, who had been ambassador to Moscow since October 1943.

According to Mullins, the Manhattan Project was so named because its secret director, Bernard Baruch, resided in Manhattan, as did many others working on the Project, including General Leslie R. Groves, the Army commander in charge of the Project. Oppenheimer chose the name "Trinity" for the test of the first explosion of a nuclear weapon, which took place on 16 July 1945 at Alamogordo in the Jornada del Muerto desert, the 17th-century Spanish name for an arid plain of volcanic rock and sand infested with rattlesnakes, scorpions and tarantulas whose temperature in summer is around 40 degrees Celsius. The fissile material in the bomb, colloquially called "the gadget", was plutonium, the same as that contained in "Fat Man", the Nagasaki bomb. The Hirosima bomb, "Little Boy", was uranium. After watching the explosion, Oppenheimer remarked: "I have become death, the destroyer of worlds".

Only one civilian was able to attend Trinity's historical test, William L. Laurence, a Lithuanian Jew whose real name was Leib Wolf Siew, who had begun his career in 1926 as a journalist at the *New York World*, a newspaper owned by Bernard Baruch whose editor, another Jew named Herbert Bayard Swope, was also Baruch's advertising agent. In 1930 Laurence went to work for *The New York Times* as a science expert. On 9 August 1945 Laurence (Siew), sitting in one of the co-pilot seats of the B-29, witnessed the dropping of the atomic bomb on Nagasaki. This sinister journalist was awarded the Pulitzer Prize in 1946 for his eyewitness account of the atomic blast.

Truman became the new President of the United States on 12 April 1945, and when he took office he was advised on all matters relating to the atomic bomb by the National Defence Research Committee, chaired by James Bryant Conant, a chemist whom Churchill had asked in 1942 to develop the anthrax bomb for dropping on German cities. Conant was US ambassador to Germany between 1955 and 1957 and there, with the help of Otto John, arranged for the confiscation and burning of ten thousand copies of *The Secrets of the Federal Reserve Bank. The London Conexion*, the book by Eustace Mullins that had been published in Oberammergau (see note 29 in chapter 5). Two other prominent members of the Committee were George Leslie Harrison, a member of the Brotherhood of Death (Skull & Bones) who had been President of the Federal Reserve for thirteen years, and James F. Byrnes, one of Bernard Baruch's men in Washington who in July 1945 replaced Stettinius as head of the Secretary of State. On 25 July 1945, Harry Solomon Truman wrote in his diary:

> "We have discovered the most terrible bomb in the history of the world. It may be the fiery destruction prophesied in the age of the Euphrates Valley, after Noah and his fabulous ark.... This weapon will be used

against Japan... We will use it in such a way that military targets and soldiers and sailors will be targeted and not women and children. Although the Japanese are savage, ruthless, cruel and fanatical, we as leaders of the world for the common good cannot drop that terrible bomb on the old capital.... The target will be a strictly military one..... It seems to be the most terrible thing ever discovered, but it can be made the most useful."

At 08:17 on 6 August 1945, the uranium bomb dropped from the B-29 *Enola Gay, named* after Enola Gay Haggard, mother of pilot Paul Tibbets, was finally exploded 584 metres above the city of Hiroshima, in order to achieve maximum explosive effect. Some 80,000 people were killed in the act; but months later the death toll had risen to 140,000. Many thousands of them were children sitting in classrooms at the time of the explosion. In *Hiroshima's Shadow*, which is considered to be one of the best books on this historic event that has forever marked the whole of humanity, it is established that in the end 750,000 people, including the dead, the wounded and those sickened by radioactivity, ended up as victims of the two atomic bombs.

The next day, 7 August 1945, *The New York Times* appeared with a three-line front-page headline, each line taking up the entire page: "First Atomic Bomb Dropped on Japan; Missile Equals 20,000 Tons of TNT; Truman Warns Enemy of 'Rain of Ruin'". In successive issues, articles began to appear in the paper by the future Pulitzer Prize winner, William L. Laurence, who, in addition to his newspaper payroll, was paid a supplementary salary by the War Department to work as public relations for the atomic bomb. Laurence denied in his articles that there had been any radioactive effects on the victims of the bombs.

Wilfred Burchet, the London *Daily Express*'s envoy to Hiroshima and author of one of the chapters of *Hiroshima's Shadow*, wrote an honest account in mid-September 1945, far removed from Laurence's prefabricated reports. Burchet begins the chapter with these words. "I would never have thought when I entered Hiroshima, only four weeks after the incineration of the city, that it would be a turning point in my life, that it would influence my entire professional career and my conception of the world." Here are some excerpts from his first chronicle:

> "In Hiroshima, thirty days after the first atomic bomb destroyed the city and shook the world, people are still dying mysteriously and horribly. Hiroshima does not look like a bombed city. It looks like a gigantic steamroller has passed over the city and crushed everything. I write these facts as dispassionately as I can in the hope that they will serve as a warning to the world.... When you arrive in Hiroshima, you can look around and for twenty-five or thirty square miles you can hardly see a building. You get an empty feeling in your stomach at the sight of such manmade destruction.... My nose detected a peculiar smell, unlike

anything I had ever smelled before. It is something like sulphur, but not exactly. I could smell it when I passed near a fire that was still burning or at a point where they were still recovering bodies from the ruins. But I could also smell it where everything was deserted. They believe it emanates from the poisonous gases coming from the earth penetrated with the radioactivity released after the uranium bomb exploded.... From the moment this devastation was wrought upon Hiroshima, the people who survived have hated the white man. It is a hatred whose intensity is almost as dreadful as the bomb itself.... On the day I was in Hiroshima, a hundred people died. Of the 13,000 seriously injured by the blast, a hundred have been dying every day and will probably all die. Another 40,000 people suffer less serious injuries...".

These were provisional figures given by the police, which were later revised to 130,000. A month later, there was still no way of knowing how many people were still in ashes and how many would die from the effects of radiation. The journalist visited some ramshackle hospitals accompanied by Dr Katsube, whose diagnoses had no precedent on which to base them. Of the reference in his *Daily Express* article to "hatred of the white man", Wilfred Burchet explains that he felt it in the reactions of relatives and of the patients themselves, whom he beheld with oozing third-degree burns, bleeding eyes and jaws, and hair falling on the floor, where they looked like "black haloes" near their beds: "The victims and their family members," he wrote, "looked at me with a burning hatred that cut me like a knife." Dr Katsube felt it too and told him in English: "You must leave. I cannot take responsibility for your life if you stay any longer." As he took his leave, the last words of Dr. Katsube, who thought Burchet was American, were, "Please report what you have seen and tell your people to send some specialists who know about this disease, with the necessary medicines. Otherwise everyone here is doomed to die".

Hiroshima's Shadow contains the text of the communiqué that the Swiss Consulate sent from Tokyo to the State Department on 11 August 1945: "The Swiss Consulate has received a message from the Japanese Government. On August 6th American planes dropped bombs of a new type on the residential district of Hiroshima, killing in one second a large number of civilians and destroying a large part of the city. Not only is Hiroshima a provincial city without any protection or special military facilities of any kind, but none of the neighbouring regions or cities constitute a military target". It took twenty-five years for this Swiss Consulate document to be published.

Eustace Mullins transcribes excerpts from the text *Reflections of a Hiroshima Pilot*, a work in which pilot Ellsworth Torrey Carrington, a flight lieutenant co-piloting the *Jabit III*, offers some very interesting information. Sarcastically, he writes, for example: "After the first bomb was dropped, the bombing command was very fearful that Japan would surrender before the second bomb could be dropped, so our people worked twenty-four hours a day to prevent this misfortune". This pilot confirms that when the atomic bombs were dropped Japan was completely devastated and already a defenceless country. Admiral William D. Leahy, Chief of Staff under Roosevelt and Truman, in his *I Was There* (1950) honestly acknowledged: "My impression is that as the first to use the atomic bomb we adopted an ethical pattern similar to the savagery of the dark ages. I had not been taught to wage war in that way, and wars cannot be won by sacrificing women and children".

Eager to experiment with a second bomb, a plutonium bomb, the mass murder perpetrated three days earlier in Hiroshima was repeated in Nagasaki on 9 August 1945. The initial target was Niigata, but because of rain it was changed to Kokura. Kokura was flown over by the B-29 *Bockscar*, but it was completely covered by clouds and visibility was zero. Commander Charles Sweney then decided to drop the bomb on Nagasaki. At 11:02 "Fat Man" exploded 560 metres above the ground. Due to the 3,000 degree temperature, one square kilometre (the epicentre) was completely disintegrated to the ground. In another two kilometres, a 1,500-kilometre-per-hour wind ripped houses from the ground and trees and people were thrown four kilometres away. Subsequently, the black mushroom of the atomic satan rose to a height of almost twenty kilometres as fallout rained down on the city. Immediately 70,000 people died in Nagasaki, but in the following weeks the number of victims rose to 170,000. In addition, 60,000 people were injured.

On the same day, 9 August, President Truman radioed the nation and said: "The world will realise that the first atomic bomb was dropped on a military base at Hiroshima. This was because we wished in this first attack to avoid, as far as possible, the killing of civilians." In the days that followed, US planes dropped thousands of leaflets over towns and cities warning: "We are in possession of the largest explosive ever designed by man, equal to the entire arsenal that two thousand B-29 aircraft can carry. We have begun to use this new bomb against your people. If you have any doubts, ask about what happened at Hiroshima and Nagasaki." On 15 August the Emperor declared Japan's unconditional surrender.

Statements by top US military leaders leave no doubt as to the inappropriateness of the use of nuclear terror. Air Force Chief of Staff Curtis LeMay acknowledged that the decision to drop the atomic bombs on Hiroshima and Nagasaki had nothing to do with ending the war. Brigadier General Carter Clark went a little further in his confession: "We had beaten them to a pulp and forced them into a miserable surrender just by sinking their merchant marine and starvation. We didn't need to do it and we knew it. We used them as an experiment for two atomic bombs." As has been demonstrated in these pages, the propaganda excuse that nuclear terror was resorted to in order to avoid an invasion that would have cost a million American soldiers' lives is untenable. Years later, President Truman was asked whether he had any doubts or misgivings about the use of atomic bombs on Japan. His response was that it was done "in defence of freedom".

It remains to be added that the "hibakusha", the Japanese word for people who survived the atomic bombs, had to face a miserable life: they were disfigured by burns or with protruding scars, lost their hair, suffered from cataracts in their eyes, developed blood diseases or some form of cancer. Women who were exposed to radiation had children with abnormally small heads, which meant irreversible impairment of intelligence. In 1951 Japan signed a treaty with the United States in which it waived any claim to compensation for the "hibakusha" in exchange for the Americans' withdrawal. Only in 1957, twelve years after the atomic holocaust, did the Japanese government decide to enact a law granting free medical care for 360,000 victims who were still alive. In 1968 the government announced special financial aid for the "hibakusha", but by 1976 only a third of them had received the announced compensation.

PART 5
THE MORGENTHAU PLAN.
HALF OF EUROPE FOR COMMUNISM

Throughout this work it has been emphasised that communism, as early as the founding of the Bavarian Enlightenment by Adam Weishaupt, was a doctrine conceived by the bankers. The abolition of the concept of patriotism and of nations themselves, the idea of world revolution and the creation of a universal society came about long before Marx wrote the *Communist Manifesto* for the League of the Righteous ("Bund der Gerechnet"). The alliance between the Illuminati and the Frankists of Jacob Frank, a sect to which Europe's most important financiers belonged, was sponsored by Mayer Amschel Rothschild, the founder of the dynasty. By 1830 the doctrinal basis of communism was already established in Europe and America, where in 1841 Clinton Roosevelt published *The Science of Government, Founded on Natural Law,* a work updating Weishaupt's ideas and advocating a dictatorship to establish a new social order. Heinrich Heine, whose source of information was James Rothschild, announced years before the *Manifesto* appeared that communism was waiting for an order to enter the scene. On the other hand, Moses Hess declared that socialism should be made under the red Rothschild flag. Rabbi Antelman believes that Moses Hess, the introducer of Marx and Engels into Freemasonry, is the key to understanding the Illuminati-Communist-Zionist conspiracy. It was Hess who proposed to transform the "Bund der Gerechten" into a communist party.

The World Revolutionary Movement had thus been financed from its inception by the international Jewish bankers, who had set their eyes on the immense resources and wealth of Tsarist Russia. It has been seen how a legion of Jewish agents working for these bankers, the most conspicuous of whom was Trotsky, led the revolution in Russia, which was financed and sponsored by Jacob Schiff, Alfred Milner, Felix Warburg, Otto Kahn, Olof Ashberg, Bernard Baruch, J. P. Morgan, Guggenheim, etc. The failure to spread the communist revolution to Germany, the death of Lenin and Stalin's ability to displace Trotsky, the man who was to take power in Moscow, allowed national communism to take hold in the USSR. Despite this, the international bankers, who had been planning to seize global power since the creation of the Illuminati, had not given up their aims. The lack of any scruples and the ruthless terror of communism had enabled them to steal on an epic scale. The plunder of Russia through Jewish agents, the surreptitious control of its vast resources and the systematic elimination of economic competitors and political opponents were accomplished with unprecedented speed. It was simply a matter of putting covert agents back at the helm of the Soviet Union who could serve them better than Stalin.

All the plots to displace him having failed, after the Moscow trials and the Spanish civil war, Stalin increased his distrust of the capitalist countries and as a consequence came the surprising Ribbentrop-Molotov pact. Simultaneously, while Stalin was eliminating the Trotskyites and gaining a foothold, in the United States, Franklin Delano Roosevelt, a pawn of the international bankers and Zionism, was placed in power. An Illuminati Mason of the 32nd degree of the Scottish Rite, Roosevelt, who held the grandiloquent title of "Sublime Prince of the Royal Secret", was, as it turned out, surrounded for twelve years by socialist and Zionist Jews who controlled the US government during his three terms in office. Big captains like Felix Frankfurter, Louis D. Brandeis, Bernard Baruch, Henry Morgenthau and others flooded the Administration with their intermediaries and front men. When in June 1941 Hitler invaded the Soviet Union, the United States rushed, as we have seen, to come unconditionally to Stalin's support. Never mind the democide of communism perpetrated over twenty-five years, nor the extermination by starvation of seven million Ukrainians (Holodomor), nor that Stalin's regime was a ruthless dictatorship, nor that he had eliminated Trotsky, nor that he had occupied half of Poland, Estonia, Latvia and Lithuania, nor that he had invaded Finland in a war of conquest. None of this was to be taken into account, for it had already been conceived to expand communism into the heart of Europe in order to be able to control it again by stealth, as had happened with Lenin and Trotsky. To this end, covert agents were kept in the chamber who could in due course replace Stalin and his clique, the most important of whom was the crypto-Jewish Lavrenti Beria.

A disturbing secret document

Between 14 and 24 January 1943, the Casablanca Conference was held in Morocco, which Stalin declined to attend. A month later, Roosevelt made his intentions known to the Soviet leader in the following letter. At Casablanca Roosevelt and Churchill took a momentous decision: to prolong the war. To this end, they declared that they would only accept Germany's unconditional surrender, which would force the Germans into desperate resistance. It was in Casablanca that it was agreed to increase the appalling mass bombing of civilian populations. The demand for unconditional surrender made it clear that Germany's annihilation was intended, and derailed all efforts by those seeking a way to end the war, including Spain.

Curiously, it was the Spanish Foreign Ministry that first became aware of the true intentions of President Roosevelt and his clique with regard to Europe and the world. A document dated 20 February 1943 in Washington, the so-called "Zabrousky document", reached the hands of General Franco, head of state, at a time when Spanish diplomacy was working to mediate in the world conflict and was seeking the support of other neutral countries. The document, a secret letter from Roosevelt to a Jew surnamed Zabrousky who served as a liaison between him and Stalin, was a bitter blow for Spanish diplomats, who, in agreement with the foreign minister, Francisco Gómez-Jordana, Count of Jordana, hoped that the United States would implement a policy quite different from the one proposed by Roosevelt in the text sent to Zabrousky.

The letter was first published in the book *España tenía razón 1939-1945 (Spain was right 1939-1945)*, published in 1949 by Espasa-Calpe. The author of this work, José Mª Doussinague, was during the Second World War Director General of Foreign Policy at the Ministry of Foreign Affairs. Six years later, in 1955, Mauricio Karl (Carlavilla) reproduced the text in full in the prologue to *Yalta*, a book that presented in Spain the documents published by the US State Department on the Yalta Conference. Subsequently, Count Léon de Poncins also transcribed the Zabrousky document in two of his works: in *Freemasonry and the Vatican* (1968) and in *Top secret. Secrets d'Etat anglo-américains* (1972), a book later published in English under the title *State Secrets*. Léon de Poncins, who describes the text as extremely important, alludes to the fact that the document was practically unknown outside Spain and notes that the Spanish government kept its source secret. Doussinague, however, reveals in *Spain he was right* that it was a woman of deep Christian feeling who 'wanted to help stop the ruin of the world' who leaked the text to the Spanish government, for which he publicly thanks her. Doussinague comments that Spain had been plundered and lacked the gold and resources to set up the very expensive information services that the great powers had, which did not prevent them from "through one channel or another" receiving "the most secret news and the most confidential documents".

Léon de Poncins expressed his absolute conviction that the Spanish Government was certain that the Zabrousky document was authentic, since its policy and the speeches made by its leaders since then did not fail to take it into account. Moreover, the agreements reached in Teheran and Yalta were in conformity with the ideas expressed in Roosevelt's letter. When Doussinague was Spain's ambassador to Rome, Léon de Poncins met him personally in the Eternal City and inquired about the famous letter. Without, of course, revealing any diplomatic secrets, Doussinague made some very apt comments which Léon de Poncins reproduced in *State Secrets*: "The authenticity of the document," explained Doussinague, "is clear simply from its context. Who among us - unless he was a prophet, who would have been accused of being a crackpot - could have imagined in advance that Roosevelt, acting in his right mind, was about to hand over more than half of Europe and Asia to the Soviets, secretly and without getting anything in return?" Since the document is little known, it is copied in full.

"The White House - Wahington, 20 February 1943".

"My dear Mr. Zabrousky, as I had the pleasure of expressing verbally to you and Mr. Weis, I am deeply moved that the National Council of Young Israel has been kind enough to offer me as mediator to our common friend Stalin, in these difficult times when any danger of friction between the United Nations - achieved at the cost of so much renunciation - would have fatal consequences for all, but mainly for the Soviet Union itself.

It is therefore in your interest and ours to iron out the differences, something which is proving difficult in dealing with Litvinov, whom I have been obliged to warn, much to my regret, that 'those who pretend to fight with Uncle Sam may regret the consequences', both in domestic and foreign affairs. For their pretensions with regard to Communist activities in the States of the American Union are already intolerable in the extreme. Timoshenko was more reasonable on her brief but fruitful visit, and pointed out that an interview with Marshal Stalin might be the quickest means of a direct exchange of views, which I consider increasingly urgent, especially remembering how much good came out of Churchill's talks with Stalin.

The United States and Great Britain are prepared - without any mental reservation whatsoever - to give the USSR absolute parity and a vote in the future reorganisation of the post-war world. To this end, it will - as the British Premier sent word to it from Adana, sending it the preliminary draft - be part of the leading group within the European and Asian Councils. It is entitled to this not only because of its extensive intercontinental position, but above all because of its magnificent and by all accounts admirable fight against Nazism, which will deserve all the plaudits in the history of civilisation.

It is our intention - and I speak for my great country and the mighty British Empire - that these Continental Councils should be composed of the whole of their respective independent States, albeit with equal proportional representation.

And you - my dear Zabrousky - can assure Stalin that the USSR will be, for this purpose and with equal power, on the Board of the said Councils (of Europe and Asia), and will also be a member, like England and the United States, of the High Tribunal which is to be set up to settle disputes between the various nations, and will also be equally involved in the selection and preparation of the international forces and the arming and command of these forces, which, under the orders of the Continental Council, will act within each State, in order that the most wise postulates for the maintenance of peace, according to the spirit of the League of Nations, may not again be frustrated, but that these inter-State entities and their attached armies may impose their decisions and make themselves obeyed.

This being so, this high leading position in the Tetrarchy of the Universe should satisfy Stalin to the point of not reiterating pretensions which create insoluble problems for us. Thus, the American Continent will remain outside all Soviet influence and under the exclusive control of the United States, as we have promised our continental countries. In Europe, France will return to the English orbit. We have reserved for France a Secretariat with a voice but no vote, as a reward for its present resistance and as a punishment for its former weakness. Portugal, Spain, Italy and Greece will develop under England's protection towards a modern civilisation which will lead them out of their historical collapse.

We shall guarantee the USSR an outlet to the Mediterranean; we shall accede to its wishes regarding Finland and the Baltic countries, and we shall demand that Poland adopt a sensible attitude of understanding and compromise. Stalin will have a wide field of expansion in the small and unenlightened countries of Eastern Europe - always taking into consideration the rights due to Yugoslav and Czechoslovak loyalty - he will fully recover the territories temporarily taken from Great Russia.

And most important of all: after the partition of the Reich and the incorporation of its fragments into other territories to form new nationalities detached from the past, the German threat will definitely disappear and cease to be a danger to the USSR, to Europe and to the whole world.

There is little point in discussing Turkey any further. He must understand this, and Churchill has given President Inönü the necessary assurances on behalf of our two countries. The move to the Mediterranean should satisfy Stalin.

On Asia, we agree with your claims, barring further complications that may arise later. On Africa, what need is there to argue? France will have to be given something back and compensated for its losses in Asia. Egypt will also need to be given something, as has already been promised to the Wafadists (nationalist party). As for Spain and Portugal, they will have to be compensated in some way for their necessary renunciations in the interests of a better universal balance. The United States will also participate in the distribution by right of conquest and will necessarily claim some vital point for their sphere of influence. That is only fair. Brazil, too, must be granted the small colonial expansion that has been offered to it.

Convince Stalin - my dear Mr. Zabrousky - that, for the good of all and for the speedy annihilation of the Reich (although all this is only a general outline presented for study), he must give way on the colonisation of Africa, and on his propaganda and intervention in the centres of labour in America. Convince him also of my absolute understanding and of my full sympathy and desire to facilitate solutions, for which the personal interview I propose would be very convenient.

And these are all the issues.

As I told you at the time, I was greatly gratified by the kind terms of the letter which informed me of your decision and the desire you expressed to offer me on behalf of the National Council a copy of that treasure which is the greatest in Israel, the Torah Scroll. Of my acceptance, this letter gives you the proof; to those who are so loyal to me, I respond with the utmost confidence. Please be so kind as to express my gratitude to the high body over which you preside, recalling the happy occasion of your XXXIst anniversary banquet.
I wish you every success in your translation work".
"Very sincerely yours,

Franklin D. Roosevelt".

As the text points out, it is a sketch, a working proposal designed for later analysis. Nevertheless, the value of this letter, written two years before the Yalta agreements, is undeniable because it shows that those who had forced the world war had a global plan at the beginning of 1943 that was quite similar to the one that ended up being implemented. The first relevant fact is that the mediation between Roosevelt and Stalin was offered by the "National Council of Young Israel", an organisation of Orthodox Jews clearly connected to Zionism. The fact that the intermediaries between Roosevelt and Stalin were Jewish is further evidence of the enormous influence they exercised over the president and of the responsibility of these Jewish circles for the disastrous Yalta Agreement that allowed the spread of communism in Europe and Asia. Significantly, Roosevelt acknowledges in the letter that the activities of the Communists in the United States were already so brazen that he could no longer tolerate them. The extent to which Communist agents had infiltrated the Administration and the structures of power without problems will be seen later. Sufficiently eloquent is also the use of the nominal syntagma "Tetrarchy of the Universe" to refer to the power that would be wielded by the supposed masters of the post-war world. The "Sublime Prince of the Royal Secret" did not want to deprive himself of showing his authority by using these terms with clear Masonic connotations.

Between 28 November and 1 December 1943 Roosevelt, Churchill and Stalin met for the first time to finalise decisions on the continuation of the war. The meeting was held at the USSR Embassy in Tehran. Some of the issues outlined in the letter to Zabrousky were discussed, although they were only to be finally resolved at the Yalta Conference. The informality of the talks between the Big Three was one of the characteristic features of the Teheran Conference. Stalin, in consideration of Roosevelt's paralysis and in order to spare him travel, proposed to the American president that he should be a guest of the Soviets and offered him accommodation in his embassy, the venue of the conference. In this way he succeeded in bringing the Americans closer to him and distancing himself from Churchill, who was helplessly aware of Stalin's manoeuvre. When Churchill proposed a dinner between the two of them to Roosevelt, the American president replied that he did not want Stalin to feel that he was being ignored. There was no rigour or methodology to the meetings and Roosevelt himself admitted that it was political chumminess. In reality, Stalin made only the necessary compromises. In Teheran, Stalin made an avalanche of demands to Roosevelt and Churchill, including the placement of puppet governments in Eastern Europe and the new borders of Poland, which would be definitively assumed at Yalta. Stalin had already announced that he intended to annex the eastern Polish territories to the Soviet Union and proposed that Poland should be compensated by territorial cessions to the detriment of Germany. The Oder-Neisse line as a land border between Poland and Germany was implicitly accepted, since the main issue was Germany, whose future division was the subject of several proposals.

The treatment of the Nazis after their defeat was also considered. In this regard, Elliott Roosevelt, the US president's son, who travelled with his father to Tehran, famously told the story. In his book *As He Saw It*, he wrote that the subject of how to deal with the Germans was brought up to everyone's surprise in the toasts of a magnificent banquet at which "Stalin," Elliott Roosevelt reveals, "had shared vodka of 100% alcohol content," while Mr. Churchill "had stuck to his favourite brandy. Rising to propose his umpteenth toast, Stalin said: "I propose a toast to the swiftest possible justice for all the war criminals of Germany, justice before a firing squad. I drink for our unit to eliminate them as soon as we capture them, all of them, and there must be at least 50,000 of them." Churchill then quibbled: "The British people would never support such mass murder." The premier advised that appearances should be kept up and they should be subjected to legal trials. According to President Roosevelt's son, his father then interjected into the ensuing discussion and sardonically proposed. "Perhaps we could say that instead of summarily executing 50,000, we should set the figure at a lower number. Shall we leave it at 49,500?" In reality, Churchill's objections were just posturing, for, as has been seen, he had no qualms about gassing Germans, nor did he have any qualms about authorising the bombing of Dresden, Hamburg and so many other cities where civilians were slaughtered by the hundreds of thousands.

The *Morgenthau Diary*. The Morgenthau Plan for Germany

On 24 June 1934, Congressman McFadden, whose speeches have been presented in chapter eight, revealed in Congress who Henry Morgenthau was. We borrow his words in order to proceed to the introduction of this character:

> "... Through marriage he is connected with Herbert Lehman, Jewish governor of the State of New York, and through marriage or otherwise he is related to Seligman, proprietor of the large international banking firm

of J. & W. Seligman, who during the Senate investigation was proved to have tried to bribe a foreign government. Morgenthau is linked with Lewinsohn, the international Jewish banker, and also with the Warburgs, who jointly control Kuhn, Loeb & Co, the International Acceptance Bank and the Bank of Manhattan, and has, in addition, many other businesses and interests here and abroad. These bankers caused a $3 billion deficit in the US Treasury and still owe this amount to the Treasury Department and the US taxpayers. Morgenthau is also connected with the Strausss family and is also related or associated with several other members of the Jewish banking world in New York, Amsterdam and other financial centres."

Henry Morgenthau Jr. was one of the Jewish tycoons who accumulated the most power during Franklin D. Roosevelt's twelve years in office. Secretary of the Treasury from January 1934 to July 1945, he financed the war by issuing 'war bonds'. Morgenthau wrote a diary known as the *Morgenthau Diary*, which was published in Washington in November 1967 by the Government Printing Office. It is an excerpt of more than 1,650 pages compiled in two large volumes dealing exclusively with American policy in relation to the war, Germany and Europe. The reason for the publication was the investigation undertaken by the Internal Security Subcommittee of the U.S. Senate Judiciary Committee into Morgenthau's extraordinary activities during his years as Secretary of the Treasury.

The foreword to the publication states that Dr. Anthony Kubek, Head Professor of the Department of History at the University of Dallas, acted as advisor to the Subcommittee in the selection of the documents. He indicated that the Morgenthau Diaries condensed in the Government publication were written in eight hundred and sixty-four numbered volumes, plus additional unnumbered volumes, bringing the total to nine hundred volumes of three hundred pages each. Dr. Kubek wrote an introduction that placed the events recorded in the Diary in their historical perspective. The Subcommittee, finding that Kubek's analysis presented the facts brilliantly and with historical depth, offered the eighty-one pages of the introduction to the Senate as an informative supplement. In *State Secrets*, a work mentioned several times, Léon de Poncins presents a very pertinent selection of texts on Professor Kubek's work, which we will use to study the Treasury Department's policy towards Germany during the Second World War.

Various Morgenthau associates warned at the time that the material contained in the diaries could be compromising for many people, especially if it fell into the hands of Republicans in the context of an investigation into the Roosevelt regime. John Pehle, a Jewish lawyer in the Treasury Department, proposed to remove materials that could compromise certain individuals. The documents released by the Government necessarily reveal the enormous influence of Roosevelt's Jewish advisors, including Bernard Baruch, Felix Frankfurter, Louis D. Brandeis, Harry Dexter White, Henry

Morgenthau himself and others in cardinal political circles, who at a crucial moment were able to guide US foreign policy and determine the course of events in Europe. It is clear that Morgenthau, surrounded exclusively by Jewish collaborators and advisors, pursued a policy dictated purely by Jewish concerns without much concern for the interests of his country.

Before coming to the Treasury, Morgenthau had lived for two decades near Roosevelt's home in New York and was one of his closest friends. Although he was only Secretary of the Treasury, during the years 1934-1945 Morgenthau and Roosevelt secretly made decisions that fell within the purview of the State and War Departments, sometimes ignoring the respective secretaries. At the Quebec Conference, for example, held between 17 and 24 August 1943, Roosevelt attended in the company of Morgenthau and Harry Dexter White. There, with Churchill and Mackenzie King, Prime Minister of Canada, they agreed to begin talks on Operation Overlord, the code name for the invasion of France, and to increase operations in the Mediterranean, both decisions that directly affected the War Department. On 19 August Roosevelt and Churchill signed a secret agreement in Quebec to share nuclear technology.

Morgenthau's interference in matters within the purview of the State Department deeply irritated other members of the Administration and caused friction with Cordell Hull. In *The Memoirs of Cordell Hull*, the Secretary of State writes: "Annoyed by the rise of Hitler and his persecution of the Jews, Morgenthau often tried to induce the President to anticipate the State Department or to act contrary to our intentions. Sometimes we discovered him conducting conversations with foreign governments that were within our competence. His work in devising a catastrophic plan for the post-war treatment of Germany and his eagerness to persuade the President to accept it without consulting the State Department are outstanding examples of his meddling."

Hull notes in his memoirs the enormous importance of Harry Dexter White, a Lithuanian-born Jew who was Under Secretary of the Treasury and Morgenthau's main collaborator. Both White's father, Joseph Weit, and mother, Sarah Magilewski, were Jews who had come to America in 1885. The FBI later discovered that Harry Dexter White was a Soviet agent, the key man in "Operation Snow", whose aim was to condition U.S. strategic policy. Knowing the truth, Truman, instead of ordering his arrest, kept him on as director of the newly created International Monetary Fund, proving again that communism was an instrument of the conspiracy of the international Jewish bankers.

Professor Kubek writes in his introduction to the *Morgenthau Diary* some very interesting pages on the figure of Dexter White. According to Kubek, "White and his colleagues were in a position to exert an influence on American foreign policy that the Diaries reveal was profound and unprecedented. They used their power in a variety of ways to devise and promote the so-called Morgenthau Plan for the post-war treatment of Germany." On Harry Dexter White's status as a Soviet agent, Professor Kubek writes in his report to the Senate:

> "... What makes this a unique chapter in American history is that Dr. White and several of his colleagues, the architects of vital national policies during those crucial years, were later identified in congressional hearings as participants in a Communist espionage network under the very shadow of the Washington Monument. Two of them, Frank Coe and Solomon Adler, had spent several years working in Asia for the Chinese Communists. Many details of the extensive political espionage operations carried out by this group, especially in the area of political subversion, can be gleaned from the Morgenthau Diaries."

In the summer of 1948 Elizabeth Bentley and Whittaker Chambers, two defecting Soviet agents, testified before the House Committee on Un-American Activities (HUAC) of the Congress and offered important information about the activities of White and company. Professor Kubek confirms in his introduction to Morgenthau's Diary that White's name came up repeatedly in hearings before the Senate Subcommittee on Internal Security, where the two spies revealed the activities of the communist group within the Institute of Pacific Relations, a body that helped bring about the fall of China to communism. Subsequently," writes Kubek, "when the Subcommittee discussed subversion connections within government departments, the hearings revealed additional information about White's activities and his involvement with members of a Communist conspiratorial group within the government. Dr. White was at the centre of all this activity."

The Morgenthau Plan to de-industrialise Germany after the defeat of the war and to reduce the activities of the German people to pastoralism had a hidden agenda: to bring about rigorous and indiscriminate misery among the population as a means of delivering Germany into the arms of the Soviet Union. On 10 July 1946 Molotov declared that the Soviet Union hoped to transform Germany into a "democratic and peace-loving state, which, in addition to its agriculture, will have its own industry and foreign trade." In the light of these statements, Professor Kubek makes the following reflections: "Was Russia really planning to become the saviour of the prostrate Germans in the face of the vindictive fate that the United States had concocted for them? If this was the hidden objective of the Morgenthau Plan, what about the main organiser? Was this Harry Dexter White's purpose? Was White acting as a communist without specific instructions? Was he acting as a Soviet agent when he designed the project?" Kubek points out that anyone who studies the Morgenthau Diaries immediately sees the enormous power that H. D. White was accumulating. A week after Pearl Harbour, Kubek notes, the Treasury Department issued an order in which Henry Morgenthau announced that "the Assistant Secretary, Mr. Harry D.

White, will assume full responsibility for all matters relating to foreign relations to be handled by the Treasury Department." The awesome power that Morgenthau was delegating into the hands of a Communist agent can escape no one.

In *State Secrets,* Count Léon de Poncins extracts from Professor Kubek's introduction to Morgenthau's Diary an excerpt from the statement made in 1952 by defector Elizabeth Bentley before the Senate Subcommittee on Internal Security. The members of this Subcommittee wanted to know if there was a Morgenthau Plan for the Far East. Here is her transcript:

> "Miss Bentley: No, the only Morgenthau Plan I knew was the German one.
> Senator Eastland: Did you know who came up with that plan?
> Miss Bentley: It was due to Mr. White's influence. He was pushing for the devastation of Germany because that was what the Russians wanted.
> Senator Eastland: Do you think it was a communist conspiracy to destroy Germany and weaken it to the point where it could not help us?
> Miss Bentley: That is correct. It could no longer be a barrier protecting the Western world.
> Senator Eastland: And Mr. Morgenthau, who was Secretary of the Treasury of the United States, was used by Communist agents to promote this plot?
> Miss Bentley: I am afraid so; yes.
> Senator Smith: It was used unknowingly.
> Senator Ferguson: So you have conscious and unconscious agents?
> Miss Bentley: Of course..."

On 17 November 1952 J. Edgar Hoover, Director of the FBI, confirmed before the Subcommittee that Elizabeth Bentley's statement had been proved and corroborated by Whittaker Chambers and by manuscripts of White himself. As to whether Henry Morgenthau had been used, as Senator Smith claimed, it is clear that he was not, but that he was well aware of what was intended and approved of it, as will be seen below.

Disagreements between the Treasury Department and the State Department with regard to Germany increased as the end of the war approached. After the Bretton Woods Conference in July 1944, where Harry D. White prevailed over John M. Keynes, the British representative, and it was decided to create the World Bank and the International Monetary Fund, Morgenthau learned of the State Department's draft for Germany. Professor Kubek suggests that White may have received a copy of the document either from Virginius Frank Coe, a Jewish Communist who ended up working with Mao in China, or from Harold Glasser, another Soviet spy who like Dexter White was the son of Jewish émigrés from Lithuania. Glasser, codenamed "Ruble", had been a member of the Communist Party USA since 1933 and worked closely with White.

Henry Morgenthau was concerned about the State Department's plans and on 5 August 1944 decided to travel to London with White. On the 7th they held a meeting in southern England with General Eisenhower. They also contacted Colonel Bernard Bernstein, another Jew who was a Treasury legal officer and acted as Morgenthau's personal representative on General Eisenhower's staff. Bernstein, an extremist who was later identified by the Senate Subcommittee as an ardent supporter of the cause of communism, was the most conspicuous of the so-called "Morgenthau boys" and symbolised Morgenthau's spirit in the US military. "Only the Russians," Bernstein declared to the *Daily Worker* in February 1946, "have shown that they want to exterminate fascism and Nazism." On 12 August Morgenthau convened a meeting with several American officials in London formally interested in post-war Germany. He told them that the only way to prevent a third world conflagration was to make it impossible for Germany ever to wage war again.

The State Department, however, was unwilling to allow itself to be forced into a plan it considered absurd. When it was argued to Morgenthau that his plan was impossible simply because the countryside could not absorb so much labour, his retort was that the surplus population should be dumped in North Africa. As soon as he returned from England, the Treasury Secretary sought the intercession of his friend Roosevelt and called Secretary of State Hull to let him know that he had explained to General Eisenhower how the Germans were to be treated after the war. Morgenthau let Hull know that the commander-in-chief had assured him that "Germany would stew in her own gravy" for several months after the Allies' entry.

Eisenhower was true to his word, for in his death camps he kept millions of German prisoners "stewing in their own sauce" from April to October 1945, leaving them out in the open without shelter, medicine, water or food. At least 800,000 to 900,000 Germans died of starvation and thirst from dysentery, typhus and other diseases. This is another chapter of World War II that hardly anyone knows about because it has never been told. The Americans captured more than five and a half million German soldiers in Europe, not counting the prisoners in North Africa. On 10 March 1945 Eisenhower, so that they would not receive the treatment that the Geneva Convention required of POWs (prisoners of war), signed an order creating a new type of prisoner, "Disarmed Enemy Forces" (DEF). On the same day he told a conference in Paris that the US respected the Geneva Convention.

As a consequence of this order, the prisoners were never searched. They were kept on the bare ground despite the cold and rain and had to dig holes in the ground for shelter. The latrines were pits and wood set up next to the fences. The German prisoners remained for days without water and food: neither the Red Cross nor the population could get near the camps: the aid and food delivered by the Red Cross was returned by order of Eisenhower: the sick and wounded died without any care. From 1 May to 15

June, the camps set up along the banks of the Rhine suffered a dreadful death toll. Military doctors found that the mortality rate was eighty times higher than in any other situation known to them: diarrhoea, typhus, septicaemia (blood poisoning), dysentery, tetanus, cardiac arrest, lung inflammation, wasting and exhaustion were the causes of death recorded. James Bacque's *Other Losses* (1989) is the book where all the information can be found on this silent holocaust, one more, on which we will expand in a separate section at the end of this chapter.

Dwight David Eisenhower, son of David Jacob Eisenhower, was known at the West Point Military Academy as 'the terrible Swedish Jew', according to a 1915 West Point yearbook. Among his mentors were Bernard Baruch and Morgenthau himself. Perhaps because of this, despite his mediocre academic record and poor service record, he was passed over by military men such as George Patton and Douglas MacArthur and was promoted to general-in-chief and appointed commanding general of all Allied armies in Europe. His anti-Germanism must also have served him well in his meteoric rise. In a letter to his wife in September 1944, he wrote: "God, I hate the Germans!" James Bacque reproduces in *Other Losses* the embarrassed statement of Dr. Ernest F. Fisher, a major in the US Army: "Eisenhower's hatred, tolerated by a military bureaucracy that was amenable to him, produced the horror of the killing fields, unparalleled by anything else in American military history. Thus it was Morgenthau himself who explained how the Germans were to be treated to General Eisenhower, who showed that he hated them as much as the Secretary of the Treasury. As is well known, in 1953 Eisenhower was elected President of the United States and has gone down in history, like Roosevelt, Truman, Churchill and so many other criminals extolled by propaganda, as a champion of freedom and democracy.

Professor Kubek confirms that in the discussions between Morgenthau and White written in the Diary the plan to totally destroy the industrial resources of the Saar and Ruhr valleys appears again and again. Morgenthau stated categorically that he wanted to turn the Ruhr into "a ghost region". President Roosevelt was not at all opposed to this, for when the second Quebec Conference was held between 11 and 16 September 1944, he presented the Morgenthau Plan to Churchill and defended it. Roosevelt had invited Stalin, but Stalin declined the invitation, perhaps fearing that concessions would be demanded of him as his troops prepared to penetrate Eastern Europe. Stalin would no doubt have welcomed Roosevelt's willingness to dismantle Germany industrially and turn it into an agricultural country; but Churchill was beginning to question the disadvantages of allowing Russian imperialism to extend into the heart of Europe. He therefore argued that Germany might be necessary to establish a European balance. Nevertheless, on 15 September 1944 Roosevelt and Churchill signed the following declaration, which implied acceptance of the Morgenthau Plan:

> "It is only fair that the devastated countries, particularly Russia, should have the right to seize the material they need to compensate for the losses they have experienced. The Ruhr and Saar industries are therefore to be rendered unusable and closed down. It is accepted that these two regions will be placed under the supervision of a body under a world organisation charged with overseeing the decommissioning of such industries and preventing them from being brought into operation by subterfuge. This programme of eliminating the war industries presupposes that Germany would be converted into an agricultural country."

When the Morgenthau Plan and its acceptance by the Allied leadership was made public on 24 September 1944, despair grew in Germany as it became clear where the unconditional surrender agreed at Casablanca was leading. Consequently, there was an appeal to resistance through the media: the radio reported day and night that Germany would become a country of starving peasants if it surrendered.

In the United States, Stimson and Hull, the Secretaries of War and Defence who opposed Morgenthau, reacted when they learned that the President had endorsed the Treasury Secretary's plan in Quebec. Stimson submitted a memorandum to Roosevelt, rejecting the plan to turn Germany into an agricultural country, and Cordell Hull called the proposed policy for Germany "catastrophic". It was then decided to use a section of the press to counter-attack, with one article claiming that the British had been bought to accept the Morgenthau Plan. The interdepartmental confrontation escalated over the months, as evidenced by the entries in the *Morgenthau Diary, which* show that the Secretary of the Treasury felt strengthened by Churchill and Roosevelt's approval of the plan.

Convinced that they were going to get their way, Morgenthau and White were able to integrate the main features of their plan into the military orders issued by the Joint Chiefs of Staff (JCS). JCS/1067, which General Eisenhower received as soon as he entered Germany, concerned post-surrender control activities and reflected the hard-nosed philosophy of revenge outlined by Morgenthau, White and their team of Jewish Treasury officials. JCS/1067 of 22 September 1944 became an official watered-down version of the Morgenthau Plan that remained in effect for almost three years, until it was replaced in July 1947 by a new JCS policy directive.

As soon as Franklin D. Roosevelt's new victory was confirmed in the November 1944 elections, Harry Dexter White and his team of Jewish Communists in the Treasury renewed their efforts to implement the programme for the permanent destruction of Germany. Through various channels, White gathered information on the directives that other Departments were preparing in order to counter them. However, among the military and in certain Allied political circles, voices were increasingly insistent that German industry was needed to supply aid to devastated regions throughout Europe. Informed of these initiatives, on 10 January 1945 Morgenthau submitted a stern memorandum to President Roosevelt in which he stressed the Treasury's fears of a new militarism emerging in Germany, boldly questioned the arguments of those who opposed his Plan, and accused them of opposing a weak Germany out of fear of Russia and communism. A month later the facts were to prove that these fears were not unfounded, for Stalin's first demand at Yalta was the dismemberment of Germany.

The Morgenthau Plan had been hovering over the Big Three at the Yalta Conference; but when Roosevelt returned to the United States, he found that the State Department had drawn up its own programme for post-war Germany. The new Secretary of State, Edward Stettinius, replacing Cordell Hull, who had resigned in November 1944, submitted a draft to the President on 10 March outlining occupation policy without consulting the Treasury at all. This State Department memorandum was a reasonable replacement for the JCS/1067 directive that had so pleased Morgenthau and White, and was based on the idea that Germany was necessary for the economic recovery of Europe. When Morgenthau saw a copy of the memorandum, he was furious. Professor Kubek records his words to Stettinius: "I have the feeling that this is a completely different philosophy..., with which I cannot agree".

In his introductory work to *Morgenthau's Diary*, Professor Kubek notes that Morgenthau was convinced that approval of the State Department's plan would mean the complete defeat of his project, so he instructed his colleagues to prepare a paragraph-by-paragraph rebuttal of the document in order to demonstrate that the State Department's memorandum differed from the philosophy of the already accepted secret instruction JCS/1067. An emergency meeting on 19 March 1945, at which Dexter White and Jewish advisers Coe and Glasser advised him on how to approach President Roosevelt, was recorded in the Diary. The next day Morgenthau rushed to the White House to confirm Roosevelt's support. Roosevelt had a date with death in three weeks and was already suffering from mental lapses. On 21 March, an interdepartmental meeting began to discuss the State Department's plan. The discussions lasted until the 23rd and ended in a resounding triumph for the Treasury. Morgenthau exultantly informed his colleagues that the President had been persuaded to withdraw the State Department's 10 March memorandum. We copy below a very significant paragraph from Kubek's introduction as reproduced in Léon de Poncins' work:

> "For White and his associates the President's action was a victory of profound importance..., but success would not be complete, Morgenthau added, until certain people in key positions had been removed from the

Government. This concluding remark encapsulates a remarkably unconscionable excerpt from his political philosophy and includes some of the harshest language to be found in the Diaries: 'It is very encouraging that we have the President's backing.... The State Department people tried to get him to change it and couldn't. Sooner or later the president will have to change it. Sooner or later the President will have to clean his house. I'm talking about the mean people.... They are supporters of Herbert Hoover (pre-Roosevelt President) and Herbert Hoover got us into chaos and they are fascists at heart.... They are a malicious people and sooner or later they have to be rooted out. It was those people who fought us without rules.' The State Department was deeply disappointed by the President's rejection of its 10 March memorandum."

In another very interesting excerpt, Kubek highlights notes in *Morgenthau's diary* about a meeting Bernard Baruch had on 21 April 1945 with the War Cabinet. Baruch is acting in his capacity as adviser to President Truman (Roosevelt died on 12 April). He is asked about his position on the German problem. According to Morgenthau, Baruch replied that his recent trip to Europe had strengthened his idea of the decentralisation of Germany and that the Treasury plan was too soft and its author was almost a sissy. In the Diary, Morgenthau reports some harsh words from Baruch to a State Department representative named Clayton, who seems to offer him some resistance. The financial wizard threatens him severely, telling him that he will "cut his heart out if he doesn't behave himself". According to the Diary, Baruch told Clayton in public that he either understood the German issue or it was in his interest to "leave town". Morgenthau wrote with evident satisfaction that Baruch was adamant: "All that is left for me to live for," Baruch declared, "is to see that Germany is de-industrialised and that this is done in the proper way and I will not allow anyone to stand in my way." After commenting that Baruch was moved to tears, Morgenthau noted that he had "never seen a man speak as harshly as he did". Morgenthau wrote that he "had the impression that Baruch realised the importance of maintaining a friendly relationship with Russia". It is shocking to see the extent of Baruch's arrogance and thuggishness, capable of behaving like a Mafia capo to threaten and intimidate a senior State Department official who dared to disagree politically. Baruch, as we know, in addition to being a personal friend of Roosevelt, had acted as a political advisor to American presidents since the time of Woodrow Wilson. His power had been omnipotent and remained so with the arrival of Truman. The fact that he considered the Morgenthau Plan too soft gives an idea of the visceral hatred of the German people that nestled in the guts of America's most powerful Jews.

With Truman's accession to the Presidency, the State Department slowly tried to regain control of the reins of American foreign policy, as the influence of the Treasury slowly began to wane after the death of Morgenthau's fraternal friend Roosevelt. Step by step, the principles inspiring his plan for Germany lost support within the Administration to the point that on 5 July 1945, the day before Truman was due to travel to Europe to attend the Potsdam Conference, it was announced in Washington that Henry Morgenthau had resigned after eleven years as Secretary of the Treasury. Admiral Leahy revealed that Morgenthau intended to attend Potsdam and threatened to resign if he was not included in the American delegation, so his resignation was accepted. This did not, however, prevent Colonel Bernstein and other "Morgenthau boys" from hanging on to their posts after their boss's departure. At the end of 1945, some 140 Treasury "specialists" still held important positions in the German military government and continued to implement the secret directive JCS/1067.

The treatment of Germany in the period of initial control was the main issue discussed at the Potsdam Conference in July. The Allied leaders came imbued with the spirit of the Morgenthau Plan, and the agreements adopted departed little from its broad outlines. The Potsdam agreement contained a clause authorising each of the heads of the four zones to take action to prevent famine and disease. However, it has already been shown that in the American zone, General Eisenhower's inhumane actions led to the deaths of nearly one million prisoners. On the other hand, the Allies had agreed at Yalta to hand over all Soviet citizens to Stalin, so that Russian anti-Communists who had taken refuge in the American, French and British zones of Central Europe, as well as refugees from satellite countries such as Hungary, Bulgaria, Romania and others, were arrested. The forced repatriation to the USSR of fifty thousand Cossacks against their will has already been discussed in chapter eight. In all, more than two million unfortunates whose fate was deportation or death were handed over to the Soviets. This was a despicable act, committed by countries claiming to defend freedom.

Since the JCS/1067 instructions were virtual orders, US administrators in the American zone could not fail to implement them. Soon journalists and international observers realised that the policy in the American zone was absolutely insane. As White had anticipated, the situation in Germany for three years was desperate. The cities, into which an unceasing stream of millions of refugees from the East flowed, remained a heap of ruins. Had the Treasury plan, designed to quarantine the entire population of a defeated nation and plunge it into misery, been implemented as Morgenthau, White and their clique of communist Jews had designed it, the greatest genocide in history would have taken place. Even so, as had happened in Eisenhower's death camps, of the seventeen million Germans driven from their homes, another two million died inhuman deaths on their pilgrimage to the West. There will be an opportunity to recount this later.

All these facts make it possible to prove for the hundredth time that from its inception communism was an ideology put at the service of the Jewish bankers' plan for international domination. Adam Weishaupt, Jacob

Frank, Moses Hess, Karl Marx, Israel Helphand (Alexander Parvus), Trotsky, Lenin, Zinoviev, Kamenev and all the main leaders of the Bolshevik Revolution were Jewish agents who dedicated their lives to the cause of international communist revolution. Thus, the fact that the very large group of Jews who acted under Morgenthau and White were at the same time Communists is not a novelty or an exception, but a confirmation of the rule. There is no doubt that the Morgenthau Plan was psychopathologically anti-German. Douglas Reed considers in *The Controversy of Zion* that what happened to the Germans was Talmudic revenge, and this was corroborated in *The Hidden Tyranny* by Benjamin H. Freedman, the Jewish billionaire convert to Catholicism who claimed that Roosevelt was manipulated by Talmudic Jews. The pertinent question is whether the Morgenthau Plan was not only anti-German but also pro-Communist. Two undeniable facts suggest that it was: the Plan was in line with Stalin's wishes for Germany, and Harry Dexter White and his aides were Soviet agents. Professor Kubek ends his 81-page introduction to *Morgenthau's Diary* with this paragraph:

> "Never before in American history has an unelected stealth bureaucracy of anonymous high-ranking officials exercised power so arbitrarily or cast such a shameful shadow over the nation's future as did Harry Dexter White and his associates in the Treasury Department under Henry Morgenthau. What they attempted to do in their bizarre contortion of American ideals and how close they came to success is demonstrated by these documents. But this is all that is known for certain. What priceless American secrets were transmitted to Moscow through the clandestine communist tunnels will probably never be known. And how much damage these sinister men did to the security of the United States remains, at least for the moment, a matter of conjecture."

It can be concluded, therefore, that a group of Jews placed in essential circles of power determined the American government and played a decisive role in directing American policy in their interests. There is no doubt that they intended to inflict as much damage as possible on the German people as a whole and to further the establishment of communism in Europe, a goal that was largely achieved at Yalta. The *Morgenthau Diary* shows that an elite of Jews who dominated finance controlled as usual the political power, from which they secretly worked to achieve their aims, which included the disintegration of European Christian societies through revolutionary doctrines such as international atheistic communism. Their other major aim was the creation of the Zionist state. To achieve this, they needed the persecution of European Jews, to whom, having lost their property and homes, the promised land of Israel would be offered. Henry Morgenthau, after having been one of the leaders of the Bretton Woods Agreements that led to the creation of the World Bank and the International Monetary Fund, became after his resignation a financial advisor to Israel, where in 1948 a rural community ("kibbutz") was named in his honour "Tal Shahar", which in Hebrew means, like Morgenthau in German, "morning dew".

The Yalta Conference

In 1955, the Americans brought to light the official documents of the Yalta Conference, which until then had remained secret. The State Department acknowledged, however, that important parts had been omitted. In the same year AHR published the texts in Spain in two volumes entitled *Yalta*, so they can be read in Spanish. John Foster Dulles, the Secretary of State, disguising the hidden reasons of political interest behind the publication, explained at a press conference that it was intended to inform public opinion in the interests of truth and historical accuracy. Both the government and the British press criticised Foster Dulles' manoeuvre: *The Times* found that the decision had been "taken at the wrong time and for clumsy reasons". The *Daily Mail* called the publication "a diplomatic blunder of the first magnitude". In the United States, some newspapers strongly criticised the decision. The *New York Daily News* accused the State Department of wanting to cloud international relations. The *Daily Mirror* demanded to know how many pages and words had been omitted and for what reasons. From Jerusalem, Eleanor Roosevelt, on an eight-day visit to her Zionist friends in Israel, assured that her husband would never have released the documents.

Before arriving at Yalta, Churchill and Roosevelt met in Malta to discuss the situation in Europe and the Pacific, but as at Tehran, Roosevelt was reluctant to meet alone with the British prime minister for fear that Stalin might think that his Western allies were allied against him. Those who did meet on 1 February were his foreign ministers, Secretary of State Edward Stettinius and Foreign Office Secretary Anthony Eden. Both reportedly agreed to disapprove of Poland's well-known territorial demands, as expressed by the provisional puppet government in Lublin, but their opposition was watered down at Yalta. On 3 February Roosevelt and Churchill flew to the Crimea. The American president received special treatment and stayed in the Tsar's room in the Livadia Palace, the central venue for the meetings. Stalin arrived on Sunday 4 February 1945, the opening day of the Conference where the future of millions of people in the post-war world was to be determined. The Red Army had entered Warsaw and Budapest and the Germans were already resisting in their own territory under impossible conditions. The destruction of Dresden was at hand. Meanwhile, since the end of January, Japan had been unsuccessfully asking the Soviets to mediate with the United States to sign an armistice.

During the week-long Conference, the Big Three delegations held four types of meetings: plenary sessions, foreign ministers' meetings, chiefs of staff meetings, and leaders' meetings, which were either trilateral or bilateral. As early as 4 February, for example, the Soviets and Americans met at 4 p.m. in "petit comité". Roosevelt was accompanied by Charles "Chip" Bohlen, a diplomatic expert on the USSR who was supposedly only acting as an interpreter. Stalin was accompanied by Molotov and his interpreter, Vladimir Pavlov. Already at this meeting Roosevelt confessed that he was more bloodthirsty than in Teheran and that he expected Marshal Stalin to propose again a toast to the execution of 50,000 German officers. Stalin replied by confirming that they were all more bloodthirsty. After discussing the military situation on the two fronts. Roosevelt enquired about Charles De Gaulle's interview with Stalin, and Stalin commented that he did not find him a complicated person, although he was deluded by his pretensions. Stalin asked whether France should have an occupation zone and for what reasons. Both Molotov and Stalin were not at all clear about this, but over the course of the week the Soviets eventually made this concession for the sake of other priorities on which they did not intend to compromise.

Poland and Germany were the main topics of discussion. The creation of the UN, Japan, the Balkans, the Middle East and the Europe Stalin called "liberated" were the other major topics. The Polish question was discussed for the first time in a plenary session that began at 4 p.m. on Tuesday 6 February in the Livadia Palace. The British and Americans began by accepting the Curzon Line without further problems, thus legitimising the invasion and annexation of 1939. On these territories of over 181,000 square kilometres lived 10,640,000 people, according to the 1931 census, whose wishes or opinion were irrelevant to the champions of freedom. All they dared to ask of Stalin about these territories was that he would consider ceding Lvov to Poland. Churchill asked him for "a gesture of magnanimity which would be acclaimed and admired." Britain's position on Poland was pathetic throughout the Conference. The country that had provoked the war by refusing to accept that the Danzig Germans could rejoin the Reich, was now handing millions of Poles over to communist totalitarianism. In London, Poles in exile had expected everything from the British, so Churchill recalled that he had gone to war to protect Poland against German aggression and declared that the British had no material interest in the country, but that it was a question of honour, which was why "his Government would never be content with a solution which did not leave Poland as a free and independent state... mistress of her own house and director of her soul". Churchill then added that Britain "recognised the Polish Government in London, but had no intimate contact with it." He asked whether it would be possible to form an interim government with the men in it until another one emerged from an election. Stalin asked for a ten-minute break for the obvious purpose of preparing his reply.

To the question of honour, Stalin replied that for the Russians it was not only a question of honour but also of security. To the question of the magnanimous act, he recalled that the Curzon line had been drawn by Lord Curzon and Clemenceau. "Should we then, he asked, be less Russian than Curzon and Clemenceau? As to the creation of a Polish Government on the pass of the Government of the exiles in London he said, "They call me a dictator and not a democrat, but I have enough democratic feelings to refuse to create a Polish Government without the Poles being consulted; the question can only be settled with the consent of the Poles." Stalin then recalled the interviews held in the autumn in Moscow between Stanislaw Mikolajczyk, representative of the London Government, and the Poles in Lublin, where the Polish Communist Government under Stalin's own auspices resided, which, he intimated to Churchill, had at least "a democratic basis at least equal to that of Charles De Gaulle." From this first approach, it was thus clear that rather than borders, the insoluble problem was going to be the existence of two Polish governments.

In order to better understand the discussion on Poland at Yalta, it is necessary to consider briefly a few facts. The Polish government in exile had expressed to London and Washington the need for East Prussia to be incorporated into the Poland that would emerge with the Allied victory. After the German attack in June 1941, Stalin supported this idea without revealing that he coveted the northern half, including Königsberg, for himself. On 15 March 1943, at a dinner in Washington attended by Hopkins, Roosevelt and Eden agreed to accede to the Poles' request. Hopkins called Litvinov, the ambassador to the United States, the next day to confirm this. Litvinov then reminded Roosevelt's adviser that the USSR would keep the part of Poland taken as a result of the Ribbentrop-Molotov Pact. Upon learning of the Soviet claims, the Poles in London appealed to their Western allies for help. This created an embarrassing situation for the British, who were about to approve the annexation of half of Poland's pre-war territory when they had supposedly gone to war to guarantee Poland's territorial integrity. At the Tehran conference, despite Polish reluctance, neither Churchill nor Roosevelt resisted Stalin, and the idea of compensating the Poles at the expense of the Germans was born. In other words, without consulting anyone and in order to please the Soviet dictator, they decided to move the borders 240 kilometres westwards, completely ignoring the rights of the millions of people affected.

Despite promised compensation, the Polish government in exile could not accept the renunciation of half of its territory in the east. Moreover, the relations of the Poles in London with the Soviet Union had been steadily deteriorating after the discovery of the Katyn graves in the spring of 1943. As discussed earlier in this chapter, General Sikorski, President of the Government in Exile, requested an investigation by the International Red Cross, the results of which showed that Beria and Stalin were responsible for the massacre. The Soviets, in addition to feigning indignation, took the opportunity to accuse Sikorski of working for Hitler and broke off relations with the Polish government in London. On 4 July 1943 a bomb planted on Sikorski's plane killed the cumbersome character and Mikolajczyk became his successor[11]. In this way, Stalin quickly took advantage of the situation, for in one fell swoop he pushed the non-communist Poles aside and formed a tailor-made Polish government in Moscow, which, unlike Sikorski and Mikolajczyk, would be ready to approve the surrender of eastern Poland to Soviet communism.

In the summer of 1944 the Red Army began to dislodge the Germans from Poland and occupy the country. In its wake came the Polish Communists from Moscow, who rushed to assume real authority on the ground while the London-protected Poles could do nothing from a distance. The president of the Polish government-in-exile, Stanislaw Mikolajczyk, had visited Roosevelt in June, and both the American president and Churchill pressed him to travel to Moscow and appeal directly to Stalin. On 27 July 1944, the same day that newspapers announced an agreement between the Soviet government and the Polish Communist Committee of National Liberation allowing the Committee to assume "full direction of all matters of civil administration", Mikolajczyk travelled to Moscow to meet with Stalin and Molotov.

The Poles in London were already doomed, for the most that could be offered to them was a position in the communist-formed government. Churchill understood this at once and warned them that the best thing they could do was to forget the Katyn massacre and try to collaborate with Stalin, otherwise they would be ruled out as players in the Poland of the future. The first prerequisite for understanding with the Russians was to capitulate on the issue of the eastern border. On the morning of 14 October 1944, only a few months before the Yalta Conference, Churchill and Eden, who were in Moscow, summoned Mikolajczyk to the British Embassy in order to press him to accept the Curzon line without Lvov or Galicia. Alfred M. de Zayas reproduces in *Nemesis at Potsdam* a good excerpt from the interview, which allows us to appreciate, as this author rightly points out, what level of tension or pressure on political power can reach:

"Mikolajczyk: I know that our fate was sealed in Tehran.

---

[11] Roland Perry's *The Fifth Man*, which will be discussed in more detail in the next chapter, provides some very interesting facts about Sikorski's assassination. According to this author, Donald Maclean, one of the Soviet spies known as the "Cambridge Five", knew that Sikorski would travel to Gibraltar in July to meet with other exiles. After taking off from the Rock in a Liberator carrying his daughter and two British servicemen, Victor Cazalet and Brigadier John Whiteley, the plane exploded at an altitude of 300 metres. Colonel Victor Rothschild, the third Baron Rothschild, appointed during the war as security inspector by Guy Liddell, was appointed to undertake the investigation demanded by the Poles. His findings indicated that there had been an explosion on board, indicating that it was not an accident, but an act of sabotage.

Churchill: He was saved in Tehran.

Mikolajczyk: I am not a person completely lacking in patriotic sentiment to give up half of Poland.

Churchill: What do you mean when you say that you are not devoid of patriotic spirit? Twenty-five years ago we reconstituted Poland although in the last war more Poles fought against us than with us. Now we are preserving them again so that they do not disappear, but you do not want to play the game. You are completely crazy.

Mikolajczyk: But this solution does not change anything.

Churchill: Unless you accept the frontier, you are out of the question forever. The Russians will raze your country to the ground and your people will be liquidated. They are on the verge of annihilation.

Eden: If we can reach an understanding on the Curzon Line, we will reach an agreement with the Russians on all other issues. You will get a guarantee from us.

Churchill: Poland will be secured by the three Great Powers and certainly by us. The American Constitution prevents the President from committing the United States. In any case, you are not giving up anything because the Russians are already there.

Mikolajczyk: We lose everything.

Churchill: The Pinsk Marshes and five million people. Ukrainians are not part of his people. It saves its own people and empowers us to act forcefully.

Mikolajczyk: Should we sign this if we are going to lose our independence?

Churchill: You have only one choice. It would make a big difference if you agree.

Mikolajczyk: Would it not be possible to announce that the Big Three have decided on Poland's borders without our presence?

Churchill: We will get sick and tired of you if you go on arguing.

Eden: You could say that in view of the statement made by the British and Soviet governments, you accept a de facto formula, under protest if you like, and put the blame on us. I understand the difficulty in saying that it has been done with your will.

Mikolajczyk: We lose all authority in Poland if we accept the Curzon line, and besides, nothing is said about what we could get from the Germans.

Eden: I think we could do it. We could take the risk. We could say what you guys are going to get."

At this point, Churchill went to fetch a draft of the declaration stipulating Polish acceptance of the Curzon Line and explained to Mikolajczyk that the Germans would be furious if they knew what they intended to take from them, and that their resistance would be even greater. This ended the meeting, which resumed in the afternoon. Churchill showed up in a bad mood and with increased impatience. Mikolajczyk informed him that having reconsidered, his government could not accept the loss of almost half of the territory in the east without having heard the opinion of the Polish people. With extreme harshness, Churchill denied that they were a government, since they were incapable of making decisions. You are," he said, "heartless fiends who want to wreck Europe. I will leave you to your own problems. You have no sense of responsibility when you want to abandon your people, whose sufferings you are indifferent to. They do not care about the future of Europe. They think only of their own miserable selfish interests. I will have to call the other Poles and this government in Lublin can work very well. It will be the government. It is a criminal attempt on their part to ruin, with their 'Liberum Veto'[12], the agreement between the Allies. It is cowardice." The interview was called off with this violent accusation, as Churchill was due to attend an interview with Stalin scheduled for that same afternoon.

The next day, 15 October, Mikolajczyk met Churchill again and offered to accept the Curzon Line if Lvov and the Galician oil fields were preserved for Poland. In an outburst of temper, Churchill, before slamming the door out of the room, shouted to the Pole, "It's all over between us." Mikolajczyk, for his part, left the room without wanting to shake hands with the Secretary of the Foreign Office. It is understandable, then, that Stalin refused at Yalta to make "a gesture of magnanimity" about Lvov, for he knew that both Roosevelt and Churchill had already accepted the Curzon line and that he had no need to cede Galicia and/or Lvov. George F. Kennan, a diplomat who had served in Moscow with Bullitt and Davies, repeatedly expressed his frustration with the Allied attitude in his Memoirs. Kennan had been in the Russian capital since July 1944 with Ambassador Averell Harriman and had good information about what was being hatched at the end of the war. This diplomat was among those who thought that the United States and Britain might have opposed Stalin, since he depended on their military and economic aid.

While Moscow's negotiations were failing, the Lublin government had already recognised the Curzon Line and was consolidating its power in Poland. It did not take Mikolajczyk long to realise that it was not possible to save eastern Poland and that the only option was to obtain the greatest possible compensation in the west, at the expense of Germany. With the German lands Stalin was absolutely generous and had offered not only the border of the Oder, but even that of the Neisse Lusatius, the tributary flowing perpendicularly from Czechoslovakia on the left bank of the Oder. The Oder-Neisse border was publicly demanded by Dr. Stefan Jedrichovski, head of Propaganda of the Lublin Committee, in a long article published in *Pravda*

---

[12] By using this Latin expression, Churchill demonstrates knowledge of Polish parliamentarianism. "Liberum Veto" means "free veto" or "veto freely". This was the name given in the Polish Diet to the veto by which each deputy could oppose any decision of the assembly.

on 18 December 1944. Jedrichovski also claimed the Pomeranian capital, Stettin, located west of the Oder, which was to become a new Polish port.

Two Neisse rivers flow into the Oder on its left bank. Between the Neisse Lusatius and the easternmost Neisse, both in Lower Silesia, stretches an agricultural territory that was inhabited by about three million Germans. It escaped no one's notice that Khedrichovsky's demands reflected the Soviet government's position on Poland's western border. The first to show serious misgivings was Kennan, who warned Ambassador Harriman about the implications of the article. "I did not know then," Kennan writes in his Memoirs, "that this agreement had already been practically accepted, specifically by Churchill and tacitly by Roosevelt, at the Teheran Conference a year earlier." Six weeks before the start of the Yalta Conference, Kennan submitted a memorandum warning that between nine and ten million Germans lived in the areas claimed by the Polish Communists.

We can now return to Yalta to continue the discussions on the Polish question. At the plenary session on Wednesday, 7 February, Molotov read out the Soviet proposals on Poland. As for the borders, the Foreign Commissioner stuck to the Curzon line in the east and the Oder-Neisse border in the west with the town of Stettin for Poland, even though it was situated west of the Oder. On the Provisional Government in Lublin, he was prepared to accept the inclusion in it of "democratic leaders of émigré circles" if this contributed to its recognition by the Allied governments. Churchill rejected the term "émigrés" because, he said, "this word had originated during the French Revolution and meant in England a person who had been expelled from his country by his own people". He said that he supported Molotov's proposals on the movement of the Polish frontiers; however, in connection with the Neisse frontier he pointed out that "it would be a pity to stuff the Polish goose with so much German food that it would suffer indigestion." Stalin was quick to comment that the Germans fled when his troops arrived, but Churchill observed that there was then the problem of how to handle them in Germany. "We have killed six or seven million," he said coldly as if talking about animals in a slaughterhouse, "and we shall probably kill another million before the end of the war." "One or two?" retorted Stalin. "Well, I am not proposing a limitation. So, then," Churchill clarified, "there will be room left in Germany for those who want to fill the vacancies. I am not afraid of the problem of transferring peoples, so long as there is proportion to what the Poles can manage and what they put into Germany in place of the dead."

The issue of non-Communist members of the Lublin government prompted Churchill and Roosevelt to propose that democratic leaders from "inside Poland" should be included. Roosevelt raised the need for the future provisional government to organise elections and suggested that London Poles such as Mikolajczyk, Romer and Grabski should be part of the new government. The issue of borders, then, was less of a concern than that of the future Polish government, an issue on which Churchill and Roosevelt were staking their credibility. After the meeting, Roosevelt addressed the following letter to Stalin:

> "My dear Marshal Stalin, I have given our meeting this afternoon a great deal of thought, and I want to express my opinion to you quite frankly.
> As far as the Polish Government is concerned, I am very unhappy that the three great powers do not agree on the political restoration of Poland. It seems to me that it would put us in a bad light in the eyes of the world if you were to recognise one government while we and the British were recognising another, in London. I am sure that this state of affairs should not continue and that if it does continue it would only lead our people to think that there was a split between us, which is not the case. I am determined that there should be no rift between us and the USSR. Surely there will be a means of reconciling our differences.
> I was very impressed by some of what you said today, particularly your determination that the Russian rearguard should be safeguarded in its movement towards Berlin. You cannot and we cannot tolerate an interim government which would cause your armed forces such a disruption. I want you to know that this is a matter of great concern to me.
> You can believe me when I tell you that our people look with a critical eye on what they regard as a rift between us at this vital stage of the war. Indeed, they say that if we cannot come to an agreement now that our armies are converging on our common enemy, we will not be able to understand each other on even more vital things in the future.
> I must make it clear to you that we cannot recognise the Lublin Government as it is now composed and that it would be considered a regrettable beginning to our work here if we were to part company with an obvious divergence on the matter.
> You said today that you were ready to support any suggestion that would offer a chance of success in solving this problem and you also mentioned the possibility of bringing some of the members of the Lublin government here.
> I understand that we all feel the same anxiety to settle this matter. I would like to comment a little on your proposal and suggest that we invite here to Yalta at once Mr. Bierut and Mr. Osubka-Morawski from the Lublin Government and also two or three Poles who, according to our reports, would be advisable. Osubka-Morawski of the Lublin Government and also two or three from the following list of Poles who, according to our reports, would be advisable as representatives of other elements of the Polish people in the formation of a new temporary government which all three of us could recognise and support: Bishop Sapieha of Cracow; Vincent Witos; Mr. Zurlowski (Zulawski); Professor Buyak (Bujak) and Professor Kutzeba. If as a result of the presence here of these political leaders we could jointly agree with them on a provisional government in Poland, which would certainly include some political leaders from abroad

such as Mr. Mikolajcvzyk, Mr. Graber and Mr. Romer, the U.S. Government and, I believe, certainly also the British Government, would be prepared to dissociate themselves from the London Government and to transfer their recognition to the new provisional government.
I do not think it necessary to assure you that the United States will never lend its support to any Polish provisional government which is inimical to its interests.
It goes without saying that any interim government that might be formed, as a result of our conference here with the Poles, should undertake to call free and democratic elections in Poland at the earliest possible date. I know that this is entirely in keeping with your desire to see a new democratic and free Poland emerge from the mire of this war.

Yours sincerely Franklin D. Roosevelt".

Although it has been shown throughout these pages that cynicism, hypocrisy and shamelessness were consubstantial to this American president throughout his political career, Roosevelt's last words are truly insane, to say the least. One imagines Stalin, a ruthless dictator if ever there was one, laughing his head off after reading Roosevelt tell him that he knows he wants to see "a new democratic and free Poland". The substance of the letter is, of course, a concern to save face in the face of a public opinion that was soon to see how at Yalta its leaders had surrendered half of Europe to communism.

At the plenary session on the 8th, Molotov acknowledged receipt of Roosevelt's letter. He insisted that it was impossible to ignore the existence of the Lublin or Warsaw Government, "which was at the head of the Polish people and enjoyed great prestige and popularity in the country". Any agreement should therefore be reached on the basis of its enlargement, which he reiterated his readiness to discuss. On borders, the Soviets did not budge. The British premier began by saying that, according to his reports, the governments in Lublin or Warsaw did not represent the overwhelming mass of the Polish people, and reiterated that "if the British Government were to sweep away the London Government and accept the Lublin Government, there would be an irritated outcry in Britain." He recalled that on the Western fronts a Polish army of one hundred and fifty thousand men had fought bravely and that they would not accept "an act of betrayal of Poland". Increasingly uncomfortable, Churchill shrugged off the borders and declared that he accepted the Soviet point of view; but he insisted that "a complete break with the legitimate Government of Poland, recognised during the war years, would be an act subject to the severest criticism in England". That said, he seized on the need to call an election on the basis of universal suffrage and assured that Britain could then recognise the government born of the elections.

Roosevelt endorsed the proposal and argued that, if there was agreement on it, the only problem was "how Poland would be governed in the interval". Stalin intervened to confirm that, indeed, they and the British had different briefs. He acknowledged that for years the Poles had hated the Russians,, but that the old feelings had disappeared and that his impression was "that the expulsion of the Germans by the Red Army had been received by the Poles as a great bank holidays." He accepted the idea of expanding the Provisional Government. Roosevelt then asked directly how long, in the Marshal's opinion, it would be before elections could be held in Poland. Stalin replied that, barring a catastrophe at the front, they would be possible within a month. The President immediately proposed to refer the matter to the Foreign Ministers for consideration. If Roosevelt and Churchill really believed that in just one month, in the middle of the war, elections could be held with the participation of the exiles, one would think they were just two pipsqueaks; however, the facts show that they were two seasoned politicians.

In order to lighten the mood, Stalin hosted a dinner for the delegations in the evening at the Yusupovsky Palace. The host, in excellent humour and in high spirits, created an extremely cordial atmosphere. As many as forty-five toasts were made: to the armed forces, to the countries, to the military leaders, to the friendship of the three powers.... The most cloying eulogies were given by Stalin, who proposed a toast to the British Premier, "the bravest government figure in the world". The Marshal said that he "knew of few examples in history where the courage of one man had been so important for the future of the world and that he drank to Mr. Churchill, his friend, fighter and courageous man". In his reply, Churchill toasted Marshal Stalin "the mighty leader of a mighty country who has withstood the shock of the German machine, broken his sword and driven tyrants from his soil." For his part, Roosevelt, in response to a toast from Stalin, said that the atmosphere at the dinner "was that of a family."

At the plenary meeting the next day, Friday, 9 February, the Polish issue began to get on track when the Soviets decided to allow Mikolajczyk to take part in the elections because, Stalin said, "he was leader of the Peasants' Party, which was not a fascist party." Roosevelt appealed to the six million Poles living in the United States for assurances of free elections. Stalin then accepted a statement read by Roosevelt which spoke of "interim authorities, broadly representative of all elements of the population and the obligation to create as soon as possible, through free elections, a Government responsible to the people." The minutes of H. Freeman Matthews, assistant to the Secretary of State, reproduce this dialogue:

> "Churchill: I want this election in Poland to be first of all. It must be like Caesar's wife. I don't know, but they say she was pure.
> Stalin. So they say, but in reality he had his sins.
> Churchill: I do not want the Poles to be able to question the Polish elections. The issue is not just one of principle, but of practical politics.
> Molotov: We owe this to the Poles. We are afraid that if we do not consult with them they will regard it as a lack of trust on our part.

At this point Roosevelt proposed that the foreign ministers finish polishing the declaration and suggested moving on to the issue of the liberated zones. Clearly, the Soviets had already decided to make things easier on Poland, in order to avoid embarrassing the British and Americans in the eyes of public opinion at home. The elections, like Caesar's wife, had to be pure; but Stalin had already warned about Caesar's wife....

At the foreign ministers' meeting, the text to be presented at the end of the conference was finally agreed upon. In short, it was decided that the established government in Poland would broaden its base and be reorganised with the inclusion of democratic leaders from Poland itself and from abroad. The new government would be called the "Polish Provisional Government of National Unity". Mólotov and the two ambassadors in Moscow, Sir Archibald Clark Kerr and Averell Harriman, were authorised to mediate with each other to make possible the formation of such a government, which would be obliged to call free elections as soon as possible on the basis of universal suffrage and secret ballot. Once these requirements had been met, the three governments would recognise the results. As for the borders, the final document agreed that the Curzon line, with slight adjustments of five to eight kilometres in some regions in favour of Poland, would be the eastern boundary. On the western Oder-Neisse border, although implicitly accepted, final approval was postponed to the Potsdam Peace Conference.

In reality, the good intentions expressed with regard to Poland were valid for the rest of the European countries occupied by the Soviets. Only very naïve politicians, and this was not the case, could have been confident that, after allowing the Red Army to reach the Brandenburg Gate, democracies would emerge in a Europe surrendered to communism. It is therefore not acceptable or credible that Roosevelt and Churchill expected a dictator like Stalin to become a democrat at the drop of a hat, so it is appropriate to speak of betrayal of the nations of Eastern Europe. After Potsdam, the Yalta agreements on the establishment of freely elected democratic regimes were systematically flouted. In Poland, the main opponents were murdered throughout 1945. Instead of the elections promised by Stalin, a fraudulent referendum was held in 1946 which consolidated the Communists in power. By the time elections were called on 19 January 1947, virtually all opposition parties had been declared illegal. A pro-government National Unity Front composed of the Communists and their allies inevitably won. Mikolajczyk's Peasant Party could do little. Accused of being a foreign spy and facing arrest, Mikolajczyk left the country. The few remaining opponents followed his example. Different versions of what happened in Poland were experienced in what were soon to be called satellite countries.

The idea of the dismemberment of Germany, of which the cession of East Prussia, Silesia, Pomerania and eastern Brandenburg to Poland was part, had been decided long before Yalta. In October 1943, shortly before the Tehran Conference, foreign ministers had agreed in Moscow to set up a European Consultative Commission. The proposal came from the British, who wanted this consultative body to deal with all European issues of common interest related to the war. At the end of 1943 such a Consultative Commission was set up in London, and on 14 January 1944 it held its first working meeting. Even then, the British presented detailed proposals for the future zones of occupation of Germany, which, with few differences, were eventually implemented. On 18 February the Russians accepted the London plans.

On 1 May 1944 John Winant, the American ambassador who had replaced Joe Kennedy, received instructions from Washington accepting the boundaries of the eastern zone, which shows that everything was decided while the Red Army was still fighting with the Vehrmacht on Soviet territory, i.e., well in advance. As we have seen, Morgenthau, Dexter White and their cast of Jewish Communists were working to ensure that Germany would end up in the hands of the Soviets. Stalin contemplated at Yalta the possibility of condemning the entire population to forced labour so that they could meet the reparations of $20 billion, half of which was to be received by the USSR. It was established that the three powers would occupy parts of Germany and that a Central Control Commission based in Berlin would control the administration. As for France, Stalin reluctantly agreed that if the British and Americans wanted to cede part of their zones to him, he could become a member of the Control Commission if he wished. At Yalta, however, the agreed dismemberment was not announced, as it was decided to wait for unconditional surrender and the Peace Conference.

It is not possible to devote space to talks on the UN, the Middle East or Japan. We will end, therefore, by highlighting a conversation that took place at a tripartite dinner held at 9 p.m. on 10 February at the Vorontsov villa. It was attended by Roosevelt, Churchill and Stalin alone, accompanied by their respective foreign ministers and interpreters. During the meal the subject of the Middle East was raised and in this context Stalin said that the Jewish problem was very difficult and that they had tried to establish a homeland for the Jews in Birobidjan[13], but that they had remained there for two or three years and then dispersed to the cities. President Roosevelt, who

---

[13] Settlement of Jews in Birobidjan had begun in the 1920s. During the 1920s, the government moved Jews to the region to expand security in the Soviet Far East. On 28 May 1928, the Birobidjan District was established, and it was in that year that the mass emigration of Jews began, coming from Belarus, Ukraine and even the United States. After the Japanese occupation of Manchuria in 1931, settlement in Birobidjan intensified. On 7 May 1934, a Decree of the Central Executive Committee of the USSR made the Birobidjan District a Jewish Autonomous Region. Stalin thus created the Jewish state of Birobidjan in Siberia, which was similar in size to Israel. Some 30,000 Jews arrived in the Autonomous Region during those years.

knew that the Jewish leaders would accept no territory other than Palestine and that Churchill, like him, was working for Zionism to establish the Jewish state after the war, publicly stated that he was a Zionist and asked Marshal Stalin if he was too. Stalin, no doubt surprised by the question, said that he was, but recognised the difficulty. Later, in reviewing Stalin's assassination, there will be occasion to return to Stalin's relations with the Zionists.

Part 6
Immune Crimes and Massacres against the German People

The crimes that the victors committed against the German people are not generally known. As we have been denouncing, for more than seventy years lies and the falsification of reality have prevented the people of Europe and the world from learning about the tragedy of the Germans. The uninterrupted propaganda and the fraudulent version of events disseminated in schools and in the media have been relentless, making it almost impossible to change the perception of history that points to Germany as solely responsible for the Second World War, for which it deserves no clemency and eternal condemnation. A neglected episode is the deportation imposed on Germans living in USSR-occupied parts of Europe, who were systematically banished from their homes and lands, regardless of whether or not they were members of the NSDAP.

In addition to the areas of Germany evicted and handed over to Poland, millions of ethnic Germans were persecuted and/or unceremoniously expelled from the countries where they had lived before the war. Poland, Romania, Yugoslavia, Hungary, Czechoslovakia, the Soviet Union, Estonia, Latvia, Lithuania, not forgetting the city of Danzig, expelled the ethnic German population. In all, some 19,000,000 people lost everything, for if they did not flee, they were expelled to Germany, where the desolation and misery of a devastated country awaited them. Many could not reach the British, American and French-controlled areas, and settled in Austria and communist Germany. Some two million died during their pilgrimage west, victims of hunger, exhaustion, cold and disease. These expulsions, the largest population transfer in history, will be discussed in Chapter XI: "I am not afraid," Churchill had declared at Yalta, "of the problem of the transfer of peoples". Before dealing with this colossal tragedy in the first part of the next chapter, the crimes and massacres committed against the Germans in the last months of the war and the early post-war period must be described.

The Nemmersdorf Prelude

The flight for their lives was a prelude to the mass expulsions or population transfers that followed after the end of the war. In October 1944, Nemmersdorf in East Prussia was a foretaste of what was in store for the Germans if they did not abandon the towns taken by the Red Army. On 16 October the Soviets launched an offensive that allowed them to penetrate into Reich territory for the first time. On 19 October they occupied Gumbinnen, and a day later the 25th Armoured Brigade entered

Nemmersdorf, a town of just over 600 inhabitants ten kilometres southwest of Gumbinnen. With the German fortified defensive line broken, the Soviets could have pushed west and north-west unopposed, but they did not. Although General Budenny, commander of the 2nd Armoured Army Corps, ordered the immediate advance, the Brigade did not move for a day and a half, allowing the Germans to deploy two Panzer divisions, one on each side of the Soviet penetration. On 23 October the pincer closed on the rear of Budenny's Corps, which after losing a thousand tanks and seventeen thousand men fell back and on 27 October had to go on the defensive.

Following the success of the Wehrmacht's vigorous counter-offensive, which drove the Russians out of their territory, General Hossbach's troops recaptured Nemmersdorf. The events of 20 and 21 October in this East Prussian town were so horrific that its name was to be forever imprinted on the collective memory, for it became a symbol. When the facts became known, it triggered a mass flight of German citizens, not only from East Prussia, but also from Silesia and Pomerania. Entering Nemmersdorf, the soldiers found in the streets the bodies of old women and children decomposing with brutal wounds to their faces and skulls. The women showed obvious signs of having been raped en masse before being murdered. Houses were looted, razed and burned. On the way out of the village, tanks had driven over the wagons of refugees fleeing the village.

On 5 July 1946, German and Russian servicemen, as well as Belgian, French and British prisoners of war, testified before an American court in Neu Ulm about the events at Nemmersdorf. Dr. Heinrich Amberger, a lieutenant in the reserves, gave an affidavit in which he confirmed that the column of refugees was run over by tanks, which drove over people and wagons. According to this witness, the civilians, mostly women and children, were crushed to such an extent that they were flattened on the asphalt. On the edge of a street," said this German, "sat a cornflower hunched over with a bullet in the back of her head. Not far from her lay a baby a few months old, killed at close range with a shot in the forehead.... A group of men, unmarked by mortal wounds, had been killed by the blows of shovels or gun butts. Their faces were completely smashed. One man had been nailed to the door of a farmhouse."

Alfred M. de Zayas reproduces in *Nemesis at Potsdam* chilling excerpts from these statements at the Neu Ulm tribunal, which were later presented by the defences at the Nuremberg trials. The cruelty and ruthlessness of the Soviet troops is striking in the account of Karl Potrek, a civilian from Königsberg who had been conscripted and hastily sent to the Gumbinnen and Nemmersdorf area:

> "At the end of the town to the left of the road is the large tavern 'Weisser Krug'... in the farmyard, further down the street was a cart, to which four naked women were nailed through the hands in cruciform position.

Behind the 'Weisser Krug' in the direction of Gumbinnen is a square with a monument to the Unknown Soldier. Further on there is another large tavern, 'Roter Krug'. Near it, parallel to the street, there was a barn and on each of its two doors, a naked woman crucified with nails through her hands. In the dwellings we found a total of seventy-two women, including girls, and a seventy-four year old man. All dead... all murdered in a bestial manner, except for a few who had bullet holes in their necks. Some babies had their heads blown off. In one room we found an eighty-four-year-old woman sitting on a sofa... half of her head had been sliced off with an axe or a shovel. We took the bodies to the village cemetery where we laid them out to await the foreign medical commission. In the meantime, a nurse from Insterburg, a native of Nemmersdorf, arrived looking for her parents. Among the bodies were her seventy-two-year-old mother and her seventy-four-year-old father, the only man among the dead. She confirmed that all the dead were neighbours of Nemmersdorf. On the fourth day they were buried in two graves. The next day the medical commission arrived, so the graves had to be opened again so that the bodies could be examined. The doors of the barns were put up as a block so that the bodies could be spread out on them. This foreign commission unanimously established that all the women, plus girls aged eight to twelve and even a woman aged eighty-four had been raped. After being examined by the commission, the bodies were reburied".

Captain Emil Herminghaus speaks of a group of women, including several nuns, all of whom were savagely stabbed and shot. According to the captain, the army immediately invited the neutral press: Swiss and Swedish journalists, as well as some Spanish and French ones, testified to the horrific scene. In Nemmersdorf there were also French, Belgian and British prisoners of war who had not been evacuated and witnessed the behaviour of the Soviet soldiers. They later recounted their experiences in veterans' newspapers. Some British POWs confirmed after their repatriation that the lack of discipline in the Red Army was striking. During the first weeks of the occupation," reported a British prisoner interned in a camp between Schlawe, Lauenburg and Buckow, towns in eastern Pomerania, "the Red soldiers raped all the women between the ages of twelve and sixty. This may sound like an exaggeration, but it is the truth. The only exceptions were girls who managed to stay hidden in the woods or who had the fortitude to feign infectious diseases such as typhus or diphtheria.... The Reds searched for women in every house, intimidated them with pistols or machine guns and took them away in their tanks or vehicles."

Normally, one finds very few references in Russian sources to the criminal conduct of the Red Army. One of them is Alexander Solzhenitsyn, who in 1945 was a Red Army captain whose regiment had entered East Prussia in January. On page 43 of the first volume of the three-volume English edition of *Archipelago Gulag*, he writes: "Yes! We had been at war in Germany for three weeks and we all knew very well that if they had been Germans (he means Poles), they could have been quietly raped and then shot and almost had it counted as a merit of war...". Alexander Werth, a Russian-born, British-born author of some 20 works, covered the war in Russia as a correspondent *for the Sunday Times*. Werth recalls in *Russia at War 1941 to 1945* a conversation with a Russian commander, who cheekily comments:

> "Any of our compadres had only to say: 'Frau komm' (woman, come), and she knew what was expected of her.... For almost four years, the Red Army had been sex-starved..... In Poland regrettable things happened from time to time, but, on the whole, strict discipline was maintained as far as rape was concerned.... Looting and rape on a large scale did not begin until our soldiers entered Germany. Our men were so hungry for sex that they often raped old women in their sixties, seventies or even eighties - to the surprise of these grandmothers, if not really to their delight. But I recognise that it was an obscene affair."

Goebbels, the Minister of Propaganda, as he had done with the work of Theodore Kaufman, showed the German population the atrocities committed by the Soviets at Nemmersdorf. It was the first time the Red Army had encountered German civilians, and the experience was so terrible that all of Germany seemed to understand what was coming. Thereafter, the resistance of those who could fight was even more fierce, but Nemmersdorf also marked the beginning of a mass flight of civilians who neither could nor knew how to fight. Thus, as we have seen in the account of the Dresden Holocaust, by early February 1945 more than 600,000 fugitives had taken refuge in the Saxon capital alone, fleeing in terror at the news that confirmed that Nemmersdorf was not an isolated event, but the prelude to a play that was being written in every occupied city and would only conclude with the epilogue in Berlin.

Refugee massacres at sea: three forgotten sinkings

The savagery against German civilians as they fled westward was not only on the roads, where low-flying aircraft strafed the columns of fugitives as they trudged through snowdrifts on icy roads. Knowing the hardships of escape by land, hundreds of thousands of refugees headed for the Baltic ports in the hope that they could be evacuated by sea. Admirals Oskar Kummetz and Konrad Engelhardt, charged by Admiral Dönitz with launching "Operation Hannibal", were able to assemble over a thousand ships of all types in order to carry out the evacuation. All available ships in the Baltic were dedicated to this operation. Engelhardt and Kummetz used the merchant navy, the navy and even private vessels, including fishing boats. According to Alfred M. de Zayas, more than two million Germans, civilians and soldiers (mainly wounded and sick), were rescued from late January to early May 1945 in what is considered the largest sea evacuation in history. However, between 25,000 and 30,000 people, mostly civilians, perished at sea. In and near Danzig Bay, three large ships filled with refugees and wounded being evacuated to Germany were sunk by Soviet submarines.

The first of these disasters occurred on 30 January 1945, when the Soviet submarine S-13, commanded by Captain Alexander Marinesko, sank the *Wilhelm Gustloff*, a modern ocean liner built on Hitler's orders for the "Force through Joy" programme and used as a hospital ship (Lazarettschiff). For this purpose she had been painted white with a green band from bow to stern and several red crosses were visible in various places on the hull and deck. *The Wilhelm Gustloff* had sailed from Pillau (Balstik in Polish) for Mecklenburg packed with nine thousand civilians: women, children and the elderly, and some seventeen hundred military personnel: one thousand navy cadets and the rest wounded. After several hours of sailing in rough seas and temperatures close to minus 20 degrees Celsius, the deck was frozen and the lifeboats were freezing. Three torpedoes hit the liner, which sank slowly, allowing some 850 people to be saved with the help of other ships in the convoy, according to German sources.

Eleven days later, on 10 February 1945, Captain Marinesko's same submarine S-13 sank its second liner, the *General von Steuben*, a luxury passenger liner confiscated by the Navy and converted into a hospital. More than 5,200 people were on board: 2,000 civilians, as usual women and children escaping from the advancing Soviet troops; 2,700 wounded; 320 nurses and 30 doctors; and some 300 crew members. Three children were born that night on the ship, and a sense of relief was palpable among the passengers as they escaped the hell of East Prussia. Two torpedoes hit the ship, which had also left Pillau and was heading for Swinemünde. An escorting torpedo boat was able to rescue six hundred and fifty-nine survivors, the rest died in the icy waters of the Baltic.

The tragedy of the *Goya*, another hospital ship that had been built in Oslo in 1940, occurred on 16 April 1945, just as the war was ending. Its sinking made no sense, as the Soviets and Poles had already decided to expel the Germans. The ship had sailed from the port of Danzig full of refugees. The captains of these ships usually allowed far more people on board than were authorised, and they did not comply with orders to do so. This was unavoidable, as it was very difficult for them to leave so many destitute civilians who had endured all sorts of hardships ashore. In the case of the *Goya*, the passenger list was stopped when the number of passengers reached 6,100, so there were about 7,000 people on board, not counting the crew. On this occasion, two torpedoes were fired by the submarine S-3, commanded by Captain Vladimir Konovalov, which caused the ship to sink in less than seven minutes. Only 165 people survived. In *The Last Hundred Days* (1967) Hans Dollinger records the testimony of a survivor named Brinkmann, who recounts the scenes of collective terror that followed the cry of "Every man for himself". In 2003, the wreck of the *Goya* was found at a depth of eighty metres.

In the course of the evacuation operation in the Baltic, thirteen hospital ships were deployed, four of which were sunk, and twenty-one wounded transports, eight of which ended up at the bottom of the sea. The USSR had expressly refused to recognise the German "Lazarettschiffe" and attacked them throughout the war as if they were legitimate military targets, a war crime that must surely have been "peccata minuta" for the Soviets, who had for decades disregarded the most elementary human rights and ignored international conventions. The sinkings of *the Wilhelm Gustloff* and the *Goya* are considered to be the two worst naval disasters in history in terms of loss of life, a fact that few people are aware of. On 9 May 1945, after Germany had already capitulated, the last sinking took place: the small 500-ton tanker *Liselotte Friedrich*, carrying more than 300 refugees, was torpedoed from an aircraft and sank near Bornholm, Denmark. At least fifty people lost their lives.

Königsberg

The East Prussian capital, Königsberg, held out until 9 April 1945. The evacuation by sea from the Baltic ports near the city depended to a large extent on this. In the Yalta agreements, Königsberg, the old capital of the Teutonic Knights, had been given to Stalin as a gift, so the Soviets set about administering it and acted ruthlessly from the outset. As a lesser evil, the entire German population was to be deported, although there was also the option of exterminating much of it. On 9 April there were an estimated 110,000 Germans left in Königsberg, but when the Soviets counted the number of deportees in June there were only 73,000. Giles MacDonogh, from whom this information comes, recounts in *After the Reich* the Red Army's entry into Königsberg. Among the main sources cited for the capture of the city of Kant is *Ostpreussisches Tagebuch: Aufzeichnungen eines Arztes aus den Jahren 1945-1947* (*East Prussian Diary: Notes of a Physician from the Years 1945-1947*), a work published in 1961 by Dr Hans Graf von Lehndorff, a surgeon who was an eyewitness to what happened.

The siege of the Prussian capital was completed on 26 January 1945, but General Lasch managed to hold out against the siege of Königsberg for two and a half months. He capitulated on 10 April, when waves of soldiers entered the city and ruthlessly attacked the population who dared to come out of the dens where they had survived the long siege: "They were beaten, robbed, stripped naked," writes MacDonogh, "and, if they were women, raped. The cries of the women were heard everywhere. Schieß doch!' (shoot), they shouted. Sisters in a hospital were raped by bloodthirsty boys, sixteen years old at the most." A large number of people chose to take their own lives to avoid the cruelty of the Soviets, who entered the shelters with their flamethrowers and set them on fire without a second thought. In his diary, Dr. Hans Lehndorff recounts the storming of his hospital by the soldiers: "The sick and wounded were thrown out of their beds, the bandages on their wounds torn off....".

On 11 April, the soldiers found alcohol, located a distillery and began setting fire to the few houses in the town that had not been damaged in August 1944 by the terrible British bombing raids. Except for the buildings that the Soviets occupied, such as the Command Headquarters and the old Gestapo barracks, the rest were razed to the ground. Dr. Lehndorff recalls that soldiers with syphilis and gonorrhoea returned to the hospital and, despite the fact that in their savagery they had shattered the dispensary, demanded treatment for their illnesses at gunpoint. Lehndorff recounts that without him present his "soulmate", whom he refers to as "Doctor", was dragged from an operating table and raped. When he saw his colleague with her gown torn to shreds, but still trying to carry on with her work of bandaging the wounded, he understood what had happened. She asked for a Bible and prepared some pills in case she needed them. The worst was yet to come, as the doctor had to resist three more attacks. Dr Lehndorff admits he was relieved when she burst into tears: "I was glad she had finally given in."

Once the city had been burned and the orgies were over, the citizens were grouped together to start marching to the camps. Dr Lehndorf was one of those who left Königsberg on 12 April on one of the expeditions. Lehndorff wrote in his *Tagebuch* (diary) that before leaving the hospital a patient with a head wound was raped countless times without her being aware of it. According to his testimony, all those who were wounded or considered too old were killed in their beds or in the ditches. During the 25-kilometre march, the soldiers, with the help of communist Polish auxiliaries, dragged the women out of the column with shouts of "Davai suda" ("Come on, woman!").

Some sources mentioned by Giles MacDonog claim that the Russians tied young Hitler Youth members to horses and they were torn limb from limb. Inhabitants of villages near Königsberg suffered the same fate. One witness who managed to flee to the east reported that a poor village girl was raped from eight in the evening until nine in the morning by members of a tank squadron. Another source, Josef Henke, reports in *Die Vertreibung* (*The Expulsion*) on the experiences of survivors, which include all kinds of atrocities. One narrator explains that after witnessing the murder of a married couple by a shot in the back of the head, she was captured and raped twenty times before being locked up with eight other women, including a fourteen-year-old girl, in a cabin in a forest, where they were all raped for a week. Another survivor says that after a man was killed, he was thrown into a pigsty to be eaten by pigs.

Two million women raped

According to the Russian commander quoted above, "discipline" was maintained in Poland, where "regrettable things happened" (looting and theft), but not crimes and mass rapes. While in Poland, therefore, no excesses against the civilian population were allowed, in Germany the bestial behaviour of Soviet and Polish soldiers was condoned by the commanders. The bloodthirsty Jew Ilya Ehrenburg, whose harangue entitled "Kill" has already been transcribed in part in chapter nine, played a leading role in his work as a propagandist. His repugnant articles appeared in *Pravda*, in *Izvestia* and in the newspaper *Red Star*, which was sent to the front-line soldiers at the front. As early as 1943, Ehrenburg published the book *The War*, in which he systematically incited rape and unceremonious killing. "The Germans are not human beings," wrote this sinister preacher of hatred and death, who called on soldiers to kill in cold blood:

> "...We will not get excited, we will kill. If you have not killed at least one German a day, you have lost that day..... If you cannot kill your German with a bullet, kill him with your bayonet. If there is calm on the front and you expect to restart fighting, kill a German while you are at it. If you leave a German alive, the German will hang a Russian and rape a Russian woman. If you kill one German, kill another - there is nothing more fun for us than a pile of German bodies..... Kill the Germans, this is your grandmother's request. Kill the Germans, that's your son's prayer. Kill the Germans, that is the request of your motherland. Do not fail. Don't miss the chance. Kill."

Two million German women were raped during the Red Army's advance towards Berlin, of whom more than 200,000 died, either from inhuman assaults, injuries or suicide. Some women were raped more than sixty times in a single night. Girls and young women, nuns, women of all ages, including women in their eighties, were raped incessantly. The men formed queues, sometimes led by the officers. Ehrenburg had expressly called for the tearing apart of women carrying a child in their wombs: "Among the Germans there are no innocents, neither among the living nor among the unborn.... Tear the racial pride of the Germanic women with briskness. Take them as legitimate booty."

Surprisingly, in 2008, the film *Anonyma - Eine Frau in Berlin* (*Anonyma, a woman in Berlin*) appeared, the English version of which is available on the internet. Directed by Max Färberböck, it is based on the personal diary of Marta Hillers, a repeatedly raped German journalist who spoke Russian and French. It is well worth seeing. In addition, 2010 saw the publication of Thomas Goodrich's *Hellstorm: The Death of Nazi Germany (1944-1947)*, a book that provides a full account of the silenced tragedy of so many German women who were never remembered. The interested reader can learn the lurid details and understand the extent of the horror. There is, however, a pioneering work by Dr. Johannes Kaps: *Die Tragödie Schlesiens 1945/1946 in Dokumenten* (1952), a large excerpt of which was translated into English and published under the title *Martirio y heroísmo de la mujer alemana del este (Martyrdom and Heroism of East German Women)*. It is a collection of shocking documents about rape, unspeakable bestial murders and other atrocities committed by Soviet and Polish soldiers. Some testimonies allege that the Poles were even more sadistic than their cronies.

Goodrich alleges that Americans, British and French knew that atrocities were being committed and not only did nothing to stop them, but many went so far as to participate in the orgies of sexual depravity and sadism, particularly French Moroccans. The scenes recounted by victims and witnesses in *Hellstorm* are chilling. Some soldiers, for example, were so drunk that they could not finish the act and so used the bottle, leaving many women obscenely mutilated. According to reports from the two main hospitals in Berlin (these are therefore only figures from women who were able to reach the hospitals), more than 100,000 women were raped in the capital alone, of whom 10,000 died, many of them by suicide: "Father," said one of these wretched women to her confessor, "I can't go on living. Thirty men raped me last night". Many mothers were forced to watch as their ten, eleven and twelve year old daughters were raped over and over again by scores of men; but at the same time, girls and teenage girls had to watch their mothers and even their octogenarian grandmothers being raped. Women who resisted were brutally and mercilessly tortured to death. Sometimes, after consenting to rape, soldiers would slit their victims' throats or disembowel them. Historian Anthony Beevor, author of *Berlin: The Downfall 1945*, calls what happened "the greatest mass rape phenomenon in history." Saint-Paulien, the pseudonym of Maurice-Yvan Sicard, claims in *La Bataille de Berlin*, the first volume of his work *Les Maudits* (1958), that in Greater Berlin the number of women raped was well over a million.

It has already been said in chapter eight that according to Andrei Sverdlov, son of the Jewish Bolshevik who ordered the assassination of Tsar Nicholas II and his family, there were in the Red Army three hundred and five Jewish generals during the Second World War. This was a consequence of the policy pursued by Trotsky, who had been relying on his blood brothers to shape the command structures of the Red Army. Naturally, both generals and middle commanders facilitated the mass distribution of millions of pamphlets by Ilya Ehrenburg (originally called Eliyahu) to Soviet soldiers entering Germany. Ehrenburg must surely be considered the ideologue of the rape, torture and murder of defenceless German women, many of whom became pregnant: it is estimated that some 300,000 babies were born. Many of these babies died for lack of means and care. This Jewish "philanthropist" was awarded the Stalin Peace Prize in 1952. In Israel, of course, Ehrenburg is the object of all honours. His papers are preserved there in the "Yad Vashem Holocaust Museum".

At this writing, we have learned that a new book on the indiscriminate rape of German women, *Alle die Soldaten kamen* (*All the Soldiers Came*), has just been published. For the first time, it offers an investigation into the attitude of American, British and French soldiers. Professor Miriam Gebhardt, who interviews victims and rape victims in her book, estimates that, apart from the Soviet orgy, the Allied soldiers raped some 860,000 women during and after the Second World War.

German prisoners of war
Eisenhower's death camps

In a later chapter, devoted exclusively to studying the accusations against Nazi Germany in connection with the alleged extermination of six million Jews, we will examine the German prison system. We will say only that initially there were prison camps (Straflager), labour camps (Arbeitslager) and concentration camps (Konzentrationslager), the infrastructures of which were well designed to fulfil their function. Germany was by far the country that complied best with the Geneva Convention, and therefore treated prisoners of war in accordance with international conventions, as is attested to by the reports of the Red Cross, which regularly visited the camps. The treatment of German POWs was another matter. It has been seen how Eisenhower barred the International Red Cross from his death camps, where nearly a million Germans perished in the open air. We will expand on this long-hidden historical fact in a moment.

The Soviet treatment of prisoners of war is hardly open to question: the fact that the USSR, the ally of the democracies, was one of the few countries in the world that had not signed the Geneva Convention goes some way to explaining its scandalous actions. Already in the spring of 1940 Beria had eliminated 22,000 Poles, the cream of Poland's army and intelligentsia, without anyone knowing about it. In other words, it was not possible to control the Soviets and demand that they treat the prisoners humanely and with dignity. We have seen how their own citizens were treated for decades, and we know how seven million people were starved to death in Ukraine (Holodomor). The treatment of enemy soldiers should therefore come as no surprise.

On 29 December 1941 in a German field hospital in Theodosia (Crimea), 160 wounded soldiers were killed. Some were thrown out of the windows and doused with water to freeze them. In February 1943, after the surrender of General von Paulus at Stalingrad, 91,000 German soldiers set out on foot through the snow on the so-called "death march" to the concentration camps. Half of them died from the trek, the extreme cold and the beatings. The rest were interned in a dozen concentration camps, and only 6,000 survived the inhumane conditions of internment. In Kharkov (Ukraine) in the summer of 1943, 150 prisoners were hanged in public in front of a cheering crowd. At Glowno (Poland), 2,000 German prisoners who surrendered were forced to step on landmines, and those who survived were burned with flamethrowers. These examples will suffice.

Of the three million German prisoners who fell into the hands of the Red Army, one million died between 1945 and 1953 in the Soviet Gulag. From the latter date, after Stalin's death, the International Red Cross began to press for the return of prisoners from nations that had fought against the USSR: Romania, Hungary, Italy, Japan, Finland, Slovakia, Vichy France and others including Spain. Of the more than half a million Hungarian prisoners held in Soviet camps, some 200,000 perished. The Romanians also suffered greatly from the treatment they received in the USSR camps: out of 400,000 prisoners, only half survived and were able to return to Romania.

Little could therefore be expected from the Soviet Union, a country that since 1917 had been characterised by the ruthless elimination of all opponents and by an unmitigated disregard for the lives of its own citizens, who were considered class enemies. On the other hand, something more could be demanded of countries that proclaimed themselves the defenders of freedom and democracy. It was quite unthinkable, therefore, that Dwight D. Eisenhower would ban the International Red Cross from his death camps. It is now pertinent to return to this issue in order to expand on the brief information given above in a few pages.

The first thing to note is that mass surrenders occurred on the Western Front because German commanders were convinced that the Allies would treat them better than the Soviets. On the Eastern Front, Wehrmacht units fought to the last to try to prevent many of their countrymen from falling into the hands of the Communists. It was Admiral Dönitz who ordered this strategy, which was ultimately to no avail, for, when you think about it, the slow death Eisenhower had prepared for them was one of the cruelest that could be inflicted on a human being: "I saw thousands of men huddled together," said Martin Brech, an American soldier guarding one of the camps, "soaking wet and cold, sleeping in the mud without shelter or blankets, eating grass because we hardly fed them, dying.... It became clear that not feeding them properly was our deliberate norm.... They begged, sickened and died in front of us."

The publication in 1989 of James Bacque's *Other Losses*, which proved beyond doubt what had happened, uncovered a truth that had been kept hidden. It took forty-four years for the world to learn that Eisenhower, "the terrible Swedish Jew", was a genocidal man who deliberately killed nearly a million Germans in just a few months. One can get an idea of the magnitude of this crime when one realises that these deaths far exceeded those suffered in Western Europe by the German Army in the entire war. Bacque interviewed hundreds of American prisoners, guards and officers and amassed exhaustive evidence from archives in Germany, France, Britain, Canada and the United States that enabled him to uncover the shocking story of a gigantic crime executed over nauseating quagmires that became swamps of filth, epidemics and disease.

The Germans estimated that more than 1,700,000 soldiers who were alive at the end of the war never returned home; but the Allies rejected any responsibility and pointed the finger at the Russians. Between 1947 and 1950 most reports of US prison camps were destroyed. Willy Brandt himself, the driving force behind "Ostpolitik" between 1969 and 1974, subsidised books denying the atrocities in American camps. James Bacque notes that years later Brandt refused to discuss his role in censoring and subsidising books that concealed crimes against the German people. Bacque also charges that the International Committee of the Red Cross in Geneva did not allow him to investigate the archives reporting on the British and Canadian camps, who knew what was going on in Eisenhower's death camps.

When Morgethau travelled to Europe with White in August 1944, he had the opportunity to meet Eisenhower, supreme commander of the Allied Expeditionary Force in Europe, who, as has been said, assured him that he would "cook the Germans in their own sauce". James Bacque, who in addition to the *Morgenthau Diary* and Professor Anthony Kubek's introduction used by us, cites John Morton Blum's *Roosevelt and Morgenthau*, confirms that the Treasury Secretary returned satisfied with Eisenhower's willingness, since the general promised to "deal harshly" with the Germans. However, Morgenthau told Roosevelt at the White House that the European Consultative Commission was not considering "how to deal severely with Germany in the way we would wish". In any case, Morgenthau was convinced that he would eventually impose his plan against the Germans and told the President, "Give me thirty minutes with Churchill and I can make amends for this." Roosevelt's reply, which comes from the *Presidential Diaries*[14], is not to be missed: "We must be tough on Germany, and I mean the German people, not just the Nazis. Either we must emasculate the Germans or we must treat them in such a way that they can no longer reproduce people who want to continue what they have done in the past".

These words are in tune with Theodore N. Kaufman's proposal to sterilise all Germans, which suggests that, as Göbbels and other National Socialist leaders once denounced, Kaufman moved around the White House, namely as a man of Samuel Rosenman, one of the President's most important

---

[14] In the *Morgenthau Diaries* there is a series of some 2,000 pages, the so-called *Presidential Diaries*, which record Morgenthau's interviews with FDR. In this collection of handwritten documents, in addition to their banter and "tête-à-tête" discussions, there are also ministerial meetings. These documents give an insight into the close friendship between the two Jews and the extent to which they were on the same wavelength in their hatred of the German people. The *Presidential Diaries* also contains materials relating to Harry Salomon Truman and Dwight David Eisenhower.

Jewish advisors. Even shortly before his death, Roosevelt confirmed to Morgenthau, who was in Warm Springs, Georgia, on the night of 11 April 1945, that he shared his plans. As the Secretary of State for the Treasury noted in the *Presidential Diaries*, the president's last words to him on political matters were: "Henry, I am with you 100 percent.

At the second Quebec Conference, held on 11-16 September 1944, Morgenthau had more than the half-hour he had asked for to try to convince Churchill, who had travelled to Quebec with an old acquaintance who hated the Germans as much as Morgenthau, Lord Cherwell, i.e. Frederick Alexander Lindemann, his Jewish adviser, his close friend, the ideologue of air terror over Germany. The two agreed to convince Churchill of the need to implement the Morgenthau Plan. "Morgenthau and Churchill's adviser Lord Cherwell," writes Bacque, "drew up a plan to overcome Churchill's resistance." Only Anthony Eden, Secretary of the Foreign Office, opposed the Morgenthau Plan and Lord Cherwell, the Plan's main advocate in Britain, in Quebec. In Moscow in mid-October Churchill explained the Morgenthau Plan for Germany to Stalin, who agreed. Within the British War Cabinet, however, there were doubts. Lindemann managed to anger the Foreign Secretary when he intimated to Churchill that Eden's concerns about famine in Germany were completely wrong. According to Bacque, Churchill had to mediate between the two and appease Eden, who retorted angrily.

On 10 March 1945 Eisenhower found a way to violate the Geneva Convention and prevent prisoners of war (POWs) from being treated as required by international standards. To do this, he created a new type of prisoner: DEF (Unarmed Enemy Forces). The Combined Chiefs of Staff (CCS), composed of the British and Americans, received the message in April at Supreme Headquarters Allied Expeditionary Force (SHAEF). The CCS approved DEF status only for American-held POWs, as the British refused to adopt Eisenhower's plan for their own POWs. The main conditions set out in the order were reflected in items B, C and D and were as follows:

> "(B) The Germans are responsible for feeding and maintaining the unarmed German troops.
> (C) The procedure adopted shall not apply to war criminals or other categories of wanted German personnel or other persons found among the German Armed Forces and held for security reasons. These persons will continue to be imprisoned as suspected war criminals or for military security reasons and not as prisoners of war. They will be fed, housed and thus supervised by the Allied Forces. The German authorities will exercise no control over them whatsoever.
> D) There shall be no public statement concerning the status of the German Armed Forces or unarmed troops".

On 10 March, the same day he created DEF status for German prisoners of war, Eisenhower held a press conference in Paris, at which he said: "If the Germans would reason like normal human beings, they would know that throughout history the United States and Britain have shown generosity to the defeated enemy. We abide by all the rules of the Geneva Convention". Through provision D, the violation of the Geneva Convention was kept secret, which was a prerequisite to prevent the public from learning the truth and, in the process, discovering that Eisenhower was a cynical liar. The Geneva Convention provided for three fundamental rights for the prisoners: food and shelter on the same level as the troops of the captor army; reception and dispatch of correspondence; the right to be visited by delegates of the International Committee of the Red Cross.

Clause B provided for the Germans themselves to feed and maintain their unarmed troops. However, the Morgenthau Plan stipulated that German institutions were to be dismantled, including all agencies providing social services. According to the Plan, the production of up to 500 products was to be prevented or abolished. To pretend, therefore, to shift responsibility to the German authorities was absolutely delusional, since, once the army, the government, welfare agencies, the German Red Cross and other institutions, including commercial ones, had been abolished, there were no authorities. In fact, Eisenhower knew very well that the famous directive JCS 1067 specifically laid down the policy he had to adopt in relation to each of the German institutions: he had to abolish the Army, the Central Government, the NSDAP, close schools, universities, radio stations, newspapers, prevent soldiers from talking to Germans.... The spirit and the letter of the Morgenthau Plan, as intended by Harry Dexter White, Frank Coe and Harry Glasser, the three Jewish Communists in the Treasury who had devised it, were contained in JCS Directive 1067.

On 21 April 1945 Eisenhower signed a text sent to SHAEF telling General Marshall that the new fenced enclosures for prisoners "would not be provided with shelter or other amenities." He added that the prisoners themselves should improve them "using local materials." These roofless spaces, which were called "Prisoner of War Temporary Enclosures" (PWTE), were nothing more than open fields surrounded by barbed wire. The so-called temporariness lasted for more than half a year. Eisenhower did not permit even a paltry tent to be erected; but searchlights, guard turrets and machine guns were ordered to be installed. As for the permission given to prisoners to improve the camps "using local materials" as much as possible, an order of 1 May specifically forbade the entry of materials into the enclosures. When surrendering prisoners began to be confined in these enclosures in April, there were no watchtowers, no tents, no water, no latrines, no facilities of any kind. In some camps the men were so cramped that they could not even lie down on the ground. Here, from *Other Losses*, is a description of the situation from inside a camp:

"In April 1945, hundreds of thousands of German soldiers as well as hospital patients, amputees, women assistants and civilians were imprisoned.... One prisoner in the Rheinberg camp was over eighty years old, another only nine.... His comrades were overwhelmed by hunger and tormented by thirst, and were dying of dysentery. A cruel sky poured water on them week after week. Amputees crawled like amphibians through the mud, soaked and shivering. Out in the open, day after day, night after night, they lay desperate in the Rheinberg sand or slept exhausted in their crumbling holes."

At night, spotlights shone on the men lying in their dark holes, screaming in their nightmares. One of these unfortunates, Charles von Luttichau, was interviewed in 1987/88 in Washington, D. C. by James Bacque. Luttichau's mother was American, so, convalescing at home, he decided to surrender voluntarily. He was imprisoned in Kripp, a camp near Remangen on the Rhine. The following is an excerpt from his description to the author of *Other Losses*:

"The toilets were just logs thrown over ditches next to the barbed wire. To sleep all we could do was dig a hole in the ground with our bare hands and then stick each other in the hole. We were huddled close together. Because of the diseases, the men had to defecate on the ground. Soon many of us were too weak to take off our trousers first. As a result, our clothes were infected, and so was the mud on which we had to walk, sit and lie down. At first there was no water at all, except for the rain. Then after a couple of weeks we were able to get some water from a pipe. But most of us had nothing to catch it with, so we could only take a few sips after hours of queuing, sometimes even through the night. We had to walk between the holes, on the wet earth piled up as we dug, so it was easy to fall into a hole and difficult to get out of it. In this part of the Rhine the rain in spring was almost constant. More than half the days we had no food at all. The rest we had a small K ration. I could see from the packets that they gave us a tenth of the rations they gave their men. So in the end we were getting maybe five percent of a normal U.S. Army ration. I told the camp commander that I was in breach of the Geneva Convention, but he just said, 'Forget about the Convention. You don't have any rights. Within days, men who had entered the camp in good health were dead. I saw our men dragging many bodies of the dead to the camp gate, where they were piled on top of each other and carried away in trucks.
A seventeen-year-old boy who could see his village in the distance used to cry standing at the barbed wire fence. One morning the prisoners found him shot dead at the foot of the fence. His body was hung on the barbed wire by the guards and left in plain sight as a warning. The prisoners were forced to walk near the body. Many shouted 'murderers, murderers'. In retaliation, the camp commandant withheld the already miserable rations

for three days. For us, who were already starving and could hardly move because of weakness, it was terrifying. For many it meant death. This was not the only time the commandant withdrew rations to punish the prisoners."

Almost all the survivors interviewed by Bacque agree that the lack of water was one of the most terrible things. George Weiss, a tank mechanic, recalls that they went three and a half days without water, so they drank their own urine. The taste of it," Weiss recalls, "was terrible, but what could we do? Some of the men would lick the ground to get a little moisture." Other testimonies report that among the prisoners in the camps were children as young as six years old, pregnant women and the elderly. It should be noted that there were no records in the DEF camps and that most of the records of the POW camps were later destroyed. Therefore it cannot be known how many civilians were taken prisoner.

The French Army demanded prisoner transfers from the Americans in order to use them for repair work. According to French reports, in a delivery of 100,000 who were supposed to be useful for work, the Americans transferred 32,640 women, children and old people. James Bacque highlights the disastrous situation of the French prison camps, so disastrous that they almost emulated the American. Out of a total of 740,000 prisoners received from the US Army, 250,000 died from starvation and the miserable treatment to which they were subjected. To these deaths must be added at least another 800,000 who died at the hands of the Americans, bringing the total figure to over one million.

General Patton was the only one to release a significant number of prisoners during the month of May, thus saving them from starvation. When other generals tried to follow his example and also ordered the release of prisoners, a counter-order signed on 15 May by Eisenhower aborted their attempt. Bacque confirms that within a month Patton discharged about half a million. Of the more than five million soldiers captured by the Americans in northwest Europe, nearly four million remained locked up in open-air enclosures. According to Bacque, some 2.2 million detainees had been released by 8 September 1945. Another 3,700,000 of the total number of prisoners in all the European theatres of operation were still in the camps, or had died, or their custody had been transferred to the British or the French. With the arrival of summer, weather conditions improved and suffering from the rigours of the climate eased, but famine continued to wreak havoc. In addition, in June and July prisoners with POW status were secretly transferred to DEF status. Between 2 June and 28 July the number of prisoners in the DEF camps increased by almost 600,000.

The US Government refused the International Committee of the Red Cross permission to enter the camps and visit the prisoners, in flagrant violation of the Geneva Convention. With the disintegration of the German government, Switzerland had been authorised to exercise the role of Protecting Power, which was to ensure that Red Cross reports would be received by Switzerland. In order to prevent this, on 8 May 1945, as soon as Germany surrendered unconditionally, the US State Department informed the Swiss Ambassador in Washington that Switzerland had rejected Switzerland as a Protecting Power. Once this was done, the State Department informed the ICRC (International Committee of the Red Cross) that there was no point in visits, since there was no Protecting Power. Despite this, the State Department brazenly informed Switzerland that the US would continue to treat prisoners "in accordance with the provisions of the Geneva Convention".

By contrast, two million British, American, French and Canadian prisoners were released from the German camps that spring. The Red Cross, which oversaw the operation, greeted them with parcels from its warehouses in Switzerland, where it had stored millions of them. The liberated prisoners had the opportunity to thank the Red Cross for its help with food parcels that had been arriving at the internment camps. The Germans, despite the fact that at the end of the war the German people were suffering from severe food restrictions, had supplied 1,500 calories per day to the detainees almost to the very end. Other aid had reached the camps through the mail. Ninety-eight per cent of the prisoners held in German detention centres returned home safely, according to reports issued by the Red Cross in May 1945. Their state of health was good, not only because they had had food, but also warm clothes and medicines, which had arrived regularly by mail with the acquiescence of the German authorities.

The US War Department banned German POWs from sending or receiving mail on 4 May 1945. The International Committee of the Red Cross proposed a plan in July to restore mail to German POWs, but it was rejected by the Americans. The British, however, accepted the Red Cross suggestion and in July-August re-established mail communications. Another ICRC attempt was made in late May or early June. Two trains loaded with food from their warehouses in Switzerland, where over 100,000 tons of food was in storage, were sent to Germany. One was bound for Mannheim and the other for Ausburg, cities in the American sector. Both arrived at their destination, where the officials on them were informed by American officials that the warehouses were full. The trains had to return to Switzerland with their cargo.

The first zone to allow Red Cross shipments was the British zone, but not until October 1945. The French, on the other hand, did not allow aid until December. In the Soviet and North American zones, by contrast, Red Cross deliveries were refused throughout the particularly severe winter of 1945-46. The United States military authorities, although the substantial Irish and Swiss donations were specifically marked, according to the ICRC, as being for Germany, advised the International Committee of the Red Cross delegate in Berlin to send all available aid consignments to other needy areas of Europe. Max Huber, head of the ICRC, finally decided to launch an investigation, but to little avail, since until Eisenhower was relieved in November by Lucius Clay, the US Army did not allow any benefits of any kind to the Germans. Even so, it was not until March 1946 that international relief was allowed into the American zone. The Soviets delayed their agreement until April. By then, hundreds of thousands of Germans had already died of hunger, cold and disease.

Eisenhower must surely go down in history as one of the greatest criminals of World War II. On 10 March 1945, before the great German prisoner captures took place, he created DEF status, which shows that the policy he intended to adopt was conceived in advance. In line with the requirements to treat the Germans harshly and in perfect harmony with the Morgenthau Plan, in reality a genocidal plan, Eisenhower planned to deprive the prisoners of food, water and shelter. Despite the fact that the US Army had a surplus of tents and that the Red Cross was stockpiling food in abundance in Switzerland, it was decided to lock the Germans in open-air PWTEs (Temporary Prisoner of War Enclosures) and to prohibit the distribution of food and Red Cross medical care. This amounted to condemning hundreds of thousands of Germans to death. The only general who more or less understood what was happening and dared to disagree was George Smith Patton, who would eventually be killed in December 1945.

The assassination of General Patton

Eisenhower knew that he could be the subject of some kind of investigation by a Congressional or Senate Committee, so he had demanded loyalty from his subordinates. This fear of Eisenhower's is reflected by Patton in his personal diary: "After lunch General Eisenhower spoke to us very confidentially about the need for solidarity in case any of us might be called before a Congressional Committee.... He outlined a form of organisation. Although none of us exactly agreed, it was not sufficiently opposed to our views to preclude general support." Eisenhower not only had to avoid a Congressional investigation for all that was being covered up in the American zone of occupation, but he had to avoid disagreements with generals like Patton himself, who represented the honour of the Army and the simplicity and generosity of the American people. Patton's prestige was recognised by the Germans themselves, who considered him one of America's military geniuses.

His thoughts on the treatment of Germans were expressed when answering a question put to him by a military judge. Patton confirmed that in his speeches to the troops he emphasised "the necessity of proper treatment of prisoners of war, both to their lives and their property". Considered his country's finest soldier in World War II, he was admired by his soldiers, to whom he spoke bluntly: he encouraged them to kill as many Germans as they could on the battlefield, "but don't put them up against a wall and kill them. Do it while they are fighting." Martin Blumenson quotes the following words of General Patton in *The Patton Papers*: "When a man has surrendered, he should be treated exactly according to the rules of ground combat and in exactly the same way as you would like to be treated if you had been stupid enough to surrender. We Americans don't punch people in the teeth when they are beaten." As will be seen below, Patton deplored Eisenhower's policies against the Germans and the victors' treatment of Germany: "What we are doing," he denounced, "is completely destroying the only modern state in Europe so that Russia can swallow it whole."

Patton was about to occupy Czechoslovakia and Germany when he was ordered to halt the offensive because it had been agreed at Yalta that the Soviet Union should occupy this part of central Europe. In order to prevent their advance, Eisenhower gave Montgomery the fuel for his tanks. After the war, Patton was appointed military governor of Bavaria and dared to say bluntly that Stalin would not have occupied half of Europe without Roosevelt's support. When he discovered that his country had colluded with the Soviet Union, Patton publicly denounced this collusion. This caused him many problems and made him many enemies, both in the United States and in the USSR. His views were written down in his diary and in letters to his family and friends, many of which are contained in *The Patton Papers*.

It is likely that Patton, who despised without exemption everything the Soviet Union stood for, never fully understood why half of Europe was being surrendered to communism. Clearly, from his military logic, he had no acceptable explanation. He had fought to liberate Europe from Nazism and considered that leaving it in Stalin's hands was tantamount to failure, especially as he was convinced that the Red Army could be pushed back to its borders if the moment was seized. On 18 May 1945 Patton wrote in his diary that the American Army could beat the Russians with the greatest of ease. Two days later he wrote a letter to his wife repeating the same idea: "If we have to fight the Russians, now is the time. From now on we will become weaker and they will become stronger". Soon his views and his derogatory words towards the Soviets reached the ears of his enemies and detractors.

On 21 July 1945, after visiting the ruins of Berlin, he wrote to his wife: "Berlin has saddened me. We have destroyed what might have been a good race and are close to replacing them with brutal Mongols. And the whole of Europe will be communist. It is sad that during the first week they entered Berlin, all the women who ran were shot and those who didn't were raped. If they had been left to me, I could have taken it." Naturally, had Patton been allowed to take Berlin the savage assaults, murders and rapes would have been avoided. The reference to the Mongols has to do with the fact that the Soviet troops who occupied the Reich's capital were plentiful in Mongolian soldiers, which is why several historians speak of German women being raped by "Asiatic hordes". Patton insists in his diary on respect for the German race. In another entry on 31 August, he wrote: "The Germans are really the only decent people left in Europe. It is a choice between them and the Russians. I prefer the Germans.

Nor were the Jews a saint of his devotion. In fact, he was repulsed by them. It seems clear to us that Patton did not quite understand the real reasons why the world had been drawn into the most devastating war in history, so he watched in amazement as a swarm of Jews from Russia and Poland began to invade Germany as soon as hostilities ceased. While awaiting arrangements for their transfer to Palestine, they were housed in the Displaced Persons (DP) camps that the Americans had built for them. Their behaviour and lack of hygiene in these camps disgusted Patton. On one occasion, Eisenhower insisted that he accompany him to a Jewish religious service, an experience he recorded in an entry in his diary on 17 September:

> "It turned out it was the Yom Kippur holiday, so they gathered in a big wooden building they call a synagogue. It fell to General Eisenhower to make a speech for them. We went into the synagogue, which was packed with the most stinking pile of humanity I've ever seen. When we got halfway through the ceremony, the chief rabbi, who was wearing a skin similar to that worn by Henry VIII of England and a very dirty embroidered surplice, came to see the general.... The stench was so terrible that I almost fainted and in fact about three hours later I ruined my lunch as a result of his reminiscence."

In another entry, also in September, Patton recorded his indignation at the favourable treatment Washington was demanding for the Jews. He was ordered to remove Germans from their homes to house Jews: "Evidently," he wrote, "the virus of Semitic vengeance against all Germans set in motion by Morgenthau and Baruch is still at work. Harrison (a State Department official) and his associates say that German civilians should be removed from their homes for the purpose of housing Displaced Persons." In reality most of these Jews who were intended to be housed were not displaced persons, but groups who voluntarily entered Germany. Despite his disagreement with official policy, which led him to defy JCS 1067, Patton tried to carry out orders that did not violate his conscience: "We have received orders today," he noted in another entry, "telling us to give special housing to Jews." In another letter to his wife, he insisted on deploring the treatment of Germans: "I have been to Frankfurt to attend a conference of the civil government. If what we do to Germans is freedom, then give me death. I cannot see that we Americans have stooped so low. It is Semitic, and I am sure of it." It seems clear that by this time Patton had already associated the Communists with the Jews.

Patton's views were by now unacceptable, so a press campaign was mounted to discredit him. The harassment began with accusations that he was too soft on the Germans; but an incident in August 1943 in the Sicilian campaign was soon seized upon. There he slapped a slacker named Charles H. Kuhl with his gloves because he thought he was playing sick. In the hospitals there were a large number of them who pretended to be sick in order to avoid combat. In order to accuse the General of anti-Semitism, a New York newspaper reported that when Patton slapped the soldier, who was Jewish, he had called him a "cowardly Jew", which was not true. At a press conference on 22 September, the general realised that some reporters were provoking him to make him lose his temper. The same day he wrote in his diary: "In the press there is a very obvious Semitic influence. They are trying to do two things: first, to implement communism, and second, they are trying to make all businessmen of German lineage without Jewish ancestors lose their jobs.... They have lost their sense of justice and think that a man can be fired because someone says he is a Nazi." To his wife, too, he explained what had happened at the press conference: "Before you receive this letter, I will probably be in the headlines, for the press is keen to say that I am more interested in restoring order in Germany than in hunting Nazis."

The press outcry against Patton was soon seized upon by Eisenhower, who on 28 September, after reproaching him for his views, decided to replace him as military governor of Bavaria and remove him from command of the Third Army. On 7 October, in a sad ceremony, Patton bade farewell to his subordinates with these words: "All good things must come to an end. The best thing that has happened to me so far is the honour and privilege of having commanded the Third Army." His new appointment was command of the Fifteenth Army in a small barracks in Bad Nauheim. On 22 October he wrote a long letter to General James G. Harbord, who had returned to Bad Nauheim. Harbord, who had already returned to the United States. In it Patton bitterly condemned the implementation of Morgenthau's policy; Eisenhower's pusillanimous and cowardly conduct in the face of Jewish pretensions; the marked pro-Soviet bias in the press; and the politicisation, corruption, degradation and demoralisation these things caused in the Army.

Finally, on 9 December 1945, near Mannheim, the Cadillac in which General Patton was travelling crashed into a two-ton Army truck that crossed the road unexpectedly. The impact was not fatal, as both the driver, Horace Woodring, and his chief of staff, General Hobart Gay, nicknamed "Hap", got out of the car with only minor scratches; however, Patton was shot in the neck, but not seriously. On the way to the hospital, the vehicle that had rescued the general was rammed again by another heavy military truck. This time Patton's injuries were more serious; but he made it to the hospital alive, from where he was able to contact his wife in the United States. She asked him to get him out of the hospital urgently because they wanted to kill him: "They are going to kill me here". And so he did. On 21 December 1945 Patton was pronounced dead of an embolism. Not only did the Army not undertake any investigation into the "accidents", but no questions were raised about his "embolism". The American hero's body was never repatriated to the United States. No autopsy was performed.

The assassination of General George Patton became one of the most covert events in military history. Although his file at the National Archives in St. Louis runs to over 1,300 pages, only a few pages refer to the accident. Five reports made at the scene disappeared shortly after they were filed. Although Patton's driver stated that the first truck was waiting for them on the side of the road, none of the truck drivers were arrested and none of their names were revealed. Later, Ladislas Farago, a former intelligence agent, reported that the driver of the first truck was Robert L. Thompson, who was spirited away to London before he could be questioned. Thompson was not authorised to drive the truck and, in violation of the rules, had two mysterious passengers in the vehicle.

In 2008, author Robert K. Wilcox published *Target: Patton: The Plot to Assassinate General George S. Patton*, exposing the plot to eliminate the general. The attack is reconstructed thanks to the location of a person directly involved, the Lebanese Jew Douglas Bazata, an agent of the OSS (Office of Strategic Services), the predecessor of the CIA, who was interviewed by Wilcox before his death in 1999. It was Bazata himself who fired a low-velocity projectile at the general, wounding him in the throat. According to Bazata, the order to silence Patton came from the head of the OSS, General William Joseph ("Wild Bill") Donovan, considered the father of the CIA, who had close relations with the communists. According to Bazata, Donovan's words were: "We have a terrible situation with this great patriot. He is out of control and we must save him from himself and prevent him from ruining everything the Allies have done." Bazata confirmed that many people hated Patton and revealed to Wilcox that he was hired by Donovan, who offered him $10,000 to stage the accident. Once hospitalised, Patton was kept in isolation and died a surprising death as he was recovering. According to Bazata, the American secret services allowed Stalin's agents to kill him with an injection[15]. The embolism was thus allegedly caused by introducing a bubble of blood into the bloodstream and hitting a vital organ, something anyone can do with a syringe after a brief medical apprenticeship.

---

[15] The collaboration between the OSS (Office of Strategic Services) and the NKVD began to take shape in December 1943. At that time, Donovan travelled to Moscow to organise cooperation between the two secret services during the war. As Herbert Romerstein and Eric Breindel explain in *The Venona Secrets*. On 23 December, Donovan met with Pavel Fitin, head of the NKVD's Foreign Intelligence unit, and even offered to provide him with names of American agents operating in Nazi-occupied Europe in order to improve cooperation. Romerstein comments: "Offering the names of agents to another intelligence service had never been done by an experienced intelligence officer before. Fitin naturally welcomed the proposition and suggested using American facilities in Germany and France.

Brother Nathanael Kapner, a Jewish convert to (Orthodox) Christianity, reports on his *Real Jew News!* page that Bill Donovan, although he passed as being of Irish origin, was allegedly a crypto-Jew, since his mother, Anna Letitia "Tish" Donovan, was probably Jewish. Brother Nathanael links Donovan to the inner circle of Jews who advised Franklin D. Roosevelt. In particular, he believes that the premise of her Jewish identity is strengthened by her role as an assistant to Judge Samuel Rosenman at the Nuremberg trials, where Donovan made it clear that she felt more than just sympathy for Jews.

Jewish terrorism

In 1969 a prominent Zionist named Michel Bar-Zohar published *Les vengeurs* (*The Avengers*), a book that has already been cited in this chapter in discussing the murder of Wilhelm Gustloff, the NSDAP leader shot in his home by the Jewish terrorist David Frankfurter. More than twenty years after the events he uncovers in his work and when the Holocaust religion had already begun to spread worldwide after the Six Day War, Bar-Zohar, the official biographer of David Ben Gurion, Shimon Peres and Isser Harel, legendary head of the Mossad, reveals in the first part of the book, 'Revenge', that as soon as the war ended in Europe, groups of Jewish terrorists set about assassinating alleged Nazi leaders and planned to poison German citizens en masse. This author presents the criminals as heroic avenging knights acting in the name of a justice for which they are accountable only to God. Evidently, to their God, Yahweh, the God who has chosen the Jews from among all the peoples of the earth. In this way, the terrorists, most of them Zionists who in the late 1960s held prominent positions in Israel, become at once policemen, prosecutors, judges and executioners who act from an unquestionable moral superiority, with unparalleled integrity and, of course, with total impunity.

Thanks to this shameless work, it became known that certain Jewish groups, with the aim of exacting "Jewish revenge", murdered thousands of Germans, many of whom, according to them, were SS criminals. The first group presented by Bar-Zohar is an autonomous Jewish brigade that in late May 1945 sought to enter Germany from Italy at the head of a British column travelling in Dodge vehicles. On their cars, in addition to the Israeli flag, carried the following inscription: "Deutschland kaputt! Kein Volk, kein Reich, kein Fuhrer! Die Juden kommen!" (Germany broken! No people, no empire, no leader! The Jews are coming!). A few kilometres from the border, a counter-order from the British command was issued and the brigade, made up of Jewish officers affiliated with the Haganah (the embryonic military organisation of the future Zionist army), was sent to Tarvisio, near Trieste. Shortly before their arrival, Bar-Zohar reports, attacks on Germans had taken place in the town, Nazi houses had been set on fire and German women had been raped. It is implied that the perpetrators of these acts were Jewish soldiers in Tarvisio, and although the culprits were not discovered, the brigade command was concerned that such disorderly violence could harm the Jewish cause. It was necessary to "channel the feeling of vengeance that nestles in all the Jewish soldiers of Tarvisio," writes Bar-Zohar, "and it is for this purpose that the leaders of the Haganah decided to entrust the right to shed blood in the name of the Jewish people to a group of men who were particularly confident and known for their moral qualities.

The leader of the Jewish brigade was a Haganah chief, Israel Karmi, who in 1969 had become commander-in-chief of the Israel Military Police. He and Shalom Gilad are Bar-Zohar's main sources of information in this part of the book. According to a secret report by Gilad kept in the Haganah archives in Israel, Karmi was taking orders from Shlomo Shamir, alias "Fistouk", a future army general. American and Palestinian Jews working inside the Allied intelligence services provided information on future victims. Gilad's secret report recounts an action in which he took part, which, in our opinion, casts doubt on the criteria for selecting victims and, as in this case, on the reliability of the sources of information:

> "Once, I remember, we arrested a Pole who had collaborated with the Nazis. We served him a good meal, suitably watered, and then said to him. We know you are a Pole, not a German, we also know that you did what you did because you had no choice. We don't want to hurt you, but to prove to us that your conscience is pure, you will sit down and give us a list of criminals you know and tell us where we can find them.

According to Bar-Zohar, the frightened Pole wrote down a list of several dozen names of Germans. Subsequently, the author confirms, these people accused by the Pole were executed by the avengers of the Jewish brigade.

Within the brigade, 'a second group of avengers' was formed by order of the Haganah, but as a precautionary measure, neither commando knew of the existence of the other. Marcel Tobias, who was part of this second group, told an Israeli journalist in 1964 that the Jewish Brigade's avengers toured towns and villages in northern Italy, Austria and southern Germany for months and only stopped their actions when rumours began to circulate and families of missing Nazis went to the British authorities to complain about the whereabouts of their relatives: usually the terrorists, who wore British army uniforms, would pick up those selected from their homes on the pretext of taking them to British Command to give evidence. Local people or military patrols began to find dead bodies on the edge of forests, on the side of roads, even at the bottom of a pond. There were even strange deaths among the sick in the hospital in Tarviso and disappearances ("escapes") in prisons when there were Jewish guards from the brigade.

In the autumn of 1945 another Jewish unit, the "German battalion", joined the brigade in Tarvisio. This battalion had been formed in Palestine from German Jews who had come to the Holy Land under the Haavara Agreement. The German battalion, Bar-Zohar explains, was born out of the "Palmach", a Haganah shock force commanded by Yitzhak Sadeh. The German battalion, "Deutsche Abteilung", was thus a Palmach commando made up of volunteers who mastered the techniques and terminology of the Wehrmacht and wore German uniforms. Its leader, Simon Koch, known as Colonel Avidan, and some of the members of the battalion, which was based in Camporosso, two kilometres from Tarvisio, were integrated into the Avengers' command. Their triangle of operations was Tarvisio, Innsbruck and Judenburg, but they also made raids into Germany. Bar-Zohar again quotes Gilad's report to recount the visit of a young member of the "Deutsche Abtelung", the son of a Christian and a Jew, to his mother's home near Stuttgart:

> "He found his mother and sister well, but they refused to speak to him. He then asked them where his father was. They eventually replied curtly that he was dead. He continued to ask them and they confessed that he had been killed by the Germans. The young man wanted to know who had killed his father. Since his mother and sister refused to answer him, he threatened them with the machine gun and they gave him the names and addresses of those responsible."

Finally, as the relatives of the executed persons insisted that the authorities should be held responsible, the British High Command decided it would be better to move the Jewish brigade away from Tarvisio and sent it to Belgium, then to Holland, and later to France. In these countries, the vigilante avengers continued the executions of former Nazis and also penetrated into Germany to kill alleged criminals there. "How many Nazis, Bar-Zohar asks, were executed by the Jewish brigade?

> "Estimates vary, which is understandable since most of the avengers only knew about the operations in which they personally participated. Marcel Tobias thinks that 'more than fifty' Nazis were executed. Others quote much higher figures. According to Gilad, the commando operated almost every night for six months, so that it would have carried out about one hundred and fifty executions. To this figure should be added the Nazis who were discovered among the supposedly sick in the hospital in Tarviso, who were put to death. Another credible avenger told me: 'Between two and three hundred people'".

In the chapter entitled "The Bread of Death", Bar-Zohar interviews Beni, Jacob and Moshe in a kibbutz. In early 1945 they were in Lublin, where the communist government formed in Russia by Stalin had been installed.

An organisation was set up there that worked to enable tens of thousands of Jews from Central and Western Europe to travel to Palestine. Multiple Zionist organisations had this goal as soon as the war ended. In the section "Zionists and the Evian Conference" it has been seen that international Zionism refused to resettle Jews in other countries, as it wanted them to emigrate to Palestine. Instead of seeking to spare its people suffering, Zionism wanted them to be persecuted. This is a fundamental premise of the syllogism, which could be formulated as follows: If Jews are not persecuted, they will not emigrate to Israel. If Jews do not emigrate to Israel, the Zionist state will not come into being. Ergo, if Jews are not persecuted, the Zionist state will not be born.

In the early spring of 1945 the Zionist group in Beni was devoted, writes Bar-Zohar, to the constructive task of "concentrating and leading to safety the survivors of the camps who were wandering in rags, starving, and helping them to take the road to Palestine". To prove the perfect organisation put in place by Zionism at the end of the war, we reproduce an excerpt of interest:

> "At first, Beni and his companions planned to gather a few hundred men. Very soon their plans were exceeded. Thousands and thousands of exhausted, destitute, disoriented Jews caught up with them and hitched themselves to them. They lead and discipline this miserable herd. They form the 'Eastern European Survivors' Division', a real military unit, the only way to give a modicum of cohesion to this tide of poor people fresh from despair. And so the division sets out, crosses Poland, enters Romania. Special detachments took charge of supplies, while others sent in advance prepared the cantonments for the stages.
> - We also had a secret mission service," Jacob told me,. "I was the head, because I had served in the NKVD. I was the head, because I had served in the NKVD and had files, archives, lists of names... their aim was to punish former collaborators.
> It was in Bucharest, at the end of a long journey, that the leaders of the division met the first Jewish emissaries from Palestine.
> - We had planned,' says Moshe, 'to buy a ship in Constanza on the Black Sea, put all the people on it and sail to Israel. The project was too small for us. We knew that the Palestinian brigade of the British army was in northern Italy, and we decided to join it.

In short, Germany's unconditional surrender had not yet taken place and the operation was already underway to bring to Palestine "thousands and thousands of exhausted Jews", who had lost everything as a result of Nazi persecution and were therefore ready to travel to the Promised Land, as planned.

Once this first mission was accomplished, half a hundred members of the Lublin group, of whom eight were young girls, entered Yugoslavia and from there went on to Italy. The men of Simon Koch's "Deutsche Abteilung" welcomed and supported Beni's group, which soon became involved in terrorist activities under the secret code name "Nakam", which means revenge in Hebrew. In July 1945 they began preparing to enter German territory. The leaders of the Nakam group studied three projects, of which the first, called A, was communicated to only a few. "A lot of time and money were devoted to the implementation of the project," confesses Beni, who more than twenty years later describes the plan as "diabolical". Bar-Zohar reproduces Beni's words: "It was about killing millions of Germans. I mean millions, in one fell swoop, without distinction of age or sex. The main difficulty was that we only wanted to hit Germans; however, on the territory of the Reich there were Allied soldiers and residents of all the nations of Europe, liberated from labour camps, escaped from concentration camps. Moreover, some of our people were not determined to carry out such a terrible act, even against the Germans....".

Plan A having been discarded, it was decided to implement Plan B, which consisted of killing some thirty-six thousand members of the Schutzstaffel (defence or protection squads), known as the SS, who had been assembled in a camp near Nuremberg. We had decided," explains Jacob, "to poison the 36,000 SS, and I was in charge of the execution of the project. First I got two of my men hired inside the camp: one as a driver and one as a storekeeper. Later others were hired as office employees. One of our girls was assigned to the broadcasting service." As soon as it was ascertained that the bread distributed in the camp came from an industrial bakery in Nuremberg, it was decided that the bread would be used to liquidate the Germans, although care had to be taken not to kill the camp guards at the same time. Samples of the bread were taken to laboratories where chemical engineers experimented with various poisons. Neither Beni nor Jacob would reveal the location of these laboratories, which Bar-Zohar places in France and near Tarvisio. The poison was not intended to act too quickly, so, after various tests, it was decided to put arsenium in the layer of flour with which the bread was sprinkled.

In April 1946 the preparations were ready: the Nakam group was assisted in the camp by American soldiers of Jewish origin who were responsible for surveillance, and several men had also been brought into the industrial bakery. It was planned to poison about 14,000 loaves of bread, which required six hours of work and five men. "Two men were also needed to stir the mixture in the cauldron, because the arsenic had a tendency to separate from the other ingredients. We had decided to act on a Saturday night for two reasons: on Sunday the bakery was closed and the time between the preparation of the bread and its transport to the camp was twenty-four hours longer. The night of 13 to 14 April 1946 was therefore chosen". In the end, a series of circumstances prevented the operation from being a complete success. On Saturday morning, as a result of a quarrel with the management, a strike broke out among the workers, who at noon left the factory and locked the doors. In the evening, a storm broke out and a gust of wind tore off a wooden shutter, breaking window panes. This alerted the factory guards, who called the police.

One of the avengers explains that they had foreseen that if they were discovered they would pose as thieves, so they hurriedly scattered the poisoned loaves in the warehouse and fled. On Monday 15 April, poisoned loaves and untouched loaves were delivered to the camp. One loaf of bread was distributed to five or six prisoners, thousands of whom suffered violent colic. The text of the Bar-Zohar continues: "According to rumours reported in the newspapers, twelve thousand Germans are said to have been victims of arsenic bread and several thousand are said to have died. These figures are exaggerated. According to the estimates of the avengers, four thousand three hundred prisoners are said to have felt unwell. A thousand were rushed to American hospitals. In the days that followed, between seven and eight hundred died. Others, suffering from paralysis, died over the course of the year. In all, the avengers put the death toll at 1,000." The operation was considered a failure, as the initial plan was to liquidate thirty-six thousand German prisoners and they only managed to kill three percent.

During the summer of 1946 the Nakam group continued to murder detainees in the camps. Dressed in American, British or Polish uniforms, they presented themselves with false orders and had prisoners delivered under the pretext of transferring them to other camps. According to them, these were former members of the SS or Nazi dignitaries who were executed as soon as they left the camp. *Les Vengeurs* records many more actions that were carried out, as well as projects that were abandoned because they were demanded by the Zionist leaders, who always prioritised the creation of Israel: "Paradoxically," writes Bar-Zohar, "it was the creation of the State of Israel more than anything else that influenced the reduction of this Jewish vengeance". Sources that this author prefers not to uncover revealed to him that there were plans to set fire to several German cities and to poison the populations of Berlin, Munich, Nuremberg, Hamburg and Frankfort. "Technically it was not impossible. Poison had to be introduced into the water tanks. Again, the major difficulty was how to avoid affecting soldiers of the occupation forces and non-German refugees sheltered in these five cities." On how to get the poison, *Les vengeurs* says that a scientist from an overseas country agreed to supply it to the avengers.

Since Hitler's rise to power in 1933, various Jewish leaders and organisations had threatened to destroy Germany completely. Samuel Untermayer was the first to call for a "holy war". Theodore Kaufman outlined in *Germany must perish* the project to exterminate the German race by sterilisation. The Morgenthau Plan, as has been explained, involved the genocide of the German people. His henchman Eisenhower, after annihilating a million prisoners in his death camps, would have gladly collaborated with the Secretary of the Treasury if Morgenthau had remained in office. Michel Bar-Zohar's work proves once again that the hatred of the Jewish leaders for Germany and Germans was boundless.

CHAPTER XI

The Decisive Post-War Years

Part 1
Germany, a Nation on the Brink of the Abyss

Many of the Germans who left their homes and became refugees when the Red Army began the offensive that was to take them to the capital of the Reich did so with the intention of eventually returning. None of them knew at the time of the Allied plans to amputate their provinces and expel those who had risked staying. Many of these fugitives therefore chose to face the risks of the occupation of their towns and cities and tried to return to their homes in the east when the war ended with Germany's unconditional surrender. In most cases these attempts were thwarted by the Polish and Russian authorities, who either prevented them from returning or detained them. The men who were detained usually ended up in labour camps in the USSR and were never heard from again. Those who succeeded in their attempt to return found their homes destroyed or already occupied by Russians or Poles, although there were also some who were fortunate enough to enjoy a few months in peace in their villages until they were finally expelled without compensation.

Some authors have sought to exonerate the Western countries from the expulsion of fifteen million people on the grounds that at Potsdam they declared themselves in favour of limiting population transfers and, in any case, doing so in an orderly fashion. They forget that Churchill and Roosevelt imposed the Curzon Line on the Poles to satisfy Stalin's territorial demands and promised to compensate them with German territories in the West. Neither Roosevelt nor Churchill at Yalta opposed the mass expulsions of Germans, but acquiesced: "I am not afraid of the problem of the transfer of peoples," Churchill declared at the plenary session of 7 February, "so long as there is proportion as to what the Poles can handle and what they put into Germany in place of the dead". It is pure hypocrisy, therefore, to try to shift the responsibility for the largest population transfer in history only onto the countries that carried out the expulsions, since not one real measure of pressure was taken to prevent them.

It has already been said that the spirit of the Morgenthau Plan was in the making at the Potsdam Conference, held at Cecilienhof Palace between 17 July and 2 August 1945. Morgenthau, who tried to be in Berlin with

Truman in the American delegation, resigned as Secretary of the Treasury on 22 July; but this did not mean that his criminal plan was buried. In fact, many of the policies that were adopted, for example the de-industrialisation programme, were related to his proposals. Also, as noted above, Eisenhower's treatment of German prisoners was a consequence of the Treasury Secretary's request. Honest people in the United States and Europe noted that the conditions initially imposed on Germany were those contained in the Morgenthau Plan, even though it had been officially abandoned. A year after the end of the war, this fact was still strongly denounced by US Senator Henrick Shipstead, quoted by Alfred M. de Zayas in *Nemesis at Potsdam*. On 15 May 1946, Shipstead made a very severe criticism of US occupation policy in the Senate. Shipstead considered "the Morgenthau Plan for the destruction of the German people an eternal monument of shame to America".

The expulsion of the Germans, an unprecedented population transfer

Over the centuries, the migration of Germans to Central and Eastern Europe had been a constant. As a result, millions of ethnic Germans, known as "Volksdeutsche", lived outside the borders of the Reich. Germans living in Germany were called "Reichdeutsche". These included those living in the eastern provinces of Silesia, East Prussia and Pomerania. Some clear-headed voices had warned long beforehand that the idea of mass expulsions of the German population after the war was madness. The more sensible ones considered it obvious that the deportations could not be carried out under conditions, and this was increasingly accepted by more and more people. To begin the transfers of German populations from the countries of Europe at a time when the Reich was devastated and famine and disease were a plague was, more than madness, a crime, for it would mean a new catastrophe to add to the cataclysm already ravaging the whole of Germany. Unfortunately, those who had no other interest than to hurry in order to gain time and implement their plans against the German people prevailed.

As noted, the mass displacement of Germans began as soon as the Red Army conquered the areas where they had traditionally lived. Millions fled on their own or were evacuated during the retreat of the German army. Millions, however, had chosen not to leave their homes and to remain in their villages. For these, the expulsion began as early as spring 1945, months before the Potsdam Conference began. Then, only the Soviet authorities and the provisional governments of Poland and Czechoslovakia could have prevented it. Instead, they deliberately accelerated the expulsions, despite American and British pleas not to take unilateral decisions and to wait until an international agreement was reached among the Allies. While the Western Allies thus opposed premature deportations, the Soviet Union had an interest in promoting them. The expulsions in East Prussia, Pomerania and Silesia therefore began months before the end of hostilities. The Soviet occupation forces encouraged Poles to evict Germans from their homes in these provinces. Excessive evictions were common, and many Germans who had resisted leaving their land and belongings were forced to abandon everything and march west.

In Czechoslovakia and the Sudetenland, where Field Marshal Ferdinand Schörner still occupied and defended the German-inhabited areas, the savage expatriations began as soon as the German army was disarmed. Before that, however, came the brutal massacre in Prague, where some 42,000 native Germans (Volksdeutsche) and another 20,000 anti-Nazi officials and refugees (Reichdeutsche) were living. At 11 a.m. on 5 May, a pre-organised anti-German uprising broke out in the Czech capital. After the distribution of weapons, Czech flags appeared in the streets and an indiscriminate massacre of Germans and Austrians began. After the radio station was occupied, the slogans: "Death to the Germans!" "Death to all Germans!" "Death to all occupiers!" were given. These orders were carried out to the letter, and for days there was no mercy even for women and children. Many distinguished ethnic Germans from Prague were killed. Giles MacDonogh, in *After the Reich*, cites more than half a dozen names of prominent professors, scientists and other personalities who were unceremoniously hanged. He also describes the massacre at the Scharnhorst School on the night of 5 May, where "men, women, children and even babies were shot in groups of ten in the courtyard". According to this author, in Prague's Strahov Stadium, the Czechs rounded up between ten and fifteen thousand prisoners and "organised a game in which five thousand prisoners had to run for their lives while the guards shot them with machine guns. Some," MacDonogh continues, "were shot in the latrines. The bodies were not removed and those who used the toilet had to defecate on their dead compatriots".

During the night of 6-7 May 1945, German troops left Brüx. On the same day, Soviet soldiers entered the city and a wave of looting and rape began, followed by multiple suicides: some sources estimate that 600 people took their own lives. The terror in this city continued for months. In Prague, negotiations between the Wehrmacht and the Czech National Council were unsuccessful, and some 50,000 wounded and sick soldiers were not allowed to be evacuated and left to their fate. On 9 May the Red Army appeared in Prague and crowds of Czechs attacked the ethnic German population: beaten with iron bars or stoned with cobblestones, men and women died in the streets before the cheering masses. As a rule, SS men were shot in the back of the head or in the stomach. Some SS men were hung by their feet from lampposts and their bodies set on fire; a female Wehrmacht auxiliary was stoned and hanged. Many witnesses," writes MacDonogh, "testified that not only soldiers but also boys and girls were hanged and set on fire.

In the midst of this vortex, Edvard Benes, the Grand Master of Czech Freemasonry, arrived in Prague from London on 13 May. He was greeted by Rudolf Slánsky, the Jewish-born communist leader, with living torches: bodies of Germans hanging by their feet burned on rows of lampposts and panels in St. Wenceslas Square. Thousands of prisoners were concentrated in the Military Prison, the Riding School, the Ministry of Education and other buildings. Many Czechs who had lived peacefully with the Germans were also mistreated and accused of collaboration, especially women who had had ethnic German mistresses. Many Czechs risked their lives trying to protect friends and acquaintances. According to MacDonogh, when some order began to be restored after 16 May, between a dozen and a score of people died daily from torture in the stadium and were taken out in a manure wagon. Thousands of Germans were buried in the Wokowitz cemetery.

In the weeks following the capitulation, tens of thousands of Sudeten Germans were placed on the borders of Germany and Austria. On 30 May 1945, the ruthless expulsion of 30,000 Germans took place in Brno (Brünn in German), the capital of Moravia. Victor Gollancz, one of the few Jewish authors (and there were some) who took pity on the Germans, denounced the events in Brno in *Our Threatened Values* (1946). It quotes an article that appeared on 6 August 1945 in London's *Daily Mail*, in which the journalist Rhona Churchill, who had an English friend married to a German, recounted the events:

> "... Young revolutionaries of the Czech Home Guard decided to 'purify' the city. Shortly before nine o'clock in the evening they paraded through the streets ordering German citizens to stand at the door of their houses at nine o'clock with only one suitcase per person, ready to leave the city forever. The women had ten minutes to wake up and dress their children, put some things in the suitcases and go out into the street. There they were ordered to hand over all their jewellery, watches, furs and money to the guards. They were allowed to keep their wedding rings. They were then led at gunpoint out of the city towards the Austrian border. It was pitch dark when they arrived. Children sobbed, women staggered. Czech border guards pushed them towards the Austrian guards. Then more trouble started. The Austrians did not accept them and the Czechs refused to readmit them. They were shaken into a camp where they spent the night. The next day Romanians were sent to guard them. They are still in that camp, which has become a concentration camp. They only receive the food that the guards give them from time to time. They have received no rations... A typhus epidemic is now spreading among them and it is believed that a hundred die daily...".

In addition to this account by the *Daily Mail* journalist reproduced by Gollancz, there are much harsher accounts by survivors of what has been called the "Brno Death March" and also the "Death March to Pohrlich".

These testimonies make it possible to reconstruct more precisely how the events took place. They are collected in *Documents on the Expulsion of the Sudeten Germans: Survivors Speak Out*, edited in German in 1951 by Dr Wilhelm Turnwald and translated and edited in English in 2002. The following information is taken from this English edition, which is available on the Internet. According to the witness M. v. W., some of the expellees called the march "Corpus Christi procession", which lasted the whole day. After being evicted from their homes during the night of 29 May, the Germans were concentrated in the courtyard of a monastery on the outskirts of the city, where they spent the night in fear, unable to rest. In the rain, endless processions set out from there at 9 a.m. on the morning of the 30th for the Austrian border. In the columns were old people taken from the old people's home, the sick from the hospitals and children. After having spent the previous night on their feet, the weakest began to faint after having walked ten miles. Those who straggled were beaten with truncheons and whips; those who could not go on were shot. Some were taken to a camp near Raigern, where again many were beaten to death. Arrival in Pohrlich, a little more than halfway to the border, took place on the night of Corpus Christi. Most of the deportees dropped exhausted. The next day those who were able to walk continued their deportation journey to the border, but some six thousand people remained in Pohrlich, housed in a car factory and grain warehouses.

Those who were unable to continue the march were, of course, the weakest, among whom the elderly and women with small children predominated. M. v. W., a Red Cross nurse, stayed with them in Pohrlich. Among the harrowing accounts of this health worker was that of a woman in her thirties, who was found lifeless on the floor with two children, "a three-year-old and a baby several weeks old". The woman had committed suicide with poison and "her face was already blue. The baby was also dead, for his mother had pressed him to her breast until he was dead." A Czech gendarme asked the nurse what had happened. We now give the floor to this witness:

> "I replied that she had probably poisoned herself. He cursed her, calling her a Nazi whore and a filthy sow for committing suicide, and ordered me to 'throw the sow in the latrine with her bastard'. When I protested that I was a Red Cross nurse and, bound by my promise, could not obey such an order even if it killed me, he hurled insults like 'German pig' and 'German whore' at me. He then called three other women, whom he intimidated more easily because they did not dare to reply against his threats. The names of these women were Agnes Skalitzky, a 63-year-old widow from Leskau, Franziska Wimetal, in her 30s, and a third woman whose name he did not know. These women were forced to throw the body of the mother and her child into the open latrine. The detainees in the camp were then ordered to use the latrine so that 'the sow and her bastard would disappear from sight as soon as possible'. And this is what

happened. Days and even weeks later, the baby's little head and one arm of the mother could still be seen sticking out of the filth."

According to this account, night after night the women, even those who were ill and over 70 years old, were raped in the camp two or three times a night. There follows an allusion by this nurse to her own rape:

"I witnessed how a soldier decided to rape an eleven-year-old girl. The terrified mother tried to defend her and finally offered herself to save her daughter. The soldier beat her until she bled, but she still held on tightly to the girl. I intervened when the soldier threatened the mother with his revolver. Since I speak a little Russian, I was able to reproach the soldier and he finally let her go. Shortly afterwards, the partisans called me and I went to a door. There I was handed over to the same man who had dragged me to the sugar refinery, where I was raped by five Russians. When I decided to commit suicide and looked for the means to do so, I witnessed the suicide of an elderly couple, who hanged themselves in an empty grain elevator...".

The dead were buried very shallow in mass graves near the Pohrlitz camp, so that the stench of decay could be smelled everywhere. Only after 18 June did the wretched begin to be evacuated from Pohrlich, where seventy to eighty people had died daily, many from typhus: "The first to leave Pohrlich," says Giles MacDonogh, "were the sick, who were taken out and dumped in the marshy bogs near the Thaya River near the Austrian border. In this way they agonised to death. The bodies were photographed and shown in film newsreels in Britain and the United States. The Czechs replied that they had been killed by the Austrians.

This case, which may appear to be an example of inhumane deportation and unspeakable treatment, is a true reflection of the barbarity that characterised the expulsions of Germans throughout 1945. The Czech militia and the army of Svoboda, a communist general appointed defence minister by President Benes, were also engaged in moving large numbers of Sudeten Germans to the Soviet zone of Germany during the month of June. At the same time, the Benes government was trying to obtain the approval of the Western Allies to give the deportations a semblance of legality. Benes had travelled to Moscow on 27 March 1945 and had agreed to hand over the Ministries of Defence, the Interior, Information, Agriculture and Public Education to communists or communist sympathisers. He had also bowed to Stalin's demands for the elimination of Czech agrarians and Catholic populists.

According to documents on the Potsdam Conference, when Churchill argued that it would be necessary to think about where the Germans would go, Stalin said in all seriousness that the Czechs had already evacuated all the Sudeten Germans to the Russian zone of Germany, which was not true, as there were still at least two million Sudeten Germans and several hundred thousand anti-Nazi refugees from the Reich. In any case, however, Stalin's comment confirmed that a large number of Germans had indeed already been expelled to the Russian zone, which did not worry the Soviet dictator at all.

The issue of the transfer of the German populations of Poland, Czechoslovakia and Hungary came to the fore in Potsdam during the session on 21 July. There was no agreement on the number of Germans still living east of the Oder-Neisse line. Truman spoke of the nine million who were supposedly living there in 1939; but Stalin replied that many had died during the war and that the rest had fled. The Generalissimo brazenly emphasised that there was not a German left in the territory to be ceded to Poland. The Polish delegation was invited to express its views and estimated that there were only 1.5 million Germans left in the territories in question. The Poles felt that once the harvest was over, these Germans would voluntarily agree to leave. In reality, no less than four million were still there and, in addition, another million were trying to return, which both Russians and Poles were well aware of. It was therefore intended that Truman and Churchill/Attlee, whose occupation zones in Germany were full to overflowing, should consent to an additional transfer of five million people from Polish-administered territories.

Churchill, who learned on 25 July that he had lost the elections held on 5 July, had to accept that Labour's Attlee would replace him as head of the British delegation in Berlin. Thus, of the three leaders who had divided up the world at Yalta, only Stalin remained. In any case, the Churchill of Potsdam was not the same as the Churchill of Yalta, for he had begun to realise that limits had to be placed on communism, which was not only going to impose itself in the European countries occupied by the Red Army, but was threatening to establish itself in Italy, Greece and France, where the communist parties were calling strikes, intensifying their activities and even announcing in 1948 that the Red Army would be welcome. During the session on the 21st, Churchill opposed the Polish-Soviet plan and not only sought to limit the expulsions, but proposed that some of the refugees who had fled to the west be allowed to return east of the Oder-Neisse line.

At the session of 22 July, Churchill, who had cheerfully defended the principle of population transfers at Yalta, insisted that His Majesty's Government could not accept Polish claims and pleaded moral scruples. "We could accept," he said, "a transfer of Germans equal in number to the number of Poles transferred from east of the Curzon line, say two or three millions; but a transfer of eight or nine millions of Germans, as it appears from the Polish request, would be too much and entirely wrong." Despite these serious objections, however, the Western Allies finally approved the transfer of Germans. Article XIII of the Potsdam Treaty was finally worded as follows:

"The three Governments, having considered all aspects of the question, recognise that the transfer to Germany of the German populations or elements thereof remaining in Poland, Czechoslovakia and Hungary will have to be undertaken. They agree that such transfers should take place in an orderly and humane manner."

The acceptance of the German expulsion implicitly recognised the inability of the Western Allies to oppose the USSR and Poland unless, as General Patton had suggested, they were prepared to confront Stalin in order to push the Red Army back to its pre-war borders. In the case of Czechoslovakia, the Sudeten German "final solution" had already been accepted in advance. Before the Yalta Conference, the US State Department had estimated that 1.5 million people would be expelled; but during the Potsdam Conference, the number was put at 2.5 million, to which should be added another 800,000 anti-Nazi refugees who were not supposed to be transferred. One of these, Bruno Hoffman, recounts how he was forced to leave his home in Gablonz in one of the expulsion documents quoted above. His account begins: "Since my wife and I had never been supporters of Hitler's regime and my wife had been interrogated by the Gestapo in 1942 for anti-fascist activities, we did not believe that anything could happen to us". In the end, all these Germans also ended up being expelled simply because they were Germans. So there is no room for subterfuge of any kind: it was the consent of the Western Powers that made the expulsions legal, and this was publicly acknowledged by numerous British and American authors, such as Anne O'Hare McCormick, the first woman to win the Pulitzer Prize for Journalism in 1937. A foreign correspondent for *The New York Times*, in an article published on 13 November 1946, Anne O'Hare referred to the expulsions as "the most inhuman decision ever taken by governments dedicated to the defence of human rights".

The Western Allies needed, however, to regulate and monitor population flows into their areas as much as possible, since they were responsible for the livelihoods of the deportees. The incessant and unscheduled influx of millions of destitute people could only aggravate the chaos that already existed in the Germany they occupied. They therefore decided to call for a moratorium on expulsions and introduced clauses in the aforementioned Article XIII of the Treaty warning of their disruptive or harmful effects. Thus, while the first paragraph had formally approved the deportations, the third expressly requested that they be temporarily halted so that the occupying powers could examine the problem they created. Stalin, in deference to his allies, accepted the introduction of these "humanitarian" paragraphs and agreed that the foreign ministers should meet to work out a programme to regulate the flood of Germans into the various zones of occupation. This was only an empty gesture, for at no time was there any serious consideration of suspending the deportations and granting the moratorium. The Soviet authorities in Poland and Czechoslovakia took no steps to prevent the governments of these countries from continuing to pour Germans into their zone of occupation. Only Hungary respected the moratorium and halted the expulsion measures until January 1946.

With the Potsdam Conference over, the Western Allies thought they would have a few months to try to mitigate the disaster before the winter of 1945-46 arrived, a period when, if shelter and food were not provided for the deportees, deaths could rise en masse from cold, hunger and disease.. The Polish and Czechoslovak governments appeared to formally accept the suspension of the expulsions, but this was only an appearance, as the Poles issued a statement announcing that they needed to get rid of the Germans from the city of Stettin and Silesia, as they intended to proceed with the immediate reconstruction of these areas. Under this pretext they continued to bring Germans into the Soviet zone. Of course, the deportees did not wish to remain in a communist Germany, so most of them tried to continue marching westwards with the aim of reaching the British and American zones. Faced with this evidence, the British urgently proposed to the Soviets and Americans that they jointly ask the Poles to stop the expulsions immediately. The text of the proposal is dated 9 September 1945. Extracted from volume 2 of *Foreign Relations of the United States*, it is transcribed in part by Alfred M. de Zayas:

> "... despite the request made to them by the three governments following the Potsdam Conference, the Polish authorities continue, at any rate by indirect means, to expel the remaining German inhabitants of the German territories handed over to the Polish administration. The difficulties created for the Control Commission, which are already formidable as a result of previous expulsions, are thus increasing daily".

Several reports from American officials in Czechoslovakia confirm that the Bene" government did not prevent repeated abuses and harassment of Germans from continuing, but encouraged them. This led to a disorganised resumption, if it had ever stopped, of the mass movement of German civilians into the American zone of occupation. In the background, Benes feared that the British and Americans might eventually oppose the expulsions, and so he pursued a policy of fait accompli. Serious outbreaks of violence occurred in Sudeten-inhabited towns.

Two days before the end of the Potsdam Conference, on 31 July 1945, a particularly serious pogrom took place in Aussig, a town on the Elbe. In the early hours of the morning, soldiers of the Svoboda Army who had arrived in Aussig during the night attacked ethnic Germans, recognisable by the white armbands they wore on their arms. In 1977, the book *Jews in Sovoboda's Army in the Soviet Union* was published about this army, highlighting the important role that Jews from Czechoslovakia played in Ludvík Svoboda's army during World War II. Its author, Erich Kulka, undertook the research on behalf of the "Institute of Contemporary Jewry" of the Hebrew University in Jerusalem. Little was known until the publication of this work about the actions of Jews in Svoboda's army.

The pogrom began at around 3 p.m. The trigger was an explosion in an ammunition depot northwest of the city in Schönpriesen. It was triggered by an explosion in an ammunition depot in the north-west of the city, in Schönpriesen. This incident was used as a pretext for the Aussig massacre, where a crazed Czech militia known as the Revolutionary Guards ("Revolucni Garda"), who had been committing atrocities since the beginning of May, entered in a frenzy. These fanatics, who had arrived by train from Prague, mass-murdered German civilians, bludgeoning them indiscriminately with iron bars and stakes. The exact death toll could not be established: estimates vary between 1,000 and 2,700 victims. The criminals herded people over the new Elbe bridge and threw everything from babies with prams to old people into the river. Those who tried to float to safety were mercilessly shot. In Pirna, a town in Saxony near Dresden, some fifty kilometres from Aussig, floating corpses were rescued and eighty bodies were buried there alone. This is the testimony of Therese Mager:

> "I ran to the Elbe bridge and saw how hundreds of German workers coming from their bricklaying jobs were thrown into the Elbe. Even women and children with their prams were thrown into the stream by the Czechs. Most of them wore black uniforms with red armbands. They threw women and children who could not defend themselves from the twenty-metre high bridge into the water. The mass pursuit of the Germans lasted well into the night. From every street and street corner we could hear people screaming and crying. Neither the Czech authorities nor the Russian occupiers did anything to prevent the slaughter. Numerous Germans rescued from the water were machine-gunned...".

The most macabre thing," writes Alfred M. de Zayas, "is that this pogrom against the German population was used by the Czechoslovak government as an argument to induce the Western Allies to accelerate the pace of expulsions. By now, hundreds of thousands of Sudeten Germans were interned in camps awaiting expulsion. Those who remained in their villages and towns lived in constant fear of arrest. President Bene¨ publicly called for the "liquidation" of the Germans. In his words, it was necessary to "cleanse the Republic". It is undeniable that the criminal harassment of the German populations in Europe has to be seen as a paradigmatic case of large-scale ethnic cleansing. It should be noted, moreover, that the areas which the Czechoslovak government was going to re-annex in order to confiscate property and de-Germanise had for seven hundred years been populated by Germans.

On 15 September 1945 *The Economist* of London denounced the situation: "Despite the Potsdam declaration calling for a pause in the disorderly and inhuman expulsions of Germans, the forced exodus from the provinces of East Prussia, Pomerania, Silesia and parts of Brandenburg, which had a population of about nine million in 1939, continues". In the same report, the London paper also alluded to the situation in Czechoslovakia, where "the expulsion of three and a half million Sudeten Germans is also continuing." *The Economist* called on the Council of Foreign Ministers to put an end to this "appalling tragedy" and noted that millions of people were wandering in the occupation zones "with virtually no food or shelter." The article claimed that the major urban centres were already overcrowded before the arrival of the deportees and warned: "The inevitable result will be that millions will die of starvation and exhaustion".

Foreign Secretary Ernest Bevin was questioned in the House of Commons on 10 October 1945. One MP, Bower, asked the minister whether the government had protested to Poland about "the atrocities inflicted on German women and children in connection with their expulsion". Bevin replied in the affirmative, but in reality the demarche had gone no further than a note of protest to the Polish ambassador in London, which was to no avail. Three days later, on 13 October, *The Economist* again demanded a halt to the expulsions. Unfortunately, the reality of the situation showed day by day that the efforts were fruitless and nothing was achieved. On 19 October Bertrand Russell wrote in *The Times*: "In Eastern Europe our Allies are now carrying out mass deportations on an unprecedented scale, and in an apparently deliberate attempt to exterminate many millions of Germans, not with gas, but by depriving them of their homes and food, leaving them to starve to death in a slow and agonising manner". Captain Alfred E. Marples, a Conservative MP who would later become Minister of Transport, on 22 October 1945 announced the following in the House of Commons: "According to a recent report of the International Red Cross, protests against the disorganised deportations of Germans have had no effect, and refugees continue to pour into Berlin, where thousands are dying in the streets."

Three days later, on 25 October, a delegation led by Sir William Beveridge and including seven members of Parliament, four bishops, the publisher Victor Gollancz and other prominent figures visited Prime Minister Attlee. The meeting was reported *in The Times*, which on 26 October reported that the VIP committee had requested that "in view of the imminent danger of death by starvation and disease to millions of human beings", Her Majesty's Government should negotiate with the Russian, Polish and Czechoslovak governments "to stop at once and throughout the winter the expulsions of Germans from their homes in Eastern Europe ". Thus, on the eve of what was a harsh winter, in which entire families were to freeze to death and daily rations were only 1,000 calories, the moratorium provided for in Article XIII of the Potsdam Treaty was not being observed, and the deportations had not only not been stopped, but were being publicly announced.

At the end of October 1945, the Polish authorities in Breslau, at the demolition ceremony for the statue of Kaiser Wilhelm I, one of the few remaining German monuments, announced that 200,000 Germans still in the city would be forced to leave for one of the German occupation zones. The Jewish mayor, Stanislav Gosniej, announced in his speech at the demolished monument that four thousand Germans were leaving the city every week and that within half a year Breslau would be Poland's second city. In Breslau, Beria had placed Jews at the head of the organs of repression. The Jewish writer John Sack, author of *An Eye for an Eye. The Untold Story of Jewish Revenge Against Germans in 1945. The Untold Story of Jewish Revenge Against Germans in 1945*), reports that the head of the police, Shmuel "Gross", who used the Polish name Mieczyslaw "Gross", and the head of the department for Germans, were Jewish. According to this source, from which we will drink hereafter, the chief of police in Katowice, Pinek Piekanowski, and those in Kielce, Lublin and Stettin, as well as the head of the Internal Security Corps of the Polish Army, were also Jewish.

Finally, the Allied Control Council decided to work on a plan to rationalise the expulsions. The aim was not to stop the expulsions, but to ensure that the transfer of populations was carried out in a more orderly fashion and under better conditions. The plan was already outlined on 20 November 1945. At that date, it was estimated that, after more than half a year of savage deportations, three and a half million Germans still remained in the areas administered by the Polish authorities. It was anticipated that two million of them could be admitted by the Soviets and the rest would be transferred to the British zone. As for the Germans in Czechoslovakia, it was estimated that two and a half million remained in the country, most of them in the Sudetenland region, one million seven hundred and fifty thousand would go to the American zone and the rest would be allocated to the Soviets. As for the half million Germans in Hungary, they would all be admitted to the American zone of occupation. It was also planned to transfer 150,000 Germans from Austria to the French zone. The plan estimated that all population transfers could be completed by August 1946.

Alfred M. de Zayas notes that more than two million Germans lost their lives during or as a result of the displacements. The following is an excerpt from his account, taken from *Nemesis at Potsdam*, which is one of the main sources for what we have been writing:

> "More than two million Germans did not survive their displacement. Probably one million perished in the course of military evacuations and during the flight in the last months of the war. The rest, mostly women, children and the elderly, died as a result of the ruthless methods of their expulsion. Of course, not all transfers were carried out in a brutal manner. The transports to the western areas during the summers of 1946 and 1947 were relatively well organised and the number of deaths decreased substantially. On the other hand, the 1945 expulsions, the means of

transport in general, and most of the movements to the Soviet zone of occupation were catastrophic in method and consequences".

This author divides the expulsions into three phases: those before the Potsdam Conference, which he describes as "savage expulsions"; those from the period after Potsdam until December 1945; and those of the years 1946-47, which was the period of the "organised" transfers (his own quotation marks). It can be said, however, that the deportations of 1945 were all beastly; women and children were loaded onto trains like cattle. The journey could take several days, during which no food was provided. Children who died during the journey were thrown out of the windows. At the arrival stations, numerous corpses were routinely removed from the wagons. On 24 August 1945, the British *News Chronicle* published a report by its Berlin correspondent, Norman Clark, in which the journalist recounts the arrival in Berlin of a train from Danzig. The text, despite its considerable length, is reproduced in full in the above-mentioned work. Here are some eloquent excerpts:

> "... The train from Danzig had come in. This time the journey had taken seven days; sometimes it takes longer. Those people in the cattle cars, and hundreds lying on the bales of their belongings on the platforms and in the station hall, were the dead, the dying and the starving abandoned by the tide of human misery that daily reaches Berlin, and the next day will return to catch a train to another city in a desperate search for food and relief. Thousands more - up to 25,000 in a day - trek to the Berlin slums, where they are stopped and barred from entering the overcrowded city. Every day between fifty and a hundred children - a total of five thousand already in a short period of time - who have lost their parents or have been abandoned are picked up at the stations and taken to orphanages or in search of foster mothers.
> ... According to a low estimate - given to me by Dr. Karl Biaer, the anti-Nazi now installed as head of the Berlin Social Welfare Committee - there are 8,000,000 homeless nomads wandering in parts of the provinces near Berlin. If you take the Sudetenlanders expelled from Czechoslovakia and those on the move from anywhere, the figure of those who cannot be provided with food amounts to at least 13,000,000.... What has just aggravated the problem and made it insoluble is the continuation of the expulsions of Germans from their homes by the Poles...".

One last example will provide a definitive understanding of how savage and ruthless the expulsions could be. In the monthly *The Nineteenth Century and After*, the British journalist Frederick Augustus Voigt reported in November 1945 on the arrival in Berlin of a train from Troppau (Czechoslovakia), on which men, women and children had travelled for eighteen days in open cattle cars. Of the 2,400 people who left Troppau, almost half, 1,50, died en route.

Although the deportations were scheduled to end in the summer of 1946, they continued until 1947. Although they were to be "organised" by 1946, the sight of the deportees was moving to all those who looked at their tragedy from a Christian point of view. In March 1946, the *Manchester Guardian* published a sad chronicle by its correspondent in Lübeck: it described the arrival in the British zone of German civilians from Poland, entering the Hanseatic city on board overcrowded trains, where it was impossible to sit down to rest, as the deportees were packed together standing up. In the first transport, a seventy-three-year-old man and an eighteen-month-old child arrived dead; in a second transport, the dead numbered three. Although rations were to be provided for the expellees, on the first train each person had received half a slice of bread for the entire journey. The *Manchester Guardian* journalist described the miserable physical condition of the refugees, on some of whom the marks of ill-treatment were still visible. Most of the women, British doctors who examined the deportees confirmed, had been raped, including a ten-year-old girl and a sixteen-year-old girl. In general, the age of the deportees was over fifty, although there were many elderly people in their eighties, including a number of cripples and paralytics.

As a new winter approached and the expulsions continued, the military authorities, in order to avoid the disaster of winter 1945-46, in which thousands of people had died of cold or frostbite, succeeded in cancelling several train movements. Unfortunately, more than half the days of the winter of 1946-47 dawned with temperatures below freezing. Snow and frost were constant. It is considered to have been the coldest winter in living memory. At Christmas, trains from Poland arrived frozen. Thirty-five deportees died on one train and another 25 required amputations. The delegation of the International Committee of the Red Cross (ICRC) in Warsaw, noting that in January 1947 the convoys of deportees were arriving in Germany in deplorable conditions, brought the problem to the attention of the Polish Ministry of the Interior. Despite his efforts, the deportations did not stop, and only a few deportations of people who were not in internment camps were suspended. At least the fact that the receiving authorities had information about the number of people they were going to receive and their dates of arrival allowed for better organisation, which helped to save lives. In the "organised transfers" the various countries involved in the ethnic cleansing of Germans deported some six million people.

Little can be known about what happened to German prisoners and civilians in the Soviet Union. It has already been said that the USSR had not signed the Geneva Convention and was therefore exempt from any international control. Nevertheless, it is certain that more than a million German soldiers died in the Soviet Gulag. As for German civilian casualties in Russia, Alfred M. de Zayas estimates that there were between 1.5 and 2 million people.

In addition, the Red Cross tried to establish a presence in other European countries where German civilians were also persecuted. From March 1945 onwards, the International Committee of the Red Cross made representations to gain access to internment camps in Romania, but was repeatedly refused permission. In Hungary, some visits were authorised in November 1945 and January 1946. As a result of these inspections, the ICRC delegation submitted a number of requests to the Hungarian government to improve conditions for the detainees. As for civilians interned in camps in Yugoslavia, the ICRC received private appeals and reports that conditions of internment were poor, since, in addition to food shortages, hygiene and the treatment of detainees were appalling. The Red Cross could do little to improve the situation of the civilians and had to be content to focus on its work to help prisoners of war (POWs). The treatment of the ethnic German minority in Yugoslavia was another typical case of ethnic cleansing. Recently, the International Criminal Tribunal in The Hague has been examining crimes related to ethnic cleansing committed during the Balkan wars at the end of the last century, but no one has ever bothered to denounce the persecution of German civilians in half of Europe after the Second World War.

In 1939, according to data published in 1967 by the German Federal Ministry for Expellees, some two million Germans lived in south-eastern Europe, i.e. in Yugoslavia (537,000), Hungary (623,000) and Romania (786,000). Settled along and near the Danube, they were known as "Donauschwaben" (Danube Swabians). Most of them were descendants of settlers who had arrived in this fertile region of Europe in the 17th and 18th centuries, i.e. after the liberation of Hungary from the yoke of Turkey. Seen as exponents of Christian civilisation in the face of the Islamisation of the Balkans and Europe, they were appreciated in Austria and the Austro-Hungarian Empire. Everything began to change for them in 1919 as a result of the disastrous Treaty of Versailles.

At the end of World War II, the communist regime of Josip Broz Tito, a crypto-Jew whose real name was Josif Walter Weiss, and Moses Pijade, another Jew who was the grey eminence and the real strongman, was installed in Yugoslavia. A decree of 21 November 1944 deemed the Germans "enemies of the people" and they were deprived of their civil rights and their property confiscated without compensation. A law enacted on 6 February 1945 stripped them of their Yugoslav citizenship. The Reich authorities had been evacuating 220,000 Germans; but by the end of May 1945, more than two hundred thousand ethnic German Yugoslavs were still at home and were arrested and taken prisoner. Of these, 63,635 died between 1945 and 1950 from malnutrition, exhaustion and disease. Some 100,000 small businesses: factories, shops, farms and various trades were confiscated. In addition to the number of civilians, some 70,000 German soldiers died in captivity in Yugoslavia as a result of ill-treatment, executions, reprisals and forced labour in mines, road construction, shipyards, etc. The German soldiers had surrendered in the 1950s. German soldiers had surrendered to the British in southern Austria, but London handed over 150,000 prisoners of war to Tito's communist regime on the pretext that they would later be repatriated to Germany.

De Zayas comments in his work that forty-odd years after the expulsions from their homes, the fairs of East Prussians, Pomeranians, Silesians and Sudeten Germans were attended by several hundred thousand expellees. Their leaders spoke of the right to keep their legal claims alive through peaceful means, for there were people in the Federal Republic of Germany at the time who considered it a danger to peace in Europe to raise the issue. Old people are still alive today who remember the tragedy of the expulsions. In 2012, Erika Vora published *Silent no More*, in which she collects multiple accounts of octogenarian and nonagenarian women who were children in 1945 and survived the deportations. Frederick A. Lindemann, Lord Cherwell, the Jewish ideologue behind the massive bombing of German working class homes, is reported to have said that "to have one's own house destroyed is the most damaging thing to morale". In the preface to *Silent no More*, Erika Vora quotes the humanist Albert Schweitzer, theologian and philosopher, who considers being expelled from one's own home to be the cruelest offence to human rights. We end with some of his questions: "What does it mean to have a home? What does it mean to be expelled from the place where generations of your ancestors worked hard for centuries? What does it mean to be thrown out onto the frozen streets with a child in your arms and be left homeless and without rights? What does it mean to be separated from your helpless child? What does it mean to see death everywhere and to fear being attacked at any moment? What does it mean to never again be able to return to the resting place where you and your loved ones found peace?"

Jewish criminals in concentration camps

As for the internment camps, it must be explained that people who were not allowed to stay in their homes were locked up in them. The International Committee of the Red Cross found it extremely difficult to visit them in order to distribute aid to the detainees. Even in the few camps where it was allowed entry, mostly in Czechoslovakia, conditions were considered unsatisfactory and this was recorded in reports submitted to the Bene¨ government in Prague. In Poland, the distribution of Red Cross relief was not allowed in almost any camp. Only the relatives of the internees were allowed to deliver parcels, which were usually opened by the guards, who would tear them apart to keep the best and hand over the rest. Only in June

1947, despite repeated demands, was the delegate of the International Red Cross Committee allowed by the Polish authorities to visit some camps, but by then most of the detainees had already been expelled.

Heinz Esser, a German doctor who survived the terrifying conditions of internment at the Lamsdorf camp in Oberschlesien (Upper Silesia), published in 1949 *Die Hölle von Lamsdorf: Dokumentation über ein polnisches Vernichtungslager* (*The Hell of Lamsdorf: Documentation of a Polish Extermination Camp*), a 127-page booklet denouncing all the cruelty and ruthlessness of the Poles who controlled the camp. Interested readers who read German can still purchase this work, of which there are several editions. Reading it confirms that Lamsdorf was indeed an extermination camp, as 6,488 out of an inmate population of 8,064 died from starvation, disease, forced labour, physical and mental torture, beatings and ill-treatment. There were 828 children in the camp, of whom those over the age of ten had to carry out the hardest and most inhumane work: 628 died. The camp commandant, Ceslaw Gimborski, a young Jewish man in his twenties, demanded that the prisoners work on a diet of two to three hundred calories a day. The list of dead Germans was passed to him daily, and his usual question was: "Why so few? The Lamsdorf guards, who according to Dr. Esser all suffered from venereal diseases, were true psychopaths who, drunk, continually raped the females in the camp. Sometimes these degenerates forced the women to drink urine, blood and eat excrement, among other atrocities.

A chilling episode about the Lamsdorf camp is reported in two different sources: Heinz Esser in the above-mentioned work and also the Jewish author John Sack in *An Eye for an Eye*. Sack, who has already been quoted above, was a veteran journalist of more than fifty years who wrote several books, most notably *An Eye for an Eye*, subtitled *The Untold Story of Jewish Revenge Against Germans in 1945*. The book caused an uproar, for Sack denounces in it that the Polish communist concentration camps were run after the war by Jews who tortured and killed tens of thousands of German civilians: "I learned," Sack writes in the preface, "that in 1945 a great number of Germans were killed: not Nazis, not Hitler's henchmen, but German civilians, men, women, children, babies, whose only crime was to be Germans". We therefore choose Sack's version, which appears on pages 130-131:

> "During the war, the SS had buried some Poles, five hundred bodies, in a large meadow near Lamsdorf, but Ceslaw had heard that there were ninety thousand, and ordered the women of Gruben to dig them up. The women did so, and began to gag as the bodies appeared, black as sewer substance. The faces were corrupt, the flesh was glue, but the guards shouted to the women of Gruben: 'Throw yourselves in with them!' The women did so and the guards shouted: 'Embrace them, kiss them, make love to them!' With their rifles they pushed behind the women's heads

until their eyes, noses and mouths penetrated the slime of the Poles' faces. The women who pressed their lips together could not scream, and those who screamed had to taste something nauseating. Spitting, vomiting, the women emerged at last, with debris on their chins, on their fingers, on their dresses, with moisture seeping into the fibres. Sprayed with the stench they returned to Lamsdorf."

Dr. Esser's account adds that there were also men digging in the pit and emphasises that the stench of putrefaction emanating from the women was so unbearable that at night it permeated all the rooms and the entire camp. The terrible stench lasted for weeks, as there were no showers. Sack confirms that sixty-four of the Gruben women died. Given the need to cover up such ferocity, it is understandable that the Red Cross was denied access to the camps.

In *An Eye for an Eye* John Sack explains that the largest camp in Poland was Potulice, built by Jews near the Baltic Sea for thirty thousand would-be oppressors. Every night the commandant would go to a barrack, shout "Attention!" and force the detainees to sing a humiliating song. When they had sung, he would start beating them. When they had sung, he would start beating them with the stools, often killing more than one. In the same camp, Jewish guards would take Germans out of the camp at dawn and make them dig a grave near a forest, throw a portrait of Hitler into it and force them to weep. They were then ordered to strip naked and had liquid manure poured over them. Sometimes, "the guards would take a toad," writes Sack, "and shove the thick thing down the throat of a German, who would soon die. According to this source, the death toll in Potulice was enormous. In the Myslowitz camp, a hundred Germans died every day. In Grottkau, writes the Jewish author, "the Germans were buried in potato sacks, but in Hohensalza they went directly into the coffins, where the commandant saw them off. At Blechhammer the Jewish commandant did not even look at the Germans and they died without being examined." Sack gives the figure of 1,255 camps for Germans awaiting deportation in the area controlled by the Department of State Security and claims that in each of them between twenty-five and fifty percent of the detainees died.

In charge of State Security was Jakub Berman, a Warsaw Jew who had headed Polish Communist Party Intelligence. Berman had taken refuge in Moscow after the German invasion of 1939, and Stalin had appointed him to the government that marched to Lublin with the Red Army. In Warsaw he was Beria's man, so he had direct communication with Moscow. John Sack reports on a visit by Jakub Berman to Kattowice, where another Jew, Pinek Piekanowski, was also in control of security. Berman was accompanied by Wladyslaw Gomulka, who was married to a Jewish woman, and two other Jewish ministers. Gomulka acknowledged that he had problems with the Red Cross and tried to get Piekanowski to authorise inspections of the camps. The reply was: "I don't respect the Red Cross". The angry dialogue, reproduced in *An Eye for an Eye*, shows that Gomulka was not capable of asserting himself against his subordinate: "If you order me to let the Red Cross through, I will." Gomulka's words were, "No, I will not order you." Berman, who had been quiet listening to the scuffle finally said slowly: "Comrade, we have your word that the Germans are being well treated."

In Gleiwitz, the camp commandant was a young Jewish woman, Lola Potok, the main protagonist of John Sack's play, who argues that Lola and her colleagues had come out of Auschwitz unscathed, so they tortured and murdered Germans to take revenge. Most of Lola Potok's fifty foremen were Jews, some of whom were women who enjoyed torturing German prisoners. Lola's trusted assistant was named Moshe Grossman. The director of all the camps and prisons in Silesia was Chaim Studniberg, a twenty-six year old Jew whose hatred of the Germans was pathological. For the Lamsdorf camp, Studniberg had personally chosen Czeslaw and the ten young Jews who constituted his team of criminals. Other Polish Jewish members of the terror apparatus reported in various sources are: Henryk Chmielewski, Jan Kwiatowski, Josef Jurkowski, Jechiel Grynszpan, Karol Grabski, Berek Einsenstein, Adam Krawiecki, Pinek Maka, Shlomo Singer, Stefan Finkel, Adela Glikman, David Feuerstein, Aaron Lehrman, Mordechai Kac, Salek Zucker, Hanna Tinkpulwer, Nahum Solowic, Albert Grunbaum and many others whose names we leave unmentioned and which the reader can find on the *Raport Nowaka* website (a report by Polish researcher Zbigniew Nowak).

Among the major Jewish criminals featured in John Sack's book is Shlomo (Solomon) Morel, appointed by the Soviet occupiers as commandant of the Zgoda camp in Schwientochlowitz, where most of the interrogators were also Jewish. Morel, who according to Sack had been Lola Potok's lover, personally killed a child by smashing his head against a wall. In December 1989 a Commission for the Investigation of Crimes against the Polish Nation put his case in the hands of Piotr Brys, a prosecutor in Katowice, who summoned Morel for the first time on 27 February 1991. On 24 November of the same year, the newspaper *Wiésci* publicised the case. Days later, the prosecutor confronted Morel with a Polish woman, Dorota Boreczek, who at the age of 14 had been with her mother in Schwientochlowitz. Fearing that things might get complicated, Shlomo Morel took a plane and landed in Tel Aviv in January 1992, but his pension could not be paid in Israel, so he returned in June. At the time, documents from the Archives of the Federal Republic of Germany were in the hands of investigators. John Sack quotes some statements from the reports: "The commander was Morel, a bastard ("Schweinehund") without equal". "The commandant, Morel, appeared. Sticks and whips rained down on us. They broke my nose and beat my ten nails which turned black and later fell off." "The commander, Morel, arrived. I saw him with my own eyes kill many of my fellow prisoners." Faced with the evidence that he was to be tried, Morel flew back to Israel, where he was living in June 1993.

With the dissolution of the Soviet Union, Morel was charged with crimes against humanity by the Polish National Institute of Memory. In 1998 and 2004, Poland requested extradition to Israel,, which refused on both occasions and denied Morel's crimes. The Zionists claimed that an anti-Semitic conspiracy had been set up against him. Another extradition requested by Poland, in this case to Britain, was that of Helena Wolinska, a Warsaw-born Jew who held the rank of lieutenant colonel. Twice, in 1999 and 2001, the British refused to extradite her, justifying their refusal on the grounds of Wolinska's age and the length of time that had elapsed since the alleged crimes took place. The obstructionist attitude of Israel and the UK contrasts with the unconditional willingness of the German authorities. While Israel protects and honours known Jewish criminals and accuses those who have uncovered and claimed them of anti-Semitism, in Germany, elderly nonagenarians continue to be prosecuted and tried for the simple fact that they served in Auschwitz. In 2015, for example, at the time of writing, Oskar Gröning, a ninety-three-year-old former accountant at the labour camp, awaits trial in detention for alleged war crimes.

Angela Merkel, the Jewish-born chancellor, attributes "eternal responsibility" to Germany, yet she prefers to ignore the massacres of all kinds committed against German civilians. While scholars who try to revise history are accused of being revanchists, anti-Semites and neo-Nazis, the official historiography insists on repeating the same lies ad nauseam and concealing the historical truth. In an article published by the Institute for Historical Review analysing the fate of the ethnic German Yugoslavs ("Volksdeutsche"), Tomislav Sunic asks: "Why are the sufferings and victims of some nations or ethnic groups ignored, while the suffering of other nations and groups receive exaggerated attention and sympathy from the media and politicians?" The question is rhetorical for those of us who know the answer, but it still deserves to be asked.

What happened in Poland, where absolute control of the police and internment camps was in the hands of unscrupulous Jewish criminals, also had its version in Hungary, Romania, Yugoslavia and other countries where tens of thousands of Jews released from concentration camps, supposedly for extermination, were welcomed with open arms by the communist occupation forces and integrated into Beria's repressive police apparatus.

At the same time, a steady stream of Jews was pouring into Germany, which was to serve as a springboard for channelling illegal immigration to Palestine. Lieutenant General Sir Frederick Edgeworth Morgan, head of operations of the UNRRA (United Nations Relief and Rehabilitation Administration) in Germany, denounced the existence of a secret organisation behind the arrival of so many 'ruddy, well-dressed, well-fed' Jews who were handling a lot of money. In January 1946 the British general caused a scandal when he bluntly denounced at a press conference that a Zionist organisation was secretly working with Soviet aid to facilitate the "exodus" of European Jews to Palestine. Frederick E. Morgan wrote a memoir in 1961 entitled *Peace and War: A Soldier's Life*, from which this quote is taken:

> "I have been able to assemble a full and reasonable assessment of the way in which the UN agency was being skilfully used to promote what was nothing less than a Zionist campaign of aggression in Palestine. Defying the prohibition of the British Mandate, reluctant as ever to employ decisive measures, the Zionist command, admirably well organised, was employing every means to force immigration into the country without regard for the hardship and suffering of the immigrants, few of whom seemed to have any spontaneous enthusiasm for the Zionist cause. The whole project evidently had Russian connivance, if not actual support, since its success would lead to the elimination of British authority in a vital area of the Middle East."

General Morgan's denunciation, based on information received from military intelligence, unleashed a storm in the press, which was quick to label his comments as anti-Semitic and demand his resignation. Since he did not resign "motu proprio", he was dismissed by the head of UNRRA, who was the Jew Fiorello La Guardia, former mayor of New York.

In total, according to Giles MacDonogh, there were nearly 200 Jewish DP (displaced persons) camps in the Allied occupation zones, most of which were in the American zone. The most famous camp was Landsberg (Bavaria), where they edited the *Landsberger Caytung* (*Landsberg Newspaper*), which provided information in Yiddish about the Nuremberg trials. By the end of 1946 there were more than 200,000 Jews in Allied camps in Germany and Austria. MacDonogh comments in *After the Reich* that in Bad Ischl, a spa town in the Austrian region of Salzkammergut, there were riots in the summer of 1947 over the favourable treatment of Jews in the distribution of milk quotas. The Jewish displaced persons had been placed in a hotel, which was surrounded by rioters who stoned it, shouting: "Get out, you dirty Jews! Hang the Jews! The American authorities sentenced one of the rioters to 15 years.

As General Patton denounced before he was assassinated, being a Jew in post-war Europe became a great privilege. Rabbi Judah Nadich confirmed this fact on 4 February 1949 in the South African newspaper *Jewish Times*. Judah Nadich, a lieutenant colonel who acted as Eisenhower's Jewish advisor, stated that the American general personally gave orders for preferential treatment to the Jews, who were placed in special camps and given more food rations than other displaced persons. In addition to evicting Germans from their homes, which outraged Patton, to give them to Jews entering Germany en masse, hundreds of Jewish journalists returned and took over the media in the occupied areas, where special Jewish police forces controlled the stations. They obtained food rations without having to queue like the others and were immediately provided with travel passes to give them freedom of movement. The black market monopoly was in their hands. In addition, as has seen, they organised the deportations in the Baltic countries, Poland, Austria, Hungary, Yugoslavia and Czechoslovakia, where the Czech communists put them in charge of the expatriation of Sudeten Germans.

Nuremberg's disastrous set-up

Much has already been written about the Nuremberg trials, enough to stop them being referred to with the slightest respect. In Spain, however, Alberto Ruiz Gallardón, Minister of Justice, in order to satisfy the demands of Jewish associations, proposed making it a crime to deny facts that "had been proven by the Nuremberg Tribunals". In October 2012, a few days before presenting the changes to the reform of the Penal Code to the Council of Ministers, Gallardón met with the president of the American Jewish Committee, David Harris, and the president of the Jewish Communities of Spain, Isaac Querub, who expressed their satisfaction. Predictably, legal circles with a modicum of professional decorum described the proposal as "extravagant" and considered the reference to the crimes proven at Nuremberg to be "far over the top and unnecessary". Certainly, it takes a great deal of ineptitude and ignorance or a great deal of impudence to attach any legal value to the sinister masquerade enacted at Nuremberg. Whichever way you look at it, Nuremberg was a macabre farce, a consummated vendetta by international Jewry, one more since 1933 when its leaders declared "holy war" against Germany when Hitler had not yet taken any action against German Jews. Authors such as Douglas Reed, Louis Marschalko, Joaquín Bochaca and others have no hesitation in describing what happened in the Bavarian city as "Talmudic revenge".

When in 1939 Roosevelt, Baruch and company decided to make the atomic bomb, their initial intention was to drop it on Germany. Then, as we have seen, a string of Jewish leaders came up with successive extermination plans: Theodore N. Kaufman (*Germany must perish*), Henry Morgenthau (Morgenthau Plan), Frederick A. Lindemann (ideologue of aerial terror), Dwight D. Eisenhower (the genocidal death camps), and the avengers hailed by Michel Bar-Zohar. All of them intended to inflict as much damage as possible on the German people, on the German nation as a whole. Already in the post-war period, as we have just seen, a troop of ruthless Jews set about torturing and murdering hundreds of thousands of Germans in the prison camps in Poland. There was still one more show for the gallery, a travesty of justice dressed up in high ethical principles and higher moral values: the Nuremberg trials.

While they were taking place, it should not be forgotten, the entire population of the Sudetenland, East Prussia, Pomerania and Silesia was being persecuted, arrested, interned in camps and deported under the conditions described above, resulting in the deaths of more than two million people (Alfred M. de Zayas gives the figure of 2,211,000 and Gerhard Ziemer 2,280,000). At the same time, those who had been members of the NSDAP, which numbered some thirteen million, were politically persecuted in Germany. For having belonged to a political party, any citizen could be arrested and interrogated before ending up in a "democratic prison".

Nahum Goldmann, who was both president of the World Jewish Congress and the World Zionist Organization, boasts in his memoirs that the Nuremberg Tribunal was the brainchild of the WJC, the organisation he chaired, which is confirmed by various sources. The WJC was not only the father of the creature, but also played an important shadow role throughout the entire trial. Nahum Goldmann had already hinted at the plan for the trials in his opening speech at the Pan-American Conference of the World Jewish Congress in Baltimore in 1941. Between 1942 and 1943 the WJC devoted itself to carefully studying and refining the project, which was presented to the US government. Naturally, Roosevelt and his entourage of Zionist advisors received it with enthusiasm. Already at the Tehran Conference in November 1943, the Big Three discussed the subject. In *Memories: The Autobiography of Nahum Goldman,* this Zionist leader writes the following:

> "The World Jewish Congress set up the Institute of Jewish Affairs, where preliminary work was done with two main aims: to ensure that Nazi criminals would not escape punishment and to obtain maximum compensation from defeated Germany. It was at this Institute that the idea of punishing Nazi criminals was conceived, an idea that was taken up by some great American jurists, notably Supreme Court Justice Robert H. Jackson, and implemented at the Nuremberg trials. The idea of prosecuting and convicting military leaders for crimes against humanity was completely new in international justice. Many jurists, unable to see beyond the concepts of conventional jurisprudence, were hesitant or strongly opposed. Also, the principle that one cannot be convicted for a crime not contemplated by the law at the time it was committed and the fact that subordinates cannot be punished for obeying superior orders appeared as counter-arguments. But these arguments were outweighed by the importance of exacting punishment for the monstrous Nazi crimes against Jews and gentiles. It had to be established that national sovereignty is not a justification for infringing the most basic principles of humanity, and that obedience to a superior is not an acceptable pretext for individual and mass crimes. From this point of view, the Nuremberg Trials were a momentous event in the history of morality and international justice. Not only did they prove their merit in bringing major Nazi criminals to justice, but they also served as an effective warning and deterrent for the future. Under the leadership of Jacob and Nehemiah Robinson, the World Jewish Congress put all its intellectual and moral

effort into the preparatory work for these trials, and it is one of the triumphs of the Roosevelt administration that it accepted these principles with conviction despite the misgivings of some influential Allied circles, especially in England."

Two Jewish officers in the US Army, Colonel Murray C. Bernays, a prominent New York lawyer, and Colonel David "Mickey" Marcus, a fanatical Zionist. Bernays, a prominent New York lawyer, and Colonel David "Mickey" Marcus, a fanatical Zionist, played decisive roles in organising the Nuremberg trials. According to the ADL (Anti-Defamation League), Bernays, a Lithuanian-born, naturalised American Jew, planned the entire legal and procedural framework. His was the proposal to try not only private individuals, but also organisations such as the SS, the NSDAP and the Gestapo. Historian Robert Conot considers him to be the "influential spirit who led the way to Nuremberg". The second, Marcus, was a key manager of US policy in occupied Germany. Since he had been appointed head of the War Crimes Section, it was he who selected almost all the judges, prosecutors and lawyers for the Nuremberg Military Trials (NMT). Arthur Robert Butz tracks him down and in *The Hoax of the Twentieth Century* reveals that by the end of 1947 Marcus had left the US Army and was acting as supreme commander of Jewish forces in Jerusalem.

In January 1945 Roosevelt appointed Judge Samuel I. Rosenman, one of the most conspicuous Jewish Zionists of the Brain Trust, as his personal representative on war crimes. After the Yalta Conference, Rosenman travelled to England in order to begin negotiations that were to lead to the establishment of a legal system to cover the proceedings of the Nuremberg tribunals. The result was the London Agreement ("London Agreement"), which was to serve as the basis on which the trials could begin. When Roosevelt died on 12 April 1945, Rosenman was working in the English capital. Truman asked him to travel to San Francisco, where the United Nations Conference was to be held. There, Judge Jackson and Rosenman drafted a document that was presented and approved at the Conference. The agreement provided for the establishment of an International Military Tribunal (IMT) to try the top Nazi leaders. By June 1945, Jackson and Rosenman were back in London, where, in the company of Murray C. Bernays did the groundwork for the establishment of the IMT. After completing his mission, Bernays returned to the United States in November 1945 and left the Army.

The London Agreement thus preceded the opening of the trials and was made public on 8 August 1945, but the details of the sessions did not become known until four years later. Only then did it become clear what the disagreements and concerns of some of the negotiators had been. Conscious of their own crimes, the victors wondered what the Tribunal's response would be if the German defence raised the issue of wars of aggression and crimes committed by other nations. It was logically envisaged that the Tribunal would have to deal with American and British aerial terror against defenceless cities. On the other hand, it was unclear how military personnel or individuals could be legally charged and convicted for acts that were not considered crimes under existing law. Later, US Supreme Court Justice William O. Douglas wrote: "I thought then and still think now that the Nuremberg trials were cynical. The law was created ex post facto"[16].

Moreover, it was sarcastic that the Soviet Union should seek to sit on the future international court, since it had participated in the partition of Poland and initiated wars of aggression against Finland and other states, and should therefore be among the defendants and not among the judges. The British delegation also considered the possibility of the defendants' lawyers arguing that the occupation of Norway had been in self-defence, since there was evidence that Britain had planned the invasion of the Scandinavian country in advance. In short, the United States, Britain and the USSR, the winners of the war, after having resorted to atomic terror, an absolute evil of a satanic nature, after having murdered millions of civilians with saturation bombing in Europe and Japan, after having committed unspeakable crimes of all kinds, pretended to ignore their atrocities and set themselves up as champions of morality and justice.

Justice Jackson found the formula to overcome all these pitfalls: a clause inserted in the statutes would limit the scope of the Tribunal, which could only consider acts performed by the defendants. In other words, criticism and/or discussion of the victors' actions were formally prohibited. When the defence of the defendants sought to present certain facts, the response of the presiding judge was invariably: "We are not interested in what the Allies may have done". Thus a body of law was established which became the Constitutive Act of the IMT (International Military Tribunal), which opened its sessions on 20 November 1945 and closed, after four hundred and seven sessions, on 30 September 1946.

Among other legal aberrations, Article 9 stipulated that claiming to be following orders was not an excuse. In other words, soldiers and officers were supposed to disobey their commanders, which is unthinkable in any army in the world, let alone in wartime. Another article, Article 19, specified that "the court "shall not be bound" by technical rules of evidence... and shall accept any evidence which it considers to be of probative value". On this basis, the murkiest statements and the most dubious "evidence" provided by Soviet and American commissions of "enquiry" were accepted as valid. A significant example, for example, is document USSR-54, a detailed report issued by a Soviet commission of enquiry which "proved" that the Germans

---

[16] Ex post facto is a legal term that refers to a law that changes the legal status of an act committed prior to the enactment of that law. In other words, a law that is given a retroactive character in order to make an act a crime that was not a crime at the time it was committed.

had murdered thousands of Polish officers in the Katyn forest. To finish off the "evidence", the Soviets produced three witnesses who "confirmed" that Germany was responsible for the massacre. It is generally acknowledged today that some of the most important documents presented at Nuremberg were fraudulent.

It should be made clear that the major trial held in Nuremberg after the war against the Nazi leadership, the one that captured the attention of the world's media, is known as the IMT ("International Military Tribunal"). Already at this trial the Allies raised the accusation that Jews had been exterminated, although apart from affidavits and testimony, no other evidence was presented. Between 1946 and 1949, the Americans conducted twelve other trials at various locations in their zone of occupation. These are known as the NMT ("Nuremberg Military Tribunal"). At these, one main responsible person was chosen to present the twelve cases, which included the concentration camps (Oswald Pohl), the Einsatzgruppen (Otto Ohlendorf), the case of I. G. Farben (Karl Krauch), etc.

In the main trial, although by persuasive methods many people were forced to sign affidavits and testify against their superiors, most of the Nazi leaders were not tortured, as they were too prominent and it was considered that they should appear in good condition before the court and the international press. The exception was Julius Streicher, editor of the newspaper *Der Stürmer*. It has been said that he was so badly vilified that he was even forced to eat excrement and drink water from the W.C. In chapter eight we have already seen that Streicher was tortured by black and Jewish soldiers who spat into his mouth and forced him to swallow the spittle. He was whipped and beaten on his genitals and all over his body with impunity, because the court ignored the complaint of his lawyer, Hans Marx.

In the other trials (NMT) torture was commonplace. Mark Weber, director of the Institute for Historical Review, in a comprehensive and well-documented essay entitled *The Nuremberg Trials and the Holocaust*, cites more than half a dozen sources confirming, for example, what happened at Dachau. A US Army commission of enquiry that included Pennsylvania Judge Edward van Roden and Justice Gordon Simpson of the Texas Supreme Court found that defendants at Dachau were brutally tortured through beatings, testicular beatings (ruined in one hundred and thirty-seven cases), smashed teeth, matches burning under fingernails, months of solitary confinement, food deprivation, and threats or reprisals against families. Minor trials were held in Dachau, supervised by the War Crimes Section, whose head was the Zionist Marcus, Israel's future general. A journalist who attended the Dachau tribunal hearings, shocked at what was happening in the name of justice, left his post and eventually testified before a US Senate investigative subcommittee that the most brutal interrogators had been three German Jews.

In *After the Reich* Giles MacDonogh reveals that there were also many Jews among the interrogators in Britain. Among the team of interrogators and Nazi hunters was Robert Maxwell, the famous press magnate and Mossad agent. Maxwell, a Jew of Slovakian origin, was actually called Ján Ludvik Hoch. According to MacDonogh, the War Crimes Investigation unit was full of German and Austrian Jews who could interrogate the accused in their own language. Among others he mentions Peter A. Alexander, a bank clerk in Vienna; Major Frederick Warner, who in Hamburg had been Manfred Werner; Lieutenant Colonel Bryant (actually Breuer); Peter Jackson (formerly Jacobus), who was responsible for the arrest of Auschwitz commandant Rudolf Höss; Anton Walter Freud, grandson of Sigmund Freud, who captured and interrogated Dr. Bruno Tesch, whose company manufactured the famous Zyklon B gas; Fred Pelican (born Friedrich Pelikan); Sergeant Wieselmann...

Joseph Halow, a young Army reporter who reported on the Dachau trials in 1947, recalls in the article, 'Innocent at Dachau', published in the *Journal of Historical Review,* that the American investigators who presented the cases before the Dachau military tribunals were "Jewish refugees from Germany who hated Germans". Among the most brutal interrogators was Lieutenant William R. Perl, a Prague-born Zionist Jew who had immigrated to the United States in 1940 and enlisted in the US Army. Perl was a protégé of Zionist leader Vladimir Jabotinsky and had been involved in intensifying the illegal immigration of Jews to Palestine. He was assisted in his interrogation team by other Jews as ruthless as him, including Frank Stein, Harry W. Thon, Morris Ellowitz.... Hallow reports on the case of Gustav Petrat, a twenty-four year old soldier who served as a guard at Mauthausen, who after being savagely beaten and beaten ended up signing a false report against him, as he was asked to do, and was hanged in 1948.

A scandalous, tragicomic case in Dachau is recounted by Freda Utley in *The High Cost of Vengeance* (1949) and also by Arthur R. Butz in his aforementioned work: Joseph Kirschbaum, a Jewish investigator on Perl's team, brought a Jewish witness named Einstein before the Dachau court of justice to testify that the defendant Menzel had killed his brother. To general astonishment, Menzel recognised the alleged victim, sitting quietly in the courtroom, and warned the court. Kirschbaum, put on the spot, shouted angrily at the witness: "How can I take this pig to the gallows if you are so stupid as to bring your brother before the court." According to the Hungarian nationalist writer Louis Marschalko, author of *The World Conquerors* (1958), two thousand four hundred of the three thousand officials who participated in the Nuremberg farce were Jews.

The colonel who acted as head of the War Crimes Section in Dachau was another Jew, A. H. Rosenfeld. A ploy put into practice by Rosenfeld was the mock trials ("mock trial"). When a prisoner refused to cooperate, he was taken to a room where investigators dressed in US Army uniform sat around a black table. In the centre of the table was a crucifix; on the sides were two candles. There was no other lighting. In this gloomy atmosphere, the "tribunal" proceeded to enact the farce, which concluded with a mock sentencing. Once "convicted", the prisoner was promised that if he cooperated with the accusers and provided evidence, he could be pardoned. When Colonel Rosenfeld left his post in 1948, he was interviewed by a journalist who asked him if the stories of mock trials, in which false death sentences were handed down, were true. His answer was: "Yes, of course. Otherwise we wouldn't have been able to make those birds sing.... It was a trick, and it worked like a charm."

Frederick John Partington Veale argues in *Advance to Barbarism* that if the Nazis' guilt was so evident, the outcome of the trials would have been the same if the victors had invited prestigious international jurists from non-belligerent countries: Swiss, Swedish, Portuguese, Spanish, Argentinian, who would no doubt have agreed to face the investigations and preside over tribunals composed of neutral judges. The hypocrisy of Nuremberg was denounced by jurists of integrity who, despite having been recruited by the US Army, condemned in writing the judicial vengeance that was being perpetrated. One of the judges in the I. G. Farben case dared to denounce that there were "too many Jews in the process." Harlam Fiske Stone of the US Supreme Court expressed his disappointment at the way Justice Jackson had agreed to conduct the Nuremberg trial. Mark Weber quotes as saying: "Jackson is leading his lynch mob in Nuremberg. I don't care what he does to the Nazis, but I hate to see the pretense that he is running a court according to the common law". The American judge Charles F. Wennerstrum of the Iowa Supreme Court publicly protested loudly against the travesty of justice being enacted in Germany. In texts published in February 1948 in the *Chicago Tribune*, a gentile-owned newspaper, he wrote:

> "If I had known seven months ago what I know today, I would never have come here.
> Obviously, the victor in a war is not the best judge of war crimes. However one tries, it is impossible to convince the defence, its counsel and those it represents that the tribunal is trying to represent the whole of humanity rather than a country that has appointed its members. What I have said about the nationalistic character of the courts applies to the prosecution. The high ideals heralded as the motive for the creation of these tribunals have not been seen. The process has failed to maintain objectivity, away from vindictiveness, away from personal convictions and ambitions. It has failed to seek to establish precedents that could have helped the world avoid future wars.
> The whole atmosphere here is unhealthy. Linguists were needed. Americans are particularly poor linguists. The lawyers, civil servants, interpreters and researchers who were hired had recently become

Americans and their training was steeped in European hatreds and grievances (a clear reference to Jewish immigrants).
[...] Most of the evidence in the trials was documentary, culled from the huge tonnage of captured files. The selection was made by the prosecution. The defence had access only to those documents that the prosecution considered relevant to the case. Our court introduced a procedural rule that when the prosecution presented a summary of any document, the entire document should be made available to the defence to test the evidence. The prosecution protested vehemently. General Taylor put the court to the test and called a meeting of all the presiding judges for the purpose of overturning this rule. This was not the attitude of an officer conscious that justice must be exacted from the courts.
Also abhorrent to the American concept of justice is the prosecution's reliance on self-incriminating reports signed by defendants while incarcerated for more than two and a half years, who were interrogated without their lawyers present. Two and a half years in prison is a form of pressure in itself.
The lack of appeal leaves me with the feeling that justice has been denied. [...] They should go to Nuremberg. They would see there a courthouse where ninety percent of the people are interested in the prosecution. The German people should be given more information about the trials and the accused should have the right to appeal to the United Nations."

Following the publication of these words, General Taylor accused the judge of making comments "subversive to the interests and policies of the United States". It seems clear to us, however, that Wennerstrum avoids mentioning Jews in his criticism in order to avoid further trouble. He evidently knew that they predominated in all the accusations and that they were driven by blind hatred and an immoderate desire for revenge, which, as the judge points out, had nothing to do with justice. As for Wennerstrum's comment about the tons of documents, Arthur R. Butz, Mark Weber and other sources confirm that the Allies thoroughly scrutinised Germany for any papers that could be used to incriminate the National Socialist regime. Government archives were completely ransacked. The documents of the NSDAP and related organisations, those of industries and private companies, those of official and private institutions were also seized. The confiscated archives of the Foreign Ministry alone amounted to almost 500 tons of paper. More than a million pages of documents on the Jewish policy of the Third Reich were sent to the United States and are in the National Archives. Most significantly, not a single document confirming the existence of an extermination programme was found in all this vast amount of information.
From this enormous quantity of papers the "American" staff selected only two thousand documents which it considered the most incriminating for the Nuremberg trial. Only the prosecution had access to the German documents held by the Allies, and defence lawyers were prevented from

selecting their own materials. Historian Werner Maser in *Nuremberg: A Nation on Trial* (1979) noted that at Nuremberg "thousands of documents that could apparently incriminate the Allies and exonerate the accused disappeared". This author charges that important specific documents that were claimed by the defenders were not found. "It is clear," says Maser, "that the documents were confiscated, withheld from the defence or even stolen in 1945." One of the documents of paramount importance that was withheld from the defendants' lawyers was the secret supplement to the German-Soviet Pact that divided Eastern Europe into two spheres of influence. To top it all off, the "Association of Persons Persecuted by the Nazis" launched a propaganda campaign and succeeded in getting former concentration camp inmates barred from testifying for the defence lawyers.

At the tribunal which from 20 November 1945 tried the top Nazi leaders, the United States was represented by Judge Robert H. Jackson and ten assistants. The chief prosecutor for Great Britain was Attorney General Sir Hartley Shawcross, assisted by Lord Chancellor Jowitt and eleven assistants. France was represented by Robert Falco, advocate of the Court of Appeal, and Professor André Gros, a specialist in international law. Representing the Soviet Union was General Iona T. Nikitchenko, Deputy Chairman of the Moscow Supreme Court, who was assisted by two assistants. The verdict was pronounced on 30 September 1946. Twelve defendants: Göring, Ribbentrop, Keitel, Kaltenbrunner, Rosenberg, Frick, Frank, Streicher, Sauckel, Jodl, Seyss-Inquart and Martin Bormann (in absentia) were sentenced to death. For Hess, Funk and Räder the sentence was life imprisonment. Schirach and Speer got twenty years; Neurath, fifteen; Dönitz, ten; Hans Fritzsche, Hjalmar Schacht, the representative of international high finance, and Franz von Papen, who never became a member of the NSDAP, were acquitted.

The star of the Nuremberg IMT was not any of the Nazi hierarchs, but SS Colonel Rudolf Höss, the prosecution witness who on 5 April 1946 signed an affidavit, or affidavit written in English, from which the story of the extermination of millions of Jews at Auschwitz was based. Rudolf Franz Ferdinand Höss, after being tortured by British officials, signed a confession in which he incriminated himself and admitted that two and a half million people had been murdered in Awschwitz in the labour camp's gas chambers. Höss's statement to the Nuremberg tribunal marked the climax of the trial, and his confession is considered the key Holocaust document and the most important evidence presented about the much-vaunted extermination programme. Arthur Robert Butz's *The Hoax of the Twentieth Century* provides evidence and arguments that lead to the conclusion that Höss lied to save himself. We will return to the subject of this startling confession at a later date.

The main defendant before the IMT in Nuremberg was Hermann Göring, who for many years had been the Reich's second man. Göring vehemently denied that there had been an extermination programme during the war: "The first time I heard about this terrible extermination was here in Nuremberg". German policy, he said, was to expel Jews, not to kill them. Nor, as far as he knew, did Hitler know anything about a policy of extermination, he said. Reportedly, more than three-quarters of the personnel who swarmed Nuremberg: jurists enrolled in the US Army, journalists, interpreters, translators and various civil servants were Jews. Their presence was overwhelming. On one occasion, Göring recognised them on one of the podiums in the audience and, unable to restrain himself, pointed to them and said, "Look at them, no one can say we have exterminated them all!" Göring, Ribbentrop and Rosenberg all insisted that the tribunal had no legitimacy or authority and that British and Americans were equally guilty of having broken international law. When the defendants were shown a Soviet film of German atrocities, Göring, at times appalled by some of the images, sneered, yawned and said that the Russians did not exactly have a reputation for morality. His mockery was already unstoppable when the film showed images of the slaughter of Polish officers in the Katyn pits.

General Alfred Jodl, Chief of Operations of the Armed Forces High Command and one of Hitler's closest military advisors, never lost his temper and behaved like the soldier he was. When asked about the alleged plan to exterminate the Jews, he declared: "I can only say, fully conscious of my responsibility, that I never, neither in hints nor in words spoken or written, heard anything about an extermination of the Jews.... I never had any private information about the extermination of the Jews. I give my word, as sure as I sit here, that I heard all these things for the first time at the end of the war."

Another of those sentenced to death was Ernst Kaltenbrunner, who from early 1943 was head of the RSHA (Reichssicherheitshauptamt), the Reich High Security Department, which comprised the Gestapo (Geheime Staatspolizei), the Secret State Police; the SD (Sicherheitsdienst), the Security Service; and the Kripo (Kriminalpolizei), the Criminal Police. In February 1944, a Hitler decree ordered that all political and military intelligence functions were to be taken over by the RSHA. Mark Weber comments in the essay quoted above that Kaltenbrunner knew that whatever he said would be condemned. Weber reproduces Kaltenbrunner's statement to the court: "The colonel in command of the British prison where I was being held has told me that I will be hanged anyway, regardless of the outcome. Since I am fully aware of this, all I want to do is to clarify some fundamental things that are wrong here." At one point in the interrogation he was accused of having personally ordered the gassing of the prisoners: "Witness after witness, through testimony and affidavit," the accuser reminded him, "have said that the deaths by gas chamber were executed on Kaltenbrunner's general or specific orders." The reply from Kaltenbrunner, who along with Papen and Seyss-Inquart went to mass regularly, was, "Show me one of these men or any of these orders. It is quite impossible." The accuser insisted: "Practically all orders came from Kaltenbrunner." Rebuttal: "Absolutely impossible." Before dying on the gallows, Dr. Ernst Kaltenbrunner bid farewell to this world with the following words: "I loved my fatherland and the German people with all my heart! Good luck, Germany!"

A particularly indignant case demonstrating the abuse of Nuremberg was that of Rudolf Hess, the prisoner of Spandau, who, after risking his life to achieve peace with Britain, was sentenced to life imprisonment and died ill in his cramped cell on 17 August 1987 at the age of ninety-three. The prison regime he was subjected to was infamous, as he was only allowed one 15-minute visit a month and even had his correspondence censored. The British historian A. J. P. Taylor, author of *The Origins of the Second World War,* told Hess's son: "Hess came to this country in 1941 as an ambassador of peace. He came with the intention of restoring peace between Britain and Germany. He acted in good faith. He fell into our hands and was unjustly treated as a prisoner of war. After the war, we should have released him. Instead, the British Government handed him over to the IMT for sentencing.... No crime against Hess could ever be proved." Buried in the Bavarian town of Wunsiedel, on 20 July 2011, the evangelical "Christian" community refused to allow his relatives to extend the lease of his grave to prevent it from becoming a place of pilgrimage. His body was cremated and his ashes were thrown into the sea.

After hearing his death sentence, Joachim von Ribbentrop insisted that his lawyer had not been able to exercise his rights normally and that he had not been allowed to defend and explain Germany's foreign policy. Ribbentrop reminded the court that they had submitted a request for the handing over of evidence, which had been refused. He also said that half of the three hundred documents submitted by his defence had not been admitted without any explanation as to why they had been refused. Neither the correspondence between Hitler and Chamberlain nor ambassadorial reports or diplomatic minutes were accepted. Ribbentrop pointed out that only the prosecution had been given access to the Foreign Office files and that the defence had been deprived of this right. Finally, he expressed his indignation at the biased use of incriminating documents selected by the prosecution, which, by contrast, had consciously withheld exculpatory reports and documents and denied them to the defence.

The executions of the Nazi leaders and German Army generals took place on 16 October 1946, the day on which Jews celebrate the holiday of "Hoshanah Rabbah", i.e. the "Day of Jewish Judgement" for the nations. Douglas Reed writes in *The Controversy of Zion* that with the choice of this date Western leaders gave the conclusion of World War II the appearance of a vengeance exacted specifically on behalf of the Jews. The following is an excerpt from Reed, taken from the aforementioned work:

"Certain symbolic acts evidently had the significance of establishing the authorship, or the nature, of revenge. These acts of the highest symbolism were the reproduction, after almost thirty years, of similar acts performed during the revolution in Russia: the Talmudic boast left on the wall of the room where the Romanovs were executed and the canonisation of Judas Iscariot. After the Second World War the Nazi leaders were hanged on Jewish Judgement Day 1946, so their execution was presented to Jewry in the form of Mordechai's revenge on Haman and his sons. Then, in the Bavarian village of Oberammergau, where the world-famous Passion Play had been performed for three centuries, the actors of the main parts were put on trial before a communist court for 'Nazi activities'. Those playing Jesus and the apostles were found guilty; the only actor acquitted was the one playing Judas. These things do not happen by accident, and the revenge on Germany, like the previous one in Russia, was thus given the stamp of a Talmudic revenge...".

In chapter two it was stated that the executioner who on 21 January 1973 guillotined King Louis XVI was a Jewish Freemason named Samson. As Douglas Reed recalls in the above quote, the assassins of the family of Tsar Nicolas II were also Jews. It is significant that, again, the henchmen who executed those convicted by the Nuremberg IMT were Jews. *Stag Magazine* (Vol. 3, No. 1, December 1946) revealed that the chief executioner, American Sergeant John Clarence Woods, was Jewish. Woods was assisted by Joseph Malta, who according to some sources was also Jewish. Woods explained to the press that he had made the Nazi leaders' agony last as long as possible, and Malta declared fifty years later, in 1996, that it had been a pleasure. It has already been noted in chapter eight that these executioners botched the hanging of the Nazi hierarchs with the deliberate aim of prolonging their agony. The noose tightened around Ribbentrop's neck for almost twenty minutes before the former Reich Foreign Minister expired. General Alfred Jodl, who like General Keitel shouted: "Alles für Deutschland. Deutschland über alles" ("All for Germany. Germany above all!"), needed fifteen minutes to die. Julius Streicher was sentenced to death without having committed any crime: his crime was to edit a newspaper, *Der Stürmer*, which harshly attacked Jews. His agony lasted for fourteen minutes, and as he made his way to the gallows, he said: "This is the Purim Festival of 1946".

During Purim, Jews celebrate one of the great avengers of their history. According to the Book of Esther, the Jew Mordechai managed to win the will of King Ahasuerus of Persia (probably Xerxes) over his niece Esther without revealing her racial origin. Once the Persian queen was displaced and became queen, Esther accused the prime minister Haman, who had denounced the existence of a people scattered throughout the provinces who did not accept the laws of the empire like other peoples. Haman, a sworn enemy of the Jews, and his ten sons were hanged. Mordechai took his place as prime minister and ordered the massacre of all the enemies of the Jews from India to Ethiopia, 75,000 in all according to the Book of Esther. The king thus became a historical symbol of a puppet ruler in the hands of the Jews. The precept of celebrating and remembering throughout all generations, in every family and in every city the feast of Purim has been kept for twenty-five centuries. It is a religious duty to drink to drunkenness to commemorate the historic slaughter, and this is done in synagogues all over the world. Thus, while for Christianity the greatest feast is the birth of Christ, whose greatest teaching is "love one another", Jewry's greatest feast is Purim, a feast of hatred and revenge.

In addition to the twelve secondary trials (NMTs) organised by the US government between 1946 and 1949, the British also held trials in Lüneburg and Hamburg, and the Americans themselves in Dachau. Subsequent Holocaust-related trials have been held in West Germany, in the United States and in Israel, where in 1961 the famous trial that sentenced to death Adolf Eichmann, abducted in Buenos Aires in 1960, took place in Jerusalem. Regarding the NMTs, it should be stressed that torture was used again and again to obtain sworn statements and testimony. Mark Weber in "The Nuremberg Trials and the Holocaust", an article published in 2002 in the *Journal of Historical Review*, summarises some of the cases. He mentions, for example, the case of Josef Kramer, commandant at the Bergen-Belsen and Auschwitz-Birkenau camps, and other defendants in the so-called Belsen trial, conducted by the British. Some of them were tortured mercilessly to the point that they even asked to be killed.

Volumes 12 and 14 of the Nuremberg Military Tribunal contain case number 12, "Wilhelmstrasse", also known as the Ministers' or United States v. Weizsäcker, the politician who personified the case as the leading figure. In this trial, the testimonies of the main prosecution witnesses were obtained through physical and psychological torture. The American lawyer Warren Magee was able to obtain the transcript of the first interrogation of Friedrich Gaus before the trial. Surprisingly, despite the exasperated protests of Robert Kempner, the Jewish prosecutor, the judge allowed attorney Magee to read the interrogation document, during which Kempner had threatened to hand Gaus over to the Soviets and have him hanged. Gaus implored the interrogator to think of his wife and children, but Kempner assured him that he could only be saved by testifying in court against his former colleagues. After four weeks in solitary confinement, increasingly desperate, Gaus agreed. Mark Weber, who draws on several sources to recount this episode, writes: "By the time Magee finished reading the irrefutable transcript, Gaus was sitting with both hands on his face, utterly crushed". During the Wilhelmstrasse trial, Hans Lammer, head of the Reich Chancellery between 1933 and 1945 and Hitler's legal adviser, was asked whether he still believed that there had never been a programme to exterminate the Jews. His answer was: "Yes, I do. For at least I have never heard of such a programme. The programme could not have existed..... I never heard of mass murders and about the cases I did hear about, the reports were allegations, rumours.... The fact that individual cases occurred in one part or another, the shooting of Jews during the war in one city or another, about this I read and heard something. This is quite possible.

Another telling case of the perversion that framed the trials is that of SS General Oswald Pohl, who during the war was head of the WVHA (Wirtschafts-Verwaltungshaupamt), the Main Office of the Economic Administration, an extensive body whose function was to supervise various economic aspects of SS work, mainly related to the availability and work of prisoners in the concentration camps. The camp commandants reported to the Inspectorate of Concentration Camps, headed by General Glücks, who reported to Pohl, who then passed the reports on to Himmler. Pohl was captured in 1946 and taken to Nenndorf, where British soldiers tied him to a chair and beat him unconscious. The beatings were repeated and he ended up losing several teeth. He was then handed over to the Americans, who interrogated him for more than half a year in four-hour sessions. In all, Pohl endured some 70 interrogation sessions without ever having the right to a lawyer or any other assistance. He was never charged with anything specific and it was never made clear to him why he was being interrogated. His trial, United States v. Oswald Pohl, is the Concentration Camps case, number 4, and is contained in volumes 5 and 6 of the NMT.

In November 1947, Oswald Pohl was sentenced to death by an American military tribunal. After learning of his sentence, he described the emotional treatment he was subjected to in a report that was published in Germany. Mark Weber, who quotes from it, notes that at Nuremberg the Americans did not subject him to physical torture like the British, but subjected him to more brutal psychological torture. The American interrogators, most of them Jews, accused Pohl of murdering 30 million people and condemning 10 million to death. The Jewish accusers knew they were lying and were only trying to break his resistance. "Since I am not emotionally tough," Pohl wrote, "these diabolical intimidations had an effect, and the interrogators got what they wanted: not the truth, but enough statements to serve their needs." Pohl was forced to sign self-incriminating affidavits that were used against him at trial. "As a result of the fierce physical abuse in Nenndorf and my handling in Nuremberg, emotionally I was a completely broken man," Pohl claimed in his report, "I was 54 years old and for thirty-three years had served my country without dishonour, and was not conscious of any crime." Pohl was hanged on 7 June 1951. In his final plea to the court he expressed his faith that one day blind hysteria would give way to a just understanding.

Despite the fact that in the 21st century there are still incompetent people who, like Minister Ruiz Gallardón, continue in their ignorance to appeal to the parody of Nuremberg justice, most jurists know that what happened was unheard of, unacceptable, the antithesis of Justice. Already at the time, both in Europe and in America, there were numerous voices denouncing and deploring what was happening in Germany. On 5 October 1946, in a speech in Ohio, Senator Robert A. Taft, reputed to be the conscience of the Republican Party, denounced the spirit of revenge that prevailed at Nuremberg. Revenge," he said, "is almost never justice. The hanging of the eleven convicted men will be a stain on our history which we shall long regret." Mississippi Congressman John Rankin on 28 November 1947 delivered these words to the US Congress: "As a representative of the American people I wish to say that what is taking place in Nuremberg, Germany, is a disgrace to the United States.... Representatives of a racial minority, two and a half years after the war, are at Nuremberg not only hanging German soldiers, but trying German businessmen in the name of the United States". Another Congressman, Lawrence H. Smith, representing Wisconsin, on 15 June 1949 told the House, "The Nuremberg trials are so revolting that we should be forever ashamed of this page of our history."

The full picture of the immorality and brazenness of Nuremberg is given by Mark Lautern in *Das letzte Wort über Nürnberg* (*The Last Word on Nuremberg*). He writes that in the intervals between sentences or executions, the Jews, who dominated the scene and were omnipresent, traded American cigarettes, porcelain, silver, gold, furs and works of art. One was a watch specialist, another smuggled works of art. *Das letzte Wort über Nürnberg* is currently unavailable; but it is a source for Louis Marschalko in *The World Conquerors*, from which the following quotation from Lautern is taken:

> "But it was not only the black market that turned the area around the Nuremberg Tribunal into a den of Europe. Even more horrible was the moral degradation that originated there. The orgies that foreign employees held in private flats and hotels often caused outrage throughout the district. The number of young women employed by the Court grew steadily. Among them were both Germans and foreigners, attracted by the maelstrom of depravity and corruption. Sexual incontinence and the most disgusting perversion predominated in these circles. Unlimited scandals proved by copious evidence provided material for years for certain newspapers and magazines."

Propaganda, denazification, punishment and looting

Tens of thousands of prisoners died in German concentration camps at the end of the war because of the famine and epidemics that ravaged the entire territory of the Reich. The German population itself was a victim of the hardships brought about by the progressive collapse of the country: cities were destroyed, energy resources were scarce, and hunger and disease ravaged the population. In these circumstances it became impossible to feed the prisoners, who in the labour camps had ingested some fifteen hundred calories before the collapse. It is not a question of seeking justifications for the existence of the camps. It is, of course, reprehensible that people were arrested on racial or ideological grounds and imprisoned in concentration or labour camps; but the Americans did exactly the same with their citizens of Japanese origin, who were interned in squalid internment centres. At the end of the war they even imprisoned their best writer, Ezra Pound, for having denounced the real culprits of the world catastrophe, a story to which we could devote more attention if we had the space. The British also imprisoned people who sympathised with fascism or National Socialism. The ideological persecution and crimes committed in France after the war would also deserve a separate chapter.

It would be absurd to deny the crimes of one side in the bloodiest and deadliest conflagration known to mankind. Undoubtedly the Nazis committed atrocities and there were among them fanatics of the worst kind. They showed their worst face in the war against the Soviet Union. The Einsatzgruppen, for example, shot partisans en masse who fought viciously against the German army, including Jews, gentiles and civilians of both sexes who gave them cover. After the invasion of the Soviet Union in 1941, Hitler himself warned that the war in Russia would not be fought according to the rules of traditional warfare and granted Himmler power to "act independently on his own responsibility". Nor did the activities of the partisans provide for any restrictions whatsoever, and they too unceremoniously liquidated the soldiers who fell into their hands. We shall return to the subject of the Einsatzgruppen later.

As we have seen throughout these pages, the United States, Britain and the USSR had all committed unspeakable crimes that delegitimised them from every point of view. Despite this, the first thing the victors did was to organise a propaganda campaign that exonerated them of any responsibility and blamed everything on Germany. From the outset, they sought to create a sense of guilt among the German people, which they fully succeeded in doing, as it persists to this day. The Allies presented themselves as liberators, exemplary democrats, defenders of human rights, and began to re-educate the defeated to accept that National Socialism was the most perverse ideology that had ever existed. Billboards with pictures of skeletons, charred bones, hanged prisoners in uniform and starving children appeared in German cities in the American occupation zone. Above the picture was the question "Who is guilty? A second poster contained the answer: "This city is guilty! You are guilty!". The next step was propaganda films recorded in concentration camps such as Belsen or Buchenwald, where many prisoners had died of starvation and disease and many of the survivors were living skeletons.

While in some camps prisoners continued to die daily, instead of immediately evacuating the survivors to alleviate their suffering, the Allies turned the camps into a macabre tourist spectacle for journalists, congressmen, senators and the more or less morbidly curious. German citizens were forced to visit Buchenwald, where among the main attractions were the crematorium, the famous lampshades made in theory from tattooed skins, the shrunken heads, and so on. All this was supposedly the work of Ilse Koch, the wife of the camp commandant, Karl Koch. The bodies of the dead were left lying around for days for visitors to see. There was even a tour of the concentration camps.

The outrageous thing is that while the liberators held themselves up as an example of respect for the dignity of human life, instead of leading by example, they had their own camp route, the Eisenhower death camps, where in the same area they kept millions of German POWs out in the open, of whom they managed to starve, freeze and epidemic nearly a million to death. At the same time, hundreds of camps were operating in Poland and Czechoslovakia where tens of thousands of German civilians were to die and were treated like animals. Moreover, as we have seen, the saviours of the German people and champions of human rights allowed millions of ethnic Germans to be driven from their homes and deported under inhumane conditions. On the other hand, the camps of the communist allies continued to function as smoothly as ever. For decades, millions of human beings died in them without anyone ever remembering these dead. Significantly, there are hardly any photos of the Soviet Gulag and its victims.

While seeking to re-educate the population, JCS 1067 imposed destruction rather than construction, resulting in inhumane treatment of people. Although the Morgenthau Plan had been officially abandoned, its spirit and policies remained in force for a long time after the war. Membership of the NSDAP was an insurmountable obstacle preventing citizens from finding work and living in peace. Hundreds of thousands ended up in prison, as the famous JCS directive 1067, the result of Morgenthau's revenge plans, called for punitive measures for those who had been National Socialists. Of the NSDAP's estimated 13 million members, 8 million were still in the party at the end of the war. This mass membership must be seen as a result of the social policies that the Nazis had promoted in Germany. We have already seen that unemployment, which had tormented the working classes for decades, was brought to an end; housing was made available to the population as a way of stimulating and rewarding the birth rate; bank interest rates were practically eliminated; tourism and travel for the working classes were encouraged; in short, social conditions were created which won majority recognition for the NSDAP's policies.

In order to exclude Nazis from public life, thirteen million questionnaires ("Fragebogen") were printed, consisting of twelve pages and 133 questions to be answered by those looking for a job in order to survive. No group was exempt from the "Fragebogen" filter. Depending on the degree of membership or sympathy for the party or a related organisation, it was determined whether the subject was "guilty", "committed", "moderately committed", "sympathetic".... A doctor, for example, could not practise his profession if he had belonged to the NSDAP. Most of the civil servants had belonged to the party, so that the purge of the administration jeopardised its functioning. The questionnaire included questions such as what one had voted for in 1932, whether one had confidence in Germany's victory, whether one had scars on one's body.... The questionnaires warned that "false information would lead to prosecution by the courts of the Military Government". Only after returning the completed form and after it had been checked by the occupation authorities was it possible to enter the labour market, provided one had passed the screening. If not, there was no possibility of working and no possibility of getting a ration card. The worst thing was that one could be considered a criminal for having been a National Socialist and sent to prison. Depending on your qualifications, you got different ration cards and were eligible for certain jobs.

On food rationing, Victor Gollancz reported, for example, that in March 1946 the population of Hamburg received only 1,050 to 1,591 calories a day, i.e. four slices of dry bread, three medium-sized potatoes, three spoonfuls of oatmeal, half a cup of skimmed milk, one slice of leftover meat and a pinch of fat. Infant mortality was ten times higher than in 1944. In February 1946, 257 children were born in Dortmund, forty-six of whom died. Giles MacDonogh writes: "Politicians and soldiers like Sir Bernard Montgomery insisted that no food be sent from Britain. Starvation was a punishment. Montgomery said that three-quarters of the Germans were still Nazis". In the drive to impose collective guilt, even those who had opposed Nazism paid the consequences of the vindictive policy imposed on Germans as a whole.

In Bavaria, General Patton appointed Fritz Schäffer, known to be anti-Nazi, as Minister President, but he was eventually dismissed because Schäffer did not hate all Nazis. It has already been seen that Patton himself fell out of favour because he did not share the policies of hatred and revenge that flowed from JCS 1067. MacDonogh explains that in the Ruhr "all the mining engineers were sacked by Nazis. There were then explosions that claimed hundreds of lives - including Englishmen - and General Templer concluded that the Military Government were acting like fools". According to this author, by September 1946 in the American zone 66,500 Nazis had been sent to prison and in the British zone 70,000. In Nordhein-Westfalen two and a half million cases had been examined and many men and women were locked up for years in terrible conditions. Of the Russians, MacDonogh writes: "They believed firmly in collective guilt and that any German could be deserving of punishment and even death. They put Germans to work and gave them the bare minimum to survive. They investigated half a million cases in their area."

When one realises that the Allies were incapable of dignifying the lives of the population and had no desire to feed them at all, their claim to have come to Germany as liberators is indeed offensive. Victor Gollancz, who notes that prisoners in Belsen received 800 calories, reports in *In Darkest Germany* (1947) that in early 1946 the British authorities in Germany proposed lowering the daily ration to 1,000 calories. The Americans then provided 1,270 calories, while the French were already at 950. In the work cited above, Gollancz recounts his visit to Hamburg, a city which after being totally destroyed by criminal saturation bombing had no housing to accommodate the population, so that seventy thousand people were living in shelters and cellars in appalling conditions. Many Germans," MacDonogh writes, "were at first prepared to see the Allies as liberating angels, but were soon disappointed when they realised that the very humane soldiers arrived laden with propaganda and hatred of civilians.

At the same time, the redeemers of the German people engaged in robbery as rarely before in history. All governments were involved in plundering the country. Even the British Royal Family had no qualms about keeping Göring's yacht, the *Carin II*, for their own enjoyment. It should be noted that the bulk of the Anglo-American forces did not enter Berlin until Friday 6 July 1945, giving the Soviets more than two months head start in plundering the Reich's capital. The communists, experts since the Bolshevik Revolution in conscious theft, planned the operation not only in Berlin, but throughout their occupation zone like true experts. Two and a half million works of art of various kinds, including 800,000 paintings by Rubens, Fra Angelico, Luca Signorelli, Zurbarán and Murillo, were shipped to Russia. In addition, some five million tons of equipment and materials of all kinds, mostly from the dismantling of factories, were seized. Of great importance was the theft of valuable military, scientific and industrial secrets, as well as German invention patents. Joaquín Bochaca, who in *Los crímenes de los buenos* provides interesting figures and data on the looting of Germany, gives the figure of 346,000 patents confiscated. Bochaca points out that a crushing demonstration of the servitude of the government of the Federal Republic of Germany came years later, when it was forced to recognise an astronomical debt to Israel, a state that did not even exist.

Part 2
Failure of the World Government's Plan Based on the Monopoly of Atomic Violence

"Our post-war programme depends entirely on the ability to terrorise the world with the atomic bomb. These words by Secretary of State Edward Stettinius addressed to Soviet agent Alger Hiss, who was acting as Roosevelt's adviser at the San Francisco Conference, are definitely revealing. Delivered in April 1945, months before Truman ordered the first atomic bomb to be dropped on Hiroshima, they clearly reveal that the US plan was to preserve the nuclear monopoly in order to impose an international government or federation that it would guard through its monopoly of atomic violence. To achieve this goal, it was essential to obtain the consent of the other powers, especially the USSR, which knew from the outset, through its network of agents, including Dexter White and Alger Hiss, what the Americans' plans were.

If the strongman in the Soviet Union had been Trotsky, the agent of the illuminati bankers, everything would have been easier, since the one in charge of presenting the plan of the global government based on the monopoly of atomic terror was Bernard Baruch, the all-powerful Jew who had arranged the release of Lev Davidovich Bronstein when he was arrested in Canada, the banker Trotsky dreamed of taking control of Russia's finances: "What we need here is an organiser like Bernard Baruch", Trotsky once said. But in the USSR Stalin was in charge, the man who had viciously persecuted all Trotskyists, who had ordered Trotsky's assassination and who wielded power with an iron fist. As had been the case since Lenin's death, the nuclear monopoly affair showed that Stalin was a character they could not quite control.

One of the first to publicly call for the much-heralded World Government was Emery Reves, a Hungarian-born Jew who as early as 1945 published *Anatomy of Peace,* a book that would be translated into twenty-five languages and published in thirty countries, in which he called for an end to state sovereignty in favour of an international or global government. This "pacifist" was convinced that the existence of sovereign nations was anti-peace and ensured future wars. According to him, nation-states were an anachronism that had to be overcome: "We cannot have democracy," he said, "in a world of independent nations". Soon Albert Einstein, another "pacifist" who had given Roosevelt the letter calling for the manufacture of the atomic bomb, was quick in an interview to applaud the project, which he called "the political answer to the atomic bomb".

On 1 February 1946 *The Bulletin of the Atomic Scientists,* the publication of the scientists who had brought the world into the nuclear age, publicised the plan for the World Federation of Reves: "If Russia or other countries," the article said, "cannot be persuaded to join the Federation at once, it must be created at any rate by the nations who are willing to accept the scheme". On 15 February 1946 *The Bulletin* published a further article insisting that the scientists who had made the bomb considered a world government necessary. In its issue of March 1, 1946, *The Bulletin* announced the appearance of the book *One World or None*, written precisely by the Jewish scientists, mostly international socialists, who had made or encouraged the making of the uranium and plutonium bombs.

It is clear that the proponents of the notorious New World Order were using scientists to clothe their long-standing project of gaining absolute control of the planet in pacifist and humanitarian ideas. For their part, the Jewish scientists who had asked Roosevelt to build the atomic bomb for use against Germany were seeking to clean up their image and show that they were aware of the danger. Therefore, they hypocritically lent themselves to be used and, as if they were not responsible for anything, they now appealed to the politicians to implement the old Illuminati project in order to avoid the biblical Armageddon, i.e. the end of the world announced in the Old Testament and in the Apocalypse. In reality, they were acting as a team. Once again, under the façade of progressive and philanthropic ideas, the need was presented to create the World Government for all mankind and to do away with states and outdated patriotic sentiments. At this point, it is of interest, before moving on, to reflect on the historical moments in which we have encountered the same idea throughout this narrative we have been producing.

The origins of the project come from the Talmud. It has already been seen in chapter three that the Zionist Michael Higger dedicated to the Hebrew University of Jerusalem his work *The Jewish Utopia*, published in 1932. It reviews the Zionist plan for world domination, to be achieved when "all the treasures and natural resources of the world will be in the possession of the righteous (Jews) in fulfilment of Isaiah's prophecy". The idea of financing and directing the World Revolutionary Movement (WRM) to gain control of the world's resources and wealth arose with the Rothschilds as early as the late 18th century. Their agent Adam Weishaupt (Spartacus) founded the Bavarian Order of the Illuminati on May 1st and adopted as his symbol the pyramid with the All Seeing Eye. The abolition of governments, private property, the inheritance, religions, patriotism and the family were the sect's goals for the "Novus Ordo Seclorum" or New World Order. The Illuminati instilled in their followers that universal happiness would be achieved by the abolition of nations and the union of humanity in an international society. The union of the Illuminati and Jakob Frank's Frankists, sponsored by the Jewish bankers behind the MRM, preceded the appearance of the *Communist Manifesto* (Karl Marx and Moses Hess came from Frankist families), written by Marx for the League of the Righteous ("Bund der Gerechten"), a secret Illuminati organisation.

As we have seen, the aims of communism coincided with those of Weishaupt, but were now explicitly concretised. The proletariat and force were to be used by the international bankers to conquer the world: the world dictatorship of the proletariat was to be achieved by overthrowing the established order through terror and violence: the end justified the means. When in 1860 Adolphe Cremieux, Grand Master of the Grand Orient of France, founded the Universal Israelite Alliance, he announced in the founding manifesto that the time was approaching "when all the riches and treasures of the world shall be the property of the children of Israel". In the *Protocols of the Sages of Zion* the plan for World Government is again concretised and detailed: "When we have struck our great blow, we will say to all peoples: everything was going very badly for you, you are all exhausted with suffering. We are going to abolish the cause of your torments, namely: nationalities, frontiers, diversity of currencies". In short, the idea of "universal brotherhood", of an "invisible king", of the "unification of mankind", of a League of Nations aiming at world unity were clichés expressed over and over again by Jewish and Zionist ideologues. "We will have a world government whether they like it or not. The only question is whether we will achieve it by conquest or by consent." These words of the illuminati banker Paul Warburg, the great architect of the Federal Reserve, uttered on February 17, 1950 before the US Senate, are further proof that behind the idea were the usual conspirators.

Bernard Baruch presents plan for Global Governance

Two Jews, Bernard Baruch and David Lilienthal, the latter in contact with Dean Acheson, the undersecretary of state, were the authors of the plan for World Government that the US government tried to impose on Stalin. Baruch, who according to the *Encyclopaedia Judaica* served at Versailles as President Wilson's personal economic adviser and had been adviser to five American presidents, was appointed by Truman to present it to the UNAEC (United Nations Atomic Energy Commission). The plan had been laid out in advance and discussed in the pages of *The Bulletin of the Atomic Scientists*, a fortnightly publication founded in late 1945 by two Jewish scientists, Eugene Rabinowitch and Hyman H. Goldsmith, of which Baruch and Lilienthal were editors. Robert Oppenheimer, the "Dark Prince", on 1 June 1946 published in issue 12 of the *Bulletin* an article entitled "The International Control of Atomic Energy", in which he commented on the project of Baruch, his mentor. Oppenheimer, the "destroyer of worlds", announced the meeting of the United Nations Commission, supported the creation of an Atomic Development Authority, advocated that countries should cede some of their sovereignty, and appealed to the United States to agree to lose "the monopolistic position of technical advantage in the field of atomic energy". As is well known, Oppenheimer had been closely watched by the FBI because of his relationship with the Communist Party. Consequently, he favoured a solution of compromise and convergence with the USSR.

Finally, on 14 June 1946, Baruch presented the plan to the UNAEC. In his introductory remarks he presented the dilemma: the choice was between world peace or world destruction. "Science has wrested from nature a secret so great in its potentialities," Baruch said, "that our minds shrink in fear from the terror it creates." Under the Baruch Plan, the Atomic Development Authority would oversee the development and use of energy, direct nuclear facilities capable of producing bombs, and inspect research for peaceful purposes. Illegal possession of the atomic bomb was prohibited. Violating countries and those interfering with inspections would be appropriately punished. A Security Council would be responsible for punishing and imposing sanctions on nations that violated the terms of the plan. A very important point concerned the right of veto. The Baruch Plan stipulated that members of the UN Security Council would lose the right of veto in all matters concerning sanctions against nations engaged in prohibited activities. Only when the plan was in place would the United States begin the process of destroying its nuclear arsenal.

Meanwhile, the Americans pressed ahead with their nuclear test plan at Bikini Atoll. Only two weeks after the project was presented to the UNAEC, Operation Crossroads began, which called for several atomic detonations, each with a yield of 21 kilotons. The first, "Able", was carried out on 1 July 1946; the second, "Baker", on 25 July. A third, "Charlie", was planned, but was cancelled because of the tremendous radioactive contamination generated by "Baker".

A second UNAEC meeting had taken place on 19 June, at which Andrei Gromyko, ambassador to the United States and representative to the United Nations, presented the USSR's proposal. Gromyko expressed that his country was not prepared to give up its right of veto in the Security Council, which the Soviet ambassador said was already very favourable to the United States. Gromyko, who undoubtedly must have had information about Operation Crossroads, argued that for the plan to have any credibility, the sanctions announced in Baruch's report should be imposed immediately. It also called for the exchange of scientific information. Moreover, they were unwilling to allow international inspections of their facilities. From the outset, the communists understood the plan as allowing the United States to maintain its nuclear monopoly. The Soviet press denounced it as "an attempt to establish America's atomic world domination." On 1 July 1946, the same day the first test was carried out at Bikini Atoll, *The Bulletin*, which had become a platform for debate on World Government and the control of atomic energy, reproduced Baruch and Gromyko's texts before the UNAEC.

Since the emergence of the Bavarian Illuminati sect, the conspiracy to establish the World Government envisioned by Adam Weishaupt had been diversifying and structuring itself into different tendencies. Among the main ones were communism, Zionism, British imperialism (used from the beginning as a tool of global power by the Rothschilds), Fabian socialism, etc. The common denominator, the cross-cutting element, was that the conspiracy to establish the World Government had a common denominator, the common denominator was the common denominator of the world government. The common denominator, the cross-cutting element that permeated them all was the Jews. Communism, the most genuine faction of the conspiracy, did not support the Baruch Plan in 1946. Communism had apparently become with Stalin an expansionist national communism controlled from Moscow and had escaped the initial control of the times of Lenin and Trotsky. As has been said, if Trotsky had defeated Stalin in his struggle for power in Russia, two theoretically parallel ideologies would have paradoxically converged after World War II and the World Government would have been established at last by consensus, for the Judeo-Bolsheviks had been a most effective instrument of the conspiracy of the international Jewish bankers. In the USSR, however, Stalin was still in charge, and he had come to power by supplying his Trotskyist enemies with the same medicine they had used to eliminate their opponents. In reality, the problem was not insoluble: it was a question of putting a new Trotsky in power. To this end, both in Russia and in the occupied countries of Eastern Europe, the struggle for power would soon begin. The problem was not communism, but communism led by Stalin. "Stalins come and go," Krivitsky had told his friend Reiss, "but the Soviet Union will endure."

Fabian socialists, including Bertrand Russell, H.G. Wells, Arnold Toynbee... were among the advocates of the World Government. On 1 October 1946, Bertrand Russell published a long three-page article in *The Bulletin* entitled "The Atom Bomb and the prevention of war". In it he noted that the negotiations with Stalin had reached an impasse and that the agreement with the Soviet Union was becoming more complicated. Russell made it abundantly clear that the monopoly of nuclear violence should be the exclusive prerogative of the World Government:

> "It is absolutely clear that there is only one way of permanently preventing major wars, and that is the establishment of an international government with a monopoly of powerful armed forces. When I speak of an international government, I mean one that really governs, not a friendly façade like the League of Nations or a pretentious pretence like the United Nations as at present constituted. An international government, if it is to be capable of preserving peace, must have the only atomic bombs, the only factory to produce them, the only force, the only warships, and, in general, whatever it takes to make it irresistible. Its atomic personnel, its air squadrons, its warship crews and its infantry regiments must be solidly composed of men of different nationalities; there must be no possibility of national feeling developing in any unit

larger than a company. Every member of the international armed force should be carefully trained in loyalty to the international Government."

Russell was evidently mindful of Machiavelli's political thought on the need for the monopoly of violence to be in the hands of the prince: "The monopoly of armed force is the most necessary attribute of international government". In a far from conciliatory tone, Russell advised the Americans and British that if, having made it clear that their aim was international cooperation, they did not get the cooperation of the Soviet Government, they should not allow themselves to be believed to be for peace at any price. At a given moment," he wrote, "having completed their plan for an international government, they should offer it to the world and enlist maximum support.... If Russia would willingly accept, all would be well. If not, it would be necessary to press the bear, even to the point of risking war, for in this case the Russians would almost certainly agree. If Russia does not agree to the formation of the international government, there will be war sooner or later. It is therefore wise to exert all the necessary pressure".

At the end of 1946, the Atomic Energy Commission (AEC) was set up in the United States, which took over all nuclear matters and brought civilian control of atomic manufacturing plants. Also at the end of 1946, Stalin definitively rejected the Baruch Plan on the grounds that it implied submission to Washington. From this point on, relations between the two countries deteriorated and the Cold War began shortly afterwards. The rejection of the Baruch Plan, however, did not necessarily imply, far from it, the renunciation of the World Government that had been tried to impose on mankind for so long; although, at the very least, a good opportunity to achieve it had been lost.

The scientists who made the atomic bomb shared with the Jewish politicians and tycoons of the Brain Trust the same desire to crush Nazi Germany. When Einstein proposed the bomb to the American president in a letter, he did so with the idea that it would be used against Germany. This was also the intention of Roosevelt, Baruch, Morgenthau, Rosenman, etc., in launching the Manhattan Project. Apart from their anti-German sentiments, most of the Jewish physicists, including Einstein, were Zionists, which meant that their allegiance to one state or the other was very relative, if not non-existent. Many of them, like Oppenheimer, favoured a world authority based on internationalist principles that transcended ideas of national allegiance. Some were committed to communism and remained willing to work for it. Indeed, it was Jewish scientists who helped the USSR build its atomic bomb.

Oppenheimer would eventually be accused of spying for the Soviet Union, which he was able to do thanks to the privileged position he held as a member of the General Advisory Board of the Atomic Energy Commission (AEC), whose first chairman was David Lilienthal. One of Lilienthal's first tasks as chairman of the AEC was the appointment of the members of the Advisory Board. The first choice was his friend Oppenheimer, who would also be appointed director of the prestigious Institute for Advanced Study at Princeton University, where Albert Einstein reigned supreme.

On 4 January 1947, his plan having finally failed, Bernard Baruch resigned as US representative to the United Nations Atomic Energy Commission. His replacement was another Jew considered anti-Communist, Lewis Lichtenstein Strauss, a man whom Felix M. Warburg had introduced to the Kuhn Loeb & Co. bank, where he had made his fortune. Although he had been a member of the Executive Committee of the American Jewish Committee, it appears that he was not a Zionist, but a supporter of the assimilation of the Jews in the countries where they lived. Strauss soon became aware of Oppenheimer's communist activities and a slow process of estrangement between the two began.

Doubts about Oppenheimer's loyalty to the US, which had arisen as early as 1942, were completely dispelled in March 1947: the FBI learned for certain that Oppenheimer was informing on the USSR and reported his activities to David Lilienthal and Lewis Strauss. Both were friends of his and did not want to believe the reports that he was an infiltrator. Nor were the members of the ACS Council willing to doubt his loyalty, so in the summer of 1947 they decided to retain him as chairman of the General Advisory Council. Nevertheless, Lewis Strauss became suspicious and his relations with the Dark Prince deteriorated. A significant development was Oppenheimer's falling out with Edward Teller, the Jewish physicist who had continued at Los Alamos to work on a new version of the nuclear fusion bomb: the thermonuclear bomb, or H-bomb, which they called the "Super". From his position as chairman of the AEC Council, Oppenheimer recommended that the government not spend money on the project. By July 1947, the United States possessed thirteen nuclear fission bombs and the USSR was pursuing the manufacture of its own bomb. Oppenheimer was apparently trying to prevent Teller from succeeding in making a more powerful and destructive atomic bomb, which would tip the balance back in the US's favour.

In 1949 Lewis Strauss became convinced that Oppenheimer was not only trying to boycott or delay the production of the hydrogen bomb, but that he had violated national security. Rumours of Oppenheimer's disloyalty grew, and the government consequently decided to appoint Strauss as AEC chairman, replacing David Lilienthal, Oppenheimer's close ally. Distrust was evident on several levels: Senator Joseph McCarthy had begun an investigation into Oppenheimer's relations with the Communists, and the air force brass demanded his replacement. Finally, in December 1953, the House Joint Committee on Atomic Energy sent a letter to the FBI and the AEC stating that between 1939 and 1942 Oppenheimer had spied for the Soviet Union and that since 1942 he had been an agent who, at the direction of the Soviets, influenced the military, atomic energy issues, intelligence and diplomacy in the United States. Before the Senate began another investigation, Lewis Strauss demanded his resignation as chairman of the AEC's General Advisory Council. When Oppenheimer refused, Strauss ordered a trial, which took place from 5 April to 6 May 1954. Oppenheimer ended up in retirement at Princeton, where Einstein chaired the Institute for Advanced Study, a think tank funded by the Rothschilds through one of their many secret foundations. Oppenheimer's case is part of a vast espionage plot in favour of the USSR, of which everything related to the atomic bomb is now of interest.

Communist Jews hand over atomic bomb secrets to USSR

At the end of World War II, the Americans estimated that it would take the Soviets seven to ten years to build their own atomic bomb. This meant that the United States could for this time have an unattainable nuclear monopoly. When it became known that on 29 August 1949 the USSR had detonated its first nuclear bomb, codenamed "Joe" in honour of Josef Stalin, it came as a major surprise to some. The Russian bomb was an exact replica of "Fat Man", the plutonium bomb tested in the Dead Man's Day desert and dropped on 9 August 1945 on Nagasaki. Many voices began to denounce that there were traitors, operating from within, who were plotting against the United States.

It is a proven fact that the invasion of Soviet spies into FDR's Administration reached staggering heights during his three terms in office. The most relevant cases of Communist agents - Alger Hiss, Harry Hopkins, Harry Dexter White - have already been mentioned and will be the subject of attention in the following pages. Alger Hiss, a member of the American delegation at Yalta, was supported there by Dean Acheson, one of the driving forces behind the recognition of the USSR in 1933. Acheson, Dexter White's companion at Bretton Woods, Under-Secretary of State from 1945-47 and Secretary of State from 1949-53, repeatedly ignored FBI reports that pointed to Communists infiltrating the State Department. Roosevelt himself scorned the efforts of whistleblowers within the Administration.

In 1940, when the USSR had attacked its Eastern European neighbours, Martin Dies, a Democratic congressman from Texas who chaired the House Committee on Un-American Activities from 1938 to 1945, warned Roosevelt that there were thousands of communists and communist sympathisers on the government payroll. Roosevelt told him: "I don't believe in Communism any more than you do, but there is no problem with Communists in this country. Several of my best friends are Communists..... I do not see the Communists as a present or future threat; in fact I see Russia as our best ally for years to come. As I told you when you started your research, you should limit yourself to Nazis and Fascists.

Although I don't believe in communism, Russia is much better off and the world much safer under communism than under the Tsars". Absurdly, instead of considering the warning of the Chairman of the Committee investigating Communist espionage on behalf of the Soviet Union, Roosevelt, the world leader who claimed to stand for the values of freedom, democracy and human rights, justified the Communist totalitarianism of the USSR, a bloodthirsty regime that had eliminated more people in a single week than the Tsars did in the entire 19th century. Roosevelt's words can only be understood if one considers that communism was an instrument of the Hidden Power and that he was an agent of this Power which had launched the MRM (World Revolutionary Movement), had implanted communism in Russia and was going to impose it in China, as will be seen in this chapter.

The instability in the early post-war years in the State Department, a Ministry with a reputation for conservatism, shows that the plan for the US to hold world leadership alone through a monopoly on atomic terror was not unanimous. Edward Stettinius, who had taken office on 1 December 1944, was replaced in June 1945 by James F. Byrnes. A few weeks later, Under Secretary of State Joseph Grew, a veteran in the diplomatic corps who had tried to avoid war with Japan, resigned after two months of press attacks that labelled him a reactionary and demanded his resignation. Grew's replacement was Dean Acheson, a "progressive" who became the dominant figure in the Department and led to the departure of all Grew's allies. Although some sources portray Acheson as anti-Soviet, he promoted a policy of conciliation with Moscow and worked closely with Alger Hiss until 1946 when Hiss was forced to resign after being exposed as a Soviet spy. Byrnes did not remain Secretary of State for long either. As Truman writes in *Years of Decisions* (Vol. 1 of his Memoirs), Byrnes announced to him that he was "tired of babying the Soviets". Byrnes, in favour of removing Hiss from the Department, of burying the Morgenthau Plan for Germany for good, and increasingly opposed to Stalin, threatened several times to resign. Finally, on 21 January 1947, the White House accepted his resignation. Byrnes resentfully left the administration, and Truman replaced him with George C. Marshall. In Truman's administration, as in Roosevelt's, there were thus many "friends" of the Soviet Union, where Beria was manoeuvring in the shadows to replace Stalin. Among those in favour of converging with communism and sharing nuclear technology with the USSR was Robert Oppenheimer, who had made no secret of his interest in a convergence with the USSR. The extension of communism throughout Asia, with China as a key player, was part of the internationalists' plans. The transfer of atomic secrets to the Soviet Union must be seen in this context.

The "Venona" documents, decrypted in 1948, confirmed the truth of the FBI's claims about Soviet espionage on the atomic programme. Published in 1995 by the NSA (National Security Agency), they show that the Kremlin received information about the secret British-American atomic bomb project as early as 1941. "Venona" is the code given to the secret communications of Soviet spies intercepted by the United States. In addition to these documents, there are now other sources that make it certain that Beria not only received information about the Manhattan Project and the research at Los Alamos, but also about the work being carried out by the British. In *The Venona Secrets,* Herbert Romerstein, a Jewish author who cannot hide a certain Trotskyite whiff, confirms that the first information the Soviets had about the atomic project came from London on 25 September 1941. It was a report on a meeting held nine days earlier by the British Uranium Committee. The source of the information was an agent codenamed "List". Romerstein, citing Pavel Sudoplatov's *Special Tasks* as a source, notes that "List" was in fact John Cairncross, the private secretary to Lord Hankey, who chaired the British Uranium Committee. Cairncross, who some authors claim was the "fifth man" in the Cambridge Group, denies in his memoirs that he was the source who informed Moscow.

Before going any further, it should be said that the famous Cambridge spy group consisted of five agents: Donald Maclean, Guy Burgess, Kim Philby, Anthony Blunt and a fifth man. In 1994 Roland Perry published a book entitled *The Fifth Man,* in which he states categorically that the fifth agent of the 'Cambridge Five' was not Cairncross, but Nathaniel Mayer Victor Rothschild (1910-1990), better known as the third Lord Rothschild, a triple agent who reportedly worked for the British MI5, the KGB and the Mossad. Burgess and Maclean were discovered in 1959, Philby, whose code name in Venona was "Stanley", was discovered in 1963. In 1979 it was Margaret Thatcher herself who denounced to Parliament that Blunt was a Soviet spy. Anthony Blunt, the fourth man, was reportedly recruited by MI5 in 1940 and was curator of the royal paintings collection and personal adviser to the Queen, for which he held the title of Sir to the Crown. In the 1960s Blunt used to spend Christmas holidays at the Cambridge home of Victor Rothschild. According to MI5 documents made public in 2002, Moura Budberg, an old acquaintance in this work, revealed as early as 1950 that Blunt was a communist, but was ignored. Roland Perry's book provides very interesting information about the activities of Victor Rothschild, about whom he writes the following:

> "The third Lord Rothschild was camouflaged as the fifth man thanks to his powerful position within the Establishment. The immense wealth of his banking dynasty embedded him in the power elite more than any other member of the Group of Five. It was a perfect cover and served as his protection. He appeared to embody the British establishment of the 20th century and it was unthinkable that he could be a traitor. However, closer examination showed that he had other loyalties.... Rothschild was more loyal to his Jewish heritage than to anything English. He proved it by his prolonged devotion to the affairs of his race.... He was never more committed to his native country and its established order. Indeed, when

he had to choose between race and country, he chose race more than once."

Considering that the World Revolutionary Movement had been financed by members of the Rothschild dynasty since the creation of Weishaupt's Illuminati, it is entirely consistent that a Rothschild was dedicated to the task of consolidating and expanding communism, one of the two systems controlled by the Occult Power.

Among the members of the British delegation who worked with Oppenheimer on the Manhattan Project were two Jewish physicists very close to Victor Rothschild, Rudolf Peierls and Otto Frisch. Both worked in Birmingham. The former claimed that the nuclear chain reaction was possible, so Fermi's experiment in Chicago in 1942 would have been in part the demonstration or confirmation of Peierls' theories. The latter designed the first atomic bomb detonation mechanism in 1940. Both were supported by Sir Mark Oliphant, another Australian-born Jew who was a professor of physics at Birmingham University. In the spring of 1941 Oliphant authorised his colleagues to hire Klaus Fuchs, who was by then an agent working in England for Soviet military intelligence (GRU).

There is some controversy about Fuchs' origins: some sources claim that he was Jewish, but others deny this on the grounds that his father, Emil Fuchs, was a Protestant theologian. A member of the Communist Party since 1930, Fuchs had left Germany after Hitler came to power and settled in England, from where he was sent to the United States to work on the atomic bomb. Klaus Fuchs was not identified as a spy until September 1949, when the British arrested him after receiving FBI reports based on analysis of the Venona documents. Peierls, Frisch and Fuchs submitted a memorandum on the radioactive properties of the bomb and its feasibility, which was delivered by Oliphant to the British government. According to Roland Perry, MI5 received a copy of the document and Victor Rothschild allegedly passed it to Beria through an agent named Krotov who worked at the British Embassy.

As we have been recounting, suspicions about Julius Robert Oppenheimer's disloyalty were a constant almost from the time he was appointed scientific director of the Manhattan Project. The first FBI report on Oppenheimer is dated 28 March 1941. It states that in the autumn of 1940 he had participated in a meeting at the home of Haakon Chevalier, a conspicuous Marxist, which had been attended by prominent communists such as Isaac Folkoff and William Schneiderman. The former, referred to as "Uncle" in Venona, had been one of the founders of the California Communist Party and served as a liaison with Soviet intelligence. The second, codenamed "Nat", was listed as a leader of the California Communist Party. The FBI recorded numerous references to Oppenheimer in which he was repeatedly referred to as a secret member of the Communist Party. One of these reports reads: "In December 1942, Julius Robert Oppenheimer was the subject of discussion between Steve Nelson (a Jew named Steve Mesarosh who had participated with the Lincoln Brigade in the Spanish Civil War) and Bernadette Doyle, Organizing Secretary of the Communist Party of Alameda County, California. Steve Nelson then reported that Dr. Hannah Peters had visited him to tell him that Dr. Oppenheimer could not be active in the party because of his work on a special project...". In May 1943, a similar reference further elaborates on the same circumstance: again Bernadette Doyle informs a Soviet agent, John Murra, that Mrs. Oppenheimer and her husband were "comrades" and that Robert Oppenheimer was working on a special project at the Berkeley Radiation Laboratory. Doyle tells Murra that Oppenheimer "was a member of the party, but he was to take him off the mailing lists he handled and was not to be mentioned at all."

As early as 10 March 1942, Beria had suggested to Stalin the creation of an atomic bomb committee composed of scientists, politicians and intelligence officials. Pavel Sudoplatov, a veteran of the NKVD, was in charge of coordinating the data and reports sent by agents from the United States, England and Canada. In *Special Tasks* (1994), cited above, Sudoplatov, who in February 1944 was appointed by Beria as head of Department "S", which united NKVD and military (GRU) intelligence in order to secure the Soviet atomic bomb project, claims that Oppenheimer provided them with secret information on the development of the atomic bomb. According to this source, the information came to them through Lisa Zarubina, the wife of the "rezident" Vassiliy Zarubin[17], who had operated first from the San Francisco Consulate and later from Washington. Zarubina[18], a Bessarabian-born Jewess whose real name was Liza Rozensweig, travelled frequently to California and was in direct contact with Oppenheimer's wife, Kitty. Jerrold and Leona Schecter also claim in *Sacred Secrets* that Elizabeth Zarubin was able to obtain important information about the secrets of the atomic bomb.

---

[17] A "rezident" was a spy who resided in a foreign country for extended periods of time and was in charge of the intelligence operations of a "Rezidentura", the Soviet name for an organisation headed by one or more rezidents. There were four Rezidenturas in the United States, three of them legal and one illegal. The three legal ones operated from the Soviet Embassy in Washington, and from Consulates in New York and San Francisco.

[18] This Soviet spy, who between 1923 and 1928 worked in the Vienna Rezidentura, was also known as Lisa Gorskaya and was able to speak Yiddish, Romanian, Russian, German, French and English. In 1929 she worked in Turkey with Yakov Blumkin, the Jewish terrorist who, on Trotsky's orders, assassinated Wilhelm Mirbach, the German ambassador to Russia, on 6 July 1918 in order to incite Germany to resume the war. As has already been recounted in another chapter, Blumkin sold Hasidic manuscripts stolen from the Central Bookshop in Moscow in Turkey to finance Trotsky. One of the Jewish secretaries of the physicist Leó Szilárd, the writer of the letter proposing to Roosevelt the manufacture of the atomic bomb, had been recruited by the Tsarubina.

On 26 April 1996, two years after the publication of Sudoplatov's book, an article based on sources in the SVR, the successor to the KGB, appeared in the newspaper *Pravda,* confirming that documents obtained from Oppenheimer and other Western scientists were still in the Soviet secret archives. *The Venona Secrets* reproduces the following excerpt from the article:

> "It is no secret that first-hand information about the nuclear reaction experiment carried out in 1942 by the Italian physicist E. Fermi in Chicago was obtained through scientists close to Oppenheimer. The source of this information was a former member of the Comintern, G. Kheifitz, our 'Rezident' in California and former secretary of N. Krupskaya (Lenin's wife). It was he who informed Moscow of the fact that the development of the nuclear bomb was a practical reality. At that time, Kheifitz had established contact with Oppenheimer and his circle. In fact, Oppenheimer's family, in particular his brother, had links with the then illegal Communist Party USA on the West Coast. One of the places for illegal meetings and contacts was the home of the socialist Madam Bransten in San Francisco. It is precisely there that Oppenheimer and Kheifitz met. For our intelligence, people who sympathised with the communists were extremely valuable for making contacts.... Madam Bransten's salon operated from 1936 to 1942. The Soviets financed it. Kheifitz helped to deliver the funds for its financing."

Like most of the agents involved in atomic espionage, Gregory Kheifitz was Jewish, as was Louise Rosenberg Bransten. Both were lovers. Kheifitz headed the San Francisco Rezidentura from 1941 to July 1944. His code name was "Kharon". In 1948 he was arrested by the KGB during the campaign against the Jewish Anti-Fascist Committee, which will be studied later in the context of the Stalin assassination. Louise Bransten, a wealthy Communist from California, had divorced Richard Bransten, a wealthy Communist writer and publisher who had inherited a coffee importing business founded by her father, Morris J. Brandenstein. Richard Bransten would later become a successful Hollywod screenwriter. In 1947 Louise married another Jewish communist, Lionel Berman, and was renamed Louise Berman. Madam Bransten's salon", mentioned in the quote, served as a cover for Kheifitz to recruit agents.

The Venona code was not cracked until April 1948, but the FBI had been investigating Communist infiltration of the Berkeley Lab, one of the centres linked to the Manhattan Project, since the early 1940s. The initial investigation, called COMRAP ("Commintern Apparatus"), eventually resulted in a memo that by 1944 was nearly 600 pages long and contained some 400 names. As it grew, the FBI decided to create a new file for atomic espionage CINRAD ("Communist Infiltration of the Radiation Laboratory").

By 1942 the FBI had sufficient evidence of Oppenheimer's disloyalty that a separate file was created for him.

Another very important source of information and supply of materials on the work at Los Alamos was the aforementioned Klaus Fuchs, who, it has been said, worked in England for the GRU (Soviet military intelligence), although his spy work in the United States was directed by the NKVD. Fuchs arrived in America in September 1943 as a member of a British mission sent to work on "Enormous" (the atomic bomb project). His contact was a Jewish communist named Harry Gold, who had been recruited by Jacob Golos[19], another Jewish agent who until his death in 1943 was Elisabeth Bentley's lover. Recall that Bentley and Whittaker Chambers were the defectors who revealed to the FBI the extent and complexity of Soviet espionage in the United States. Harry Gold, "Gus", and Klaus Fuchs, "Rest" and also "Charles ", met for the first time on 5 February 1944 in New York, specifically in Manhattan. Further contacts took place on 25 February and 11 March 1944. On both occasions Fuchs gave Gold materials about his work on "Enormous". At the 11 March meeting the dossier was fifty pages long. The courier Harry Gold occasionally met Fuchs at the home of the physicist's sister, who lived in Cambridge, Massachusetts.

In June 1944, Fuchs handed Gold a document entitled "Fluctuations and Performance of a Diffusion Plant", which was copied from an original text dated 6 June. Harry Gold's boss was NKVD Lieutenant Colonel Semyon Semyonov (born Aba Taubman), another Jew known to the FBI as Semen Semenov whose code name was "Twen". From August 1944 Klaus Fuchs worked at Los Alamos under the orders of Hans Bethe, the Jewish physicist who headed the Theoretical Physics Division at Los Alamos and was present in the desert of Dead Man's Day when the Trinity test was carried out. After the atomic genocides perpetrated on the populations of Hiroshima and Nagasaki, Fuchs continued to work and spy at Los Alamos, where Edward Teller was working on the hydrogen bomb.

---

[19] Jacob Golos, a Trotskyite Jew of Ukrainian origin, had participated in the 1905 revolution in Russia, led by Trotsky and Parvus. In 1910 he came to San Francisco and in 1919 was one of the founders of the Communist Party of the USA. In 1926 he returned to the USSR, but was recalled by his American comrades and returned to America, where by 1933 he was working for the NKVD. Elisabeth Bentley met him in 1938 and, in addition to becoming his mistress, agreed to work as a Soviet spy. However, already in September 1939 Pavel Fitin, during World War II head of the NKVD's Foreign Department, reported to Beria that among all the Trotskyist organisations, the American one was the most powerful in both membership and financing. The same report warned that Jacob Golos, one of the most important spies in the US, could not be trusted. Since his knowledge of the network was extensive, Fitin recommended that he be ordered to return for the purpose of arrest. Before the year was out, Pavel Fitin insisted to Beria about the Trotskyist activities of Golos, who was a US citizen and did not accept the "invitation" to return to Moscow.

In 1946, the McMahon or Atomic Energy Act was passed in the United States, prohibiting the transfer of information on nuclear research even to Britain. This did not prevent Fuchs from continuing to supply important documents to the USSR on Operation Crossroads at Bikini Atoll. From late 1947 to 1949 he gave Alexander Feklissov, the NKVD agent who took over Semyon Semyonov's spy network, the main theoretical studies for the creation of the hydrogen bomb, which was to help the Soviets build their own fusion bomb, thus neutralising the advantage of the "Super".

In 1948 the FBI confirmed that Fuchs was a member of the Communist Party and began to link him to his sister Kristel's contacts with a Soviet agent codenamed "Gus". In 1947 the FBI had also discovered that Kristel's husband, Robert Heineman, had been a Communist since 1936. In 1949 FBI agents were already certain that Klaus Fuchs, who had already left the United States, was "Rest", so they travelled to London with photographs of alleged spies for interrogation. In May 1950 Fuchs identified Harry Gold and the Americans, although on 5 October 1944 the Soviets had changed his code name to "Arno", finally learned the identity of the spy called "Gus" in Venona. This enabled Harry Gold to be arrested. His statements led to the arrest of Julius and Ethel Rosenberg, two other famous Jewish spies.

In his autobiographical *My Silent War*, Kim Philby, who after his exposure had taken refuge in the Soviet Union, lamented that Fuchs had failed to keep his mouth shut. Fuchs not only confessed his own part in the affair," Philby wrote, "but identified his contact in the United States, Harry Gold. Through Gold, who was also chatty, the chain inexorably reached the Rosenbergs, who were duly electrocuted." The Rosenbergs have been the only Jewish spies sentenced to the electric chair. Klaus Fuchs was sentenced to fourteen years, but served only nine years in prison and ended his days in communist Germany. Harry Gold received a thirty-year sentence in 1951, but was released in 1965.

Harry Gold's statements led to the identification of David Greenglass, who worked on the Manhattan Project at Los Alamos. The son of Jewish immigrants from Russia and Austria, he had married Ruth Printz, also of Jewish origin, in 1942. In the same year they both joined the Young Communist League. Greenglass was the brother of Ethel, who since 1936 had been a member of the YCLUSA (Young Communist League USA), where she met Julius Rosenberg, the organisation's leader, and married him in 1939. David Greenglass' arrest on 15 June 1950 was the trigger for a series of arrests. The Rosenbergs, alarmed at the foreseeable consequences of Harry Gold's interrogation, were planning to leave the country. Julius Ronsenberg tried to convince the Greenglasses to flee and even offered them $4,000, but they ran out of time. On 17 June Rosenberg was arrested, followed by his wife Ethel.

Having introduced these four characters, let us now look at the extent of their espionage activities. In 1942 Semyon Semyonov recruited into the

NKVD Julius Rosenberg, who was already working as an inspection engineer for the Army Signal Corps at the Fort Monmouth laboratory. Secret military projects related to electronics, radar, guided missiles, anti-aircraft systems, etc. were being researched there. The espionage at Fort Monmouth was investigated in 1953 by the vilified Joe McCarthy, a patriot who is blacklisted in history because he dared to expose the conspiracy, which led him to confront the Hidden Power behind it. In *Blacklisted by History. The Untold Story of Senator Joe McCarthy*, a work by M. Stanton Evans that vindicates the figure of the senator who "hunted witches", explains in detail the espionage plot at Fort Monmouth (New Jersey), where Julius Rosenberg, Morton Sobell, Joel Barr, Al Sarant and Aaron Coleman, all Jews, were part of a network of Soviet and/or Zionist spies. How Joe McCarthy's career was ended will be discussed elsewhere in this chapter. When Semyonov was recalled to Moscow in 1944, Julius Rosenberg reported to Alexander Feklissov, to whom he handed over hundreds of reports classified as "top secret". In 1945 the Army discovered Julius Rosenberg's communist affiliation and he was dismissed from Fort Monmouth, but no further action was taken.

According to the intercepted Venona documents, Julius Rosenberg, whose code name was "Liberal", became the head of a spy ring himself. In addition to recruiting his wife and brother-in-law, Julius recommended Ruth Greenglass, "a smart and clever girl". Since David Greenglass worked at Los Alamos, he was tasked with getting hold of a diagram of a lens that was to be used to detonate the bomb. Greenglass was to take the diagram of the explosive lens out of the lab and deliver it to J. Rosenberg. *The Venona Secrets* reproduces the following message from December 1944, issued by the New York Rezidentura, which could be deciphered in 1948:

> "Osa' (Ruth Greenglas) returned from a trip to see 'Kalibr' (David Greenglass). Kalibr' expressed his willingness to help explain the work being carried out at Camp 2 (Los Alamos) and reported that he had thought about the issue before. Kalibr' says that the camp authorities were openly taking all precautionary measures to prevent information about 'Enormous' from falling into Russian hands. This is causing great discontent among progressive workers.... In mid-January 'Kalibr' will be in 'Tiro' (New York). Liberal' (Julius Rosenberg), referring to his ignorance of the problem, expresses his wish that our man should meet 'Kalibr' for personal questioning. He assures us that 'Kalibr' will be very happy about the meeting. Do you consider such a meeting advisable? If not, I will be obliged to draw up a questionnaire and give it to 'Liberal'. Let him know if you have any questions of priority interest to us".

Despite the increased security measures at Los Alamos referred to in the text, therefore, Greenglass obtained the diagram of the essential lenses that caused the bomb to detonate.

Two other Jewish agents in the Rosenberg circle were Mike and Ann Sidorovich. Mike Sidorovich, after participating in the Spanish Civil War in the Lincoln Brigade, had returned to the United States in February 1939. He had previously worked for Soviet intelligence and expressed his willingness to resume contact with the NKVD. In October 1944 Rosenberg recommended him and his wife Ann, also a close friend, to join the spy group. The New York Rezidentura reported them to Moscow. The report, apart from mentioning Mike's time in Spain and his political inactivity for three years, said that Julius Rosenberg and Sidorovich had been friends since childhood. Ann Sidorovich was reported to be a dressmaker who could open a shop as a cover. Moscow was asked whether Mike Sidorovich, whose code name was "Linza", should be used to assist Rosenberg or "Yakov", the code name of William Perl, another important Jewish agent of the Soviets whose real surname was Mutterperl.

Initially, when authorising the draft, Moscow assigned the Sidorovich couple to Rosenberg's circle, but soon after the New York Rezidentura sent them to Cleveland, Ohio, where William Perl lived. Since Mike Sidorovich was a photographer, he helped Rosenberg photograph stolen documents. The Rosenbergs planned for Ann Sidorovich to travel to New Mexico to collect the atomic data that David Greenglass had stolen from the lab. However, perhaps because they were finally assigned to Perl, she was unable to make the trip and Julius Rosenberg used Harry Gold as a courier. It was this circumstance that led in 1950, after the testimony of Klaus Fuchs and Harry Gold himself, to the FBI reaching out to the Rosenberg circle. At the trial, which began on 6 March 1951, Gold confessed that he had met Greenglass in his Albuquerque flat and had given him information about the bomb project.

Julius Rosenberg acted as a direct link between Soviet Intelligence and the leader of the Communist Party USA, Earl Browder. In addition, he was continuously recruiting new agents for his superiors. In 1944, while still working in the Army Signal Corps, he was sent for ten days to Washington, where he took the opportunity to visit Max Elitcher, a Jewish friend with whom he shared a Communist ideology. He had thought of him to photograph documents, as he was an excellent photographer. When the Venona code was cracked in 1948, Elitcher was identified. In 1951 he was presented as the first witness for the prosecution: after having agreed with the prosecutor on the best terms for himself, he gave testimony that was very damaging not only to Julius Rosenberg, but also to Morton Sobell, who had fled to Mexico with his wife Helen, a Jew like him, whose maiden name was Levitov. From Mexico they tried to cross into Europe, but on 16 August 1950 they were stopped by armed men who handed them over to the FBI at the border. Alexander Feklissov, Rosenberg's Soviet boss, confirmed in *The Man behind the Rosenbergs* (1999) that Morton Sobell, an electronics engineer, had been recruited as a Soviet spy in the summer of 1944. Max

Elitcher accused Sobell of microfilming secret information for Rosenberg, for which he was sentenced to thirty years in prison, of which he served almost eighteen, much of it on Alcatraz.

The judge who sentenced the Rosenbergs and Morton Sobell, Irving R. Kaufman, was also Jewish. Here, from *The Venona Secrets*, is an excerpt from the sentence handed down on 5 April 1951:

> "I consider your crime worse than murder..... I think that their conduct in placing the atomic bomb in the hands of the Russians years before they could make it, as predicted by our best scientists, has already, in my opinion, caused the Communist aggression in Korea, resulting in more than 50,000 dead, and who knows whether millions of innocent people will pay the price for their treachery. Indeed, with their disloyalty they have undoubtedly altered the course of history to the detriment of our country. No one can say that we do not live in a constant state of tension. Every day we have evidence of their treachery everywhere, for the actions of our country's civil defence are aimed at preparing us for an atomic attack."

There was yet another group of Jewish Communists who carried out atomic espionage on behalf of the Soviet Union without ever being arrested. Among them was the youngest agent, Theodore Hall, a nineteen-year-old whose real name was Theodore Alvin Holtzberg. Thanks to his skills in mathematics at Harvard University, Hall was one of the young scientists recruited to work on the Manhattan Project at Los Alamos, where he participated in experiments with the "Fat Man" implosion device and also helped calculate the uranium mass of "Little Boy". His code name in Venona was "Mlad", the Russian lexeme for the word "young". He arrived at Los Alamos in 1944. In November he went on leave to New York, where he shared a flat with Saville Sax, another young Jew who was a member of the YCL ("Young Communist League"). According to Herbert Romerstein, when Hall explained to his colleague what kind of work he was doing, Sax convinced him to pass information to the USSR about the experiments at Los Alamos. In order to contact Soviet Intelligence, they considered offering themselves to Earl Browder, the leader of the Communist Party, who was in fact deeply involved in Soviet espionage in the United States. Browder's secretary was wary of a teenager offering important secrets and, fearing that he might be an FBI agent, turned him down. Eventually, contact was made through Sergey Kurnakov, "Bek", who was both a correspondent for *the Daily Worker* and a Soviet intelligence agent. The New York Rezidentura informed Moscow about the case and Kurnakov initially became a courier for Ted Hall, who sent the information to him through Saville Sax.

Hall and Sax gave Kurnakov reports and lists of personnel working on the atomic bomb project. Among Hall's friends at Los Alamos was Samuel Theodore Cohen, a young Austrian-born Jew working on the study of neutron behaviour at "Fat Man". Years later, Sam Cohen would be considered the father of the neutron bomb. In March 1945, the NKVD confirmed to the New York Rezidentura that "Mlad's" reports were received with great interest. In May of the same year, the Rezidentura sent a new report to Moscow in which Hall revealed the experimental sites and the names of the heads of each research group. Only Oppenheimer was listed under a code name: "Veksel". In 1950, the FBI suspected that Hall had been involved in Soviet espionage, but although he was questioned in March 1951, they were unable to charge him. In 1962 Ted Hall and his family settled in England. It was only when the National Security Agency published the Venona documents in 1995 that it became known that Saville Sax and Theodore Hall had been Soviet agents. Three years earlier, in 1992, the appearance in Russia of documents on atomic espionage had revealed that "Charles " and "Mlad" had alerted the USSR about the Trinity test. In Venona, these code names corresponded to Fuchs and Hall.

The recipient of the reports that Hall delivered to Sax was no longer Kurnavov, as he was replaced by another agent of the New York Rezidentura, Anatoli Jacob Yakovlev, alias "John" according to the FBI, who had identified him in connection with the Fuchs, Gold and Greenglass cases. Sax himself stepped down as courier, and the task was taken over by a legendary communist spy, Lona Cohen, whose maiden name was Leontina Petka, the daughter of Polish Jews who had emigrated to the United States. Lona had married Morris Cohen, another New York-born Jew of Russian origin, in 1941. Morris Cohen had been a member of the Lincoln Battalion and was known as Israel Altman, which was the name on the stolen passport he used to enter Spain. Cohen had been recruited into the NKVD while recovering in a Barcelona hospital from wounds received in 1937 on the Aragon front. Lona travelled regularly to New Mexico in search of reports supplied to him by "Perseus", who could not be identified, although it has been suggested that he was Ted Hall himself. The National Security Agency never identified who was behind "Volunteer" and "Lesley". It is now known that they were Morris and Lona Cohen.

Part 3
The Imposition of the Zionist State in Palestine

In the preceding pages we have noted that after the Second World War the world was a turbulent place in which nations, exhausted by the catastrophe they had experienced, were trying to catch their breath. A totalitarian ideology whose brutality had been evident since its triumph in Russia dominated half of Europe and half the world, as it was to gain a foothold in China and other Asian countries. In these circumstances, the old colonies were preparing to take advantage of the "power vacuum" to rebel against the metropolises and fight for their independence. The explosion of the atomic bombs had drastically changed not only the conditions of war, but also those of peace. The fact that a superbomb was being produced that could wipe out all life forms in one second in 130 square kilometres around ground zero and severely burn people and animals in 750 square kilometres gives an idea of the new situation created on the planet. It was under these international circumstances that the Zionists finally succeeded in imposing the state of Israel on the world in Palestine.

The partition plan for Palestine, Resolution 181, adopted by 33 votes to 13 with 10 abstentions, divided Palestine into six regions: three of them (56% of the total area) were to form the Jewish state; the other three with the enclave of Jaffa (43.35%) were to form the Arab state. Jerusalem and its environs (0.65%) were to be an "international zone" to be administered by the UN. The first glaring injustice of the partition plan was that Jews owned only 6.6% of the land allocated to them. In the Arab state, which included 552 Arab villages and 22 Jewish villages, there would be 725,000 Arabs and only 10,000 Jews. In the proposed Jewish state, 498,000 Jews were to live in 183 villages and 497,000 Arabs in some 274 villages. The partition, as can be seen, was profoundly biased in favour of the Jews, to whom the best lands were given, and could only lead to confrontation, which was exactly what the Zionists had planned and prepared for.

Zionist pressures both inside and outside the United Nations were unprecedented. In the United States, the coercion of congressmen and senators together with the propaganda campaign in the media broke all records. As usual, those who tried to defend the rights of the Palestinian people were accused of anti-Semitism, as if the Palestinians were not Semites. Blackmail and bribery were used not only against individuals, but also against nations, as microphones were placed in the delegations of the countries in order to know in advance the direction of the vote and to be able to exert pressure and blackmail those who were going to vote against the partition plan. Finally, on the night of 29 November 1947, the vote was taken. While in Tel Aviv the Zionists greeted the news of partition euphorically with dancing and singing, in the Arab world there was an explosion of anger in all the capitals of the Arab League. In Damascus, the US and Soviet delegations were attacked. In Jerusalem, too, there were numerous scenes of violence. The Arab High Committee called a three-day general strike, which was plagued by incidents. It was all in vain, for although it was not proclaimed until 15 May 1948, the State of Israel was actually born in November 1947.

Some historical events before 1936

Throughout this book, some of the keys to understanding how the usurpation of land from the Palestinian people came about have been provided. In the first chapter it was explained that the Zionists are not Sephardic or Sephardic (Semitic) Jews, but are mostly Ashkenazi or Ashkenazi (descendants of the Khazars), so none of their ancestors come from Palestine. It has also been seen that the prophecies and messianic dreams of some kabbalists caused some Jews, especially Hasidim, to travel to Palestine as early as the 18th century. In any case, their numbers were not significant: in the early 19th century there were only a few thousand Jews in the Holy Land. There has also been talk of the Rothschilds being asked to buy Palestine from the Ottoman Sultan and of the pro-Zionist nationalism of Moses Hess, the teacher of Karl Marx, whose work *Rome and Jerusalem* is considered the theoretical genesis of Zionism.

The idea of the Rothschilds using their wealth to restore a Jewish kingdom in Palestine gained momentum after the Damascus Affair. Gradually this banking dynasty, apart from financing projects in Jerusalem and elsewhere, became more committed and began to promote the founding of colonies in Palestine, working with Zadok Kahn and Michael Erlanger, members of the Central Committee of the Universal Israelite Alliance, famously founded by Grand Master Adolphe Isaac Crémieux. One of the first colonies was "Rishon le Zion", located south of Jaffa. In 1895 Theodor Herzl, Paris correspondent of the *Neue Freie Presse* of Vienna, insisted to the Rothschilds that the only way to solve the Jewish problem was for them to leave Europe and found their own state. In February 1896 Herzl published *Der Judenstaat (The Jewish State)*, which immediately aroused great interest. The book defended the thesis that if Palestine were chosen as a place to settle the Jews, they would form a kind of wall against Asia: "we would be the advanced sentinel of civilisation against barbarism". In June 1896 Herzl travelled to Constantinople to meet Sultan Abdul Hamid II, who refused to receive him. In his *Journal,* Herzl writes the reply the Sultan gave him: "The empire is not mine, it belongs to the Turkish people. I cannot cede any part of it. Perhaps, on the day when the empire is divided up, they will have Palestine for free. But it is our corpse that will be divided up". In these circumstances, Herzl succeeded in convening the first Zionist congress on

29 August 1897, which was attended by some two hundred delegates from all over the world.

In the face of Zionism's growing organisation, one of the problems that the national resistance movement in Palestine faced from the outset was the quasi-feudal structure of Palestinian society, in which the great families were unable to organise politically and converge in a unified national front. However, until the emergence of Zionism, the Palestinians, despite the collaboration of the landlords with the Ottoman authorities and the prevailing social hierarchy, were well cohesive and the non-Zionist Jews living among them, mostly in Jerusalem, were well integrated and accepted by the diverse Palestinian society. Jerusalem, Haifa, Gaza, St John of Acre, Nazareth, Jaffa, Jericho, Nablus, Hebron were thriving cities. The hillsides were carefully worked by the terraced system and the citrus fruits, olives, grains and other products of Palestinian agriculture were known and valued throughout the world. Manufactures, textiles and handicrafts completed the commercial activity. Initially, Palestinians were unwisely tolerant of the early Zionist settlements, but by the early 20th century they began to realise the danger and rejection took place.

In 1903, despite Turkish and Palestinian opposition to Zionism, there were about thirty Jewish settlements in Palestine, most of which were subsidised by Edmond de Rothschild. Palestinians began to see the Zionist settlers as "undesirable aliens" and opposition grew over time. In 1904 Israel Zangwill, a Fabian socialist who advocated a world government in which his race would play a determining role, came up with a slogan that would become popular: he called for "a land without a people to a people without a land". This Jewish nationalist, who was otherwise internationalist and in favour of suppressing other nationalisms, thus established one of the myths on which Zionism justified the theft of the land from the Palestinians, a people whose ancestors, the Canaanites, had inhabited it long before the first Hebrews made their presence felt in Canaan. Zionists have since cultivated this idea in order to present Palestine as a remote and desolate place that could be safely taken over. This meant denying from the outset the Palestinian identity, their nationhood and, of course, any legitimacy over the land they inhabited and owned. Ralph Schönman, a Jewish author who denounces Zionism, writes the following in *The Hidden History of Zionism* in relation to this objective:

> "What distinguishes Zionism from other colonial movements is the relationship between the settlers and the people to be conquered. The stated purpose of the Zionist movement is not merely to exploit the Palestinians, but to disperse and dispossess them. The aim is to replace the indigenous population with a new settler community, to eradicate the farmers, artisans and inhabitants of Palestine and to replace them with an entirely new working population composed of the settlers. By denying

the existence of Palestinians, Zionism aims to create the political climate for their extirpation, not only from their land, but from history."

In 1908 the anti-Zionist newspaper *Al-Karmal* was founded, and in 1911 an anti-Zionist party called the National Party was born in Jaffa, whose aim was to oppose the Zionists, not because they were Jews, but because they were foreigners motivated by a colonisation project. Thus came the First World War. The British tried to get the Sherif of Mecca, Hussein, the only Arab prince descended from the Prophet who could issue a fatwa justifying a holy war against Turkey, to support them. Lord Herbert Kitchener, the British commissioner in Egypt, promised the Sherif Hussein in writing that Britain would guarantee his help against any foreign intervention. After consultation between Hussein and the Arab nationalists in Syria and Palestine, Anglo-Arab negotiations began and were recorded in eight letters between Hussein and Sir Henry MacMahon, the High Commissioner in Cairo. This correspondence took place between July 1915 and January 1916. As is well known, convinced of the reliability of the British promises, on 5 June 1916 the Sherif Hussein called on the Arabs to revolt, events that have become known to the general public in the West thanks to the epic of the famous Lawrence of Arabia, which was made into a film.

A few months earlier, in the spring of 1916, Georges Picot, a representative of the French Foreign Ministry, and Sir Mark Sykes of the Foreign Office drew up a secret draft agreement dividing the Near East into five zones. Known as the Sykes-Picot agreement, it was ratified on 6 May 1916 by Paul Cambon, the French ambassador in London, and Edward Grey, Secretary of State at the Foreign Office. The boundaries drawn by the European diplomats narrowed the scope of the promises made to the Sherif Hussein and were to shape the future of the Arab world. In December 1916 the government of Herbert Henry Asquith, who had been prime minister since April 1908, fell. We refer the reader to chapter seven, where we have recounted how, just as peace was about to be made with Germany, David Lloyd George, Secretary of State for War, backed by a media campaign against Asquith, manoeuvred to isolate the prime minister and take control of the government after making a deal with a delegation of American Zionists to bring the United States into the war. On 7 December 1916 Lloyd George became Prime Minister of the United Kingdom and Lord Balfour was appointed Foreign Secretary. The Zionists had received assurances that Britain would launch a campaign to conquer Palestine. On 2 November 1917 the famous *Balfour Declaration* was made.

In chapter eight we have also seen how the San Remo Conference in April 1920 established the British Mandate for Palestine, which was confirmed in July 1922 by the Council of the League of Nations. It is pertinent to recall that the San Remo Resolution was seen by the Zionists as obliging the British to cede sovereignty over Palestine to them. Lord Curzon, opposed in 1917 to the Balfour Declaration, was at San Remo the Secretary of the Foreign Office and vigorously defended the second part of the text, which referred to the need to guarantee the rights of Arabs and Christians, whom the British and French diplomats referred to as minorities when in fact they constituted the bulk of the population of Palestine, since in 1920 it was the Jews who constituted a very small minority. All this has been dealt with in some detail in the first part of chapter eight, so we shall now confine ourselves to reproducing in full the text of the *Balfour Declaration*, in reality a letter from the Foreign Office Secretary to Lord Rothschild:

> "Dear Lord Rothschild,
> I have pleasure in forwarding to you, on behalf of His Majesty's Government, the following statement of sympathy with Jewish Zionist aspirations, submitted to and approved by the Cabinet.
> The Government of H.M. considers favourably the establishment in Palestine of a National Home for the Jewish people and will use its best endeavours to facilitate the realisation of this objective, it being understood that nothing will be done which may prejudice the civil and religious rights of the non-Jewish communities in Palestine, as well as the rights and political status enjoyed by Jews in any other country.
> I would be grateful if you would bring this statement to the attention of the Zionist Federation".

On 19 November 1917 Lord Balfour acknowledged in a parliamentary interpellation that there had been "no official information to the Allies on the subject". Despite this, Balfour said, and I quote: "Her Majesty's Government believe that the declaration in question will be approved by them". However, weeks later, in December 1917, Stéphen Pichon, France's foreign minister, outlined in the Chamber of Deputies the French position of "internationalisation of Palestine", a fact that seemed to ignore the *Balfour Declaration*. Pichon considered that Turkish rule should be replaced by "an international regime based on justice and freedom" and not by a British or French administration. This position provoked an immediate reaction from the Zionists. Nahum Sokolov, the London-based secretary general of the World Zionist Congress, immediately went to Paris at the head of a large delegation. Baron Rothschild also contacted G. Clemenceau, who had just begun his second term as Prime Minister of France on 16 November.

On 9 February 1918 Sokolov had an interview with Pichon, which resulted in a communiqué announcing that Britain and France were in complete agreement on all matters concerning Jewish settlement in Palestine. On 14 February 1918 Pichon wrote a letter to Sokolov reiterating his support for the Declaration. In December 1918 it was Clemenceau himself who offered Lloyd George to renounce France's "rights" in Palestine in exchange for a solution to the Rhineland problem and British recognition of "France's exclusive influence over Syria". On 31 August 1918, US President Woodrow Wilson sent a letter to Rabbi Stephen Wise endorsing the Declaration. The tragedy of the Palestinian people, still unfinished, began to unfold. In 1949, Arthur Koestler, then a Zionist who had attended the proclamation of the State of Israel, in the essay *Analyse d'un miracle: naissance d'Israel* wrote the following about the *Balfour Declaration*: "It is a document by which one nation solemnly promises to another nation the territory of a third nation; although the nation to which the promise is made was not a nation, but a religious community and the territory, at the time it is promised, belonged to a fourth nation, Turkey". Comments would be superfluous if Koestler did not use the noun miracle: clearly there was no miracle, but an unmistakable demonstration that the Zionists were able to impose their will to inconceivable extremes.

After the San Remo Conference, the British Mandate over Palestine began. At Chaim Weizmann's request, a Zionist Jew and member of the Liberal Party, Herbert Samuel, was appointed high commissioner. He arrived on 1 July 1920 and began to take measures to encourage Zionist colonisation: the creation of the Jewish National Fund, the granting of the electricity monopoly to the Zionist Rosenberg, the granting of powers to the Zionist Organisation to encourage Jewish immigration, etc. Palestinian protests against Jewish immigration were continuous, and on 1 May 1921, violent anti-Zionist and anti-British riots broke out in Jaffa for several days. Bichara Khader in *The Sons of Agenor* cites various sources to quantify the number of victims of the incidents and gives the following toll: 157 dead and 705 wounded on the Palestinian side and about 100 dead on the Jewish side, figures that give an idea of the tension caused by Herbert Samuel's policies. The violence of the riots provoked a reaction from the British government, which on 3 June 1922 published a document known as the 'White Manifest',, which qualified the Zionists' aspirations and announced restrictions on immigration.

Palestinians tried to organise themselves politically and held as many as seven congresses between 1919 and 1928. The first, held on 15 February in Jerusalem, had approved the rejection of the *Balfour Declaration,* union with Syria and full Palestinian independence within the framework of Arab unity. However, the ineffectiveness of this form of political opposition soon became apparent due to the rivalries and the diversity of positions that were expressed. This was helped by the ability of the British to create a so-called 'moderate' current within the Palestinian movement. As a result, the Palestinian national movement failed to structure itself properly and an impasse was reached.

Meanwhile, illegal immigration continued. Zionism knew that only through immigration was it possible to transform a country inhabited by Arabs into a Jewish state. From 1920 to 1932, 118,378 new immigrants landed in Palestine[20]. The peak period was between 1924-26, the famous 'Aliyah' of Polish Jews suffering from Poland's anti-Semitic policies. In 1931, according to a census of that year, there were 1,035,821 inhabitants in Palestine, of whom 759,712 were Muslims, 174,006 Jews, 91,938 Christians and 10,101 unclassified. The percentage of Jews had risen from 11% in 1922 to 17.7%. However, things were not going according to plan, as many of these immigrants did not find the living conditions sufficiently stimulating to settle, so that between 1924 and 1931 almost a third of the immigrants who had entered Palestine left after having been there for some time. In fact, in 1927 there were more departures than arrivals.

The riots and clashes escalated in 1928, when the Zionists, in order to change the status quo of access to the Western Wall, tried to buy land and real estate in the vicinity. The Palestinians reacted and, on the initiative of the Muslim Supreme Council of Hajj Amin al-Husseini, founded the 'Committee for the Defence of the Al-Aksa Mosque'. For their part, the Jews, at a congress in Zurich in 1929, stressed the importance of the Wailing Wall and in August paraded through the streets of Jerusalem. The Palestinians responded a week later with another demonstration. On 23 August, serious riots finally broke out and spread from Jerusalem to Jaffa, Haifa and Safed. Zionist settlements were attacked and hostilities continued for a week. The numbers of dead and wounded on both sides give an idea of the severity of the riot: 133 Jews were killed and 339 wounded; Palestinians were 116 killed and 232 wounded. Palestinian women, seeking to resist immigration and colonisation, held their first national congress on 26 October of the same year.

The explosive situation led the British to set up a commission of enquiry, the so-called 'Shaw Commission', whose report concluded that the cause of the outbreaks was the Arabs' fear of being dispossessed of their land and of being dominated by Zionist Jews. In addition, Sir Henry Hope Simpson, an expert sent by London to assess the facts on the ground, presented a report in which he concluded that Palestinian workers were being discriminated against and that Zionist organisations were using "diabolical" methods to get Jewish immigrants into Palestine. In 1930, protests resumed and the authorities decreed a state of emergency in Nablus.

The British Government, on the basis of the Shaw Commission report and Hope Simpson's memorandum, published a new White Paper on 21 October 1930. It stated that His Majesty's Government had "a double commitment, to the Jewish people on the one hand, and to the non-Jewish population on the other". Zionists reacted indignantly. In protest, Chaim Weizmann resigned from the presidency of the Zionist Organisation and the

---

[20] The figures given below are taken from Bichara Khader's *The Sons of Agenor*, the work cited above, who in turn draws primarily from Mark Tessler's *A History of the Israeli-Palestinian Conflict* (1994).

Jewish Agency. Felix Warburg resigned as chairman of the Agency's administrative committee. Despite this, Weizmann put pressure on Prime Minister Ramsay Mac Donald, who on 31 February read a statement to the House of Representatives addressed to Weizmann in which he effectively annulled the White Paper. One passage read: 'No suspension or prohibition of Jewish immigration in any form is prescribed or contemplated by His Majesty's Government.... The statement of His Majesty's Government does not imply a prohibition of the acquisition of land by Jews..." The Arabs regarded this declaration as "the black book", since it effectively repudiated the White Book.

In any case, the atmosphere in Palestine did not invite European Jews to leave the countries in which they lived and to leave their homes. Figures show that immigration stagnated completely between 1928 and 1931. Despite all the efforts of Zionist organisations, only 16,445 Jews entered Palestine in these four years as a whole. It was thanks to the Haavara Agreement, signed between the Nazis and the Zionists on 25 August 1933, that Palestine experienced a substantial demographic and economic boost. As discussed in chapter eight, Hitler facilitated the transfer of tens of thousands of German Jews' wealth to Palestine, laying the groundwork for the creation of the future state of Israel. Between 1933 and 1936, the years of maximum 'Nazi' collaboration, 178,671 Jews immigrated to Palestine. It is estimated that between 60,000 and 80,000 of them came from Germany and thus entered Palestine under optimal conditions. Probably unaware of the scope of the Haavara Agreement, Jamal Husseini, the founder of the Palestinian Arab Party, in an interview in London in May 1937, stated, and I quote:

> "The Zionists have a lot to thank Hitler for. Zionism received a major setback after the 1929 uprisings and in 1931, in fact, more Jews were leaving Palestine than were coming in. It should be said that the Nazi revolution saved Zionism. A resurgence of Judaism began in Germany and young Jews headed for Palestine. A Zionist newspaper clearly stated that a Nazi Government in every European country would help Zionism enormously."

The struggle for land was decisive during these years. The Zionists counted on British support on the ground to initiate the conquest of "a land without a people for a people without a land". However, the Zionist fallacy ran up against a stubborn reality from the outset: the Palestinian people existed and owned the land, were fully aware of its value and did not want to part with it. The Zionist leadership concentrated much of its efforts on multiplying settler settlements. The Jewish National Fund allocated large sums of money to the purchase of rural areas, and the British administrative machinery did all it could for the Zionists. However, the final results of this land-grabbing policy were a failure. In 1922 the Zionists owned 71 settlements, the equivalent of 594,000 dunums (59,400 hectares). By 1931 they had one hundred and ten settlements and 1,068,000 dunums. More than 85 per cent of the land had been bought from large landowners, absentees or residents, resulting in the eviction of 20,000 Palestinian farming families. Nevertheless, at the time of partition in November 1947, the Zionists owned only 6.6% of the total area of Palestine, or 15% of the arable land.

The situation between 1936 and November 1947

The loss of land and continued oppression by the British and Zionists heightened the Palestinian people's awareness of the fate that awaited them. On 13 September 1933, serious riots broke out in Jerusalem and were brutally suppressed. In protest, Arab leaders demonstrated on 13 October and again the British used excessive violence, resulting in 32 dead and 97 wounded, including the octogenarian leader Musa Jazem al-Husseini. The revolt spread across the country the next day. Finally, in November 1935, the leaders of five Arab parties formed a united front to negotiate with the British High Commissioner, to whom they proposed the creation of a legislative council with a British president,, appointed by London. The council's function would be to advise and assist the British authorities. Also in November 1935 came the revolt of Sheikh Izzidim al-Kassam, an Arab leader who believed that only 'armed revolution' could liberate Palestine from Anglo-Zionist colonialism. Al-Kassam had formed pockets of resistance and founded a secret organisation of Muslims, mostly peasants and workers, who vowed to lay down their lives for the homeland. This entity was organised in such a way that it had a section for the purchase of weapons, a training unit, an espionage group and a propaganda department. On 12 November, the "fedayeen" (militiamen or fighters) decided to launch a revolutionary action and took up positions in the village of Yabed, near the port of Haifa. The British army dealt with them well, and on 21 November Izzidim al-Kassam was killed along with other fedayeen. His figure became a symbol of Palestinian resistance and today there is an Islamist military cell in Gaza named after him. The Izzidim al-Kassam brigades are unanimously recognised among Palestinian resistance groups.

The spring of 1936 saw the rejection of the legislative council proposal suggested by the Palestinians. The British Parliament once again bowed to the Zionists' protests and rejected the bill. It was in this context that the great popular uprising took place and lasted for three years until 1939. Civil disobedience and armed insurrection were the forms adopted by the revolt. On 15 April 1936 two Jews were murdered and the situation began to deteriorate rapidly. Daily clashes spread throughout the territory. The nationalists in Nablus formed a National Committee, which was joined by the six main Palestinian parties. On 25 April this Committee became the Arab High Committee, which was chaired by Mufti Hajj Amin al-Husseini.

The Committee decreed a general strike to force the British to accept Palestinian demands. A congress was held on 7 May, attended by 150 delegates representing all sectors of the population. It was then decided to stop paying taxes and endorsed the general strike throughout Palestine, which was to last half a year.

As usual, the British reacted with extreme severity and unleashed a campaign of repression. Those considered to be organisers or sympathisers of the strike were arrested. Across the country houses were demolished by detonating explosives. On 18 June 1936, much of the city of Jaffa was destroyed by the British authorities, leaving 6,000 people homeless. Numerous homes were also destroyed in the communities surrounding the city. Martial law was declared on 30 July. At the end of August 1936, clandestine armed groups from neighbouring Arab countries began to enter Palestine. The revolt could be said to have taken on the tinge of a social revolution, revealing the frustration and confusion of the poorer classes of the population. The influence of the notables, in the middle classes and in the middle classes of the population, was a major factor in the revolt. The influence of the notables, which was waning in the face of the spontaneity of the uprising, mainly led by the peasantry, was not able to redirect the situation for another six months. Alarmed by the scale and duration of the strike, the British invited the most prominent Arab leaders in the Middle East to London in an effort to seek mediators with the Arab High Committee. Finally, on 11 October 1936, the Committee appealed for calm and ordered an end to the strike as of the following day. A month later, on 11 November, the General Command of the Arab Revolution in southern Syria-Palestine issued a communiqué calling for "an end to hostilities, in order not to poison the atmosphere of the ongoing talks on which the nation places all its hopes."

In order to find out what had happened, Britain sent a commission of enquiry to Palestine at the end of the year, headed by Lord Peel. Only under pressure from the Arab sovereigns in the area did the Palestinians agree to air their grievances before the so-called Peel Commission, which produced a document published on 7 July 1937. It analysed the first fifteen years of the Mandate. Essentially, it drew two conclusions about the causes of the revolt: the Palestinian people's desire for national independence and the fear that the Zionists would establish a colony on their land. The Peel Report also detailed other underlying factors: the spread of nationalist sentiment outside Palestine; increased Jewish immigration from 1933 onwards; the ability of Zionists to influence British public opinion and gain government support; lack of confidence in London's intentions; fear of continued purchases of land from absentee landowners, leading to the expulsion of peasants who had worked the land; British prevarication in relation to consideration of Palestinian sovereignty. Finally, the Peel Commission report summarised the demands in three points: immediate cessation of Zionist immigration; a halt and ban on the transfer of Arab land ownership to Zionist settlers; and the establishment of a Palestinian-controlled democratic government. Another important aspect was the recommendation, for the first time, of a partition of Palestine in order to achieve a final settlement. The Peel Commission awarded 85 per cent of the territory to the Arab state and proposed only the coastal areas north of Tel Aviv and the Galilee hills for the Jewish state.

A month later, the 20th Zionist Congress was held in Zurich. Since Zionism had envisaged that the future Jewish state would encompass the whole of Palestine, they wanted nothing in principle to do with the Peel Commission's proposals. In 1938, a year after the publication of the Peel Report, David Ben Gurion was to present to the World Council of Poale Zion, the forerunner of the Labour Party, a report reflecting his true intentions: "The limits of Zionist aspirations include southern Lebanon, southern Syria, the entire West Bank and the Sinai". However, Chaim Weizmann assured Congress that the partition idea was "a step in the right direction" to begin with. Ben Gurion then decided to support Weizmann's strategy, and Congress authorised talks with the British government.

At the same time, fighting in Palestine flared up again and on 26 September the British commissioner of the Galilee district, Andrews, who was accused of preparing the transfer of the region's Arab population, was assassinated. The British authorities responded by disbanding the Arab High Committee and its local organisations. Several of its members were arrested and others fled to Damascus, where the political leadership of the revolution was located. Again the situation became explosive and in late 1937 London decided to send an additional 20,000 troops to deal with the revolt.

Ralph Schönman denounces that Zionist forces were integrated into the British intelligence services, who then began to rely on the Zionists as their enforcement arms. From October 1938 onwards, seventeen British infantry battalions seized the Old City of Jerusalem and ruthless repression began: hangings, collective punishments, mass destruction of population centres, arrests, bombing of insurgent villages. The revolution," writes Bichara Khader, "was drowned in blood. At the end of 1938, an estimated 2,000 people were sentenced to long prison terms. In Acre prison alone, 148 Arabs were hanged. Five thousand houses were destroyed and almost fifty thousand people were arrested". At the end of 1938 London found the idea of partitioning Palestine impracticable and rejected it definitively. It then proposed a conference to which it invited representatives of the Jewish Agency, the Palestinians and Arabs from neighbouring states.

The London Conference, chaired by Neville Chamberlain, began on 7 February 1939 and concluded late in March. The positions remained irreconcilable, and the Chamberlain government set out its resolutions in another White Paper prepared by Sir Malcolm MacDonald and published in May, which included the Arab demand for the creation of a state for Arabs and Jews within ten years. MacDonald's White Paper set a ceiling for immigration of 75,000 people in five years, after which time Jewish immigration would be subject to the agreement of the Arab majority. Churchill's reaction has already been discussed in the previous chapter. After meeting Chaim Weizmann, he staged a protest in Parliament on behalf of international Zionism and accused the Chamberlain government of violating the promise made in the *Balfour Declaration*.

A new Zionist congress was held in Geneva on 16 August 1939, at which Weizmann and Ben Gurion indignantly denounced the British betrayal. By the end of 1939, with the Second World War already underway, Zionist leaders announced a counter-offensive to establish the Jewish state even if it meant entering into conflict with the British. In the US, the publication of the White Paper predictably exasperated the Zionists, who "forced" Roosevelt to make a verbal protest. But if Zionism rejected MacDonald's White Paper, which they also considered a "black book", the Palestinians did not take a positive view of it either, considering that ten years was too long a period for the creation of the Arab state. Moreover, they no longer trusted the British.

Since in 1941 it looked as if Germany might win the war, both sides contemplated turning to Hitler for help. In the face of London's hesitation and indecision, Revisionist Zionism set out to fight the British. In late 1940 a meeting took place in Beirut, where the Vichy government was still in control, between Otto von Hentig, head of the German Foreign Ministry's Orient Department, and Naftali Lübentschik, a member of the Stern Group, set up by Abraham "Yair" Stern. Lübentschik proposed creating a front against Britain. A document dated 11 January 1941, "Proposal of the National Military Organisation (Irgun Zvai Leumi) concerning the solution of the Jewish question in Europe and the participation of the NMO (National Military Organisation) in the war on the side of Germany", was transmitted by the Reich Embassy in Turkey. The Irgun, following a split from the Haganah, had been formed in 1931 by Jabotinsky, the founder of Revisionist Zionism. The Stern (Lehi) Group claimed to represent the true essence of the Irgun. Since the Zionists had already signed the Haavara Agreement with the Nazis, the terms of the document reiterated the ideas that had already enabled collaboration in 1933: it called for the evacuation of the Jewish masses from Europe to settle in Palestine, noted common interests and the possibility of understanding, and proposed to link the future Jewish state to the Reich by treaty. The Germans were undecided, so in December 1941, after the British had taken Lebanon, Stern sent Nathan Yalin-Mor to Turkey, but British intelligence had already been alerted and he was stopped on the way.

For his part, Amin al-Husseini, the exiled mufti of Jerusalem, sent a letter to Hitler on 20 January 1941 requesting his help against Britain, "this bitter and cunning enemy of the true freedom of the peoples." On 28 November 1941 came the interview between the Führer and the Mufti, who told Hitler that the Arabs would be "Germany's natural friends because they have the same enemies as Germany, especially the English, the Jews and the

Communists." Al Husseini called for Germany to make a public statement supporting the independence and unity of Palestine, Syria and Iraq, since "it would be very useful for the purpose of propaganda on the Arab peoples." Hitler, who did not see that such a statement was timely, after having been the Zionists' chief collaborator from 1933 until the outbreak of the war, after having fertilised Palestine with wealthy German Jews through the Haavara Agreement, cynically proclaimed his opposition to the Jewish national home in Palestine, which, he told the Mufti, was "a centre, in the form of a state, in the service of the destructive influence of Jewish interests."

In February 1942 the British discovered Abraham Stern's hiding place in Tel Aviv and killed him. Many members of the organisation were then arrested. Isaac Shamir replaced Stern as head of Lehi and was one of those responsible for the response that was prepared for the British. On 6 November 1944, Lehi members assassinated Lord Moyne, Minister of State for the Middle East and a close friend of Churchill's, in Cairo. At the trial the assassins claimed that they had killed Lord Moyne because of the policy towards Jews outlined in MacDonald's White Paper. This attack was to mark the beginning of the terror campaign against Britain to provoke its exit from Palestine. The British authorities issued wanted posters with the photos and names of a dozen Irgun and Lehi terrorists, including Menachem Beguin, the future prime minister of Israel from 1977-83 and Nobel Peace Prize winner in 1978, and Isaac Shamir, the mastermind of the assassination attempt on Lord Moyne, who would also become prime minister of Israel from 1983-84 and from 1986-92.

Zionist leaders made it clear during the World War years what they intended to do with the Palestinian people. Ralph Schönman quotes, for example, the words of the head of the Jewish Agency's Colonisation Department, Joseph Weitz, the man most responsible for the organisation of the settlements, who in 1940 wrote: 'It must be clear to us that there is no place for the two peoples in this country. We will not achieve our goal if the Arabs are in this small country. There is no way out but to transfer the Arabs from here to the neighbouring countries. All of them. There must not be a village or a tribe left." With these ideas in the chamber, they were arming themselves to proceed to the conquest of Palestine by force when the time came. In June 1945, as soon as the war in Europe was over, the Zionists hastened to petition Britain for the establishment of the State of Israel. In August 1945, the World Zionist Conference was held in London, where they demanded that "an immediate decision be taken to make Palestine a Jewish state". It demanded that the Jewish Agency be given "full authority to transfer to Palestine as many Jews as it deems necessary".

In this context the Attlee government had only two alternatives: either to abandon the decision passed by Parliament in 1939 or to renounce the Mandate and withdraw from Palestine. The second option was the desire of Zionism, as it would allow them to expel the native inhabitants, who were unarmed. The problem arose with the appointment of Ernest Bevin as Foreign Office Secretary, a trade unionist who had been Labour Minister during the war and who enjoyed nationwide prestige. It seems that the monarch himself, George VI, asked Prime Minister Attlee to appoint him to the post, as he considered him to be the best man and the strongest politician in the post-war circumstances. Although a Labour Party member, Bevin was anti-communist. Douglas Reed in *The Controversy of Zion*, a work we have often quoted, writes the following about Bevin:

> "He was a sturdy man, with the energy and air of the countryside in his bones and muscles and his traditional courage in his blood; but even he was psychically broken in a few years by the ferocity of relentless defamation. He did not allow himself to be spiritually intimidated. He realised that he had to deal with an essentially conspiratorial enterprise, a conspiracy of which revolution and Zionism were linked parts, and he may have been the only one among the politicians of this century to use the word conspiracy, which was as defined in the dictionary clearly applicable to the case. He told Dr. Weizmann bluntly that he would not be coerced or persuaded into any action contrary to Britain's interests. Dr. Weizmann had not experienced such warnings, at this high level, since 1904, and his indignation, which manifested itself through the world Zionist organisation, gave rise to the continued mistreatment of Mr. Bevin which then ensued."

Bevin did not share the Zionist schemes and announced that he did not accept the approach that the Jews should be removed from Europe. Naturally, the power of international Zionism was capable of ruining the policies of the new UK Foreign Secretary, and a campaign was launched across the board: as usual, Bevin was accused of anti-Semitism; Churchill, from the Conservative opposition, accused him of harbouring "anti-Jewish sentiments"; the Anti-Defamation League invented a new defamatory term: "Bevinism".

The Zionist offensive was forged in the United States, where there was a succession of Jewish presidents. Roosevelt, surrounded by communists and/or Zionists, had already in 1938 conceived the idea of expelling the Arabs from the Holy Land. His Jewish advisers had even calculated that the operation could cost the taxpayer some 300 million dollars. Roosevelt, the world champion of democracy, had no problem asserting to his collaborators that Palestine should belong exclusively to the Jews and that there should be no Arabs left. On 24 July 1945, shortly before Churchill lost the election, Harry S. Truman, the new US president, wrote to Churchill to tell him that American public opinion was against restrictions on Jewish immigration to Palestine. On 16 August 1945, Truman was questioned about his government's attitude on the matter. "The American position," he replied, "is that we want to let as many Jews into Palestine as possible." Days later, on 31 August, the American president suggested in a letter to Prime Minister Attlee that the British government should grant 100,000 visas to Jews from Austria and Germany. However, Truman himself admits in *Years of Trial and Hope* that in September 1945 he received a memo from the State Department advising that the US should "refrain from supporting a policy tending to encourage mass immigration into Palestine during the interim period".

Meanwhile, after the war, clandestine immigration took place on a massive scale and reached unprecedented levels. Hundreds of thousands of Jews from Russia and Eastern Europe (Khazars) were trafficked by Zionist organisations to the Holy Land. There, increasingly prepared for the big moment, the Zionists already had a real army, the Haganah, and a host of militias, including the Palmach, the elite force of the Haganah, the Irgun and the Stern. In addition to harassing the weakened Palestinian population with little political leadership, these militias increased sabotage and bombings, and on 28 January 1946 the British enacted extraordinary legislation to try to curb Zionist terror. To little avail, as terrorist actions not only did not diminish but increased: between 16 and 17 June the Palmach and Stern blew up nine bridges and attacked railway warehouses in Haifa.

Faced with this new wave of terror, the British military went on the attack: they occupied the offices of the Jewish Agency, seizing important secret documents, and raided and arrested some 2,700 suspects, including Zionist leaders. It was in this context that the famous bombing of the King David Hotel in Jerusalem, which served as army headquarters, took place. On 22 July 1946, Irgun terrorists, whose leader was Menahem Beguin, the future Nobel Peace Prize winner, detonated 350 kilos of explosives from underground, destroying all seven floors of the hotel's south wing. The brutal attack killed 91 people.

One of the most famous propagandists for Zionist terror against the British and the Palestinians, Ben Hecht, a journalist, novelist, playwright, film director, producer and author of some seventy screenplays, for which he was called the "Shakespeare of Hollywood", placed a full-page advertisement in major US newspapers addressed "To the terrorists of Palestine". The text read: "The Jews of America are with you. You are their champions... Every time you blow up a British arsenal or blow up a British train or rob a British bank or attack with your guns and bombs the British traitors and invaders of your land, the Jews of America have a little party in their hearts." This fervent Zionist so outraged the London Government with his apologia for terrorism that his works were boycotted in England. Douglas Reed denounces in *The Controversy of Zion* this fanatical Jew's hatred of Jesus Christ, which suggests that he was a Talmudist. "One of the most excellent things ever done by the people," wrote Hecht, "was the crucifixion of Christ. Intellectually it was a splendid act. But they didn't get it quite right.

You know, what I would have done would have been to send him to Rome to feed the lions. They could never have made a saviour out of mincemeat."

While Bevin sought a face-saving solution to defend Britain's interests in the Middle East, where it only controlled the Suez Canal after losing its position in Egypt, Truman resumed his pressure: on 4 October 1946 he insisted that Britain should allow 100,000 Jews to be received in the Holy Land. The American president further noted that his country was prepared to help establish a "Jewish commonwealth in Palestine". Bevin was irritated by Truman's repeated badgering, which came at a time when he was trying to bring Jews and Arabs to the table in order to reach a compromise. In brief, the plan presented by Bevin was as follows: Palestine would be divided into two cantons and Britain would be the mandated power for five more years. In the first two years, four thousand Jews would be allowed to immigrate each month (96,000 in two years). After this time, no further entries would be allowed without consultation with the Arabs, although the final decision would be made by a British High Commissioner and the UN Trusteeship Council.

Bevin's efforts and the UK's future in the Middle East were doomed in Switzerland. Terrorism as a means to end the British Mandate in Palestine was approved at the 22nd Zionist Congress in Geneva in December 1946. Thereafter, Zionist leaders ceded the initiative and control of events to the terrorist leaders of the three armed groups until the first objective of pushing the British out of Palestine had been achieved. The Congress appointed David Ben Gurion as the head and coordinator of all Jewish Agency armed activity. Thus the ambushes intensified and hundreds of soldiers were killed in various ways. The situation was untenable. On 14 February 1947, Jews and Palestinians flatly rejected Bevin's last proposal and, disappointed, he finally surrendered. On 18 February he announced in Parliament in London: "Her Majesty's Government has been faced with a conflict of irreconcilable principles.... We have decided to ask the United Nations to propose a solution." On 23 February 1947, a major debate on Palestine took place in the House of Commons. Bevin said publicly that the attitude of the United States had led to the failure of its policy and reproached President Truman bitterly for his obstinacy in demanding the entry of 100,000 Jews into the Holy Land before the question was fully settled.

On 28 April 1947, the UN General Assembly was convened in extraordinary session to examine the British request for the transfer of the Palestinian file. By Resolution 106 the Assembly set up the UNSCOP (United Nations Special Committee for Palestine), which began its work on 26 May. Britain warned that it would withdraw from Palestine if other powers, clearly alluding to the United States, made its administration impossible. On 8 August 1947 General Marshall, who had been the new Secretary of State since the beginning of the year, informed the government that a British withdrawal "would provoke a bloody struggle between Arabs and Jews". A week later, on 15 August, Undersecretary of State Robert A. Lovett warned of the danger of a consolidation of anti-US sentiment among Arab and Muslim peoples. The fact that 1948 was an election year in the United States prompted Robert Hannegan, one of Truman's campaign managers, to recommend to the president on 4 September 1947 that he make a political statement and respond to British threats by requesting the admission of 150,000 Zionists into Palestine. Hannegan said that this new demand "would have a great influence and a great effect in raising funds for the National Committee of the Democratic Party."

A new figure was suddenly to become the leading critic of US policies in favour of Zionism. On 17 September 1947, James Forrestal, a wealthy banker who had served his country out of patriotism during the war, stepped down as Secretary of the Navy to become America's first Secretary of Defence. Forrestal fought a battle behind the scenes that was to cost him his life. On 29 September 1947, Forrestal, as Secretary of State for Defence, asked the President at a Cabinet meeting that the Palestine issue not shape national interests and that it be taken out of the election campaign. Truman's response came at the next Cabinet meeting on 6 October. He rejected Forrestal's suggestion with these words: "Mr. Hannegan brought up the Palestine question. He said that many people who had contributed to the Democratic campaign were pressing hard and demanding assurances from the Administration about definite support for the Jewish position on Palestine." From this moment Forrestal understood that Truman was determined to capitulate to the pressures of the Zionists, who felt that the United States was not doing enough in the United Nations General Assembly to secure the votes of other countries in favour of the partition of Palestine.

While Forrestal was fighting a losing battle both inside the Democratic Party and in the White House, the date of the vote was approaching. Chaim Weizmann was undoubtedly a very high official of Zionism, the highest; but above him were the big shots in the United States: Bernard Baruch, Henry Morgenthau, Felix Frankfurter and others, whose support was the greatest guarantee for the success of his efforts. Other powerful Jews moved within the Democratic Party, including Senator Herbert Lehman, whose father had been one of the founders of the banking firm Lehman Brothers. Lehman had been the first director general of UNRRA between 1943 and 1946 and had used this UN agency to smuggle Jews from Eastern Europe to Palestine. On 19 November 1947, Weizmann asked President Truman that the United States support the inclusion of the Negev (where they intended to build the Dimona nuclear power plant later) in Zionist territory, as this district was considered of great importance. In his autobiography, *Trial and Error*, Weizmann writes: "He promised me that he would immediately inform the American delegation".

In short, the power of Zionism in the United States was unstoppable and Truman proved to be an exemplary and disciplined president. All those in the State or Defence Departments who, like Forrestal, opposed the Zionists' designs for economic, strategic or military reasons were accused of anti-Semitism. Alfred Lilienthal, a Jewish friend of the Palestinian people who early on became an implacable critic of Zionism and the state of Israel, denounced in *What Price Israel?* (1953) that economic blackmail was used to silence people with different opinions and that there was a moral lynching of those who disagreed with the Zionists. What happened to James Forrestal is the best example.

The officially "suicided" Secretary of Defence wrote very interesting entries in *The Forrestal Diaries* on Zionism's methods of controlling and manipulating governments. Forrestal witnessed the underground struggle from the autumn of 1947 to the spring of 1948 to bring about the creation of the Zionist state in Palestine. As mentioned above, on 29 September 1947, Forrestal, who had secret information provided by the Intelligence Service, asked Truman to resist Zionist pressures on Palestine. Forrestal, in conflict with very powerful enemies, submitted a memorandum on 21 January 1948 analysing the consequences of submission to Zionism for US foreign policy. On 3 February 1948 Forrestal had lunch with Baruch. In his diary he wrote: "I had lunch with B. M. Baruch. He took the position of advising me to keep out of this particular matter, as I had already been identified, to a degree that was not in my own interests, by my opposition to the United Nations policy on Palestine. This is an example of high-level bullying.

Douglas Reed recounts in *The Controversy of Zion* his own experience when he travelled to the United States in early 1949. He noted with bewilderment that the press and radio were launching "poisoned attacks" on the Secretary of Defense. On 9 January 1949 it was reported that Truman "would accept Forrestal's resignation within a week". On 11 January it was insisted that the resignation "had already been accepted". In reality, it was all part of the pressure campaign. Finally, on 31 March, Truman dismissed him. Admitted to Bethesda Naval Hospital on 2 April, Forrestal, according to the official version, committed suicide on 21 May 1949. "Coincidentally", on the very day he was due to leave because he had been discharged, he jumped from a tenth-floor window. Among his personal effects was a scrapbook of newspaper attacks on him. It was not until 2004 that the report of his death was revealed; but his relatives immediately declared that he had been murdered, as suicide was an unacceptable act for him. At his funeral Truman described him as "a casualty of war".

From partition (29/11/1947) to the proclamation of Israel (14/5/1948)

At the beginning of this third part of the chapter we have already detailed the outcome of the vote on 29 November 1947, how the land was divided up and what the population figures were in the two states envisaged.

Two days later, on 1 December, the first meeting of the Truman Administration was held, at which Undersecretary of State Robert Lovett confessed that "never before in his life had he been under so much pressure as in the last three days". Lovett explained that Liberia's vote in favour had been obtained through the Firestone Rubber and Tire Company, which held the concession on these raw materials in the country. The company's representative was instructed to put pressure on the Liberian government, which was planning to vote against, to change its vote. It is known that the pressure consisted of blackmail.

On 21 January 1948 Fames Forrestal, in his eagerness to support the State Department's resistance to Truman's policy, submitted a memorandum analysing the dangers of a misguided policy: "There is hardly any segment of our foreign relations of greater importance or of greater danger," Forrestal wrote, "to the security of the United States than our relations in the Middle East." Elsewhere in the text he warned of the need to avoid "permanent damage to our relations with the Islamic world." At the State Department, Under Secretary Lovett, after reading Forrestal's report, set about presenting another memo that had been prepared by the Department's Planning staff. In it, the President was told that the partition plan was not feasible and that the United States was not committed to supporting it if it could not be implemented without the use of force. It was also stated that it was against US interests to supply arms to the Zionists while denying them to the Arabs. Robert Lovett added that the State Department was "seriously embarrassed and disavowed by Niles' activities in the White House after he had gone directly to the President on Palestinian issues". Subsequently, the undersecretary complained that Niles had called him from the White House "expressing the hope that the embargo on arms sales to the Zionists would be lifted." David K. Niles, a Russian-born Jew, had been Roosevelt's adviser for Jewish Affairs. He and Judge Samuel Rosenman, who has already been featured, were primarily responsible for Truman's actions that had placed Bevin and the London Government in an untenable position, as denounced by Byrnes, former Secretary of State.

The entry James Forrestal wrote in his diary on 3 February 1948 deserves to be transcribed at length, for on that day he was visited by Roosevelt's son and later had lunch with the omnipotent Bernard Baruch. Taken from the first edition of *The Forrestal Diaries*, it follows:

> "Visit today of Franklin D. Roosevelt, Jr. who came with a strong defence of the Jewish State in Palestine and saying that we should support the 'decision' (the inverted commas in the term are Forrestal's own) of the United Nations.... I pointed out that no 'decision' had yet been taken by the United Nations, that it was only a recommendation of the General Assembly, that any implementation of this 'decision' by the United States would probably not result in the need for a partial mobilisation, and that I thought the methods which had been used by persons outside the

executive arm of the Government for the purpose of blackmailing and coercing other nations in the General Assembly constituted a scandal. He expressed ignorance of the latter point and returned to his general exposition of the Zionists' case.

He made no threats, but he made it very clear that the fanatics in this cause were acting in the belief that they could defeat the government's policy on Palestine. I replied that I had no power to make policy, but that I would be derelict in my duties if I did not point out what I thought of the consequences of a particular policy which might endanger the security of my country. I told him that I was only directing my efforts to take the issue out of politics, i.e. that the two parties should agree not to fight for votes on this issue. He said that this was impossible, that the nation was already too compromised and that, moreover, the Democratic Party stood to lose and the Republicans to gain by such an agreement. I told him that I was obliged to repeat to him what I had said to Senator McGrath in response to the latter's remark that our failure to support the Zionists might mean the loss of the States of New York, Pennsylvania and California - that I thought it was time for someone to consider whether it was the United States that we might lose.

I had lunch with B. M. Baruch. After lunch, the same question came up with him. He took the position of advising me not to be too active on this particular issue, as I had already been identified, to an extent which was against my interests, by my opposition to the United Nations policy on Palestine. He said that he himself did not approve of the actions of the Zionists, but he immediately added that the Democratic Party could only lose if it tried to change the policy of our Government, and he said that it was an unfair thing to let the British arm the Arabs and that we would not supply similar equipment to the Jews."

One might wonder who it was that had identified Secretary Forrestal for his opposition to the Palestine policy. Following Baruch's warning, a press smear campaign against the Defence Secretary was progressively orchestrated. The attacks reached extreme levels of inclemency and within a year James Forrestal was removed from the government. There can be little doubt, as stated above, that his death in April 1949 was an assassination.

The concerted moves by the State and Defence Departments were embodied in a statement by Warren Austin, the US ambassador to the United Nations. On 24 February 1948 he stated: "The United States does not believe that force should be used to support a recommendation of the General Assembly". He then added that partition did not seem a viable option. On 25 February, the *New York Post* published an article by Rabbi Baruch Korff in which he claimed that Austin's words were "pure and simple anti-Semitism." Zionist organisations were quick to organise a massive letter and telegram campaign: some 100,000 letters of protest reached the White House.

In March 1948, violence in Palestine continued to escalate, making it clear that the State Department's warnings that the partition plan was unworkable were well-founded. Ambassador Austin announced a shift in US policy on 19 March. Noting that the Assembly resolution could not be implemented peacefully, he proposed that the partition proposal be suspended, that a truce be arranged and that a UN "trusteeship" be installed after the end of the Mandate. This had been the State Department's proposal in its January memorandum. The Zionists were furious: in addition to being anti-Semitic, some accused the United States of being "diabolical cheats". At the same time, however, they decided to step up terrorist actions on the ground.

In April 1948 Ernest Bevin, the Foreign Office Secretary, was fighting a lonely battle against the Conservative opposition and the majority of the Labour Party, whose members did not support him. In these conditions Bevin decided to wash his hands and throw in the towel. The end of the British Mandate was initially set for 1 August 1948, but in April the Zionists learned from their contacts in London that the British were planning an early withdrawal and decided to take action. On 9 April 1948, the famous massacre of Deir Yassin, a village less than five kilometres west of Jerusalem, took place. This massacre has gone down in history as the first in a series of genocidal actions perpetrated throughout 1948. Deir Yassin is part of the collective memory of the Palestinian people because of its significance and the psychological effect it had, for, as intended, it succeeded in terrorising the Arabs and triggered the mass flight of the residents of the area that the UN had allocated to the Jews. Paul Eisen, a Jewish friend of the Palestinian and German people who courageously fights against Zionism, founded the association "Deir Yassin Remembered" to honour the memory of the victims of the massacre.

In the early morning hours of 9 April the village was attacked by terrorist commandos of the IZL (Irgun Zwa'i Leumi) and the Lehi (Stern Group), led by Menahem Begin and Benzion Cohen. They killed 254 men (many of them elderly), women (some of them pregnant) and children. The adult men were working the land when the criminals entered the village. Some wounded men were arrested and, blindfolded, handcuffed and with bloody clothes, were loaded onto trucks and taken to Jerusalem, where they were paraded through the streets to the applause and jeers of the Zionists in the city. After the parade, they were taken back to Deir Yassin, lined up against a wall and murdered. Jacques de Reynier, head of the International Red Cross, was alerted to what was happening in Deir Yassin and asked to meet the commander of the Irgun detachment, who told him the story that the villagers had been ordered to evacuate their homes 24 hours in advance by loudspeakers. Those who did not "got the fate they deserved". This senior Red Cross official immediately went to the village with an ambulance and a pick-up truck. Ralph Schönman reproduces Jacques de Reynier's account in *The Hidden History of Zionism*:

"... I reached the village with my convoy and the firing stopped. The band (Irgun) wore uniforms with helmets. They were all young men, some even teenagers, men and women armed to the teeth: revolvers, machine guns, hand grenades and also cutlasses in their hands. A beautiful young woman with criminal eyes showed me hers, still soaked in blood; she displayed it like a trophy.... I tried to enter a house. A dozen soldiers surrounded me with their machine guns pointed at my body. Their officer forbade me to move. The dead, if there were any, would be brought to me, he said. Enraged as never before in my life, I told those criminals what I thought of their conduct and threatened them with everything that came to my mind, then I pushed them aside and entered the house. The first room was dark, everything was in disorder, but no one was there. In the second, amidst smashed furniture and all sorts of debris, I found some bodies, cold. The 'clean-up' there had been done with machine guns and hand grenades. It had been finished off with knives, anyone could see that. The same in the next room, but as I was about to leave, I heard something like a sigh. I looked all around, turned the bodies, and finally discovered a small foot, still warm. It was a girl of about ten, mutilated by a hand grenade, but still alive.... Everywhere was the same spectacle. There had been about four hundred people in the village, about fifty had escaped with their lives. The rest had been deliberately murdered in cold blood....

Back in my office I was visited by two gentlemen in civilian clothes who had been waiting for me for an hour. They were the commander of the Irgun detachment and his deputy. They had prepared a paper which they wanted me to sign. It was a statement that I had been received very courteously by them and that I had obtained all the facilities requested for the accomplishment of my mission and that I thanked them for the help I had received. Since I showed them my doubts and started arguing with them, they told me that if I valued my life, I would do well to sign immediately. The only option I was left with was to convince them that I did not value my life in the slightest".

The Irgun took photographs of the murdered people and distributed them to the Arab population with an inscription on the back: "This will happen to you if you don't disappear". Racial cleansing was the main objective, as a future ethnically pure Jewish state was intended. The Deir Yassin massacre had the desired effect. In less than two weeks 150,000 Arabs vacated their villages and fled to Jordan and Gaza. They were the first Palestinian refugees. This mass flight, which would later increase scandalously, was due to the hierarchical and patriarchal structure of Arab society. Christian Zentner writes in *The Postwar Wars*: "The subservience of the peasant to the landlord and of the Bedouin to the families of the sheikhs determined the mass exodus of Arabs, for the flight of one family dragged with it hundreds or even thousands of people. Lenni Brenner reports in *The*

Iron Wall: Zionist Revisionism from Jabotinsky to Shamir Begin's statements, boasting and bragging about the effects of the massacre:

> "A legend of terror spread among the Arabs who panicked at the mere mention of our Irgun soldiers. It was worth half a dozen battalions to Israel's forces. Arabs throughout the country panicked beyond measure and began to flee for their lives. This mass flight soon turned into an uncontrollable mad stampede. Of the 800,000 Arabs who lived in present-day Israel, only about 165,000 are still there. The political and economic significance of this event can hardly be overestimated".

On 12 April, Arab guerrillas wanted to avenge the Deir Yassin massacre and attacked a column of vehicles that early in the morning set out from the new part of Jerusalem towards Mount Scopo, where the Zionists had the Hassada clinic and the Jewish University. Between the new part, largely inhabited by Jews, and Mount Scopo lies the Arab Old City. The strip between the Old City and Mount Scopo and the surrounding land also belonged to the Arabs, so the convoy would inevitably have to pass through Arab territory. A Haganah armoured vehicle served as escort and led the way. Behind it followed an ambulance with the red Star of David, two armoured buses, a second ambulance and three truckloads of food and medicine for the hospital. A second armoured escort vehicle closed the column. At a narrow spot on the road at the foot of the hill, the assault took place with grenades, rifles and Molotov cocktails. The coaches were set on fire and the occupants who tried to leave were shot by the attackers, whose numbers were increasing as Arabs from the old district of Jerusalem and nearby towns came to seek revenge and targeted the doctors and nurses in the convoy. Seventy-seven were killed and missing. They included the director of the hospital, a university psychology professor and three professors.

On 19 April the Zionists began their campaign of occupation and ethnic cleansing of Palestinian cities with the capture of Tiberias. On 20 April, faced with the passivity of the British troops, they decided to take large-scale action, using the troops of the Haganah, which, unlike the Irgun, was militarily organised and was in effect an army. The target was the port city of Haifa, which had a population of 158,000, mostly Arabs. The Haganah attack came from the Jewish quarter on Mount Carmel, which overlooked the city. The Arabs had no armed forces in the city and only the British could defend them, but they were ordered not to intervene in the fighting. As a result, there was virtually no resistance, and within two days the Arabs decided to ask the British to negotiate the surrender of Haifa. The commander of the British forces acted as an intermediary between the Zionists and the Palestinians. While in almost all the towns conquered by the Zionists the indigenous population was evacuated, in Haifa, despite the fact that the port had been allocated to the Jewish state in the partition plan, almost a quarter of the inhabitants were able to remain in the city. In any case, the number of Arab refugees continued to grow and before the unilateral proclamation of the Zionist state had reached three hundred thousand.

Days later, on 25 April, the Haganah attacked the area where the ambush against the medical convoy had taken place, i.e. the region between Mount Scopo and the Jewish district of Jerusalem. Within three hours the entire territory was in Jewish control. Since according to the partition plan it belonged to the Arabs, units of the Jordanian Arab Legion, British-trained and trained professional troops commanded by British officers, attacked the Zionists, but were defeated and lost three tanks. Given the symbolism and importance of Jerusalem, the thrice holy city, the British were finally ordered to intervene. Three companies equipped with artillery pieces, mortars and machine guns were thrown into the fray. Finally, after heavy fighting, the Haganah was forced to evacuate the sector it had occupied. The British decided to declare the area east of Jerusalem a military zone and barred Jews and Palestinians from entering.

On the same day, 25 April, the city of Jaffa was also attacked. The UN partition agreement provided for the Arab state to have at least one port. The port city of Jaffa was therefore of vital importance to the Palestinians. Tel Aviv, built in the previous decade by the Jews, was close to Jaffa, so the Zionists, disregarding the UN resolution, set out to conquer the city, which held out until 12 May 1948. There is a first-person account of how Ramla, near Jaffa, fell. In Ramla, located very close to Lod and sixteen kilometres southeast of Jaffa, lived Jalil Wazir, then a boy of twelve. Known as Abu Jihad, Wazir was a co-founder of Fatah[21] with Yasser Arafat and for many years the second in command of the PLO. Journalist Alan Hart, author of *Arafat. A Political Biography* (1989), interviewed Abu Jihad before he was assassinated. The following is taken from that interview in Hart's book:

> I remember, as if it were yesterday, the day the Zionist forces attacked Jaffa," Abu Jihad told me. The Arabs in the city sent us cars and trucks to Ramla. Help for Jaffa', they shouted, 'help for Jaffa'. I remember the men and women of Ramla getting into the vehicles. One man was carrying a very old gun and several knives and sticks. At that time we helped each other. We knew that the Jews could come for Ramla and Lod if they captured Jaffa. And that's exactly what happened. In one night they surrounded Ramla, which they did without difficulty, because the Jordanians retreated without fighting. We were alone and surrounded.

---

[21] Fatah, born in 1957, was the largest and most influential of the liberation organisations that created the PLO (Palestine Liberation Organisation), founded in 1964. From 1957 to 1965, Fatah consisted of a network of secret and clandestine cells. Arafat (Abu Amar) and Wazir (Abu Jihad) were the two organisers of the network. Abu Jihad was assassinated in Tunisia by an Israeli commando in April 1987.

Our people couldn't fight; they had nothing to fight with. The commander and a municipal delegation visited the Jewish commanders. Our commander told them: 'Very well, you can enter the city, but you must not harm the people or take prisoners, and you must allow the people to stay in their homes and live their lives normally."

Naturally, the Zionists intended exactly the opposite. So, when they found that the inhabitants of Ramla and Lod did not flee, they subjected both cities to artillery fire. A storm of shells fell on Ramla. Wazir's house in the Christian quarter of Ramla was destroyed. Amidst the explosions, he and his family made their way to the Catholic church, where men, women and children spent two whole days huddled together. When the Jews entered the city, Jalil Wazir climbed to the top of the church: "With my own eyes I saw the Jewish soldiers shooting at the women and children who were still in the street. I can't forget it. Then I watched as they entered our houses kicking, breaking doors and shooting. Sometimes they pushed people out and then killed them. In the church, people were crying. They were saying: 'Deir Yassin, Deir Yassin'. We were sure we were going to be killed en masse."

When the soldiers entered the church street, the priest went out to meet them with a white flag and returned with the Jews, who began to separate the people. All the men between the ages of fourteen and fifty were taken to detention camps. Only the oldest men, women and children were left in the city, and they were allowed to return home. Two days later, they were ordered over the loudspeaker to leave their homes and gather at various points along the road, where they spent three days waiting for buses to take them to Ramallah. On the second day, the elders were ordered to start walking to Ramallah. On the third day, the buses arrived and on one of them, Khalil Wazir boarded with three brothers, one of whom was a baby, three sisters, his mother, his grandmother and his aunt. However, the torment was not yet over, with fifteen kilometres to go to reach the city, the people were forced to get off and walk the rest of the way:

"So we started walking. We had to walk slowly. Some of the women were too old and sick and had to stop every few minutes to catch their breath and rest. Some of the other women who were more able to walk were exhausted from carrying their children in their arms. At night the Jews attacked us with their artillery and mortar bombs. At first we took cover behind some rocks. Then, when we saw that the attack continued, we all started to cry and panic... and we had to run and run towards Ramallah. I can't forget what happened. Some mothers abandoned their children, they were too exhausted to carry them anymore. Even my aunt told my mother to leave some of her children behind. My mother had three on her. My aunt told her, 'You can't run with three children on your back. They will kill you. Leave two of them behind and we will send help when we get to Ramallah'. My mother refused. Then she said, 'Jalil, do you think you could take one of your sisters and run?' I said, 'Yes,' and I did. Some children were left behind because there was no one to take them. Others stayed behind because their mothers died. To this day I have not been able to forget it."

Some 60,000 people were expelled in the refugee caravans that were directed towards Ramallah from different parts of Palestine. Other localities met the same fate as Ramallah and Lod. Safad was occupied on 8 May, where some 10,000 Arabs were ethnically cleansed to leave the town in the hands of just over 1,000 Jews, and on 12 May, the same day that Jaffa was surrendered, the Arab town of Bissan also fell. In the midst of the Zionist orgy of terror and oblivious to the humanitarian disaster it was causing, the British, in breach of their obligations, announced on 14 May 1948 that they were ending their Mandate in Palestine. As agreed at the UN, after the British withdrawal, which was to take place on 1 August, a commission would be responsible for enforcing the agreed partition. Following the UN takeover, elections would be held in both states and then the UN would hand over power to the respective governments.

Unilateral proclamation of independence and war of conquest

Before the British announced that they were disengaging from the Mandate of Palestine, the Zionists had already occupied most of the Arab cities and expelled their inhabitants. On 14 May, the same day that Sir Allan Cunningham, the last British High Commissioner, left the Holy Land aboard the cruiser *Euryalus*, the Haganah began the assault on St John's in Acre, which fell on the 17th. From the outset, then, the facts show that the Zionists never had any intention of submitting to UN plans. In *The Fatal Triangle: The United States, Israel and Palestine* Noam Chomsky quotes the words of Beguin, who in 1948 declared: "The partition of the homeland is illegal. It will never be recognised. The signing of the partition agreement by both institutions and individuals is invalid. It will not bind the Jewish people. Jerusalem was and will always be our capital. Eretz Israel will be returned to the people of Israel. All of it. And forever."

To violate Resolution 181 with impunity, however, required the complicity or passivity of the nations that had won the world war. Once again, what happened in the United States demonstrates the extent to which Jewish lobbyists wielded real power. On 13 May 1948 President Truman received a letter from Chaim Weizmann announcing that at zero hours on 15 May the provisional government of the Jewish state was to take office. The letter indicated that it was expected to be quickly recognised. The text of the letter is reproduced by Weizmann himself in *Trial and Error*. It follows an excerpt quoted in *The Sons of Agenor* by Bichara Khader:

"... The leadership which the American Government exercised under your inspiration made possible the establishment of a Jewish State.... It is for these reasons that I very much hope that the United States, which under your leadership has done so much to find a just solution, will promptly recognise the provisional Government of the Jewish State. The world, I think, will find it especially fitting that the largest democracy in existence should be the first to welcome the newest in the family of nations".

B'nai Brith President Frank Goldman appeared at the White House on the morning of 14 May 1948 and was received by Truman. In 1947 the members of the New York lodge, whose president was Lester Gutterman, had individually contributed $50,000 to the Haganah. After the proclamation of independence, B'nai Brith sent ship after ship loaded with $4,000,000 worth of supplies to Haifa. Goldman evidently intended to make sure that Truman would not fail. The next visitor that morning was Eliahu Epstein, the Jewish Agency's representative in Washington, who handed the President formal notification that Israel would be proclaimed that same day at 18.01 (US time).

On the afternoon of 14 May 1948, the Jewish National Council met in the great hall of the Tel Aviv Museum. The members of the Jewish Agency were seated on a rostrum. Above their heads was a large framed portrait of Theodor Herzl. The chairman of the Council, David Ben Gurion, stood up and all present sang "Hatikwah", the song of hope, which was to be Israel's anthem from then on. Ben Gurion then proceeded to read the Declaration of Independence, which ended with these words: "We, members of the National Council, representatives of the Jewish people of Palestine and of the international Zionist movement, have gathered in solemn assembly. On the basis of the national and historical law of the Jewish people and the resolution of the United Nations, we proclaim the foundation of the Jewish State in the Holy Land, whose name shall be Israel". The Executive Committee of the Jewish Agency became the first government of the new state.

Eleven minutes after the proclamation, i.e. at 18.11 US time, Charlie Ross, the President's press secretary, read the terse communiqué signed by Harry Solomon Truman: "This Government has been informed that a Jewish State has been proclaimed in Palestine and recognition has been requested by the provisional Government of that State. The United States recognises the provisional Government as the de facto authority of this new State of Israel". Recognition thus took place without delay, as Weizmann had requested. The meeting at the Tel Aviv Museum was still going on when the Zionists received the news. It was an unprecedented display of speed that has not been surpassed to date. The US delegates to the UN, who had not been informed, could not believe it, since they had submitted a draft international trusteeship for Palestine which was under consideration by the General Assembly. After a few moments of confusion, they contacted the White

House and received confirmation that the news was true. Months later, when Chaim Weizmann visited the US president as the first president of the State of Israel, Truman acknowledged that the recognition was "the proudest thing in his life".

On 15 May 1948 troops from Syria, Lebanon, Iraq and Jordan entered Palestine. It was the beginning of the first Arab-Israeli war (1948-1949). The Secretary General of the Arab League, founded in March 1945, sent a telegram to the United Nations expressing his astonishment at the Zionists' decision, which was against the law. It denounced the fact that the Jews had taken possession of almost all of Palestine and justified the intervention: "The Arab states have been obliged to intervene in order to ensure peace and security, to restore order in Palestine, and also to fill the vacuum left by the British". Actually, the troops were supposed to protect the sectors handed over to the Arabs according to the partition plan and only invaded these territories. However, the preparation and equipment of the soldiers was very poor. Moreover, they lacked a central command that could coordinate their actions. Syria and Lebanon had only recently gained independence and their armies numbered only 8,000 men. Egypt's King Farouq had more troops, but they were unprofessional and equally ill-equipped. Only the Arab Legion of King Abdullah of Transjordan was a truly well-armed and organised military force, having been trained by the British, who were still in command. Its general was John Glubb, "Pasha". The commanders and officers under him were also British. Only the Arab Legion was able to stand its ground; the other Arab armies were defeated on all fronts by the Haganah. The Arabs were ignorant of the most elementary infantry tactics, they charged in droves firing old spiked guns and acted foolishly, for they went to meet enemy fire because they were carrying a sura of the Koran blessed by the mufti.

The most significant clash between the Haganah and the Arab Legion occurred in Jerusalem. The partition plan had left a corridor between the Holy City and the sea so that the Arabs and the international authorities residing there would have a free exit to the coast. The Zionists marched on Jerusalem and attacked the Arab district from the Tel Aviv road; but not only did they fail in their attempt to take the Old City, they also lost the Jewish quarter nestled in this old part of Jerusalem. It was a painful defeat, as for the first time in history all Jews without exception were expelled from the historic part of the city. The Jewish Quarter was occupied by troops of the Arab Legion and its inhabitants, some 2,000 in number, were forced to leave. The Jews left on 28 May 1948 through the Zion Gate and were taken captive to Transjordan under Red Cross surveillance.

On 29 May, as the last Jews were leaving Old Jerusalem, the ceasefire proposal put forward by the Security Council was accepted. War operations were to be suspended for a period of four weeks, during which time a mediating commission would try to bring an end to the hostilities. During the truce, no new troops were to enter Palestine and no war materiel was to be brought in. Failure to comply with the terms of the armistice would lead to appropriate sanctions. The Swedish Count Folke Bernadotte, a relative of the Swedish Royal Family and for many years an official of the international Swedish Red Cross, was appointed chairman of the UN mediation commission. Folke Bernadotte announced on 7 June that the truce would begin at 6 a.m. on 11 June.

Bernadotte's choice was well accepted by the Zionists, since at the end of World War II, as a representative of the Red Cross, he had interceded with Himmler on behalf of thousands of Jews, a fact that had brought him international prestige. Like James Forrestal, Count Bernadotte kept a diary which was published after his death. In it he noted that after accepting his peace mission, he stopped in London on his way to Palestine and visited Nahum Goldman, then vice-president of the Jewish Agency and representative of the Zionist state, who assured him that "the State of Israel was now in a position to assume full responsibility for the actions of the Stern Gang and the members of the Irgun". Comforted by these words, Bernadotte arrived in Egypt, where he met the prime minister, Nokrashi Pasha, who told him that he "recognised the extent of Jewish economic power, since it controlled the economic system of many countries, including the United States, England, France, Egypt itself and perhaps even Sweden". Bernadotte did not note in his diary any objection to the reference to his country. Nokrashi Pasha also told him that the Arabs "did not expect to be able to escape this domination", but added that they could not accept that they wanted to achieve it through force and terrorism and would resist.

The Zionists accepted the ceasefire before the Arabs did, although they had no intention of honouring the agreement. The truce would allow them to decisively reinforce their contingents, as thousands of well-trained Jews arrived from Europe who did not need military training. In addition, Czechoslovakia sent substantial supplies of arms, a decisive contribution that had begun in March, following the Communist coup in Prague, which in February 1948 had bloodlessly overthrown the Bene" government.. The coup had been orchestrated by the communists in Prague, who in February 1948 had overthrown the Bene" government. The coup had been orchestrated by Jewish communists acting under the leadership of Lavrenti Beria. The strongman of the conspiracy was the Jew Rudolf Slansky (Rudolf Salzmann), general secretary of the Communist Party of Czechoslovakia, the criminal who in 1945 had welcomed Benes with living torches hanging from lampposts.

It is worth noting that the most prominent Jews who came to power in Prague after the February 1948 coup were arrested in November 1951 and in subsequent months. Accused of being Zionists, they were tried in November 1952 and executed on Stalin's orders. As had been the case in the Moscow trials of the 1930s, the Western media called the trial that opened on 20 November 1952 a farce and accused Stalin of anti-Semitism for purging Jews from the Communist party apparatus in Eastern Europe. The truth is, however, that as soon as control of the Czechoslovak government was in their hands, Slansky and company were quick to send shipments of armaments to the Zionists in Palestine. In addition to Slansky, the following Jewish Communists came to power under Beria's protection: Vladimir Clementis, Minister of Foreign Affairs, whose role was paramount in the arms smuggling operations to the Israelis; Bedrich Reicin, appointed Deputy Minister of Defence; Bedrich Geminder, Slansky's right-hand man and a leading figure in the Comintern; Josef Frank, Slansky's deputy and Deputy Secretary General of the Communist Party; Rudolph Margolius, Deputy Minister of Foreign Trade; Stefan Rais, Minister of Justice in April 1950; Artur London, Deputy Minister of Foreign Affairs; André Simone (actually Otto Katz), head of the Foreign Ministry Press Department, a propagandist who came to use some twenty pseudonyms and whose role in the Spanish Civil War has already been discussed; Otto Fischl, deputy finance minister, who admitted at the Prague trial that he was a Jewish nationalist and collaborated with the Israeli secret service; Ludwig Frejka (actually Ludwig Freund), economic adviser to Klement Gottwald, president of the Republic; Evzen Löbl, deputy minister; Vavro Hajdu, also deputy minister; and many others who held less important posts. Later, in September, the Zionists ruling Czechoslovakia would form a brigade of Czech Jews that was moved to Palestine.

Unlike the Jews, the Arabs were hesitant to accept the truce, convinced that it was in Israel's interest. Moreover, by June the number of Palestinian fugitives and displaced persons had risen to more than 600,000, who longed for a Zionist defeat so that they could return home. In Jordan and Egypt, it was argued that it was the Jews who had to be forced to comply with UN decisions and to allow the expellees to return. Finally, a decision by the British government forced the Arabs to accept the UN truce: the British announced that they were withdrawing their officers from the Arab Legion. Christian Zentner's *Post-war Wars* quotes Major Glubb Pasha: "The withdrawal of the British officers was a severe blow to the Legion. Among them were the chiefs of staff, two brigade and four regimental chiefs, as well as the entire artillery command. And since the artillery had been organised three months earlier, there were no Jordanian officers capable of replacing them. The British officers were the backbone of the edifice until 1948, without them the whole thing would collapse....". Finally, then, the Arabs gave in and the fighting more or less ceased.

Despite an express UN ban, the Jewish communists in Czechoslovakia sold the Zionists not only small arms, but also artillery, tanks and even aircraft, both fighters and bombers. The deliveries included weaponry captured from the Germans at the end of the World War, such as 98 K rifles, M 42 assault machine guns, anti-tank bombs and M-109 fighters. The material was transported by air from Czechoslovakia to Palestine with a stopover in the Greek territory dominated by General Markos, leader of the communist guerrillas fighting the civil war in Greece. Material was also sent to Yugoslavia, whose leaders were the Jewish communists Tito and Pijade, and from there continued by ship to the ports of Haifa and Tel Aviv. Thus, well armed, when hostilities resumed on 9 July 1948, the Zionists launched a ten-day offensive that took them from victory to victory : Nazareth, the birthplace of Jesus Christ, was conquered and the whole of Galilee was in Jewish hands. On 19 July, Count Bernadotte made every effort to bring about a new truce, for not only were the civilian population fleeing in disarray, increasingly terrified by the ethnic cleansing practised by the Jews, but also the Arab troops, who were unable to cope with the Haganah. On 29 July the Swedish mediator managed to stop the fighting again for another four weeks.

The UN delegate and the commission he chaired, comprising French, American and Belgian representatives, were determined to make the Israelis comply with the UN resolution, namely: the borders of the Zionist state were to be as envisaged in the 'recommendation' of 29 November 1947; Jerusalem was to be internationalised under UN control; the UN should reaffirm and guarantee the right of expelled Arabs to return home. During August, discussions between the Swedish mediator and Zionist leaders festered. The Jews disagreed with Count Bernadotte and first used the tactic of demonstrating with loudspeakers outside the UN delegation building; then they held up posters and leaflets against the UN representative and his negotiating commission; finally, on 17 September 1948, they killed him on a Jerusalem street. When one of the parties assassinates the mediator, the person to whom the utmost respect and consideration is due because of the difficulty of his mission, little can be said in the face of the shock and disappointment of such a grave violation. The tribal fanaticism of the criminals, however, was made clear to international opinion. In this case, moreover, there was the aggravating circumstance that Count Folke Bernadotte had rescued some twenty thousand Jews from the hands of the Nazis, which demonstrates the esteem in which the Swedish nobleman held the Jewish people.

At around 5 p.m. on 17 September, three UN cars left government headquarters with the intention of driving through Jerusalem. As the three vehicles were driving along the road from Katamon to Rehaviah, a "jeep" with four men in addition to the driver blocked the road. The assassins, wearing Afrika Korps uniforms, jumped to the ground and fired their automatic weapons at the three cars. One of the terrorists headed towards the car in which Count Bernadotte was travelling. In the front seat were Colonel Begley, who was driving the jeep, and Captain Cox, the Belgian delegate. Behind them were Bernadotte's assistant, the Swedish General Lundström, seated at the window through which the gunman approached, in the centre was the French Colonel Serot, and on the other side was Count Bernadotte. The shots killed Colonel Serot on the spot. Folke Bernadotte, seriously wounded by gunshots to the head, died as soon as he arrived at the hospital. The three cars of the delegation were riddled with bullets. It later emerged that the jeep used by the criminals had been stolen some time earlier by the terrorists of the Stern Gang.

General Lundström, who escaped the attack unharmed, declared the next day, 18 September, that "the deliberate assassinations of two senior international officials constituted a breach of the truce of the utmost gravity and a black page in the history of Palestine for which the United Nations would demand full justification". General Lundström was wrong: there was no demand made on the Zionists. The pressure mechanisms that had been operating behind the scenes since the *Balfour Declaration* once again worked to perfection. The assassination of the UN mediator had not the slightest repercussions: the Zionists ignored Count Bernadotte's proposals: they conquered and retained whatever territories they wanted, rejected the Palestinians' right of return to their homes and proclaimed that they would not allow Jerusalem to be internationalised.

The Times of London went so far as to blame the Swedish mediator for what had happened, since the proposal to internationalise Jerusalem "undoubtedly incited certain Jews to kill Count Bernadotte". Of course, the Zionists continued with their accusations of anti-Semitism against all those who championed the Arab cause, which was the most outlandish of sarcasms, since the real Semites were the Palestinians and the Zionists were overwhelmingly Ashkenazi Jews (descendants of the Khazars). The impunity of the Zionists has been a constant since : the state of Israel has never complied with a single UN resolution and since 1948 has acted uninterruptedly outside international law without the slightest problem.

As for the terrorists who murdered the international mediator, two Stern members named Yellin and Shmuelevitz were sentenced four months later to eight and five years in prison by a special court of justice. When reading the sentence, the presiding judge said that "there was no proof that the order to kill Count Bernadotte had been given by the leadership". In other words, as usual, the terrorists acted on their own. In *The Controversy of Zion* Douglas Reed writes the following about what happened to the convicted men: "The two men (according to the Jewish Telegraph Agency), 'in view of the fact that the Council of State was expected to approve a general amnesty, paid little attention to the judicial process', and within hours of being sentenced were released to be escorted in triumph to a popular reception."

Bernadotte's successor was an American diplomat, Ralph Bunche, who protested out of obligation and without much energy: the presidential election was about to take place and Jewish votes and money were essential for Truman. Moreover, the United States presided over the Security Council. In these circumstances, the Zionists resumed their war of conquest and seized Beersheba, a city that was to be part of the Arab state according to the partition plan. The Security Council ordered a ceasefire on 22 October 1948 and the withdrawal of the Jews to existing positions on the 14th, a week before the offensive. Naturally, the Israelis, while accepting the ceasefire, ignored the order to withdraw and continued their policy of fait accompli with impunity. In February 1949 they resumed their attacks on Egyptian forces. Between March and April the Arab states were forced to accept an armistice sealing their defeat. The Jews had conquered 1,300 square kilometres destined for the Palestinians, including fourteen towns and 313 villages, whose inhabitants had fled en masse to avoid the ethnic cleansing announced after the Deir Yassin pogrom: "this will happen to you, if you don't disappear". The 56% of the territory granted to the Jewish state when the Zionists owned only 6.6% of the land had become 74% of the total area of Palestine.

After the end of the first Arab-Israeli war, the Palestinians realised that what had happened was a catastrophe, "al-Nakba", and they have been repeating it until today. Political Palestine disappeared from the map, as King Abdullah of Transjordan annexed the West Bank, the left bank of the Jordan, now called the West Bank, and the Gaza Strip was taken over by the Egyptian military administration. Between November 1947 and December 1951, some 850,000 Palestinians, three quarters of the total population, became refugees, whose inalienable aspiration to return gave rise to the second great concept of the Palestinian people's epic, "al-Awda", the right to return, symbolised by the transmission from generation to generation of a key to the house that their ancestors had to leave behind when they were expelled by the Zionist Jews. These exiles have settled in refugee camps in Lebanon, Jordan, Syria, the West Bank and Gaza, where they have survived in destitution. In November 1948, the United Nations launched an aid programme for Palestinian refugees, which on 8 December 1949 was replaced by Resolution 302, which created the United Nations Relief and Works Agency (UNRWA), responsible for distributing food rations and providing schooling for the children.

Killings and ethnic cleansing

Plan Dalet (Plan D) was activated in early April 1948 and aimed to seize, clear and destroy Arab villages in areas designated by the command. The first area chosen was the rural villages in the Jerusalem mountains and was implemented between April and May 1948. It was "Operation Najson", carried out by Palmach units, and was to serve as a model for the future. The Alexandroni Brigade was in charge of attacking the coastal villages. The Golani brigade was ordered to clear the eastern Galilee on 6 May. In 2008, the book *La limpieza étnica de Palestina*, by Ilan Pappé, who was exiled from Israel in 2007 because of the boycott he suffered for his criticism of Zionism and his defence of the rights of the Palestinian people, was published in Spanish. We advise the interested reader to read the work of Professor Pappé, whom some of his detractors accused of being "a Jew who hates himself because he is a Jew", a common slander that Jews who maintain their dignity and put their status as human beings above ethnicity often have to endure.

Since Ilan Pappé's case is very significant, it is worth explaining the origin of his academic ostracism in Israel. He recounts it himself in his article "Israeli academic boycott: the 'Tantura case'". In the late 1980s Pappé taught a course at the University of Haifa on the Israeli-Palestinian conflict. The course aroused the interest of student Teddy Katz, who, encouraged by Professor Pappé, decided to undertake research on the fate of the village of Tantura on 23 May 1948. In 1998 Katz submitted his master's thesis to the University of Haifa, which concluded that 225 Palestinians had been killed in Tantura: twenty were killed during the battle, the rest executed after the village surrendered. His grade was a very high 97% (Professor Pappé notes that he would have given it 100%).

At the end of January 2000, the daily *Ma'ariv* interviewed Katz and some veterans of the Alexandroni brigade, although others confirmed the research data, refused to admit the massacre, filed a libel suit and demanded compensation of one million shekels. "If you research Israeli history," writes Professor Pappé, "contradicting the Zionist narrative, you suffer reprisals." The pressures from the university and from his own family caused a depression in Katz that nearly cost him his life. He finally agreed to sign a letter of apology retracting his statement and admitting that there had been no massacre in Tantura, although he quickly regretted it. The investigation confirmed ethnic cleansing and Judge Pilpel closed the case. However, the university demanded the annulment of the qualification and accused the student of fabricating the evidence and Professor Pappé of supporting him.

After three days and three nights listening to the recordings of the young Katz with the testimonies and evidence, Pappé realised that he could not defend the monstrous events in Tantura. He decided to make a summary and post it on the university's website. He also proposed to discuss the matter with other experts, but the University considered that its role was not to seek the truth but to defend Zionism, and rejected the proposal. In this way Professor Pappé discovered that his university had systematically manipulated history. Thus," Pappé continues, "subjected to a de facto boycott, I became a pariah in my own university. Friends and colleagues cancelled invitations to courses and seminars that had been sent to me before the Tantura affair broke out, exposing the brutal nature of Israel's ethnic cleansing in 1948". Ilan Pappé's commitment and determination to spread the facts led to him being declared "persona non grata".

Unfortunately, there are no university theses that make it possible, as in the case of Tantura, to document with absolute rigour the massacres carried out by the Zionists. Some authors, such as the aforementioned Ralph

Schönman, have, however, published witness statements or information published in the Israeli media. On 28 October 1948, the massacre of Al-Dawayima, a few kilometres east of Hebron, took place. The horror of the massacre became known through the statements of a soldier who participated in the events, which appeared in the Hebrew-language newspaper *Davar*, published by the General Federation of Workers in the Land of Israel. The soldier claimed that between eighty and a hundred people were killed; however, other sources suggest that the number was higher. In *The Hidden History of Zionism*, Schönman publishes this excerpt from the soldier's testimony:

> "... They killed between eighty and one hundred Arab men, women and children. To kill the children they broke their heads with sticks. There was not a house without bodies... One commander ordered a soldier to take two women inside a building that he was about to dynamite.... Another soldier boasted that he had raped an Arab woman before shooting her in the head. Another Arab woman with her newborn child was forced to clean the place for a couple of days, and then she and the baby were shot. Polite and well-mannered commanders considered 'good guys'... became common criminals, and not in the heat of battle, but as a method of expulsion and extermination. The fewer Arabs left, the better."

There is also a report on this massacre dated 14 June 1949, submitted by the Ramallah Congress of Arab Refugees to the Technical Committee of the United Nations Conciliation Commission for Palestine. From this report it is known that the population of Al-Dawayima was about six thousand, as about four thousand people had taken refuge there before the massacre. Since this document is available, it is reproduced almost in its entirety:

> "...The reason so little is known about this massacre, which in many ways was more brutal than the Deir Yassin massacre, is because the Arab Legion (the army that controlled that area) feared that if the news was allowed to spread, it would have the same effect on the morale of the peasants as Deir Yassin had, namely that it would cause another wave of refugees.
> In order to assist the Arab delegations meeting in Lausanne, a brief account of the massacre is presented here. This report is taken from a statement made under oath by Hassan Mahmoud Ihdeib, the Mukhtar (chief) of Al-Dawayima. I have personally interviewed the Mukhtar and found him to be a reasonable and calm man, not given to exaggeration.
> He reports that half an hour after noon prayer on Friday 28/10/48, he heard the sound of gunfire in the western part of the village. On investigating, he observed a troop of about twenty armoured vehicles approaching the village of Qubeida - on the Al-Dawayima road - a second troop approaching from Beit Jibril, and other armed vehicles approaching

from Mafkhar-Al-Dawayima. The village had only twenty guards, who were stationed on the western side.

When the vehicles were half a kilometre from the village, they opened fire with their automatic weapons and mortars and advanced on the village in a semi-circular movement, thus encircling it from the west, north and south. A section of the armoured vehicles entered the village firing their automatic weapons. The Jewish soldiers jumped out and scattered through the streets of the village firing indiscriminately at everything in sight. The villagers began to flee the village while the older ones took refuge in the mosque and others in a nearby cave called Iraq El Zagh. The shooting went on for an hour.

The next day, the Mukhtar met with the villagers and agreed to return to the village that night to find out the fate of those who had remained. He reports that in the mosque were the bodies of about sixty people, mostly the elderly men who had taken refuge there. His father was among them. He saw a large number of bodies in the streets, bodies of men, women and children. Then he went to the cave of Iraq El Zagh. He found at the mouth of the cave the bodies of about eighty-five people, again men, women and children.

The Mukhtar took a census of the villagers and found that 455 people were missing, 280 of them men and the rest women and children.

There were other casualties among the refugees, the number of which Mukhtar was unable to determine.

The Mukhtar expressly reports that the people were not forced to surrender and that the Jewish troops met no resistance.

There is no point in mentioning that this brutal, unprovoked attack took place during the truce".

It would be of little use to go on stating cases and recounting the same facts over and over again. Ethnic cleansing continued not only in 1948 and 1949, but throughout the years that followed. In the early 1950s the Gaza refugee camps were subjected to various massacres. The same decade also saw massacres in West Bank villages. Of these, the best known is that of Qibya, where in October 1953 seventy-five civilians, men, women and children, were murdered in cold blood in their homes during the night. The man most responsible was Ariel Sharon, the future prime minister of Israel,, who began to forge his reputation as a murderer. Among Sharon's most internationally known crimes were the massacres at Sabra and Chatila, the refugee camps in southern Lebanon, where on 16 September 1982 at least 2,400 people, all of them women, children and elderly people, were exterminated on Sharon's orders. A Belgian court in 2001 upheld a lawsuit brought by a score of survivors, and in Europe several committees organised the Campaign for Justice for the Victims of Sabra and Chatila. As always, the crimes of the Zionists went unpunished, as Ariel Sharon was never brought to trial.

Schönman provides a list of Arab villages destroyed by Israel in all districts of Palestine, which was compiled by Israel Shahak, president of the Israeli League for Civil and Human Rights and author of *Jewish History, Jewish Religion*, a book repeatedly cited. The figures give an insight into the scope of "al-Nakba". Before 1948 there were a total of 475 villages in Palestine, of which only 90 remained in 1988, i.e. 385 villages were destroyed, razed to the ground, as the Israeli government undertook systematic destruction. Sometimes trees were subsequently planted on the sites of villages or hamlets in order to erase all traces of their existence; often a new village was built where the Arab village had once stood. Shahak reports that the list is incomplete because it is impossible to find numerous Arab communities. This is because official Israeli data gives the name "tribes" to more than forty Bedouin villages, a ploy that allows them to reduce the number of permanently established Palestinian communities. Some 93% of the land in the State of Israel is now controlled by the Israel Lands Administration, governed by the guidelines of the Jewish National Fund. In order to live on the land, rent it or work it, one must prove Jewish parentage from at least four generations. Even in order to work on a kibbutz (agricultural community), racial purity must be proven. In the case of Christian seasonal workers related to Jewish women seeking kibbutz membership, they must convert to Judaism. Christian candidates for kibbutz membership through conversion," writes Professor Shahak, "must promise to spit when they pass a church or a cross in the future".

The Zionist Nuclear Golem

From the outset, the Zionists decided that the Jewish state, erected on land usurped from the Palestinian people, had to possess the atomic bomb. Roland Perry confirms in *The Fifth Man* that, months after the proclamation of Israel, Victor Rothschild was involved in founding a special department of nuclear physics at a scientific institute in Rehovot, where in 1934 Chaim Weizmann had established the Sieff Institute, which was to become in November 1949 the Weizmann Institute of Science. According to Perry, his goal was to manufacture the atomic weapon for Israel. This plan became the best-kept secret and the most fervent wish of the founders of the new state.

Perry claims that Victor Rothschild was fully involved in atomic espionage through his contacts with Jewish physicists working in nuclear research and reports on several trips by the third Baron Rothschild to the United States, where in 1947 he held meetings with Lewis Lichtenstein Strauss, the chairman of the Atomic Energy Commission (AEC), with whom he had a personal friendship. Lewis Strauss organised a dinner in his honour, to which he invited scientists and military personnel. Rothschild brought up the subject of exchanging information on atomic secrets, which worried the Americans, who wanted to maintain their nuclear monopoly for as long as possible. Strauss, according to Perry, did not allow Rothschild access to AEC information, although the Soviets sometimes obtained it through their spy network.

Victor Rothschild tried to keep abreast of all developments in nuclear research in order to relay information to the Weizmann Institute, where the Dimona nuclear reactor in the Negev desert was already being considered. Under a modified guise of concern about the spread and dangers of nuclear weapons," Perry writes, "he was able to maintain contact with the appropriate scientists around the world. He began this official and legitimate process at the end of World War II, becoming an expert on collateral damage, which enabled him to oversee the Manhattan Project. He continued in the 1950s, even attending conferences on nuclear arms control organised by British atomic scientists." Rothschild briefed Israeli Intelligence leaders, of which he was part as he was a secret Mossad agent, on scientists who could be of use, where the necessary technology might be and how it could be obtained and financed.

The time was ripe for the atomic bomb during the Suez crisis. In Egypt, after the defeat in the war against the Jews, a series of events led to Colonel Gamal Abdel Nasser becoming President of the Republic. On 23 July 1952, a bloodless palace revolution led by a group of officers deposed King Farouq, who went into exile. On 18 July 1953, the Republic was proclaimed, with General Mohamed Naguib as its first president. In November of the same year Colonel Nasser, whom Naguib had appointed vice-president, deposed the general and became the strongman of the Egyptian revolution. He himself drafted a constitution designating him as "Rais" (leader). In 1956 came the moment of the big decision. On 26 July, in a three-hour speech, Nasser announced over the radio the nationalisation of the Suez Canal and its technical installations. The properties of the Anglo-French company that operated it were to be confiscated and compensation paid. An Egyptian state-owned company would manage this important waterway, the country's largest source of revenue, which had hitherto gone to a foreign company. The Egyptian people were entitled to the profits from the operation of the canal and Egypt would be able to pay for the construction of the Aswan Dam.

In Britain and France, the reaction was business as usual. The British press described Nasser as "the Hitler of the Nile". As is well known, it has become commonplace to turn anyone who opposes the designs of the powers that won the war into a new Hitler (the quintessential monster). In France, Nasser's decision was compared to Hitler's troops entering the Rhine. The French foreign minister, Christian Pineau, rushed to London to seek a common strategy. Anthony Eden, the British Prime Minister, asked the United States to put pressure on Egypt to get Nasser to renounce nationalisation. The French and British immediately contemplated military intervention. France, in addition to the usual arms supplies, rushed two dozen of the modern Mystère fighter-bombers to Israel. The US response was not as expected, and France and Britain decided to act on their own.

Egypt appealed to its sovereignty rights over the canal and, since it was still at war with Israel, argued that it had no reason to allow enemy ships to ply the canal, as the British had done with German ships during World War II. The UN démarches proved unsuccessful and on 14 September 1956 the Western technicians left their jobs and were replaced by Egyptian pilots. In addition to the economic importance of the Suez Canal, through which oil flowed, there was the political role that Nasser, a pan-Arabist leader, could play and should be overthrown. Since his rise to power in Egypt, Israel had been considering waging a pre-emptive war and occupying the Gaza Strip, from where the Palestinian fedayeen operated.

Between 1948 and 1956 the Security Council had several times condemned Israel's aggressions against its neighbours, with whom it maintained permanent tension. On 10 October 1956 the Zionists launched an unexpected attack on Jordan that resulted in heavy casualties. Britain had a pact of alliance and mutual support with Jordan, so King Hussein, fearing a major Israeli offensive, asked the British for help. Jordan only obtained condemnation of Israel as an aggressor nation from London through its delegate to the UN Security Council. King Hussein then contemplated allowing Iraqi troops into Jordan to deal with a possible war with Israel and was also willing to join forces with Egypt.

It was in these circumstances that the Zionists decided to offer to wage war for France and Britain. Shimon Peres, then head of the Ministry of Defence, whose chief of staff was Moshe Dayan, had frequent meetings with ministers in the government of Guy Mollet, a socialist who had long been vice-president of the Socialist International. His main contact was Maurice Bourgès-Maunoury, the Minister of Defence, to whom he had access through Abel Thomas, Director General of the Ministry of the Interior, where Bourgès-Maunoury had been Minister before becoming Minister of Defence. Peres' dealings with Bourgès-Maunoury yielded the expected result, as France pledged to supply Israel with the first nuclear reactor for Dimona in exchange for Israel's attack on Egypt.

The following year, for a brief period of three and a half months, between 13 June and 30 September 1957, Bourgès-Maunoury became prime minister of France and had the opportunity to fulfil his commitment to Peres, as his foreign minister, Christian Pineau, signed a top-secret agreement with Shimon Peres and Asher Ben-Nathan, a Mossad agent in Israel's defence ministry. Through this agreement, the French undertook to provide Israel with a powerful 24 megawatt reactor, the technical assistance to know how to operate it, and some uranium. This secret pact was known to only a dozen people, including, according to Perry, Victor Rothschild. The small print of the document included the delivery of equipment that was to enable the Israelis to produce nuclear-fuelled weaponry. In the same year, 1957, French engineers began construction of a six-level underground construction site in the Negev desert, where the two-storey reactor was to be installed. As for Bourgès-Maunoury, after leaving the Presidency of the Council of Ministers, he became Minister of the Interior.

On 14 October 1956, General Maurice Challe and Labour Minister Albert Gazier, commissioned by Prime Minister Guy Mollet, arrived secretly in London by plane and met Prime Minister Eden, to whom they explained the plans they had hatched with the Zionists. The idea was to find out how the British would react if Israel attacked Egypt. The British ambassador in Paris had already informed the British government that France had supplied seventy-five Mystère jets to Israel, which would allow it to dominate the airspace of the Near East. London, without knowing exactly what the deal was about, realised that something very important had been hatched between the French and Israelis. The plan was that Israel would quickly penetrate the Sinai in order to reach the Suez Canal. France and Britain would then present both sides with an ultimatum demanding the withdrawal of troops from the area. Since Egypt would not agree, London and Paris would have the pretext to occupy the canal militarily in order to preserve it from the instability of war. They would thus appear to the public as peacemakers seeking to protect a waterway of international interest. The United States was not informed, but the US secret service informed President Eisenhower on 15 October that the Israelis had mobilised their troops and had more Mystère aircraft at their disposal than the twelve officially supplied by France.

As a diversionary ploy, Israel maintained a dialectical offensive against the Jordanians through the press, thus pointing to Jordan as the future theatre of war. At the same time, the world's attention was focused on Hungary, where on 23 October the Hungarian people had begun a rebellion against communist tyranny, which was to be put down in blood and fire by Soviet troops. In these circumstances, the "Sinai campaign" began on the night of 29-30 October 1956. In addition to air superiority, the Israelis had 250,000 troops at their disposal compared to 75,000 Egyptian troops. The attack took the Egyptians by surprise, as they were expecting the offensive on Jordan. As for the rest of the world, the disappointment was significant in the United States, which had been kept on the sidelines. On 30 October, a telegram was received in Washington from Guy Mollet, explaining that Britain and France had made a "solemn appeal" to Israel and Egypt to withdraw their troops from the canal zone and end hostilities. Shortly afterwards, a message arrived in Washington from British Premier Eden, which included the word "ultimatum" of twelve hours to both sides and the announcement that Franco-British troops would occupy the canal zone.

On 31 October, British bombers took off at dusk from Cyprus and attacked Egyptian air bases, whose aircraft were almost completely destroyed on the ground. Further waves of bombers attacked Cairo, Alexandria, Port Said and Ismailia. On 1 November Egypt broke off diplomatic relations with Britain and France. On 2 November the full General Assembly met in New York. Eisenhower, of course, refrained from condemning the Jews for their aggression against Egypt, but the Americans put forward a ceasefire proposal, calling for Israeli troops to withdraw and for arrangements to be made for the resumption of shipping traffic in the canal. The proposal passed by 65 votes to 5. The USSR voted in favour. After its show of force in Hungary, it would have been absurd to seek to condemn the two US allies at the UN. By the afternoon of 4 November Hungary had been fully occupied and the Sinai Peninsula was in Israeli hands, including Sharm El-Sheikh at the southern tip of the peninsula and the island of Tiran at the entrance to the Gulf of Aqaba. The Gaza Strip, filled with Palestinian refugees, was fully occupied for the first time.

As if the ceasefire did not apply to them and concerned only the Egyptians and Israelis, the British and French, claiming that they could not leave a military vacuum while a UN force was being formed, prepared to intervene as planned. On 5 November London and Paris deployed airborne troops to the area and seized Port Said. On 6 November, more British troops from Malta landed in Port Said and the French occupied Port Fuad. Joint forces began the advance on the west bank of the canal. The fighting was observed by the Israelis from the other side without intervening, as they had already fulfilled their objectives. However, both the Soviets and the Americans had realised that they had an ideal opportunity to end Franco-British influence in the Middle East and played their cards in the crisis in order to take their place in the future.

Moscow warned Eden, Mollet and Ben Gurion that it was prepared to use "all available means" to stop the aggression, a clear reference to nuclear weapons. Bulganin, chairman of the Council of Ministers, proposed to Eisenhower to act in unison to "expel the aggressors"; but the US president rejected the option on the grounds that the UN was already preparing to send troops to guarantee peace. On 6 November, the USSR raised the tone of its threats and, through Khrushchev, declared that it would attack the aggressor countries with rockets. US intelligence noted that many Soviet fighter planes were heading for Syria via Turkey, theoretically with the aim of intervening in the conflict. Aware of the gravity of the situation, Eisenhower told the Committee of National Defence: "If the Soviets attack France and Britain, we will have to go to war". Finding that Washington would not support them in their venture, the French and British were forced to halt operations against the Egyptian forces. By 7 November, a tense peace had settled over the Suez Canal.

Ultimately, France and Britain had miscalculated the scope of their adventure and when the UN expeditionary force, comprising soldiers from Indonesia, India, Brazil, Colombia and the Scandinavian countries, turned up, they had to withdraw from Egypt. Their failure was evident and Nasser, despite the defeat, emerged as the victor, as he succeeded in his aim to have the canal nationalised. The consequences of the debacle were many and varied: Prime Minister Eden was forced to resign and Britain was plunged into a serious political crisis. The Suez Canal, blocked by the sunken ships, was closed for half a year, leading to shortages for European countries and rising oil prices. The American oil trusts benefited from this and increased their sales in Europe. Nasser became a hero to the Arabs and an example of resistance to other countries. The USSR was seen by Arab public opinion as a true friend and was able to lay the foundations for its future influence.

Another winner in the aftermath of the Suez crisis was Israel. Despite being the country that had initiated the aggression, it initially refused to withdraw from Sinai and the Gaza Strip. It was only in March 1957 that pressure from the Americans, who threatened an economic boycott, succeeded in swaying the Zionists. To make them accept the UN decision, as the French and British had done, they had to be offered compensation, including the opening of the Gulf of Aqaba, which the Egyptians were blocking at the Straits of Tiran. They were thus able to turn the port of Eilat, their outlet to the Red Sea at Aqaba, into one of the most modern in the region. The UN guaranteed free access to the port of Eilat and set up a checkpoint with UN troops at Scharm El-Sheikh, a key point in the Gulf.

But the greatest achievement of the Zionist state was the creation of its nuclear Golem, whose existence today is an undeniable threat to the whole world, for it is an element of mass destruction in the hands of a supremacist state where racial hatred is at the basis of education. According to Jewish law, only the sacrifice of a Jew is a sin, so gentiles can be slaughtered like animals. Talmudic law states emphatically that only the Jew is human and that non-Jews are beasts in human form. More than half a century after its manufacture, the Zionist nuclear Golem still exists in hiding, unchecked by the international community. The equating of Israel's nuclear power with the Golem is a metaphor used to designate the danger of an uncontrolled monster.

The legend of the Golem is currently very popular among Israelis. It is likely that Mary Shelley, the author of *Frankenstein*, had it in mind when writing her famous novel. Its origins date back to the 16th century, when Rabbi Judah Loew created the Golem to defend the Jewish community in Prague from attack because, as elsewhere in Europe, Czech Jews were accused of practising ritual crimes and the emperor was asked to expel them. Rabbi Loew made a figure out of clay and inserted a scroll with the secret name of God into its mouth. Thus was born the Golem, an automaton of enormous strength that obeyed its creator. During the Sabbath, the rabbi would take the scroll out of its mouth and immobilise it. One Sabbath he forgot to do so and marched to the synagogue. Soon neighbours arrived, terrified that the Golem, enraged, was tearing everything apart. When Loew arrived at his house, he found it in ruins, his animals had been slaughtered in the courtyard. The rabbi managed to hypnotise the monster and extract the scroll from its mouth. The Golem fell and Loew never encouraged it again. According to legend, the Golem is still kept in the attic of the Prague synagogue.

The world learned that Israel had been making atomic bombs for a quarter of a century thanks to the testimony of Mordechai Vanunu, the Israeli nuclear technician who, after converting to Christianity, revealed in 1986 to *The London Sunday Times* the secret that the political elites had known since John F. Kennedy. Vanunu was kidnapped by the Mossad in Rome, tried and sentenced to eighteen years in prison, of which he spent eleven in solitary confinement. After serving his sentence, he tried to leave the country, but was not allowed to do so. On 22 April 2004, he applied to Norway for a passport and political asylum. On 11 November 2004, three weeks after he told *al-Hayat*, a London-based Arabic-language newspaper, that he believed John F. Kennedy had been assassinated because he tried to stop Israel from making nuclear weapons, he was arrested by Israeli police on the premises of the Anglican church in Jerusalem, where he had been living since his release. Since then he has been confined to a flat and cannot leave the country.

In February 2015, after more than five decades of feigning ignorance, the US Department of Defence finally released a secret 1987 report by the Institute for Defense Analyses confirming that Israel possesses atomic bombs. While all countries have been obliged to sign the Nuclear Non-Proliferation Treaty (NPT), which means that they are subject to regular inspections by the International Energy Agency, Israel has never signed it and, consequently, its nuclear Golem has never been inspected, no one knows what its destructive power is, what its dimensions are. Ever since Vanunu warned of the existence of the monster and the danger it posed to the world, Israel has acted in this area, as in all others, outside international law. Only President Kennedy dared to stand up to Zionism, and we know how that ended: on 22 November 1963 he was assassinated in Dallas.

Avner Cohen, a professor specialising in Israel's political strategy and nuclear history, published *Israel and the Bomb* in 1998, a work that caused him many problems. Since then, this work has been an inescapable reference. Cohen amply demonstrates that President Kennedy confronted David Ben Gurion and made it clear that under no circumstances would he consent to Israel becoming a nuclear state. Cohen's book implies that the Zionist state would probably not be a nuclear power today if Kennedy had still been alive. On 16 June 1963, JFK sent a letter to Ben Gurion which, according to the Israeli professor, contained an explicit and unusually harsh message: the threat that an unsatisfactory solution on the nuclear issue would jeopardise the US government's commitment and assistance to Israel. Since Kennedy's death, no other US president has ever again exerted the slightest pressure on Israel's nuclear programme.

Given that so far no one has ever been able to see the Zionist nuclear Golem or have the slightest control over it, it is clear that the world is virtually hijacked by an unacceptable threat. The fear that some Talmudic fanatic, drunk on racial hatred, will come to power in Tel Aviv and activate the monster is real and permanent. Dr. Martin van Creveld, a Rotterdam-born Jew, professor until 2007 at the Hebrew University of Jerusalem and later at Tel Aviv University, an expert in military history and military theory, made some extremely worrying statements to the prestigious Dutch weekly *Elsevier* in September 2003. The interview took place in Jerusalem and was conducted by Ferry Biedermann. The interviewer asked about a plan to deport all Palestinians and Martin van Creveld replied that it was quite possible. These two questions and answers followed:

> "Biedermann: Do you think the world would allow this kind of ethnic cleansing?
> Creveld: It depends on who does it and how fast it happens. We have several hundred nuclear warheads and missiles and we can launch them against targets in all directions, perhaps even Rome. Most European capitals are targets for our air force.
> Biedermann: Would Israel then become a rogue state?
> Creveld: Let me quote General Moshe Dayan. Israel must be like a rabid dog, too dangerous to be disturbed'. I think it would all be futile at this point. We will try to prevent things from going to this extreme if possible. Our armed forces, without however, are not the thirtieth strongest in the world, but the second or third strongest. We have the capacity to take the world with us. And I can assure you that this will happen, before Israel goes down."

Of course, despite Creveld's execrable assumption that Israel contemplates European capitals as possible targets, the greatest risk is to Arab and Muslim countries in the Middle East and Near East, most of which have suffered the consequences of the Zionist state's aggressive policies since 1948. Israel Shahak, whose views we hold in the highest regard, confirms that Israel does not seek peace, nor has it ever sought it. In 1997 Professor Shahak published the book *Open Secrets: Israeli Foreign and Nuclear Policies*, in which he warns against the myth of the supposed differences between the secular Zionist parties. Shahak argues that the Israeli lobby in the United States supports Israel's expansionist policies in order to impose itself throughout the Middle East. Shahak points out that Israel's nuclear policy constitutes a real danger that few dare to imagine.

Part 4
In the United States, "Witches".
In China and Korea, Communism

"I think that the Communist conspiracy is simply one branch of a much larger conspiracy". With these words of Bella Dodd, a member of the National Committee of the Communist Party USA until her defection in 1949, Willard Cleon Skousen begins his work *The Naked Capitalist* (1962). Dr. Bella Dodd published *School of Darkness* in 1954, in which she acknowledged that the goals of communism were the attainment of power and the destruction of Christian civilisation, although millions of naive idealists were convinced that its purpose was to help the poor. Cleon Skousen worked in the FBI under Edgar Hoover (FBI Director from 1935 to 1972) during the years when the extent of Communist penetration of the Administration was discovered. John Edgar Hoover reported the extent of the conspiracy to President Truman by submitting several memos. Skousen confirms in his book that the FBI director was astonished that despite his reports, the Truman administration did not react.

In February 1950, when China had already fallen to Communism and the Soviet Union had its own atomic bomb thanks to treachery and espionage, Senator Joseph "Joe" McCarthy appeared on the scene and began a titanic struggle and denounced the deep Communist penetration of the Administration. McCarthy arguably took over from the seven-year chairman of the Congressional Committee on Un-American Activities, Martin Dies, whom Roosevelt famously advised to forget the Communists and focus on the Nazis and Fascists. Joe McCarthy (1912-1957), an honest and committed patriot, today figures on the dunghill of his country's history. The official historiography has managed to sully his name and uses the term "McCarthyism" to refer to a dark period in the history of the United States. Joe McCarthy is portrayed the world over as a hysterical man who unleashed a "witch hunt", an "anti-communist crusade", without evidence. However, the Venona documents and other research prove beyond doubt that the communist conspiracy was far-reaching and that Senator McCarthy was right, and he should be removed from the blacklist of history and rehabilitated as a hero who had the courage to stand up to powerful occult forces that he himself could not have imagined.

The defections of Elizabeth Bentley and Whittaker Chambers, the two Communist spies, were instrumental in enabling the FBI to begin to unravel the web of Communist espionage in the United States. Chambers, whose defection in 1938 is linked to the struggles between Trotskyists and Stalinists, and Elisabeth Bentley, who in August 1945 offered herself to the FBI to act as a double agent, testified in 1948 before the Congressional Un-

American Activities Committee and their testimonies triggered the persecution and arrest of numerous Communist agents. Some of the characters and events that will be discussed in this fourth section of the chapter have already appeared in the course of our work, but we will now give them the space they deserve, so that their true dimension can be more fully understood. Harry Dexter White, Alger Hiss and Harry Hopkins held such trusted positions in the Roosevelt and Truman governments that it is hard to believe that their actions were not known to their superiors. The most incredible case is that of Dexter White, the Lithuanian-born Jewish economist who had joined the Treasury Department in 1934 under Jacob Viner, another Jewish economist who was a personal adviser to Henry Morgenthau.

Harry Dexter White as head of the International Monetary Fund

In studying the Morgenthau Plan, the decisive role played in its drafting by Dexter White and his team of Jewish communists has been seen. It has also been pointed out that the Morgenthau Plan for the de-industrialisation of Germany was ultimately designed to create an economic vacuum in Europe which could be exploited by the Soviet Union. White's role in the decisive post-war years and the discovery of his espionage activities on behalf of communism will now be discussed. On 30 April 1946, almost six months after being informed by the FBI that Harry Dexter White was a Communist agent, President Truman sent him a letter congratulating him on his service to the nation and on his confirmation by the Senate as Executive Director of the International Monetary Fund. In this letter, Truman said he regretted his departure from the Treasury Department. My regret is tempered," he wrote, "by the knowledge that you are leaving the Treasury only to assume new duties at the International Monetary Fund.... In that position you will be able to carry forward the work which you so ably began at Bretton Woods.... I am sure that in your new position you will add merit to your already distinguished career at the Treasury."

Seven and a half years later, on 6 November 1953, US Attorney General Herbert Brownell Jr. publicly declared in a speech in Chicago that former President Truman had appointed Harry Dexter White to a position of the highest importance knowing without a doubt that White was a communist agent. Naturally, this allegation caused a considerable stir. In order to defend himself against the Attorney General's allegation, Truman appeared on 16 November on a television programme broadcast simultaneously to the entire nation by all four of the country's major television companies. The next day, 17 November, Brownell appeared before the U.S. Senate Investigating Committee and gave an explanation of the charge made against Truman on 6 November. On the same day, J. Edgar Hoover, Director of the Federal

Bureau of Investigation (FBI), also appeared before the Committee chaired by Senator Joe McCarthy and gave a detailed report on the matter. Both Brownell and Hoover were extremely harsh on former President Truman and made well-founded recriminations against him. Attorney General Brownell also responded on 17 November 1953 to former President Truman's televised address to the nation. Brownell made a report to the Senate Subcommittee on Internal Security. An excerpt of this speech is given by Léon de Poncins in *State Secrets*. The following text is taken from that work:

> "Since April 1953, this subcommittee has been holding a series of hearings for the purpose of exposing the plans of Communist agents infiltrating the United States Government. The work of this subcommittee has rigorously documented the result of the successful penetration of Communist espionage into our Government during World War II and subsequently.... The Justice Department has been preoccupied since the new Administration took office with cleaning up the government. One of the most important and vital problems is to remove all persons of questionable loyalty and to prevent future communist infiltration of the United States Government. Among other speeches and articles, I gave a speech in Chicago on 6 November in which I publicly discussed the problem of Communist infiltration of the Government and the steps taken by the Eisenhower Administration to deal with the problem. In that speech I referred to the Harry Dexter White case and the way it was handled by the Truman administration on the basis of the established facts and the reports of the Justice Department.
> It has been said that I hinted at the possibility that the former US president was disloyal. I did not intend that this conclusion should be drawn.... I specifically said that I thought that the ignorance of the evidence in the White case was due to the refusal to face the case on the part of non-Communists in positions of responsibility and the persistent delusion that Communism in the United States Government was a red herring, and that the manner in which the proven facts about White's disloyalty had been ignored is typical of the blindness suffered by the former Administration in this matter. When this subcommittee completes its investigation, I believe it will conclude, as I did, that there was a refusal on the part of Mr. Truman and others around him to face the facts and a misconception that Communist espionage in high places in the Government was a mirage. And I think will conclude that this attitude may have done great damage to our nation.
> The Truman administration was informed at least as early as December 1945 that there were two spy rings operating within the Government.... White took over his duties and became the U.S. Executive Director of the International Monetary Fund on 1 May 1946. What did the White House know about his espionage activities before this date? On 4 December 1945, the FBI transmitted to Brigadier General Harry H. Vaughan, military assistant to the President, a report on the general aspects of Soviet

espionage in the United States.... It was a secret and very important report of some seventy-one pages. It covered the whole subject of Soviet espionage in the United States during and after World War II. It specified many names and described numerous Soviet espionage organisations. Harry Dexter White and the spy ring of which he was a member were among those profiled in the report. No responsible person who read it can deny that the summary was an adequate warning of the risk posed by White's appointment to the International Monetary Fund or his continuation in government.

Copies of this report were sent to a group of government and Truman administration officials, including the Attorney General. It would be difficult to understand how, under any circumstances, a document on such sensitive and dangerous matters could not have been brought to the attention of the President. But in addition, I have here a letter from J. Edgar Hoover to General Vaughan dated November 8, 1945. As you know, General Vaughan has testified before this subcommittee that by agreement with Mr. Truman, when the FBI had information considered of importance to the President, it was referred to him. Vaughan testified that he knew that such a report was submitted to the President.

The attorney general then read the letter in which the FBI chief drew Vaughan's attention to the importance of the accompanying report. The document listed the names of the spies who held positions of responsibility in the government. Among others mentioned were Harry Dexter White, Gregory Silvermaster, George Silverman, Frank Coe, Laughlin Currie, Victor Perlo, Maurice Halperin. All of them, except Laughlin Currie, were Jewish and would be denounced in 1948 by Wittaker Chambers, which confirmed that the information contained in the 1945 memo to the White House was correct. This document stated that Dexter White had acted since 1942 as a spy. Edgar Hoover noted that if White was appointed director of the International Monetary Fund he could exert great influence in all matters relating to international finance, adding that he could not keep him under surveillance because the offices of the International Monetary Fund were considered neutral territory and consequently FBI agents could not enter them. Herbert Brownell reported that handwritten reports by Dexter White to the Soviets had been recovered in the autumn of 1948 and were in the possession of the Justice Department. The Attorney General ended his remarks by referring to former President Truman's appearance on major television channels:

> "...However, in the light of Mr. Truman's speech on television last night, it now seems to be admitted that on February 6, 1946, the day White's appointment was confirmed by the Senate, Mr. Truman had read the most important of the reports, to which I have referred, and that shortly thereafter, although he had the legal right to ask that the appointment be

revoked, he signed it and allowed him to take office as of May 1 with full knowledge of the facts referred to by the FBI. It is of course extraordinary to learn from Mr. Truman, in the light of his latest statements, that he signed White's appointment with the idea that it might assist in his arrest.... It seems to me even more extraordinary to know that Mr. Truman was aware in 1946 that a spy ring was operating within his own administration, when for so many years since then he has been telling the American people exactly the opposite. It certainly seems to me that this explanation of White's appointment - that is, that he was appointed and allowed to remain in office for more than a year to help the FBI catch him as a spy - raises more questions than it answers."

The entire US press followed the hearings of these high-ranking officials before the Senate Internal Security Subcommittee in detail and gave full coverage of their statements in their editions. The texts reproduced by Leon de Poncins in *State Secrets* are regularly taken from journalistic sources. Thus, for example, the Paris edition of the *New York Herald Tribune* reported on 19 November 1953 on Edgar Hoover's statement of the previous day. The FBI director confirmed that as early as the beginning of November 1945, Elisabeth Bentley and Whittaker Chambers had already agreed with Harry Dexter White's denunciation and that the investigations had been able to prove that the information of the two communist defectors was correct. Hoover claimed that when they learned that, despite his memorandum, White's name had been sent to the Senate for confirmation of his appointment as Executive Director of the IMF, they decided to submit to President Truman a new 28-page document with the information consolidated from Bentley's and Chambers' statements, which was delivered to General Vaughan on February 4, 1946. The FBI Director told the subcommittee that between November 8, 1945, and July 24, 1946, seven communiqués on espionage activities in which White's name was particularly mentioned had been delivered to the White House. During the same period, two reports on Soviet espionage were sent to the Treasury Department and six others on the same subject were sent to the Attorney General. Hoover also referred to Virginius Frank Coe, another of Morgenthau and White's men in the Treasury Department who was Secretary of the IMF from June 1946 to December 1952. The FBI director recalled that Frank Coe had invoked the Fifth Amendment and refused to answer the subcommittee's questions concerning White, which had led to his dismissal from the IMF.[22]

---

[22] The Fifth Amendment to the US Constitution provides that no one shall be compelled to testify against himself or herself, not only in trials but also in police interrogations. However, invoking the Fifth Amendment before a Congressional or Senate investigating committee and refusing to answer is tantamount to acknowledging involvement in the matter in question, often with political repercussions.

One of the copies of Edgar Hoover's report also found its way into the hands of Secretary of State James F. Byrnes, who, he later recounted, went to see Truman the same day he read the report, to whom he expressed his dismay and asked what he intended to do. According to Byrnes, the President said that he too was shocked by the information. Byrnes suggested withdrawing the nomination even though it had already been confirmed by the Senate. Truman could have either rejected the nomination or demanded White's resignation. Byrnes suggested both possibilities, but the President did not follow his advice.

The cases of Harry Dexter White and Frank Coe are extremely significant, for they confirm the words of Bella Dodd and what we have been arguing in this work about the true nature of international communism as an instrument of the illuminati bankers. Dexter White was not simply a communist spy, but the agent of a wider conspiracy whose aim was the establishment of a global or international power. If this is not so, how can it be explained that White was one of the founders of the World Bank and to a large extent the father of the International Monetary Fund, for it was he who as early as 1942 drafted the first draft of this financial body. Both institutions were approved at the Bretton Woods Conference and are the pillars on which the economic system was built. The form and functions of the IMF were determined in 1944 at Bretton Woods, where White was the economist who, thanks to the political and economic power of the United States, was able to impose his plan on Keynes'. It was White who argued that the IMF should be a dollar-based institution. Proof that Dexter White was not an agent of Stalin but of the Hidden Power that sought control of the Soviet Union after the war was his insistence that the USSR should be part of the IMF even though its economic principles ran counter to commercial and financial freedom. Although Keynes and others opposed the Soviet Union's participation in the Bretton Woods Conference, White succeeded in getting it invited. Stalin, however, proved again that he was not the man the international financiers wanted at the helm of the USSR, for a year later he decided that his country would not join the International Monetary Fund.

The Venona documents fully demonstrate that Harry Dexter White was what is known in professional circles as "an agent of influence". He was part of the circle of Nathan Gregory Silvermaster, a Russian-born Jewish economist who was with White at Bretton Woods and led a group of spies who operated primarily within the Treasury Department and the Economic War Council. Elisabeth Bentley, who had already informed the FBI in 1945 that Dexter White was a Soviet agent, testified in 1948 before the House of Representatives Committee that White passed information to the Soviets through Silvermaster. The Venona documents establish that White, whose code names "Lawyer", "Richard" and "Jurist" changed over time, passed information during World War II to Soviet Intelligence, whose top man was Lavrenti Beria, the Jewish agent who would preferably succeed Stalin.

Silvermaster, "Robert", used White's power and influence in the Treasury to infiltrate more Soviet agents, one of whom was Harold Glasser, "Rouble", who operated within another spy ring whose leader was another Jewish Communist, Victor Perlo, so Silvermaster requested that Glasser be reassigned to his group. On 31 March 1945, Secretary of State Stettinius invited White to join the US delegation to San Francisco for the Founding Conference of the United Nations. White then passed on information about the US delegation's discussions.

On 19 June 1947, Harry Dexter White resigned as Executive Director of the IMF. President Truman wrote him a letter in which he expressed his high appreciation and regard for his work and added that he "would not hesitate to call on him from time to time for assistance." Shortly thereafter, on 15 August 1947, White was questioned for the first time by the FBI. He admitted then that he had known Silvermaster since 1934. He acknowledged that, as government employees, they were colleagues and that they met frequently at Silvermaster's house, where they played instruments: Silvermaster, the guitar; his wife Helen, the piano; William Ullman, another Treasury official who lived with the Silvermasters, played the drums; and White, the mandolin. White stated that Silvermaster had never asked him for confidential information and that "it would be a surprise and a great shock to learn that Silvermaster was involved in espionage." In August 1947, the NSA (National Security Agency) had not yet cracked the Venona code, whose intercepts would confirm that what Elisabeth Bentley had revealed was absolutely true. Finally, on 13 August 1948, Harry Dexter White testified before the House Un-American Activities Committee (HUAC) and denied Chambers' and Bentley's accusations. Shortly after testifying, White suffered a heart attack and died on 16 August 1948.

The cases of Harry Hopkins and Alger Hiss

Harry Hopkins, married to a Hungarian immigrant of Jewish origin, Ethel Gross, with whom he had three children, died on 29 January 1946. There was no suspicion of his loyalty to the United States during his lifetime. Appointed by Franklin D. Roosevelt to administer the Lend-Lease programme, an instrument that allowed massive military and economic aid to be provided to the Allies, Hopkins became an all-powerful figure during the war. Particularly significant is the fact that aid to the USSR through the Lend-Lease programme was provided unconditionally through the intervention of Hopkins, President Roosevelt's most trusted confidant who lived in the White House from early 1940 until December 1943. His case seems to be a witch's case, for it is absurd to accept that Hopkins could have done what he did for communism and the USSR without arousing anyone's suspicions. No doubt this would have been impossible without Roosevelt's constant support. It would be necessary to know to what extent the "Big Boy" (as some American communists nicknamed FDR) was aware of all the manoeuvres and actions of his right-hand man.

It is only recently that it has been concluded that Harry Hopkins was a Soviet agent. The fact that he died in 1946 without being discovered meant that his activities simply passed into history. It should be noted that, despite having been decrypted in 1948, the Venona documents only became accessible when the NSA began publishing them in 1995. It was after this date that several historians and researchers began to write about them, and it is surprising to note that most of them agree that Harry Hopkins was agent "19". Unanimity is not absolute: John Earl Haynes and Harvey Klehr, authors of *Venona: Decoding Soviet Espionage in America*, believe that "19" was Laurence Duggan of the State Department. Since their thesis is in the minority, we will stick to the conclusions of Herbert Romerstein and Eric Breindel in *The Venona Secrets*, which are shared by military historian Eduard Mark and M. Stanton Evans, among other authors who have published books on Venona at the time.

In any case, it is pertinent to know some very interesting information before reviewing the data that point to Hopkins as agent "19". On 1 February 1943, the company Chemator Incorporation received an order in New York from the Soviet Government for 100 kilos of uranium oxide, 100 kilos of uranium nitrate and 11 kilos of uranium metal. The company had already supplied small quantities of chemicals to the USSR under the Lend-Lease programme. This was the first time the Soviets intended to buy uranium, so the company asked the authorities for permission. In March, the Soviets ordered tons of uranium. Almost seven years later, on 5 December 1949, shortly after the Communists detonated their first atomic bomb, Major George Racey Jordan, who had helped ship the uranium material to the Soviet Union, first from Newark (New Jersey) and then from Great Falls (Montana), testified before the HUAC (House Un-American Activities Committee), which was investigating the shipment of uranium to the USSR in connection with the atomic espionage affair. Jordan confirmed the uranium shipments and testified that Harry Hopkins told him by telephone to speed up the shipments. Two days later, on 7 December 1949, Lieutenant General Leslie Groves, in charge of the Manhattan Project, also testified before HUAC. General Groves testified in Congress that he complained to the executives working on the Lend-Lease program, who told him that "there was great pressure on us to go under the Lend-Lease program, ostensibly to give the Russians everything they could conceive of. There was great pressure to give them these uranium materials. We didn't want this material shipped," Groves insisted, "but they (the executives) came back and back. As is well known, Hopkins, FDR's friend and adviser, ran the Lend-Lease programme.

In 1952, Major Jordan published *From Major Jordan's Diaries*, *which* contains his statement to HUAC. Jordan accuses Hopkins of having acted against US interests to help the Soviets, to whom he passed nuclear secrets. The book claims that in 1943 Harry Hopkins secretly sent a plane to Russia with black suitcases containing documents related to the atomic bomb. Major Jordan reiterates in his testimony before the Congressional Committee about several deliveries of uranium ordered by Hopkins without being recorded in written records. According to experts, the mixtures of refined uranium shipped to the USSR were more than sufficient to produce an atomic explosion. Despite the appearance of this book and the scandal it caused, no one thought at the time that Hopkins was a Soviet agent. It is very difficult to explain how it is possible that in 1943, in the midst of the atomic bomb-making process, when the FBI was suspicious of Oppenheimer and other scientists working at Los Alamos, Hopkins was able to proceed with the delivery of uranium to the Soviets despite the objections of the military authorities. This fact alone should have been enough to remove his confidence. Nevertheless, Hopkins remained indispensable to Roosevelt, with whom he was at Yalta, and, had he not died, to Truman, whom he helped prepare for the Potsdam Conference.

According to the Venona documents, the Jew Isaac Akhmerov, an 'illegal rezident' in the United States during World War II, was Harry Hopkins' contact. Akhmerov, an OGPU agent since 1930, had travelled to the United States after serving in China in 1934. His wife Elena joined him; but in 1936 Akhmerov met Helen Lowry, granddaughter of Earl Browder, the leader of the Communist Party USA, who had been recruited by Soviet Intelligence. Helen was commissioned to assist Akhmerov in a house in Washington that was to serve as a safe meeting place. In 1939 they were married. Helen, Isaac Akhmerov's former wife, returned to Moscow, where she became secretary to the ominipotent Beria, supreme chief of the police and secret service (NKVD) from 1938. The newlyweds were recalled to Moscow in the summer of the same year, where Helen was granted Soviet citizenship. In September 1941, shortly after Hopkins' first trip to Moscow, they were both sent back to the United States. Isaac Akhmerov re-established the illegal rezidentura and became the chief spy in this organisation of secret agents. In December 1945 Helen and Isaac Akhmerov returned to the USSR.

One of the deciphered messages that researchers consider to be decisive in establishing that Harry Hopkins worked for the Soviets was issued by Akhmerov from New York on 29 May 1943. In it he revealed that "19" had reported on discussions between Roosevelt and Churchill at which he was present. Military historian Eduard Mark refers to this meeting between the American president and the British premier as the "Trident Conference". It was a secret conference, as there are no records of the discussions in the official archives of the State Department. Significantly, only Soviet reports of it are available. Eduard Mark argues convincingly that no one but Hopkins could be trusted enough by Roosevelt to be present at a secret, tête à tête meeting with Churchill.

In any case, Hopkins did not need to cover up his relations with the Soviets, as his leading position in official relations with the USSR allowed him many legal, face-to-face encounters. Since 1942 he had publicly maintained intimate contact with General A. I. Belyaev, chairman of the Soviet Government Purchase Commission. Two Venona messages from Washington to Moscow sent in March and April 1943 contained messages from Hopkins which Belyaev passed on to his bosses. Hopkins was in regular contact with Andrei Gromyko, who in August 1943 replaced Litvinov as USSR ambassador to the United States. After Yalta and Roosevelt's death, Truman sent Hopkins to Moscow in May 1945 to meet with Stalin. Under Secretary of State Charles Bohlen, considered a diplomat close to Hopkins, made a written record of the meeting. Instead of pressing for free elections in Poland, as supposedly intended by the US, Hopkins told Stalin that "the United States would desire a Poland friendly to the Soviet Union and in fact desired friendly countries along the Soviet borders". To which Stalin replied, "If that is so, we can easily understand each other in relation to Poland."

As for the case of Alger Hiss, a protégé of Supreme Court Justice Felix Frankfurter, FDR was warned before World War II that he was an important spy for the Soviet Union. The information came from Whittaker Chambers, who had defected since 1938. Roosevelt rejected the allegations and would not even investigate them. In 1948 Chambers testified before the Congressional Committee and it then became definitively clear that one of the most prominent men in the State Department, President Roosevelt's trusted adviser at Yalta, who played an important role in the work for the founding of the UN, was a communist agent. Whether Alger Hiss was Jewish or not is in doubt. In one of the tapes used against President Richard Nixon in the Watergate case, Nixon says: "The only non-Jews in the Communist conspiracy were Chambers and Hiss. Many believe Hiss was. He may have been in part, but he was not in a religious sense. The only non-Jews. Everybody else was Jewish. And all hell broke loose on us."

In *Blacklisted by History*, the aforementioned work on the struggle of the ill-fated Senator McCarthy, M. Stanton Evans writes: "If White and Oppenheimer were proof of indifference to security standards, the Alger Hiss case was even more so. This was, of course, the most famous of all espionage cases. It was also the case which demonstrated the willingness of the Truman administration not only to ignore security in Intelligence, but to harass the witnesses who supplied it." This attitude of the Administration was echoed by the press, which began to launch a campaign that eventually equated the persecution of Communist spies and agents with a witch-hunt. Not everyone in the government, however, shared the immobility. In early 1946, after receiving continuing FBI reports based on the testimony of Chambers and Bentley, Secretary of State Byrnes realised that Hiss had to be removed from his Department, prompting the resignation of the Soviet spy. However, when in the summer of 1948 the two defectors' statements reached the public eye, the White House and the Justice Department, instead of attacking and discrediting Hiss, turned to harassing Chambers.

The strategy against Chambers was recorded in a White House memo signed by George Elsey, assistant to President Truman. On 16 August 1948, Elsey addressed to Clark Clifford, Truman's adviser introduced to the White House by Samuel Rosenman, the report with the guidelines agreed upon in a meeting with Attorney General Tom C. Clark. It suggested that the Justice Department "should make every effort to establish whether Whittaker Chambers is guilty of perjury". The next point called for "Investigation of Chambers' confinement in mental institution". In other words, it was suggested that it be investigated whether Chambers had been confined in a mental institution. On 20 August, the FBI dismissed the thesis that Chambers might be insane. In a letter to Attorney General Clark, Edgar Hoover reported, "With regard to Whittaker Chambers, there is no indication in the files of the 'Bureau' or in the records of the New York office that Chambers was ever committed." Despite all this, the effort to discredit Chambers and bring charges against him persisted; but in November 1948 he produced before HUAC papers and microfilms which constituted irrefutable evidence that Hiss was lying. These documents were instrumental in subsequently sending Alger Hiss to prison.

Nevertheless, the efforts to save Hiss and convict Chambers did not cease: the deputy attorney general, Alexander Campbell, reacted to Chambers' testimony before the Congressional Committee by sending a note stating: "It would be desirable that an immediate investigation be made in order to verify whether Chambers has committed perjury. In this connection, photostatic copies of these documents should be obtained together with a copy of the testimony given by Chambers". Stanton Evans indicates that more such notes came into Hoover's possession. He has located them in various volumes of the FBI's Hiss-Chambers file. Another dated 2 December 1948 insisted that the Justice Department wanted "an immediate investigation by the 'Bureau' to determine whether Chambers had committed perjury." After instructing his agents to proceed as directed, Hoover noted in the margin, "I cannot understand why so much effort is being made to incriminate Chambers in order to exonerate Hiss." He later remarked again, "I wonder why they don't act against Hiss as well." Stanton Evans can't help a sarcastic aside and writes: "It was - is - an excellent question."

The Congressional Committee was chaired by Robert Stripling, who had the backing of a Republican who would become US President years later, Richard Nixon, "assassinated" by the press in the Watergate frame-up[23]. Both were determined to uncover the truth. When Stripling and Nixon

---

[23] The Nixon administration tried to pressure Israel to comply with UN resolutions and withdraw from territories occupied during the Six Day War. After the Yom Kippur War

discovered the Administration's plans, they protested indignantly and warned that such an attitude was outrageous. Thus Truman and company had to resign themselves. Senator Joe McCarthy discovered years later in his investigations that the State Department had unfavourable information on Hiss as early as 1946, which confirmed Chambers' allegations. On 16 December 1948 Alger Hiss, charged with perjury, pleaded not guilty. His first trial was declared a mistrial on 10 July 1949. He was retried and convicted of perjury on 20 January 1950 and received a five-year prison sentence. Hiss was released from prison in November 1954. Despite so much evidence, Truman continued to defend the communist spy to the end. In 1956, *U.S. News & World Report* reprinted a television interview with the former President in which Truman insisted that Nixon had investigated "a red herring". The interviewer asked him the question: "Do you believe that Hiss was a Communist spy? His answer was, "No, I don't."

Venona proved that Chambers had not lied and Hiss did. According to Chambers, in the autumn of 1936 a new Soviet agent appeared on the scene from whom he received orders. This individual introduced himself as "Peter"; although Chambers later learned from Walter Krivitsky, who as we know fled to the United States in late 1938, that Peter was in fact Boris Yakovlevich Bukov, known as Boris Bykov and also "Sasha", a Jew who had worked with Krivistsky in the GRU (Military Intelligence Service), so it

---

in 1973, King Feisal of Saudi Arabia embargoed oil shipments to the US, Canada and the Netherlands in retaliation for their support for Israel. Nixon understood that allowing the Jewish lobby to direct foreign policy was against his country's interests and in early 1974 he defended a compromise reached with Yasser Arafat for a peace agreement. He sent General Vernon Walters to the area, who returned to Washington convinced that the Palestinians accepted the mini-state formula and wanted to live in peace with Israel. Secretary of State Kissinger derailed the talks and prevented Walters' future contacts with the PLO. In June of the same year, shortly after Kisinger sabotaged the Nixon-PLO dialogue, the US president travelled to the Middle East. Nixon's visit to Saudi Arabia ended with what diplomats considered a sensational message. In his farewell speech, Feisal made an unexpected reference to Nixon's problems in Watergate and domestic politics, breaking the custom that a leader of one country never interferes in the domestic affairs of another. Here are the king's exact words from the official Saudi Ministry of Information statement: "What is important is that our friends in the US are smart enough to support you, to stand by you, Mr President, in your noble efforts, almost unprecedented in the history of mankind, efforts whose aim is to secure peace and justice in the world.... And anyone who opposes you, whether at home or abroad, or who opposes us, your friends in this part of the world, obviously has one purpose in mind, and that is to bring about the division of the world, the misguided polarisation of the world, to create a discord that will never lead to tranquillity and peace in the world." Nixon reportedly told his interlocutor that he was prepared to explain to his people that Israel and its American friends controlled foreign policy. On 9 August Richard Nixon resigned under pressure from the Watergate scandal and on 25 March 1975 King Feisal was assassinated. The Saudis interrogated Ibn Musa'ed, the assassin, for ten weeks and are known to have found out that he had a girlfriend in America who was a Mossad agent, who disappeared without trace after the assassination.

is very likely that he was a Trotskyite. By the time Bykov arrived, Chambers had only received documents on three occasions, but with the new agent, who wanted to meet personally some of the infiltrators within the Roosevelt administration, the deliveries were expedited. In the spring of 1937 Alger Hiss travelled to New York to meet Bykov. Chambers picked up Hiss near the Brooklyn Bridge station and they travelled by train to Brooklyn, where they met Bykov near the Prospect Theatre. The three took the underground and then a taxi to make sure they were not being followed and travelled to Chinatown in Manhattan, where they ate at the Port Arhur restaurant. Since Bykov's English was poor, he spoke in German and Chambers translated his words for Hiss, who pledged to increase State Department document releases. Chambers explained to the FBI how the transmission of materials worked: on pre-arranged nights, he would visit Hiss at his 30th Street home, where Hiss would take the papers out of a zippered suitcase and put them in another zippered suitcase and take them to his flat, where he would photograph or microfilm the documents with a Leica camera and other equipment supplied by Bykov. The originals were returned to Hiss and the microfilms and photocopies were handed over to Bykov. Some of these documents retained by Chambers were provided to the FBI when he defected.

A message from the Wahington Rezidentura sent to Moscow on 30 March 1945 was decrypted by the NSA in 1969. It shows that Alger Hiss, "Ales", was then in contact with Isaac Akhmerov, the illegal rezident to whom Harry Hopkins also passed information. This message confirmed that Hiss had remained linked to military intelligence (GRU) while all the other infiltrated spies had been transferred to the NKVD. After the Yalta Conference, where Hiss acted as a special adviser to President Roosevelt and received much military information, he travelled to Moscow with Secretary of State Stettinius, where he was reportedly officially decorated by Vyshinsky. Alger Hiss's wife, Priscilla, and his brother Donald, also a State Department official, were also Soviet spies. Alger Hiss died in 1996. On 30 December 1996, Herbert Rommerstein and Eric Breindel, authors of *The Venona Secrets*, published an article in *The New Republic* entitled "Hiss: Still Guilty" in which they provided new evidence of Alger Hiss's guilt.

"Such an immense conspiracy": China's surrender to communism

Among the most momentous events of the decisive post-war years, the surrender of China to communism is perhaps the most significant. On 14 June 1951 Joe McCarthy delivered a lengthy speech to the Senate,, in which he bitterly denounced the events of October 1949. Here is a brief excerpt that is highly significant of the senator's indignation and bewilderment:

"How can we account for our present situation unless we think that men in high positions in this Government are concerted to throw us into disaster? This must be the fruit of a great conspiracy, a conspiracy on a scale so immense as to dwarf any such enterprise in history. A conspiracy of such black infamy, that, when it is finally exposed, its directors will forever deserve the curse of all honest people.... What can be made of this unbroken series of decisions and actions that have contributed to the strategy of defeat? They cannot be attributed to incompetence. If Marshall were simply stupid, the laws of probability would indicate that part of his decisions would have served the interests of this country...".

In order to adequately explain what happened in China, it is necessary to go back to May 1919 and place ourselves in the Hotel Majestic in Paris. In chapter eight it has been explained that in the context of the Peace Conference Colonel Mandell House organised a meeting at which the founding of a series of global bodies linked to the Round Table, the secret society founded by Alfred Milner to which the Rothschilds and Astors among other illuminati families belonged, was conceived. Representatives of Morgan, Rockefeller and other international bankers sent to Europe then set up the RIIA (Royal Institute or International Affairs) and the CFR (Council on Foreign Relations). The reader will recall that the financial elites also devised the IPR ("Institute of Pacific Relations"), whose main function was to be the conduct of affairs in the Pacific area. The IPR finally came into being in 1925, sponsored by Wall Street capitalists, and its objectives included the spread of communist ideology, although in theory it was to be a forum for discussion of Asian problems and their relations with the West. The IPR, a private, non-tax-paying association, was funded mainly by Morgan, Rockefeller and other Wall Street banks and firms. The IPR endowed itself with two organs of expression: the quarterly *Pacific Affairs*, whose editor was the crypto-Jew Owen Lattimore, and *Far Eastern Survey*, published by the IPR's American Council, whose executive secretary was Frederick Vanderbilt Field, known as "the Communist millionaire". In 1937 another press organ emerged, *Amerasia*, a monthly publication whose role was of the first order. The *Amerasia* project, approved by the IPR, was owned by the Jewish communist Philip Jacob Jaffe and Vanderbilt Field himself. US policies in China were ultimately imposed by the IPR, as will be seen in the pages that follow.

In his famous work *Tragedy and Hope*, insider Carroll Quigley acknowledges that the IPR was responsible for China's fall into the communist camp and refers to the investigation into the matter undertaken in 1951 by the Senate Internal Security Subcommittee (SISS), created on 21 December 1950, which was the congressional equivalent of the House Un-American Activities Committee (HUAC). Quigley explains that the SISS sought to demonstrate that China had fallen into the hands of communism due to the deliberate action of a group of academics with expertise in the Far

East controlled and coordinated by the Institute of Pacific Relations. At this point, Quigley implies that these agents would have done little without the backing they had, adding: "The influence of the Communists on the IPR is well established, but the Wall Street sponsorship is less well known". He explains that the IPR was made up of ten independent national councils based in as many countries concerned with Pacific affairs. The IPR's headquarters and its American Council were located in New York, where they worked interlinked. Between 1925 and 1950," Quigley reveals, "each spent some two and a half million dollars, provided primarily by the Rockefeller and Carnegie foundations. The annual financial deficits were borne by "financial angels, almost all connected with Wall Street". In addition, private individuals assiduously contributed large sums of money to meet research, travel and other expenses.

With this in mind, a brief look at the historical process in China that began at the beginning of the 20th century is necessary to better understand the final outcome. Hatred of foreigners was the driving force behind the revolutionary process. The humiliating presence throughout the 19th century of powers such as Britain, France, Russia, Japan and Germany prompted nationalist revolutionaries to start fighting in the cities. Sun Yat-sen, a doctor hunted by the imperial police, fled abroad and from the US and London laid the foundations of the KMT (Kuomintang). During World War I, the Allies got China to declare war on Germany in 1917 in exchange for promises they reneged on. On 4 May 1919 students demonstrated in Peking outside foreign embassies and set fire to several buildings. Meanwhile, the Communist International sent agents to China in an attempt to steer the revolutionary nationalist movement back onto the path of communism.

A United Front was initially organised between the Chinese Communist Party, founded in July 1921, and the Kuomintang (National People's Party) nationalists of Sun Yat-sen, who was a Freemason and married to a Chinese woman of Jewish origin, Soong Ching-ling, of the Chinese Jewish ethnic group of the Tiao Kiu Kiaou[24]. Known as Madame

---

[24] To learn more about the Tiao-Kiu Kiaou, there is a work that can be read in English: *El comunismo chino y los judíos chinos*, by Itsvan Bakony, who in turn draws mainly from another source: *The History of the Jews in China*, by S. M. Perlmann. The *Enciclopedia Judaica Castellana* and the *Jewish Encyclopedia* also provide interesting data, according to which Chinese Jews were prominent in agriculture, commerce, the judiciary and the army. According to these sources, the presence of Jews in China dates back to time immemorial. Marco Polo refers to the powerful commercial and political influence of Jews in China. During the 19th century, the Tiao-Kiu Kiaou Jews engaged in the opium trade in Shanghai and Honk Kong in collusion with the British and the Jewish banker Elias David Sassoon. All indications are that their collaboration with the Communists was very significant, as many of the leaders were Tiao-Kiu Kiaou. Jean Lombard writes in *The Hidden Face of Modern History* that Chinese Jews worked on the development of Freemasonry and Chinese secret societies. According to this author,

Sun Yat-sen, Soong Ching-ling worked closely with Mao after the establishment of communism. Also Sun Yat-sen's secretary and right-hand man was a Jew named Morris Cohen. It was the Fourth Congress of the Communist International (November/December 1922) that proposed the alliance between communists and nationalists. Lenin sent as ambassador to China Adolf Abramovich Joffe, the Jew who had headed the Soviet delegation to the Brest-Litovsk peace negotiations with Trotsky. As is well known, Joffe, a staunch Trotskyite, committed suicide in 1927 as a way of protesting Trotsky's expulsion from the party. On 26 January 1923, Sun Yat-sen and Adolf A. Joffe issued in Shanghai the declaration that sealed a collaborative alliance for the period 1924-27. At the time, some Chinese from the wealthy classes were coming to communism by way of radical nationalism. Joffe was joined by another Jew, Jacob Borodin (Grusenberg), who became a political adviser to the Kuomintang, which he tried to Bolshevise. At the First Kuomintang Congress in January 1924, many communists were placed in advantageous positions in the party. After Sun Yat-sen's death in 1925, Borodin targeted as his successor Chiang Kai-shek, who like Sun Yat-sen was a high degree Freemason and also married a Tiao Kiu Kiaou of the Soong family, sister of Sun Yat-sen's wife. The coalition period was fraught with controversy and dissension between the two parties.

After a stay in Moscow in 1927, Chiang Kai-shek came to the conclusion that the Soviets intended to use the young Chinese Communist Party as an instrument of their foreign policy. Hostilities began on 12 April 1927 with an anti-communist coup by Chiang Kai-shek, and on 28 April there was the storming of the USSR Embassy in Peking. Thousands of CCP members accused of being disloyal to China were liquidated. Heinz Neumann, another Jewish Trotskyite who represented the Comintern in Spain and who would be purged by Stalin in 1937, organised a communist rebellion in Nanjing that failed. The United Front was definitively broken. The Trotskyist internationalists had from the beginning attached great importance to the triumph of communism in China, so these events of 1927 served as a trigger for Trotsky to launch a campaign against Stalin and to try to regain power. Trotsky, Zinoviev and other Jewish leaders of the Trotskyist opposition accused Stalin of incompetence and led a conspiracy against him which failed and ended, as already mentioned, with Trotsky's confinement in Alma Ata in 1928.

A long civil war was to begin in China which was to end with the triumph of Mao Tse-tung in 1949. In a speech delivered on 1 August 1927 at the Plenum of the Central Committee, Stalin announced it in these words: "Let us now proceed to the second stage of the revolution in China. Whereas the first stage was characterised by the fact that the revolution was directed

---

"Mao himself and some of his collaborators in the Communist Party and the Red Army pass for Tiao-Kiu-Kiaou."

mainly against foreign imperialism, the distinguishing feature of the second stage is that the revolution will now be directed directly against internal enemies." However, the Soviet advisors had to leave the country, the CCP lost all the cities and remained only underground in the countryside. In Mao's home province of Hunan, he had organised peasant leagues on behalf of the Communist Party and the Kuomingtang. It can be said that while Chiang Kai-shek liquidated urban communism, Mao Tse-tung managed to save peasant communism. At the end of 1929 Britain, the United States and France recognised the newly formed Nationalist government of Chiang Kai-shek.

During the 1930s many agents of the Communist International working surreptitiously for the Trotskyist internationalists, many of whom were Americans, entered China. Simultaneously, activities of Chinese Communists developed in the United States, the most famous of whom was Chi Chao-ting, married to an American Jewish Communist named Harriet Levine who was a cousin of Philip Jaffe. Chi wrote articles for the *Daily Worker* under the pseudonym R. Doonping in which he accused Chiang Kai-shek of being a counter-revolutionary who had betrayed the Chinese revolution in 1927. Chi Chao-ting went on to earn a doctorate in economics from Columbia University and worked for the Central Committee of the Communist Party of the USA. He was also very active in the American Friends of Chinese People, an organisation that promoted aid to the communists and had a publication, *China Today*, to which Madame Sun Yat-sen was a contributor. Prominent American Communists in the organisation included Frederick Vanderbilt Field, Philip Jaffe, Thomas A. Bisson, Max Granich, Owen Lattimore, Anna Louise Strong and Grace Hutchins. With the exception of Vanderbilt Field, all of them were Jewish. By 1936, Chi Chiao-ting was already a member of IPR's International Secretariat in New York and a contributor to *Far Eastern Survey* and *Pacific Affairs*. In 1937 he became an associate of *Amerasia*. Two other Chinese Communists very active in the Institute of Pacific Relations and its publications who later held prominent positions in Communist China were Chen Han-seng and Hsu Yung-ying.

In China, Generalissimo Chian Kai-shek launched successive annihilation campaigns in the early 1930s against Mao's communists, who could only find respite thanks to the Japanese invasion of Manchuria. In October 1934, after successive defeats, Mao's peasant soldiers began the legendary "long march" to avoid being encircled and annihilated. For a year the forces commanded by Mao Tse-tung marched almost without interruption, harassed and pursued by hundreds of thousands of Kuomingtang soldiers. They covered more than ten thousand kilometres on foot, a distance twice as long, for example, as the distance from Lisbon to Moscow. They crossed eighteen mountain ranges, twenty-four rivers, several deserts and swamps. Political instructors left soviets in the towns and villages they passed through and formed guerrilla units. Of the one hundred thousand men who made up Mao's forces, eighty thousand died of hunger, cold and exhaustion, when they were not drowned in the rivers or thrown into the ravines. According to Christian Zentner, Mao also had to overcome internal enemies, comrades who tried to kill him, because he was not the man chosen by Stalin, who sought to replace him with someone he trusted more. In Moscow, Mao Tse-tung was never considered the head of the party. Everything suggests that Stalin's man at the time may have been Chang Kuo-tao, head of the Fourth Army, officially superior to Mao within the CCP, whom he tried several times during the "long march" to eliminate. This fact is highly significant, since the American Communists did bet from the beginning on Mao Tse-tung, who according to Jean Lombard was a Tiao Kiu Kiaou.

In October 1936 Moscow concluded that a new United Front between the Kuomingtang and the CCP was necessary to defeat the Japanese, the external enemy. The Communist Party USA and Mao Tse Tung himself shared the idea; but not Chiang Kai-shek, for whom the Japanese were a lesser evil and who considered it a priority to defeat the Communists, the enemy within that sought to eliminate him and his system. In a memorandum dated 18 May 1954 and entitled *Potentialities of Chinese Communist Intelligence Activities in the United States,* John Edgar Hoover, the director of the FBI, reveals that in June 1937 important American Jewish Communists linked to the IPR visited Mao in Yenan. Among them were Philip Jacob Jaffe, Agnes Jaffe, Thomas A. Bisson and Owen Lattimore. In a letter, Mao let Earl Browder, the Communist leader in the United States, know that he was getting information about affairs in the United States from "various American friends and other sources."

Significantly, in the spring of 1941 one of these "American friends" of Mao, Professor Lattimore, was to be appointed by Roosevelt as adviser to the Nationalist leader Chiang Kai-shek in Chungking, the wartime capital of free China. Thus the IPR made a first-rate strategic contact in a particularly sensitive place: Owen Lattimore evidently heard and saw everything that could be of interest in developing the strategy for the triumph of Mao and communism in China. As an adviser to Chiang Kai-shek, Lattimore travelled sporadically to San Francisco to serve as head of the Office of War Information (OWI) Pacific Coast.

Ultimately, at the end of 1937, it was secretly agreed to establish the Second United Front in order to oppose the Japanese. The Communists reportedly promised the Kuomintang four things: they renounced the agrarian reorganisation they were carrying out; they guaranteed that they would not overthrow the Kuomintang by force; they accepted new democratic regional governments in the border territories where soviets had been established; they agreed to transform the Red Army into a national revolutionary army. During this new United Front period, *China Today* and the American Friends of the Chinese People directed all their propaganda artillery against Japan and ceased attacks on Chiang Kai-shek. In December 1937, the China Relief Council was formed in the United States to organise fund-raising for China relief projects. Among the directors of the Council were Philip Jaffe and Chi Chao-ting, both members of the IPR and *Amerasia*.

The period of the Second United Front was marked in the United States, according to Edgar Hoover's memorandum, by the infiltration of the Roosevelt government by agents working to achieve communist objectives in China. Edgar Hoover mentions Lauchlin Currie, Michael Greenberg, Harry Dexter White, Solomon Adler and the *Amerasia* group, who according to the FBI report had access to classified government documents. Special mention is again made of Chi Chao-ting, who theoretically acted during this period on behalf of the Chiang Kai-shek government, which he represented in 1944 at the Bretton Woods Conference.

After the Japanese attack on Pearl Harbour, things began to change in China, and mistrust again marked the relations between Chiang Kai-shek and the Communists, who were able to use the war as an opportunity to strengthen themselves. It was clear to Chiang Kai-shek, advised by Owen Lattimore, the IPR strategist, that, just as Poland had been a casus belli for Britain in 1939, China had been a casus belli for the Americans, who had supported it to contain Japanese conquest. By 1944, however, the Communist forces of Mao Tse-tung and Chou En-lai had an independent power base in their fiefdom of Yenan, commanded their own armies and were preparing for the decisive moment. Moreover, two Communist agents who passed for senior American officials, the diplomat John Stewart Service and Solomon Adler, close to Harry Dexter White in the Treasury, had joined Owen Lattimore in Chungking. To complete the trio, Chi Chao-ting was placed next to the Minister of Finance in the Kuomintang. All of them were supposedly in China to help the Nationalists, but in reality they hated Chiang Kai-shek and were working in the shadows for the triumph of communism. In Chungking, Solomon Adler, John Stewart Service and Chi Chao-ting lived together in the same house. In connection with the IPR affair in China, Elisabeth Bentley would testify to the SISS on 14 August 1951 that Solomon Adler was a member of Silvermaster's group and that she was the courier between them. Bentley confirmed that Harry Dexter White was also receiving information from Adler.

In the *Morgenthau Diary: China*, there is a message from Solomon Adler to Harry Dexter White, who evidently discussed it with Secretary of the Treasury Henry Morgenthau, as Morgenthau noted the conversation in his Diary. The communiqué was produced in February 1945 and in it Adler argues that they should only support Chiang if he really tries to promote a coalition government with Mao. The way to press for this, according to Adler, is to use the power of the Treasury and withdraw financial aid to Chiang, especially a previously promised credit of $200 million in gold.

Santon Evans reproduces excerpts from Solomon Adler's text to Dexter White in *Blacklisted by History*:

> "There seems to be no alternative for the Treasury but to adopt a negative policy towards China. We should continue to send as little gold to China as possible. Because this gold will not be used effectively to combat inflation.... We should be tough and slow in approving army spending in China. There is no need to have a bad conscience in this respect, for the Chinese deceive us at the slightest opportunity.... We should deny Chinese demands for goods in loans and leases in civilian matters under the guise of combating inflation.... We should keep a close watch on Chinese funds in the United States."

These words certainly show what plans the Treasury was preparing to adopt in February 1945. Stanton Evans comments: "This strategy, laid out by one Communist agent to another Communist agent, was to become official US policy toward China within months". This author quotes words Henry Morgenthau wrote in his Diary, "I love these letters from Adler." Evans adds, "White would make sure that Treasury Secretary Morgenthau saw the Adler memos and selected Stewart Service reports. Morgenthau would take the message to the White House, where he had direct access to FDR, his long-time neighbour in New York's Hudson Valley. Since Lauchlin Currie, on the White House 'staff', received updated reports from Service, each memo could be cited as confirmation of the other."

As for the efforts to combat the Japanese, the reports reaching Washington differed widely depending on the source. While diplomat Stewart Service reported that only the Communists were fighting the Japanese and that Chiang Kai-shek was doing nothing, General Albert Wedemeyer claimed the exact opposite. Wedemeyer, a military expert who had been in China in command of the fight against Japan for many months, published years later the book *Wedemeyer Reports* (1955). According to this source, the Chinese Communists contributed very little in the fight against the Japanese and had been of no help: "There were no Chinese Communist forces - writes Wedemeyer - fighting in any of the important battles of the Sino-Japanese war". On the basis of reports passed to him by his Intelligence service, the general wrote in the work cited above, "I learned that Mao Tse-tung, Chou En-lai and other Chinese Communist leaders were not interested in fighting the Japanese because their main concern was to occupy the territory that the Nationalist forces evacuated in their retreat."

In the spring of 1945, the US Ambassador to Chungking, General Patrick Hurley, who had been Secretary of War from 1929 to 1933, told his superiors in Washington that he did not trust a diplomat under his command, John Stewart Service, and asked that he be recalled from service at the Embassy. By the end of 1944 Service had returned to the United States on a two-month leave of absence. During the visit, in addition to meeting

Lauchlin Currie and Dexter White, he met with people who had been under FBI surveillance, such as Grace Granich, a Jewish-born Communist who had been Earl Browder's secretary; Andrew Roth, a Hungarian-born Jew who had been an IPR investigator and was a lieutenant in the Far East Division of the Department of Naval Intelligence; Rose Yardumian, another Jewish woman of Armenian origin in charge of the IPR office in Washington and an old friend of the Lattimores. In John Service's absence, Ambassador Hurley had time to peruse dispatches and communiqués sent by the diplomat, who was supposedly working for him, and did not like them at all. Here is one of them, reproduced in fragments by M. Stanton Evans, particularly contrary to the official line of the Embassy:

> "Our relations with Chiang Kai-shek apparently continue on the unrealistic assumption that he is China and that he is necessary to our cause..... In the present circumstances, the Kuomintang depends on American aid for its subsistence. But we do not depend on the Kuomintang at all. We do not need it for military reasons.... We need not fear the collapse of the Kuomintang Government..... We do not need to support the Kuomintang for international political reasons..... We do not need to support Chiang in the belief that he represents pro-American or pro-democracy groups.... We don't need to feel grateful to Chiang.... There may be a period of some confusion, but the eventual advantages of a collapse of the Kuomintang will outweigh it."

When John Service returned to Chungking at the end of January 1945, Pat Hurley had already decided that he did not want him at the Embassy. In addition to showing his hostility, the ambassador announced that he had requested his replacement. In the spring, Washington granted the request, and without any farewell ceremony Service was sent back to the United States. On 12 April he was in Washington, where Andrew Roth put him in touch with Philip Jacob Jaffe, editor of the pro-communist newspaper *Amerasia*. The meeting between the two took place at the Statler Hotel. Jaffe had been under close surveillance for some weeks, including wiretapping, bugging and monitoring of his movements. As if the first meeting with Granich, Roth and Yarmudian had not been enough, after this meeting Service began to appear in FBI files. On 11 May 1945, the FBI sent the White House an eighty-page memorandum related to the *Amerasia* case. It contained the April movements of Philip Jacob Jaffe, John Service, Andy Roth, Mark Gayn (another Jew whose real name was Julius Ginsberg) and Emmanuel Larsen (of the State Department). When declassified, the *Amerasia* file consisted of more than twelve thousand pages. In June the FBI arrested John Service and other State Department officials on charges of espionage, but Lauchlin Currie ensured that he was not ultimately charged.

On 24 April 1945 Mao Tse-tung in a report to the Seventh National Congress of the Chinese Communist Party referred to the necessity of eliminating the Japanese aggressors externally and the Kuomintang internally. Mao pointed to the resumption of civil war. From this point on, it can be seen in greater detail how Mao Tse-tung was able to defeat Chiang Kai-shek and proclaim the People's Republic of China. Harry Dexter White and Solomon Adler's sabotage of the gold loan discussed above can be said to have been the trigger for the plan. In 1951 Freda Utley published *The China Story*, in which she analyses US policy in China since 1945. She refers to a speech delivered in Washington on 11 April 1950 by Colonel L. B. Moody of the Artillery Corps. Moody charged that the US Government had continuously denied military aid to Chiang Kai-shek. On 16 July 1951, Moody published a lengthy article in *The Freeman* magazine detailing shadowy efforts to deny military aid. In the summer of 1945, this army specialist inspected a surplus of munitions intended for delivery to the KMT (Kuomintang). Colonel Moody alleges that the officials who handled these materials went to great lengths to ensure that they were not delivered. The munitions were under the control of the Federal Economic Administration, the successor to the Board of Economic Warfare. When the supplies were to be delivered to Chiang, Moody wrote, "the FEA did everything it could to block or delay the shipment of this essential material, probably through Embassy officials". According to the colonel, of the 153,000 tons of ammunition, Chiang received only two percent, "the rest was dumped in the ocean or otherwise disposed of." Rifles captured from the Germans that were supposed to be for the generalship were tapped. "A small consignment was sent," Moody notes, "but the project was cancelled on orders from Washington."

In the autumn of 1945 John Carter Vincent was appointed director of the Bureau of Far Eastern Affairs. This diplomat, like John Stewart Service before him, was to play a decisive role. Coinciding with his appointment was the resignation of Patrick Hurley, the American ambassador to China, who, since the Service episode, had become an obstacle to plans to undermine Chiang and favour the Communists. Pat Hurley began to see that more Foreign Service officers were involved in the strategy, but his comments were considered rantings and he himself was labelled a braggart and a boaster. Unaccustomed to being mistreated and faced with an obvious campaign to discredit him, Ambassador Hurley resigned at the end of November 1945. His replacement was the famous General George Marshall, the man who suddenly lost his memory on 6 December 1941 and did not know where he had been for the twelve hours before the Japanese attack on Pearl Harbour.

It should be noted that Stalin had pledged at Yalta to declare war on Japan three months after the defeat of Germany. This was basically a nice gift from Roosevelt, as it was an invitation for the Soviets to set foot in Manchuria, whose ports and railways were of vital importance. After the dropping of the atomic bomb on Hiroshima, Moscow ordered the start of the operation in Manchukuo (Manchuria), Japan's satellite state. It was a blitzkrieg, in true German style, as the Soviet Army achieved one of its most brilliant victories in three weeks. Logically, this surrender of Manchuria to Stalin was in favour of the establishment of communism in China.

There are all sorts of interpretations of what happened after the Japanese defeat. Since the Kuomintang had no troops in Manchuria, fifty thousand US Marines had landed in China and American planes flew Chiang Kai-shek's soldiers to Manchuria to participate in the capitulation of the Japanese, who had surrendered to the Soviets. It then became clear once again that Mao was not Moscow's man, for Stalin, who had been ruthless in his occupation of half of Europe, agreed to hand over the important industrial zone of Manchuria to Chiang Kai-shek and allowed the Kuomintang to occupy the key cities in northern China. It seems clear that if he had trusted Mao Tse-tung he would never have acted in this way.

In November 1945, through the statements of Elisabeth Bentley and Whittaker Chambers, the FBI was able to establish that, surprisingly, the parallels were converging: all the espionage networks they were investigating appeared to be interconnected. On 27 November, the FBI presented President Truman with a new 50-page memorandum on Soviet espionage in the United States, which brought together information on COMRAP ("Comintern Apparatus"), CINRAD ("Communist Infiltration of the Radiation Laboratory") and *Amerasia*. This report would become famous years later when Richard Nixon read it in part before the investigating committees. Among the names that appeared in this overview of communist infiltration were: Oppenheimer, Silvermaster, Hiss, Currie, Bransten, Kheifitz, White, Service, Adler, Glasser... among others less relevant.

On 20 December 1945, supposedly on a mission to get Mao and Chiang to agree to form a unity government, General Marshall arrived in China, where he was received by General Wedemeyer. In September 1945, the American ambassador, Patrick Hurley, had brokered a first meeting between Mao Tse-tung and Chiang Kai-shek. Fight or coalition were thus the only two options when the Japanese capitulated. By then, however, everything had changed in favour of the Communists: in 1937 the CCP had forty thousand members; in 1945, one and a half million. In terms of regular soldiers, it had grown from eighty thousand to more than nine hundred thousand. In 1937 the Chinese Communists dominated a territory of twelve thousand square kilometres with two million inhabitants; in 1945 their domain was ten times larger with more than 95 million inhabitants. Nevertheless, Chiang Kai-shek was convinced that he could defeat communism with the help of his American allies. However, the threat to cut off aid to Chiang Kai-shek if he did not join forces with the communists was tantamount to putting the handle of the frying pan in Mao's hands, who, to prevent Chiang from being assisted by his supposed American allies, had only to prevent the formation of the unity government.

General Marshall's main mentor in China was John Carter Vincent, a diplomat who was an IPR leader infiltrated into the State Department, a colleague of Owen Lattimore and a close ally of John Stewart Service and Lauchlin Currie. In November 1945, before Marshall travelled to China, Vincent presented him with a memorandum on the situation, which, along with two other reports signed by Truman himself, served as his guide. It was about Chiang Kai-shek's acceptance of the agreement with "the so-called communists" (Vincent's terms). From the outset it was clear that if Chiang did not accept the approach, the United States would suspend its aid to the generalissimo: "A China disunited by civil war," Truman said in a letter, "cannot realistically be regarded as a suitable place for American aid". To top it all off, Solomon Adler, was among Marshall's top economic and financial advisers. Truman's attitude to the Dexter White case was repeated with Solomon Adler, who had been Treasury representative in China in 1944. The FBI knew that in Chungking Adler had lived with Chi Chao-ting and John Stewart Service in the same house. Despite Edgar Hoover's repeated reports that he was a Communist agent, President Truman not only kept him at the Treasury, but promoted him, increased his pay and appointed him to key positions. In 1946 he was an adviser to General Marshall. In 1947 he was tasked with providing background information on China to General Wedemeyer. From December 1947 to February 1948 he discussed with the State Department questions of technical and financial aid to Chiang Kai-shek. Naturally, being a henchman of the international communist conspiracy to strangle Chiang, he advised cutting off aid to the Chinese Nationalists.

Only in May 1950, after Senator Joseph McCarthy burst onto the scene, did Solomon Adler, with his mission accomplished, consider it prudent to leave the Treasury and travel to England, from where he fled to China in order to work for the communist regime he had helped to establish. Service, Vincent, Adler, Currie, Lattimore were just the tip of the iceberg. Stanton Evans quotes historian Maochun Yu, who based on his study of Chinese sources writes: "When George Marshall was in China, Communist penetration of American media was rampant. Many Chinese typists and interpreters employed by the OSS and OWI (Office of War Information) were secret agents working for Yenan. As has been revealed in recent materials published in China, they stole documents, organised secret activities, provided incorrect data and fed American intelligence agencies in China with falsified information."

Nevertheless, during the first months of 1946 the KMT nationalists were winning the war and did not understand why the Americans were trying to force them to make a pact with the communists instead of helping to defeat them. Indeed, Marshall's first decision was to ask for a truce, which the Communists logically accepted, since they were losing. Another Chinese author quoted by Stanton Evans, the communist Jung Chang, in a text entitled "Saved by Washington" writes the following:

> "Marshall was to render a monumental service to Mao. When Mao had his back against the wall in what can be called his Dunkirk at late spring 1946, Marshall exerted strong and decisive pressure on Chiang to stop the persecution of the Communists in northern Manchuria.... Marshall's 'diktat' was probably the most important decision affecting the outcome of the civil war. Reds who lived through that period, from Biao to Army retirees, comment privately that the truce was a fatal mistake on Chiang's part."

In July 1946, Marshall stepped on the accelerator in order to reach the goal he had been set. The general warned Chiang that his orders were to achieve "peace and unity" and that if the fighting did not stop he would have to suspend aid to the KMT. Unconcerned that no one was putting pressure on the Communists, all responsibility for the continuation of the civil war was placed on the Nationalist side. Joe McCarthy would refer to these moments in 1951. According to the senator, General Wedemeyer had prepared a sensible and intelligent plan that would have kept China as a valuable ally, but it was sabotaged, which McCarthy considered high treason. In a speech on 14 March 1951, he declared that General Marshall, now ill and weakened, had in fact been duped by the conspirators:

> "When Marshall was sent to China with secret orders from the State Department, the Communists were then locked in two areas and were fighting a losing battle; but because of those orders the situation was radically changed in favour of the Communists. In pursuance of those orders, as we know, Marshall seized all arms and ammunition from our allies in China. He forced passage into Manchuria through the Nationalist-controlled Kalgan Mountains in order to give the Communists access to the equipment and the vast quantities of arms captured from the Japanese. There is no need to explain to the country how Marshall tried to force Chiang Kai-shek to form a coalition government with the Communists."

The arms embargo began in the summer of 1946 and was decisive. Not only were the Nationalists prevented from buying arms and ammunition, but they were also prevented from receiving those shipments that had already been purchased. For the blockade to be complete, the embargo was coordinated with the British, who were the Nationalists' most likely alternative. This policy continued until the early summer of 1947, although it was pursued through clandestine methods in the months that followed. Freda Utley explains in *The China Story* that Chiang Kai-shek tried for a year to have the embargo lifted in order to buy ammunition that could not be sold to anyone else, as it had been manufactured during World War II according to previously agreed requirements. According to this author, the State Department initially allowed the Chinese government to buy three weeks' worth of ammunition, and a further small grant was made to the Nationalists when in 1947 US Marines leaving China were ordered to leave six days' worth of 30mm calibre ammunition. Freda Utley again quotes Colonel Moody, who estimated that in December 1947 the ammunition held by the Nationalist government was sufficient to fight for little more than a month.

In early 1948, concern over what was happening in China prompted the US Congress to press for $125 million in economic assistance, which was supposed to alleviate Chiang Kai-shek's military emergency. Again, agents of the conspiracy were able to manoeuvre in the shadows to delay the aid. On 5 April, the Chinese ambassador in Washington made the first request for compliance with the law passed by Congress. For two months the Chinese pleaded in vain to be allowed to place their supply orders with the funds provided for that purpose. The requested munitions could only be obtained from government "stocks"; but Truman at first authorised only commercial transactions. General Claire Chennault, longtime commander of the Air Force in China, testified that a first shipment was allowed in April but did not reach Shanghai until December. Admiral Oscar Badger, who in the summer of 1948 was part of a group of American observers in North China, confirmed General Chennault's testimony. The KMT forces knew that Congress had voted the aid and were eagerly awaiting it so that they could engage in decisive battles. Unfortunately, not only was the delivery delayed, but only ten percent of what was expected arrived. Admiral Badger added that, in addition, the material supplied was defective in many respects. For the KMT forces," Badger said, "it was the straw that broke the camel's back.

Early in 1949 came the definitive episode which proved that Grand Master Truman was fully in on the conspiracy game. President Truman, Dean Acheson, a member of the newly appointed Secretary of State of the CFR (Council on Foreign Relations), and other well-placed figures in the Administration decided, despite Congressional approval, to suspend all military aid to Chiang Kai-shek. To justify the move, they argued that the KMT's cause was already lost. When Republican Senator Arthur Vandenberg learned what was intended, he threatened to denounce it publicly. In order to avoid debate, Truman cancelled the order; but Acheson, reports Stanton Evans, instructed his subordinates in the State Department: "It is desirable that shipments be delayed whenever possible and that this be done without formal order".

In the end, all the measures and tricks to bring about the defeat of Chiang's Nationalist government bore fruit, and the KMT forces were forced to leave the mainland and land on Formosa. However, instead of ending the struggle against him, Acheson was determined to pursue the generalissimo to liquidate him for good. As soon as Mao Tse-tung's Communists seized power in October 1949, a conference took place at the State Department at which Philip Jessup, a member of the IPR Governing Council and also a member of the CFR, was the keynote speaker. It was decided that the fall of China was not the end of the process, but merely the beginning. It was agreed that further communist advances in the region were to be expected and the recommended policy for the United States was to stand aside and allow them to happen. Specifically, the "experts" on Asia recommended that Mao's communists be allowed to invade Formosa. In mid-November Acheson advised Truman to recognise the new Beijing regime and to dissociate himself completely from Chiang Kai-shek on Formosa. These policy directives were public, but other anti-Chiang manoeuvres only became known decades later. There were, for example, a number of plans in the State Department to do Mao's work and get Chiang out of Formosa: military intervention was considered, and even a coup against the generalissimo was considered.

Stanton Evans reveals in *Blacklisted by History* that these clandestine machinations against the anti-communist leader were not new and that during World War II there had already been plans to eliminate him. Specifically, he points to General Joseph Stilwell, nicknamed "Vinegar Joe", as the central figure. Stilwell, assisted by none other than John Service, was on Chiank Kai-shek's General Staff during World War II. According to Vinegar Joe's aide Frank Dorn, the general ordered him in 1944 to devise a plan to remove Chiang from the scene by assassinating him. Dorn wrote that General Stilwell told him that "The Big Boy (Roosevelt) was fed up with Chiang and his temper tantrums." Frank Dorn speculates that the idea may have come from Harry Hopkins. Stanton Evans writes that the whole plot might have been called into question if it had not been confirmed in 1985 by Eric Saul, OSS archivist. According to Eric Saul, there is a record of the plan in the archives of this unit (which predated the CIA), but it was not carried out because the order did not arrive.

As for the plan to remove Chiang by means of a coup in Formosa, there are written reports in the State Department confirming this: the candidate to lead the coup was a KMT dissident, a general named Sun Li-jen. In mid-January 1950, Acheson declared that neither Formosa nor Korea were in his defence plans. Also early in the year, Philip Jessup toured Asia to gather accurate information. He was in Tokyo and also in Taipei. On his return he reported on his visit to Chiang. His words are reported in *Foreign Relations of the United States*: "The Generalissimo's house is located high up in the mountains, about twenty minutes' drive from the centre of Taipei. There was a sentry box with a sentry at one of the many bends in the mountain road, and we saw a few soldiers in the vicinity, but no large military presence". No doubt these observations could be extremely useful if there was any thought of getting rid of Chiang by commando action.

All that has been said so far confirms the existence of the "vast conspiracy" denounced by Senator Joseph McCarthy. Between 1945 and 1950, a series of agents serving the interests of the behind-the-scenes financiers of international communism succeeded in having China handed over to Mao Tse-tung. If action had been taken against them in 1945, as advised by the reports supplied by John Edgar Hoover's FBI, the catastrophe in China could probably have been avoided. The fact that Solomon Adler, instead of being purged, was sent to China with General Marshall in 1946 is a crucial episode. Also crucial was Chi Chao-ting's role as a Maoist agent infiltrating the KMT (Kuomintang) until his fall in 1949. Like Solomon Adler, Chi fled to Beijing after his mission was completed. Lauchlin Currie is the third character who should have been unmasked in 1945 but was not. Elisabeth Bentley's statements, confirmed by the Venona documents, place Currie in the Silvermaster circle and make it clear that he was one of the most important Communist agents within the government, as his China portfolio and his influence in the White House were of paramount importance. To these three main captains, Senator McCarthy would attach in 1950 more than a dozen other important names who, on the Federal Government payroll, worked closely with them to establish communism in China.

The *Amerasia* case, although it originated in the Roosevelt era, was the one that most compromised and exposed Truman, for it all unfolded under his nose and with his approval. *Amerasia* was a monthly magazine linked to the IPR, founded in 1937 by Philip Jaffe and Frederick Vanderbilt Field. It featured relevant analysis and information on the situation in Asia and America. It was in the early 1950s that, thanks to Senator McCarthy's perseverance, the investigation into espionage and the leaks of secret documents delivered to *America* from various government departments, especially the State Department, was deepened. Finally, much later, in 1970, the Senate Internal Security Subcommittee published a two-volume report, *The Amerasia Papers: A Clue to the Catastrophe of China*. M. Stanton Evans begins Chapter 28 of his valuable book on Joseph McCarthy with these words on the importance of the investigation led by the Wisconsin senator:

> "If McCarthy had done nothing else during his turbulent heyday in the Senate, his role in blowing the lid off the *Amerasia* scandal would deserve the plaudits of a grateful nation. This was not only because of the intrinsic significance of the case, but because it was the gateway to other unthinkable revelations from the darkest recesses of the Cold War.
> And there should be no doubt that it was McCarthy who bore the burden - constantly hammering away at the case, digging up security reports on Service, and putting pressure on *Amerasia*'s people and their accomplices. Hoover and his agents knew the facts - they knew far more than McCarthy did - but they had to fight their fight behind the scenes, in

a secret war of fighting reports. These internal efforts were not enough to prevent the Tydings Committee (anti-McCarthy) and Truman's Justice Department from peddling a false version of the story. It was McCarthy who would arouse public anger and the necessary outcry so that the security problems implicit in the case could be exposed and properly remedied.

It was not just a simple matter of Service-Jaffe and the documents passed between them, or even the dirty list of federal crimes committed by *Amerasia*'s technicians. The deeper significance of the case lay in all that lay behind it that would need to be uncovered for it to be aired publicly. Going after *Service/Amerasia*, McCarthy was stretching the visible edges of a huge web - much longer than we knew - that stretched across the federal government and had grander aims than the papers that reached Jaffe, important though those papers were."

It also took until 1950 for Joe McCarthy to denounce before the Senate the role played by the IPR in the fall of China. When such a respected body was attacked by Senator McCarthy, his enemies were shocked. Senator Clinton Anderson asked incredulously: "Does Senator McCarthy intend to convey the impression that in 1935 and 1936 the Institute of Pacific Relations was under Communist control?" Although the IPR was not publicly exposed until the 1950s, the FBI knew as early as 1945 that the *Amerasia* group was working hand in hand with the IPR, which served as its cover. On 6 June 1945, with the authorisation of the Attorney General who ordered the investigation, Edgar Hoover's agents searched *Amerasia*'s headquarters and found nearly eighteen hundred documents labelled "top secret" that had been stolen from government files. In his early Senate speeches, McCarthy pointed out that prominent IPR members were linked to *Amerasia* and linked them to sinister US policy in China.

The research on the IPR featured the prominent figure of Edward C. Carter, a former official of the YMCA (Young Men's Christian Association), an association that sought to spread Christian values, which are obviously antithetical to communist atheism. Carter, who had been a member of the IPR since its founding in 1925, was secretary general of the organisation from 1933 to 1946 and vice-president from 1946 to 1948. After being the subject of McCarthy's investigations, it was established that Frederick Vanderbilt Field and Joseph Barnes became his closest aides. He was soon joined by Owen Lattimore, who took over as editor of the IPR's flagship *Pacific Affairs*. Despite his supposedly Christian roots, Carter was noted for his services to communism, an ideology that worked against Christianity wherever it gained a foothold. According to the communist *Daily Worker*, Carter was during the war chairman of the National Committee for Medical Aid to the USSR; according to the FBI, he chaired the Russian War Relief Fund and was also chairman of the Board of Directors of the Russian-American Institute, an organisation that the US Attorney General's Office had classified as subversive. Louis Budenz, editor of the *Daily Worker*, testified before investigative committees that Carter was a member of the Communist Party.

In 1951, the Senate Subcommittee on Internal Security (SISS) chaired by Pat McCarran seized the IPR records thanks to the enquiries of Senator McCarthy, who discovered that the files were located at an Edward Carter farm in New England. These documents included correspondence between senior IPR officials and members of the Administration, as well as memoranda, minutes of meetings, and reports of agreements with government representatives. The SISS interim findings established that both Communist Party USA and Soviet officials viewed the IPR as an instrument of communist policy, propaganda and military intelligence, used to guide US policy in the Far East in favour of communist objectives.

Senator McCarthy pointed to the leading role played by Owen Lattimore, a member of the CFR and the IPR Council, in ruining Chiang Kai-shek's Nationalist cause and strengthening the Yenan Communists. Joe McCarthy alleged that Lattimore had an office in the State Department which gave him access to the highest levels of the executive branch. In the FBI files, where Lattimore had been considered a communist since May 1941, the Wisconsin senator's theses were fully confirmed. Most of the entries in the "Bureau" register bore the entry "Owen Lattimore, Espionage-R." The "R" in the heading stood for "Russian". In 1948, Edgar Hoover's men questioned Alexander Barmine, a former Soviet intelligence officer, who informed them that General Berzin, head of Military Intelligence (GRU) purged in 1938 after his time in Spain, had told him that Owen Lattimore was a Soviet agent who had been commissioned to set up a commercial cover for Soviet espionage in China. Alexander Barmin's statement, quoted by M. Stanton Evans, is on file with the FBI:

> "The informant recalls that Berzin then told him.... 'We already have the organisation. Berzin told him that the organisation was called the 'Institute of Pacific Relations' and was the base of the network in China.... At that time Berzin mentioned the fact that the two most promising and brightest men that Soviet Military Intelligence had in the IPR were Owen Lattimore and Joseph Barnes."

Philip Jessup, one of the most prominent pro-communist agents of the IPR, of which he chaired its investigative committee, was also indicted by Senator McCarthy. At the behest of Secretary of State Acheson, Jessup organised and conducted a conference of experts on the Far East to discuss what course US policy should take after the debacle in China. Months earlier, in March 1949, he had become an important figure in the State Department, having been appointed Ambassador-at-Large. Jessup, to whom Dean Acheson entrusted the conduct of China policy, chaired the committee that drafted the "White Paper", which was presented in August 1949. In it, the

United States washed its hands of China, renounced defending the freedom of the Chinese people and declared the Communists the victors of the civil war. When the White Paper was published, the fighting was still going on and Chiang Kai-shek's forces were still in control of southern China, so Louis A. Johnson, the Secretary of Defense who had replaced the "suicidal" James Forrestal on 28 March 1949, and General Claire Chennault argued that the document would be a final blow to the Nationalists and begged that it not be published.

General Albert C. Wedemeyer, the last American commander-in-chief in the Chinese theatre of operations, confesses in *Wedemeyers Reports* that he had assured Generalissimo Chiang Kai-shek that his country would help the Chinese Nationalists establish a democratic form of government after the war. The US ambassador to China, John Leighton Stuart, wrote on 17 March 1948 that in desperation all groups blamed America for its stubbornness in demanding structural changes and reforms rather than delivering the promised aid, on which "the survival of democratic institutions depended." Freda Utley reproduces some words of the ambassador written on 31 March 1948: "The Chinese do not want to become Communists; however they see the tide of Communism advancing irresistibly. In the midst of this chaos and paralysis, the Generalissimo stands out as the only moral force capable of action". The Chinese people's panic at being handed over to a Communist dictatorship like that suffered by the Russians was repeatedly warned by Leighton Stuart: "We would therefore recommend," he wrote on 10 August 1948, "that American efforts be directed towards preventing the formation of a coalition government, and our best means be used to that end, and, if possible, aid to the present Government be increased." In his *Fifty Years in China* (1955) John Leighton Stuart denounced the State Department's responsibility for the "great catastrophe" and rejected the White Paper as historically worthless because it distorted reality. Similarly, Kenneth Colegrove, Professor of Political Science at Northwestern University, had harsh words for Dean Acheson and his White Paper: "one of the most false documents ever published by any country".

The crimes and atrocities of communism in China could be written about at length, for they are unparalleled. Robert Conquest, the British Sovietologist quoted throughout this book, puts the human cost of communism in Russia at between 35 and 45 million lives, an estimate that the authors of the *Black Book of Communism* put at 20 million. Despite the magnitude, these figures are doubled or tripled in China. Professor Richard L. Walker of the University of South Carolina puts the number of victims of Mao Tse-tung's regime at 64 million. In this case the figure coincides with the one given in *The Black Book*, which is 65 million. Suffice it to consider that during the Great Leap Forward campaign alone, between 1958 and 1961, there was a famine in China that caused between 18 and 32.5 million deaths. The Communist Party, led by Mao Tse-tung, embarked on a social, economic and political campaign to transform the country into a socialist society through agrarian collectivisation and industrialisation. Private farms were banned and, as in Russia, those who opposed them were considered counter-revolutionaries. The Great Leap Forward became an unprecedented catastrophe that killed tens of millions of people. Dutch historian Frank Dikötter argues that the basis of the campaign was violence and terror, which led to the largest mass slaughter in history. The Cultural Revolution was to follow. Zeng Yi, a Chinese dissident writer, explains in his *Scarlet Memorial: Tales of Cannibalism in Modern China* (1996) that during the years of the Cultural Revolution the Chinese communist leaders instructed the masses to demonstrate their class consciousness by eating the organs and flesh of their enemies. Cannibalism, however, according to the great writer Lu Xun, was one of the worst practices in Chinese civilisation. The illuminati banker David Rockefeller, whose clan collaborated since the late 19th century with the Rothschilds and other Jewish bankers in the communist conspiracy, in statements to *The New York Times* published on 10 August 1973, referred to Mao's regime of terror as "one of the most important and successful in the history of mankind."

And more of the same in Korea

Contrary to Stalin's predictions and wishes, Mao Tse-tung had won the longest civil war in modern history in China. Until 1948, Moscow had maintained diplomatic relations and cooperation agreements only with Chiang Kai-shek's China, so the CCP had received aid not from the USSR but from its American friends. Stalin's agents within the Chinese Communists had been reporting anti-Soviet tendencies among the Maoists and Stalin had no control whatsoever over what was happening in China, although, naturally, neither side was interested in a break-up. Despite the mutual distrust, in early 1950 Mao came to Moscow to sign a Sino-Soviet Friendship Treaty. In his biography *Stalin. Breaker of Nations*, Robert Conquest states that during this visit the Chinese leader asked for the atomic bomb and Stalin refused. Nevertheless, Mao verbally recognised Stalin as the leader of world communism and, according to Conquest, as a gesture of goodwill, Stalin denounced his chief agent within the CCP Politburo, Kao Kang, Beria's man, whom Stalin was then beginning to distrust, as will be seen at the end of the chapter. Significantly, Kao Kang remained in the Politburo without problems. Numerous texts on "relations with the Central Committee of the Chinese Communist Party" were found in the documents seized from Beria after his arrest. Most of them were reports written by Beria himself or sent by Kao Kang, who had begun his collaboration with Beria in the winter of 1940 and lasted until the arrest of his boss in the summer of 1953. Kao apparently committed suicide in early 1954, although another version suggests that he was arrested and shot.

In January 1950, Secretary of State Acheson announced that Korea, Formosa and other territories in the area were no longer within the US defence perimeter, which, at the very least, was an invitation to the spread of communism. At Potsdam, it had been agreed to divide the Korean peninsula into two zones along the 38th parallel. The north was occupied by the Red Army and the south by the United States. In the north, a communist regime under the tutelage of Moscow had been consolidated, and in the south an anti-communist or capitalist regime. In March 1950, Kim Il Sung, the North Korean communist leader who had a deep admiration for Stalin, appeared in Moscow. Sung asked for permission to invade the Republic of Korea, i.e. the southern peninsula, and requested support for his plans of conquest. A meeting of the Politburo, attended by Kim Il Sung, was convened and the plan was given the green light.

So, at 4 a.m. on 25 June, the North Korean communists crossed the 38th parallel and launched the attack. Despite incredible disagreements, Tokyo-based US General Douglas MacArthur came to the aid of the South Koreans. MacArthur succeeded in stopping the surprise attack in the suburbs of Seoul and launched an all-out counteroffensive in a strategic manoeuvre that demonstrated his military genius. Although Truman strictly forbade American bombers to attack targets in North Korea and no military action across the 38th parallel, the North Korean Red Army was severely defeated and retreated northward in chaos and disorder. Some 150,000 communist soldiers were captured. On 29 September General MacArthur reinstated the South Korean government in Seoul. On 4 October 1950 the UN Plenary Assembly agreed that UN troops (South Koreans, Americans, British and a newly joined Turkish brigade) would "continue their advance northward in police action against the aggressors... to re-establish a single Korean state". On 19 October Pyongyang, North Korea's capital, was attacked and in mid-November the Americans reached the Yalu River, the border between Korea and Manchuria. The North Korean communists had been defeated and their army destroyed.

On 19 November, thousands of Chinese Communists began to cross the Yalu into Korea. As soon as MacArthur became aware of the massive troop movements in Manchuria - almost 900,000 fighters were being mobilised - he proposed to destroy all the bridges over the Yalu River by intensive aerial bombardment in order to make the invasion virtually impossible. Astonished, General MacArthur received an order preventing him from destroying the bridges and attacking Chinese bases beyond the Yalu River. The order came from the ineffable General Marshall, who had recently, on 21 September 1950, been appointed Secretary of Defence. MacArthur protested indignantly and reported that aerial reconnaissance showed that the invasion was total. Biographers and authors who have written about this famous American general report numerous angry texts and statements. MacArthur tells of a mortally wounded squadron leader: "Only a stump was left of one arm and his mouth was foaming with blood. He whispered in my ear: 'Whose side are Washington and the UN really on? On the same day, MacArthur told General Hickey, his chief of staff, "Surely this is the first time in military history that a troop commander has been forbidden to use arms in defence of his soldiers and his positions."

By 28 November the UN armies were fleeing south: the Turkish brigade had been engulfed by the red tide, the British brigade was almost annihilated, and the Americans, closely pursued, made the longest retreat in their military history. On 29 November General MacArthur proposed the intervention of Chinese Nationalist forces. From Formosa, Chiang Kai-shek pleaded to be allowed to intervene to liberate his country, but was prevented from making any move. Weather further complicated the situation, as by mid-December snowstorms made movement difficult and temperatures had dropped to minus 35 degrees Celsius. According to some American historians, there was no more frustrating war in American history than the Korean War. General MacArthur was not allowed to announce to the American people that the country was engaged in a new war and that the enemy was Red China. The losses of American soldiers were heavy, with the commander of the Eighth Army, Walton Walker, killed in action. When the first reports of army casualties reached the country, Congressman Joseph W. Martin wrote to MacArthur to find out first-hand why so many soldiers were dying when the war was supposedly won. On 20 March 1951, the general wrote from Tokyo to the congressman and frankly explained his views. "It seems to be extremely difficult for some," MacArthur said in a passage, "to understand that it is here in Asia that the Communist conspirators have decided to play their trump cards for global conquest..."

On 6 April 1951, Congressman Martin, during a debate on the Korean War, read General MacArthur's letter aloud in its entirety to the entire House of Representatives. On 11 April, enraged, Truman forced the Joint Chiefs of Staff to remove MacArthur from command on military grounds. It was argued in the text that confidence in his strategy had been lost. The public and congressional reaction to the news of the general's dismissal was overwhelming, and a great controversy ensued with serious accusations against Truman, whose approval rating was declining. After eleven years out of the country, Douglas MacArthur immediately returned to Washington. On 19 April 1951, he made his last public appearance before Congress, where he delivered a farewell speech, interrupted thirty times by standing ovations.

As for the war, it lasted another two years and killed more than a million people. In 1953, after Stalin's death, an armistice was signed that maintained the division of the country into two states with a border very similar to the one that existed in 1950, before the North Koreans made the first invasion. What was never said was that Jessup, Lattimore, Jaffe and other Institute of Pacific Relations strategists infiltrated into the State Department and the Administration had originally envisaged that the entire

Korean peninsula should be taken over by communism. This had been implicitly accepted in the White Paper and in Dean Acheson's statement confirming that Korea and Formosa were outside the scope of US action.

"Witches" and "warlocks" plotting against McCarthy

Senator McCarthy and many others in America and around the world could not understand how it was possible that, after having fought against Japan to maintain China's freedom, 600,000,000 people could be shamelessly handed over to the Communist bloc. For years, congressmen and senators had realised the seriousness of the situation. There was a widespread outcry that communists who could harm national security were being protected in high positions in the Administration and that despite repeated allegations nothing was happening. Joe McCarthy's appearance on the scene in February 1950 and his decision to expose individuals was therefore welcomed by those who understood the seriousness of the betrayal and demanded accountability and punishment for the traitors.

However, the task the senator set himself was the work of giants, and he was only one man with all the limitations and weaknesses of human beings. In 1953, FBI Director J. Edgar Hoover, having witnessed three years of the Wisconsin Senator's titanic struggle, described him in a report to the press: "McCarthy is a former Marine. He was an amateur boxer. He's Irish. Combine all of this and you have a vigorous individual who will not be overpowered.... He is certainly a controversial man. He is serious and honest. He has enemies. Wherever you attack subversives of any kind... you run the risk of being the victim of the fiercest and most vicious criticism that can be made." Two more touches to add to this description: during his time in the Navy, he was in the Pacific and was an intelligence officer. He flew two dozen missions photographing targets from the back seat of dive bombers or as a tail gunner on regular bombers.

Among his immediate enemies was President Truman, who was quick to dismiss McCarthy's accusations as lies. So did prominent politicians, the State Department, the media, all manner of so-called experts, academics and various opinion leaders. For more than three years, Joe McCarty was a kind of American Quixote who, unlike the ingenious nobleman of La Mancha, was not a bit mad, but lucidly sane. His many opponents tried to falsify reality and said that he saw witches where there were indeed herds of treacherous Judeo-Marxists. McCarthy, like the immortal Cervantes character, was an idealist, a man of integrity who dreamed of "undoing wrongs" and uncovering the truth, an impossible dream that would turn into the worst of nightmares. Although our space is already limited, we will outline his struggle to unmask the enemies of America and of Christian civilisation.

It all began on 9 February 1950, a Thursday, in Wheeling (West Virginia). At the Republican Women's Club, a series of lectures by Senator Joseph McCarthy, a virtually unknown politician in the Republican minority in the Senate, was scheduled for that month. His exposé of the infiltration of the State Department by some fifty Communists received scant attention; but the local *Wheeling Intelligencer* ran it on its front page, so the all-powerful global Associated Press sent a brief note to its clients, and days later several newspapers carried the story for their readers. On 20 February McCarthy gave a speech in the Senate and, in addition to persisting in his denunciation, alluded to a struggle between atheistic communism and Western Christian civilisation. McCarthy criticised President Truman's neglect of the *Amerasia* scandal and mentioned among others the John Stewart Service. Without naming names, he referred to 81 cases of Communist infiltrators in the State Department and other departments. Thus, for example, No. 1 was an employee of the Under-Secretary of State. Regarding case 28, he said: "This individual has been in the State Department as a Foreign Service officer since 1936". During the debate some senators pleaded with McCarthy to provide the names associated with the numbers. He responded that he was willing to go before an investigating committee and reveal the identity of each number, believing it was wrong to make them public on the floor of the Senate. Thus was born the Tydings Committee, which opened its public sessions on 8 March 1950. Thus began the McCarthy era in American politics.

From the outset, the sessions turned into harassment of Senator McCarthy, who was tried to lose his temper as he was aggressively interrupted more than a hundred times during his presentation. Instead of showing interest in investigating the allegations, it soon became apparent that the main concern was to question the senator, which provoked outrage among some Republicans. Tired of seeing his colleague being harassed, one senator protested in this way:

> "Mr. Chairman, this is the most unusual procedure I have seen since I have been here. Why not treat the Senator from Wisconsin in the normal way and allow him to make his report as he chooses, instead of subjecting him to cross-examination before he has had a chance to state what he has to say? I think the Senator from Wisconsin should be accorded the courtesy that all Senators and all witnesses are accorded to proceed with the statement in his own way and not have it torn to pieces before he has had a chance to utter a single continuous sentence.... I don't understand what the game is being played here...".

Finally, McCarthy said that he was presenting leads, excerpts and names of suspects who should be followed up and investigated as mandated by the Senate. Senators Tydings, Green and McMahon, however, saw it exactly the other way around: it was McCarthy who was to prove his charges. They would act as a kind of jury to judge on the evidence presented. In other words, they would forgo investigating the reported cases. In any case, McCarthy offered more evidence than expected and often associated the names he presented, for example John Stewart Service, with *Amerasia* and the IPR, a body he wanted to make clear was a problem for US security and should be subject to close scrutiny.

After this initial session, the hearings began. The dynamic was as follows: McCarthy would present his charges, the committee would summon the accused, who would deny everything, denounce the senator from Wisconsin as a scoundrel or a lout, and present a bunch of endorsements from eminent persons, all of whom declared that the accused was a patriot and an honest public servant. The Committee then, without exception, accepted the statements as "facts" and regarded the replies as conclusive rebuttals. The cases of Philip Jessup and Owen Lattimore may serve as examples. Jessup returned from Asia and gave the sub-committee an extensive summary of his background and career. He then mentioned relevant people who trusted his decisions and showed his indignation at McCarthy's absurd accusations. From the point of view of the Committee chaired by Tydings, this was more than enough to deliver a favourable verdict for Jessup. Owen Lattimore was treated with inordinate courtesy. He asked if he could read without interruption and was assured by Tydings that he could. Lattimore proceeded to lay out a huge report of some ten thousand words, contained in about thirty pages, which took two and a half hours to read. Unlike Senator McCarthy, Lattimore was only interrupted by the attentions of the President: "Doctor," said Tydings solicitously, "if at any time you would like to rest for a minute, your presentation is long, please do not hesitate to ask me. After finishing his soliloquy on his life, career and writings, Lattimore launched a fierce attack on McCarthy.

A few days later, Louis Budenz appeared before the committee. It was a proceeding not planned by Tydings, but by McCarthy, who had the opportunity to counter-attack with the subpoena of this witness who had been a member of the Politburo of the CP USA and editor-in-chief of the *Daily Worker*. Budenz had defected in October 1945, about the same time as Elisabeth Bentley. His information was exhaustive, for he knew very well who was who in the organisation. The Democratic members who had been quietly listening to the Jessup and Lattimore monologues were stunned. Budenz testified that members of the PC leadership had assured him that Lattimore was an agent of the party and should be treated as such in the *Daily Worker*. He recalled the propaganda work and services Lattimore had provided. His statement raised hackles. The silk cloths with which Democratic senators had preserved Lattimore and Jessup became boxing gloves. Despite the storm of sceptical and insulting questions with which the witness was pummelled, Budenz's statement was devastating.

McCarthy, nicknamed "Tail-gunner Joe" by the press, nevertheless enjoyed public support, as polls showed, and was a popular figure. He was quick to unearth the *Amerasia* scandal, which had been buried twice before his arrival. The affair involved crimes, theft of official documents, perjury, cover-ups and other security-related offences. During Sessions, the Justice Department's intention was to bury it a third time. Senator Tydings began by considering the matter a trifle. However, the FBI knew of the Justice Department's complicity in past dealings to bury the whole scandal and had wiretaps and other documents on record to prove it. In any case, the Bureau was an arm of Justice that had an obligation to keep its mouth shut in public matters on controversial issues, as it acted on the orders of the Attorney General's Office. However, if its agents were called before the Senate, the FBI's subordination, culture of silence and traditional discretion did not oblige them to perjure themselves in order to protect Department officials who had committed crimes.

This situation led to conflict, as attempts were made to muzzle Edgar Hoover's men in order to continue the cover-up. To minimise the case, the evidence was rejected and the documents were deemed unimportant. Two senior officials, John Peurifoy of the State Department and Peyton Ford, assistant to Attorney General Howard McGrath, took it upon themselves to feed these arguments to the newspapers. Peurifoy soon went a step further, issuing a press release accusing McCarthy of being a compulsive liar and attributing to Hoover words that encouraged a lack of concern about the Amerasia affair. When he learned that words were attributed to him that he did not say, the FBI Director protested to the Assistant Attorney General, who was unmoved, and Edgar Hoover put his protest in writing to Howard McGrath. Testimony before the Senate Subcommittee attributing unsaid words and reports to the FBI Director irritated Hoover greatly.

The idea that the whole thing was a storm in a teapot was gaining ground in the press, prompting a reaction from Republican Bourke Hickenlooper. Hickenlooper, a member of the Senate Subcommittee, issued a press release insisting that many of the papers recovered from *Amerasia* concerned military and strategic matters that could have influenced the war in the Pacific or been of great value to the communist in Yenan in their struggle for control of China. Hickenlooper described some particularly important documents, such as, for example, the location of naval units in the Pacific in November 1944 or messages from Roosevelt to Chiang Kai-shek. The replies and counter-replies in the newspapers made it clear that the Justice Department intended to cover up the case. After lengthy and repeated hearings concerning *Amerasia,* by the end of June 1950 Millard Tydings and company were determined to write a report that would put an end to an affair that had only just begun. On 7 July the last meeting took place, and by 17 July the Subcommittee had drafted the report that was delivered to the Senate.

Parallel to the public sessions in the Senate, behind the scenes there was a frenzy of activity going on outside the cameras to ensure that the

McCarthy allegations were closed without further consequences. In theory, confirmation of many of the issues raised by the Wisconsin Senator's allegations could be found in the State Department files; but there were many people who wanted them to remain inaccessible, which was to be a source of conflict and argument. The Truman administration had refused in March 1948 to allow Congress access to data that the government wanted to withhold, allegedly for reasons of state. McCarthy considered this "law of silence" to be a cover-up for crimes, and insisted that the requested files should be requested. Since Senate Resolution 231, under which the Subcommittee operated, explicitly stated that the records should be obtained and studied by the Subcommittee, the tug-of-war between the Senate and the Truman Administration dragged on for several months. McCarthy argued that if his allegations about the disastrous state security situation were false, the President could easily prove it by turning over the records. On 4 May, Truman announced that he was denying the Senate access to the requested documents, and a "stalemate" ensued. After much back and forth, it was agreed that the release would be restricted and only some records would be made available. McCarthy and his staff alluded to rumours that the records were being stripped. On 21 June, Tydings announced that the FBI had informed him that all materials collected by the Bureau relating to the loyalty of those under investigation were still at the State Department, some of which were being examined by the committee. Senator McCarthy asked the FBI Director in writing to confirm Tydings' assertion. Edgar Hoover asked Mickey Ladd, an agent he trusted, whether the verification announced by Tydings had been made. The next day Ladd replied: "We have not examined the State Department records file by file.... We have never made any such comment to Senator Tydings." Accordingly, Hoover, in an unusual move, wrote a letter of reply to Senator McCarthy on 10 July 1950, published in full by Stanton Evans in *Blacklisted by History*, the primary source for the lines we have been writing:

> "My dear senator:
> I have received your letter dated 27 June 1950 in which you ask whether the Bureau has examined the 81 loyalty files which members of the Tydings Committee have been scrutinising and whether such examination by the FBI has revealed that the files are complete and that nothing has been removed therefrom.
> The Federal Bureau of Investigation has not conducted such a survey and is therefore not in a position to make any report as to whether the State Department's files are complete or incomplete.
> For your information, the Federal Bureau of Investigation provided Mr. Ford, at his request, with a record of all loyalty materials on the 81 cases in question provided to the State Department. For your information, I am enclosing a copy of Mr. Ford's letter to Senator Tydings, which I have obtained from the Attorney General.

Yours faithfully
J. Edgar Hoover".

In our opinion, the fact that Joe McCarthy wrote to the FBI director indicates that he was suspicious of Tydings and of any moves the Truman administration might make to "clean up" the State Department files. This letter shows that Hoover and McCarthy were on the same page. Of course, the Bureau was well aware that the conspiracy the senator was trying to expose to the public existed, as they had been investigating it for more than a decade. On 22 March 1947, President Truman had signed Executive Order 9835, known as the "Loyalty Order", which created the LRB (Loyalty Review Board), a Board supposedly designed to investigate and root out Communist influence in the Federal Government. This was intended to silence critical voices accusing the Democrats of being soft on communists. Some three million people were investigated; but only 300 civil servants were dismissed. In reality, all this paraphernalia was designed to mitigate Truman's discredit in the run-up to the next election and at the same time to limit the FBI's role in order to avoid a so-called "witch-hunt".

As McCarthy's struggle with the Truman administration festered, suspicions that the State Department was "cleaning out" files on people who should have been expelled were confirmed. For example, McCarthy managed to get hold of the minutes of a meeting of the LRB held on 14 February 1951, which discussed loyalty cases in the State Department, including that of John Stewart Service, and what should be done with them. In the discussions, some members clearly expressed concern about the Department's clearance of many suspects. LRB Chairman Bingham said in relation to the exchange of views on the matter: "I think it is fair to say that the State Department, as you know, has the worst record of all the Departments in the actions of this Loyalty Board.... It has found no one guilty under our rules. It is the only Department that has acted in this way". These words are unmistakable, for they are not from McCarthy or any Republican member of the Council, but come from the Chairman of the LRB created by Truman.

Any government official under investigation had the option to resign. If he or she did so, the investigation was stopped immediately and the process had no consequences. Often, an employee who had resigned from one department was later hired in another. Joe McCarthy was understandably outraged at this farce. I think we ought to know," Senator McCarthy protested, "how many of those who resigned have obtained positions in another department. Take the case of Meigs (Peveril Meigs had been McCarthy's No. 3 case before the Senate). While under investigation, he resigned from the State Department. He went into the Army and got a job. Whether or not he had access to classified matters, I don't know. His Loyalty Council ordered after a hearing that he be cleared of the charges. I wonder how many cases there are analogous to this one." For three years, chicanery of all sorts to obstruct Senator McCarthy's work was the norm; but in 1952, after a period of twenty years of Democratic terms, there was the election victory of the Republicans which, theoretically, was supposed to change some things.

In the early months of 1953, it seemed that the big break came for Senator Joseph McCarthy, who was easily re-elected in Wisconsin. Under the new circumstances, McCarthy became chairman of the Senate Government Operations Committee and also of the Permanent Subcommittee on Investigations (PSI). In addition, he retained his seat on the Senate Appropriations Committee, which controlled the budgets of executive departments. Some of his bitterest enemies, such as William Benton, the Connecticut senator who in 1951 even introduced a resolution to expel McCarthy from the Senate, or Millard Tydings himself, failed to win re-election. The new US President, Eisenhower, had placed Richard Nixon, who had backed McCarthy during the years of bitter struggle with the Democrats, as his vice-presidential running mate. This augured that the Senator could count on significant support. Not everything was to be as easy as it might seem, however, for the president's guard included a number of influential advisers who despised McCarthy. It should not be forgotten that Eisenhower, "the terrible Swedish Jew", the man responsible for the death camps, Morgenthau's and Baruch's man, was a domestic who was part of the international cabal of conspirators.

But if McCarthy had enemies among Republicans, he counted among his Democratic friends the Kennedy brothers, loyal and solid supporters. Such was the harmony between Robert Kennedy and Joe McCarthy that Bob asked him to sponsor his first son. Joseph "joe" Patrick Kennedy, patriarch of the clan, wanted his son Robert to be McCarthy's chief counsel on the new committee he was chairing; but mistakenly, to avoid the usual accusations of anti-Semitism, McCarthy announced on 2 January 1953 that 26-year-old Jewish Roy M. Cohn would be chief counsel to the Permanent Subcommittee on Investigations (PSI). Cohn, son of New York Supreme Court Justice Albert Cohn, admitted that he had been appointed by Senator McCarthy because he was Jewish. There was a growing rumour, evidently spread by themselves, that McCarthy hated Jews. Naively, he wanted to prevent these slanders from hindering his work. At the same time, the fact that Joseph Kennedy was considered an anti-Semite must have helped in the election.

The press campaign on Cohn's behalf was led by George Sokolsky, an influential Jewish columnist whom Cohn called "rabbi", and Richard Berlin, the Jewish president of the Hearst Corporation, both purported anti-Communists. Most of the print and broadcast media maintained an intense campaign against the Wisconsin senator, who craved some media coverage. In the end, McCarthy sold his soul to the devil, for in exchange for Cohn's nomination he had the support of the Hearst Group newspapers. Republican Senator Everett Dirksen confirmed: "Cohn was put on the Committee by the Hearst newspapers, and Joe dares not lose that support. Cohn, a homosexual who died of AIDS in 1986, brought onto the staff another young Jewish billionaire heir, G. David Shine, who had avoided military service and the Korean War. Shine volunteered to work for free, so McCarthy did not object to his inclusion in the team. In time, this signing would prove to be decisive in the course of events. To make it all the more clear how wrong McCarthy's steps were, it should be added that Bob Kennedy and Roy Cohn had a deep enmity that bordered on contempt. Suffice it to say that when in the early 1960s Robert Kennedy became attorney general, he tried to put Cohn in jail.

It is not possible to follow in detail the meandering plot of events that brought McCarthy down. We will recount only a few of the episodes that those plotting against him used to precipitate his bitter defeat. Prominent among McCarthy's principal enemies was Maurice Rosenblatt, a Zionist Jew who acted as a lobby agitator and was an agent of the "sorcerers" who ran the operations behind the scenes. Already in the early 1940s this so-called left-wing activist had been the catalyst for a mobilisation against the HCUA (Congressional Committee on Un-American Activities) chaired by Martin Dies. Rosenblatt then became the head of a group called the "Coordinating Committee for Democratic Action", which accused all those who criticised Roosevelt's pro-communist policies of fascism. In the McCarthy era, Rosenblatt reappeared as head of the NCEC (National Committee for an Effective Congress), a group he founded in 1948 whose main thesis regarding the senator from Wisconsin was that Joe McCarthy was a new Hitler who had to be eliminated before he could spread fascism in the United States. With the advent of the Republican Administration in 1953, the NCEC gained access to the White House through Paul G. Hoffman, another Jew who was a close friend and advisor to Eisenhower. Hoffman, the chief administrator of the Marshall Plan, later married Anna Rosenberg, a Hungarian-born Jew who had served in various capacities under Roosevelt and between 1950 and 1953 was Under Secretary of Defense under Truman, an appointment much criticised by Senator McCarthy. Maurice Rosenblatt had in Paul Hoffman an important colleague right next to the president.

In June 1953 McCarthy, in an attempt to smooth things over between Bob Kennedy and Roy Cohn, appointed Joseph Brown Matthews, known as J. B. Mathwes, director of research for the PSI, the Permanent Subcommittee of Inquiry which he chaired. Matthews, involved for years on numerous Communist fronts, broke disenchanted with the party and was to become one of the most famous anti-Communist experts. In 1938, before the Dies Committee, he reported on the activities of numerous organisations covertly controlled by the party and had become an example of a collaborating communist defector. Months before being signed by McCarthy, Matthews had written an article for *The American Mercury* entitled "Reds in Our

Churches", which, fatally, was published shortly after his appointment. McCarthy's enemies saw the article as an opportunity to provoke a crisis in the senator's team and launched a full-fledged campaign. The article began with the words: "The largest support group for the Communist apparatus in the United States today is composed of Protestant priests. It then went on to denounce odd groups, such as the "People's Institute of Applied Religion", which promoted Marxism in rural churches, and *The Protestant* magazine, which specialised in fierce anti-Catholic vituperation and thinly veiled red propaganda.

Rosenblatt and company immediately began their campaign through journalists, liberal activists and clergy. All were outraged by the Matthews-McCarthy tandem, whom they accused of being anti-Protestant bigots. The power of Rosenblatt's group was demonstrated by the extent of the attacks in the press and by the reaction they were able to orchestrate among the Democratic senators on McCarthy's subcommittee. Such was the strength of the pressure groups that they even succeeded in getting President Eisenhower to attack Senator McCarthy, who soon found himself cornered and with no alternative but to fire Matthews. Eisenhower's words were designed by his advisers to do as much damage as possible. Stanton Evans reports the journalistic account of Joseph Alsop, who revealed at the time what happened in the White House. Eisenhower has finally broken off hostilities with Senator Joseph McCarthy," Alsop wrote, "through the decisive statement denouncing the libel against Protestant clergymen perpetrated by McCarthy's favourite investigator, J.B. Matthews." Alsop added that the real interest of the statement consisted of a vital background fact: "The White House vigorously sought the opportunity, indeed created the opportunity, to deal this severe blow to the Senator from Wisconsin."

One of the prestigious journalists who worked closely with Rosenblatt's NCEC was Drew Pearson, the same one who had years earlier seized on Patton's incident with a Jewish soldier in a hospital to accuse the general of anti-Semitism. Pearson, a flunky who according to some sources was a crypto-Jew, wrote several poisoned columns. In one he claimed that both Matthews and McCarthy were Catholics, which was not true, as Matthews was a Protestant, and that both were engaged in an indiscriminate attack on the nation's Protestant churches and in deliberately fomenting religious hatred for political reasons. The fallout from the whole set-up was very serious for the McCarthy-chaired PSI, as Democratic members of the subcommittee demanded further apologies. When the whole thing degenerated into a confrontation with McCarthy and his Republican colleagues, they decided to boycott the sessions until the end of the year. Robert Kennedy also walked out of the debates, but later returned as an advisor to the Democratic senators. In the end, the "lobbyists'" strategy had paid off: McCarthy, a bigot who not only persecuted communists but also slandered and discredited the Protestant Church, had his fight adulterated,

President Eisenhower had been biased against him, and the senator from Wisconsin had been damaged in the eyes of public opinion.

Another chapter in the unequal struggle that our American Quixote waged against his hulking enemies originated at Fort Monmouth, a research laboratory of the Army Signal Corps. The episode began when McCarthy, in the spring of 1953, received an enigmatic call offering him important security documents. McCarthy met with the mysterious informant, an intelligence officer, who handed him a confidential memo about a secret investigation the FBI had turned over to the Army. This was to become one of the longest and most complex enquiries, and one that caused endless problems. The document was a compendium of a report dated January 1951. The subject was the security breach at Fort Monmouth, an Army laboratory in Eatontown, New Jersey. Later in one of the Senate sessions it was revealed that the FBI had investigated thirty-four workers at the facility, most of them Jews. The investigations lasted from the summer of 1953 until the spring of 1954, when they were suddenly halted because of the Army's incredible accusations against McCarthy for illegal activities.

It has already been mentioned in the pages on atomic espionage that in 1945 the Army had dismissed Julius Rosenberg from Fort Monmouth when it was discovered that he was a communist. The other members of the circle of Soviet and/or Zionist agents had continued to work and spy in the laboratory. McCarthy's investigations confirmed that Monmouth had for years been an information leak and security debacle. Among other relevant aspects, the senator's staff discovered that the complex and its associated facilities were highly security-related and that the indolence and irresponsibility at the highest levels of the military had been scandalous. The investigations revealed serious negligence in the handling of official papers. Among the top undercover agents still at the lab when the PSI (Permanent Subcommittee on Investigations) hearings began, Joe McCarthy's team named Aaron Coleman, a Jewish Communist who was at the facility until September 1953. When he was finally fired, classified documents taken from Fort Monmouth were found at his home. On 8 and 19 December 1953 he appeared before the Subcommittee and despite multiple evidence of his relationship with Julius Rosenberg (sentenced to death) and Morton Sobell (sentenced to thirty years in prison) and of his espionage activities, he was never charged in court. Another Jewish agent, Nathan Sussman, who had spied for Julius Rosenberg, testified during the PSI hearings that Coleman, Rosenberg, Sobell, Al Sarant and Joel Barr, all Jews linked to the Fort Monmouth laboratory, were communist agents.

At the start of McCarthy's investigation, Fort Monmouth had for ten years been a nest of Communist agents. Six other Jews accused by McCarthy of being communists were Jack Okun, Barry Bernstein, Samuel Simon Snyder, Joseph Levitsky, Harry Hyman and Ruth Levine. The first, Jack Okun, was Aaron Coleman's roommate and had been expelled from Fort

Monmouth for security reasons in 1949. Despite having access to the documents Coleman kept in the house, Okun successfully appealed the decision and the Loyalty Review Board (LRB) allowed his readmission to the Pentagon and his resignation was later accepted. This was one of the reversals in security cases that alerted McCarthy and his aides. Similar was the case of Barry Bernstein, a senior official at the Evans Signals Laboratory, where he held a particularly sensitive position with secret clearance. In 1951, Bernstein had been questioned at Monmouth on security grounds and after being examined by a First Army security board was suspended from his duties. He immediately appealed to the Pentagon, the decision was reversed and he was reinstated; but, unlike Okun, he did not resign and was still in his post when the McCarthy hearings began. A third case was that of Snyder, who in late 1952 had been expelled from the Signal Laboratory by a regional council of the First Army. He, too, had managed to get the Pentagon to allow his reinstatement and then resigned.

Hearings before the Subcommittee chaired by McCarthy showed that numerous components of the Rosenberg-Sobell group were still at Monmouth in the early 1950s. Joseph Levistsky had worked at the Signals Laboratory and then at the Federal Telecommunications Laboratory, where he had had access to classified Army projects. When asked by McCarthy if he was part of the Communist conspiracy while handling sensitive information for the government, Levistsky pleaded the Fifth Amendment. Samuel Snyder also invoked the Fifth Amendment. It should be considered that when an incriminated person invoked the Fifth, it indicated that he could not answer the charges without incriminating himself. In other words, an appeal to the Fifth Amendment was understood to connote guilt, even if the defendant could not be charged in a criminal prosecution. Working with Levitsky until 1951 at the FTL (Federal Telecommunications Lab) was Harry Hyman, who had been identified as a Communist agent by two people, Lester Ackerman and John Saunders, both former Communists. Here, from *Blacklisted by History*, is an example of how the interrogations were conducted:

> "McCarthy: Have you ever discussed espionage with members of the Communist Party?
> Hyman: I decline to answer for the reasons given above (Fifth Amendment).
> McCarthy: Have you ever handed over government secrets to anyone who was known to you as an espionage agent?
> Hyman: I decline to answer for the same reasons.
> McCarthy: Did you make 76 calls to the Federal Telecommunications Laboratory in Lodi, New Jersey, between 24 January 1952 and 21 October 1953 for the purpose of receiving classified information and for the purpose of delivering it to an agent or agents of espionage?
> Hyman: I refuse to answer for the same reasons".

This session took place on 25 November 1953. Senator McCarthy asked numerous questions related to espionage and referred to hundreds of telephone calls to military and scientific facilities. On each occasion Hyman invoked the Fifth Amendment. Another prominent security breach suspect was Ruth Levine, who had worked for a decade at the CTF, where she rose to a high position with secret clearance. When the Joe McCarthy hearings began, Levine was still employed, even though several witnesses had testified that she was part of a communist cell operating within the CTF. She too, like her colleagues, refused questions and pleaded the notorious Fifth.

McCarthy was initially supported by Robert Stevens, who had been appointed Secretary of the Army by Eisenhower on 4 February 1953. Stevens was an anti-Communist who, as soon as he took office, held a briefing on the Army Loyalty and Security Programme. His first interest was in what steps had been taken to prevent disloyal individuals from infiltrating the institution and what had been done to ferret out and expel suspects. He first contacted Edgar Hoover, the director of the FBI, and asked his advice. He then sent a telegram to Senator McCarthy and offered his help in the investigation he had undertaken. When on 10 February 1953 McCarthy announced that there was clear evidence of espionage at Fort Monmouth. Stevens instructed General Kirke B. Lawton, the post commander: "Cooperate! Make it easy for them to question whoever they wish.

General Lawton had arrived at Fort Monmouth in 1951 and had identified security problems, but had failed to act effectively, hence his willingness to cooperate was sincere. On 15 October 1953, he appeared in executive (non-public) session before the Senate Subcommittee. The following is an excerpt from his conversation with McCarthy, reproduced by Stanton Evans:

> "McCarthy: Would you say that since you took office and especially in the last six months you have been working to eradicate the accumulated security risks in the Signal Corps and that you have put a considerable number of them on hold?
> Lawton: That's a question I'll answer yes, but don't go back six months.... Effective results have been seen in the last two weeks. I have been working for the last twenty-one months trying to achieve what has been achieved in the last two weeks.
> McCarthy: Would you say that in the last few weeks you have had more effective results?
> Lawton: Absolutely, more than we've had in the last four years.
> McCarthy: Can you tell us why it is only in the last two or three weeks that you have been able to achieve effective results?
> Lawton: Yes, but I'd better not say it. I know very well, but I work for Mr. Stevens".

Although it was not a public hearing, an enemy of McCarthy's, John Gibbons Adams, the Army's general counsel considered "Mrs. Rosenberg's people" (people close to Under Secretary of Defense Anna Rosenberg), attended the hearing and informed Stevens that Lawton had acknowledged to the PSI that McCarthy had achieved more in two weeks than he had in two years. These remarks did not please Secretary Stevens, much less others above him, who sought to harass McCarthy on the grounds that he was unjustifiably attacking the Army. The undercover work of McCarthy's enemies was to provoke changes in the positions of those in the Army who supported the investigation. Thus Secretary Stevens, who undoubtedly wanted to clean up Monmouth and collaborate with the Wisconsin senator, soon found himself caught up in the conflict and increasingly pressured by his superiors. General Lawton had shown in the hearings the greatest willingness to help the Subcommittee, so that a week after his October appearance he was praised by McCarthy, who thanked him for the stand he was taking. Lawton responded: "Yes, but this position will cost me my promotion. And I'll be lucky if I survive much longer here at Fort Monmouth."

His words were prophetic, as his promotion was indeed rejected and within a year he was relieved of his command. After his 15 October speech, the general, in addition to being reprimanded for cooperating and talking more than necessary, had been pressured by John G. Adams to complete his purge at Fort Monmouth. G. Adams to finish his purge at Fort Monmouth. Later, at one of the McCarthy hearings in April 1954, General Lawton explained that he had received a call from Adams in October 1953 in which Adams said, and I hope you see clearly that you must withdraw certain cases which you have recommended for dismissal because of security risks. Lawton's response was, "I will not. Let the secretary take the responsibility." Clearly, then, a tug-of-war was being waged among the military. By the end of 1953, Robert Stevens was beginning to rectify the situation, stating that the Army was not aware of any espionage at Fort Monmouth at the time.[25]

---

[25] Getting rid of Lawton became a goal. Only the fear that Senator McCarthy would expose the harassment of the general to the public and provoke an unwanted reaction held back those who wanted to get rid of him. In an attempt to subdue Lawton while he was in command at Fort Monmouth, he was told to stop attending McCarthy's sessions and to stop collaborating with him. As had been done with Ezra Pound or James Forrestal, an attempt was made to make him look sick. He underwent a medical examination, without specifying for what illness, and was sent to Walter Reed Hospital. Those who visited him saw no signs of ill health. Secretary Stevens, for his part, reported in his statements that General Lawton remained in charge of Monmouth in order to keep McCarthy at bay. As early as the spring of 1954, the Wisconsin Senator's staff was made aware that if the General appeared before the PSI he would subsequently be punished by the loss of benefits to which he was entitled for his Army service. Finally, in the summer of 1954, he was removed from command at Fort Monmouth and retired from active duty at the end of August.

A second general, Ralph W. Zwicker, a World War II veteran who commanded Camp Kilner, another Army installation in New Jersey, was to serve as a tool to stop Senator McCarthy's investigations against Communist infiltration and direct them against him. Zwicker's behaviour and indignity contrasted with the honest attitude adopted by General Lawton. In late January 1954 a member of McCarthy's committee, George Anastos, telephoned General Zwicker for information about a security-related case at Camp Kilner involving a Medical Corps employee. Zwicker must have hesitated at first, for he replied that he would return the call himself, which he did an hour later. The general gave Anastos the name of the suspect, a Jewish communist named Irving Peress, and added that he worked as a dentist. The next day, General Zwicker telephoned again to confirm that Dr. Peress, who had earned the rank of captain in the Korean War, had been promoted to major and expected to be discharged with full honours. This dentist, it turned out, had been an organiser of communist groups who had perjured himself when he joined the army, having signed a statement swearing that he had no connection with communism.

McCarthy was outraged to learn that, having learned that Peress was part of a communist cell, the White House had ordered his promotion to major and the expediting of his retirement. When Peress appeared before the Senate Permanent Subcommittee on 30 January 1954, he repeatedly invoked the Fifth Amendment to avoid answering questions such as: Did you recruit military personnel at Camp Kilner for the Communist Party? Did you hold Communist Party meetings in your home with military personnel at Camp Kilner? Is there a Communist cell at Camp Kilner of which you are a member? Did you organise a Communist cell at Camp Kilner? Obviously, refusing to answer in order not to incriminate himself after having signed an affidavit denying his membership in the Communist Party was proof that he was a perjurer.

This was the understanding of Senator McCarthy, who promptly wrote a letter, hand-delivered to the Pentagon, urging that Peress's honorable discharge be cancelled and that he be retained in the Army so that he could be court-martialled. Since Secretary Stevens was away in Asia, the letter found its way into the hands of John G. Adams, the Army's general counsel. In 1983, Adams published a book, *Without Precedent*, in which he claims to have precipitated McCarthy's downfall. In his own words, this was his reaction to receiving the senator's letter: "I decided not to do what McCarthy asked, and instead let the dentist go. In short, to hell with McCarthy". Thus, on 2 February 1954, one day after receiving the letter, General Zwicker signed Irving Peress out of the Army with full honours.

Exasperated, McCarthy redoubled his efforts to find out how he could be so brazen. More than a few in the Army shared the view that the Peress case was an embarrassment that showed how easy it was to evade security. On 13 February, James Juliana, one of McCarthy's investigators, went to

Camp Kilner to meet with Zwicker, who told him that he had objected to honorably discharging Peress. Juliana returned convinced that the general shared her criticism of the Army's lax handling of security cases. It was then decided that Zwicker should appear at an executive hearing on 18 February to find out who had ordered Peress to get off scot-free and through the front door. Senator McCarthy showed up exhausted and irritable, as his wife had been in a car accident and had not slept all night. His aides wanted to postpone the hearing, which, given the tension of the hearing, would have been best.

The day before, on 17 February, General Counsel Adams had visited General Zwicker and had instructed, perhaps bribed, him not to reveal the name of the person who had ordered the Communist agent's honourable retirement. John Adams himself recounts the meeting in *Without Precedent*, though without going into much detail: "We were anxious to make Zwicker understand," Adams wrote, "that neither names nor further security details were to be revealed. To everyone's surprise, when a well-informed and cooperative witness was expected, Zwicker was evasive, verbally sparred with McCarthy, changed his testimony three or four times, and refused to answer questions about Irving Peress's bizarre career and grotesque discharge. All this infuriated Senator McCarthy, who could not accept the General's claims of ignorance. He perjured himself when he said he knew nothing of Peress's connections with the Communists, since he himself had disclosed to George Anastos in late January that he knew about the case. [26]

Unusually irritable from accumulated fatigue, McCarthy's nerves betrayed him, and he confronted General Zwicker as if he were an accusing prosecutor. It was a grave mistake, perhaps the one his enemies were waiting for. McCarthy asked Zwicker if he thought a general who knowingly covered up for a Communist agent should be removed from command. Zwicker replied that he did not think that was sufficient reason to remove a general. The former Marine reacted angrily and said: "Then, General, you should be

---

[26] There are documents published in 1955 by a Congressional Committee, the McClellan Committee, which demonstrate the perjury of General Zwicker, who had expressed himself in writing in terms very similar to those of McCarthy. On 21 October 1953, Zwicker had written to the Commanding General of the First Army: "This officer (Peress) refused to sign the certificate of loyalty, and refused to answer questions concerning his affiliation with subversive organisations by appealing to constitutional privilege..." Of Peress' presence in the Army, Zwicker said, "it is clearly at odds with the interest of national security." Days later, on 3 November, when Zwicker learned of Peress's promotion, he sent a second letter to the First Army insisting that Peress was a Communist agent: "An investigation completed on April 15, 1953 established that this officer was a known and active Communist in Queens N.Y." These words he had written only three months before he swore before Joe McCarthy that he knew nothing about Peress's relations with communism. It is not surprising, then, that McCarthy's colleagues thought Zwicker would be a useful witness and that the senator, perplexed, was exacerbated by the general's change of heart.

removed from command. Any man who has received the honour of being promoted to general and claims that he would protect another general who has harboured communist agents does not deserve to wear the uniform, General." It was the ammunition needed by those who sought to liquidate the senator from Wisconsin. Immediately, the press made a big fuss about McCarthy's harsh treatment of Zwicker. Among other things, he was said to have "insulted the uniform" and to have accused a decorated wartime general of "protecting subversives".

From this point on, the final campaign to destroy Joe McCarthy began, and he was no longer able to resume his work. An uninterrupted series of charges was hurled against him and members of his staff, who had to devote all their time and energy to refuting or disproving the continuous barrage of allegations. In the press, the flow of propaganda across the country was already a steady crescendo that did not cease until McCarthy was censured and rebuked by his own colleagues in the Senate. Secretary Stevens would not allow General Zwicker or other military personnel to continue testifying.

Paul Hoffman, at whose California residence President Eisenhower was vacationing, which gives an idea of the close friendship between the two Jews, telephoned Stevens to congratulate him on the decision, a congratulation which, of course, was shared by Eisenhower, to whom Hoffman was his closest adviser. From the President's entourage, John Adams was ordered to gather information on the conduct of Roy Cohn and David Shine, the two Jews whom Sokolsky and the Hearst group had placed alongside Senator McCarthy. The assignment was justified by the fact that during the investigation at Fort Monmouth, Cohn had come into conflict with the Army because of his romantic partner. Homosexuality was a taboo subject in the military at the time. The relationship between the two and Cohn's erratic behaviour were to be used to further destabilise McCarthy and provoke his definitive break with the army.

On 21 January 1954, John Adams had held a meeting in the office of the Attorney General, Herbert Brownell, which was attended among others by Eisenhower's Chief of Staff, Sherman Adams, a Mason of high rank. A briefing on the Monmouth enquiry took place there, at which Counselor Adams charged that Cohn was trying to profit for Shine and had even threatened the Army by using his position on Senator McCarthy's investigative team. Sherman Adams asked the counselor to submit a written report, which he did the next day. The text he wrote, excerpts of which he leaked to the press, provided a chronology of events regarding Cohn's activities and Shine's treatment of McCarthy's views and actions.

On 10 March, on the basis of this report, the Army publicly made a series of charges, the gist of which was a complaint about Cohn, who, with McCarthy's acquiescence, allegedly used his power on the Senate Subcommittee to curry favours for Shine. This was the genesis of a series of hearings between April and June 1954 in which McCarthy had to defend himself against the Army's allegations, which, based on the chronology presented by Counsel Adams and Secretary Stevens, accused him and Cohn of dishonest lobbying. McCarthy defended himself by arguing that the Army was trying to paralyse the investigation within the Army and discredit the PSI over which he presided. The hearings were televised and some twenty million people watched the spectacle daily. For the duration of the hearings, which produced some three thousand pages of printed transcripts, Senator McCarthy was removed from the PSI presidency. His place was temporarily taken by Republican Karl Mundt.

Joe McCarthy was saddened to find that Secretary Stevens, who had initially supported him, was acting under orders from Eisenhower's entourage. Stevens testified for fourteen days and explained the Army's charges against McCarthy-Cohn; but he was unconvincing in justifying the alleged threats to the Army attributed to both men. During the hearings, Senator Everett Dirksen, a member of the McCarthy Subcommittee, testified that General Counsel John Adams and Gerald Morgan, an aide to Eisenhower, had approached him on 22 January 1954 with the pretense of suppressing part of the McCarthy investigation. Dirksen claimed that Adams had mentioned to him that the Army had a file on Cohn and Shine and had dropped the threat that the dossier could be very damaging if aired on the front pages of the newspapers. At this point, John Adams realised that he had no business being Eisenhower's scapegoat and revealed that members of Eisenhower's staff had ordered him to compile the chronology on Cohn and Shine in a meeting in the attorney general's office the day before he went to Dirksen.

It was clear, then, that the White House was implicated in the conspiracy against McCarthy and in the cover-up of subversion in the government. On 17 May, with the obvious aim of preventing an investigation into his own role, Eisenhower issued an order claiming for himself a constitutional principle that the President could prohibit his subordinates from revealing any information to Congress. On 27 May McCarthy exaperatedly alluded to Eisenhower's "gag order" and urged federal officials to come forward with any information about corruption or subversion in the government. On the gag order, he reminded: "The oath that every member of the Government takes to protect and defend the country against all enemies, foreign and domestic, far outweighs any presidential security order." The White House response came the next day. Eisenhower's press secretary released a statement to the press, again comparing McCarthy to Hitler. A comparison that appealed to a number of high-profile columnists who henceforth also used it.

Then Joseph Welch appeared on the scene. A histrionic figure whose perfectly measured and calculated performance was just what the media needed to complete the harassment and demolition of Senator McCarthy. Joe Welch, a lawyer who acted as counsel to the Army, has gone down in history thanks to his superb performances, broadcast on television. This infamous character actor's acting skills were confirmed in 1959 when he took on the role of a judge in *Anatomy of a Murder*, a Hollywood film directed by Otto Preminger. In the words of Stanton Evans, "Welch treated the whole thing as a melodrama in which fact and reason were unmistakably secondary to image and impression. Much of what he said and did was directed to his conception of the trial as a soap opera." With utter disregard for the truth, for example, Welch lied undeterred before television cameras and declared that part of the FBI report giving the names of more than thirty subversives operating at Fort Monmouth was "a carbon copy of exactly nothing" and, despite the fact that Bureau Director Edgar Hoover had said he wrote the report, Welch alluded to the document as a "perfect forgery." On another occasion, he accused McCarthy of producing a doctored photo as evidence. It was a genuine photo showing Shine, Stevens and Colonel Jack Bradley, which had been cropped and enlarged to make it clearer. The media accepted Welch's version and ignored McCarthy's explanations.

On 9 June 1954 McCarthy alluded to a lawyer in Welch's firm, Fred Fisher, who had been a member of the National Lawyers Guild, an organisation that the US Attorney General's Office had considered a Communist Party stronghold. Fisher, in addition to being a Communist, was probably a Zionist: he died years later in Tel Aviv where he had gone to give a lecture sponsored by the Israeli Bar Association. Welch's counter-attack was an onslaught that has been repeatedly reproduced in books and videos:

> "Until this moment, Senator, I don't think I had fully understood your cruelty and folly. Fred Fisher is a young man who went to Harward Law School, came to my firm, and is beginning a brilliant career with us.... I would never have imagined that you could be so irresponsible and so cruel as to injure this boy..... I fear that he will forever bear the scar that you have unnecessarily branded him with. If it were in my power to forgive you for your reckless cruelty, I would do so. I consider myself a gentleman, but your forgiveness will have to come from somebody else."

McCarthy tried to delve into the background of the National Lawyers Guild and to retort with a louder "tu quoque" to refer to the allegations and the damage Welch himself had tried to inflict on the reputation of his collaborators. Welch refused to listen and insisted on the insults to Fisher:

> "Let's not go on murdering this boy, Senator. Haven't you got any sense of decency left, after all? Haven't you any sense of decency?"

After calling the senator indecent in front of the television cameras broadcasting the hearing, Welch burst into tears and was applauded by the audience on the Senate floor. On the way out of the courtroom, Welch cried again in front of the cameras of press photographers. The newspapers agreed in highlighting the great humanity shown by Joe Welch, a man shocked by McCarthy's vileness, who would never have been expected to be so petty as to ruin Fisher's career with his accusations. The fact that the senator's charges were true was of no interest to the media: radio, television and newspapers, traditionally in the hands of Jewish owners obedient to royal power, had conspired to take McCarthy down and would not stop until they did. Scott Speidel of Florida State University, in an article entitled "How the Jewish Marxists in America Destroyed Joe McCarthy"considers that the press "has not poured so much hatred on a public figure since Adolf Hitler".

The next step of the anti-McCarthy plotters was to secure a Senate conviction in order to discredit him definitively and ruin his political career and reputation forever. The Democrats were not enough to do this, for in the public eye it was desirable to bring in Republican senators who would vote against him in order to avoid the impression that it was a partisan fight. The top picks were Arthur Watkins, a Republican senator from Utah who was to chair a special Senate committee to study the charges against McCarthy, and Ralph Flanders, a senator from Vermont, who, in a savage attack on his colleague on the Senate floor, had accused him, Cohn and Shine of being a trio of homosexuals. Nor had Flanders shied away from drawing similarities between McCarthy and Hitler, which had become commonplace. Days after peppering the martyred McCarthy with these diatribes, Flanders listed as many as thirty-three specific charges against him, which were to be the basis of his censure. Some of the charges were so bizarre that some Republicans asked him where they came from. Without the slightest modesty, Flanders admitted that they had been given to him by the NCEC (National Committee for an Effective Congress), whose alma mater was the Zionist Jew Maurice Rosenblatt, an avowed enemy of the Wisconsin senator and one of the main agitators against him. Rosenblatt had extracted the NCEC material and Flanders had merely read it to the Senate. Thus began the road to McCarthy's Calvary, which was to end with the vote that crucified him on 2 December 1954.

Thus, the Senate hearings against McCarthy were conducted under Republican control, although some senators in the party were still with him and did not support censure. During the years when Joe McCarthy stood up to Truman, he could at least count on the backing of a majority of his party's senators; but with a Republican president in the White House pushing against him, the split had occurred. The NCEC's mainstay in Eisenhower's entourage was once again Paul Hoffman, who acted as a veiled transmission belt between Rosenblatt's committee and the White House, whose influence was decisive in the rejection.

So brazen was the NCEC's leadership in the campaign to censure McCarthy that it underwrote the financial expenses of Flanders and company. Stanton Evans reproduces a budget of the organisation to cover expenses from June 25 to August 10, 1954, amounting to $23,650, $3,500 of which were advertisements in three Washington newspapers. The same author writes the following about the connection between Rosenblatt and Hoffman: "Behind the scenes, Hoffman had supported Rosenblatt's effort with financial contributions. In the midst of the censorship battle, however, he publicly showed his connection by stressing the political linkage between the NCEC and the White House. Shortly after Flanders introduced his resolution against McCarthy, the NCEC drafted and Hoffman signed a widely publicised telegram urging support for the censure motion."

Arguably, by the end of September, many of McCarthy's remaining supporters threw in the towel when they saw the fight as lost. Although some of his staunchest friends, Senators William Jenner, Herman Welker and a few others, denounced what was going on, his Senate colleagues expelled him from their own Committee in November. Finally, on 2 December 1954, the Senate condemned him for "conduct contrary to the traditions of the Senate". The result of the vote was 67-22. The fact that among the votes of condemnation there were 22 cast by Republicans made it possible to argue that both parties had censured the Senator from Wisconsin, who became a person to be avoided.

McCarthy was locked for four years in a death struggle he could never win. His enemies included two US presidents, the universal media empire and, ultimately, the covert tyranny that had been financing communism since its inception, whose lobbies spanned the entire political and economic spectrum. Joseph McCarthy died at the age of forty-eight on 2 May 1957, thirty months after being censured. He apparently sought the false refuge of drink. According to some, the emptiness and exclusion to which he was subjected sapped his will to live. Others argue that he drank himself to death. In the decades that followed, the falsifiers of reality, in the service of the Occult Power, took it upon themselves to throw his name into the dustbin of history, where those who have dared to denounce the manipulation and crimes that a cabal of conspirators exercise over humanity are placed.

PART 5
THE CONTROL OF COMMUNISM
BERIA AND THE ASSASSINATION OF STALIN

The figure of Stalin, Iosif Vissarionovich Dzhugashvili, is one of the most impressive in history. During his almost thirty years of merciless power in Russia, he proved to be a formidable policeman of incommensurable cunning and malice, who knew how to get rid of all those who tried to take him out of the way. His ability to confront Trotskyism and what it represented, his tenacity in systematically eliminating his enemies, his intelligence to manoeuvre and resist as an absolute dictator are astonishing when one considers that, except in the years of the World War, he was confronted by global forces of the Hidden Power who sought to replace him with one of their agents. However much the official historiography ignores it, Stalin was aware that the Trotskyite opposition intended to take advantage of Hitler's rise to power to provoke war with Germany and regain control of the USSR. Trotsky had no qualms about publicly stating that in the event of war he and the opposition would remove Stalin from power and then organise the defence that would allow the final victory [27].

The fact that among all the great murderers of communism - Trotsky, Lenin, Yagoda, Kaganóvich, Beria, Mao Tse-tung and so many others - only Stalin is criticised in the eyes of international opinion is extremely revealing. Yagoda, Kaganóvich and Beria, three Jews who rank among the greatest criminals of all time, are not even known to the general public. Trotsky and Lenin, whose crimes in no way detract from those of their co-religionists, remain emblematic and respected figures in supposedly progressive circles around the world. As for Mao Tse-tung's terrible massacres in China, they are neither remembered nor denounced. Only Stalin's crimes are exposed with some regularity by the media, whose propaganda has focused for

---

[27] Isaac Deutscher, a Polish writer and historian of Jewish origin considered a Trotskyite, wrote biographies of Stalin and Trotsky. In *Stalin,* he writes: "In the supreme crisis of the war, the leaders of the opposition, had they still been alive, could indeed have acted under the conviction, true or false, that Stalin was conducting the war in an incompetent and fatal manner. From the beginning, they could have opposed the agreement with Hitler. Had not Trotsky foreseen such an action against Stalin in his 'Clemenceau thesis'? Let us imagine for a moment that the leaders of the opposition had survived and witnessed the defeat of the Red Army in 1941 and 1942, with Hitler at the gates of Moscow and millions of soldiers imprisoned by the Germans, with the people in the grip of a dangerous moral crisis such as that which occurred in the autumn of 1941, at a time when the future of the Soviets hung in the balance and Stalin's authority was at its lowest ebb. It is possible that they would then have tried to overthrow Stalin". That was precisely the plan that was exposed in the Moscow trials. That was the initial idea when the Jewish Wall Street bankers financed Hitler.

seventy years on exposing to exhaustion the intrinsic evil of Nazism and the unparalleled suffering of the Jews.

The elimination of numerous Trotskyist Jews, who since Lenin's death had been gradually displaced from power, was an extraordinary show of force on the part of Stalin, the only "bad guy" in international communism. The Moscow trials, described by the world press as "show trials", demonstrated to those who wanted to see the reality that there were all kinds of manoeuvres to dislodge Stalin from the Kremlin. After World War II, the issue of his replacement as head of the USSR gradually resurfaced, especially as it became clear that he had no intention of ceding his omnipotent power to anyone. When Stalin realised that, as before the war, Jewish agents were again scheming in the shadows to get rid of him, he stuck to his old methods and resumed the policy of arresting and murdering his opponents. Accusations of anti-Semitism surfaced everywhere. However, the words of Heinz Galinsky, chairman of the Berlin Jewish Community, put the problem in its proper terms: "Unlike Nazi anti-Semitism," Galinsky declared, "Communist action against the Jews is not of a racial character, but of a political character. In other words, Stalin did not persecute Jews because they were Jews, but because those who sought to destroy him were Jews working for the occult forces that had financed communism from the beginning.

After the Second World War, intrigues to succeed Stalin, led by some of the leaders of the Central Committee and the Politburo, soon began. The leading figure in the conspiracy was Lavrenti Beria, a Georgian like Stalin. As People's Commissar for Internal Affairs, a post he held from 25 November 1938, he had control of the police and the secret service, the NKVD, which gave him the levers he needed to seize power after the longed-for demise of the incombustible master of the Kremlin. Almost all scholars, as will be seen, agree that he was the main suspect in Stalin's assassination. Before going on to describe the struggle that unfolded, a review of the figure of Beria, one of communism's most brutal and ruthless mass murderers, is obligatory.

Lavrenti Pavlovich Beria

When Stalin decided to do battle with the Zionist and/or Trotskyist Jews who questioned his leadership in the countries of Europe "liberated" by the Red Army, also began to distrust the Jews who remained in prominent positions in the USSR itself. Adburahman Avtorkhanov, a specialist on the Stalinist period, writes in *Staline assassiné. Le complot de Béria* that Stalin was convinced that Zionist spies were infiltrating everywhere and saw them as potential conspirators. According to this author, Stalin studied the family trees of Communist Party members up to the second and even third generation, trying to discover Jews among their ancestors. It was in this way that he discovered that Beria's mother was listed as a Georgian Jew. Since, as has been said, among Jews it is the mother who confers ethnicity, Lavrenti Beria was therefore Jewish. His mother, Tekle, who was born in Uria Sopeli, a village inhabited by Jews, gave birth to him on 29 March 1899 in Merkheuli, a village in Abkhazia, a region of Georgia inhabited by the Mingrelians, an ancient Caucasian tribe.

At the age of sixteen, Beria made an eight-hundred-kilometre train journey from the Black Sea to the Caspian Sea, to cosmopolitan Baku, where he studied at the Higher School of Mechanics and Construction, known as the "Technicum". There he came into contact with Marxist revolutionary students who called for the overthrow of the Tsar, such as Vsevolod Merkulov, whom he befriended and became one of his trusted men, Mir Djaffar Bagirov and Evgeny Dumbadze, whom he would assassinate years later; but at the same time he became a confidant of the Ojrana, the Tsarist secret police. Thaddeus Wittlin states in *Commissar Beria* that when the Provisional Government headed by Prince Lvov was formed in Russia in February 1917, "Beria thought it wiser to be on good terms with both sides and began to play with two cards"; that is, at the age of eighteen, by which time he was behaving like an adult, he began to work for both the Ojrana and the Bolshevik conspirators, whose leaders considered Beria one of their own.

After the October revolution, following Lenin's declaration guaranteeing the right to self-determination, Azerbaijan, Georgia and Armenia, the three Caucasian countries, proclaimed themselves independent. However, the Soviets soon reacted in Azerbaijan, whose Caspian oil wells were being exploited by international companies, and on 25 April 1918 they set up in Baku the Council of People's Commissars, called the Baku Commune, which tried to impose the dictatorship of the proletariat throughout the country. Stalin declared that Baku was to be "the fortress of Soviet power in Transcaucasia". Then came the reaction of the Mussavatist nationalists, supported by the British. The fighting in the capital was extremely fierce, and the battles were fought street by street. At the end of July 1918, the Bolshevik government in Baku ceased to exist. Soon British regiments under the command of General Lionel Charles Dunsterville entered Baku and occupied the city, whose port was the centre of the oil emporium. The 26 commissars of the Baku Commune were imprisoned. A provisional government, calling itself the "Central Caspian Dictatorship", was formed, which, in the hands of the Azeri Mussavatists, lasted until April 1920. It was during these years that Beria came into contact in Baku with the British intelligence services, for whom he worked from 1919 onwards.

Nikita Khrushchev confirmed on several occasions that Beria was a British agent. Both the aforementioned A. Avtorkhanov and Anton Kolendic, author of *Les derniers jours. De la mort de Staline à celle de Beria (March-December 1953)*, refer to the circumstances in which Khrushchev publicly disclosed Beria's membership in British espionage. Kolendic reproduces

Khrushchev's remarks at the closing dinner of the 22nd Congress of the CPSU, held in 1961 in Moscow, at which he was re-elected General Secretary of the party. On that occasion, Khrushchev gave his version of how Beria's arrest took place during the Politburo meeting on the night of Saturday 21 to Sunday 22 June 1953: "I have seen many things in my life," the General Secretary declared, "but I will never forget that white, exhausting night...". The following is taken from Kolendic's book, in which Khrushchev recounts at the dinner in October 1961 how in 1953 he accused Beria before his comrades in the Politburo of having worked for the British:

> "-... Therefore, comrades, I propose that we should first of all take up the discussion of the case of Comrade Beria....
> All approved, some loudly, others with applause, some nodding their heads...
> Beria, alone, was troubled, surprised, simply caught off guard. He was sitting next to me and he grabbed my arm amicably, murmuring:
> - But what's the matter with you, Nikita, what evil spirit is driving you? What do these jokes mean?
> I pushed his arm away and in a loud voice, so that everyone could hear, I answered him:
> - Pay attention, you'll understand!
> I then stated:
> - What is happening today in East Berlin, the fact that Lavrenti Beria has betrayed and sold out the interests of the Soviet Union, is not by chance, not even a simple mistake. No! It is Beria! I would like first of all to remind you of the Central Committee Plenum of 1937. On that day, a member of the Central Committee, comrade Grisha Kaminski, had provided evidence that Beria, who was then a candidate for the Politburo, had worked for British espionage and had collaborated with the Mussavatist groups, and that his case was therefore not up to the party, but to the General Prosecutor of the Republic. What happened, comrades? Instead of opening an investigation, Beria was elected to the Politburo and Grisha Kaminski disappeared after the plenum without a trace. He was never heard of again."

Beria's simultaneous collaboration with the Soviets and the Mussavatist nationalists was probably a requirement of his work for British Intelligence. In *Staline assassinated*, Avtorkhanov confirms Beria's relationship with the Azeri nationalists and recalls that already in the Secret Report to the 20th Congress of the CPSU, which was not part of the official reports and resolutions issued by the Congress because it was delivered in closed session on 25 February 1956, Khrushchev reported on the denunciation of Beria by the People's Commissar for Health, Grisha Kaminsky. On that occasion Khrushchev was more precise and revealed that, as soon as the Central Committee plenum was over, Kaminsky was arrested and shot.

At the end of 1919 the British left the area and left Azerbaijan in the hands of the Mussavatists, who were recognised as the only legal government in the country. The Soviets wanted nothing to do with Lenin's right to self-determination for the peoples, and as soon as the British left and the nationalists were left without their protection, they began to prepare a coup d'état. At dawn on 20 April 1920, the Soviet XIth Army commanded by Kirov and his aide-de-camp, Komandarm Gekher, entered Baku and seized the city. On the same day, members of the Government of the Azerbaijan National Republic were arrested and executed in the Bailov prison yard. The Red soldiers were given carte blanche to act against the bourgeoisie.

In *Commissar Beria,* Thaddeus Wittlin writes: "Soon the windows and doors of the houses of the rich were broken down, convents were demolished and ransacked. Nuns were forced to dance naked before being raped and shot. Many homes of the bourgeoisie and the wealthy classes were ransacked, and their women were also raped". During the night of 20-21 April the flames of the burnt houses lit up the capital, and at dawn the bodies of its inhabitants, bayoneted or stabbed to death, lay charred in the ruins. Beria, true to his principle of standing with those in power, took a central role in the repression unleashed by his Bolshevik friends. Having been in contact with the nationalists as a British agent, he was in a position to provide blacklists of people who had collaborated with the Azerbaijani government.

The terror, which lasted six days, has gone down in history as the "Week of Annihilation of the Bourgeoisie". All officers of the Azerbaijan National Army were arrested and imprisoned. The officers were also taken from their homes, loaded into trucks and driven to prison. The Bailov prison was so overcrowded," writes T. Wittlin, "that there was not even room to sit on the floor. Men, women and children, young and old, healthy and sick, had to stand upright, crowded together. Not only the cells, but also the corridors and the rooms, the toilets, the laundry, the storerooms and the infirmary were full. All these places were turned into mass cells". Soon, however, the prison was evacuated. The detainees were taken by boat to the island of Nargen, where the mass murders began, executed by machine-gun platoons which, without discrimination of age or sex, fired on groups of a hundred or two hundred people lined up next to previously opened ditches, into which the bodies fell. Two small steamers made two or three trips a day from the port to the island. The operation, directed by Serge Ordzhonikidze, was carried out by the Komsomol (Communist Youth) in Baku, whose main leaders were Dumbadze, Bagirov and Dekanozov, assisted by Lavreni Beria, whom T. Wittlin points out as one of those responsible for the massacres: "The lists and other documents prepared by Lavrenti Beria - says Wittlin - contained the names and addresses, as well as the alleged charges against the persons whom Beria considered and described as enemies of the Soviet regime".

Beria never believed in God or Marx. Scholars agree in describing him as a cold, calculating man devoid of ideology. In fact, while uncertainty about the final outcome persisted in the Caucasus, Beria gradually positioned himself close to those in power; but from May 1920 onwards it became clear where he belonged, and he became a communist for good. At the October 1961 dinner mentioned above, Khrushchev had this to say about him: "Beria was never a communist, but a calculating and selfish careerist who saw in our party the ideal way to realise his plans as a megalomaniac, a criminal and a spy". Be that as it may, in May 1920 Beria began a career that over thirty-three years was to make him the most feared and powerful man in the USSR after Stalin. It was Ordzhonikidze who, seeing Beria's talent during the days of massacres on the island of Nargen, offered him a position as a chekist with the rank of deputy chief of the Secret Operations Section, a position that came with the directorship of Bailov prison, where he set up his office.

There he gained experience as an interrogator and torturer. There are testimonies from this period about how he proceeded with the girls during interrogations: in addition to slapping them, he forced them to lie face down on the floor, to take off their shoes and to pull up their skirts until their underwear was exposed. Beria would put one foot on the victim's neck and use a riding crop to whip her buttocks and legs. His biographer, Taddeus Wittlin, who during 1941-42 met a woman in the Vorkuta detainee camp who had been tortured by Beria, writes the following:

> "The whipping of the girls excited Beria sexually, and not only because they were half-naked in front of him. There is no doubt that a half-naked girl is a turn-on for a young man of twenty-one, as Lavrenti Beria was at the time. But that was not the main reason why Beria was affected: after a few lashes the victim's body would turn purple, begin to bleed in places, and finally, when the girl was unable to bear the pain any longer, the call of nature had to be obeyed. The sight of the excrement was not pleasant and neither was the smell. The real reason for Beria's pleasure was the victim's youth. The more abandoned and young and innocent the girl was, the more desirable and exciting she became and, consequently, the greater the pleasure experienced by Beria. Despite being a mature, strong man endowed with an animal voluptuousness, Beria had lived an austere, spartan life, and until then his sexual experiences had been limited".

Within a few months, as a reward for his work in Bailov Prison, Anastas Mikoyan and Ordzhonikidze, his most powerful friends, proposed Beria's promotion to the post of head of the Department of Secret Operations and vice-chairman of the Azerbaijan Cheka. His progression continued in 1921, and in July, after the fall of Georgia to the Soviets, Stalin personally ordered Ordzhonikidze to appoint Beria, whom he had met in Tiflis, as head of the Georgian Cheka. It was not, however, until November 1922 that he settled in the Georgian capital, where the Cheka headquarters were located in the state prison on Olginskaya Street. He took with him the most important files and documents from his secret archive. He was soon confronted with the hostility of many Georgians to the Soviet regime: Menshevik networks, Batumi dock workers, thousands of workers in the Chiatura coal and manganese mines, officers of the former nationalist army and pro-independence groups were at the centre of the nationalist and anti-Bolshevik movement. Beria began by quietly arresting intellectuals and opposition leaders. Initially, he had allowed the activities of the opponents in order to defeat them and take credit for them.

In the spring of 1923, in Sukhumi, the capital of Abkhazia, Beria killed a person with a shot to the temple for the first time. The episode is recounted at length in *Commissar Beria*. The victim was a grocer named Ierkomoshvili, for whom Beria's mother had worked. He and his wife had helped Tekle financially so that their son, whom they called "Lara", could study in Baku. Instead of gratitude, Beria felt hatred and resentment towards them, so he decided to accuse the merchant of anti-Soviet activities and imprisoned him. Convinced that "her dear boy" would free her husband, Maro Ierkomoshvili came forward to intercede. Beria interrogated the merchant in the presence of his wife Maro. After slapping the woman and punching her twice in the face in front of him, he ordered the guard to take the prisoner away again. Beria then went down to the cellar. According to T. Vittlin's account, "he ordered the policeman accompanying him to stay outside and entered the cell. He took the pistol out of its holster. He took the pistol out of the holster, cocked it, put it to the old man's temple and pulled the trigger. He then walked out. This first execution was paradigmatic, since Beria always executed his victims with the utmost calm and without the slightest excitement or emotion, as if it were an unimportant and unimportant act.

Beria had information about preparations for an uprising organised by an underground National Committee led by the nationalist general Valiko Dzugheli. The date was set for 25 August 1924, so two days earlier he ordered the arrest of General Dzugheli. In view of this, Colonel Cholokashvili attacked the Red Army barracks on the 24th. Many fishermen, peasants and students joined the patriots, and fighting broke out in the capital and other major cities. In Tbilisi, Soviet troops abandoned the barracks and left the city. Within ten days, however, the rebels began to give way and those who did not flee to Turkey were captured. The prison camps, many of whom were wounded, quickly filled up, and Beria, whose interrogations served to continue to accumulate data and names for his famous archive, began to order executions, which lasted several months. Truckloads of condemned prisoners left the state prison at night. They would be driven to a clearing on the outskirts of Tbilisi, where they were shot in groups of fifty or even a hundred near pre-prepared ditches. *The Black Book of Communism* gives the figure of 12,578 people shot from 29 August to 5 September 1924. Beria frequently attended these summary executions and watched until the dead were buried. In the spring of 1925 the mass murders ended. Beria, lord of life and death, had become the most feared man in Georgia.

Both Anton Kolendic and Thaddeus Wittlin's works on Beria's private life, a taboo subject that was never reported on, offer some insight into the fact that he was a criminal in every sense of the word. The latter recounts in *Commissar Beria* how he chose his wife Nina. When Tekle died in the village of Merkheuli in the summer of 1929, Beria travelled to Abkhazia in his special luxury train, consisting of three Pullman cars: one served as a sleeping car, another had a bar and restaurant, and the third was a fully equipped saloon. On the way back to Tbilisi, the train was parked on a siding at Sukhumi station, where Beria stopped for a few days to take care of business. Since he lived on the train, a beautiful sixteen-year-old girl approached him in the central terminal building, convinced that the all-powerful Cheka chief, her fellow countryman, could intercede for her recently arrested brother. Beria invited her up to the luxurious sleeping quarters in the sleeping car and asked the girl to undress. After slapping her, he raped her. He then locked her in and went to the restaurant car for dinner and vodka. When he returned, he spent the whole night with her. At dawn, before leaving, he ordered breakfast for two. During the days he stayed in the city, he kept his young prisoner on the train. Finally, he decided to take her with him to Tiflis and make her his wife.

Anton Kolendic writes that the private life of "the sword of the Revolution", a nickname given to him by Stalin himself, "was particularly well protected and kept secret. No one could penetrate it and no one had the courage to do so". It was only when Beria was arrested in June 1953 that some dared to denounce his dirty tricks. Khrushchev recounts that days after Beria's arrest, Malenkov confessed to him that the head of his guard addressed him with these words: "I have just heard that Beria has been arrested. I must tell you that he has raped my beautiful daughter, a girl of fifteen. One afternoon he went out on an errand. My flat is next door to Beria's. Some guy accosted her and forced her to go. Some guy accosted her and forced her to go to Beria's place. He was waiting for her and persuaded her to have something to eat with him. He made her drink and when she dozed off, he raped her." Soon similar statements began to come in, recounting rapes of girls and women whom Beria, always in the same way, fed, made drunk and raped. It must be ruled out that Malenkov and Khrushchev invented a string of slanders against the fallen enemy, since, as Kolendic writes, "a dossier was compiled with more than two hundred individual reports on the depravities, perversions, and intimate relations with girls, young women and women". In all cases, the testimonies made very harsh statements that usually ended with the same argument: "Until now I did not dare to say anything to anyone, let alone complain or accuse, because...".

As the evidence showed that Stalin had established himself as Lenin's successor, Beria methodically worked out his strategy to curry favour with him. In honour of the Soviet dictator, he named the son he had with Nina Joseph. Although he actually hated Stalin, whom he considered a crude and vulgar fellow who reeked of cheap black tobacco, he did not hesitate to behave in a servile and shabby manner in order to win his trust. In November 1931, the Central Committee in Moscow appointed him first secretary of the Georgian Communist Party. Beria travelled to the capital to thank Stalin personally for his confidence. Since the questionnaire he had to fill out required him to say how long he had been a member of the party, Stalin suggested that he put the date 1917. From then on, Beria became an enforcer of Kremlin policy in the Caucasus. In order to please Stalin, he then projected a panegyric on Stalin: *Early Writings and Activities of Stalin: On the History of the Bolshevik Organisations in Transcaucasia*, a work that turned Stalin into a hero of the Revolution and a god of communism, in which historical truth was the least important thing.

During the 1930s, therefore, Beria laid the foundations for his rise to the leadership of the NKVD, which in 1934 became the successor to the Cheka, of the GPU and the OGPU. The assassination of Kirov, the Moscow trials and the purge of Trotskyism and the Red Army were the events that tested his loyalty to Stalin. Beria then decided that he must carry out a new purge in Transcaucasia in order to show the supreme leader that he could count on him to liquidate the undesirables. When Yagoda fell, he had aspired to take his place, and Yezhov's appointment was a disappointment to him, but he was patient and waited for his chance. Yezhov was not unaware that, as long as Beria continued to lie in wait, his position as Commissar of the Interior and Director of the Secret Police was not secure, so he set several traps for him in order to liquidate him, but he did not succeed. On 28 July 1938 Stalin called Beria personally and without further explanation ordered him to report to Moscow. Beria came to suspect that Yezhov was behind the affair and could be arrested. He knew that Yezhov hated him and had him on his blacklist. He thought that he might have prepared some denunciation against him that could serve to convince Stalin of the need to get rid of him. Proof of his distrust is the order he gave to Bogdan Kobulov, one of his closest collaborators, to destroy his secret files if he did not return.

On his arrival in Moscow, General Alexander Poskrebyshev, Stalin's personal secretary and head of the Special Section of the Secret Department of the Party Secretariat, was waiting for him at the Kazan station. Poskrebyshev, who was part of the so-called "secret cabinet", was a man of the dictator's utmost confidence, and had on occasion been used by him to eliminate prominent people without trial. Beria was not entirely reassured until he realised that his destination was the Kremlin. There, Stalin announced to him that he had decided to transfer him to Moscow in order to place him in the Lubyanka alongside Commissar Yezhov. His post was to be that of deputy commissar, which made him number two in the Commissariat. The fact that the boss had chosen him as a deputy to the man who had tried to eliminate him was interpreted by Beria as a sign of endorsement. Stalin had undoubtedly brought him out of Tiflis to become Yezhov's replacement. On 25 November 1938 Beria became the new Commissar for Internal Affairs and head of the NKVD. Yezhov was made Commissar for Water Transport, a step backwards in his career that was evidence of his fall from grace.

The first thing Beria did as the new head of the NKVD was a radical purge of the Cheka apparatus: all collaborators and many officials acting under Yezhov, whose days were also numbered, were arrested. Thousands of old Chekists were shot or sent to labour camps. The policy of destroying his opponents and placing his followers in key positions enabled him to bring the whole country under his control in a short time. As he came to power, Beria demonstrated his ability to organise and optimise the work and output of the prisoners under the control of the Higher Administration of the Forced Labour Camps, GULAG ("Glavnoye Uprovlenye Lagerey"). The aim was for the communist state to use the enslavement of millions of its own citizens to produce at the lowest possible cost. It set specific standards for each brigade of workers and went so far as to establish as many as fourteen types of food. The worst kitchen, number one, was for the punished, who received a piece of bread and a bowl of watery soup. The "champions" at work were deserving of the best meal, number fourteen. Admittedly, the system worked perfectly. With millions of slaves working for a little food in mines and forests, building roads, canals, railways and tunnels, productivity not only improved, but increased significantly.

Commissar Beria's power grew progressively in all areas. As commander-in-chief of the Special Divisions of the NKVD Forces, he had a very strong and disciplined army, equipped with the most modern weapons, including aircraft and tanks. He was also head of the Special Missions Section, which had the network of spies deployed all over the world. He was ultimately responsible for the so-called Mobile Group, used to assassinate and kidnap defectors, Trotskyists and other enemies of the USSR abroad[28].

---

[28] Two little-known assassinations that deserve mention are those of Georges Agabekov and Evgeny Dumbadze. The latter, after having been a Chekist in Tiflis, escaped to France in disillusionment and in 1930 published in Paris his Memoirs, "Na Sluzhee Cheka i Kominterna" (In the Service of the Cheka and the Komintern). In the book he described Beria as a bloody criminal and genocidal. Dumbadze was found dead in his modest flat in the French capital. According to the official version, he committed suicide by inhaling gas from his kitchen. Also in 1930 Agabekov, who had been head of the Eastern section of the OGPU, published a book in Russian which was translated into English, French and German under the title *OGPU. The Russian Secret Terror*. We have located two copies published in 1931 by Brentano's Publishers in New York, both priced at around 300 euros, which is why we have not purchased them. We can say, however, that Agabekov

Inside the country he persecuted and eliminated intellectuals who were a nuisance: besides being the censor of the press, he was the dictator of all culture offered to the people: theatre, literature, the arts were under his control and supervision.

Thaddeus Wittlin explains that Beria not only lived for his work, but he also indulged in whatever pleasures he could get his hands on. His agents abroad sent him photographs and pornographic films, which he kept locked in his home office in Katchalov Street in Moscow. With his assistant, Colonel Sarkisov, he sometimes went in his black "Packard" to Dostoyevsky Street, where there was a secondary school named after the great writer. Stopped near the Army Theatre, Beria would watch the young women leaving the building from behind the curtains of the car. His favourites, writes Wittlin, were "girls of fourteen to fifteen, somewhat plump, with round faces, rosy cheeks, innocent eyes, smooth complexion and full lips". Having chosen the prey, the colonel then went to fetch the girl, who was placed in the back seat of the vehicle. Once at the Lubyanka, the car would stop in the courtyard, next to the entrance leading to Beria's offices. Wittlin, who probably uses as a source the above-mentioned dossier with more than 200 documented cases, recounts different variants of the degenerate commissar's actions. Let us take a closer look at a few examples:

> "He explained to the little girl that she must undress and satisfy her physical desires in the way he liked and which he explained to her in detail. If she did not do so, her parents would be arrested that very night and sent to labour camps in the farthest reaches of Russia, and the same would happen to her brothers and sisters. The fate of her loved ones depended on her. She would give the child a few seconds to make a decision. When the girl gave in and knelt in front of him, stark naked, he would force her to commit an act of sodomy. Beria watched the girl's tear-stained face and took a peculiar pleasure in forcing such acts of sexual perversion on an innocent child. Sometimes he was not satisfied with this and, extremely aroused, he would throw the victim to the ground and fall on her to rape her and destroy her virginity.
> At other times, instead of taking the girl to his office at the Lubyanka, he would take her to his house on Katchalov Street. There he would invite her for a glass of wine. He would make her drink, and when the girl became drowsy from the effects of the alcohol, Beria would possess her. The presence of his wife in the house did not stop Beria in his excesses. The house was spacious, had many rooms and two entrances, and his wife had strict and definite orders not to enter her husband's office under any circumstances".

---

describes Soviet espionage methods in the East, in France, the US and Germany. As for Beria, he referred to him as a narrow-minded policeman who knew very little about the Communist Party. Beria's men tracked down the defector in Brussels, where he was living on a false passport, and assassinated him.

Beria was addicted to vodka and cognac, so he had a large cupboard full of bottles. According to Wittlin, "the more powerful he felt, the more pleasure he took in drinking, especially as he was fortunate in that no matter how much he drank he always stayed sober and realised what he was saying or doing. Never in a state of drunkenness," adds the biographer, "did a single word escape him for which he had to repent". In other words, instead of clouding his mind, the vodka cleared it and allowed him to question with greater sharpness and clarity of thought. On his interrogation techniques, Wittlin provides ample information. In addition to an iron fist, Beria kept in his drawers a whole range of cocks and truncheons of all sizes. In one of his jacket pockets he often carried one of these instruments with which he could kill a man with a single blow. With his hand in one of the pockets of his jacket," writes this author, "Beria would stand behind the detainee at a distance of two or three paces. With lightning speed, he would take out of his pocket his hand, armed with a kind of small, special truncheon, and, with the precision of the most experienced slaughterer, strike the prisoner behind the right ear. The man fell dead instantly. Since the ordinances specified that secret executions were to be carried out with a shot to the back of the head, when Beria left the cell he ordered a soldier to go in and put a bullet in the victim's head. Wittlin adds that Beria kept a mannequin or dummy in his house with which he practised striking with the greatest precision.

From March 1939 Beria was a member of the Politburo. It was then that he decided to convince Stalin of the need to get rid of Yezhov, the "bloody dwarf". Forced to resign as Commissar of Water Transport, Yezhov, after being tried in secret, was shot in April 1940. During the same year, Beria committed some of his best-known crimes, such as the massacre of Poles in the Katyn Forest and the elimination of thousands of nationalists in the Baltic republics. Less publicised is the murder of Red soldiers retreating from the Finns. Since Chapter Ten has already recounted Beria's role in the massacre of the Polish officers and also the terror unleashed in Estonia by Jewish agents acting under his orders, it now remains to give a concise account of how he organised the "barrier detachments" to prevent the retreat of soldiers fleeing from the enemy.

As a member of the High Defence Council, Beria asked Stalin to persuade the generals to hand over separate Red Army units to him,, which would be integrated into his Security Forces. The military reluctantly agreed to the demand, and Beria invented a slogan: "The Soviet soldier never retreats". So he decided to create units of infamous memory that would treacherously shoot without warning soldiers who retreated or surrendered to the enemy. Beria's criminal method was first applied on the Finnish front by the NKVD special troops, who, incredible as it may seem, murdered their own compatriots trying to get to safety from the ambushes of the Finnish patriots.

Later, during the war against Germany, the death penalty by public hanging was instituted both in the rear and at the front. Faced with the alternative of a rope around the neck from the hands of the Chekists or a bullet in the chest from the German lines, the latter was usually chosen. In the Supreme Defence Council, Stalin called for the formulation of the principles of the attitude to be adopted towards Russian soldiers captured by the Germans. Beria clearly stated that "only traitors, spies and enemies of the Soviet Union could surrender to the fascists". This implied that all those who surrendered to the enemy deserved death. At Beria's suggestion, Stalin signed an order that was read out in all units. It proclaimed that any soldier taken prisoner would be considered a deserter, whose punishment would be a court martial and execution if he returned to the Red Army.

The military never forgave Beria for these crimes against his own soldiers. Anton Kolendic quotes General Georgy Zhukov's indignant words to Malenkov and Vorochilov at the Politburo meeting in the autumn of 1953: "Do you know that out of 1,700,000 of our men, out of our soldiers taken prisoner during the war and who returned alive from captivity, you have killed more than a million? As for the families of the soldiers, the entire family of anyone who went over to the enemy was threatened with arrest and deportation. Thus, Beria's units arrested and deported hundreds of thousands of relatives of officers and soldiers who had been taken prisoner. Beria also issued a circular to the guard units in the hundreds of forced labour camps, ordering that in case of evacuation from the area all detainees were to be executed with machine-gun fire.

Capable of all kinds of double-dealing, this Mephistophelian character, perverted and ruthless, but at the same time extremely cunning and intelligent, was during the years of World War II the primary contact for the international conspirators allied with Communism, who, as we have seen throughout this book, operated mainly in the United States and Great Britain. Documents exist to prove that Beria was an agent of the British. What is not known is the extent of his complicity with foreign intelligence services during the fifteen years he was the Soviet Union's strongman.

His close collaboration with Allen Dulles is well known. Between 1941 and 1945 he was head of the American secret services in Europe, so his contacts were official. Both Allen Dulles (future director of the CIA) and his brother John Foster Dulles (future Secretary of State) were part of the select group that in 1919, at the Hotel Majestic in Paris, helped "Colonel" Edward Mandell House to set up the Round Table organisations, the secret society founded by Cecil Rhodes and the Rothschilds. Consequently, both belonged to the CFR (Council on Foreign Relations). Associated with Morgan and Rockefeller, two of the bankers who had financed communism, the Dulles brothers were part of the conspiracy.

As head of the Secret Service as a whole, espionage and counter-espionage, Beria supervised all USSR diplomacy, including the ambassadors, as his agents operated in the Embassies, chambers of commerce and consulates.. As head of Propaganda, the Communist parties in the US, Britain and France followed his instructions. Beria had secret access to the most influential people, who were surely betting on him as Stalin's successor. He was the ultimate recipient of information supplied by Harry Dexter White, Alger Hiss, Harry Hopkins and other double agents infiltrated into the upper echelons of the American Administration, who ultimately worked for the conspirators who had forced the world war.

As head of Atomic Energy Development, Beria received reports from R. Oppenheimer, from K. Fuchs, from N. Bohr, from Bruno Pontecorvo, an Italian physicist of Jewish origin whom in 1949 he helped to escape to Russia via France and Finland, as well as from other Jewish physicists and spies who, as we have seen, worked for international communism. The "Cambridge Circle" was also in close contact with Beria. One of the "Cambridge Five", Kim Philby, a senior British Intelligence officer, passed on valuable detailed information to him. A double agent in the service of London and Moscow, Philby went on to become head of the Counter Intelligence Service in the United States and was one of the organisers of the CIA. Two other members of the group, Guy Burgess and Donald McLean, fled in 1951 to the USSR with Beria's help. Not forgetting the "fifth man", Victor Rothschild. In *The Fifth Man*, Roland Perry reveals the name of the agent Beria used as a liaison for the five British spies: Yuri Modin. In the book, Perry claims that in 1947 Beria, urged by Stalin to obtain more information about the atomic bomb, even sent letters to the Jewish physicist Niels Bohr, asking him for reports on the latest research. Bohr replied that the Americans refused him access.

The struggle for power and control of communist parties and communist countries

On 8 February 1945, during the Yalta Conference, Beria attended a dinner at the Koreiz villa during which he was introduced to Roosevelt, Churchill and the other members of the US and British delegations invited by Stalin. He was not seen again in the following days. Half a year later, in Potsdam, there was excitement among the Americans and British attending the Peace Conference. It was widely believed that Beria would be part of the Soviet representation, and more than a few wanted to meet this figure, who was widely tipped as Stalin's successor. Beria, however, did not show up, which came as a surprise, as no one was unaware that he was the most powerful man in the USSR.

After the end of World War II, Beria was promoted to the rank of Marshal of the Soviet Union. In March 1946 it was decided that the People's Commissariats would be renamed Ministries, in the style of the Western, and Beria became Minister of Internal Affairs, Minister of State Security and

Deputy Chairman of the Council of Ministers of the USSR. True to his strategy of portraying himself as a loyal and submissive admirer of Stalin, Beria had been preparing an edition of the dictator's complete works and had collected speeches, reports, letters and even telegrams of the great leader in order to publish *Stalin's Complete Works* in several volumes. The first of the volumes appeared on 2 November 1946. On the surface, then, everything seemed to indicate that Beria accepted the undisputed leadership of the great Stalin; but we shall see below how he was quietly taking steps and moving his innumerable pieces in order to become the new leader of the Soviet Union as soon as the opportunity arose.

The first disagreements between the Politburo leaders arose over the Yugoslavia of Josip Broz Tito and Moshe Pijade, the two Jews who had been supported by Churchill and Roosevelt at the Yalta Conference. Jules Moch, a Jew and former socialist minister of Léon Blum, whose nephew he was, after spending some time in Yugoslavia at the invitation of Tito, whom he considered a close friend, published *Yougoslavie, terre d'expérience* in 1953, an enlightening work on the events in Yugoslavia. Moch reveals that Stalin, despite requests, refused to send arms, money or aid to Tito during the war. According to Moch, Stalin, who would later accuse Tito of Trotskyism, was in favour of the return of King Peter, but Churchill and Roosevelt gradually abandoned General Draza Mihailovic and the patriots fighting the Germans. Instead, they helped Tito from the beginning. At Yalta, Stalin asked what was holding up the formation of a unified government in Yugoslavia. It was Molotov who, at the meeting of foreign ministers at the Vorontsov villa on 10 February 1945, demanded, on Stalin's instructions, that telegrams be sent to Tito and Subasic, prime minister of the monarchist government in exile, to hasten to put into effect the agreement drawn up at Yalta for the formation of a unity government.

Georgy Malenkov was the first to warn the Politburo that Tito, Pikhade and the Bulgarian Jew Traycho Kostov were "Trojan horses" that the Trotskyist internationalists intended to introduce into the communist orb that Stalin aspired to control from Moscow; But Andrei Zhdanov, Stalin's father-in-law, since his son Yuri was married to his daughter Svetlana Aliluyeva, questioned Malenkov's accusations and did not accept the thesis that they were Trotskyists or agents of Anglo-American imperialism. These two men, Malenkov and Zhdanov, were the leading contenders to succeed Stalin, so it was clear to Beria that, if he wanted to reach the top, he had to take advantage of the differences between the two favourites to get rid of both of them. Throughout the war, Malenkov had served as the practical First Secretary of the CPSU in tune with Stalin. At the Central Committee plenum in March 1946, Malenkov replaced Zhdanov, who had held that post continuously since 1934, as secretary of the Committee, and became a member of the Politburo, which seemed to strengthen his position vis-à-vis Stalin.

Sovietologist A. Avtorkhanov argues in *Staline assassinated* that Zhdanov, who according to some sources was a Jew and was actually called Liphshitz, wrote a report on Marshal Zhukov, Malenkov's protégé, which enabled him to win back Stalin's confidence and to regain his position as secretary of the Central Committee in July 1946. According to this author, the report on Zhukov, commander-in-chief of the ground troops and the top defence official after Stalin, accused the Marshal of aspiring to become the Russian Bonaparte. This slander deeply disturbed the dictator, who had read similar theses in the Western press and was already suspicious of this military man, who had become a hero to the Russian people during the war. Zhdanov not only succeeded in getting Stalin to send Malenkov to Turkestan, but he also made General Khosif Shikin, one of his closest collaborators, head of the Military Section of the Central Committee, to the detriment of Zhukov. Two other protégés of his also occupied important posts. The first, Nikolai Voznesensky, was appointed Stalin's deputy in the government. The second, Aleksei Kuznetsov, became secretary of the Central Committee for Security and the Army. These manoeuvres and Malenkov's loss of influence alarmed Beria, who advocated the return to Moscow of Malenkov, who had not been removed from the Politburo, and tried to deploy his power against Zhdanov and his group.

In this struggle for power, Stalin's plan to subject all the countries of Europe under the influence of the USSR to his dictates and to Moscow's influence played a decisive role. In *The Permanent Revolution* Trotsky had written that "Stalin's National Socialism degraded the Communist International". It was again this very issue that served as the trigger for the revolt against Stalin and his plan to Sovietise Eastern Europe. In early 1947 Tito and Georgi Dimitrov, the Bulgarian communist who had been secretary of the Communist International between 1934 and 1943, held a secret meeting in the Slovenian town of Bled. They signed a protocol providing for the federation of Bulgaria and Yugoslavia, which Albania could later join. The president of the future Union of South Slav Socialist Republics would be Dimitrov; Tito would chair the Council of Ministers and Kostov would be deputy to the presidency. As soon as the plan became known, Moscow opposed the project. Since the Red Army occupied Bulgaria, Dimitrov apparently accepted the rebuke. Tito, for his part, showed no sign of life. Discussions on the matter within the Politburo once again revealed the disagreements between Zhdanov and Malenkov. In Malenkov's opinion, Comrade Zhdanov did not seem to have understood that it was the Western powers themselves who had recognised at Yalta that these European countries came within the sphere of influence of the USSR.

A conference of the leaders of the European communist parties was held in Szklarska Poreba (Poland) from 22 to 27 September 1947. The Soviet representatives were Zhdanov and Malenkov, who carried the proposal for the creation of Cominform (Information Bureau of Communist and Workers'

Parties), the organisation that was to replace the Communist International (Comintern), which had been dissolved by Stalin during the Second World War. Officially, Cominform was established on 5 October 1947 and its headquarters were set to be in Belgrade. In addition to the parties of the communist bloc, the French Communist Party and the Italian Communist Party were also founding members. The task entrusted to Cominform was to coordinate the activity of the communist parties on the basis of mutual agreements. It was also agreed that the Information Bureau would publish a *Bulletin*. As early as October, Pavel F. Iudin, a Jew who was perfectly in tune with Beria, went to Belgrade to organise the publication of the paper in four editions: Russian, English, French and Serbo-Croatian. The masthead of the bulletin was *For a lasting peace, for a people's democracy*.

But it was not all understanding. Mauricio Karl (Carlavilla), in *Malenkov*, a work published in Madrid in 1954, offers a very significant piece of information that does not appear in any of the works we have been studying. According to this now forgotten Spanish Sovietologist, Zhdanov had taken Josif Shikin, the general who had replaced Zhukov in the Military Section of the Central Committee, to Poland as an observer. According to Carlavilla, Zhdanov was ordered in the middle of the conference to send Shikin to Moscow as a matter of urgency. The general travelled by plane and returned the next day with a military plan that envisaged the integration of the armies of the satellite countries into the Red Army, which was tantamount to depriving the national armed forces of their independence. After the document was read out in plenary, Zhdanov asked for its approval, but one of the two Yugoslav representatives, Edvard Kardelj, actually called Kardayl, also known as "Sperans" and "Kristof", a Jew of Hungarian origin who served as Yugoslavia's foreign minister between 1948 and 1953, argued that as delegates they were not authorised to sign any military agreement and suggested that the session be adjourned until instructions were given in one direction or the other. Again according to Carlavilla, the second Yugoslav, Milovan Djilas, flew to Belgrade with the draft proposal and returned the same evening with Tito and Pijade's reply. "I regret to announce," Kardelj announced, "that the Central Committee of the Yugoslav Communist Party does not approve of the proposed military protocol and orders us not to sign it."

Although Yugoslavia's refusal to sign the military protocol was a serious setback, Zhdanov, the main driving force behind the Cominform idea, moved in November 1947 to the third place in the Politburo, held since January 1946 by Beria, who slipped back to fifth place. Since number two was Molotov, a man of the old guard who did not count as a possible successor to Stalin, it must be understood that Zhdanov was the clear favourite. Malenkov, who in January 1946 was in fourth place, had been pushed down to ninth. The creation of the Cominform practically coincided with the launching of the Marshall Plan, which did not exclude the USSR, let alone the so-called people's democracies of Eastern Europe. Stalin, however, rejected the aid, because he understood that what was really intended was the political and economic domination of Europe. In his view, the aim was to finance and strengthen communism in the countries of Eastern Europe, but to the benefit of American imperialist interests and to the detriment of the power Moscow wished to exert over them. Naturally, Stalin saw the Balkan federation project sponsored by Dimitrov and Tito as part of the strategy to undermine his authority over the communist parties and countries.

On 21 January 1948, Dimitrov, despite having been warned by Moscow, insisted at a press conference in Sofia that the Balkan federation was desirable and necessary. *Pravda*, under Zhdanov's control, reported the Bulgarian leader's words with comments that seemed to endorse the idea. Malenkov did not miss the opportunity to denounce Zhdanov and warn Stalin that the project was conceived as a counterweight to the power of the USSR, and that the line taken by Zhdanov was leading to the strengthening of the Ketrifuge tendencies in Eastern Europe. On 28 February, *Pravda* published an editorial statement, according to Avtokhanov drafted by Stalin, in which he made it clear that the fact of having published the Sofia press conference did not imply that the paper in any way accepted Comrade Dimitrov's views: "It is possible," Dimitrov had said of the great project, "that in the beginning the federation will include Yugoslavia, Bulgaria and Albania and that later Romania, Poland, Czechoslovakia and perhaps Hungary will join.

In addition to the Marshall Plan, the other major issue that coincided with the creation of the Cominform was the UN vote on the partition of Palestine. Despite the USSR's support for the resolution, Stalin was soon accused of anti-Semitism. A few facts will help to contextualise this accusation. Since the triumph of the October Revolution, Lenin, Trotsky, Zinoviev, Kamenev and company decided to execute anti-Semites: the mere fact of possessing a copy of *The Protocols of the Elders of Zion* could mean a death sentence. During the prolonged honeymoon with Roosevelt's Zionist government, Stalin, advised by Beria, authorised the creation of a Jewish Anti-Fascist Committee, chaired by Solomon Mikhoels, director of Moscow's famous Yiddish theatre, which made several trips to London and New York. Jews living abroad, especially in the United States and England, sent money and all kinds of aid. Beria placed as deputy chairmen of the Committee Viktor Alter and Henrik Ehrlich, two Polish Jews who before the war headed the "Bund" (General Union of Jewish Workers in Poland). At the head of the Jewish Anti-Fascist Committee were also Solomon Lozovsky, an avowed Zionist who in 1936 had organised the workers in Barcelona, and Polina Zhemchúzhina, Molotov's Jewish wife. Hundreds of Jewish intellectuals engaged in intense propaganda activity within the Committee. Among the most prominent were Ilya Ehrenburg, the poets Samuel Marshak and Peretz Markish, the pianist Emile Guilels, Vassili Grossman and the physicist Piotr Kapitza, one of the fathers of the Soviet atomic bomb. In February 1944, Mikhoels and others signed a letter proposing to Stalin the creation of an autonomous Jewish republic in the Crimea, despite the fact that the Jews already had a 'national state' in Birobidzhan in the USSR. It is undeniable that Jewish activism in journalistic, literary and artistic circles was predominant. In early 1945, the publication of the *Black Book* on Nazi Atrocities against the Jews, a work by Peretz Markish sponsored by the Jewish Anti-Fascist Committee, whose editors were Ilya Ehrenburg and Vassili Grossman, was banned. The reason for the ban was the biased view of the historical facts: the main argument was that the German invasion of the USSR had had no other object than the annihilation of the Jews. Throughout 1946 and 1947, the Zionist and nationalist tendencies of the Jewish Anti-Fascist Committee were more than evident, as evidenced by its pressure on Stalin to vote in favour of the creation of the State of Israel.

Once the Zionist state was created in Palestine, things suddenly changed, as Stalin began to realise that, both in Russia and in European countries, there were numerous Jews working against him. Convinced of the existence of a "Zionist plot", he soon ceased to trust those members of the old guard who were married to Jewish women, and they were not few in number. On 19 December 1947 several members of the Jewish Anti-Fascist Committee were arrested and an investigation began which was to continue for four years, until August 1952. Among those arrested was Mikhoels, whom Stalin held in high esteem and in 1946 had distinguished with the Order of Lenin. The dictator had accumulated evidence that the Jewish Anti-Fascist Committee chaired by Mikhoels was an American espionage centre. After the arrest of the famous Jewish actor, an international press campaign was unleashed, as usual, demanding his release. Shortly after his release from prison, on 13 January 1948, he died in a car accident: "Unfortunately," Beria confessed in 1953 before his execution, "upon his release from prison, Mikhoels was so disturbed that he began to drink and met his death in a car accident". This statement denying the assassination almost certainly confirms that Beria, obeying Stalin's orders, was forced to arrange the accident to prove his loyalty. Documents published on the occasion of the 22nd Congress of the CPSU contain statements by Security officials which reveal the preparations for and execution of the "car accident". Stalin ordered national funerals to be held, as befitted an artist holding the Order of Lenin.

At the beginning of 1948, then, the so-called "Zionist plot" and the dissidence of some European Communist parties were matters of the greatest concern to the dictator of the USSR. Malenkov and Molotov agreed that Tito and Pikhade had to be called to order, so they conceived the plan to invite them to Moscow. The invitation was extended, but the Yugoslav leaders suspected the worst and did not accept it. However, on Tuesday, 10 February 1948, two delegations of Bulgarians and Yugoslavs showed up at the Kremlin and were received by Stalin himself. The source for the discussions is *Conversations with Stalin*, by Milovan Djilas, who attended the meeting. On the Soviet side, besides Stalin, Molotov, Zhdanov, Malenkov and Sushlov took part. The Bulgarians were Dimitrov, Kolarov and Kostov. The Yugoslav representatives were Kardelj, Bakaric and Djilas himself.

The first to speak was Molotov, who sharply criticised Bulgaria and Yugoslavia for making alliances and planning to federate without even consulting them. Stalin interrupted to warn Dimitrov that abroad Moscow was interpreted as approving what he said at his press conferences. As an example he related an interview with Polish visitors to whom he had asked the following question: "What do you think about Dimitrov's statement?" The answer was that it was a reasonable proposition. "They thought," said Stalin, "that Dimitrov had made the statement with the full agreement of the Soviet Government." The tone of the accusations escalated, and Molotov added that they knew of contacts between Bulgaria and Romania to form a federation. Dimitrov apologised, saying that they had spoken only in general terms. Again Stalin interrupted indignantly: "It is false, for agreements were reached for a customs union and for a coordination of industrial plans." Relying on Stalin's accusation, Molotov asked, "And could you explain to us what a customs union and a co-ordination of economic plans mean, if not the creation of a single state?" Dimitrov tried to excuse himself by admitting the mistake: "We may have been wrong, but even these mistakes in foreign policy are instructive for us." According to Djilas, in a violent and sarcastic tone of rejection Stalin intimidated him, "Ah, you are instructive!".

At the same time, Beria, who never missed a chance to take advantage of the situation, decided that the time was ripe for a move of his own. The Czechoslovak leaders, the Freemasons Benes and Masaryk, also did not feel comfortable in the Cominform designed by Stalin. Beria saw an opportunity to prove his effectiveness to the big boss by removing them from the Cominform for good and placing in power men he trusted. In the same month of February 1948, he organised a conspiracy in Czechoslovakia which has gone down in history as the "Prague Putsch". At Yalta it had been decided to hand Czechoslovakia over to the Red Army; however, on 6 May 1945 American tanks appeared in the suburbs of Prague. General Patton broadcast a message from his headquarters announcing that his armoured forces would take the city the next day. Thousands of women prepared to welcome the Americans with flowers. Finally, as we know, on 9 May, the Red soldiers entered, and behind them came Beria's Secret Police forces. Thus, the Nazi occupation was followed by the Communist occupation. Later, at the Potsdam Conference, the expulsion of two and a half million Germans was accepted. Beria's instrument for the "final solution" of the Sudeten Germans was the leader of the Czech Communists, the Jew Rudolf Slansky, whose real name was Rudolf Salzman. In February 1948, Beria again used him to carry out the coup d'état. The time had come to get rid of the two

Freemasons, Benes (the president) and Masaryk (the foreign minister), whom the communists had allowed to prosper for almost three years.

Slansky, General Secretary of the Communist Party, surrounded himself with a clique of Jews whose names and positions have already been cited in the third part of this chapter. Their immediate priority was to supply arms to the Zionists who were waging their war of conquest in Palestine. The fact that the ports of Tito's Yugoslavia and Pijade were used to ship important consignments from Czechoslovakia proves once again that Stalin was not seeing visions when he denounced the "Zionist plot", but was stating actual facts. In 1951 Stalin eventually ordered the arrest of fourteen Czech communists, eleven of whom were Jews. We will comment below on some of the statements made by some of these Jews, who were sentenced to death at their trial in 1952. As for the fate of Benes and Masaryk, the former had made things easier for Slansky/Salzman and remained in Czechoslovakia, where he died in September of the same year. Masaryk had a worse fate. On 9 March 1948 he visited Benes to tell him that he intended to escape to London the next day, which he was not allowed to do. Beria got information about the interview and that same night two of his "gorillas" visited Masaryk in his office in Czernin Palace, the Foreign Minister's residence, and killed him. It seems that they tried to drown him in the bathtub in the bathroom. After losing consciousness, he was thrown out of the window into the courtyard. Officially, he committed suicide by throwing himself out of the window, the problem with this version is that he did not forget to close it.

In an attempt to redress the situation created by the Yugoslav-sponsored federation plans, which involved Bulgaria, Romania and perhaps Albania, it was decided to convene all heads of government for a new meeting of the Cominform, whose headquarters remained, however, in Belgrade. Informal negotiations began, and Tito, who did not want to leave his country, put forward a "report on the international situation" presented at the first Conference by Zhdanov, according to which foreign affairs were the responsibility of the foreign ministers. After these contacts with the Yugoslavs failed, the first act of rupture came from the USSR Politburo, which informed Tito on 20 March 1948 that the Soviet Union was withdrawing its military technicians and civilian experts from Yugoslavia because of the "lack of hospitality and trust" shown by the Yugoslav government. There followed an exchange of communiqués full of mutual recriminations which only served to highlight the differences. In a letter dated 27 March, the Soviets accused the Yugoslavs of being Trotskyites and reminded them that Trotsky had been a renegade in the service of international capitalism. Tito personally wrote a letter on 13 April deploring the tone and content of the text sent by the CPSU.

Finally, during the second half of June 1948, the second Cominform Conference was held in Bucharest. According to Carlavilla, a plan by Malenkov to assassinate Tito, who may have been tipped off by a member of the Politburo, perhaps Zhdanov, fell through at this time. In Romania, under Soviet pressure, the attending delegations agreed to condemn Tito's regime for breaking away from Soviet orthodoxy. Traycho Kostov, who had received Tito in Sofia a few months earlier, had agreed with the Yugoslav ambassador, Colonel Obrad Cicmil, that Bulgaria would support the Cominform thesis for tactical reasons. Colonel Cicmil informed him that the Yugoslav press would launch a press campaign against him to make his opposition to Tito more credible. Yugoslavia was expelled and the headquarters of the Information Office was moved to Bucharest. The Politburo decreed during the Cominform meeting the beginning of the blockade of Berlin, which began on 24 June 1948. These events were proof of the distrust between the winners of the war and the end of the honeymoon between the USSR and its Western allies.

From this point on, the struggle for power and for control of the communist parties intensified, culminating in the assassination of Stalin in early March 1953. The first victim was Zhdanov, who died on 31 August 1948. A member of the party since 1913 and of the Central Committee since 1930, his position after displacing Malenkov seemed unbeatable; but Beria, who used the tactic of speaking well of him in front of Stalin, and Malenkov knew how to exploit all his mistakes in the Yugoslav affair, which so unsettled the dictator that he even considered military intervention. As early as 29 June 1948, after Yugoslavia's expulsion from the Cominform, the first indications of the fall from grace of Zhdanov, whose friends and colleagues in the Kominform were accused of "Titoism", appeared in *Pravda*. Zhdanov himself reportedly opposed expulsion from Yugoslavia. This angered Stalin, who replaced him with Malenkov as second secretary of the Central Committee, i.e. as Stalin's deputy. Two months later, Zhdanov's heart, without ever having suffered the slightest symptom before, suffered a sudden attack. No autopsy was performed, and four doctors of the highest prestige: Yegorov, Vinogradov, Mayorov and Vasilenko signed the death certificate. There is little doubt today that Beria was behind the disappearance of Zhdanov, who died of poisoning. As usual, on 2 September, the assassins paraded at the funeral, paying their respects at the coffin surrounded by flowers.

After Zhdanov's elimination, all his followers and collaborators gradually fell, which is further proof that his death was no coincidence. In his biography of Beria, Thaddeus Wittlin explains the matter perfectly: "Beria was too clever to start such an important action with Stalin's consent alone; there were other people who were still very powerful and he had to ask them to stand by his side. The most important was Malenkov. Even though Beria hated Malenkov, whom he considered his rival, he asked him to join him and take part in the plot. It was not difficult to convince him. Malenkov, who had once been defeated by Zhdanov, was his enemy." The purge of Zhdanov's men was organised by Viktor Abakomov, who on

Beria's instructions prepared what has gone down in history as the "Leningrad Case". Among those arrested and sent to prison or concentration camps were, among many others, the men Zhdanov had placed in important positions: Nikolai Voznesensky, Politburo member and head of the State Planning Commission; his brother Alexei, rector of Leningrad University; Aleksei Kuznetsov, secretary of the Central Committee for Security and the Army; Lieutenant General Josif Shikin....

In early September 1948 Golda Meyersohn arrived in Moscow. This famous Zionist was to serve as Israel's ambassador to the USSR. She was greeted by a throng of cheering Jews. Some ten thousand people held a service in the Moscow Choral Synagogue, around which thousands of Soviet Jews crowded, shouting "the people of Israel live". On 8 November, Polina, a leading member of the Jewish Anti-Fascist Committee and Molotov's wife, gave him a warm diplomatic reception. Robert Conquest writes in his biography of Stalin that these public and private displays of Zionism and Jewish sentiment were the last straw for the dictator. On 20 November 1948, the Politburo ordered the dissolution of the Jewish Anti-Fascist Committee. Its publications, the main one being the Yiddish newspaper *Einikait*, were banned and many of its members arrested. A press campaign began, accusing the Jews of being "rootless cosmopolitans" who were dedicated to the destruction of the country's values. In order to expose the identity of this group of so-called international conspirators, who were accused of not understanding Russian culture, the original Jewish names began to appear in brackets next to the false Russian names they had adopted.

At the end of 1948, Stalin demanded from Beria the arrest of Polina Molotov, who was arrested on 21 January 1949 on charges of having "lost documents containing state secrets". The fact that Polina Zhemchúzhina was a fervent Zionist is beyond doubt. Before World War II, she had travelled to the United States as head of the Soviet Union Cosmetic Trust. Roosevelt's wife, a Zionist like herself, had received her at the White House, where they spent an entire afternoon together. Polina had a brother in America named Samuel Carp, who had left Russia in 1911 and had become a multi-millionaire thanks in large part to profits from trade with the Soviet Union. Stalin was deeply suspicious of Polina and her activities: he considered her a bourgeois Zionist and an enemy of the people. After his wife's arrest, Molotov, who went to Stalin and agreed to Polina's arrest, was short-lived as foreign minister, being replaced by Andrei Vyschinsky. Molotov, however, was not completely sidelined and was appointed deputy chairman of the Council of Ministers.

If he was to continue to enjoy the boss's confidence while working in the shadows to replace him, Beria, the dictator's indispensable instrument in all matters of repression and security, could do no other than show submission and obey the directions of the great Stalin, whom he supposedly regarded as the undisputed leader of the USSR. Stalin was convinced that the rebellion of the European communist parties was linked to the Zionist plot, so that the two issues were interrelated and fed back on each other. Throughout 1949, this became increasingly evident, as will be seen, since the leaders spearheading the dissent in all countries were Jewish. In *Les derniers jours. De la mort de Lenin a celle de Beria,* Anton Kolendic devotes chapter 12, entitled "Some of Beria's archives", to the case of Bulgaria. After Beria's arrest in June 1953, his archives were seized and documents written by Stalin were found, some of them related to the case of Georgi Dimitrov and Traycho Kostov. These texts show how the Bulgarian crisis unfolded from Yugoslavia's departure from the Cominform in June 1948 to the trial of Traycho Kostov in June 1949.

The Bulgarian crisis

Before the Cominform Conference in Bucharest, Malenkov announced to Kostov, Vice-President of the Council of Ministers and General Secretary of the Central Committee of the Bulgarian Communist Party, that he was to represent his country at the Cominform meeting which was to put a stop to Tito and Yugoslav ambitions. Having taken this step, Traycho Kostov felt strengthened and on Saturday 26 June 1948, at the extraordinary session of the Bulgarian Politburo, he launched a merciless attack on Dimitrov, whom he blamed for all the mistakes of the party since its foundation in 1919. He accused him of "personally pursuing, despite Comrade Stalin's formal warnings, the obsolete and compromising, indeed openly anti-Soviet, policy of forging a collaboration with Tito and his imperialist agents, which was evidenced by the openly friendly telegram sent the day before to Tito." The abject attitude of the Jew Kostov is evident, for it was an obvious indignity to appeal to a strictly personal telegram to accuse his compatriot of being a "Titoist"[29]. Kostov had a reputation as a brilliant and ambitious politician; however, his actions revealed his duplicity and showed that he was capable of betraying his closest comrades for personal gain. The Bulgarian comrades were astonished, for it was the first time that Dimitrov, a great figure of the defunct International (Comintern) and leader of the Bulgarian working class, had been openly attacked. Traycho Kostov, aware of the existence of Soviet agents within the Bulgarian Politburo, was trying to hide behind Dimitrov to prove his loyalty to Moscow. A few days later, at the beginning of July, a plenary session of the Bulgarian Communist Party Central Committee was held at which the Cominform resolution against Yugoslavia was unanimously accepted.

---

[29] Kolendic explains in a footnote that on 16 June 1948 President Tito had sent a telegram to Dimitrov, who was turning sixty-six, to congratulate him on his birthday. On 25 June Dimitrov had replied, "I thank you with all my heart for your congratulations."

Dimitrov's health was not at all good, which is perhaps why Kostov's attacks at the Politburo session and the criticisms levelled against him at the Central Committee meeting so overwhelmed him that he fell ill. As soon as Stalin heard of his illness, he ordered "Dimitrov to be transported urgently to a sanatorium in order to ensure his treatment. Avoid all worry and activity. Let him take care of himself and rest. Dimitrov was transferred to Moscow and Traycho Kostov then began to prepare for the convening of a party congress in order to take full control of the party. Nevertheless, Dimitrov received a long official report signed by Kostov, which was personally taken to Moscow by Georgi Tchankov, a member of the Bulgarian Politburo. With the permission of his attending physicians, Dimitrov decided to fly to Sofia, where during the first half of December 1948 he worked tirelessly on documents for the congress and, above all, on the general report which was to define Bulgaria's orientation.

Before Dimitrov's return to Bulgaria, Kostov had sent Stalin a telegram signed on behalf of the Bulgarian Government by himself as acting president. In it he asked for exceptional aid in the form of interest-free credits, a long-term loan and the urgent delivery of raw materials and consumer goods beyond all expectations in order to stabilise the situation in Bulgaria. In the margin of this telegram Stalin wrote: "Why has the chosen solution been rejected? This is an opportunity to implement it without any problems." The official reply reached the Bulgarian Government through the Soviet Embassy in Sofia: "In reply to your request for assistance expressed in the first telegram, the Government of the USSR is ready to give you satisfaction and expects the Government of the People's Republic of Bulgaria to send a plenipotentiary delegation as soon as possible." Traycho Kostov was exultant, but he soon had to tone down his euphoria, as reports from Dmitri Ganev, head of the Bulgarian delegation to Moscow in November 1948, indicated that the Russians were backing down. According to Ganev, Anastas Mikoyan, deputy chairman of the Council of Ministers who headed the Russian negotiating team, was missing. Ganev wrote in a report: "It is rumoured in the Ministry that there will be no treaty, because our government, like that of Yugoslavia, will betray the Soviet Union and go over to the camp of the imperialists". Before the start of the congress, on 12 December 1948, Kostov sent a grim note insisting on the need to hasten the signing of the economic and trade treaty by 1949.

The congress began with a six-hour speech by Dimitrov, who read his report to the delegates. This was followed by Traycho Kostov, who was re-elected party secretary. Amidst applause and cheers he presented his report on the new programme of the Bulgarian Communist Party. Pavel Iudin attended the congress in the company of Mikhail Sushlov, the official delegate from the Soviet Union. The two drew up a report in which they noted "... demonstrations directed against the Soviet Union in the form of frenzied applause in favour of Traycho Kostov, particularly motivated by his skilfully masked anti-Soviet statements." These denunciations definitively decided Moscow to break with the Bulgarian leadership. On 13 January 1949, through Mikhail Bodrov, the new Soviet ambassador in Sofia, Stalin sent Dimitrov a personal letter in which he asked him "... to restore order in Sofia, to replace those responsible for the deterioration of relations... and in the first place the long-standing shameless Trotskyite Troycho Kostov...."

Dimitrov immediately convened the Politburo, which met at his residence. After reading out Stalin's letter, the first to speak was Vulko Tchervenkov, a Stalinist married to Dimitrov's sister Elena, who was not only Minister of Culture but also a Moscow agent infiltrating the government. Dimitrov rudely interrupted him, saying that there were older and more intelligent people, and gave the floor to Vasil Kolarov, the foreign minister who had been his collaborator during the years when he chaired the Comintern. Kolarov, troubled, was hesitant, but ended by saying that everyone agreed with Comrade Stalin, although perhaps the matter needed to be studied and explained to the Soviet comrades. The Minister of Economics, Petko Kunin, called for a meeting of the Council of Ministers, a proposal which was accepted, and defended Kostov's position on the economic treaty. However, Stalin's warning was not ignored, and it was decided to suspend Comrade Kostov as secretary of the Bulgarian Communist Party. On Kolarov's proposal, Tchervenkov provisionally assumed the post pending the final decision to be taken by the Plenum of the Central Committee.

The next day, 14 January, Dimitrov called an extraordinary meeting of the Council of Ministers, which focused on relations with the USSR and the problem of Moscow's refusal to sign the economic and trade treaty for 1949. Since Beria had a source of information within the Council in Tchervenkov, Stalin asked him for a report on the speeches of the ministers. In this way he learned of the anti-Soviet statements of Kunin, the Minister of Economics, and Ivan Stefanov, the Minister of Finance. The Council asked Dimitrov to intercede urgently with Comrade Stalin to prevent the collapse of all his plans. Dimitrov then sent a telegram to the dictator begging for his personal intervention to get the treaty signed. Anton Kolendic, in the above-mentioned chapter of his work on the Beria archives, regrets that there is no record of the Politburo discussions on this telegram from the Bulgarian government. Surprisingly, Ganev telephoned Dimitrov to announce that the Russians had given in. On 18 January 1949 in Moscow, Mikoyan and Ganev solemnly signed the "Treaty on Trade and Economic and Commercial Cooperation for 1949".

Despite the success of the signing of the agreement, the situation of Traycho Kostov, directly accused by Stalin of being a Trotskyite, had not changed. Tchervenkov, supported by Kolarov, Vladimir Poptomov and Georgi Damianov, formed a commission to examine Kostov's work and activities, which ruled against him and proposed that he be removed from all his functions in the party and in the government. The report of this commission was read before the Politburo, before which Kostov made a self-criticism that was accepted by the majority. It was then decided to pass judgement on the future of Traycho Kostov to the Plenum of the Central Committee, a decision which meant a defeat for Tchervenkov and the pro-Russians. On 11 February 1949 Dimitrov chaired the Central Committee Plenum with the Kostov case as the key issue. Petko Kunin later declared that Dimitrov had suffered an attack of the liver in the morning and that just before the plenum the doctors had given him a large quantity of opium to ease the pain, so that he attended the session drugged.

Naturally, all attention was focused on Kostov's speech, which was widely applauded, as usual. Then came his main detractors, Vulko Tchervenkov and another Central Committee member, Tsola Dragoitcheva, who, like Tchervenkov, was a Moscow agent. Both are listed in Beria's secret documents under the codenames "Spartacus" and "Sonia". Dragoitcheva launched an unmitigated attack on Kostov, whom she loudly accused of being "a traitor, an enemy, an anti-social element." There were loud protests and a considerable tumult was organised, so that amidst the whistles of the protesters Dimitrov withdrew the floor from Comrade Dragoitcheva. Finally, the Plenum of the Committee decided by a large majority to annul the provisional decision of the Politburo to sanction Kostov and confirmed him in his functions in the party and in the government.

Georgi Dimitrov was badly bruised after the eventful meeting, and in the evening he suffered from dizziness and nausea, and the Russian doctors who were looking after him concluded that he should be taken back to the USSR for the treatment he had begun before returning to Bulgaria. On 12 February he left on a Soviet plane for Moscow, from where he never returned, dying on 2 July 1949. On 3 July *Pravda* announced that he had died "near Moscow, in the intensive care centre in Barvikha, as a result of a long and painful illness (liver, diabetes)". Naturally, there were all sorts of speculations encouraged by the Western press and, although there is no evidence, it was taken for granted that Dimitrov did not die a natural death. In this case, however, the disease existed, so it would not be entirely unreasonable to accept the official version.[30]

---

[30] This was not the first time that Stalin held Dimitrov in Moscow. When Soviet troops entered Bulgaria on 8 September 1944, despite the demands of the Central Committee and the requests of Dimitrov himself, Stalin, claiming that the situation in Bulgaria was not yet consolidated and that he feared for Comrade Dimitrov's life, did not allow the famous Bulgarian communist to return. The reasons for his refusal were, of course, quite different: since he did not fully trust Dimitrov even then, Stalin kept him for a few months in order to establish a network of Russian and Bulgarian NKVD agents in Bulgaria. Finally, on 6 December 1945, fifteen months after the formation of the government, Dimitrov arrived in Sofia. With him came his irreplaceable secretary since 1938, the Jew Jakob Mirov-Abramov. According to Ivan Karaivanov, a senior official of the Communist International, before becoming Dimitrov's secretary, Mirov-Abramov had first been

After Dimitrov's departure, Kostov resumed his functions as chairman of the Council of Ministers. However, open resistance to his decisions arose in the Secretariat of the party and in the Politburo, most of which were boycotted. Vulko Tchervenkov shouted in his face at a Politburo meeting that he would not work or collaborate with him, since he was "an enemy and an agent of the foreigner." On 10 March 1949 Stalin and Molotov signed a long letter on behalf of the Soviet Government, addressed to the Chairman of the acting Council of Ministers of Bulgaria, i.e. Kostov. The letter, full of accusations, warnings and threats, was delivered to Vasil Kolarov by the Soviet Ambassador Bodrov. In the letter Stalin severely criticised the Bulgarians for their anti-Sovietism, regretted that anti-Soviet demonstrations were permitted and that within the government and the party there resided "enemy, anti-Soviet elements and imperialist spies such as Kostov, Kunin, Stefanov and others." In the face of Moscow's increasingly indignant and intransigent position, it was decided to convene a new extraordinary plenum of the Central Committee for March 26 in order to force the resignation of the persons denounced by Comrade Stalin.

The Plenum of the Committee was presided over by Kolarov and Tchervenkov, who held in their hands Stalin's letter with the nominal accusations. On this occasion it was finally decided to exclude Kostov from the Politburo and to dismiss him as Deputy Minister Chairman of the Council of Ministers and Chairman of the Economic and Financial Committee. Once out of the party and out of government agencies, Kostov was appointed director of the National Library. Finally, on 20 June 1949, he was arrested together with Kunin and Stefanov. On the instructions of Stalin, who demanded a written statement from Kostov himself, Beria ordered his henchmen to torture him properly. Once he had written and signed a lengthy confession, preparations began for the trial, which, at Stalin's express wish, according to a note to Beria and Abakuomov, was to be public and "if possible, in the presence of foreign and Western journalists."

Viktor Abakuomov was an old and experienced GPU official who had worked with Yagoda and Yezhov before becoming Beria's right-hand man. He arrived in Sofia in early November 1949 with the task of organising the trial. He studied the documents and heard witnesses and defendants. The trial was held in December in the great hall of the Army Club. The three main charges against Kostov were: capitulation to the Bulgarian fascists in 1942, espionage for the British Intelligence Services, and organising a plot with the Yugoslav leadership to form an anti-Soviet federation. Before the international press, Kostov appeared a hero as he denied the charges and denied most of the statements he himself had drafted and signed, which were contained in the indictment, read out in full in court. After accepting that the

---

secretary to Trotsky and then to Zinoviev and Kamenev. This bizarre character is said to have acted as a link between Yagoda and Trotsky.

document of some thirty thousand words containing his political biography had been written by his own hand, he denied to the court the facts contained in the indictment.

In 1934 Kostov, chief of cadres of the Balkan secretariat, met for the first time in Moscow with Tito, then known as "Walter ". In a fragment of his signing statement, he wrote the following about his relationship with the future Marshal Tito of Yugoslavia:

> "The position of the Yugoslav Communist Party was still difficult. Its leadership was challenged by strong factional struggles. It was a question of giving support to a new party leadership inside the country. The choice of Bela Kun and Valetsky, who had not yet been unmasked as Trotskyists, fell to Tito. At that time he was known under the pseudonym "Walter ". The choice of Bela Kun and Valetsky was not accidental, for as far as I could personally ascertain from materials at my disposal and from party files on "Walter"-Tito, he had adopted Trotskyist positions. In 1934, Tito spoke to me about his Trotskyist ideas and explained his concerns..... He acknowledged to me his hatred of Stalin's leadership of the CPSU. It was only thanks to the support of Bela Kun and Valetsky and the favourable reports I gave that Tito was able to travel in 1934 to Yugoslavia and assume a leading position there."

In another fragment of the written statement, Kostov referred to a visit by Kardelj, the Hungarian-born Jew who was one of Tito's confidants. In November 1944, Kardelj explained to Kostov Tito's grand strategy for Eastern Europe. These are the words written by Kostov on the indictment:

> "Kardelj informed me on a strictly confidential basis that during the war the British and Americans had supplied arms and ammunition to the Yugoslav partisans on the strict condition that at the end of the war Tito would keep Yugoslavia out of the USSR and would not allow the Soviet Union to establish its influence either in Yugoslavia or in the rest of the Balkans. On this basis a formal agreement was concluded during the war between the British and Americans and Tito".

The source of these quotes is a digital magazine, *Revolutionary Democracy* (revolutionarydemocracy.org), which is published biannually in April and September in New Delhi. Founded in April 1995, the journal's materials were in XXI volumes as of April 2015. The texts cited are from a document entitled "Traycho Kostov and Tito's Plans for Eastern Europe". It reveals that in 1946 Kostov travelled to Belgrade and met Tito, whom he had not seen since 1934. In his signed statement he wrote the following about this meeting:

"I had not seen Tito for twelve years and was greatly impressed by the remarkable change he had undergone. He was pompous in his military uniform and his fingers were curled. During our meeting Tito was constantly putting on an appearance, and with his outward appearance and manner of speaking he gave himself airs of being a great personage. Tito greeted me like an old friend, but nevertheless he behaved in an arrogant manner, giving me to understand that he was not the same Tito of twelve years ago.... He thanked me for the service I had rendered him in Moscow and admitted that otherwise he would not have been able to attain the position he had reached in Yugoslavia."

The plan, according to Kostov's written confession, was for Bulgaria to join the federation of Slavic peoples as the seventh republic, making it the largest and most populous of the federation. The British and Americans had promised Tito that they would use the press, as usual, to justify their failure to comply with the Yalta agreement. It was expected that the USSR would eventually resign itself to the Federation's fait accompli. Despite Kostov's refusal to acknowledge the facts in the indictment, the witnesses who appeared confirmed one by one what he had written. The second defendant, Ivan Stefanov, the Minister of Finance, indignantly addressed Kostov with these words: "I am deeply astonished that the main organiser of this conspiracy, the one responsible for my standing before this court today, does not have the courage to admit his guilt for the crimes he has committed." Rising to his feet, Stefanov took off his glasses and looking Kostov in the face added: "It seems that Traycho Kostov wants to remain a traitor and wants to prove his cowardice to the end." The other defendants were also furious with Kostov and reproached him for bringing them into the conspiracy and then betraying them. They all accused him and gave detailed, inculpatory accounts of his activities. After he was sentenced, Kostov, realising that he had been the only one sentenced to death, sent a letter to the Politburo in which he admitted that his lengthy written statement was correct and asked for clemency. Here are some of his words:

"I plead guilty to the accusation formulated by the court and fully confirm the dispositions written by my own hand during the investigation. Realising at the last moment the impropriety of my conduct before the people's court... sincerely regretting my attitude, due to an extreme excitement of my nerves and the morbid selfishness of an intellectual... I beg you to revoke my sentence of death if you consider it possible and commute it to strict confinement for life....".

According to a Bulgarian government communiqué, Kostov was executed on 16 December 1949, two days after the end of the trial. Of the ten other defendants who were also tried, four were sentenced to life imprisonment.

Since the documents seized after Beria's fall contain the reports the NKVD had on Kostov, it is worth taking a few more minutes before leaving the Bulgarian case. In the directives written to Lev E. Vlodzimirski, head of the Specially Important Cases Investigation Section of the Ministry of Internal Affairs, Beria refers several times to statements, information and accusations against Kostov transmitted by "Sonia" and "Spartacus". The pseudonym "Spartacus" had been used by Vulko Tchervenkov since his underground work for the GPU in the 1930s and he kept it during his long collaboration as a member of the Comintern propaganda apparatus and throughout the war. The "Spartacus" reports on Traycho Kostov therefore date back to the years before World War II. "Sonia" was the second Soviet agent who from before the war sent Vlodzimirski, then special director of secret affairs, devastating reports about Kostov. Anton Kolendic states in his book that he learned that "Sonia" was Tsola Dragoitcheva from the 1978 edition of T. Dragoitcheva's anti-Yugoslav memoirs, in which it is clear that "Sonia" was her clandestine pseudonym. In 1983, these memoirs were published in French in Montreal under the title *De la défaite à la victoire (Mémoire d'une révolutionnaire bulgare)*. Kolendic states that between 1945 and 1947 he had occasion to speak with Kostov about Tsola Dragoitcheva, whom he referred to as "the wallet". As a member of the party's Central Committee, Tsola was the mistress of a chauffeur who worked at the Soviet Embassy in Sofia. The Central Committee of the Bulgarian Communist Party headed by Kostov used her as a liaison. When the second Patriotic Front government was formed in 1945-46. Tsola Dragoitcheva was part of it.

On the basis of reports in "Sonia" and "Spartacus", Vlodzimirsky drew Beria's attention in a letter to Traycho Kostov's Trotskyite past and his involvement in anti-Soviet politics, espionage and the "Titoist plot". On the Trotskyist past, we must go back to 1934-1935, when Kostov and Tchervenkov worked in the Comintern apparatus headed by Dimitrov and Kolarov. Dimitrov had entrusted Kostov with a responsible post in the Balkan Section of the International, which required the approval of the GPU, with which Kostov necessarily worked. The GPU then demanded that he "complete" the indictment against two members of the Central Committee of the Bulgarian Communist Party, Vasil Tanev and Blagoi Popov, the two Bulgarian communists who had been arrested together with Dimitrov for the Reichstag fire and tried at the Leipzig trial in 1933-34. After lengthy negotiations with the Nazis, the Soviet government had secured their release and, after receiving them in Moscow with full honours, had granted them and Dimitrov Soviet citizenship. In 1935, the GPU discovered that they were Trotskyists and summoned Traycho Kostov to "complete" the evidence that the two were preparing Dimitrov's assassination; but Kostov did not complete any accusations or fabricate any evidence against the two Bulgarian communists. This did not save them, as "Spartacus" (Vulko Tchervenko) and Vladimir Poptomov presented evidence against them and testified that Tanev and Popov "... had created a Trotskyite faction, had publicly accused Dimitrov and had threatened to kill him". Sentenced to fifteen years' imprisonment, both disappeared without trace in the Siberian Krasny camp. The GPU then began to compile a dossier on Kostov: his behaviour had caused him to be mistrusted, and he was marked in the dossier as a Trotskyite. When Dimitrov became aware of the matter, he removed him from Moscow and, on the pretext of an "urgent mission", sent him to Tsarist Bulgaria to work there clandestinely. In short, there was documentation in the GPU archives containing numerous accusations of Trotskyism against Kostov, which was used in the trial that condemned him to death.

Failed coup in Hungary

We have gone on at length about the Bulgarian crisis, but we cannot leave out the failed coup d'état in Hungary, whose preparations coincided with events in Bulgaria. The main protagonist was, once again, a Zionist Jew named Laszlo Rajk (actually Reich). John Gunzberg, writing in *Behind Europe's Curtain,* wrote that the Hungarians joked that Rajk had entered the government because someone was needed who could sign the papers on the Sabbath, thus implying that he was the only non-Jew. Gunther cited Rakosi, Gerö, Farkas, Vas, Vajda, Revai and other Jews whom he called "Muscovites". However, Laszlo Rajk's Jewishness is confirmed by the Jewish author Howard M. Sachar in *Israel and Europe: an appraisal in history* (1999). The same author also confirms that Traycho Kostov was also Jewish. Our source of information for the following lines is "The Incredible Story of Laszlo Rajk", a work that comes from *Revolutionary Democracy,* the digital publication cited a few paragraphs above. In any case, for the reader interested in finding out more, the full document of the Rajk trial is available on the internet in pdf, entitled *László Rajk and his accomplices before the People's Court.*

A few weeks after Yugoslavia's expulsion from Cominform, on the night of 10 July 1948, the body of Milos Moich, a young Hungarian of Yugoslav origin, was found in his Budapest flat by a friend. Moich lay dying in a pool of blood, but before he died he had time to reveal to the woman the name of his killer, Zivko Boarov, a press attaché at the Yugoslav Embassy. When the police arrested Boarov, a lengthy investigation began that unravelled a far-reaching conspiracy. The leads led to Laszlo Rajk, the Hungarian foreign minister; the commander-in-chief of the army, General George Palffy; the head of the Hungarian Communist Party, Tibor Szony, also a Jew; and Lazar Brankov, a diplomat at the Yugoslav legation. Through them came Tito's Interior Minister, Aleksandar Rankovic, a Jew of Austrian origin whose real name was Rankau.

Not all was uniform in Tito's Yugoslavia, and he had few qualms about eliminating those who opposed the break with Moscow. Hundreds of dissidents were liquidated, among them Arso Jovanovic, a leading partisan general murdered while trying to cross into Romania. Those inside Yugoslavia who agreed with the Cominform's pronouncement were called "informbirovtsi" ("Cominformians") and were interned en masse in concentration camps. The main camp was Goli Otov (Naked Island). According to the independent analyst Vladimir Dedijer, about 32,000 people were interned in this camp alone. The number of deaths in all the camps due to execution, exhaustion, starvation, epidemics or suicide has not been established.

One of those who passed the Cominform resolution was Milos Moich, who since the end of the war had been working as an agent in Hungary for Rankovic's secret police (UDBA). Moich made the mistake of confiding in Andras Szalai, a secret agent and member of the propaganda section of the Communist Party, who wanted to reveal Tito's plans for Hungary. Szalai immediately alerted the Yugoslav ambassador, Karl Mrazovich. How events unfolded from this point onwards is known from the statement of Moich's executioner, Zivko Boarov, who testified at Rajk's trial. Boarov explained that when it became known that Moich was planning to denounce Tito and the activities of the UDBA, diplomat Lazar Brankov informed Belgrade. Interior Minister Rankovic ordered that Moich be forced to cross the border and, if this was not possible, he was to be liquidated. Below is an excerpt from his trial testimony:

> Brankov," said Boarov, "ordered me to do it and told me that since I was a Serb and close to Moich, I had the best chance of success. At first I refused. Then Brankov and Blasich (first secretary of the Yugoslav legation) took me to Ambassador Mrazovich and told him that I refused to do the job. Mrazovich repeated the order and ordered me to carry it out. I did not dare to disobey. Mrazovich handed me his own revolver.
> So I went to Moich's flat on the evening of 10 July after making sure he was alone. We had a long conversation. I tried to persuade him to give up his intentions and tried to get him to agree to an interview with Brankov at the Embassy. If he agreed, I knew we could put him across the border. I didn't want to use my gun on him, but Moich refused all my overtures. Then I started to threaten him and told him that I was playing with his life, so a fight broke out and at one point in the fight I lost my head and shot him with Mrazovich's revolver. I went back to the Embassy and informed Brankov, as Minister Mrazovich had already left for Yugoslavia".

A year passed between the events described by Boarov and the arrests of Laszlo Rajk, Tibor Szonyi and General Palffy. Rajk was arrested at his home on 30 May 1949 and Palffy on 18 July. Before proceeding against these important figures, the police concluded that they were preparing a coup d'état which was to be set in motion by the arrest and assassination of two

Jewish Stalinist leaders, Matyas Rakosi, general secretary of the Communist Party; and Ernö Gerö, "Pedro " in Spain during the Civil War, where he was prominent in the elimination of Trostkyites. According to the plotters' plans, if the conspiracy succeeded, Rajk and Palffy were to become the new strongmen of Hungary.

General Palffy's real surname was Österreicher and he changed his name in 1934. As reported by Ithiel de Sola Pool in *Satellite Generals. A Study of Military Elites in the Soviet Sphere,* Palffy was married to a Jewish woman, Katalin Sármány. Although he was abhorred in military circles, at the end of the war he organised the Political Department of the Ministry of Defence and began his career to the top. In 1945 he was promoted from major to colonel, and in 1946 from colonel to general. In 1947 he was a personality among the military elite, coming from the Ludovika Military Academy. Military men who had not been able to advance in the previous regime because of their Jewish origins rose through the ranks between 1947 and 1948. In February 1948 Palffy was promoted to lieutenant general and became Inspector General of the Army and Minister of Defence. Palffy then surrounded himself with a coterie of friends who were Jewish or married to Jewish women, among them Lieutenant General Kalman Revai, who succeeded Palffy as Inspector General of the Army for a short period; Lieutenant General Laszlo Solym, Chief of Staff from 1948 to 1950; General Gustav Illy, a homosexual who was Inspector of Training between 1947 and 1949; General Istvan Beleznay, married to a Jewish woman. In reality, all of them were relatively young men, opportunists who had put themselves at the service of the communists in order to make a dizzying career.

Like Lavrenti Beria or Otto Katz, Laszlo Rajk was a typical Jew who aspired above all to power and moved independently of ideologies. Cold like steel, he was a political adventurer capable of playing multiple roles. Like Katz, without ideals or loyalties, he felt bound only to Zionism, the ideology of Jewish nationalists throughout the world. In 1931, after being arrested for distributing communist propaganda, he agreed to become a police spy at the University of Budapest. From then on his career began, in which he was able to play various roles as a double or triple agent, as required. The Hungarian police chief, Sombor-Schweinitzer, sent him to Spain in 1937, supposedly to report on Hungarian communists fighting in the Rakosi Battalion. He arrived in Paris with false papers that made him a Czech communist and from France he entered Spain, where he managed to become political commissar of the Rakosi Battalion. The curious thing is that Rajk was accused of being a Trotskyite and expelled from the Communist Party. In 1939, after deserting the Battalion, he fled to France, but was arrested. The French handed him over to the Germans, who interned him first in the St. Cyprien concentration camp and then in the Gurs and Vernet camps. Before the court that tried and convicted him, Rajk admitted that during internment he had close contact with Hungarian and Yugoslav Trotskyists and mentioned in particular

Vukmanovich, known as "Tempo", who had become prime minister of Macedonia, and Mrazovich, the Yugoslav ambassador in Budapest who had given the pistol to Boarov.

While interned in France, Rajk was visited by a Communist agent infiltrated alongside Allen Dulles in the OSS (Office of Strategic Services), the famous Noel H. Field, a shadowy figure, a double or triple agent who was probably a Trotskyite. Field told him that he had instructions from his superiors to help him return home. By August 1941, Laszlo Rajk was back in Hungary, where he reported to Peter Hain, the head of the political police, about his mission in Spain and his stay in France. So that the communists would not suspect him, it was decided to imprison him for a time. Thus Rajk, whose extraordinary acting ability enabled him to deceive both sides, was considered one of the best members of the Communist Party, and in May 1945 he became the organising secretary of the Communist Party in the Greater Budapest district.

In contact with Lieutenant Colonel Kovach of the American military delegation, he simultaneously collaborated with US Intelligence. Rajk was then charged with organising a faction within the Communist Party that would serve to split the party and wrest the majority from Rakosi. On 20 March 1946, Laszlo Rajk became Minister of the Interior, a crucial position that allowed him to place British and American agents in the Ministry, who were recruited in Switzerland by Allen Dulles and Noel Field. Rajk thus placed the Jew Tibor Szonyi as head of the cadre department, a key position, as this allowed him to go placing his men in the Prime Minister's office, the Foreign Ministry, the Press and Radio departments, and, of course, the Ministry of the Interior itself.

Through Lazar Brankov, who under the cover of his post at the Embassy was the head of Yugoslav Intelligence in Hungary, Rajk was supplying Tito with sensitive information through his position as Minister of the Interior. According to his testimony at the trial, it was in the summer of 1947 that he had his first meeting with Yugoslav Interior Minister Rankovic. Rajk was on holiday in Abbazia, a Croatian town on the Adriatic coast. A blonde, Hungarian-speaking woman in her thirties contacted Rajk to announce that his Yugoslav counterpart wanted to talk to him and would visit him in Abbazia. A few days later Rankovic arrived and the woman acted as interpreter between the two. The Yugoslav minister said that he had come to see him on direct orders from Tito. During the interview, the future collaboration between the two interior ministers was forged. Laszlo Rajk, with Szonyi's cooperation, began to position "suitable" people in the army and police who would support an eventual coup d'état.

At the end of 1947, Tito and Rankovic travelled to Hungary to sign a friendship pact, and there was then an opportunity to flesh out the development of the conspiracy. Rajk organised a hunt and planned a private meeting with Rankovic on the train in which they were travelling to the hunting ground. The interpreter on this occasion was Brankov. Rankovic stressed that, in revealing the plan to him, he was following Tito's instructions. During the trial, the judge asked Rajk to recount the details of the plan. In short, the plan was to organise several federations between Yugoslavia and other countries in order to break the dependence of the people's democracies on Moscow and replace Stalin's influence with that of Tito. According to Rajk, Rankovic specified that a large federation would be built under Tito's leadership. When the judge enquired about how the takeover of power in Hungary was to take place, the following exchange took place:

> "Rajk: The task in Hungary was to overthrow the people's democratic regime. Arrest, of course, the members of the government and within that...
> Judge: Who were the main enemies?
> Rajk:... and within this the most dangerous ones, Rankovic said, had to be eliminated if there was no other choice.
> Judge: Name the names of who they were.
> Rajk: By names, he thought the first of all was Rakosi, Gerö and Farkas.
> Judge: Did you mention them specifically?
> Rajk: He mentioned them and told me that I would be responsible for implementing the whole programme in Hungary, and in connection with that, explained to me how Tito assessed the situation and the forces that could be counted on.
> Judge: Did you promise Yugoslav assistance?
> Rajk: Yes, he emphasised that he could count on the support of an adequate grouping of forces; but he considered it absolutely important that in political actions, in the organisation of forces, I should depend on my own internal backing.

In the spring of 1948, Rajk met Selden Chapin, the American diplomat who had served as minister plenipotentiary to Hungary from 1947 to 1949. He asked him if he could confirm that, as Rankovic had told him, Washington approved of Tito's plan. About this interview, Rajk testified at the trial: "Chapin hesitated a little before making a statement to me, finally he did and said that he knew about this plan and that the United States would not object to the implementation of Yugoslavia's policy". So, with the help of General Palffy, who worked in the army exactly as he did in the police, Rajk worked out the plan. Even then, however, he was under suspicion, as evidenced by the fact that after a trip to Moscow in August 1948 Rajk suddenly ceased to be Minister of the Interior and became Minister of Foreign Affairs, a position which detached him from the secret police and Hungary's internal politics.

The foreign ministers of the satellite countries were conditioned and had to submit to Kremlin policy. Perhaps for this reason, in August 1948

Brankov told Rajk that Rankovic wanted to see him urgently. Since it was not convenient for Rajk to travel to Belgrade, it was Rankovic who had to travel back to Hungary. The secret meeting took place at the estate of a landowner named Antal Klein. The Yugoslav ambassador in Budapest, Mrazovich, acted as interpreter. It was Mrazovich's mistress, Georgina, a friend of Klein's and the daughter of a high-ranking city official named Gero Tarsznyas, who arranged what was supposed to be a hunt, as told in court by Antal Klein, who testified in great indignation and annoyance at the use he had been subjected to.

The secret meeting took place in early October 1948, Ambassador Mrazovic had invited Georgina, who was present at the estate and also gave valuable testimony, as she and Antal Klein identified Rajk in court. The landowner Klein stated that Mrazovich arrived at his estate accompanied by Laszlo Rajk, who was wearing a green felt coat and dark glasses. Here is the moment of identification in court:

> "Judge: What role did Laszlo Rajk play in this so-called hunt?
> Klein: I don't know Laszlo Rajk. I don't know the man; I have never seen him before. Now that I have been brought before him by the authorities, I recognise in him as the man who was present then with Mrazovich in the green felt coat and glasses.
> Judge: Do you recognise him now?

The old landowner turned, looked angrily at the entire court, then looked each of the defendants in the face. Rajk's face broke into a broad smile. "That's the one," shouted Antal Klein, pointing a trembling finger at him. As he left the courtroom, still apparently outraged that he had not been introduced and that he had driven a group of conspirators in his carriage to his hunting reserve, his discomfort was very evident.

General Palffy, who commanded the border guards, facilitated the passage of the car of Yugoslav Interior Minister Aleksandar Rankovic, who entered the country unchecked and was waiting for Rajk and Mrazovich at the guard's house, already in the hunting area of the property. Georgina, who was with Mrazovich and Rajk, who was not introduced to her and Klein. She told the judge about the meeting between the conspirators:

> "When we arrived at the ranger's hut, I saw a man in a hunter's outfit waiting there, carrying a gun. He was a man of medium height and about forty years old. Mrazovich asked me to stay in the house and prepare lunch. I was surprised that he did not introduce me to either man. Then they parleyed, walking up and down in the vicinity of the guard's house and sometimes walking away. I heard one of the men speak a Slavic language. Again and again they came close enough and I could hear. I am sure it was not Russian, maybe Serbian. The man in the green coat spoke Hungarian and Mrazovich translated between the two of them. I could

understand some words of the conversation when they were close to me, for example, Mrazovich was talking about Yugoslavia and he said that action should be taken.... Then they talked about someone called Palffy, who was to be appointed Minister of Defence. I also heard the names of Ministers Rakosi and Farkas mentioned several times. When they had finished talking they went into the hut and had a snack."
Judge: Please come here, do you recognise the person in this photograph as the one you were waiting for at the guard's house? Look at her.
Georgina: Yes, I recognise her.
Judge: Are you sure?
Georgina: Yes.
Judge: I have verified that this photo in which the witness recognises the person in question is a photograph of Rankovich, which is now included in the documentation".

It should be noted that the meeting at Antal Klein's estate took place shortly after Laszlo Rajk stepped down as Interior Minister and months after Yugoslavia's expulsion from Cominform. These two facts justify why Tito considered it necessary to execute the coup d'état as soon as possible. Rankovich therefore announced to Rajk that Tito was ready to provide further direct assistance. Once in Budapest, Rajk met with General Palffy and told him that everything had to be ready for the occupation of the vital places. According to what he told the court, by the end of 1948 everything was ready, and two experienced assassins had even arrived from Yugoslavia who began to study the habits and movements of Rakosi, Gerö and Farkas, whose arrest was to be the signal to trigger the coup. General Palffy mentioned to the court Colonel Korondy, who was entrusted with the formation of three small groups of a dozen men who were to arrest the three leaders and who were to kill them if they resisted. It was necessary for all three to be in Budapest, so a day when there was a meeting of the Politburo or the Council of Ministers was envisaged: the three could be arrested when they returned home after the sessions. Here is an excerpt from Palffy's testimony:

"Palffy: I explained orally to Rajk the outline of my plan. The substance of it was that the coup was to be initiated by ten army battalions and police units. In Budapest, some key places, first of all the headquarters of the Communist Party, the Ministry of Defence and the Ministry of the Interior, the radio station and the offices of *Szabad Nep* (party newspaper), the railway stations, the public works and some districts where resistance might arise, were to be occupied by these forces. Simultaneously, immediately after the occupation, the small groups were to arrest the three politicians mentioned above. I would command the entire armed force and Colonel Korondy would command the police

units. This was my general plan. Rajk approved it. I was then instructed to spell it out in detail.
Judge. Whose?
Palffy: From Rajk..."

The fact that the Jewishness of Laszlo Rajk, who was also a Freemason, is only revealed by Howard M. Sachar in the above-mentioned work, invites us to relate, in order to finish with the quotations from the trial, the moment when the judge enquired about his name, a fact that outraged Rajk, who interpreted that the magistrate was trying to insinuate that he was a Jew:

"Judge: How did your grandfather write his name?
Rajk: My grandfather, being of Saxon origin, spelled his name Reich.
Judge: So, your grandfather's name was Reich. How did he become Rajk? Legally?
Rajk: Yes, legally. I cannot give the exact date when it was legalised. On my baptismal certificate it is already written with 'a', i.e. Reich became Rajk. I fail to see how this can be of the slightest interest to the court. In this connection, I wish to add that I am genuinely Aryan. The Aryan law of Hungary..."

The judge did not allow him to continue and cut him off abruptly, saying that he was not interested in whether he was an Aryan or not, but only wanted to know how he had changed his name and whether he had done so legally. Rajk, who knew that the surname Reich was one of those frequently adopted by Jews who wished to hide their race, understood that the judge was hinting at his origin.

In short, Laszlo Rajk was removed from the Ministry of the Interior because Rakosi, even before Yugoslavia's expulsion from the Cominform, had realised that Stalin was displeased with him for his inaction and feared that he himself might end up under suspicion of disloyalty. According to some sources, in late 1947 Stalin reportedly told Rakosi publicly that he was blind, for he did not see what was going on under his nose. Faced with the choice between Tito and Stalin, Rakosi (actually Rosenkranz) thought of saving himself and decided to remain loyal to Moscow. Nevertheless, in February 1949 Rajk became secretary general of the People's Front for Independence. At the May Day celebration he stood on the rostrum next to Rakosi, so there was nothing to indicate that his arrest and that of his colleagues, which took place on 30 May 1949, was in the offing. Since he had ceased to be Minister of the Interior, Rajk had been under surveillance, and despite his growing popularity, Rakosi, caught between a rock and a hard place, proceeded to unleash the purge against Rajk and his accomplices, who were accused of espionage on behalf of the Western powers in order to separate Hungary from the socialist sphere.

On 15 June 1949 it was announced that Laszlo Rajk had been dismissed as Foreign Minister and expelled from the Politburo and the Communist Party for being a "Titoist", "Trotskyite" and "nationalist". On 10 September 1949, the charges were published in the world press, and on 16 September 1949, accused of organising a plot to bring Hungary under American control and receiving military aid from Yugoslavia, Laszlo Rajk, General George Palffy, Tibor Szonyi and their accomplices appeared in court. On 22 September 1949, Laszlo Rajk, Tibor Szonyi and Andras Szalai were sentenced to death by civilian courts. Yugoslav Lazar Brankov received a life sentence. In addition, a military court sentenced Palffy, Korondy and two other officers to the maximum penalty. The sentence was carried out in mid-October. Following Rajk's trial, ninety-four other persons were arrested and fifteen more were sentenced to death.

In countries such as Rumania and Albania, too, there were trials in 1949 against the so-called "pro-Yugoslav Trotskyist fractions"; but it is beyond the scope of this work to devote attention to them. In November 1949, after the Titoist or Trotskyist agents in Bulgaria and Hungary had been subdued, Stalin convened a new meeting of the Cominform in Budapest, which was chaired by Súslov. The title of the main report was: "The Yugoslav Communist Party, in the hands of assassins and spies". It accused Tito of acting against communism for the benefit of the United States of America. In an article published on 21 August 1949, Stalin himself had denounced the crimes of the Tito regime against citizens of the USSR and threatened in these words: "The Soviet Government deems it necessary to declare that it has no intention of accepting such a situation and that it will be forced to resort to other, more effective means... to defend the rights and interests of Soviet citizens in Yugoslavia and to call to order the fascist henchmen who believe that everything is permitted to them".

Undoubtedly the support of the Americans, more than evident to Stalin, was decisive in restraining a military intervention against Tito and Pijade. Tito himself, in August 1949, addressed military and party members in Skopje and reaffirmed his willingness to resist a Red Army invasion. "It might seem at first sight," he said, "that we are alone, but this is not true." On 4 September 1949, *Borba*, the party newspaper, devoted a full page to comments by Dean Acheson, US Secretary of State, and Hector McNeil, a Foreign Office diplomat, confirming that there was support in the West for Marshal Tito's efforts to maintain and defend Yugoslav independence.

In 1951, the book *Tito and Goliath*, written by the American editor and diplomat Hamilton Fish Armstrong and published in London by Victor Gollancz, appeared. It analyses the conflict between Tito and Stalin from a perspective favourable to the Yugoslav position. Hamilton F. Armstrong, a personal friend of Tito's who lived in Belgrade in 1949 and 1950 at the height of the confrontation with Moscow, shares in this work the theses of Marx's translator into Serbo-Croatian, Moshe Pijade, whom he considers "the intellectual head of the Yugoslav Communist Party and the first estatega in its struggle against the Bolsheviks". From 1928 to 1972, Armstrong was editor of *Foreign Affairs*, the journal of the Council on Foreign Relations (CFR), which places him in the sphere of the Round Table. Already the title of his book, of which we have the first edition, is quite significant: it is clear that the crypto-Jewish Tito is seen as a new David who challenges the giant philistine Goliath (Stalin). Pijade denounced in early September 1949 that Stalin's attitude towards Yugoslavia was comparable to Hitler's "racist attitude" towards small nations.

In Hamilton Fish Armstrong's view, Zhdanov represented the supporters of "an international communist community led by the USSR, certainly; but not in fear and subjugation to Stalin's designs, but animated by revolutionary fervour". The problem, then, remained the same as ever. It was not a question of condemning communism, but of denouncing Stalin's national communism, since it claimed that the control and purity of orthodoxy should be exercised from Moscow and not from the offices of the international bankers who had initially financed it. Therefore, because the aim was to regain control of international communism, Roosevelt told Martin Dies, chairman of the Committee on American Activities, to stop investigating the communists and concentrate on the Nazis. Thus, as we have seen, when Senator McCarthy took over from Dies and tried to expose how deep the tentacles of communism ran in the Administration, he was torn to shreds by the press.

As had happened in the 1930s, when the Moscow trials were held, the international press began to develop the thesis that the trials against the Jews Laszlo Rajk and Traycho Kostov were "show trials", show trials in which communist dissidents who fought against the Stalinist dictatorship were convicted. For the duration of World War II, Stalin enjoyed absolute immunity: there was no problem with him attacking Poland, Finland and other countries, wiping out the Poles at Katyn.... Nor was there a problem at Yalta, or at Potsdam, where the ethnic cleansing of millions of Germans was allowed, as has been explained. By 1949, however, plans had gone awry and, as in the 1930s, when Hitler was financed to relocate Trotsky to Moscow after a war that was to end in a draw, the problem was again Stalin.

After the shameful travesty of Nuremberg was internationally acclaimed as a model of justice, the Rajk and Kostov trials served to vindicate another communism, that of Tito and Pijade, as opposed to Stalin's "bossy imperialism". The expression, quoted by Armstrong in *Tito and Goliath*, is from Moshe Pijade, who claims to be the ideologue of true communist orthodoxy and distinguishes between the goals of international communism and Russia's national goals. In other words, instead of strengthening the national power of the Soviet Union, the mission of the satellite countries was to serve the cause of the international communist revolution, and thus they were to form the basis of ideological propaganda for the westward march of communism. Hamilton Fish Armstrong puts it in these words: "There is in all this something reminiscent of the great controversies which divided the Bolsheviks in the early years. There was, as then, a disagreement between those who were international revolutionaries and those who were determined to build socialism in one country first".

On the first anniversary of Yugoslavia's expulsion from the Cominform, *Borba*, the organ of the Yugoslav Communist Party, insisted that Tito's Yugoslavia was on the true path of Marxism: "The truth about the struggle between the Cominform and Yugoslavia," *Borba said,* "and about the principles for which our party is fighting, is growing daily in the international working-class movement and there is no reason to think that it will not succeed. Shortly afterwards, in August of the same year 1949, Tito insisted in Skopje that "the majority of the progressive peoples of the whole world" were with them. These are the statements and arguments that seem to convince most authors, for in almost all the works we have consulted the references to the trials of the "Titoists" are characterised by sympathy for the defendants and unreserved condemnation of Stalin. The first to adopt this position is Armstrong himself, since *Tito and Goliath* was perhaps the first work to offer a detailed analysis of what was being cooked up in those decisive years.

Echoing the arguments of Moshe Pijade, Armstrong criticises the Kostov trial on the basis of a text published by Pijade on 27 January 1950 in a fortnightly publication, *Yugoslav Fortnightly*, according to which Moscow was allegedly involved in negotiations on the union of Bulgaria and Yugoslavia. Armstrong, in line with Pijade's article, charges that the trial failed to mention that in late 1944 there was a meeting between the Soviets, Bulgarians and Yugoslavs in Moscow, where a draft treaty drawn up by Kostov on a hypothetical union of the two countries was presented. Belgrade's man at the meeting was Moshe Pijade himself. The Soviet representative, Vyshinsky, proposed that the first step should be a treaty of political, economic and military cooperation. He announced that the USSR would draft an outline and asked Pijade to present his own outline at the next meeting, which took place on 27 January 1945. According to Pijade, the three delegations then agreed on a final text, to which Britain objected. In any case, again according to Pijade, before the delegates left Moscow, it was agreed that in February they would meet again in Belgrade to sign the documents. The meeting did not take place, however, as Britain vetoed the federation. Armstrong writes that, despite the British veto, "the door was not closed to the idea of an even wider federation, which could integrate Albania." Armstrong himself, however, readily acknowledges that the Soviets then decided to postpone even any Bulgarian-Yugoslav friendship treaty. For Hamilton Fish Armstrong, these contacts during the war are "shattering" evidence that invalidates the trial and the accusations against Kostov. Of course, we cannot share this view, for, as we have seen, the position of Tito's and Pijade's Yugoslavia in 1949 was an undisputed challenge to the alleged authority of the USSR.

To conclude these pages on the struggle for control of the communist parties and countries, which we have taken longer than expected, we will now turn to a 1950 interview between Tito and the author of *Tito and Goliath*, which reinforces the thesis that the conspirators who had financed the October Revolution in 1917 were seeking to regain control. Armstrong notes that the Yugoslav communists had thought of the China of Mao Tse-tung, the communist leader imposed by the "Institut of Pacific Relations" (IPR) in their search for potential allies:

> "Almost every conversation I have had with Yugoslav leaders," Armstrong writes, "whether in Belgrade or abroad, has sooner or later led to China, and always the hope is that Stalin will sooner or later violate China's national interests so flagrantly that the Chinese Communists will not be able to tolerate it, will take advantage of the fact that they are physically capable of rejecting him, and will then tacitly or perhaps openly cooperate with the Yugoslav Communist Party. Their arguments for expecting this are not unreasonable".

In other words, in 1950 there existed in Yugoslavia the hope of forming an axis against the Cominform with a foothold in Belgrade. Further on, the text continues as follows:

> "Many experts in China deny that there are any political or practical differences between Chinese and Russian communism. Tito believes that these views do not take into account the fact that Stalinism is not what he calls communism and he does not believe that many Chinese would call it communism if they experienced it. Tito maintains that Chinese communists are sure that they are different from Stalinist communists simply because they are in a position to do so. His own case shows, he points out, that there are sharp differences in ideology and practice in the communist world, and that what brings them to the surface is the Stalinist refusal to recognise the right to autonomy of communist parties and communist states."

During their talks, Tito reminded Armstrong that in the 1930s Mao Tse-tung had very bad relations with the Soviets and that for a time there were two Central Committees in the Chinese Communist Party, one based in Moscow and the other led by Mao in China. Tito highlighted the fact that Mao not only managed to avoid Moscow's attempts to sideline him, but was able to organise his communist armies without Stalin's help. What neither Tito nor Armstrong say, of course, is that this was only possible because Roosevelt and Truman, prompted by the IPR conspirators, withdrew aid to Chiang Kai-shek and supported Mao Tse-tung's communists.

Stalin's "paranoid anti-Semitism"

Despite the tensions and differences of opinion during 1949, the dictator of the USSR seemed to have consolidated his grip on power after having made a clean break. In addition to imposing Moscow's dominance over the satellite countries, the Soviet Union became the world's second nuclear power that year. On 21 December 1949, Stalin's seventieth birthday, Beria, who had chaired the Atomic Energy Commission since 1946, had succeeded in presenting his boss with the achievement he had longed for. To celebrate the general's birthday, the day was declared a bank holiday, and in the evening a gala performance was held at the Bolshoi Theatre, which Stalin attended accompanied by his daughter Svetlana. The members of the Politburo and the entire Diplomatic Corps were present in the boxes of honour. During the gala dinner that followed in the Kremlin, telegrams of congratulations were read out from all over the world. Marshal Beria rose and made a speech full of enthusiasm for the work of his beloved chief. "Comrade Stalin's whole life," Beria asserted, "is inseparably linked with the great struggle for the creation and strengthening of the Communist Party and the victory of the proletarian revolution for the welfare of the working people and the victory of communism." Outside, the crowd gathered near the Kremlin walls watched in amazement as the image of the great leader appeared in the sky. Beria had prepared this new gift for the "Father of the People": a slide of Stalin in military uniform and cap and insignia of the rank of generalissimo was projected by a powerful anti-aircraft searchlight onto a black cloud overcasting Red Square. It was like an apparition of the supposed God of international communism.

Apparently, therefore, Beria, in order to maintain Stalin's confidence, remained the faithful dog executing his designs. One of the issues that repeatedly tested his abilities was the so-called "Zionist plot", which since the assassination of Solomon Mikhoels in January 1948 had only grown. After the dissolution of the Jewish Anti-Fascist Committee in November 1948 and the arrest of Polina Molotov in January 1949, the spiral of arrests of Jews, especially in Leningrad and Moscow, had continued throughout 1949. One of the most conspicuous members of the Jewish Committee, Solomon Lozovsky, was arrested five days after Molotov's wife, on 26 January 1949. It has already been said in chapter nine that Lozovsky, a leader of the Red International Trade Union together with Andreu Nin, was one of the three Jews who travelled to Spain in 1936 to organise the communist cells and prepare the creation of a revolutionary committee. Later, along with other American Zionists, he encouraged Roosevelt to enter the war. The arrest of Lozovsky, chairman of the Sovinformburo (Soviet news agency) between 1945 and 1948, had a major international impact.

Another significant event occurred on 7 July 1949, when three Jewish judges of the Leningrad court, Achille Grogorievich Leniton, Ilia Zeilkovich

Serman and Rulf Alexandrovna Zevina, were arrested and accused of taking counter-revolutionary and anti-Soviet positions. Sentenced to ten years in concentration camps, they appealed unsuccessfully, as the Supreme Court increased the sentence to twenty-five years, finding that the Leningrad court had failed to take into account that the convicts "had asserted the superiority of one nation over the other nations of the Soviet Union." This was a clear allusion to Jewish supremacism.

The investigation of the case against the defendants of the Jewish Anti-Fascist Committee lasted more than two years, during which time there was a subterranean struggle in which Stalin, as will be seen below, tried to wrest control of the security services from the all-powerful Beria. This inevitably delayed the opening of the trial, a closed trial that was not to begin until May 1952. Of the fifteen defendants, thirteen were sentenced to death. Only Lina Solomonovna Stern was spared in the end. This Latvian-born Jewess had been introduced into Stalin's entourage by Anna Alliluyeva, sister of Stalin's second wife, who had been married to Stanislaw Redens, a Cheka chief whom Beria hated. Polina Molotov, whose arrest had served Beria to weaken Molotov's position, cultivated a group of Jewish confidants and friends that included, in addition to Lina Stern, Zinaida Bukharin, wife of Nikolai Bukharin, purged by Stalin in 1938, and Miriam Svanidze, who had been married to Stalin's brother-in-law executed in 1941, Alexander Svanidze, brother of Stalin's first wife, Ekaterina "Kato" Svanidze. Tired of the machinations of this group of Jewish women, Stalin ordered their arrest, and Beria had no problem accusing Lina Stern of "cosmopolitanism", as he took revenge on Anna Alliluyeva and Stanislaw Redens, whom he considered enemies.[31]

An international campaign against Stalin was organised as skilfully as ever and he was showered with accusations of anti-Semitism. In general, the idea that Stalin behaved like a "paranoid" has taken hold, as the official historiography considers his distrust of Jews to be absurd. Thaddeus Wittlin claims that he hated them, yet the "anti-Semitic" dictator had a Jewish mistress, Rosa Kaganóvich. A son of Lavrenti Beria, Sergo, claims that Stalin had an offspring named Yura with her. The wife of Alexander

---

[31] About Stanislaw Redens, who according to some sources was also a Jew, T. Wittlin provides interesting information in *Commissar Beria*. Wittlin describes him as "one of the most cruel and brutal chiefs of the NKVD". Yezhov placed him next to Beria in Tbilisi as second-in-command in order to spy on him. As has been said, Yezhov wished to eliminate Beria, for he saw in him his worst enemy. Since, being married to Anna Alliluyeva, Redens was a relative of the dictator, Beria acted very diplomatically in his relations with the couple. He put at their disposal a luxurious villa in the spa resort of Sochi and a comfortable house with a garden in the capital. When he discovered that Stanislaw Redens liked vodka and girls," writes Thaddeus Wittlin, "he introduced him to some of his single friends who shared the same tastes. Needless to say, these guys were Beria's agents". In this way, he was trying to discredit Redens so that he would be recalled to Moscow as soon as possible.

Poskrebyshev, his lifelong personal secretary, was a Jewess named Bronislava Solomonovna Metallikova, who, accused of Trotskyism, was executed in 1941. A look at Politburo shows that in addition to Beria and Kaganóvich, who were Jewish, Molotov, Vorochilov and Andreyev were married to Jewish women, so their children were Jewish. In *Plot Against the Church*, Maurice Pinay, a pseudonym used by a group of Catholic priests opposed to the Second Vatican Council, claims that Malenkov was also Jewish. According to this source, he was the son of Maximilian Malenk, a surname considered to be Jewish. Furthermore, and here other authors agree, Malenkov was married to a sister of Nikita Khrushchev named Pearl-Mutter, who was known as "Comrade Schemschuschne". Some sources note that Khrushchev was also Jewish and his full name was Nikita Salomon Khrushchev. In *Staline Assassiné*, A. Avtorkhanov writes that Stalin "discovered that Khrushchev had a daughter whose mother was Jewish." Avtorkhanov adds that "Malenkov's own daughter had married a Jew." Certainly, if Stalin had had to be suspicious of the Jews who moved around him he would never have finished, since he was surrounded by them. What Stalin actually realised was that, inexorably, behind every manoeuvre against his policies or his leadership there were one or more Jews, which is perhaps why Avtorkhanov concludes that Stalin's anti-Semitism was "pragmatic".

It has been shown throughout this work that from the time Stalin came to power his main enemies were Trotskyist, internationalist Jews, whom he tried to eliminate, often with the help of other Jews who, even if only out of personal interest or for strategic reasons, supported him. Stalin was not unaware that Jews had played a leading role in the Bolshevik Revolution. It has already been seen that almost all the members of the first Communist government of 1918 were Jews. Moreover, all the Commissariats were from the very beginning filled by Jews from abroad. In the Commissariat of the Interior and in the Commissariat of Foreign Affairs, they held all the important posts. The same was true of the Commissariats for the Economy, Justice, Public Education, the Army, Health, Foreign Trade, etc..

Although official historians continue to pay no attention to this reality, which they either evade or shun as if it were an anecdote, there are scholars who dare to tell the truth. Alexander Solzhenitsyn, one of them, denounced what happened in Russia with these prescient words: "It must be understood that the Bolshevik leaders who seized power in Russia were not Russians. They hated Russians. They hated Christians. Guided by ethnic hatred, they tortured and massacred millions of Russians without the slightest remorse. This is no exaggeration. Bolshevism committed the greatest slaughter of human beings of all time. The fact that the majority of the world is indifferent or ignorant about this enormous crime is proof that the global media is in the hands of those responsible."

To these media denounced by Solzhenitsyn, we must add a plethora of authors and propagandists who, among the countless communist criminals, have been singling out only the "anti-Semitic" Stalin. It is these media and historians who have presented Tito, Rajk, Slansky and other communist murderers as innocent victims of the Kremlin dictator. Most sources consider it an anecdotal, irrelevant fact that it was Jews who were at the forefront of the anti-Stalin movements in all the countries of Eastern Europe; however, the facts prove time and again that this was the general rule and not a coincidence. In Yugoslavia, alongside the Jews Tito, Pijade, Rankovic and Kardelj, there was Josef Wilfan, another Jew from Sarajevo, who acted as the Marshal's economic adviser. The Yugoslav representative to the UN was Alexander Bebler, another Jew of Austrian origin. In *The World Conquerors*, Hungarian author Louis Marschalko, who errs in regarding Laszlo Rajk as a gentile sacrificed by Jews loyal to Stalin, explains in detail how power in Hungary fell into the hands of Jewish criminals, whether Zionists, internationalists or Stalinists, who carried out the persecution and elimination of Hungarians who were ill-considered for one reason or another.

In Poland, as in the other Eastern European countries, Beria's NKVD men took control and the slaughter began. As explained at the beginning of this chapter, Beria put repression in the hands of Jewish "avengers", who ran the concentration camps and preyed on Germans who were to be transferred to the West. At the time of the Cominform's creation, power in Poland was in the hands of three men: two Jews, Jakub Berman and Boleslaw Bierut, and Wladyslaw Gomulka, who was married to a Jew. Berman was a member of the Politburo and head of the Polish security organs; Bierut chaired the Central Committee of the Communist Party. Both of them, according to Gomulka, were NKVD "buds", i.e. Beria's "buds". As for Gomulka, prime minister of the Polish government at the time of the June 1948 Cominform meeting in Romania, it seems that he had expressed solidarity with Tito's delegates at the first meeting in October 1947 and that in Bucharest he opposed the expulsion of the Yugoslavs. He was then singled out as a Titoist or Trotskyite by the newspapers *Glos Ludu, Nowe Drogi* and *Pravda*, which denounced "Comrade Gomulka's Trotskyite gang". A struggle began which led to Gomulka's imprisonment in 1951. The fact that Bierut and Berman were both Beria's agents gives the Warsaw trial an added interest.

Gomulka himself gives a version of events in a memoir entitled *Mes quatorze années*. It is known from these texts that Stalin became suspicious of Beria, as he distrusted his two henchmen in Warsaw. The Sovietologist Avtorkhanov paraphrases in *Stalinne assassiné* some fragments of the version given by Gomulka in his memoirs. Stalin conceived a plan to arrest Berman and Gomulka in order to force them to testify against Beria and Bierut. Stalin wanted to know to what extent Beria was conspiring against him with the help of his Jewish protégés in Poland. In a text reproduced by Avtorkhanov Gomulka explains it this way:

"Bierut was very much afraid of Berman, for he feared that in the course of a trial, or during the investigation, Berman would be able to say the most compromising things. Thus, for example, that Beria had at a certain time fomented a plot against Stalin, and that Bierut had been involved in this alleged plot. I must say that I am not absolutely certain that this is exactly what happened, but that is how the story was told to me. Be that as it may, Bierut was constantly on guard and kept a close watch on Berman, and so did I myself at the time, since I was the first to appear in court. The scenario was as follows... Bierut determined things as long as he could, even resorting to sending false information to Moscow, for example that I was deathly ill.... Bierut thus managed to tighten the noose as much as possible and, in the end, it was Stalin's death that spared us all from this bad step".

One would think, logically enough, that the veteran Gomulka knew much more than he implies. With this quote, which states unequivocally that Stalin's death was providential, it is time to delve into the narrative of the dictator's assassination. Beria's capacity for intrigue, his boundless ambition, his extreme hypocrisy, his insensitivity to the feelings of others, put him on a par with Stalin himself, even surpassing him. His daughter Svetlana Aliluyeva wrote in *20 Letters to a Friend*: "I consider that Beria was more cunning, more deceitful, more cautious, more shameless, more determined and firmer in his actions, and consequently stronger than my father". Such was Beria's manoeuvrability, writes Avtorkhanov, that "all machinations and interrogations ended up in his hands, for his creatures were interrogated, who were interrogated by others of his creatures."

The open struggle between Stalin and Beria

Writing about Stalin's underground struggle against Beria during the last three years of his life is perhaps the most difficult task we have faced in the course of our work. This is due to contradictions, intentional omissions and the obvious bias of some of the available sources. Anton Kolendic offers texts written by Beria after his arrest and before his execution, which deserve little credence, but are sometimes useful. Nor can the texts of Nikita Khrushchev, the man who took power in the USSR after the demise of Stalin and Beria, be accepted without reservation. As for certain authors, most of them do not want to run the risk of being accused of anti-Semitism and some go so far as to deny the obvious. In his biography of Stalin, for example, Robert Conquest absurdly claims that the eleven Zionist Jews executed in 1952 after the Prague trial, all of them Beria's agents, were veteran Stalinists and fervent anti-Zionists ("needless to say," he writes in English, "they were veteran Stalinists and fervent-anti-Zionists"). We believe that the most accurate position is that of Nicolas Werth, who in the chapter of the *Black*

Book of Communism entitled "The Last Conspiracy" admits that the complexity of the facts is so great that the current state of knowledge about what happened does not allow the truth to be unravelled, so we must await access "to the presidential archives, where the most secret and the most sensitive files have been preserved".

We shall try, therefore, to present credible facts. One of them, to begin with, is the mutual fear that Stalin and Beria began to have of each other, so that their quarrel was, among other things, about saving each other's lives. Both Khrushchev and Stalin's daughter agree that Stalin feared that Beria might attempt a plot to assassinate him. According to T. Wittlin, Beria had introduced his spies into the circles closest to the "big boss". He mentions among them a Georgian woman named Alexandra Nakashidze, who had been his mistress in Tbilisi. This woman, an agent of the Security Forces with the rank of Commander, was placed as a housekeeper in Stalin's private flat in the Kremlin, where she kept an eye on what was going on in the dictator's personal circle. Using her charms, she eventually beguiled Vasily "Vasia" Stalin, the dictator's son. Beria's biographer claims that Stalin in his later years was suspicious of some of his closest associates. Fearful of assassination," writes Wittlin, "he ate only at his home in the Moscow suburb of Blizhny in Kuntsevo. But although the food was prepared for him by his old cook Matriona Petrovna and served by his maid and housekeeper Valentina Istomina, "Valechka", and both were loyal to him and loved him, Stalin demanded that every dish, and even every piece of bread served to him, be examined by a doctor beforehand".

As for Beria, when Stalin wanted to purge the Georgian Communist Party, which he controlled through his ethnic Mingrelians, he had no doubt that this was a move against him, since Stalin intended to do it without him and without Viktor Abakuomov, who since 7 May 1946 had been the head of State Security (MGB) and Beria's right-hand man. Suspicions about Abakumov and Beria had increased as a result of the arrest of the Jewish doctor Jacob Etinger in November 1950. A State Security investigator, Mikhail Ryumin, informed Beria about Etinger's connections with the Jewish Anti-Fascist Committee. Ryumin had discovered that Dr. Etinger had treated Zhdanov and General Scherbakov (the army's political commissar who died in May 1945) with malpractice with the intention of liquidating them. Abakumov, who had organised Zhdanov's disappearance with Beria, informed his boss, who reportedly ordered him to stop the investigation. Ryumin denounced him to Stalin, who in the summer of 1951 decided to take action and triggered the events that were to culminate in 1952.

On 12 July 1951 Stalin ordered the arrest of Viktor Abakomov, Nikolai Selivanovsky, Mikhail Likhachev, Mikhail Belkin and Georgiy Utekhin. These arrests were clearly directed against the unassailable Beria. On 9 August 1951, Stalin appointed Semyon Ignatiev as the new Minister of State Security. With this appointment the Ministry of State Security became independent of the Minister of Internal Affairs, i.e. of Beria. Abakuomov was arrested for obeying Beria and ignoring Stalin's orders. According to Nicholas Werth, he was first accused "of having deliberately made Jacob Etinger disappear", who died in prison. In addition, Werth adds, Abakuomov was accused of "preventing the unmasking of a criminal group of Jewish nationalists infiltrating the higher echelons of the Ministry of State Security". In October 1951 Stalin ordered Beria to arrest Lieutenant General Nahum Isaakovich Eitingon, the organiser of the Trotsky assassination who in Spain had recruited Caridad Mercader, Africa de las Heras and Carmen Brufau, the famous Hispanic agents of the NKVD. Eitingon's sister Sofia, who was a doctor, and other Jews who like him were State Security officials were also arrested and accused of being part of a Zionist plot to seize power in the USSR. Abakumov was linked to a vast "Jewish-Zionist conspiracy" linking the Jewish Anti-Fascist Committee to the so-called "White Coat Affair", officially the "murderous doctors", which will be discussed in more detail later. The trial of Abakumov, related to the crimes previously charged against Lauvrenti Beria, began in Leningrad on 12 December 1954, well after the deaths of Stalin and Beria. On 19 December 1954 he was executed.

In Georgia, at the same time as all these arrests in 1951, the "Mingrelian affair" involved an unprecedented purge of all Beria's personal friends and of all the militants in his home region. Hundreds of party secretaries in towns and districts were purged. Under the accusation of "bourgeois nationalism", Ignatiev, following direct orders from Stalin, proceeded to arrest the leaders of the Central Committee and the Georgian Government. Candide Charkviani, the first secretary of the Communist Party placed in office by Beria in 1939, had controlled the Secret Police in the Caucasus since his chief had gone to Moscow to head the Commissariat of Internal Affairs. Charkviani was abducted at night on his way home. The purge in Tiflis continued for several months, and Ignatiev had the Minister of Justice of the Republic, B.I. Shoniya, the Prosecutor General, A.M. Rapaya, and the second secretary of the Central Committee, Mikhail Ivanovich Baramiya, one of the most loyal members of the so-called "Beria gang", arrested. These facts were a serious warning and definitely alerted Beria, who began to think that Stalin was reserving for him the same fate as had befallen Menzhinsky, Yagoda and Yezhov, his three predecessors in office. In fact, he himself had done away with Yezhov after taking his place in the Commissariat of Internal Affairs.

Another move against Beria's positions was the purge of his men in Czechoslovakia, a country he had considered his personal fiefdom since the "Prague putsch". Soon after Ignatiev took over the Ministry of State Security, a wave of arrests began, among them the heads of the Czech Secret Police, who until then had reported directly to Beria. However much Stalin may be called a "paranoid anti-Semite", the facts prove once again that most of the arrested high-ranking officers were not only Jews but also Zionists, as evidenced by the invaluable help they gave in the summer of 1948 to their colleagues who were conquering Palestine. Stalin and Ignatiev acted so swiftly that those arrested felt they had been abandoned and betrayed by their protector, whom they believed to be to blame for their fall from grace. Since we have at hand *The Nine Lives of Otto Katz*, the book by Jonathan Miles cited above, we can offer some details of how the events unfolded.

Thanks to this work, we know that André Simone (Otto Katz), a communist-Zionist who was among the most versatile agents of his time, had spent several weeks in Belgrade with Tito and Pijade and had also travelled to Traycho Kostov's Bulgaria. In March 1947 André Marty, who during the Spanish Civil War had exposed numerous Trotskyists operating in the International Brigades, wrote a letter denouncing that Otto Katz, a man with no roots other than ethnic who served as the Slansky government's chief propagandist, had worked for British Intelligence. Marty linked him to Trotskyist circles. Soviet advisers travelled to Czechoslovakia and Katz was under surveillance. Jonathan Miles writes that "he began to be isolated from the party, ceased to be invited to conferences as an adviser and lost his position as foreign editor of *Rudé Pravó*". Soviet Military Intelligence informed their Czechoslovak colleagues in the StB (State Security) that they wanted a report from Katz to support the case of another suspect, Karel Sváb. On 27 January 1950, Katz admitted during his deposition that he had made many mistakes, but claimed that he had always been loyal to the Party and to Russia. In May 1950, his case was put on hold, and although he expressed his desire to travel to Germany, he was assigned to work in radio.

At the beginning of 1951, before Ignatiev's appointment, the political atmosphere in Prague had become increasingly tense. Perhaps this can be explained by the fact that it was Soviet Military Intelligence that had initiated the investigations. Some of the StB leaders were purged and in February the first arrests were made of two high-ranking Jewish officials: Vladimir Clementis, the foreign minister, and Artur London, his deputy minister. Another Jewish deputy minister, Evzen Löbl, who had been arrested earlier, provided the evidence during interrogations that Ignatiev needed to order the arrest of Rudolf Slansky (Salzmann), the secretary general of the Communist Party and leader of the Czech government, who was arrested on 24 November 1951. As will be recalled, this Jew was one of the leading protagonists in the ethnic cleansing of millions of Sudeten Germans, and his criminal actions in 1945 were countless. The first days of 1952 saw the arrest of two other Jews, Rudolph Margolius, Deputy Minister of Foreign Trade, and Ludwig Frejka (Freund), who advised the President of the Republic, Klement Gottwald, on economic matters. In all, as we already know, fourteen high-ranking officials were arrested, eleven of whom were Jews. The last to be arrested on 9 June 1952 was André Simone (Otto Katz), who was informed that both Artur London and Evzen Löbl had testified against him.

President Gottwald, who realised from the Presidency of the Republic that he had no choice but to collaborate with Stalin, travelled to Moscow to discuss the details of the Prague trial, which began on 20 November 1952 and was broadcast on radio for the eight days it lasted. Mercenaries" and "dirty gang of vipers" were among the adjectives aimed at the audience. The fourteen prisoners were accused of being "Trotskyists, Titoists, Zionists and bourgeois-nationalist traitors who under the direction of Western spy agencies were acting in the service of the US imperialists." Freda Margolius wrote a letter to Gottwald requesting the maximum sentence for her husband, a fact which, according to Jonathan Miles, petrified the foreign press, with the sole exception of the communist *L'Humanité*, which called his attitude "admirable". As usual, the Prague trial was disqualified then and is still disqualified today as a "show trial". Not a single one of the many trials with which Stalin unmasked his enemies has ever deserved the slightest credibility. They were always, therefore, rigged, parodies, inventions, etc, etc.

However, Slansky (Salzmann) admitted in court that in 1928 he joined a Trotskyist faction, that in 1930 he was recruited by US Intelligence and that during the war he also worked for the British Secret Service. He also revealed that through Moshe Pijade and British agent Konni Zilliacus he contacted and collaborated with the Titoists. Slansky linked the Masonic lodges to the Zionist organisations and corroborated that President Beneš had been a Grand Master of Freemasonry and an imperialist agent. He admitted that he had personally placed the other thirteen defendants in the positions they occupied when they were arrested. When asked by the judge to detail the infiltration of Zionists into important positions, he said that, once in positions of power, "the Zionists in turn placed other Zionists in sectors of political and economic life.... The Zionists operating in Czechoslovakia were part of an international conspiracy led by American Zionists". Here is a passage in which Slansky expresses his views on the power of Zionism in the United States:

> "The Zionist movement throughout the world is, in fact, led and governed by the imperialists, in particular the US imperialists through the American Zionists. For the American Zionists, who, as in other countries, are the most financially powerful and politically influential Zionists, are part of the imperialist circles of power in America".

We will now offer a few excerpts from Otto Katz's testimony and the reader will get an idea of where this multiple agent moved throughout his fantastic career. Prosecuted as André Simone, Otto Katz was presented as a "cunning globetrotter, a spy with no strings attached". After pleading guilty to the charges against him, the judge asked him to explain his mistakes. Katz admitted that he had worked for French, British and American intelligence services and that he had spied against Czechoslovakia. Miles reproduces this question in his book, which gives rise to a very interesting answer:

"Prosecutor: When and how were you linked to the French espionage service?
Katz: In September 1939 I was engaged with the French Minister Mandel in Paris.... Mandel maintained his own espionage service with the support of some Jewish and French capitalist tycoons".

We have already seen that Mandel, whom Paul Reynaud appointed in 1940 as Minister of the Interior for a brief period, was actually called Jeroboam Rothschild (although he did not belong to the banking family) and changed his name to Louis George Rothschild. He was one of Europe's leading warmongers. So blatant was his pro-war stance that some French politicians accused him of placing his Jewishness above the interests of France. It is very interesting to learn that, supported by Jewish capitalists, he had gone so far as to set up his own intelligence service, for which in 1939 he recruited Otto Katz, who had already put an end to his raids and missions in Spain. The prosecutor then asked, "When did you sign your commitment to collaborate with the British Intelligence Service?" Katz then went into all sorts of details and provided the names of the two people who proposed the job to him in Paris: Paul Willert and Noël Coward, who asked him to sign a document in triplicate, as Willert told him that it was customary for each agent to commit himself in writing. Both confirmed to the author of *The Nine Lives of Otto Katz* that everything Katz had stated in court was absolutely true.

At another point in the interrogation Katz explained how he was "blackmailed" by his co-religionist David Schönbrunn in New York to work for American espionage. The passage is worth quoting in full:

"Katz: "...Schönbrunn, threatening to tell the Czechoslovak Communist Party about my connection to Mandel, coerced me into working for the American espionage services....
The presiding judge: Who was Schönbrunn?
Katz: The son of a Jewish capitalist who had immigrated to the United States before the First World War. In 1946-47, Schönbrunn was in the service of the Overseas News Agency, which was an organ of the American Jewish capitalists, financed among others by the notorious warmonger Bernard Baruch. This agency is one of the most important links between American Zionists and Jewish nationalists in the United States and cooperates closely with the State Department."

The Overseas News Agency (ONA) was launched on 14 July 1940 as an offshoot of the Jewish Telegraph Agency (JTA), which had been founded in Europe by Jacob Landau. In 1921 the JTA moved its headquarters from

London to New York. Jonathan Miles explains that the OSS (Office of Strategic Services, predecessor of the CIA) recruited Katz through the ONA and reveals that Jacob Landau had visited Otto Katz in Mexico in order to get him to work for the Zionist movement by writing reports on Germany.

Katz informed the court that in the spring of 1947 he had spoken to Slansky in his office and explained his relations with the above-mentioned agencies. He then implicated Clementis and stated that the Foreign Minister had given him documents and paid him for his risky work. Clementis himself confirmed that he had leaked secret foreign policy reports and confidential documents on agreements between the USSR and its satellites to Katz. Clementis specified that he had given Katz 60,000 kroner from the Ministry's funds and that on another occasion the figure had been 50,000 kroner. The prosecutor took the opportunity to note that Clementis had financed his espionage activities with public funds. Yes," said Katz, "Clementis had financed my espionage activities.

Ultimately, in the "show trial" the Zionist Jews revealed their connections one by one. Bedrich Geminder, Slansky's main collaborator, admitted that he had regularly moved in German Zionist circles. Otto Fischl, the deputy finance minister, confessed that he had been a Gestapo agent and had collaborated with the Nazis in Czechoslovakia during the war. On his links with Zionism, Fischl testified that as an agent of the Israeli secret services he had recruited numerous Zionists for Slansky. He also admitted that from the Ministry of Finance he had brokered business deals with Israel that clearly favoured the Zionist state. Fischl, who in Israel was nicknamed "the Jewish Himmler" in order to mislead and conceal his true actions, confessed that he had facilitated the disbursement of 6 billion kronor to help Jewish emigrants. Bedrich Reicin, who had been Deputy Minister of Defence, admitted that as a Gestapo agent he had betrayed Communist leaders and that the Nazis allowed him to escape to Moscow as a reward, where he contacted Slansky's group. Ludwik Frejka (Freund), who had been head of President Gottwald's Economics Department, claimed that he had been a secret agent of the United States and revealed that he had used his position to sabotage economic relations between the Soviet Union and Czechoslovakia. Evzen Löbl and Rudolf Margolius testified that from the Ministry of Trade they tried to connect the Czechoslovak economy to the West. Both admitted that they had worked for American espionage, although the former explained that he had also worked for the British, Austrian and Israeli secret services and had collaborated with Jewish state politicians to undermine relations between Prague and Moscow.

On 27 November 1952, the presiding judge, Jaroslav Novák, rose to read the verdict. Of the fourteen defendants, Artur London, Vavro Hajdu, and Evzen Löbl were sentenced to life imprisonment; the remaining eleven were sentenced to death. In justifying the verdict, Judge Novák argued that the maximum sentence was due to "the depth of their betrayal of the people's trust, the magnitude of their wickedness and infamy, and the exceptional damage done to our society by their criminal acts.... The defendants are to such an extent enemies of the working people that it is necessary to render them harmless by extirpating them from human society." Acts of solidarity by Jewish artists and intellectuals in some European countries were to no avail, Slansky and company were hanged on 3 December. The Israeli Parliament (Knesset), in addition to its "profound horror", expressed its concern for the fate of three and a half million Jews living behind the Iron Curtain. Prime Minister Ben Gurion spoke of "the blackest of black tragedies". Tel Aviv police were forced to protect the Czech delegation, which was attacked by angry demonstrators.

The outrage against Stalin and the international campaign against his "paranoid anti-Semitism" had continued to grow, especially after another twenty-five Jews had been sentenced to death in the USSR a few months before the Prague trial. The trial of the members of the Jewish Anti-Fascist Committee had been held behind closed doors in Moscow between 11 and 18 July 1952. It was a secret trial that ended the proceedings that had begun in early 1949. On 12 August, sentenced for espionage and treason, thirteen members of the Committee were executed, among them, in addition to the aforementioned Solomon Lozovsky, a dozen so-called intellectuals, mostly writers and scientists. Ten other Jews, the so-called "saboteur engineers" of the Stalin Automobile Plant, were also executed along with them. The *Black Book of Communism* states that the summary of the Jewish Anti-Fascist Committee resulted in 125 convictions, of which 25 were death sentences and about 100 were sentences of imprisonment in concentration camps.

In connection with the Jewish-Zionist conspiracy, the White Coats affair, which also exploded in the autumn of 1952, was to be decisive. Stalin probably intended to use it against Beria, but it was Beria who was able to take advantage of it to finally assassinate Stalin. Abakumov had already been arrested and replaced by Ignatiev for having ignored the dictator's orders to arrest the Kremlin doctors. In *Les deniers jours* Anton Kolendic refers to Nikita Khrushchev's report to the 20th Congress, in which he devotes a few words to the arrest of the doctors. According to Khrushchev, in the Politburo, Stalin handed out the attestations with the doctors' confessions of guilt and said to his colleagues: "You are as blind as kittens. What would happen without me. The country would be shipwrecked because you don't know how to recognise your enemies".

Kolendic contrasts in his book the texts Beria wrote while in detention with the versions offered by Khrushchev. Combining these texts with other sources, we shall now try to summarise briefly how the arrest of the Kremlin doctors, who, once again, were almost all Jews, came about. In 1952, two hundred and thirty-six people were beneficiaries of the Kremlin medical services, which, in addition to the chief professors of the services, employed about four hundred people, including doctors, nurses, pharmacists, technical and maintenance staff. Among them was a young radiologist, Dr. Lydia Timachuk, a former State Security officer. According to Beria, she was a "sek-sot" (Sekretny Sotroudnik), i.e. a secret collaborator of Ryumin, Ignatiev's deputy, who was head of the Special Investigation section for cases against state security. Evidently resentful, Beria wrote that Dr. Timachuck was "terribly ambitious and a real whore who, during her night on duty, could parade up to three lovers." Lydia Timachuk had written to Stalin after Zhdanov's death to complain that he had been inadequately treated by doctors Yegorov, Vasilenko and Mayorov. It later emerged that these same doctors had treated Bulgarian leader Georgi Dimitrov. The dictator reportedly kept the letter in his files for future use.

About Ryumin, with whom Dr. Timachuck worked closely, it must be said that Stalin held him in high esteem and considered him "an honourable man and a communist". Ryumin considered the Jews to be a nation of spies, so he had broken off all contact with them within State Security (MGB). After Abakumov's arrest, Stalin had ordered an investigation into corruption and mismanagement within the MGB, which had led to the expulsion of many of its leaders. Stalin ordered the arrest of all Jewish colonels and generals within the MGB. According to A. Kolendic, Dr. M.G. Kogan refused a request from Ryumin, the Kremlin Security Chief, for Lydia Timachuk to become a "head doctor". When he broke the news to the doctor, he told her that it was "Jewish cooking" and added that the "Jewish riff-raff had settled comfortably in the Kremlin and made the law". We now give the floor to Kolendic, whose text goes like this:

> "Lydia then confided that she had recently overheard the Kogan brothers, both professors and heads of service at the hospital, whispering about the diagnosis of Marshal Kóniev, the sick man they cared for. She claimed to have clearly heard B. B. Kogan say to his younger brother....go drag out the diagnosis and we will send him to meet Zhdanov'. A good counter-espionage professional, Ryumin immediately ordered Lydia to write a report with all the details and to continue digging into the matter. A few days later, Lydia had written a long report, which she handed over to Ryumin."

Beria declared that he had read the report and described it as "a bunch of idiotic fabrications that a dog wouldn't have swallowed if it had been buttered". Consequently, Ryumin was ordered to have the "hysterical doctor" expelled from the Kremlin and sent to practise medicine in a women's camp. Lydia Timachuk wrote a letter from the camp to Iosif Vissarionovich Stalin himself. The second commandant of the camp had a sister working at Stalin's dacha, and it was through this channel that the letter reached the dictator. In the text, the doctor denounced "the omnipotence of the criminals and murderers who were preparing new attacks on the very leader of the people, the beloved Stalin". In this letter, Dr. Timachuk repeated all the accusations contained in the first report to Ryumin. It seems that this letter was received by Stalin without Beria's knowledge. In addition to this, he had also received another letter of accusation written by Marshal Ivan Stepanovich Koneyev, a war hero who had recently been appointed Deputy Minister of Defence of the USSR. Stalin considered that he had "terrible evidence in hand", so he presented to the Politburo the text from Koneviev, in which the Marshal denounced that a group of Jewish doctors from the Kremlin hospital were trying to poison him and claimed that he knew that "this group of American and English spies had already murdered numerous leaders, Zhdanov and others, and was preparing to kill the supreme leader himself, Stalin".

In the quotation preceding the previous paragraph, it can be seen that Dr. Timachuk had reported to Ryumin that the Kogan brothers were trying to get rid of the Marshal, who was in hospital. Naturally, Beria linked the letters of Koniev and Timachuk and tried to discredit both of them. Since he had called the doctor a "great whore", he continued along the same path and argued that Timachuck was snogging Koniev and that it was she who had aroused the Marshal's suspicions. According to other sources, Lydia Timachuk herself had also assured Stalin that the "medical murderers" wanted to kill Marshal Kóniev and told him personally "that it was his duty as an officer and party member to help unmask the gangs of foreign spies". Khrushchev also confirms in his writings that Koneyev sent a long letter to Stalin in which he claimed "that he was being poisoned with the same drugs used to kill Zhdanov" and reveals that after Beria's arrest in June 1953, Marshal Ivan Stepanovich Koneyev was appointed to investigate the case against Stalin's assassin.

Finally, on 7 November 1952, the Jewish doctor Miron Vovsi, a former chief therapist in the Red Army, was arrested for his involvement in the improper treatment of Bulgarian leader Dimitrov. Dr. Mirov was a cousin of Solomon Mikhoels, the missing leader of the Jewish Anti-Fascist Committee. During his interrogation, Mirov made a series of revelations that were to trigger the arrests Stalin had long desired. Mirov confessed that Mikhoels had acted under the direction of Anglo-American agents. At this point, the battle between Stalin and Beria was at its height, so it is not easy to understand all the events that were unfolding.

One of these, for example, was Ryumin's dismissal from his position in the MGB. On 13 November 1952, the Central Committee surprisingly removed him on the grounds that he was "unsuitable for the post". It is not known whether Stalin knew this, or whether he gave the order, but all the indications are that this was a desperate manoeuvre by Beria, whose situation was becoming increasingly compromised. On 14 November Ignatiev suffered a heart attack and was unable to return to work until January 1953. After Mirov's arrest, arrests and interrogations of the Kremlin's Jewish doctors, including the Kogan brothers, Rapoport, Feldman, Grinstein and others, had been ongoing, but Beria succeeded in placing one of his closest collaborators, Sergo (Sergei) Goglidze, at the head of the investigation. This Chekist had the unusual distinction of having been a security services boss with three interior commissars. He had become Beria's most trusted man in 1938, when, as an NKVD chief in Georgia, he betrayed Yezhov and warned Beria that he had orders to arrest him. Beria then persuaded Stalin to rescind the order. Goglidze was to be executed along with his boss in December 1953.

During interrogations, which included beatings on Stalin's own orders, the doctors confessed one after another to their guilt and their contacts with the "Joint" (American Joint Distribution Committee), an international organisation of Jewish nationalists which financed sabotage and espionage in the Soviet Union[32]. On 13 January 1953 a report in the *Tass* news agency reported the dismantling by the State Security organs of "a terrorist group of doctors whose aim was to shorten the lives of a number of public servants in the Soviet Union by means of harmful medical treatment". All the doctors, with the exception of Professors V. N. Vinogradov and P. I. Yegorov, were Jews. The information indicated that the doctors worked for two foreign information networks. All the Jewish doctors in the service of the Americans had been recruited by the "international Jewish bourgeois-nationalist bourgeois-nationalist organisation Joint". The news was published simultaneously in *Pravda* and *Izvestia*, the two leading Soviet newspapers. "A group of spies and dirty murderers, hiding behind the mask of medical professors," it was said in *Pravda*, "was discovered some time ago by the state security organs." Sovietologist Avtorkhanov believes that the *Pravda* article was written by Stalin, as it contained all the stylistic features of the dictator's prose. The text ended thus:

> "The Soviet people stigmatise with the wrath of indignation this criminal gang of murderers and their foreign masters. It will crush like loathsome reptiles these wretched mercenaries who have sold out to dollars and pounds sterling. As for the inspirers of these murderous mercenaries, you may rest assured in advance that they will not be forgotten or escape punishment, and ways will be found to uncover them and bring them to share in the severe sentence."

---

[32] Just as it has been established through Western archives that Stalin was right when he accused Trotsky of being a foreign agent, so it can be established that the accusation of "paranoid anti-Semitism" was part of a campaign to conceal the truth. The "Joint Distribution Committee" was an international Zionist organisation set up in 1914. It worked on an international scale with economic and propaganda activities on behalf of Jewry. The organisation's headquarters were located in New York, but it had representatives in almost every country. Among its most prominent leaders, Jüri Lina cites Paul Warburg. From 1938 the "Joint" began its manoeuvres in the USSR. Jüri Lina, citing the *Encyclopaedia Judaica*, states that the illuminati Felix Warburg was chairman of the American Joint Distribution Committee.

The campaign continued in successive days. No doubt to encourage people, on 21 January 1953 a decree of the Presidium of the Supreme Soviet of the USSR was published, honouring Dr. Timachuk with the highest distinction: "In view of the help she has rendered to your government in the struggle against criminal doctors," the text read, "it has been decided to award Dr. Timachuk Lydia Fedosseievna the Order of Lenin. On January 31 the *Pravda* editorial insisted on the necessity of "educating the workers in the spirit of high political vigilance" and alluded to the "criminal prosecutions in recent years against gangs of spies and subversive elements in Bulgaria, Hungary, Czechoslovakia, Poland and other countries of people's democracy." It repeated again that it was necessary "to dismantle in the USSR a gang of vile spies and abject murderers." On 6 February the paper reported that State Security had arrested groups of spies in different regions of the country. On 11 February Lydia Timachuk sent a letter to the editorial staff of *Pravda* to collectively thank the readers for the "large number of telegrams and congratulations" she had received for her denunciation of "the enemies of the Soviet people." On 18 February, *Pravda* invited the population in all regions of the country to "unmask the enemies of the people".

Most authors agree that the "White Coat Affair", like the Prague trial, was part of Stalin's life-and-death struggle with Beria, whose negligence in guarding the plot had been exposed. Both were unequalled masters in the art of conspiracy and assassination. They were true virtuosos in the skill of gaining the confidence of their chosen victim before launching at the most unexpected moment the final blow. Both undoubtedly understood that they were facing the most formidable enemy of all those they had faced in the course of their criminal careers. Avtorkhanov notes that during the campaign launched by *Pravda* they both killed two enemies who were officially killed naturally. According to this author, Beria claimed the life of General Sergei Kossynkine, commander-in-chief of the Kremlin and responsible for Stalin's security. On 17 February *Izvestia* reported on the "premature" death of this general whom Stalin had chosen from among his personal guard to fill the position of highest confidence. Kossynkine, a young man in excellent health, was fanatically devoted to Stalin and did not depend at all on Beria, whom he deeply despised. According to Avtorkhanov, the young general "had visibly underestimated Beria's abilities, which explained his premature death".

The death attributed to Stalin requires a few lines, as it concerns one of his collaborators, the Jew Lev Zakharovich Mekhlis, a lieutenant general who had been the dictator's secretary, deputy defence minister and political commissar of the Red Army. In the 1920s and 1930s, Mekhlis, one of the many Jews who surrounded and supported Stalin, became one of his favourite executioners, hence in intimate circles he was nicknamed "the shark" and also "the grim devil". In 1930 Stalin chose him to replace

Bukharin as editor of *Pravda*, from where he justified the Moscow trials and the Great Terror unleashed by his boss. In December 1937, he was instrumental in the purge of the Red Army from his post as political commissar. In an extensive article published in 2005 by CODOH (Committee for Open Debate on the Holocaust), Daniel W. Michaels reveals that in 1938 Mekhlis was nevertheless forced to justify himself when a letter arrived at the NKVD offices, stamped in New York and signed by "your brother Solomon", informing about business friends and relatives of Mekhlis in NYC. The "shark" immediately went to Stalin and argued that the letter had been sent by provocateurs seeking to discredit him. Apparently he must have convinced the dictator, for nothing was heard of it again. During the war, Mekhlis edited the Armed Forces newspaper *Krasnaya zvezda* and was responsible for other military publications from which propaganda and hatred were orchestrated, such as Ilya Ehrenburg's incitements to the mass murder and rape of German women. During the war he was closely attuned to and cooperated with Beria from his position as head of the Army Political Administration. There are testimonies that show that the troops feared and hated him because of the severe punishments and executions he ordered: "He was cold and ruthless from the bottom of his heart," says writer Konstantin Simonov. At the end of the war, he himself announced to the four winds in *Pravda* that the Generalissimo had appointed him Minister of State Control, a position of great trust which he held until December 1949, inspecting corruption and irregularities in the Soviet economy.

According to Avtorkhanov, Stalin suspected Mekhlis of being a Zionist and linked him to the Jewish doctors' plot. While awaiting the court's verdict on the "criminal doctors", he sent Mekhlis to Saratov on "an important mission". The author writes that "it was easier to arrest him quietly and without anyone knowing about it. Taken to the Lefortovo prison hospital in Moscow," Avtorkhanov asserts, "he made all the revelations Stalin needed and died on 13 February 1953". He was buried with full honours in Red Square in the presence of numerous Politburo members, marshals and ministers; but Stalin did not attend the funeral. Another of the sources cited above, Thaddeus Wittlin, agrees that Lev Mekhlis was liquidated by Stalin, but attributes this simply to anti-Semitism: "If Mekhlis had fallen victim to the Big Chief," writes Wittlin, "this meant that Stalin's anti-Semitism had grown as he had aged to such an extent that he could not bear the presence of any Jew". This author adds that Beria "understood that Mekhlis's execution was another personal warning to him because General Mekhlis, head of the Army Political Administration, had been a close associate of his."

Stalin, assassinated. Beria's coup d'état

Against those who have nurtured the thesis of Stalin's paranoia, Avtorkhanov insists that "Stalin did not kill anyone out of instinct or homicidal passion. He was not a sadist and not a paranoid". This author considers that these errors of appreciation are due to an "incorrect premise of the anthropological type." Let us look at an excerpt from *Stalinne assassiné* where this Sovietologist rejects the idea of any mental illness of Stalin:

> "In reality, all Stalin's actions, all his initiatives, all his crimes are logical, linked to precise objectives and scrupulously faithful to a certain number of principles. One does not find in his inner world the zigzags of a mentally ill person, whose spirit darkens and then regains clarity, who passes from enthusiasm to melancholy, who is capable of committing a crime today and regretting it tomorrow, as was the case with Tsar Ivan the Terrible, who was truly ill. Stalin was a political man who often used criminal methods to achieve his goals. It can even be said that he represented a hybrid unique in its kind and in history, in which political science was organically united with the art of crime, in which he surpassed all other political men. Stalin had never varied one iota in his actions, and his crimes were governed by the most rigorous principles."

Beria's biographer agrees that despite his seventy-three years, Stalin "was in a state of truly exceptional mental clarity". A few days before his death, on 17 February 1953, he received Krishna Menon, the Indian ambassador to the USSR, at the Kremlin. According to Menon, despite his age, Stalin appeared to be in excellent health. The ambassador published *The Flying Troika* in 1963, a work containing extracts from his diary, in which he noted that during the interview Stalin amused himself by sketching a pack of wolves on his notepad and expressed an idea as a commentary on his drawings that had nothing to do with the diplomatic interview. Stalin said aloud that the peasants proceeded wisely in exterminating the rabid wolves. By 1963 Krishna Menon had realised that Stalin was undoubtedly thinking of the "rabid wolves" in his Politburo. In a clear allusion to these drawings by Stalin, Stuart Kahan, nephew of Lazar Kaganóvich, published in the early 1980s a loose work entitled *The Wolf of the Kremlin*, a biography of Kaganóvich translated into English that we have little credibility with. In it Kahan claims that his uncle was part of the plot to poison Stalin, organised by some members of the Politburo including Voroshilov, Molotov and Bulganin.

The struggle within the Politburo had come to the fore at the 19th Congress of the CPSU in October 1952, shortly before the start of the Prague trial against Beria's Zionists and the arrest of most of the Kremlin's Jewish doctors. This Congress took place after a long period during which, in violation of the provisions of the statutes, the CPSU had not met. Thirteen years had passed since the 18th Congress in March 1939. Stalin countered the "Report of the Central Committee", drafted by Malenkov and approved by the majority of the Politburo, with the release on 2 October of millions of copies of his work *Economic Problems of Socialism in the USSR*. The thesis was that the United States had sought to put Germany and Japan out of action in order to seize foreign markets, the sources of raw materials and world domination. In his work *Malenkov*, Carlavilla gives a summary of Stalin's pamphlet, as well as Malenkov's full report to the Central Committee and the speeches of Marshal Bulganin, Comrade Beria, Vorochilov and Stalin's full speech. Although the study of these texts offers interesting data, we will not dwell on them, since it is necessary to deal now with how Stalin's assassination came about.

About the Congress, therefore, we will say only that during the interrogation of the members of the Jewish Anti-Fascist Committee, the names of Molotov, Vorochilov and Mikoyan had been denounced, so that Stalin had completely lost confidence in them: he regarded them as members of the Zionist plot against him and suspected them of having been Anglo-American spies. Two of Anastas Mikoyan's sons, both generals, were in prison. Nevertheless, Molotov delivered the opening speech of the Congress and Vorochilov the closing one. Although praise for the Generalissimo figured in all the speeches, Stalin's weakness and loneliness did not go unnoticed during the sessions. Beria, who had skilfully allied himself with Malenkov, was able to rehabilitate himself in front of the delegates and showed in his speech that he had a political plan. In addition to the usual panegyric to the dictator, he made it clear that the Party and its priorities were above Stalin.

From the Congress emerged a new Central Committee, which as was customary was devoted to organisational problems, such as the election of the General Secretary and the members of the Politburo. It was within this body that Stalin fought the battle for continued control of the party. Stalin offered the new Committee his resignation as General Secretary on the grounds that he was too old and too tired to combine the post with that of Chairman of the Council of Ministers. The sources we have do not agree on whether or not this resignation was accepted: Robert Conquest claims that it was rejected, as the members of the Central Committee knew it was insincere. Adburahman Avtorkhanov, on the other hand, claims that it was accepted. According to him, Stalin believed that his proposal would not be approved and had made it in order to find out who were his friends. Acceptance was, Avtorkhanov writes, "a historic defeat for Stalin".

The Central Committee, elected at the Congress by a secret ballot of the delegates, decided on the replacement of the Politburo by a new body, the "Presidium", composed of twenty-five members. The new body included the ten members of the old Politburo, including the names Stalin had challenged, plus fifteen new members, to which were added eleven alternate members. Stalin reacted with a last-minute ruse and went to the Presidium of the Central Committee to propose the election within the Presidium of a smaller body which would enable current affairs to be settled more quickly.

Thus the nine-member "Bureau of the Presidium" of the Central Committee of the CPSU was set up. In this way Stalin sought to remove Molotov, Vorochilov, Kaganóvich and Mikoyan. Initially he managed to keep Molotov and Mikoyan out of the new "Bureau", which, besides Stalin, included Malenkov, Beria, Khrushchev, Bulganin, Vorochilov, Kaganóvich and two new members: Mikhail Pervukhin and Maksim Saburov. Khrushchev later explained that in practice the group was reduced to five people: Stalin, Malenkov, Beria, Bulganin and himself, so that Vorochilov and Kaganóvich were also excluded from the core. The political-police apparatus, however, remained in the hands of Malenkov, who controlled the party, and Beria, the Minister of the Interior. Hence the latter continually manoeuvred to secure the collaboration of the former. Stalin had controlled the party through the police, but Beria understood that in order to succeed Stalin he would need the party's approval. The fact that Stalin was trying to purge the political-police apparatus facilitated Beria's conspiracy, which increasingly influenced Malenkov.

At the end of 1952, with the "criminal doctors" affair in full swing, Beria's priorities were focused on disbanding Stalin's so-called "secret cabinet". There is every indication that the arrest of Vinogradov, the dictator's personal physician, was part of Beria's strategy to isolate him. While the Jewish doctors had been arrested during the months of October and November, on 4 December, the day after those convicted in the Prague trial were hanged, Professor Vinogradov appeared at a public address, showing that he was still at large. His arrest therefore took place during December, and it was Beria who chose to include him in the Kremlin doctors' plot. The leading figure in the secret cabinet was General Poskrebyshev. To remove him, Beria, Avtorkhanov writes, "organised the disappearance from Poskrebyshev's office of secret personal documents belonging to Stalin." Avtorkhanov's source is Khrushchev's *Memoirs*. This Sovietologist considers, however, that it is possible that Beria managed to steal more important papers than the economic manuscripts referred to by Khrushchev, who quotes in his *Memoirs* these words of Stalin: "I have proof that Poskrebyshev had mislaid secret materials. No one but he could have done it. The loss of these secret documents was carried out through him. It is therefore he who has handed over the secrets that had been entrusted to him." Poskrebyshev, who had addressed the delegates of the 19th Congress and had been elected a member of the Central Committee, was confined to his native village and forbidden to leave it.

Another of the men protecting Stalin was General Vlasik, who commanded the dictator's personal guard. Vlasik was a Chekist whom Beria had long kept close to Stalin and whose loyalty was already unshakable; nevertheless, Beria succeeded in getting Stalin to order his arrest. Thanks to Stalin's daughter Svetlana, it is known that both Vlasik and Poskrebyshev were arrested at the end of December 1952:

"It may be said that in the course of this latter period even those who for decades had enjoyed my father's intimacy suddenly fell out of favour. The immovable Vlasik was imprisoned during the winter of 1952, and it was at the same time that his personal secretary, Poskrebyshev, who had served him for nearly twenty years, was dismissed".

A third obstacle was General Kossynkine, a Stalin stalwart who commanded the Kremlin guard. It has already been recounted that Kossynkine, being relatively young, died unexpectedly, as he was not known to have any health problems. On the arrest of Professor Vinogradov, Avtorkhanov writes the following paragraph in *Staline assassiné*:

"There is every reason to suppose that it was also in the context of the plan devised by Beria that Vinogradov, Stalin's personal physician, and Yegorov, head of the Kremlin medical and hospital directorate, were arrested. It was undoubtedly also as part of this plan that Yefim Smirnov, the USSR Minister of Health, who was authorised to enter Stalin's house, was relieved of his duties. A doctor whom nobody knew, a certain Tretyakov, was immediately appointed to replace him (he took office on 27 January 1953). The new Minister of Health had personal relations with Beria".

Both the executions of the Czech Zionists and the arrests of the doctors attracted the most attention in Israel, where the pro-Soviet United Workers' Party (Mapam) and the Communist Party lost the sympathy of the population and the government. Moshe Sharett, the foreign minister who was soon to become prime minister, spoke harsh words before the Knesset (Parliament) against Stalin, comparing him to Hitler. In December 1952 Arieh Kubovy, the Israeli ambassador to Prague, was accused of espionage and declared persona non grata. Kubovy was also representing his country in Poland, which also demanded his withdrawal. In early 1953, Budapest brought espionage charges against Yosef Walter, the Israeli cultural attaché, and expelled him from Hungary.

Also in January 1953, before the newly elected Eisenhower took office, a significant event took place: Churchill travelled to New York and stayed at Bernard Baruch's house, where they both met with the future US president. In the photo that recorded the meeting of this supreme troika of Zionists, the incombustible Baruch appears seated in the centre, at the top of the triangle, in a higher position than his guests. Of course, nothing of what was discussed transpired; but on 14 January, four days after Churchill's return to London, the Israeli delegation to the UN announced that it intended to raise the case of the doctors and "anti-Semitism" in the USSR at the next General Assembly.

On 6 February 1953 it was reported in the press that 160 influential Jews had been arrested in Hungary. Among those arrested were Imre Biro, father of President Matyas Rakosi's first wife; Jewish Community President Stöcker; General Gabor Peter, head of the Hungarian Secret Police, and his chief of secret service, Colonel Caspo; the director of Radio Budapest, Imre Szirmay; Judge Garay; and Professors Benedek and Klimko, among others. On 9 February, Gyula Deesi, Hungary's Minister of Justice, another Jew who held the rank of colonel in the Hungarian police, was dismissed for his merits in the investigation of the case against Cardinal Mindszenty. According to media reports in Vienna, the Justice Minister's dismissal signified the beginning of an anti-Jewish purge in the ranks of the Communist Party.

On the same day, 9 February 1953, a small explosive went off at the Soviet legation in Ramat Gan in Israel. The ambassador's wife and two other officials were wounded. The terrorists were not located and three days later, on 12 February, Moscow rejected Ben Gurion's apology, describing it as a camouflage to hide its responsibility for the attack. In addition, the closure of the USSR embassy in Israel was announced and demands were made that the Zionists close theirs in the Soviet Union as well. On 19 February, Ivan Maisky, another significant Jewish figure, was arrested, as he had been Molotov's most trusted man and was the deputy foreign minister. As will be recalled, Maisky, as ambassador in London, had become a close friend of the Spaniard Juan Negrin and his Jewish wife, who were in exile in the British capital after their flight from Spain. During interrogation, Maisky confessed that he had been recruited as a British spy by Winston Churchill. New arrests were made daily in the USSR, adding to the scope of the plot and allowing substantial progress to be made in the investigation of the conspiracy.

Consequently, it is hardly surprising that in these circumstances Stalin, against all odds, was determined to bring the Jewish doctors and their accomplices to trial as soon as possible in order to get rid of them once and for all. Throughout February 1953 *Pravda* carried on a continuous campaign which set the political atmosphere of the country on fire. Articles, reports and commentaries devoted to "assassins", "spies", "criminals", "subversive agents", "renegades" and "necessary vigilance" appeared day after day. The last deliveries took place on 20, 22, 23, 26, 27 and 28 February. The process was to begin in mid-March 1953. Some sources suggest that Stalin had planned mass deportations of Soviet Jews to Birobidzhan, but this has not been proven by any documents.

On the afternoon/evening of Sunday, March 1, 1953, eleven days after Ambassador Krishna Menon had met Stalin and judged him to be "a man of excellent health", old Matriona Petrovna, one of the few people the dictator still trusted, discovered the body of her beloved boss lying near a table on the carpet in one of the private rooms of his Kuntsevo dacha. Petrovna called for help in alarm and Stalin was placed on a sofa. At first it was thought that he had lost consciousness because of drunkenness, but the old maid was quick to conclude that Stalin was not drunk and that it was undoubtedly something more serious. It was a cerebral haemorrhage which had paralysed the right side of his body and deprived him of speech. In reality, Stalin had suffered an attempt on his life organised, if not executed, by Beria. Anton Kolendic, Thaddeus Wittlin, Adburahman Avtorkhanov, Peter Myers and Stuart Kahan, Kaganovich's nephew, among others, claim that Stalin was assassinated and that Beria was behind his death. The great unknown remains how Stalin was killed, under what circumstances the assassination took place, how the coup d'état was organised.

What is known is that Beria, Malenkov, Khrushchev and Bulganin were the last to be with Stalin. It is a proven fact that on Saturday, 28 February, this quartet dined with him at his dacha near Moscow. Since the dictator was a man who as a rule went to bed at about four or five in the morning and got up shortly before noon, it is reasonable to assume that the meeting lasted well into the early hours of the morning. It seems that Malenkov had requested the meeting on the pretext of learning Stalin's recommendations on certain questions to be discussed at the meeting of the Council of Ministers on Monday, 2 March. Among them must have been the question of the trial of the Jewish doctors: a week earlier Stalin had told the members of the Presidium Bureau that it was to take place in mid-March and had given them copies of the final indictment drawn up by Safonov, the Prosecutor General, who was a creature of Beria. Among the materials of the forthcoming trial were documents showing that the Americans had succeeded during the war in setting up espionage centres not only within the Kremlin hospital staff, but also within the Central Committee (Lozovsky) and State Security (Abakumov). According to various sources, when Malenkov, Khrushchev and Bulganin left, Beria, on the grounds that he had some personal matters he wanted to clarify with Stalin, was left alone with the dictator. As a result, he was the last person to be with Stalin before he was found on Sunday, 1 March, on the floor by Matriona Petrovna. Some scholars have highlighted the fact that Stalin's death coincided with the holiday of Purim.

More than half a dozen versions of Stalin's death have been offered by leading international figures. We reject those of Ehrenburg, Ponomarenko, and Harriman, the American ambassador, as undoubtedly biased. Nor will we offer the version given by Khrushchev in his *Memoirs*, according to which the dinner lasted until 5 a.m. on Sunday, March 1. On the other hand, we would like to point out the most daring hypothesis, the one offered by Thaddeus Wittlin in his biography of Beria. The Polish author states that Stalin and the quartet had attended a cinema performance in the Kremlin before going to dinner at the Kuntsevo dacha. His narrative tries to imagine how the events could have happened, he recreates the atmosphere and describes details or nuances with a certain literary pretension. Here is the final paragraph of Chapter 46 of *Commissar Beria*, entitled "Last Conversation":

> "It was the beginning of March, and the snow in the garden under the windows was still quite high; there was also snow on the bare branches of the trees, which were swaying in the wind. In the room the logs crackled in the fireplace, and their flames gave out blue and reddish glows. The atmosphere was warm and cosy. The Grand Comrade paced up and down the wide room with his slow, heavy, but sure steps. Lavrenti stood, with due respect, near the window. The view of the dark garden on the other side looked like a picture painted on a blue background. For a moment Stalin turned and stared at the vivid painting. With his back turned to his subordinate, the dictator showed him his broad neck and, just above it, the deadly weak spot just below the right ear and the bone behind it. A quick, precise blow with the blackjack that Beria always carried in his pocket could have the same effect that he had so often achieved with his victims in the cellars of the Lubyanka.
> The long-awaited, precise moment arrived, a moment that may never come again. Did Beria take advantage of the opportunity? No one knows for sure.

The most widespread hypothesis among the Russian people is the so-called "old Bolshevik" version, offered by Avtorkhanov in *Staline Assassiné*. This is the author's account of what happened according to this version:

> "... In the evening Malenkov, Khrushchev and Bulganin discussed with Stalin certain items on the agenda; they drank as usual quite a lot of alcohol and left relatively early. But they did not go to their respective homes and set off on the road to the Kremlin. Beria, for his part, chose to stay with Stalin as on other occasions to discuss personal matters with him. This is when a character we do not yet know enters the picture. According to one version, he was a man, Beria's aide-de-camp. According to the other, it was a woman who worked in his service. Beria let Stalin know that he possessed reports about Khrushchev of terrible gravity in connection with the affair of the criminal doctors, and he called his aide with a dossier. But before Beria could present it to Stalin, the woman had sprayed Stalin's face with a light substance, probably ether. Stalin immediately lost consciousness and she herself made several punctures and introduced a slow-acting poison into his veins. Stalin continued to be 'cared for' in the following days by this same woman, who played the role of doctor and repeated the injections in such doses that Stalin could remain alive for some time and appear to die a slow natural death."

The first to be notified was Malenkov, who in turn contacted Beria, Khrushchev and Bulganin. The four of them reported back to the dacha, and already on the morning of 2 March they called Svetlana and her brother Vassili, who found their father already unconscious and dying when they arrived. They were told that the night before Stalin had been found in his library, slumped near the sofa, and that he had been taken to his bedroom. This is how Svetlana Aliluyeva describes the scene in her letters to a friend:

> "... Unknown doctors, who had been called for the first time to the patient's bedside, were feverishly shaking, applying leeches to his neck and nape, taking cardiograms and X-rays of the lungs, while a nurse kept pricking him and one of the doctors took notes describing the evolution of the illness.... They were all arguing, going back and forth, trying hard, devising new attempts to save a life that no one could save... I suddenly realised that I knew the young doctor, that I had seen her somewhere. Unfortunately, it was impossible to know where. We nodded to each other silently, but without speaking to each other".

The dictator's attendants were therefore inexperienced doctors who were strangers to the family, who did not even know how to operate the urgently needed artificial respiration apparatus. An anaesthetist on the resuscitation team later explained that the apparatus could not be put into operation because "it was modern American equipment operating on a different voltage". This witness quoted in *Les derniers jours* adds, "Faced with the impossibility of using the artificial respiration apparatus, we alerted Professor Lukomski, who ordered massages by hand." As for the leeches on Stalin's neck, this was a primitive method traditionally used in Russian villages. On the other hand, the mention of the young doctor or nurse, who could obviously be the same person mentioned in the version of the old Bolsheviks, is certainly relevant. Another interesting aspect of Svetlana's text is the finding that on Stalin's neck and the back of his head there must have been evident traces of a bruise or bruise on which the leeches were applied. This leads us to think that perhaps the truth about what happened could be a synthesis of the two accounts we have offered. In other words, Beria could have shocked the dictator with a non-fatal blow and immediately afterwards the mysterious woman would have come in to inject him with some substance that would ensure his death shortly afterwards, so that friends and family could accept that he had died a natural death from a stroke. Several witnesses confirm that Stalin suddenly regained consciousness for an instant. Khrushchev, puerile, in his memoirs' account of this moment, claims that "he began to shake hands with each of us". Only from the point of view of stupidity can this absurd version be given credibility. In contrast, Svetlana offers the following assessment:

> "His agony was terrible... It consumed him under the gazes of all those present.... At a certain point he abruptly opened his eyes and enveloped the gaze of the people around him. It was a terrifying look, one could not

tell whether it bore the mark of madness or anger. This look penetrated us all for a fraction of a minute. And then suddenly an incompensable and terrible event occurred, which I have not yet been able to explain, but which I cannot forget. Suddenly he raised his valid arm, the left one, it was not clear whether he wanted to indicate something or whether he was threatening us. His gesture was unclear, but it looked threatening and nobody understood what he was alluding to or who he was addressing".

Svetlana Aliluyeva was well acquainted with Lavrenti Beria, who had tried to win her sympathies when she was still a child. A final quotation from her describing Beria's attitude during the last moments of the wake will serve to describe the steps Beria took to control the situation in the first moments of the coup, during which he was able to assert himself without too much difficulty:

"Only one man conducted himself in a manner bordering on indecency, and that was Beria..... Looking at him, one could see that he was inwardly overwrought..... His face did not cease to deform under the effects of the raptures that agitated him. Now, these passions could be seen at a glance: ambition, cruelty, cunning, an inordinate desire for power.... One could see him making efforts, at that decisive moment, not to appear too perfidious, and also not to let himself be won over by someone more skilful than himself.... He approached the bed and looked deeply into the face of the sick man. My father would sometimes open his eyes, but it was a look deprived of conscience..... Beria then watched him insistently: one would have said that he absorbed the brilliance emanating from the cloudy eyes.... When it was all over he was the first to rush into the corridor and was heard from the hall to shout, without being able to conceal his triumph: 'Khrustalyov, my car!'

Khrustalyov was the dictator's bodyguard, to whom Beria began to give orders as if he were already in his service. It was the first demonstration that as soon as Stalin had died, power was to pass into his hands. He also ordered Svetlana to be taken out of the bedroom. He immediately left the Blizhny dacha and hurried to his office to take control of the situation before there could be any reaction from his potential opponents. He telephoned Tretyakov, the new Minister of Health, and the Academy of Medicine and ordered the body to be transferred, autopsied, and a medical statement signed by professors and specialists to be drawn up. After this step, the body was to be taken to the Kremlin so that the public could be informed that the Great Comrade had suffered the attack while working alone in his office. Beria also contacted the commanders of several regiments and ordered armoured divisions to be ready to reinforce the Moscow garrison and to support his Secret Police battalions, which were stationed in the capital and nearby towns. In terms of information policy, he immediately ceased to publish texts denouncing the Jewish doctors' plot and forbade any display of mourning. Cinemas and theatres remained open, and funeral music was banned from the radio until the news of the death was officially announced.

On 4 March 1953 Radio Moscow broadcast a joint communiqué from the Government and the Central Committee of the CPSU, announcing that two days earlier Comrade Stalin had suffered a cerebral haemorrhage while working in the Kremlin. The father of the fatherland was unconscious and the right side of his body was paralysed. In addition to losing his speech, he was breathing badly. The bulletin was signed by nine doctors, whose names were read out by the announcer. On the 5th, when he had already been dead for three days, Beria authorised the publication of the dictator's death. On 6 March, the day after the official death, the Presidium of the Central Committee, proposed by Stalin, was dissolved and the old Politburo, which had been liquidated in October 1952, was reinstated. Beria, with the assent of Malenkov, Khrushchev and Bulganin, i.e. the quartet who had dined with the dictator on the last night, manoeuvred to oust from the Secretariat of the Central Committee the men chosen by Stalin to do away with the old Politburo.

Since there was a risk of an army uprising to defend the memory of the Supreme Commander, the leading military officers on whom Stalin relied were dismissed. Among them were Marshal Aleksandr Vasilevsky, Minister of Defence; General Artemiev, Commander of the Moscow Military Region; Lieutenant-General Sinilov, Commander of Moscow Square. All the Security Ministry cadres were dismissed and arrested, including, of course, Deputy Minister Ryumin, who had been in charge of the investigation into the "white coats-criminal doctors" affair. Marshal Beria reunited the Ministries of Security and the Interior into one and took over the command. Ignatiev was thus removed from office, but strangely enough he was not purged and managed to stay on thanks, perhaps, to Malenkov's protection. Stalin's trusted men in the main urban centres of the country were purged if not eliminated. Andrianov, First Secretary of the Leningrad Regional Party Committee and a member of the Presidium of the Central Committee, disappeared. Two other members of the Presidium, Melnikov and Patolitchev, secretaries of the Kiev and Minsk Committees, were also dismissed.

Beria sought to maintain the collaboration of Malenkov, to whom he ceded the post of chairman of the Council of Ministers of the USSR. He took second place as first deputy chairman and also retained the Ministry of the Interior. Bulganin was placed in the Ministry of Defence, which would henceforth combine the former War and Navy Ministries. As for Khrushchev, he assumed the functions of First Secretary of the CPSU Central Committee under the leadership of Malenkov, who was the General Secretary of the party. Thus the four of them held all the levers of power between them: Beria became the great strategist and Malenkov could mobilise the party and the state. Bulganin was expected to keep an eye on the army. Later, from later statements by Malenkov and Beria himself, it emerged that Khrushchev did not agree with the new distribution of functions and proposed that Marshal Georgiev Zhukov, who was highly respected by all, should enter the government as Minister of National Defence, since he enjoyed immense popularity and could strengthen the unity between the people and the army. Beria objected, arguing that his task was to continue Stalin's work and not to destroy it by raising "imaginary Napoleons". Molotov, Kaganovich, Voroshilov and Mikoyan also joined the Council of Ministers as members of the collective command. The coup d'état was still in progress.

Already on 6 March, the day after the dictator's official death, Beria appeared at the Kuntsevo dacha and ordered the staff at to pack up Stalin's personal belongings. On the same day NKVD and Secret Police officers arrived to load all kinds of Comrade Stalin's property onto trucks, which were taken to warehouses near Moscow. Beria then announced to the dacha servants that their services were no longer needed. Except for the men whom Beria had brought into the house on espionage missions, Stalin's military men and bodyguards were arrested. According to T. Wittlin, the villa was eventually "completely emptied, even stripped of its pictures and curtains, its light bulbs and electric cables. Doors and windows were sealed. Since we have the detailed account of this episode given by Anton Kolendic in *Les derniers jours*, we cannot resist quoting it. According to this author, based on Malenkov's statements, the dictator's body left the dacha in a temporary lightweight wooden coffin.

> "When the guard closed the big iron gate behind the truck again, a new NKVD colonel who had just arrived with Beria approached the personnel grouped in the courtyard and ordered everyone to assemble in front of the garage, which two servants were still cleaning. All were astonished, but accustomed to blind obedience and to carrying out orders without a word, they went one after the other to the garage. Someone had even brought Stalin's old maid, Matriona Petrovna, who, exhausted with grief, was huddled in a corner between two huge cooks. A grey-haired man in the uniform of a general of the NKVD forces who had entered the garage accompanied by some officers addressed the staff in a curt, authoritative voice. The unknown general said sternly and briefly:
> 'First: you have signed undertakings. Therefore, the first one to reveal the slightest secret about the life and death of our chief, Comrade Stalin, will be severely punished. Second: pack your bags! Be ready to leave in five minutes!'
> Meanwhile, a dozen trucks had arrived. All the servants were crammed with their belongings on board the trucks and escorted by armed soldiers to Siberia. Even the soldiers and officers of Stalin's personal guard were taken to Siberia. The same night or rather in the early hours of the

morning a platoon of the NKVD loaded into trucks all the furniture, personal belongings, every book and every picture, the smallest scrap of paper.... Everything, everything must be collected and taken to the depot' was Beria's order. When all Beria's orders were carried out, Stalin's villa was closed and sealed.

When all the personal belongings were brought to the NKVD depot, a carefully chosen group of prisoners systematically examined them under the control of the officers. They picked out every document, the smallest piece of paper, letters, photographs, notes, minutes... everything was catalogued and classified and then forwarded to Beria.

After Beria's liquidation, during a session of the Politburo, Malenkov outlined the problem of recovering all Stalin's property, not only the documents, works and letters, but also the furniture, library and personal belongings, in order to open a large museum dedicated to Stalin, as there was already one for Lenin. It was on that occasion that Malenkov recounted all these details and revealed the fact that most of Stalin's personal belongings, except for the documents and papers, were kept in the depository of the Ministry of the Interior."

On the evening of the same day, May 6, the coffin with Stalin's embalmed body was placed in the Column Hall of the Union House building, where it remained on public display for three days and three nights. The queue of Muscovites seeking to pay a last tribute to the Great Comrade stretched as long as four kilometres. On the night of 7 March, the militia and NKVD troops had to disperse rallies. The entire centre of Moscow, both banks of the Moskova River, with Red Square and the Kremlin in the centre, had been blockaded. In the course of the interventions there were deaths and injuries. According to official sources, the clashes and disorder occurred because the mob wanted to take over Red Square. The official communiqué said that "counter-revolutionary elements and imperialist spies entered the scene, stirring up the masses with slogans directed against the Soviet Government and Comrade Stalin, to which the people responded in a dignified manner. To prevent lynching and bloodshed, the organs of the NKVD had to intervene....". According to statements by foreign correspondents, on the same night, in various places in Moscow, there were mass demonstrations, real pogroms and riots, all directed against the Jews. The cries of the people indicated that the fury was motivated by Stalin's campaign against Jewish doctors. The Soviet historian Roy Medvedev, according to whom two million people came to Moscow to pay homage to the dictator, claims that there were numerous and serious clashes that resulted in hundreds, if not thousands of deaths.

Finally, on Monday 9 March, the mass funeral took place. The coffin was carried out of the Column Hall on the shoulders of the members of the new government. Beria and Malenkov were in the foreground. To prevent, supposedly, any possibility of disorder, Beria mobilised his special forces:

tanks, armoured cars and infantry troops with machine guns and flamethrowers covered the crowded streets through which the funeral procession was to pass. A show of force that unmistakably demonstrated their power to those associated with the coup. Back in Red Square, near Lenin's Mausoleum, official speeches were made by Malenkov, Beria and Molotov. Various authors confirm that Vasily Stalin, "Vassia", the dictator's son who was a general in the Air Force, broke the silence of the ceremony several times. Under the influence of vodka, not wanting to hide his indignation, Vasily publicly accused Beria of being his father's murderer and insulted him from afar. Many could clearly hear outrageous words such as "svolotch", "blad", and "suken-sin", i.e. "rascal", "son of a bitch" and "faggot". Days later, Beria summoned his colleague Bulganin, the new Minister of Defence, to whom he expressed his opinion that it was intolerable for an alcoholic like Vasily Stalin to remain General of the Air Force. Bulganin, who feared Beria, agreed. He summoned Vasily to the Ministry, where he asked him to hand over his military ID and other military documents. Thus the dictator's son was dishonourably dismissed from the Army and Air Force.

Although the autopsy report was written in such a way as to please everyone, Beria, fearing that the doctors could be dangerous witnesses in the future, decided to "dispense" with them. In *Commissar Beria* it is revealed that Professor Arseni Rusakov, one of the doctors who signed the autopsy, "died suddenly and unexpectedly". According to Wittlin, Health Minister Tretyakov was brought to Beria's office at the Lubyanka. Here is his account:

> "There he learned that he was entrusted with a new assignment: director of a huge new hospital, with two thousand beds, which had just been opened in Vorkuta, one of the largest forced labour camps in the far north. That same night, the Minister of Health was taken to a prison train, where in a cattle car, along with sixty other detainees, he met Professor Kuperin and two of the eight colleagues who had signed Stalin's death certificate with him. The other four doctors were less important, and Beria could wait, for the time being, before dealing with them."

Twelve days after Stalin's death, Beria ordered the arrest of Ryumin, the man who, on Stalin's orders, had personally tortured the Jewish doctors until they confessed. Incarcerated in Lefortovo prison, he was interrogated by Beria on several occasions. In one of the sessions, writes T. Wittlin, "Ryumin was brutally beaten by Beria, who with both fists broke the teeth of Stalin's former secretary." Interrelated with Ryumin was Lydia Timachuk, the woman who had written the letter to Stalin denouncing the criminal plan of the Kremlin doctors. On the night of 3 April, she was taken to the Lubyanka headquarters, where Beria asked her to take off the Order of Lenin that Stalin had awarded her. She was subsequently confined to a solitary cell in the basement of the prison, awaiting transfer to a forced-labour camp. On 4 April *Pravda* published the news that Lydia Timachuk had been deprived of the Order of Lenin.

On the same day, 4 April, an official statement from the Ministry of Internal Affairs appeared in *Pravda*. In it, Beria rehabilitated all the Jewish doctors, who, the announcement said, had been unfoundedly accused. In the note, Beria recalled that at that time the Ministry of State Security had not been under his control and had used in its enquiries and interrogations methods not permitted and forbidden by the laws of the Soviet Union. In other words, the chief torturer of the USSR, the man who for thirty years had made torture and murder his usual modus operandi, was now arguing that doctors had been tortured illegally. In the following days, *Pravda* continued in its news and editorials to denounce Beria's enemies. Of Ignatiev it was said that he was a man totally "ignorant of political affairs" who had been dominated by Ryumin, his deputy, "a criminal and perverted fellow."

Among the blood brothers released by Beria was also Polina Semyonovna Zhemchúzhina (née Perl Karpovskaya), the daughter of a Jewish tailor who had become Molotov's wife. This was a convenient way of gaining the loyalty of the former foreign minister, who, although he had voted for the arrest of the Jewish Anti-Fascist Committee, could only regret that his wife's involvement had been discovered. Beria himself wrote about this matter before he was executed: "I ordered that Polina Semyonovna should no longer be interrogated and that she should be sent secretly to the special women's camp. I knew that Comrade Stalin sometimes liked to prolong the lives of those condemned to death". A few days after Stalin's death, Beria personally visited Molotov at his home and delivered his wife to him safe and sound. Molotov," wrote Beria, "wept with joy like a child. It took him a good moment to be convinced of the reality of Polina Semyonovna's return.

Two other important Jews liberated by Beria were Ivan Maisky and Nahum Eitingon. Stalin's disappearance undoubtedly saved the lives of both. Maisky, who as mentioned above had been arrested a few days earlier on charges of espionage, was the man Beria had in mind as his foreign minister as soon as he consummated the coup d'état and seized power for good. Maisky, described by Beria's son as "the nimble, small Jew who looks like a mouse", was a key collaborator of Chaim Weizmann and David Ben Gurion and had played a key role in getting Stalin to agree to the partition of Palestine. When Beria was arrested, Maisky returned to prison, but was finally pardoned in 1955.

As for Nahum Isaakovich Eitingon, a lieutenant general in State Security, the Beria agent who participated in the assassination of Andreu Nin and organised the assassination of Trotsky, he had been arrested in October 1951 along with other high-ranking Jewish agents, accused of being part of the 'Zionist plot to seize power'. *The Venona Secrets* notes that the FBI learned from a wiretap on 26 February 1941 that a meeting was being arranged between Robert Oppenheimer, Isaac Folkoff, another Jewish agent who had been one of the founders of the California Communist Party, and an individual known only as "Tom", code-named Nahum Eitingon. According to the Venona documents, two of Eitingon's agents acted between 1942 and 1945 as couriers for the network that obtained US atomic secrets for Beria. Along with Eitingon, his sister Sophia, who was a doctor and was accused of working as a link between Jewish doctors in the Kremlin and the conspirators, was also arrested in 1951 and sentenced to ten years in prison. All of them were released after Stalin's removal. As in the case of Maisky, Eitingon returned to prison after Beria's execution. Before his trial in November 1957, he spent four years in Butyrka prison. Accused of conspiracy against the regime, the court sentenced him to twelve years. Finally, after the fall of Khrushchev in 1964, he was released.

Germany and the end of Beria

Since Beria's demise is linked to the events of June 1953 in the GDR, we have left for last a commentary on the events in the two Germanies in relation to Israel and the struggle for control of the Communist parties and the Cominform. Much had changed since the final years of the war when Henry Morgenthau, Harry Dexter White and other agents of international communism infiltrated the Roosevelt administration and planned to turn Germany into a country of farmers in order to facilitate the establishment of a communist regime. As a result of Stalin's irreconcilable attitude, the Plan of the Zionist Morgenthau, who by this time was already a financial adviser to Israel, was losing supporters and relations with the USSR were going from bad to worse.

Stalin had demonstrated time and again throughout his years at the helm of the Soviet Union that he was opposed to the World Government. It should not be forgotten that Hitler was initially financed to unleash a war that was to allow Trotsky's internationalists, purged in the Moscow trials, to be reinstated in the Kremlin. The first serious post-war divergence was Stalin's refusal to accept the creation of the World Government based on the monopoly of nuclear violence, whose proposal set out in 1946 in the *Bulletin of Atomic Scientists* had been drafted by David Lilienthal and Bernard Baruch, agents of the international Jewish financiers. Stalin rejected it because it implied submission to Washington, and the Soviet press denounced the United States as seeking "atomic domination of the world". Thus began the Cold War.

This was the backdrop that fostered mistrust and sparked the struggle we have been explaining for control of the communist countries in Europe. It is in this context that the creation of the Federal Republic of Germany with its capital in Bonn in November 1949, which was recognised by the Western

Allies thanks to the Petersberg Accords, must be understood. A month earlier, the German Democratic Republic (GDR) had been established. Konrad Adenauer had to overcome major differences of opinion and the opposition of the majority of the population. A small neo-Nazi party in Saxony was banned, as was the communist party. Chancellor Adenauer later began negotiations with the Zionists, which we will now summarise, as they are of interest because of their connection with the events we have been studying.

We refer to the issue of reparations, which is fully reported by Howard M. Sachar in *Israel an Europe. An Appraisal in History*. Already in 1941 Nahum Goldmann had launched the idea of Jewish reparations and during the war a committee led by Siegfried Moses had pointed out that the first beneficiary would be Israel, a state that did not even exist. David Ben Gurion demanded in 1949 that the "Bundesrepuplik" should not be allowed to come into existence until the reparations issue was settled and asked the Allies to act as mediators, but they did not see fit to mediate. Finally, in April 1951, two Israeli emissaries, David Horowitz and Maurice Fischer, reached a secret agreement with Chancellor Adenauer at the Hotel Crillon in Paris[33] and direct negotiations began. The Zionists even set up a "Reparations Department" in the Foreign Ministry. Nahum Goldmann, for his part, organised the "Conference on Jewish Material Claims against Germany".

In December 1951 Ben Gurion decided to bring the issue of direct negotiations with the Federal Republic of Germany before the Knesset. On 7 January 1952 the debate was held and on 9 January parliamentary approval was obtained to conclude an agreement with Bonn. Both the Zionist government and the Claims Conference agreed initially to demand an anticipated compensation of $1.5 billion for the Jewish community at large, of which $1 billion was to be paid in reparations to Israel and the remainder to the Claims Conference as compensation to Jewish social organisations. The "neutral" venue chosen for the start of the formal negotiations was Vassenaar, a suburb of The Hague where the "Oudkasteel", a former ducal castle turned hotel, served as the conference venue.

In this context, on 10 March 1952 the leaders of the United States, Great Britain and France received a proposal from the Soviet Union that has gone down in history as the Stalin Note, also known as the March Note. In it, the dictator of the USSR proposed the reunification of Germany with an approach that a large part of the political class, including the CDU, viewed positively, as the proposal was believed to be sincere. The basic ideas were

---

[33] After the Nazis came to power, according to Howard M. Sachar, Adenauer was removed as mayor of Cologne. To cope with his situation, he was supported by two Jewish friends in the United States, Daniel Heinemann and Otto Kraus, who regularly sent him money orders in dollars from New York. These private obligations," writes this Jewish author, "undoubtedly weighed heavily on the chancellor's conscience".

as follows: the borders would be those fixed at Potsdam; a single German government would take part in peace negotiations; the occupying forces should withdraw; political parties and organisations would be free to operate; Germany would be neutral and could not be part of any military alliance; Germany would have its own national army and access to world markets; members of the armed forces and the NSDAP not convicted of war crimes could participate in the establishment of a peaceful and democratic Germany. A cross-talk known as the "Battle of the Notes" ensued, and the offer was rejected by the Allies, which outraged many Germans on both sides of the border. The theory of a new "stab in the back" resurfaced in certain circles and among sections of the population. To understand the rejection, it should be borne in mind that as early as 1951, German military experts and Western representatives had already begun talks in Petersberg on the Federal Republic of Germany's contribution to the European Defence Community and its future membership of NATO, which was finally to take place in 1955.

Having made this necessary digression, we can return to The Hague, where on 21 March 1952 Zionists and Germans met at the Wassenaar Conference. The Israeli delegation included Felix Shinnar, a German-born lawyer who was head of the Foreign Ministry's Reparations Department, and Giora Josephthal, treasurer of the Jewish Agency. Moses Leavitt and Alex Easterman, both executives of the Jewish Joint Distribution Committee, represented the Claims Conference. On the German side were Professor Franz Böhn, Dean of the Johann Wolfgang Goethe University in Frankfurt, and Dr. Otto Küster, who had been a colleague and friend of Shinnar's in Stuttgart. In principle, the Germans accepted the obligation of financial reparations to the Jews, but sought to tie the amounts and terms of payment to the German-Allied Debt Conference, which 23 Allied delegations were negotiating with the "Bundesrepublik" in London at the same time. Hermann Abs, President of the West German Central Bank, and Chancellor Adenauer tried to postpone any engagement with Israel and the Jews until the issue of the debt to the Allied countries had been resolved. However, the German Social Democrats, whose leader was Kurt Schumacher, came to Israel's support in the Bundestag (Parliament) and appealed to 'moral obligation' towards Israel. The Foreign Affairs Committee, meeting in emergency session, gave priority to the Zionists' claims at in May 1952. Naturally, the entire press was unwavering in its support for the resolution to put the London Debt Conference in second place.

At the end of May 1952, Küster and Böhn, the two German negotiators in Wassenaar, resigned to Chancellor Adenauer, who had to impose his authority on the members of the German delegation to get them to agree to return to the Netherlands and resume talks with a new economic proposal that was presented in advance to Israeli Prime Minister David Ben Gurion. On 9 June 1952, the Zionists decided to return to the Netherlands, and on 28 June the negotiations resumed and continued until 22 August. The

Bundesrepublik government finally approved the draft agreement on 3 September, while the Israeli government approved it two days later. Franz-Josef Strauss, the chairman of the CSU (Christian Social Union), the Bavarian branch of Adenauer's Christian Democratic Union, presented a letter signed by the leaders of several parties pleading with Adeanuer to reconsider the extent of the reparations pledged to Israel; but there was no turning back.

Once again to the unanimous applause of the German and international press, Germany and representatives of Israel and world Jewry signed the agreement on 10 September in Luxembourg. Adenauer had arrived on his way to Paris, where he was on his way to sign the treaty allowing the Federal Republic of Germany to join the European Coal and Steel Community. In the Arab world, the reaction was one of outrage. The Saudi Arabian government cancelled a telecommunications equipment contract with Siemens in October. The Syrian government threatened to terminate negotiations with three German companies to expand facilities at the ports of Latakia and Tarsus if the Luxembourg Treaty was not cancelled.

Adenauer had signed the Luxembourg Treaty at a time when one third of the German population was living deplorably in squalid housing. It should be remembered that one fifth were refugees who had lost everything after being evicted from their homes and brutally transferred to the West. It is not surprising, therefore, that the Bundestag debated for six months the economic and diplomatic consequences of the agreement signed by Adenauer. On 4 March 1953, coinciding with Stalin's death, the final reading of the treaty took place in the Bundestag. The Chancellor launched harsh words against the USSR, accusing it of using "racial hatred and racial persecution as political weapons of the communist regime". Adenauer even alluded to the recent Prague trial and accused the Prague government of anti-Semitism. He concluded by expressing his hope that the acceptance of the Luxembourg Treaty would be "a German contribution to the strengthening of the spirit of human relations and tolerance in the world." A second reading took place on 18 March, just a week before the Adenauer government's term of office ended, and the Treaty was adopted by 239 votes in favour, 35 against and 86 abstentions. The text was sent to the Senate (Bundersrat) on 20 March, which ratified it. On the same day it was signed by the President of the Republic, Theodor Heuss.

While the events outlined above were taking place in the Federal Republic, Stalin, as we have seen, was waging a relentless war against the Jews in Eastern Europe and the Soviet Union who were conspiring in favour of Zionism, which for him was synonymous with capitalist imperialism. Naturally, in the GDR there were plenty of Jewish communists who prioritised Israel above all other considerations and worked as undercover agents for the Jewish state and the Zionist cause. In the GDR the first Jewish Communist to be investigated was Paul Merker, who in the summer of 1948 had published *Der Krieg in Pälästina* (*The War in Palestine*), expressing solidarity with the Jews and the Zionist state. In August 1950, denounced for espionage, he was expelled from the Central Committee and placed under house arrest. Merker, who, contrary to Moscow's official line, held the same positions as Israel's Zionist leaders, was accused of wanting to "sell" the GDR, of "strengthening Zionist and capitalist Israel", of seeking to "transfer the fortunes of the German people". Statements by Artur London, one of those convicted in the Prague trial, served to confirm the charges against Paul Merker, who at the end of November 1952 was finally imprisoned and it was announced that he would be tried. Along with him, other members of the Communist Party, all of whom were Jewish, were indicted. Among others were Alexander Abusch, Erika Glasser-Wallach, Leo Bauer, Bruno Goldhammer and Fritz Sperling.

On 20 December 1952 the Stalinist communist leader Hermann Matern published the report entitled *Lehren aus dem Prozeß gegen das Verschwörerzentrum Slansky* (*Lessons from the trial against the Slansky conspiracy centre*), which dealt a decisive blow against Merker. Hermann Matern's document denounced the "criminal activities of Zionist organisations". It stated: "American imperialism organised and implemented various espionage activities in the people's democracies with the state of Israel and with the help of Zionist organisations". This report noted that Paul Merker was part of the German branch of this international conspiracy, in which Zionism "had nothing in common with the aims of humanity", since it was a tool of US imperialism and "exclusively served its interests and the interests of the Jewish capitalists." In Matern's report, Jews were no longer "victims of fascism" but were seen as responsible for a powerful international, anti-German conspiracy.

From this moment on, fear began to spread among many Zionists who were members of the Communist Party of the GDR or who were active in social organisations and institutions. During the first two months of 1953, hundreds of Jews, supposedly communists, defected to the Bundesrepuplik. Among the most prominent defectors were the following: Leo Zuckermann, a Zionist allied with Merker in East Berlin in all matters relating to reparations, who fled with his family to West Berlin in January 1953. Between 1949 and 1950 Zuckermann had been head of the office of Wilhelm Pieck, head of state of the GDR. Julius Meyer, chairman of the Jewish community in communist Berlin. Leo Löwenkopf, President of the Jewish community in Dresden. Albert Hirsh, in charge of Jewish affairs at the Liaison Office of the Churches. He had been a delegate of the "American Joint Distribution Committee", the Jewish agency to which the Kremlin doctors belonged. Telmuth Lohser, president of the Leipzig Jewish community. Gunter Singer, president of the Jewish community of Erfurt. It is estimated that between January and February around half a thousand Jews left the GDR for the Federal Republic, fearing arrest and accusations of espionage.

Gerhardt Eisler, another Jewish agent whose position was in jeopardy, deserves special mention. This famous spy, whose name appears repeatedly in the Venona documents, was, according to Richard Nixon, head of GDR Propaganda when he was removed from office in early 1953. Eisler, described by his own sister Ruth Fischer as "the perfect kind of terrorist", was one of Beria's top men in the United States, where he ended up on trial in 1947 after enjoying the protection of Eleanor Roosevelt, a recalcitrant Zionist as we know. The government asked for $1 million bail, but the judge set it at $23,500, which was paid by the Communist Party. In May 1949 he escaped on the *Batory*, a Polish ship on which he stowed away. The United States requested his extradition to Britain and he was arrested in Southampton, but was eventually released and arrived safely in Germany, where he was employed by the University of Leipzig until he became head of the GDR Government Information Department.

This was the state of affairs in both Germanys when Beria finally got rid of Stalin. A month after the assassination, complications began in the Soviet Union, as the Politburo came under pressure from the army, whose hatred of Beria ran deep. Marshal Zhukov, who personified the general unrest and spearheaded the demands, became a dangerous enemy for Beria, who in a later confession after his arrest wrote that he had told his Politburo colleagues that Zhukov, the Russian hero of World War II, "represented the threat of a Bonapartism that wanted to silence the party". Despite all this, Beria continued to count on Malenkov's vital collaboration; but at a meeting of the Presidium (Politburo) on 9 April 1953, the group consisting of Khrushchev, Bulganin and Zhukov provoked the first serious confrontation. After a presentation by Beria on the internal political situation, his proposals were rejected and a major rift ensued. Even Malenkov, as Khrushchev later stated when referring to this historic session, sided with those who opposed Beria, who interpreted what had happened as a declaration of war.

Thanks to statements by Adenauer, it is known that during April and May 1953 representatives accredited by the German Chancellor and Beria, the new strongman of the USSR, held repeated secret meetings in order to study the possibilities of rapprochement and closer cooperation between the two Germanys. In *Les derniers jours*, Anton Kolendic provides valuable information on these meetings and on Beria's decisions and actions that precipitated his downfall. According to the author, "to form a united Germany, Adenauer would have sold his soul to the devil. He therefore authorised and encouraged contacts between his closest collaborator, Hans Gobke, Secretary of State and coordinator of the intelligence services, and Beria's representative". During the World War, Hans Gobke and Allen Dulles, Director General of the CIA, had been regular channels for Beria. While relations with Dulles were logical, as they were allies, contacts with

Gobke, in theory a Nazi official, are paradoxical and less intelligible. After the war, Gobke had collaborated with the American intelligence services and had also provided some services to Beria.

During these secret talks, the Federal Republic of Germany put forward various ways of bringing the two Germanys closer together and insisted on the need to relax the police and military regime in the GDR. He also called for the release of many prisoners. The Soviets, for their part, demanded the cancellation of plans for the future integration of the FRG into NATO. In May 1953, Beria withdrew from East Berlin and the entire GDR a large number of NKVD officers and cadres who had shown greater commitment to Stalin's policies. At the same time, he gave greater powers to local authorities and the German military police. Along with this relaxation of occupation discipline came the release of many political prisoners from Bautzen prison. All sorts of speculations and interpretations immediately arose as to the scope and purpose of these measures.

Between 16, 17 and 18 June a series of riots and demonstrations took place in East Berlin and in several cities, the interpretation of which varies greatly according to the source commenting on them. In Moscow, it was understood that Beria's unilateral measures in May had been the signal for opposition groups to prepare for insurrection and public manifestation of their anti-Sovietism. Chancellor Adenauer's own text considers that the most direct cause of the uprising was a decision by the GDR Council of Ministers on 28 May 1953 to increase the daily working day by ten percent, which meant imposing harsher production quotas without wage increases. If dissatisfaction with this measure was the trigger, it is reasonable to assume that the organisation took a long time to prepare for the uprising, which began when the workers on Stalin Avenue in Berlin stopped work on the morning of 16 June and sent a delegation to the Presidency to deliver a memorandum. Soon about a thousand people gathered in front of the building and prevented Vice-President Heinrich Rau and Construction Minister Fritz Selbmann from addressing them. The crowd greeted them with angry shouts and a hail of stones, forcing the ministers to retreat from the balcony.

Walter Ulbricht, who in 1946 had been the architect of the unification between the Social Democratic and Communist parties in eastern Germany, a union that gave rise to the SED (Sozialistische Einheitspartei Deutchlands), held the post of party secretary general in 1953 and demanded the intervention of the Soviet troop command. Instead of authorising it, Beria forbade it and ordered the Minister of State Security, General Wilhelm Zeiser, a very loyal man known in Spain as General Gómez, to issue a radio communiqué announcing that the increase in working hours had been cancelled. The Soviet units thus remained in their barracks. As dawn broke on the 17th, columns of demonstrators appeared in the streets of the capital and gathered around the government quarter, where some 40,000 people converged. The Soviet soldiers, however, remained unresponsive despite direct provocations: when they appeared they were greeted with a hail of bricks and stones, the windows of the Propaganda Office on Potsdamer Platz were smashed with stones and the building set on fire. East Berlin was soon plunged into the chaos of revolt. In the early afternoon the situation took an alarming turn when hundreds of thousands of demonstrators in Magdeburg, Brandenburg, Lepizig, Dresden, Chemnitz and other GDR cities joined the protest against the Soviet occupation. It is not possible that all this could have been organised without the omnipotent Beria, the Minister of State Security, knowing anything about it. It seems clear that the rebellion had been planned on a large scale and that Beria knew in advance what was being planned.

What happened in Moscow on the night of the 16th is not known, but everything indicates that it was the Red Army commanders who decided to act against Beria's orders. After the border crossings between the two sectors of the German capital had been tightly closed, Soviet tanks and troops moved against the crowd. The repression, which lasted until 18 June, resulted in a death toll which, once again, varied according to the source. A document on the events of 17 June in East Berlin was found among the papers in Beria's secret archives. It was none other than a report that Chancellor Adenauer presented to a meeting of the government of the Federal Republic. It refers to sources that are considered to be reliable and gives these figures: more than 500 people died in the clashes. Ninety-two demonstrators were killed "to set an example", according to the report. More than five thousand people were arrested. Other sources substantially lower the death toll, which remains uncertain.

When Beria, who was called the "bloodthirsty otter" in army circles, learned that the occupying troops had left their barracks and marched on the Berlin demonstrators despite his orders, he went without delay to Malenkov, whose office he entered unannounced. There he telephoned the Soviet General-in-Chief, who informed him that his units "had been forced to use their weapons". Beria protested indignantly and asked Malenkov to intervene immediately and summon the responsible military officers to explain themselves. Malenkov was upset and explained that Marshal Zhukov, as Chief of the General Staff of the Army, with the approval of the Minister of the Armed Forces of the USSR, Bulganin, had announced that he should give the order to intervene and prevent "imperialist provocations and anti-Soviet insurrection in East Germany." Malenkov said he had to support such a view, as the arguments were convincing. According to Malenkov, Zhukov "openly declared that without prompt and forceful intervention, he did not guarantee the future development of events for the fate of East Germany and other people's democracies." It was clear to Beria then that Zhukov, and Bulganin, who controlled the army, were determined to confront him. Since Khrushchev supported them, only Malenkov could redirect the situation that had been created.

Among the documents seized during the search of Beria's flat were three hundred wiretap reports. They show that from the session of the Presidium on 9 April, when he lost the vote, Beria knew that a faction was at war against him. A. Kolendic reproduces in *Les derniers jours* some of these texts, in which the head of the service, S. J. Tikholiubov, specifies that he has "suppressed the superfluous". From the aforementioned work, there follows a fragment of a conversation held on 6 June 1953 between Kliment Vorochilov, who was then chairman of the Presidium of the Supreme Soviet, and thus head of state according to the Constitution, and Nikita Khrushchev:

> "Khrushchev: Let us now consider a very important problem. Lavrenti Pavlovich's conduct and initiatives seriously disturb us. You saw how he behaved yesterday at the meeting... and this in spite of the decision of the Presidium....
> Vorochilov: Enough. I can only speak highly of Lavrenti Pavlovich's work and personality. All his actions have been fruitful and useful for the country and the party.
> Khrushchev: Well, well, Kliment Yefremovich, but then you don't see what Beria's aims are?
> Vorochilov: Nikita Sergeyevich, no doubt you woke up on the wrong foot today to be so furious against the whole world...".
> Khrushchev: We do not contemplate tolerating his arbitrary power any longer. There is ample evidence against him. Even about his relations with the imperialists and international espionage.
> Vorochilov: Truly, Nikita Sergeyevich, you are an imbecile ('durak') to say such stupid things. Do you understand well where we live and where we are...?"

Anton Kolendic comments that it is clear that Vorochilov, who had long been in the highest echelons of power, knew very well that the conversations were being listened to, which is why he was so cautious in his judgements about Beria, in whose dismissal, a few days later, he played a very active part.

Thaddeus Wittlin, based on comments and statements by officials of the Ministry of State Security, claims that Beria was planning to seize power and complete the coup d'état in June 1953. He explains that two Kremlin guard militiamen fired on the prime minister's car as he was leaving through the Spassky Gate, the main entrance to the Kremlin. Malenkov was unhurt, but the chauffeur was hit by bullets. The sentries claimed that the driver of the car did not respond when asked for the slogan and did not stop to show the documents. According to their instructions, the guards were obliged to shoot in such cases. Despite the immediate arrest of the perpetrators of the shooting, who were members of Beria's Security Police, suspicion began to circulate that what had happened was an attempt to eliminate Malenkov, which would have allowed Beria to immediately take up his post as Prime

Minister. Wittlin notes that Beria's enemies in the Presidium were at night in their homes watching for any noise in the street, for they knew that if at this hour a car stopped outside their door it could mean the end.

Different versions have been spread about how Beria's arrest came about. T. Wittlin offers three of them in a chapter of *Commissar Beria* entitled "The Man Who Died Three Times". The first suggests that Beria was arrested on his way to the Bolshoi Theatre to attend a performance of *The Decembrists* and executed on the night of 27 June 1953.. Here is an excerpt from this version: "Beria's black car was still driving between two tanks that protected it as if they were two powerful battleships escorting a light ship. However, the car was not driven in the direction of the Bolshoi, but to the outskirts of Moscow, where the Lefortovo prison, the best guarded prison in the USSR, was located. That same night, Beria was executed in a cell in that prison".

The second version is the information provided by the Associated Press agency, published by newspapers in Berlin, London and New York on 18 February 1954. According to it, the main Soviet leaders and diplomats from several People's Republics attended a reception given by the Polish ambassador to honour the friendship between Poland and the USSR. It was late in the evening when Bulganin and Vorochilov, who had been in Beria's official car, approached him to suggest that they leave the party. They were followed by other leaders, including the leading generals. The motorcade, led by Beria's limousine, which he had told the chauffeur that they would accompany first Bulganin and then Vorochilov, did not follow the expected route, and the driver stopped the car in the centre of the inner courtyard of the Lubyanka. When Beria saw that other cars had followed them, he asked the driver what game it was. The man who turned and pulled down the collar of his black leather coat was not his usual driver, who was also his bodyguard, but a high-ranking chief whom he knew superficially. Vorochilov then took Beria's arm and they went out. The generals had already got out of their cars and were waiting for them. On the threshold of the gate stood the prison director with two officials, who led the group into the courtroom where a panel of three judges usually pronounced summary sentences. On this occasion, Marshal Ivan S. Koniev presided over the court, accompanied by seven other members. The specific charges were: trying to seize total power; being a spy in the service of foreigners; trying to establish capitalism in Russia. According to this version, after the sentence was read, a firing squad was called for. A captain, a sergeant and two numbers of the guard took Beria to a cell in the basement and there he was executed, in the same place where hundreds of prisoners had been annihilated on his orders.

The third version is the one on which there is the strongest consensus and to which we will devote the last pages of this chapter. The third scenario of Beria's arrest is the main conference hall of the Kremlin, where on the afternoon/evening of 21 June the Presidium of the CPSU met. Earlier, at the end of May 1953, a meeting of the Presidium had been held during which the Ukrainian party leadership, committed to Khrushchev, was replaced by one loyal to Beria. After the session, Khrushchev, by his own account, went to Malenkov and the two travelled in the same car to their dachas, which were nearby. His account goes on:

> "I expressed my desire to have a serious conversation with him, but I didn't dare start because I was afraid of Beria's microphones. We walked through his garden and I said to him:
> - Listen, Comrade Malenkov, don't you understand where this is leading us? We are heading for disaster. Beria sharpens his knives.
> Malenkov responded:
> - Yes, I too have been worried for a long time, but what can we do?
> - We must resist him, prevent his anti-party tricks. We must defend ourselves...
> - What, you expect me to oppose him alone?
> - You are not alone. I am there, Bulganin also agrees. I am sure the others will join us.
> - OK, but what do you think we should do?
> - First of all, you must change the way you chair the Presidium sessions. When Beria says or proposes something, you agree immediately, without discussion, without asking the opinion of other members. You immediately proclaim the proposal accepted and move on to the next item. Don't be so submissive and don't be hasty. From now on, when Beria speaks, keep quiet and let the others express themselves. You will see that he will not have the majority. This majority is against him, but at present it is powerless because you, as party secretary and head of the Government, support him....."

Certainly, maintaining collaboration with Malenkov had long been vital to Beria, for in this way he secured the approval of the party. Therefore, once Malenkov was on board, it was easier to convince the others, i.e., Vorochilov, Kaganovich, Saburov and the others. Khrushchev writes in his memoirs that when he met Molotov to explain the need to go against Beria, the latter said: "Yes, I fully agree with you. But I still want to ask you one thing: what is Malenkov's position?" The reply was, "I am speaking to you on behalf of Malenkov and Bulganin. We have already exchanged our views on this matter."

Beria's Achilles' heel, however, was the military. His relationship with them had been scarred during the war. In 1968, an illustrated Prague magazine published an account of the hatred the army had built up against the interior minister. The author, a Czechoslovak diplomat, quoted Bulganin as a source. According to this information, in February 1953, shortly before Stalin's assassination, a group of Marshals and Generals led by Zhukov and Moskalenko had visited Bulganin, their Minister of Defence, to ask him to arrange an interview with Stalin. They wanted to reveal to him the truth about numerous criminal actions undertaken by the Ministry of the Interior and the NKVD against the Soviet Army. In front of Bulganin, the Marshals openly attacked Beria, Abakomov and even Malenkov. They claimed that during the war and after liberation this troika had killed or sent to prison and to death numerous honest officers and soldiers who had distinguished themselves during the fighting. After the dictator's death, as explained in the version that appeared in the Prague Review, Khrushchev and Bulganin convinced the military that it would be suicidal to go against both Malenkov, head of the government and the party, and Beria at the same time. When it was announced to them that Malenkov had been persuaded to join the action, it was decided that Moskalenko would draw up a detailed plan of operations.

In short, since Beria controlled the police and the Presidium guard obeyed his orders, his arrest would not have been possible without the intervention of the army. Let us read what Khrushchev wrote about it:

> "... We therefore decided to secure the participation of the army. At first, we entrusted the imprisonment and surveillance of Beria to Comrade Moskalenko, Commander-in-Chief of the Air Defence, and five other generals. Finally, on the eve of the session, Malenkov enlarged the circle to include Marshal Zhukov and a few others. In all, eleven marshals and generals. At that time it was required that all military personnel entering the Kremlin should submit to arms control, so Comrade Bulganin had to be commissioned to see to it that the military personnel with their weapons were allowed to pass. We arranged that during the Presidium meeting Moskalenko's group would wait for our call in a nearby room. When Malenkov gave the signal, his men were to enter the meeting room, arrest Beria and take him to prison."

Anton Kolendic's account of Beria's dismissal and arrest in *Les derniers jours* explains the broad outlines of the preparations for the arrest. Among his sources, he cites statements by Moskalenko himself, in which he reveals that the last meeting before the action took place on the night of 20-21 June 1953. It was attended by Minister Bulganin, Marshal Zhukov and Moskalenko himself. All details were worked out and all eventualities were examined. Moskalenko explains that they agreed on everything except one point: "What was to be done about Beria? Khrushchev and Moskalenko were in favour of liquidating him immediately; but Bulganin and Zhukov were absolutely against it. Marshal Zhukov insisted that he should be brought before a people's court and went so far as to argue that "it was necessary to keep him alive so that he could testify to the crimes of Malenkov and the others."

To justify the presence of eleven Marshals and Generals in the Kremlin without Beria suspecting and alerting the guard, on the morning of 21 June Malenkov announced by telephone through his Secretariat that in addition to the regular session of the Politburo a special team of the National Defence Committee would also be present to examine the situation in East Germany and its international implications. Zhukov, the saviour of Moscow; Ivan Koniev, Chief Inspector of the Army; Marshal Malinovsky, hero of Stalingrad; General Moskalensko, Deputy Defence Minister; were among the group of servicemen who were led into Room 3, where they waited to be ushered into the room where the Politburo members were meeting. Before the start, Beria hastened to say to Malenkov: "Georgy Maksimilianovich, we must take urgent measures against what is happening in Berlin." To which Malenkov, without taking his eyes off the papers replied, "Lavrenti Pavlovich, the session is going to begin... it is on the agenda... you can then..." According to Khrushchev, the author of the quotation, Beria said nothing, but it was noted that he was rather surprised by the unusual reaction of Malenkov, who had always shown him a servile demeanour.

The attack on Beria was initiated by Khrushchev, who, as has been recounted above, accused him of being an agent of British espionage and of having betrayed and sold out the interests of the USSR by his actions in the events in the GDR. Beria was never a communist," concluded Khrushchev, "but a calculating and selfish careerist who saw in our party the ideal way to realise his plans as a megalomaniac, a criminal and a spy." Beria rose and asked for the floor; but Bulganin jumped up, shouting that he had asked for the floor earlier, and hurled a string of grave accusations at him. Then followed Molotov, Kaganovich, Vorochilov and others. When Beria stood up again to try to defend himself, Malenkov pressed the reserved buzzer and the side doors opened wide. At this moment, with Zhukov leading the way, the marshals and generals burst into the hall with weapons in hand. Moskalenko pointed his submachine gun at Beria's back and Malenkov uttered these words: "As Chairman of the Council of Ministers of the Soviet Union, I order you to arrest Lavrenti Beria and bring him before the competent judicial authorities". Thus the military commanders took Beria away. A few days after his arrest, on 25 June, Beria wrote a letter to Malenkov with the permission of his guards in which he complained about his treatment: "Two men pulled me by the arm, while others pushed me from behind with their machine guns and pistols. They threw me like a sack in a corner of the secretariat. When my glasses fell down, I was not allowed to pick them up, even though I explained that I could not see anything. They treated me like a ferocious beast...".

Kolendic's work, which we have been using as our main source, offers a reconstruction of what happened after Beria's arrest, based on various writings, statements and information. According to most members of the Politburo, the military commanders secured control of the strategic points in Moscow and the main cities. At the same time, the heads of the organs of the Ministry of the Interior were arrested. It can be said that Beria's closest collaborators and acolytes were immediately liquidated or deactivated. The cooperative attitude of Vsevolod Merkulov, who helped Malenkov organise the purge after the first moments of Beria's dismissal, was vital. All the interior ministers and their deputies in all the republics and autonomous provinces of the Soviet Union were arrested. The armed forces of the Ministry of the Interior and the NKVD, which constituted a second army, were thus brought under control and dominated. Merkulov himself declared that about three thousand Security officers were eliminated.

The largest number of arrests and dismissals affected Beria's counter-espionage service within the army. There the purge was carried out by a special commission headed by Minister Bulganin. An intimate of Beria's since the Baku and Tbilisi years, Merkulov had been one of the organisers of the spy network within the Manhattan Project, and Beria had appointed him as Minister of State Security to replace Ignatiev. Suddenly, a few days later, he was arrested. According to a report in Pravda on 23 December 1953, Merkulov was eventually shot along with his boss. His confessions and those of the other defendants are collected in about a hundred pages.

On 10 July 1953 the first official announcement of Beria's ouster was finally made. A "communiqué of the Plenum of the Central Committee of the CPSU" was published on the front page of *Pravda*, informing that the decision had been taken to exclude Beria and that the resolution of the Presidium of the Supreme Soviet to submit to the Supreme Court of the USSR the examination of his enemy activities had been accepted. It was stated that Comrade Malenkov had submitted a report "concerning criminal activities against the Party and the State, sabotage against the security of the Soviet Union carried out in the interests of foreign capital". It was also alleged that Beria had sought "to place the Ministry of Internal Affairs above the Government and the Communist Party of the Soviet Union." When Radio Moscow broadcast the *Pravda* communiqué, there was general astonishment, both in the Soviet Union and abroad, for no one was unaware that Beria was the most powerful man in the USSR.

But if there are different versions of how Beria's arrest came about, the date of his death has also been the subject of controversy. On 16 December 1953, all Soviet radio stations issued an official communiqué, which was also published the next day by *Pravda* and *Izvestia*. It reported that the trial of the traitor Beria, an agent of international imperialism, and his accomplices had been completed and that they would soon be brought to trial. It appears, however, that the oral trial of L.P. Beria, V.N. Merkulov, V.G. Dekanozov, B.J. Kobulov, S.A. Goglidze, P.Y. Mechik and L.E. Vlodzimirsky had already taken place when the communiqué was issued, having begun on 14 December and ended the following day, when they were sentenced and executed. These Chekists sentenced to death along with Beria passed themselves off as Armenians, Georgians, etc., but various sources suggest that they were almost all crypto-Jews like Beria himself. Merkulov, for example, one of the most conspicuous members of the so-called "Beria mafia", claims to be Azeri, as he was born in Azerbaijan; but in *Plot Against the Church* Maurice Pinay, a pseudonym used by bishops opposed to the reforms of the Second Vatican Council, claims that he was Jewish.

There is, on the other hand, an official statement published on 24 December 1953 in *Pravda* and *Izvestia*, the government newspapers, according to which Beria was tried for treason, sentenced to death and executed on 23 December. However, different accounts claim that Beria was liquidated much earlier. In 1962, for example, The *Great Polish Universal Encyclopaedia*, published by the Polish communist government, gave the date of his death as July 1953. If this information were true, one would have to think that the man who appeared before the court presided over by Marshal Koniev was a double who answered the questions put to him adequately. In the oral proceedings, for example, there is a question from Koniev, the military man who, together with Dr. Timachuk, had denounced in a letter to Stalin the criminal activities of the Kremlin's Jewish doctors. Concerning Beria's actions after Stalin's death, Marshal Koniev asked: "Who gave him the authorisation to proclaim, without consulting the Minister of Defence and without the agreement of the Defence Council, a state of alert in the army and to subordinate the command of the General Staff to the special committee composed of his men and placed under his direction?" The reply was, "It obeyed the reason of state. If I had not immediately proclaimed a state of alert and first-degree alarm, who knows what would have happened? The Politburo had its head cut off, the Government did not meet until the next day, while the Central Committee had to meet with difficulty three days later..... To avoid anarchy it was necessary to act quickly....".

In any case, since there are also confessions and other handwritten texts by Beria, it is at least reasonable to assume that he was not actually executed on the spot, as other sources suggest, but that he was alive for some time and could have been interrogated. Moreover, there are witnesses and documentary evidence that a trial was held in December in which Beria was sentenced to death. It therefore seems reasonable to consider that the person who appeared in court at the closed trial could be the real Beria.

In conclusion, it only remains to outline, necessarily very briefly, Beria's approach to Mao at the request of his "international friends" to end the Korean War. Since May 1953, Beria had been in secret contact with the Americans, who wanted to convince the Chinese and North Koreans to stop the hostilities. Beria's key man in China, his special representative, was Pavel Iudin, the Jew who as early as 1947 had been sent to Yugoslavia to edit and supervise the newspaper *For a lasting peace, for a people's democracy*, the bulletin of the Cominform. This long-time collaborator, used by Beria on very important missions, had been appointed a permanent member of the Academy of Sciences and was considered the party's official philosopher. In Peking, in addition to his duties as an informer, he was in charge of editing Mao's complete works and was eventually appointed ambassador. In May 1953 he worked closely with Kao Kang, Beria's agent denounced by Stalin, who, surprisingly, had not been liquidated. According to A. Kolendic, 'at Beria's insistence, Iudin requested and obtained a daily interview with Kao Kang'. Kolendic adds that Iudin received Kang's reports and in turn passed on to him "Beria's instructions on the necessity of accepting all the Americans' conditions and ending the Korean War". Among the documents obtained after Beria's arrest were numerous texts on "relations with the Central Committee of the Chinese Communist Party". These were reports written by Beria himself or sent by Kao Kang, who was a member of the Politburo. When the Treaty of Panmunjon was solemnly signed on 27 July 1953, which marked the cease-fire and the end of hostilities, Beria was already under arrest, if not executed.

In short, as had happened to Stolypin, to Alexander II, to Nicholas II and his family, all murdered by commissioners of the Jewish conspirators who aspired to the control and usurpation of Russia's wealth, Stalin was likewise dispatched by an agent of the Hidden Power. It seems reasonable to conclude that Lavrenti Pavlovich Beria, Stalin's assassin, was the crypto-Jew of choice for those who had financed communism from its origins. He rose to prominence during the Second World War. The secret information supplied to him by Jewish agents infiltrated into the Manhattan Project and the information he received in the post-war years consolidated his power. As soon as the war was over, Beria put his men in charge of the security services in Poland, Czechoslovakia, Hungary, Bulgaria, Romania, Yugoslavia... Stalin became suspicious of him when he realised that many of these Jews delegated by Beria surreptitiously opposed his policy regarding the control of the Cominform. Once the dictator was removed, Beria tried to consolidate the coup d'état to seize power in the USSR.

Once Adenauer had completely caved in and agreed to hand over multimillion-dollar compensation to the Zionists, a united Germany that could cope with the disproportionate, almost impossible obligations assumed by the German chancellor against the opinion of his own party was desirable. This is the only way to understand Beria's erratic behaviour during the June 1953 events, aimed at surrendering the GDR and facilitating reunification, despite the fact that a year earlier the Western powers and Adenauer himself had rejected the proposal contained in Stalin's note.

OTHER BOOKS

⊘MNIA VERITAS

It does not deny, but aims to affirm more accurately. Revisionists are not 'deniers' or 'negationists'; they strive to seek and find where, it seems, there was nothing left to seek or find".

OMNIA VERITAS LTD PRESENTS:

ROBERT FAURISSON

REVISIONIST WRITINGS
I
1974-1983

Revisionism is a matter of method, not ideology

⊘MNIA VERITAS

Jewish and Zionist organisations throughout the world are experiencing a tragedy. A myth, from which they have sought to profit, is being exposed: the myth of the so-called 'Holocaust of the Jews during the Second World War'.

OMNIA VERITAS LTD PRESENTS:

ROBERT FAURISSON

REVISIONIST WRITINGS
II
1984-1989

Revisionists have never denied the existence of the camps

⊘MNIA VERITAS

"By its very nature, revisionism can only disturb public order; where tranquil certainties reign, the spirit of free examination is an intruder and causes a scandal."

OMNIA VERITAS LTD PRESENTS:

ROBERT FAURISSON

REVISIONIST WRITINGS
III
1990-1992

Every Frenchman has the right to say that gas chambers did not exist

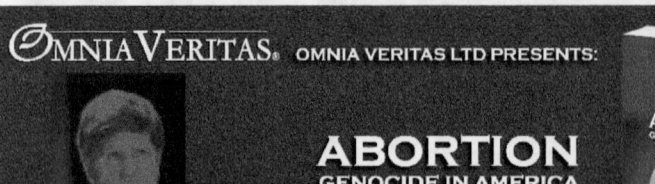

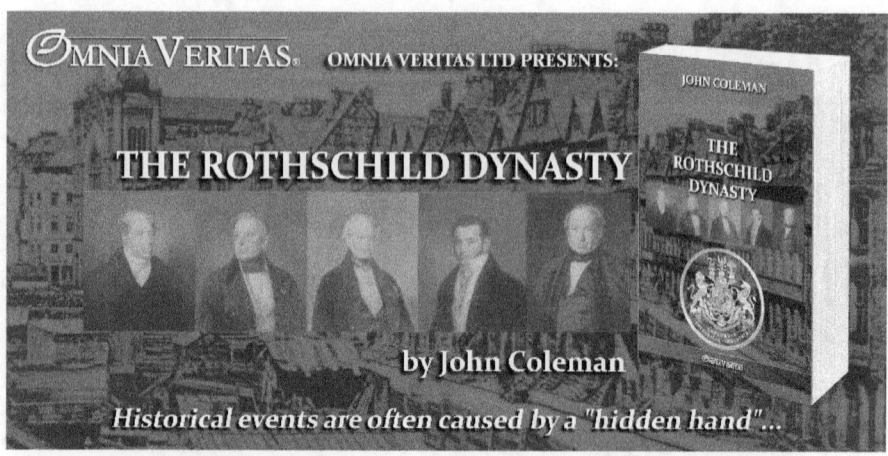

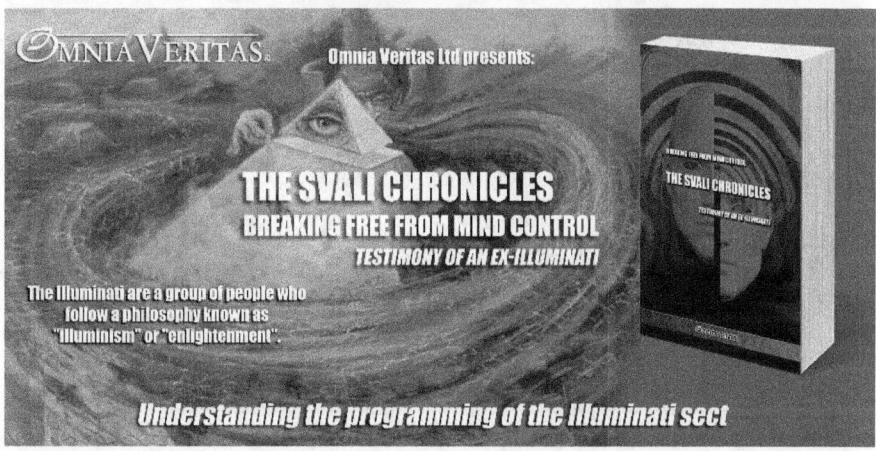

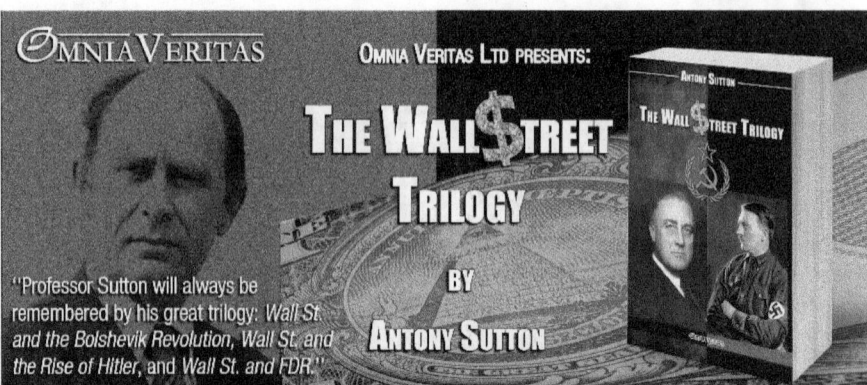

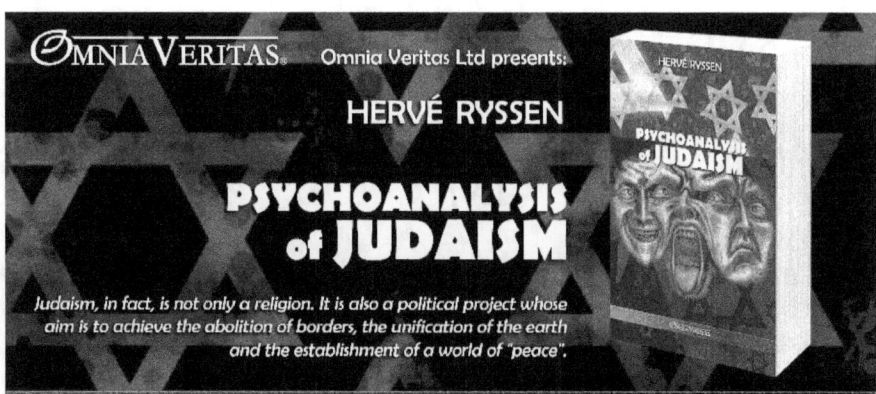

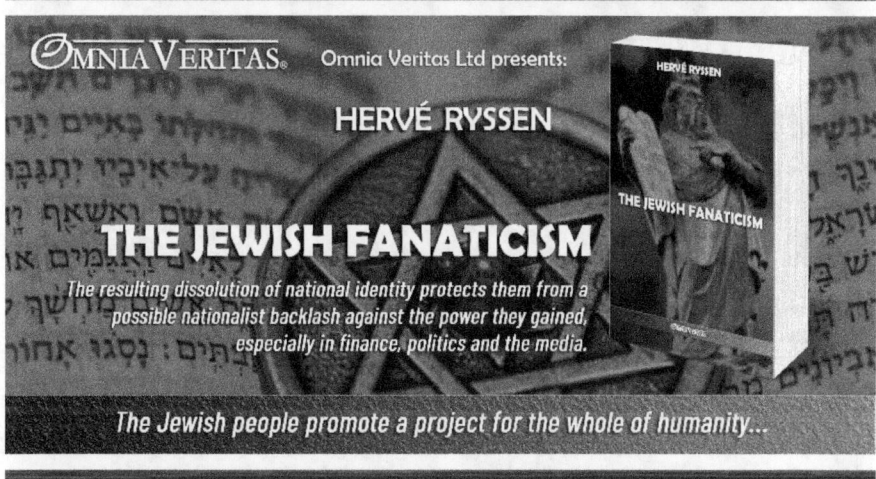

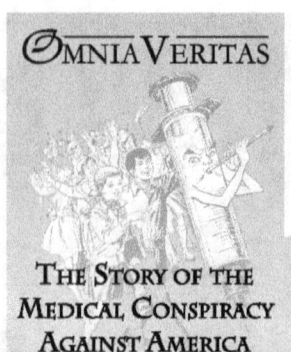
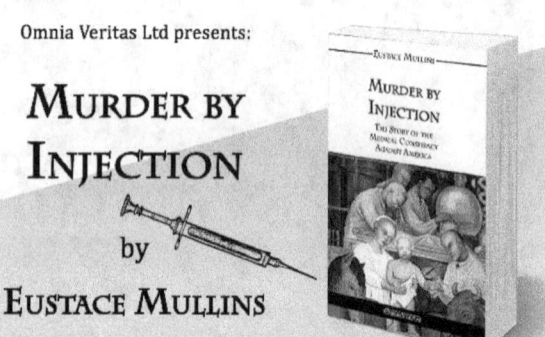
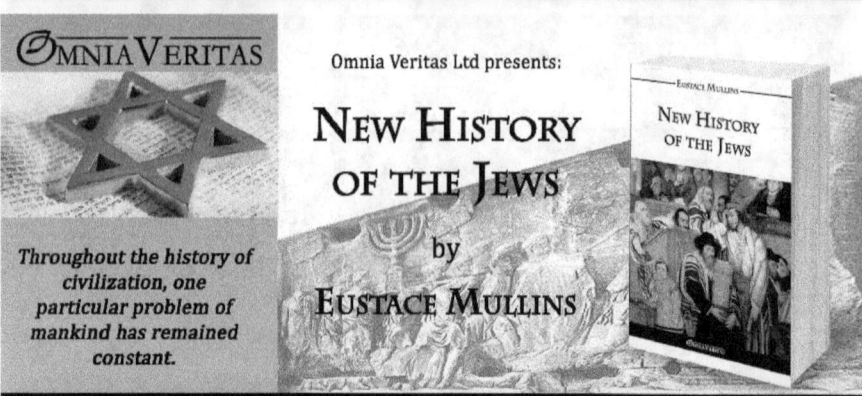

Omnia Veritas Ltd presents:

The Rape of Justice

by Eustace Mullins

American should know just what is going on in our courts

Omnia Veritas Ltd presents:

The Secrets of the Federal Reserve

by Eustace Mullins

HERE ARE THE SIMPLE FACTS OF THE GREAT BETRAYAL

Will we continue to be enslaved by the Babylonian debt money system?

Omnia Veritas Ltd presents:

The World Order

Our Secret Rulers

A Study in the Hegemony of Parasitism

by Eustace Mullins

The peoples of the world not only will never love Big Brother, but they will soon dispose of him forever.

The program of the World Order remains the same; Divide and Conquer

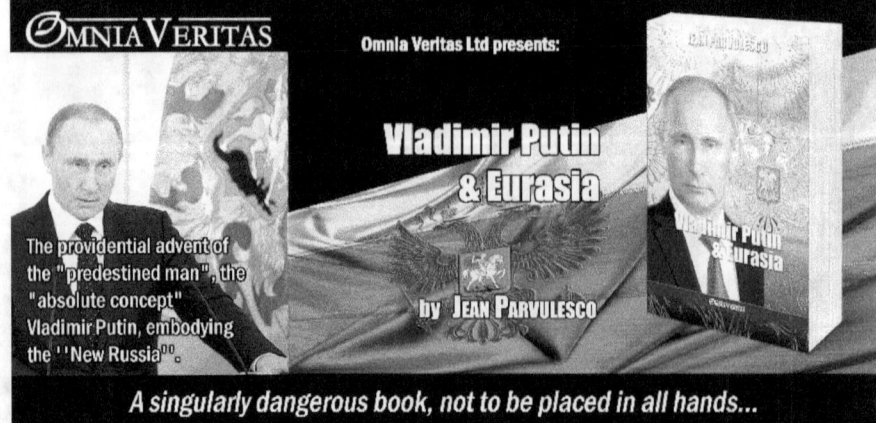

Omnia Veritas Ltd presents:

It is no wonder that Wahhabis are now the backbone of terrorism, authorising, financing and planning the shedding of the blood of Muslims and other innocents.

British enmity against Islam

Confessions of a BRITISH SPY

This document reveals the true context of the Wahhabi movement

OMNIA VERITAS LTD PRESENTS:

English Freemasonry is wealthy and capitalistic, controlling the money and rulers of the world through banking and commerce. French Freemasonry, on the other hand, is poor and communistic, attempting to control state finances through an all-powerful socialist government.

SCARLET AND THE BEAST

ENGLISH FREEMASONRY, BANKS, AND THE ILLEGAL DRUG TRADE

The Harlot's abominable cup is in the hands of English Freemasonry

Omnia Veritas Ltd presents:

ARCHIBALD RAMSAY

THE NAMELESS WAR
THE JEWISH POWER AGAINST THE NATIONS

The author describes the anatomy of the machine of the Revolutionary International which today pursues the project of supranational world power, the age-old messianic dream of international Jewry...

Evidence of a centuries-old conspiracy against Europe and the whole of Christendom...

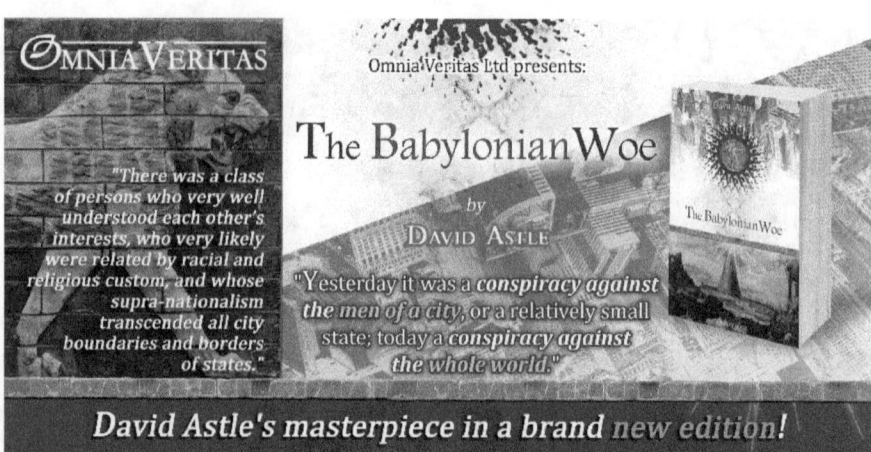

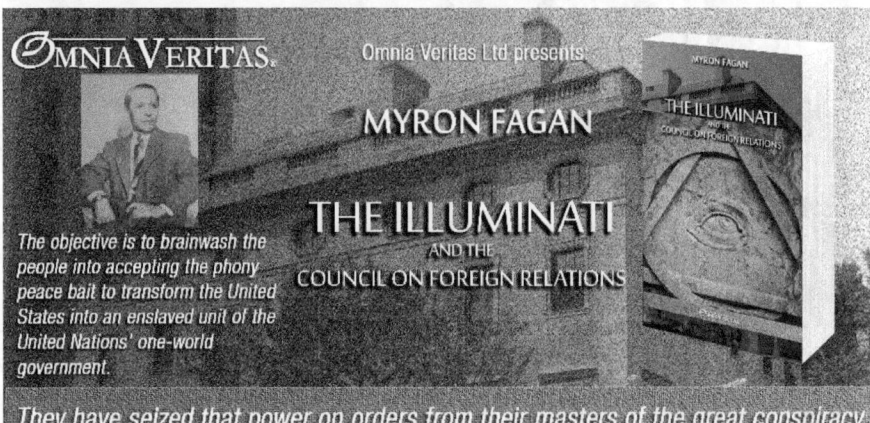

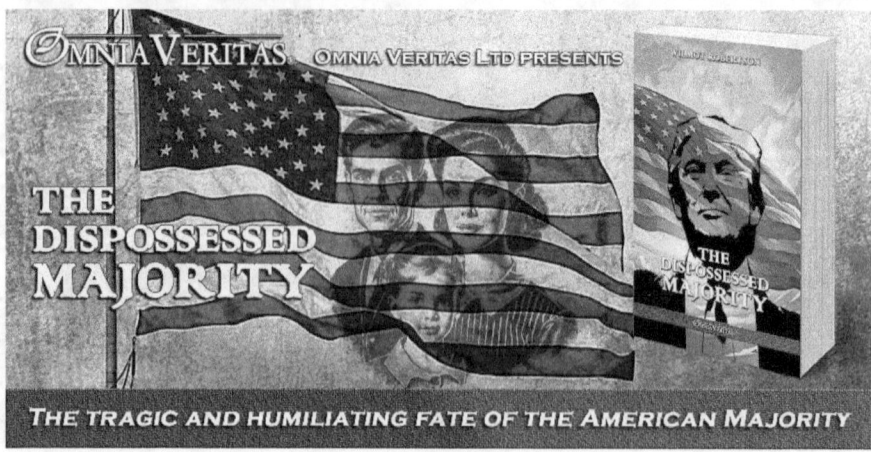

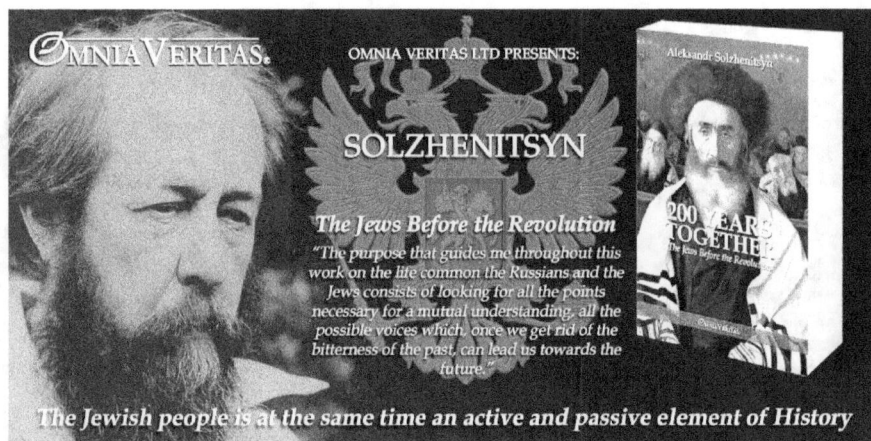
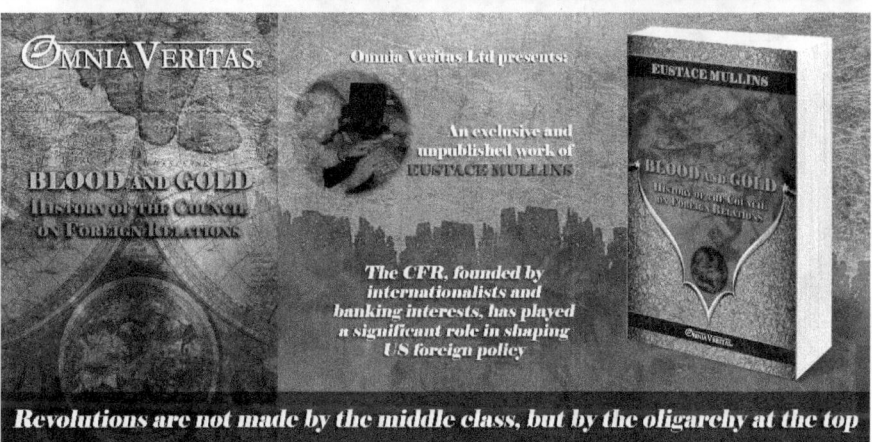
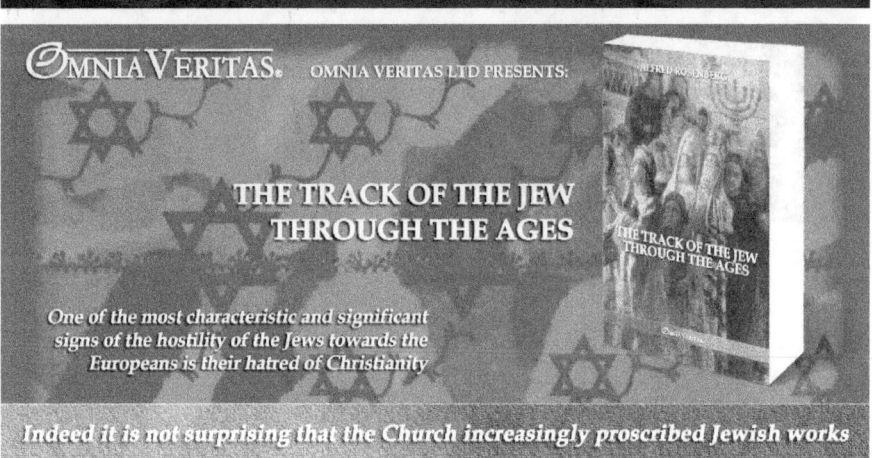

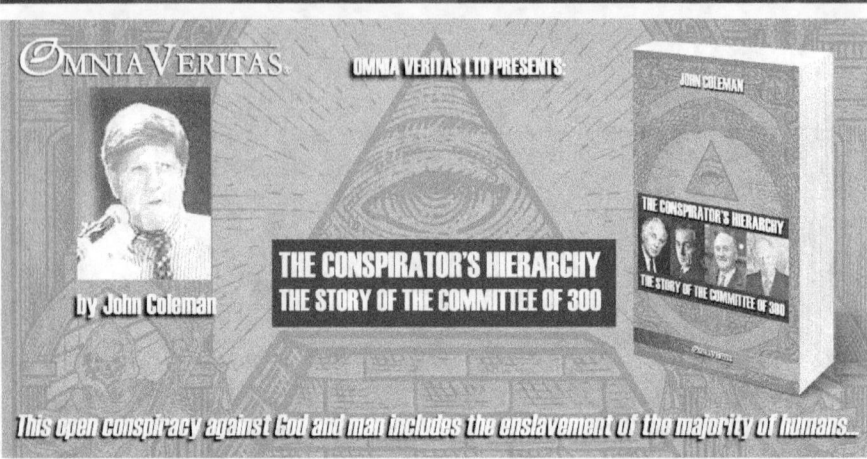

www.ingramcontent.com/pod-product-compliance
Lightning Source LLC
Chambersburg PA
CBHW060219230426
43664CB00011B/1481